HOLISTIC RESOURCE MANAGEMENT

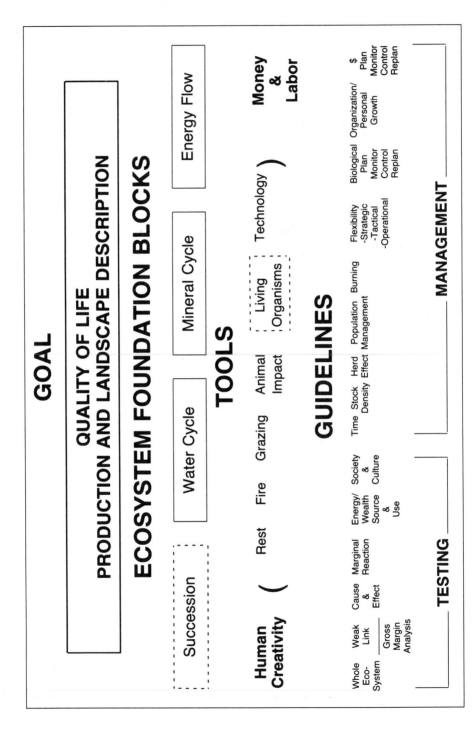

Holistic resource management model

HOLISTIC RESOURCE MANAGEMENT

Allan Savory

ABOUT ISLAND PRESS

Island Press, a nonprofit organization, publishes, markets, and distributes the most advanced thinking on the conservation of our natural resources—books about soil, land, water, forests, wildlife, and hazardous and toxic wastes. These books are practical tools used by public officials, business and industry leaders, natural resource managers, and concerned citizens working to solve both local and global resource problems.

Founded in 1978, Island Press reorganized in 1984 to meet the increasing demand for substantive books on all resource-related issues. Island Press publishes and distributes under its own imprint and offers these services to other nonprofit organizations.

Funding to support Island Press is provided by The Mary Reynolds Babcock Foundation, The Ford Foundation, The George Gund Foundation, The William and Flora Hewlett Foundation, The Joyce Foundation, The J. M. Kaplan Fund, The John D. and Catherine T. MacArthur Foundation, The Andrew W. Mellon Foundation, Northwest Area Foundation, The Jessie Smith Noyes Foundation, The J. N. Pew, Jr. Charitable Trust, The Rockefeller Brothers Fund, and The Tides Foundation.

For additional information about Island Press publishing services and a catalog of current and forthcoming titles, contact Island Press, P.O. Box 7, Covelo, California 95428.

© Copyright 1988 Allan Savory

Library of Congress Cataloging-in-Publication Data

Savory, Allan, 1935–
  Holistic resource management.

  Bibliography: p.
  Includes index.
  1. Natural resources—Management.   2. Human ecology.
I. Title
HC59.S335 1988   333.7   88-13270
ISBN 0-933280-62-9 (v. 1)
ISBN 0-933280-61-0 (v. 1 : pbk.)

Unless otherwise noted, all illustrative materials are Copyright © Allan Savory. Permission to reproduce the photograph of *Jan Christian Smuts* (Illus. 4-1) is kindly granted by *The Star*, Johannesburg, South Africa; permission to reproduce *Remnant perennial grass patch in annual California grassland* (Illus. 13-1) kindly granted by Richard King; permission to reproduce *Cartoon*, (Illus. 18-7) kindly granted by Ace Reid; permission to reproduce *Vegetated riverbank produced with cattle tramping and well-planned grazing* (Illus. 20-1) kindly granted by R. H. Vaughan-Evans; permission to reproduce *The Dixon Land Imprinter designed to rehabilitate poor rangelands* (Illus. 20-2) kindly granted by Bob Dixon; permission to reproduce *Leaking waterline turned into a waterpoint for birds, small insects, and animals. Namibia* (Illus. 21-1) kindly granted by Argo Rust, and permission to reproduce *Lincoln* (Illus. 4-2) kindly granted by AT&T Bell Laboratories.

MANUFACTURED IN THE UNITED STATES OF AMERICA

10   9   8   7

Contents

List of Plates   viii

List of Illustrations   ix

List of Figures   xv

Preface   xix

Acknowledgments   xxv

Part I: INTRODUCTION

1   What Is Holistic Resource Management?   3
2   Political and Economic Ramifications   12

Part II: THE MISSING KEYS

3   Introduction   21
4   Management Must Be Holistic   23
5   Brittle and Nonbrittle Environments   35
6   The Role of Herding Animals and Their Predators in Brittle Environments   41
7   The Time Dimension in Soil, Plant, and Animal Relationships   45

Part III: GOALS

8   Goals I: Temporary Goals to Get You Started   55

Part IV: THE ECOSYSTEM

9	Introduction	61
10	Water Cycle	63
11	Succession	73
12	Mineral Cycle	90
13	Energy Flow	95

Part V: TOOLS TO MANAGE OUR ECOSYSTEM

14	Introduction	111
15	Money and Labor	114
16	Human Creativity	121
17	Fire	125
18	Rest	133
19	Grazing	151
20	Animal Impact	173
21	Living Organisms	184
22	Technology	190

Part VI: THE GUIDELINES

23	Introduction	199
24	Time in Cropping, Grazing, Browsing, and Trampling	202
25	Time and Energy Flow	227
26	Time and Livestock Nutrition	234
27	Time and Game Management	246
28	Stock Density	251
29	Herd Effect	263
30	Whole Ecosystem	273
31	Weak Link	279
32	Cause and Effect	287
33	Marginal Reaction	299
34	Gross Margin Analysis	310
35	Energy/Wealth Source and Use	315
36	Society and Culture	320
37	Population Management	325
38	Burning	342
39	Flexibility	351
40	Biological Planning	365
41	Biological Monitoring and Control	377
42	Organization	387
43	Personal Growth	398
44	Financial Planning and Wealth Generation	409
45	Financial Monitoring and Control	435

Part VII: GOALS

46   Goals II: Setting More Permanent Goals   445

Part VIII: THE MODES OF APPLICATION

47   Introduction   461
48   Diagnostic Mode   463
49   Policy Analysis Mode   475
50   Research Orientation Mode   486

Part IX: CONCLUSION

51   The Future   497

Appendix: The Center for Holistic Resource Management   507

Glossary   509

References   513

Notes   540

Index   546

Also Available from Island Press   559

List of Plates

Plate 1. Although they have considerable knowledge of green, yellow, red, and blue, people in single, isolated disciplines are unable to manage gray (the "whole") of which they have no knowledge. Management is not even focused on gray, as the arrows indicate. This approach to management was generally recognized as a failure many years ago.

Plate 2. People in a multi-disciplinary team are focusing on gray from their perspective, as arrows indicate, but still with no knowledge of gray. Failures arising from this approach to management were attributed to poor communication owing to the jargon associated with the various disciplines, rather than a lack of knowledge.

Plate 3. To overcome communication problems, people trained in several disciplines form an interdisciplinary team which then focuses its attention on gray, as the arrows indicate. Knowledge of gray is still lacking, however. The failures arising from this approach to management have only recently been acknowledged.

Plate 4. The gray sphere represents the selection of a whole, the determination of the goal, and the application of the HRM model. Holistic management manages gray by looking outwardly from gray's perspectives at all available knowledge, as the arrows indicate. We now have knowledge of gray through selection of a management "whole" and the detailed formulation of a comprehensive goal in three parts combined with the use of a thought model to bring about that goal. Management now utilizes knowledge from all sources and disciplines.

List of Illustrations

4-1   Jan Christian Smuts (photo courtesy *The Star*, Johannesburg).

4-2   Design (courtesy AT&T Bell Laboratories).

11-1   Soil surface dominated by algae and lichens and roughened by freezing and thawing. Canyonlands, Utah.

11-2   Unsuccessful attempt to get grass established with nylon netting and woodwool as litter. Dead sticks are holding down netting (not visible). Canyonlands, Utah.

11-3   Bare soil with only tap-rooted herbs establishing under partial rest. All seedlings (see arrow) are forbs.

11-4   A short way from illustration 11-3, this bare soil appears different due to trampling by cattle. The cracks are absent and there is a soft appearance—the result of a carpet of new perennial grass seedlings between the larger old clumps.

11-5   Community establishing on concrete in nonbrittle environment. Oregon.

11-6   A neat looking orchard with newly mown grass. Pennsylvania.

13-1   Remnant perennial grass patch in annual California grassland (courtesy Richard King).

13-2   Sparse growth of grass in overirrigated hay field with excellent growth on well-drained edge (foreground). Albuquerque, New Mexico.

13-3   View of long-rested land showing sparse grass and bare ground between plants, 1982. Barlite Ranch, Texas.

13-4   Identical view as illustration 13-3, taken three years later

(1985). Grass has become more sparse and bare ground has increased under continued rest. Barlite Ranch, Texas.

13-5   View of dense complex grassland growing right up to the watering point produced by heavy animal impact and grazing, 1984. (Bare ground on left is the waterpoint.) Barlite Ranch, Texas.

17-1   Burnt shrub that has resprouted with many new stems. Arizona.

18-1   Nonbrittle grassland showing last year's old growth already fallen (see arrow) and decaying and not choking new growth. Alaska.

18-2   u.s. Fish and Wildlife Service officials inspecting dying grassland with large, bare ground spaces opening between plants. Sevilleta Wildlife Refuge, New Mexico.

18-3   Brittle environment grassland, which had developed close spacing under animal impact, showing mass deaths under rest. All plants are grey and oxidizing. Coahuilla, Mexico.

18-4   Perennial grasses dying under rest in a thirty-inch-rainfall brittle environment. All grasses are grey and oxidizing. Atlantica Ecological Research Station, Zimbabwe.

18-5   Successional shift from grassland to dense forbs and mesquite has occurred in rested patch, while overgrazed patch in foreground erodes. Coahuilla, Mexico.

18-6   Fifty years of rest in a low rainfall brittle environment. Most grass dead, bare ground and erosion extensive, and many shrubs dying. Chaco Canyon, New Mexico.

18-7   Courtesy Ace Reid.

18-8   Twelve years of rest (a high proportion of these grasses are dead and grey), Crescent Lake Wildlife Refuge, Nebraska.

18-9   Fifty years of rest, Crescent Lake Wildlife Refuge, Nebraska.

18-10   The caption accompanying this photograph, which appeared in *Along the Beale Trail*, a u.s. Office of Indian Affairs booklet published in 1938, reads: "Protected for three years by the National Park Service, this area in the Petrified Forest, for years overgrazed, proves that protection will speed recovery." Arizona.

18-11   View of the grassland in Petrified Forest National Park in 1985 after forty years of partial rest. Arizona.

18-12   A 1930s photograph of an exclosure in the Rio Puerco Valley used in 1981 in the Council on Environmental Quality report on *Desertification of the United States*. Note Cabezon Peak, which appears in the background. New Mexico.

18-13   A 1987 photograph of one of the remaining exclosures in the Rio Puerco Valley. Cabezon Peak appears in the background. New Mexico.

19-1   Ranch, stocked at conventional stocking rate, showing tendency to overgraze some areas (light patches) and overrest others (darker patches). West Texas.

19-2   Ground view of the same range as in illustration 19-1, showing close-up of overrested and overgrazed sites. Coahuilla, Mexico.

19-3   Large-scale death of perennial grasses taking place in overrested site on the same range as in illustrations 19-1 and 19-2. Coahuilla, Mexico.

19-4   Paddock grazed by three horses for one year, showing dung-free grazing area in the foreground. Longer grass in background contains much dung. New Mexico.

19-5   Chaco Canyon boundary looking through the fence to land where almost all plants have been heavily overgrazed for the last fifty years. New Mexico.

19-6   A severely distorted perennial grass, which has sent out a seed stalk flat along the ground. Zimbabwe.

19-7   Severe distortion of a normally erect perennial grass, which has been overgrazed. The knife indicates how close and flat the leaves are to the ground. Zimbabwe.

19-8   Long overgrazed, this normally matted perennial grass is surviving by forming a hedged ball. Baluchistan Province, Pakistan.

19-9   Overbrowsed and hedged perennial shrub of great age. North Yemen.

19-10   New stems growing below the old browseline once the overbrowsing has stopped. Namibia.

19-11   Close-cropped, matted leaves along the trunk of a tree suffering from severe overbrowsing. Cape Province, South Africa.

19-12   Browseline clearly showing on trees, despite a massive stock reduction. Arizona.

19-13   Severely overbrowsed stub of a bush. Arizona.

19-14   Typical bush, on the same range as in illustration 19-13, growing out well with grazing/browsing planned and livestock numbers doubled. Arizona.

19-15   During a very dry year, livestock numbers were doubled on this severely depleted rangeland, while the livestock were planned to avoid further overbrowsing/overgrazing. Illustration 19-16 is a close-up view of the plant in the lower right (see arrow). Karroo, South Africa.

19-16   Once no longer overbrowsed, this plant is flowering and seeding heavily despite the drought and increased livestock numbers. Karroo, South Africa.

19-17   Severe overbrowsing under very high numbers of large game. Rambling shrub thickets have been wiped out. Mana Pools Non-Hunting Area, Zambezi Valley, 1960. Zimbabwe.

19-18   Severe overbrowsing under reduced numbers of large game, following heavy culling. The majority of the trees have been heavily browsed to the height elephants can reach. Mana Pools National Park, Zambezi Valley, 1985. Zimbabwe.

20-1   Vegetated river bank produced with cattle trampling and well-planned grazing. Zimbabwe (courtesy R. H. Vaughan-Evans).

20-2   The Dixon Land Imprinter designed to rehabilitate poor rangelands (courtesy Bob Dixon).

20-3   Heavy animal impact has led to the immediate response in plant growth seen to the right of this fence on badly desertified rangeland. Namibia.

20-4   Extreme trampling resulting from two thousand head of cattle concentrating during a storm. Chaco, Paraguay.

21-1   Leaking waterline turned into a waterpoint for birds, small insects, and animals. Namibia (courtesy Argo Rust).

24-1   The arrow marks a severely-grazed plant after one horse had grazed for one hour. New Mexico.

24-2   Dense and vigorous grass growth after eight years of planned grazing. Igava Range, Zimbabwe.

24-3   Severe overgrazing on the same ground as seen in illustration 24-2 after four years of short-duration grazing rotation. Igava Ranch, Zimbabwe.

24-4   Severely-overgrazed plant in the foreground of illustration 24-3. Normally this plant would grow to a height of three feet or more. Igava Ranch, Zimbabwe.

24-5   Perennial grassland at the watering point in a twelve-inch-rainfall brittle environment after eight years of planned grazing. Liebig's Ranch, Zimbabwe.

24-6   View looking toward the same watering point shown in illustration 24-5 after four years of short-duration grazing rotation. Liebig's Ranch, Zimbabwe.

24-7   Complexity of community increasing on what had been essentially desert bushes and bare ground. Karroo, South Africa.

26-1   Dense, lush, and leafy growth in a complex community produced by very high animal impact from cattle moving through 101 paddocks on planned grazing. Barlite Ranch, Texas.

28-1   Low density grazing pattern seen from the air with two different stocking rates. Coahuilla, Mexico.

28-2   Two ranches at different levels of paddocking and stock density. Six paddocks per herd (left) and forty paddocks per herd (right). Grass plants on right are more closely spaced and vigorous. Chipinge, Zimbabwe.

28-3   Severe overrest resulting from rotational grazing has killed large areas of grass in the right-hand paddock. These plants are grey, oxidized, and dying and are thus ungrazed. Plants are the left are green, growing, and grazed. Igava Ranch, Zimbabwe.

29-1   A herd of two thousand animals widely scattered and calm although at high stock density on the range. Barlite Ranch, Texas.

29-2   Close-up of the soil surface between grasses in illustration 29-1. The soil is hard capped and unable to breathe.

29-3   The herd being attracted and excited to cause herd effect on the soil.

29-4   Excited animals place their hooves carelessly and raise dust.

29-5   Close of the soil surface after applying herd effect. The soil is chipped and able to breathe and succession can move forward once more.

29-6   Mobile mineral wagon with a full spectrum of trace and macrominerals. Transvaal, South Africa.

32-1   Mesquite trees have been cleared three times already on this rangeland showing both overgrazing and overresting. West Texas.

32-2   View of effective management on the left of the fence producing dense perennial grassland despite the density of the acacia trees and shrubs. Lebowa, South Africa.

32-3   Dense growth of new perennial grasses under the trees where the ground cover had been sparse the year before. Kwe Kwe, Zimbabwe.

32-4   Extension officer with his foot on one of the unpoisoned termite mounts, which is surrounded by lush perennial grass growth. Buhera, Zimbabwe.

32-5   Young, newly planted eucalyptus trees surrounded by hard capped soil, which has produced a noneffective water cycle. Buhera, Zimbabwe.

32-6   A heavy locoweed population in 1981 after years of overgrazing and partial rest had been practiced. Barlite Ranch, Texas.

32-7   A 1985 photograph of the identical area seen in illustration 32-6, showing the absence of locoweed following planned grazing with heavy animal impact. Barlite Ranch, Texas.

37-1   "Pristine" range site in New Mexico showing "desired" species of grasses but expanding bare ground and absence of any young plants for many years.

37-2   Unaware of the heavy culling that has taken place, this elephant shows little concern for humans and ignores me standing eight yards from him with a clicking camera, 1985. Mana Pools National Park, Zimbabwe.

37-3   A young winterthorn tree establishing itself where an elephant has broken the hard cap on the soil, 1985. Mana Pools National Park, Zimbabwe.

List of Figures

1-1   Holistic resource management model.

1-2   Our ecosystem viewed as four processes.

2-1   Zimbabwe: relationship of cultivated to noncultivated land as well as existing and potential irrigation.

4-1   Growth of knowledge over the past ten thousand years.

4-2   Human endeavors.

5-1   Summary of nonbrittle and brittle environments at the extreme ends of the spectrum.

10-1   The water cycle.

10-2   Effective and noneffective water cycles.

11-1   Relationship of successional complexity to relative stability.

11-2   Complex of millions of populations making up the whole.

11-3   Disruption of whole to favor one population.

11-4   Improvement in population complexity with polycultures.

12-1   Mineral cycle on range and cropland.

13-1   Basic energy pyramid.

13-2   Energy flow above and below ground.

13-3   Energy flow seen as two tetrahedrons.

13-4   Surface level that controls energy flow.

20-1   Steep stream banks—vegetated and eroded.

24-1   Relationship of grazing periods to recovery periods.

24-2   Volume of grazing governed by number of animals and time on land.

24-3   Animal days per acre concept.

24-4   Effect of increasing number of paddocks and decreasing paddock size on grazing pressure in a cell.

24-5   Effect of increasing number of paddocks and decreasing paddock size on number of animals per acre (stock density).

24-6   Necessity for planned grazing to minimize overgrazing at low paddock numbers.

25-1   Rate of immediate regrowth as affected by amount of leaf removed by grazing.

25-2   Time reserve versus area reserve for droughts.

26-1   How movement through paddocks can affect nutrition.

26-2   Four selections from each paddock.

26-3   Two selections from each paddock.

26-4   Single selection from each paddock with few paddocks.

26-5   Single selection from each paddock with many paddocks.

28-1   With new fence, time can change everywhere but stock density only changes where paddock size changes.

28-2   Low density grazing problem with rotational grazing.

28-3   Low density grazing problem largely overcome with planned grazing (plan-monitor-control-replan).

30-1   The destruction of two species of protected game animals under conventional grazing practices.

31-1   Theoretical ranch.

31-2   Annual reinvestment cycle.

32-1   Simple cause and effect.

33-1   Twenty thousand dollars to invest on basis of highest return on each additional dollar invested.

33-2   Grazing area of four thousand acres carrying three hundred cows with severe invasion of locoweed.

33-3   Fencing curve of diminishing marginal reaction per dollar.

33-4   Increasing stock density as a paddock is divided.

33-5   Conventional cattle production in many areas.

33-6   Example of cattle production planned to lower annual production costs.

34-1   American gross margin analysis.

34-2   David Wallace's gross margin analysis.

37-1   Sigmoid population growth curve.

37-2   Population age structure at various points on a sigmoid growth curve.

37-3   Desert bush population age structure - Pakistan.

37-4   Age structure of eland population before and after culling operations.

38-1   Edge effect increased with a mosaic of habitats.

39-1   Radiating grazing areas from a village.

39-2   Drought planning.

39-3   Dramatic effect of combining herds.

40-1   Principle of the biological planning chart.

40-2   Biological planning across seasons.

40-3   Assessing stocking rate.

41-1   Varying grazing/recovery periods with simultaneously differing growth rates.

42-1   Hierarchical, autocratic family.

44-1   Personal income and expenses.

44-2   Farm/ranch income and expenses.

44-3   Overall expense allocation.

44-4   Overall expense allocation with heavy debt servicing.

44-5   Selecting fences on basis of marginal reaction per dollar.

45-1   Portion of financial plan sheet.

45-2   Control sheet.

46-1   Present ranch landscape.

46-2   Landscape goal.

46-3   National park—present situation.

46-4   National park—landscape goal.

48-1   Population of desert bushes.

49-1   Annual grasshopper buildup.

50-1   Future relationship between scientific research and resource management essential for quality of life.

Preface

In 1948, I entered Plumtree School, a boarding school in the British tradition set in a delightful landscape on the border of what was then Southern Rhodesia and Botswana. When not on the rugby or cricket fields, we were encouraged to go out into the bush, a gesture of liberality that offset all my adolescent vexation with formal education. I became fanatic about the bush and the big game, and a passion to return to it drove me through a university education that qualified me for a Northern Rhodesian Game Department post at the age of 20. I had a naive dream of spending the remainder of my life in my beloved African bush among all its marvelous animals. My dream ended simply because I cared.

Once in the Game Department I began to see things as they really were and to realize that all I loved was doomed. Not for the commonly-talked-of reasons—poaching and overexploitation—but rather for our own ignorance as professional bureaucrats responsible for managing our natural resources. But professional people do not like to admit to ignorance or to raise the questions I did. It is easier to blame others while calling for more money and more staff. So began a long struggle, often very lonely, to find solutions to the deterioration I saw everywhere. Now thirty-three years later, much water has flowed under the bridge, and I can at last write about the way forward that I found.

Along the way I learned that what I saw in the destruction of wildlife reflects the condition of humanity and all other life on this planet. The wildlife problems that I first grappled with were little more than advance gusts of violent storms that will ultimately threaten the whole world.

In the 1980s, thoughtful, concerned people worldwide recognize the magnitude of the problems facing all peoples and their governments. Nowhere is the problem of environmental deterioration more apparent than in the United States. America, with her great concentration of wealth, brain-power, modern technology, and educational infrastructure, has no solutions. Despite excellent prices and the lowest input costs in the world, thousands of farmers leave the land every year, bankrupt. America's deserts continue to advance as relentlessly as those of any country. Water supplies deteriorate in volume, stability of flow, and quality. Probably no nation in the history of the world has destroyed its agricultural base of soil and water faster than America is doing.

Endless "quick-fix solutions" have, if anything, accelerated the decline. As the problems grow, the scientific efforts of individual disciplines have given way to multidisciplinary planning endeavors and finally integrated, interdisciplinary teams. Yet the decline continues. Occasionally we find isolated examples of apparent success, but on reflection we see plainly that they cannot succeed in the long run as oases on an ever deteriorating planet.

Poor land leads to poor people, social upheaval, and political unrest—even war. The frustration of concerned people rises, even in stable and relatively wealthy countries. In America, some have gone so far as to take government agencies to court because the land in their care is so obviously deteriorating. Yet blaming someone else does not help when the point is that no one knows how to manage land and keep it healthy. What scientists cannot achieve, the law certainly cannot. In the state of Nevada, where the Natural Resources Defense Council took the Bureau of Land Management to court, Judge James M. Burns saw the picture clearly and said this in his final ruling:

> At bottom . . . the primary reason for the large scale intrusion of the judiciary into the governance of our society has been an inability or unwillingness of the first two branches of government—both state and federal—to fashion solutions for significant societal, environmental, and economic problems in America. Frankly, I see little likelihood that the legislative and executive branches will take the statutory (and occasional constitutional) steps which would at least slow, if not reverse, this trend.[1]

He went on to say that for legally correct reasons he would decline the invitation to make the range management decisions in court that professional range managers could not. Recourse to the courts will not do what mankind has not known how to do for ten thousand years—stop the destruction of land under human impact—when all our modern scientific knowledge, wealth, and energy still offer no proven remedy.

For years we have attributed to ignorance the failure of civilizations now under desert sands. They did not know what we do today, nor did they have our technology. A few scientists, however, recognized that our current best attempts at management were not working. One of the first public admissions of this fact came in a statement issued at the end of an International Arid Lands Conference in 1985 sponsored by the University of Arizona, UNESCO, the U.S. Agency for International Development, and the American Association for the Advancement of Science, among others. The statement read, in part:

> An international committee of 13 arid lands scientists from nine nations have urged their colleagues to determine why years of effort to improve life in the world's dry regions have failed. Scientists must clearly tell global political leaders why those efforts have failed . . . . It has become gravely evident that with a few exceptions, the welfare of the people occupying many of the arid lands and the health of the underlying resources of air, water, soil, and biota are continuing to degrade . . . . It is not a simple matter of additional funds or of new technology or of further research along conventional lines. The central challenge is to translate our accumulated experience into approaches that see people in their environment whole, and to embody that view pervasively in new activity and policy.[2]

As the opinion of an arid lands conference, this statement unfortunately does not mention that the same situation prevails on lands of all types throughout the world, regardless of rainfall. In both developed and undeveloped countries, our resources of land, water, air, and living organisms deteriorate, and I am not aware of any place where the degradation is being halted. Small wonder that our economies, tied as they are to the health of our ecosystem (the source of all wealth), increasingly fall into crisis management.

The term *desertification* describes the deterioration of our basic land, water, and biological resources. Unfortunately, most people only recognize the process by its terminal symptom of blowing sand. They do not see the same syndrome of declining health and productivity underway in the climate of the eastern United States or Northern Europe, where sand dunes are unlikely to appear even after most life has gone.

This book answers the challenge to find an approach that treats people and their environment as one whole. I have called this Holistic Resource Management. It derives from a view of ourselves and our planet as one ecosystem functioning through four rudimentary processes—the development of living communities (succession), the cycling of mineral nutrients and water, and the flow of solar energy. It further involves the establishment of clear goals in all situations, and the use of what I have termed a "thought model" to enable us to "see the whole" we are managing.

Holistic Resource Management (HRM) applies universally, from the administration of a small family farm, to the planning for a vast national park, or the evaluation of international efforts to halt the spread of the world's deserts. Most important, it is successful. We need no longer take the narrow mechanical approach where predetermined management systems are imposed on an environment that, in our arrogance, we treat as outside ourselves.

We now operate within Nature's laws. In the light of carefully developed goals, the holistic model enables us to marshal all the accumulated knowledge of centuries. Then we can make effective plans, testing each element for its economic, social, and ecological soundness; by monitoring progress we can stay on course until the goal is reached. Although a great many mistakes have been made in the past thirty years, we have discovered most importantly how to make review and discovery part of the process. In the end we cannot fail because we will not let ourselves fail.

Throughout the following chapters I stress that our understanding of holism is newborn, and this book no more than a primitive description of our first successful flight into holistic management of ourselves and our planet. The model described here has undergone such constant evolution that I long resisted appeals to freeze it in print, as any book risks doing. However, as more people swing away from the old approaches (limited as they were by the boundaries of traditional disciplines), a book may be the best means to inspire independent minds to further develop the ideas of holism. I can only hope that a general readership will not take published thinking as dogma, but as a challenge to contribute their own ideas and experience.

Also, a book holds the promise of spreading the ideas of practical holism beyond its roots in the day-to-day management of land and into the realm of broader questions. I feel strongly that humanity's mismanagement of Nature is not distinct from many apparently unrelated problems that beset the modern world. Though the writing is addressed first to the ranchers, farmers, professionals, and policy makers who take primary responsibility for the health of our land, the questions raised affect everyone.

How, or whether, this book succeeds in advancing a new way of thinking is, of course, a subject of intense anticipation for the author. For the last eight years I have given training in Holistic Resource Management to many people and have come to appreciate the difficulty of communicating a new idea so effectively that people not only believe it, but also understand and use it successfully. Getting behind the controls of a plane on the strength of having read a book on aviation can be dangerous, and even a week of classroom discussion does not make a pilot.

In the case of holistic management, learning has tended to follow certain patterns. The majority of people attending courses have been farmers and ranchers and the government and university extension people working with them. The farmers and ranchers come eager to learn, commonly because of financial stress, and perceive an introductory course as something from which they can pick up bits and pieces of new knowledge to immediately increase their profitability. They tend to select what they want to hear, reject warnings about the importance of the "whole" and the necessity of further training, and go home to put their new ideas to work. When they inevitably strike problems, some give up and abandon the approach. Others return for further training. The latter group, whatever mistakes they may make along the way, will succeed to varying degrees.

Professional people, on the other hand, tend to express great anger, ridicule, and condemnation on their first exposure to HRM. If they persist and take a second or third course, the anger subsides and learning begins. These people, already highly trained in more conventional approaches, constantly evaluate the new ideas in terms of what they already know. The old adage that the greatest block to learning is knowledge certainly holds true and can block even the most open-minded, as I know from my own experience.

Some years ago, as a member of Parliament, I helped pass the law that enabled Zimbabwe to convert to metric standards. Though the change made absolute sense and I desired it, I have not yet succeeded in metricating myself. Many who originally opposed the move eventually did accept it and never looked back. But I still relate kilometers to miles, kilos to pounds, and liters to gallons, mentally converting every measure back to what I "know."

Some of the most closed-minded professional people who attended courses in anger (often because their superiors ordered them to go) have finally broken through because they cared enough about their work to argue every point so thoroughly that they convinced themselves. They, too, never looked back once they understood that HRM did not preclude present knowledge, but merely tested it against the "whole" before it was applied.

Until this book could be written, those who sought training could only receive it through courses. Though the recent establishment of the nonprofit Center for Holistic Resource Management (with a teaching staff) has expanded the offerings, many farmers and ranchers could never attend, either because of the expense or the time away from home. Many professionals could never attend more than one introductory course, because superiors felt one exposure, to what they termed the "new grazing system from Africa," sufficed. Perhaps this book will at last begin to fill the void of written material that has hindered people who wish to keep learning on their own.

The issues touch all kinds of people—doctors, farmers, tribespeople, politicians, artists, writers, actors, engineers, wildlifers, waiters, teachers, soldiers, preachers, industrialists, and so on endlessly. Because we and our planet are one whole, no one can succeed in the very long run unless we all do. On the other hand, most of us need to understand the concept of Holistic Resource Management only in its broadest terms. The practical application can get quite technical, but only those involved in actual land management need the greater detail. Therefore, this book has been split into two parts. This first part should satisfy the general reader's curiosity. Those practicing on farms, ranches, or in national parks, or teaching at schools and universities, will also need the companion volume, the Workbook.

I have done my best to keep this volume readable in the hope that it will hold the attention of those who most need to grasp the concept—politicians, economists, industrialists, and businesspeople. These individuals, because they control or influence government processes and the wealth of nations, control our fate. If this book is treated as only of importance to land managers, then nations will continue with crisis management of resources. Never have humans needed collaboration more than now—not only among nations but between the rural and urban societies that populate each nation.

Perhaps more than any other group I have written this book with young people in mind. The future is theirs, and our planet's fate depends upon them. When I graduated from university we had the will but not the tools. Now, if they have the will, Holistic Resource Management will indicate the best tools at any time and guide the process to success.

I would urge that you read the book once through lightly and quickly. Try to get the big picture—see the forest, not the trees. If you constantly try to relate the contents to what you already know you are likely to miss the concept. Remember, what you do not know never blocks learning, only what you already know. After a first reading, if you are one who has to actually apply holistic management then by all means read again as many times as you need, looking into every detail. Even if you have to read the book critically as a fellow scientist, my suggestion still applies—a light reading to get the picture, followed by all the critical reading you like.

Holistic Resource Management has been looked at very critically by many people. Over two thousand professional and practical resource managers have attended HRM courses over the last eight years, and all have been invited to point out any faults they could find, whether based on research, logic, or practical experience. While no glaring faults have come to light yet, many refinements have been made and the HRM model is much clearer and more easily used today because of these refinements. I will always continue to welcome criticism. In fact, I expect it to greatly modify future editions of this book. Nothing in this approach is defended by me except its simplicity.

Allan Savory
Albuquerque, New Mexico
April 1988

Acknowledgments

Anything we do in science is built on the work of thousands who have gone before us. Both from their successes and their failures we learn and thus advance. I am deeply indebted to the many who have struggled to find better ways for us to live in harmony with each other and our environment, and upon whose work I have built.

From the time I departed from the conventional thinking of my training I have been supported and helped by many people, and I welcome this opportunity to thank them. Unfortunately, the two who did the most are now deceased—Mike Fairlamb and Robbie Robertson. From the early days, when opposition to my ideas was most intense and often vicious, they remained steadfast in their support. This was not easy to give in Zimbabwe—a country ripped apart by a prolonged and bitter civil war in which I was leading one of the opposition parties. Without their open-mindedness, their concern for the nation's future, and their moral courage we would never have succeeded in finding a better way.

I would also like to thank the many farmers and ranchers scattered over five countries who loved their land and were prepared to work with me in the search for answers in those early years: in particular, Evelyn Rushmore, Bob Rutherford, Pat Bashford, Jim Sinclair, the people of Lebowa, Malcolm and Wendy Kroon, and Mike Gawler and the staff of the Liebig's Company in Zimbabwe and Paraguay.

Upon coming to America, I was greatly indebted to those first ranchers who were willing to implement the new ideas, despite considerable criticism: Charles Probandt, the Spurlock family, Earl McElroy, Mike Harrison, Mark Barrett and his staff, and soon many others.

I have also been given incredible support by a number of people in government service, in particular Don Sylvester (Soil Conservation Service),

Darrol Harrison (U.S. Forest Service), Jim Matthews and Steve Berlinger (U.S. Fish & Wildlife Service) in America; and Bob Vaughan-Evans (Agritex) in Zimbabwe.

Since forming the Center for Holistic Resource Management in 1984, I have been indebted to all of our field staff—Kirk Gadzia, Tommie Martin, Roland Kroos, Naseem Rakha, Champe Green, and Ron Moll—who have taught me so much. And without our Canadian colleague, Don Green, who has committed himself so fully to working with us on the vital human aspects of holistic management, we would not be where we are today.

This book could not have been written without the editing skills of Jody Butterfield and Sam Bingham. They have put in long hours taking my work apart, forcing me to explain more clearly and simply, and then helping me put it back together again. I could not have asked for a better team.

And lastly, I would like to thank the 777 Fund of the Tides Foundation for their support during the writing of this book, and Chuck Savitt and Barbara Dean of Island Press for their encouragement and guidance.

To Jim, Megan, Rodger, Claire, and Sarah

We lost much quality time together,
but I tried to leave you a better world

HOLISTIC RESOURCE MANAGEMENT

PART I

Introduction

1

What Is Holistic
Resource Management?

Once, while flying from Rhodesia (as my country Zimbabwe was called then) to Paraguay on a consulting assignment I was stranded for a day in Mexico City. Also stranded by the same plane holdup was a Brazilian civil engineer, and we got to talking. When I told him I specialized in resource management, he asked me what that meant. I explained that for thousands of years the productive capacity of our environment had generally deteriorated under the management of man, and no one had found a way to stop it. However, I believed I was onto a solution at last. He then said, "It must be very simple."

"Why do you say that?" I asked in some surprise.

"Because whenever there has been a major insoluble problem for mankind, the answer, when finally found, has always been very simple."

That unknown man's remark clung to me through the subsequent years as the work on this problem of environmental deterioration continued through a great many obstacles and setbacks. Time and again he proved right and now that we have finally reached the point where this book can be written, I think you will agree that the solution we've found is in fact very simple indeed.

It involves no snap judgments or any specialized knowledge, but rather the use of a "thought model" to aid our fairly simple human minds in seeing the effects of our actions on the complex processes operating in our ecosystem.

Time and again our best efforts to improve Nature have foundered on some factor we failed to consider. Perhaps it was a lack of money, or an infringement on local customs, or even some basic natural phenomenon that we did not cater for in our schemes. History shows, if anything, that any attempt to "manage" natural resources, given the complexity of our ecosystem, must consider the entire system or assume a high risk of breakdown in the long run. Nothing less than a full treatment, which includes human, biological, and financial resources, will succeed. Holistic Resource Management (HRM) provides us with a way to manage for the whole of our resources.

The HRM model (figure 1-1) can serve in the management of a national park or a national economy, a ranch or farm, or a city's water supply. It also can be used to assess resource management policies, diagnose resource management problems, and orient research toward previously unseen needs. Although it was developed in use with terrestrial resources—the land and its soil and water base—other than realizing that what we do to the land affects the oceans, we have not yet applied the model to ocean management.

The model requires the user to define a three-part goal: a *quality of life* statement; a form of *production*, which is expressed in either economic, social, cultural, aesthetic, or recreational terms; and a *landscape description* that will ensure that the goal, once reached, can be maintained indefinitely.

It will take several chapters to develop the logic of defining a goal in this way. Suffice it to say here that, however obvious it may seem on reflection, in practice the lack of a clear goal characterizes many problems of our technological age. All too often we justify drastic actions solely on the grounds that they are "technically feasible" and thus the means of attaining a goal becomes the goal itself.

When Einstein was asked, "What hopes and fears does the scientific method offer for mankind?" he answered:

I do not think that this is the right way to put the question. Whatever this tool in the hands of men will produce depends entirely on the nature of the goals alive in this mankind. Once these goals exist, the scientific method furnishes means to realize them. Yet it cannot furnish the very goals. The scientific method itself would not have led anywhere, it would not even have been born without a passionate striving for clear understanding. *Perfection of means and confusion of goals seem, in my opinion, to characterize our age.* If we desire sincerely and passionately the safety, the welfare, and the free development of the talents of all men, we shall not be in want to the means to approach such a state. Even if only a small part of mankind strives for such goals, their superiority will prove itself in the long run.[1] [emphasis added]

So also the ideas underlying holistic resource management only assume meaning and power in relationship to definite goals.

Achieving any goal of course implies a process of planning and implementation. But whenever complex interrelationships and unforeseen circumstances lie ahead, the word "plan" must become a twenty-four-letter word: *plan-monitor-control-replan.* All hope of reaching any goal without great

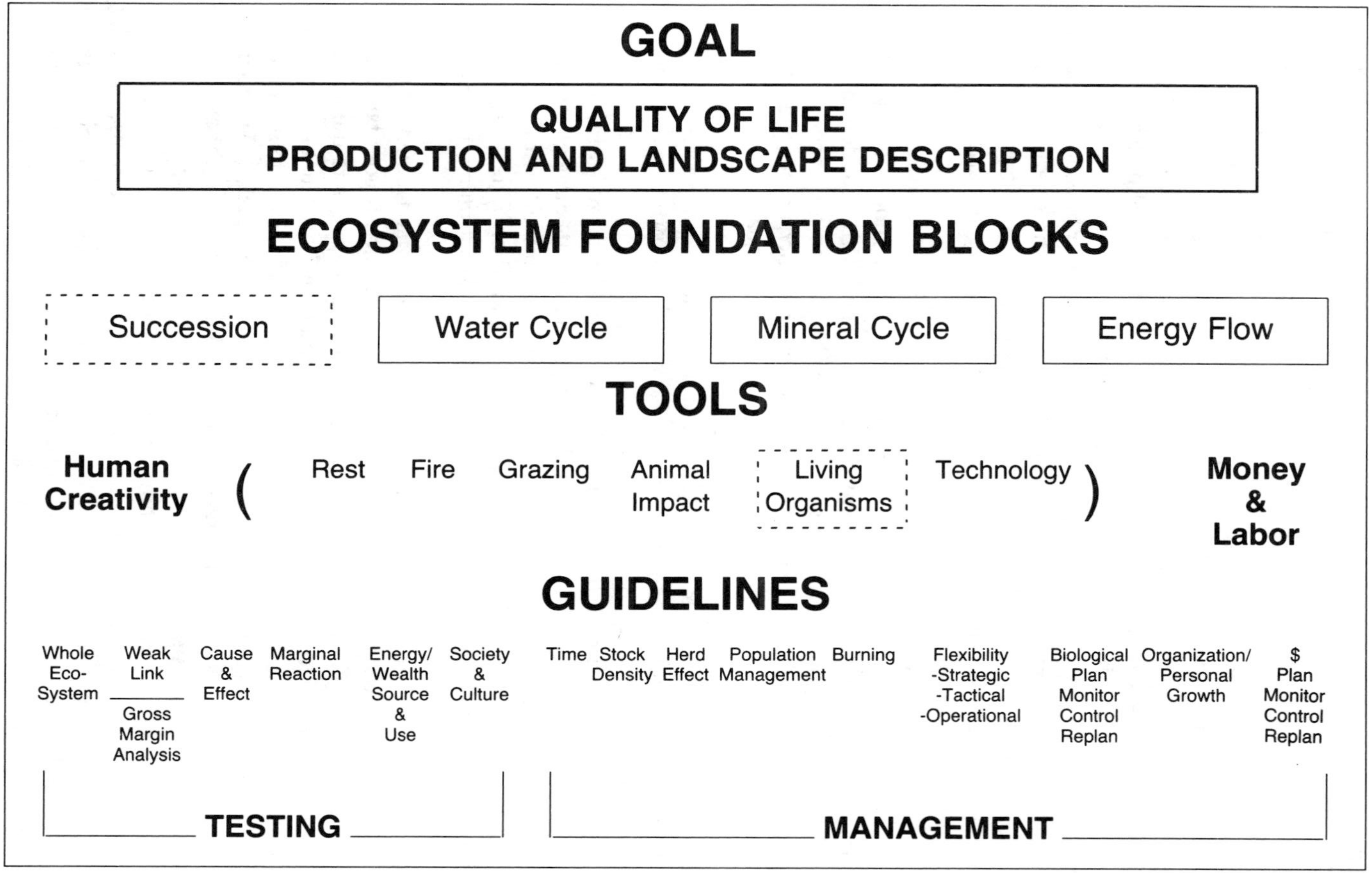

Figure 1-1. Holistic resource management model.

deviation or waste depends on this process: Once a *plan* is made it is then *monitored*. If there is any deviation from the planned route then *control* is instituted and the deviation is brought back to plan. Occasionally events go beyond our control (i.e., natural disasters such as earthquakes, hurricanes, fires) and there is a need to *replan*.

Let me illustrate this with a simple analogy. My goal is to visit a friend who lives in a house at the top of a hill. My *plan* is to use my car to get there. I start the car and move off, but clearly I have no hope of achieving my goal unless I do something more than just drive. I am going to leave the road at the first bend unless I *monitor* the road as far ahead of me as possible. Then I am going to have to *control* by turning the steering wheel in order to stay on the road. Now if all goes well and there are no earthquakes or flash floods, or my car does not break down and my monitoring and control are adequate, I will get to the house.

In real life, however, things seldom go so smoothly. I may not monitor well because I am watching the scenery and my mind wanders. I may not control well because when I stop my daydreaming and with a sudden fright realize I'm going off the road, I turn back too sharply and go off the other side. If anything does cause me to break down, hit the ditch at the roadside, or whatever, I have to *replan* to ensure that I still reach my goal. In replanning I will always be working with a changed set of resources—my car has broken down and I am now on foot, for example. I now plan to walk to the house on the hill but I still have to monitor the road ahead and turn to keep on it, and so on.

Having articulated a three-part goal and accepted the process of planning, monitoring, controlling, and replanning to achieve it, three questions nevertheless remain. What raw material do we have to work with? What tools can we use? How do we know which to use and when? The next three lines of the model—*ecosystem foundation blocks, tools,* and *guidelines*—deal with these matters.

One would suppose that the raw material in land management is the land itself, including the plants, animals, and soil. In fact, it goes beyond this to the principles and processes that govern what happens to the land. These are categorized in the four Ecosystem Foundation Blocks in the model. All goals for all land must be built upon and sustained by the foundation of the ecosystem, and there is only one ecosystem on this planet. The four foundation blocks described here exist only as four interdependent aspects of a single thing, as symbolized by the tetrahedron in figure 1-2.

Everything that happens within our ecosystem can be described in terms of *succession, water cycle, mineral* (or nutrient) *cycle,* and *energy flow.* Subsequent chapters will elaborate on each of these fundamental processes. At this stage it is enough to know that they exist and that years of research and observation have discovered much about them.

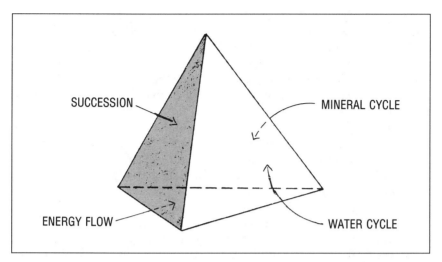

Figure 1-2.   Our ecosystem viewed as four processes.

In any living community we manage, water will cycle. We will try to ensure that the water cycle operates in a way that will produce and sustain our goal. Since almost all life forms that our goal is likely to depend upon will require water from the soil, we must ensure that water is in fact adequately present in usable form. A water cycle characterized by flood-causing run-off or excessive evaporation on the one hand, or bogs (unless cranberries are the goal) on the other, usually subverts our goals.

Similarly, the community always has a mineral cycle functioning at some level. Again, the life forms that our goal depends upon will require mineral nutrients from the soil and air, and to maintain them we must ensure that those nutrients cycle appropriately.

All living communities, together with their micro- and macroenvironment, undergo continuous orderly change as they advance from simplicity to complexity. This is called succession. Any goal will require a certain level of complexity in the communities being managed. We must manage so that the desired levels become self-sustaining. If we do not, we inevitably fall into the common pattern of relying on ever more powerful, and more expensive, technology to subdue ever recurring problems: on our rangelands the encroachment of noxious plants, grasshopper and caterpillar plagues; on our farms, insect and weed invasions; on our watersheds, increasing frequency and severity of floods and droughts—all manifestions of an impaired successional process, which we have tried, unsuccessfully, to control by direct technological intervention. *A true solution must modify the process itself, not merely attack the symptom.*

Last, self-sufficient life depends on the conversion of solar energy through green plants. For most of our goals we will want to convert as much energy as possible, both to produce the goal and to sustain it. Later chapters will emphasize the need to return to the understanding that solar energy is our most fundamental and sustainable basis of wealth. This concept was once obvious to people who lived directly from the land, but now it is largely ignored by societies grown dependent on the same solar energy entombed in oil sands and coal seams.

Our current way of life in America is not sustainable, even though we are the most technologically advanced civilization the world has ever known, because it demands an energy flow that cannot be sustained in its present form and which is damaging our planet. Because of heavy use of machinery, fertilizer, and chemicals, we consume about 9.8 calories of petrochemical energy to produce one calorie of sunlight energy in the form of food.[2] While machinery and an infusion of petrochemicals may push yields higher, they simultaneously so distort successional communities, mineral cycles, and water cycles that costs of production steadily rise with increasing unsustainability. While presuming to feed the world, America in fact bleeds it in a way that cannot go on forever.

By now you should be able to picture the goal, the planning process, and the fact that we must reach and maintain the goal on the basis of the four ecosystem processes. *It can have no other foundation.*

The tools available to achieve this *are also limited in number.* The next row in the model lists them all. In brackets between *human creativity* and *money & labor* are the words *rest, fire, grazing, animal impact, living organisms,* and *technology.* Whatever tool or combination of tools we set to work through our brains, brawn, or capital will work changes on the ecosystem as a whole, but those changes can be easier expressed, and monitored, when analyzed in terms of the four ecosystem foundation blocks.

Typically, we want to alter successional complexity and stability. We may wish to change the effectiveness of water or mineral cycles, increase or decrease energy flow. The essence of *holism,* however, is that changes in one ecosystem block affect them all. To forget that fact is to ignore the curves in the road that we must constantly monitor and correct for.

The tool line of the model has particular power because the categories embrace *all known tools available to humans in any conceivable resource management situation,* including the three broad areas that concern us most—human, biological, and financial resources. That allows us to weigh options without fear of overlooking any. In any situation we can:

- Think through which tools to bring to bear on the ecosystem processes en route to our goals, and by monitoring our progress analyze the effectiveness of each.

- Analyze past failures, including those of civilizations long gone, because all of the tools available in earlier times are included in the model.
- Use the model in a policy analysis mode and a diagnostic mode. Since any policy suggested by any country, institute, agency, or individual must involve one or more of the tools, we can assess the ecosystem processes where the policy is to be applied and deduce what is likely to happen. On a worldwide scale, the savings in avoiding doomed experiments and not sending good money after bad would amount to billions annually.
- Determine, knowing our goal and what we want the tools to achieve, where we most urgently require research, and thus use the model in a research orientation mode. Such research combined with experience and observation has already produced the *guidelines* at the bottom of the model, and it is here that the greatest changes and improvements will continue to appear.

We developed the model as a result of our search for a simple way to successfully manage a complex subject—our ecosystem. We started by gaining knowledge of what each tool *tended* to do. But how can anyone analyze the impact of a single *tendency* when many other processes and other tools may be at work at the same time? Where a cow places her hoof today begins a chain of reactions that ensures that that spot will never be exactly the same again. Because of the complex of always occurring interconnected changes, we easily could conclude that the situation lay beyond our control.

Our solution to this problem rests on the hypothesis that the tendencies of the tools, when chosen and applied according to specific guidelines, function in the ecosystem like the ripple patterns of pebbles thrown into a still pool.

It is a fact of physics that even though multiple ripples appear to create disorganized chaos on the pool's surface, the orderly ripples produced by pebbles thrown individually still exist. Each pebble does in fact impart a predictable "tendency" to the whole.

If we throw in two pebbles of very different sizes, we can see what each one's ripples tend to do and how one may overcome the other while the lesser one's ripples still have a visible effect.

As we use each of the tools, either singly or in combination, we think of them like those pebbles and ask ourselves, "Will it, when applied according to certain guidelines, start a ripple that pushes the successional process toward more complexity? How will its ripples tend to change water and mineral cycles and energy flow?"

Though there may be countervailing ripples that diminish and partially obscure the force of the ones we start, it is unlikely that the power of two ripples moving in the same general direction will combine into an entirely new and opposite force.

If our monitoring indicates that we are on track, we will continue to apply tools in the same way. If it shows deviation from the desired path, then we will have to start ripples in a new direction by applying that tool differently or applying a different tool altogether.

The guidelines as stated in the model require a good deal of elaboration before you can use them. Let it suffice here to say they will allow you to focus and control the application of the various tools in order to produce certain predictable ripples.

The tool of technology presents a particular challenge in that regard. Today we can do so many powerful things to intervene directly in the ecosystem processes that we tend not to wait for the tendency of some slower tool to have the desired effect. This has led mankind to rush in where angels fear to tread. Unfortunately when we do take direct action on any one of the processes—by applying soluble, inorganic fertilizers, clearing brush with chemicals, spraying insects, building check dams, ripping soil, or a host of other technological interventions—we often ignore the interdependence of the whole and produce more and different problems, which we again attack with another "technological solution." Inevitably this leads to the crisis management of resources that characterizes our present age.

And yet, though technology has often generated greater problems and costs, it is still a powerful tool. When a technological solution can pass what we call the testing guidelines, we should use it. To pass them it must benefit the whole ecosystem, be socially and culturally acceptable, strengthen the weakest link in the situation under management, address the cause and not the symptom of the problem, be economically sound, and reflect wise use of wealth and energy.

To summarize now how the whole HRM model is used, suppose that my goal is to build a house designed for my family that will stand forever. I have four sources of material for my foundation, in this case the four ecosystem foundation blocks. I will use all the tools at my disposal and enlist all my ingenuity and brainpower to make efficient use of labor and capital. Not being entirely familiar with all my tools, however, I turn to my instruction books—the guidelines—to learn how to use them and what they will do to my building materials. The technological tool can produce spectacular immediate results, but could have dangerous long-term effects on the building materials themselves. The guidelines help me check this out.

I work to a plan applying the tools assessed best and monitoring my progress to stay on track. When events demand it, I replan, changing the way I'm applying the tools or using different ones—whatever it takes to finish the building and achieve my goal.

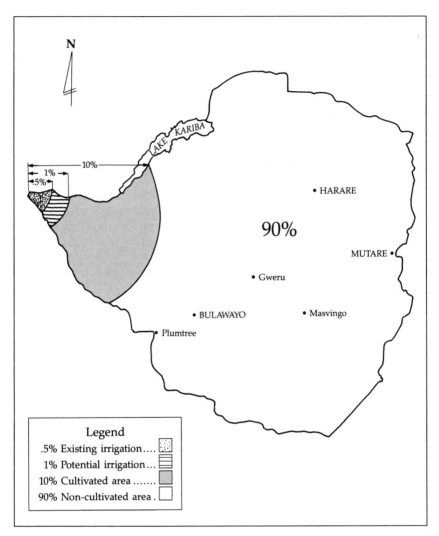

Figure 2-1. Zimbabwe: Relationship of cultivated to noncultivated land as well as existing and potential irrigation.

Too often governments perform like a team of blinkered horses all pulling in different directions, but you are forbidden by the system to remove the blinkers and get them pulling together.

Only in their mechanisms for control of finances and budgets do most governments even come close to some form of coordination. Here the economists, accountants, statisticians, and lobbyists have their day. Yet again we find narrow training, narrow reading (usually), and a tremendous focus on money, a symbol, rather than on productivity of resources, which is true wealth.

It remains to be seen what new forms of government and administration we can develop to overcome the weaknesses of compartmentalized government, but the challenge is not limited to people concerned with poor countries in deteriorating environments. The United States, blessed as it is with fertile land and a stable climate, is mismanaging its resources as thoroughly as any other country. Most of our western watersheds are desertifying—we have had dust bowls and will have them again. We are experiencing rural depression generally and its attendant urban drift. We have become painfully dependent on expensive petrochemical agriculture, and we have sacrificed much of our best land to helter-skelter development.

In all of these areas an understanding of the HRM model points toward comprehensive solutions, but only when they become the stock in trade of politicians and economists will we see real progress.

PART II

The Missing Keys

3

Introduction

If the holistic resource management model is so simple, why has it taken mankind so long to figure it out? And once discovered, why has it provoked such controversy and determined resistance by so many people?

One could draw parallels to Copernicus, Galileo, and others and have faith that one day the world will accept new knowledge readily. The fact is that although we would like to believe otherwise, even as trained scientists people still approach new knowledge in much the same way they did in Galileo's time.

The eminent British scientist W. I. Beveridge, in his book, *The Art of Scientific Investigation*, devotes a full chapter to the problem, which he states thus:

> In nearly all matters, the human mind has a strong tendency to judge in the light of its own experience, knowledge and prejudices rather than on the evidence presented. Thus, new ideas are judged in the light of prevailing beliefs. If the ideas are too revolutionary, that is to say, if they depart too far from the reigning theories and cannot be fitted into the current body of knowledge, they will not be acceptable. When discoveries are made before their time they are almost certain to be ignored or meet with opposition that is too strong to be overcome, so in most instances they may as well not have been made.[1]

Mankind still has great difficulty grasping anything but small shifts in thinking. When a new idea goes against deeply held beliefs—what people *know* rather than what people *think*—a fierce battle ensues.

When it came to understanding the causes of our ecosystem's deterioration, scientists already *knew* the answer. Their assurance that enough money and technology would put things right differed not at all from the conviction of Renaissance theologians that God caused the sun to circle the earth and not vice versa.

With the benefit of hindsight we can easily see what smaller revelations had to occur before people accepted Copernicus's theory. After people became truly comfortable with the notion of a round earth, the theory of gravity, certain advances in mathematics, and the moons of Jupiter, the movement of the planets became a simple matter too. In the meantime a number of people went to the stake.

Four such bottlenecks of understanding impeded the development of the HRM model and still impede its acceptance. That their revelation has come so late and so painfully rests on the fact that though they are each rather simple to grasp, they only become obvious when taken all together. Thus it has been difficult to discover or prove any one of them in isolation according to scientific method without accepting the others.

I call these four somewhat revolutionary insights the four missing keys. They have all been discovered separately over the last sixty years, but were ignored, forgotten, or bitterly opposed because they represented new knowledge that went contrary to the beliefs held by most people at the time they were discovered.

Earlier peoples had expressed odd flashes of insight into the principles involved, but because they were "primitive" or peasant people their opinions were discounted by the scientific community.

It has taken the last twenty-five years to discover their actual significance and to put them together successfully. We had to understand their connection to the problem of environmental deterioration and to each other in order to move forward.

The next four chapters will introduce these four missing keys one at a time, but an understanding of all four is essential to understanding the causes of the massive environmental deterioration we see today. No doubt other keys await discovery, but at this stage we know that these four represent a major advance.

The first of these discoveries—that management of resources to be successful had to be holistic—defined a need for a form of resource management modeling. The HRM model is our attempt to meet this need and it has been successful to the extent that we are able to predict results with a high degree of certainty. In short, we finally know enough to start reversing the deterioration of our ecosystem as fast as people can be trained and the new knowledge applied.

4

Management Must
Be Holistic

Of the four missing keys, the discovery that holism is *essential* in resource management is the most vital. Unfortunately it is also the most difficult to understand and more difficult still to bring to bear in actual practice. Nevertheless, we now realize that no whole, be it a family, a tribe, a ranch, a farm, a nation's economy, or any other set of resources, can be managed without looking inward to the lesser wholes that combine to form it, and *outward to the greater wholes of which it is a member.*

The concept of holism at first strikes most people as a bit too ethereal to have much use. The farmer plows out a new wheat field. The rancher clears brush. The forester sprays bark beetles. The engineer designs a dam. The economist advises a government. They put the utmost concentration and energy into their chosen tasks, never reflecting that they work within a greater whole, which their actions will affect, slowly, cumulatively, and often dramatically. In our culture, only philosophers raise this issue, because our habit of thought makes it hard to see how individuals caught up in daily life can take responsibility for the consequences; but they can. We can.

The need for a new approach to the challenge of making a living without destroying our environment goes back to prehistoric times. Paleolithic populations had no cause to reflect on such matters as long as their technology did not surpass that of other animals that used stones to break eggs and shellfish. At that early level people could not distort natural succession enough to upset ecological harmony much at all, but even down to the recent, most glorious instant of our scientific progress, the sheer bounty of our resources has allowed us to keep the old caveman attitude to any challenge:

If you have a problem, get a rock and smash it, and Nature will take care of itself.

Our scientific knowledge and the technological power to do this now soars up the steep part of an exponential curve even as the health of our natural resources has entered a breathtaking decline (figure 4-1). The symmetry of the two curves is no coincidence. Though some would argue instead that population growth, similarly exponential, accounts for the resource decline, the case of the United States disproves this. America's technology sets the pace for the rest of the world, yet millions of acres, in areas where her population has always been lowest and is declining, are desertifying at a rate that is comparable to anything I have experienced in Africa.

Figure 4-2 illustrates the same paradox another way. The first column shows areas of technological success, while the second shows areas of failure (although a few might contain apparent short-term successes). It takes no special insight to generalize about these two realms of endeavor. Every item on the left is of a "mechanical" nature in a world of human making and with clear definition. Each one on the right involves the nonmechanical world of complex relationships and wholes with diffuse boundaries. One might thus easily suspect that a deeper analysis of this difference might provide a key to understanding our failures.

The modern scientific approach to the areas in both columns goes back to the thirteenth-century work of Roger Bacon, who first distinguished experimental science from the unqualified belief in scripture and tradition. This idea developed into the formal scientific method wherein one seeks to test a hypothesis by controlling all variables of a phenomenon and manipulating them one at a time.

By the seventeenth century, scientists began to view the whole world

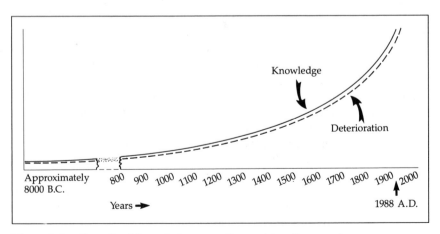

Figure 4-1. Growth of knowledge over the past ten thousand years.

Mechanical	Nonmechanical
Development of:	*Management of:*
Transport	Agriculture
—air	Rangelands
—land	Forests
—water	Air Quality
Communication	Fisheries
—radio	Water Supplies & Quality
—television	Erosion
—telephone	Economies
—satellite	Wildlife (including insects)
Weapons	Human Relationships
—conventional	Human Health
—nuclear	**EVER INCREASING PROBLEMS**
—laser	**TESTIFYING TO OUR LACK**
Space Exploration	**OF UNDERSTANDING.**
Computer Technology	
—artificial intelligence	
—robotics	
Home Building & Home	
Appliance Technology	
Energy Plants	
—nuclear	
—hydroelectric	
—etc.	
Medical Technology	
—brain scanners	
—eyeglasses/contact lenses	
—medicines	
—etc.	
Genetic Engineering	
Chemical Technology	
—soluble fertilizers	
EVER INCREASING SUCCESS	
TESTIFYING TO THE MARVELS	
OF SCIENCE.	

Figure 4-2 Human endeavors.

as a machine made up of parts that could be isolated and studied by the scientific method, and their success in areas that are in fact mechanical seemed to confirm this as fundamental truth.

Our subsequent optimism notwithstanding, in studying our ecosystem and the many creatures inhabiting it, we cannot meaningfully isolate anything, let alone control the variables. The earth's atmosphere; its plant, animal, and human inhabitants; its oceans, plains, and forests; its ecological stability; and its promise for mankind can only be grasped by observing the dynamic interrelationships that constitute its being. Isolate any part, and neither what you have taken nor what you have left behind remains what it was when all was one.

The notion that all things are connected is as old as philosophy, but in the 1920s it was given a name, holism (from the Greek *holos*), and a theoretical base by the legendary South African statesman-scholar Jan Christian Smuts (1870–1950) (illustration 4-1).

In his book *Holism and Evolution*, Smuts challenged the old mechanical viewpoint of science and in particular the notion that there could be no more in an effect than there was in the cause of it. Smuts, like modern-day physicists, came to see that the world at bottom is not substance but flexible, changing patterns. "If you take patterns as the ultimate structure of the world, if it is arrangements and not stuff that make up the world," said Smuts, "the new concept leads you to the concept of wholes. Wholes have no stuff, they are arrangements. Science has come round to the view that the world consists of patterns, and I construe that to be that the world consists of wholes."[1]

According to Smuts, matter developed when whole atoms combined to form greater molecular wholes. Life and mind likewise developed as outgrowths of lesser wholes in a continuum from matter. Individual parts did not exist in Nature, only wholes, and these formed and shaped each other.

Smuts had been greatly stimulated by Darwin's work on evolution, but went beyond it. He replaced the mechanistic concept of natural selection with that of holism, which viewed change not as random or arbitrary or governed by material (mechanical) necessity, but as an ordered striving toward unity. Holism to him was the determining force of Nature, a coordinating principle of the universe evolving from within and extending through all its aspects. The new science of the day, ecology, was simply a recognition of the fact that all organisms feel the force and molding effect of the environment as a whole. Each organism, in turn, is fundamentally a society in which innumerable members (i.e., cells) combine in mutual help, service, and loyalty to each other.

To Smuts, the connections between matter, life, and mind were ever present. "We are indeed one with Nature," he wrote. "Her genetic fibers run through all our being; our physical organs connect us with millions of

Illustration 4-1. Jan Christian Smuts. (Courtesy *The Star*, Johannesburg)

years of her history; our minds are full of immemorial paths of pre-human experience."[2]

Though Smuts's philosophy does hold the key to success in the areas where strictly experimental science and its attendant mechanical management have failed, I did not recognize how profoundly until quite recently. Like many young boys growing up in Africa during the Second World War, I idolized Smuts for his exploits as a field marshal in the Commonwealth forces; but his philosophy lay far beyond my grasp. Even though I used the word holism for years, I had to go through a long and intellectually unsophisticated school of hard knocks before I could even read his book, let alone understand holism well enough to put it to practical use. That experience is nevertheless probably worth relating for what it shows about the biases that must be overcome in our culture.

I received my scientific training in the conventional manner, which viewed events in isolation. My professors discouraged any attempt to combine what we learned in one discipline with what we covered in another, and the sanctity of research was held inviolate, even when it offended common sense.

Once a visiting lecturer from Cambridge informed us that research had shown no use for the flap of flesh behind a crocodile's ear, and that despite having the musculature to move the flap, the croc never did so. As I had kept a tame croc myself I knew I could make him move his ear flaps any day just by teasing him. When I ventured that crocs raised their flaps in response to a threat, the lecturer quickly put me down. I wasn't yet a "scientist." My observations just could not tip the scales against years of experiments in a controlled environment.

Small as this incident was, it fueled a growing disillusionment with the artificiality of any approach that isolated parts of Nature for study. The crocodile isolated from his environment was not the same animal.

Later, when I served as a research officer in both the Game and Tsetse Fly Control departments, the same kind of ambivalence led me to greatly disappoint my superiors. I never managed to set boundaries for any of the research projects I was expected to design. Common sense told me in each case that the very limitations that would make a research project acceptable scientifically also would make the results meaningless. The department of course needed research reports to justify its existence, but even under extreme pressure to do something, I could not commit myself to work that in my opinion could never lead to realistic answers to our management problems.

Later still as an advisor to private ranchers on land, livestock, and wildlife management, I encountered the same dilemma again, though in a form I did not recognize at first. They listened well to my opinion on techniques that would improve their land, but several, while making great progress toward that goal, still went bankrupt after committing scarce funds to dambuilding schemes. From my farming days I knew the risk of tying up capital in government incentive programs to build irrigation dams, as these ranchers had done, but as I was an ecologist, not a financial advisor, they ignored my friendly warnings.

That taught me that in order to help any rancher manage his land, livestock, and wildlife, I had to become involved in the financial planning to some extent. That involvement helped, but frequently other troubles cropped up that expertise in financial planning did not address. Otherwise sound operations could also fail by handling people badly or blundering along without long-range goals. This led me to add personnel management and organization to the specialties I studied.

By this time I was calling my work "holistic ranch management," but in reality it was anything but holistic. I still hadn't read Smuts and saw no need, assuming myself to have advanced beyond anything he might have written in 1926! I had a record of good results with land, wildlife, and livestock to support this opinion and had spent two five-year periods in partnership with consultants from whom I had learned much about the latest economic thinking. Nevertheless, I still got sporadic results and clearly something was missing.

Other scientists, encountering parallel frustrations, had also concluded that we often aggravated problems in resource management by approaching them from the perspective of narrow disciplines. No animal nutritionist, soil scientist, economist, or any other specialist alone had meaningful answers. Where I had accumulated knowledge in several fields and had teamed up with other experts, others also formed interdisciplinary teams of various kinds but fared no better.

Why these teams (my own included) did not work deserves a close look because many people still call their work holistic, as I once did myself, when clearly (or not so clearly) it was not. Their fundamental weakness was described in the book *Landscape Ecology* by Naveh and Lieberman (1983).

> In a computerized simulation game, Dorner (a researcher) asked 12 professionals from different relevant disciplines to propose an integrated development plan for the overall improvement of an imaginary African country, Tana. The results achieved were very disappointing: if these proposals were carried out they would worsen the lot of the people, destroy the agricultural-economic base, and create new, even more severe problems.[3]

My only criticism of this work was the need to invent an imaginary country. Tana could have been any one of my clients or any state in America or any developed country in the world using integrated planning teams. What the researcher Dorner simulated with a computer was what I had seen and experienced repeatedly in practice.

First of all specialists often communicate poorly, not only because they have different perspectives but also because they speak different languages. Often the same words in one jargon mean something else in another. Even where team members have training in several disciplines, as I myself did to some extent, the tendency is to simply swap hats and keep talking without ever being able to stand back and see the whole. In such cases, opinions acquire weight and conclusions are negotiated according to criteria that may have no relationship whatever to overall need.

I, however, did not see any of this until I undertook to explain my approach to resource management in training courses for professionals in the United States. It is a great credit to the openness of America that this happened, because my ideas departed radically from those given in the training most of these people had embraced for years. Nonetheless, the courses were very stressful events, and in struggling to teach what I knew of holism to an audience of very skeptical peers, I came to realize that I didn't understand it myself.

Finally, I read Smuts and realized wherein holism differed from everything prior in two important ways.

Since greater wholes have qualities and character not present in any of their constituent wholes (parts) *one must seek to understand the greater whole in order to understand its parts, not vice versa.*

The design in illustration 4-2 shows this well. Take a close look at it and think of it as depicting our ecosystem. This is the sort of confusing picture we saw when first trying to understand ourselves and our environment. According to scientific custom we isolated the individual squares for study, believing that if we could learn enough about each of them we would understand the whole. However, in the case of Nature, as in this pattern of squares, this leads nowhere.

Now stand well back from the pattern, squint your eyes so the squares blur into each other, and, as you now only see the interrelationships, the picture appears as a whole. It is a face, and a familiar one to most of us. If you had set out to somehow "manage" this design by paying attention only to the individual squares, anything you might have learned would have made you seem less than foolish, for no square has any meaning in isolation from all the rest.

Of course, once you see the whole in the pattern, detailed knowledge of the squares does become useful. You would need a great deal of such knowledge to reproduce, enlarge, preserve, market, or modify the work in any way, but only having first seen the whole could you even ask the right questions about the details.

I personally had tremendous difficulty in seeing why the fact that wholes have qualities not present in their parts causes the interdisciplinary approach to fail, until I actually could work it out with my own hands as a young child might.

I took four balls of kindergarten-type modeling clay in red, green, yellow, and blue, and began kneading them together until they slowly blended into a fifth color, grey. Mentally I let grey represent the world that we originally set out to understand. Close inspection of my grey ball revealed traces of the four colors I had begun with. So to understand this world of grey I would study the colors I knew to be some way involved in it, in much the same way our earliest scientists broke our natural world into what they

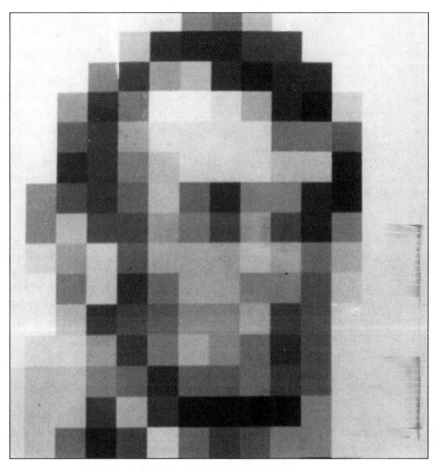

Illustration 4-2. Design (courtesy AT&T Bell Laboratories).

perceived as parts for study. Today we have thousands of disciplines but for simplicity I used four (represented by the four colors) to make my point, as shown in plate 1. Although a few hundred years of intense effort have greatly increased our knowledge of the four colors, we still have not studied grey. No matter how great our knowledge of any or all of the four colors, we could never understand (and thus manage) grey, as we had no knowledge of grey itself.

Next I pulled the four colors together as shown in plate 2 to represent a multidisciplinary team. Immediately I could see that the problem was a lack of knowledge of grey, not a lack of communication between disciplines as was previously thought.

Next I mixed (or integrated) the four colors until I had four balls, each of which contained equal divisions of green, red, yellow, and blue to represent interdisciplinary teams with knowledge of each color as illustrated in plate 3. Still no knowledge of grey! Now I could see why the interdisciplinary approach had to fail.

In practice all management decisions had to be made from the perspective of the whole under management. If we based our decisions on any other perspective, we could expect to experience results different from those intended because only the whole is reality. First, however, the whole had to be defined (bearing in mind that it always influenced, and was influenced by, a greater whole) and we had to know what we wanted to do with it (goals). Last, we needed a means of weighing up the many ramifications stemming from our actions. Because all of this was more than the human mind could handle unaided, the HRM model was developed. With it we can now take the perspective of the whole by reversing the arrows and weighing up management or policy decisions, as depicted in plate 4.

Management with the HRM model begins by defining the whole to be managed. But how does one define a whole, given Smuts's second major point that *wholes have no defined limits*? All wholes, he said, are made up of wholes and in turn make up yet greater wholes in a progression that extends from subatomic structures to the universe itself, and no whole stands on its own. To isolate a lesser whole by giving it a sharp and arbitrary definition such as farm, national economy, watershed, national park, tribe, etc. at once cripples the management of it. Although farms, economies, etc. indeed are wholes, they only exist in the context of other wholes, greater and smaller, and the boundaries are very fuzzy.

At this point a practical person might throw in the towel on holism as hopelessly academic. The idea of managing a whole that has no clear limits short of the edges of the universe is reminiscent of Archimedes's claim that he could move the earth if he only had a place to stand.

Fortunately in the case of resource management we do have a place to stand—the four ecosystem foundation blocks on the second line of the HRM model. They apply to all wholes, greater and smaller, so that any definition of an intermediate whole in terms of their condition will fit properly in the larger context.

This exercise of analyzing a piece of land or a country or some other whole in terms of mineral cycle, water cycle, succession, and energy flow will turn up in many contexts throughout the rest of this book. Most of us nevertheless need a down-to-earth example to make sense out of this notion. Here is one borrowed from a German writer named Heinrich von Kleist, who sometime in the early 1800s interviewed a famous puppeteer.

How, von Kleist wanted to know, can a normal person possibly manage the body and each individual limb of a marionette so that it moves harmoniously like a real person instead of like a robot? How does the puppeteer learn that when he moves the puppet's leg forward, he also has to tilt its head slightly, bend the torso, and shift both arms in opposite directions?

The puppeteer answered that von Kleist had not understood the actual challenge, which was both simpler and more elegant. Of course no human could produce natural gestures by pulling any number of individual strings. No matter how skilled the puppeteer, the result would still look mechanical. On the other hand a skillfully designed marionette had a center of gravity, and simply moving that would bring about all the other gestures automatically, just as a human, when taking a step, automatically moves all the other parts of his body in order to stay in balance.

In the matter of resource management, the ecosystem as defined by the four processes on the second line of the HRM model is the puppeteer's center of gravity. The manager who defines the whole within his realm of responsibility and formulates goals in terms of the four basic processes will automatically handle details properly in the context of greater and lesser wholes without having to worry over much about abstract philosophy.

The rest of this book and the companion workbook will deal with what this means in terms of what you will do after breakfast this morning. But before moving on, take a moment to reflect on the points made here and how they are built into the HRM model.

First, management must look outward from the standpoint of particular wholes and goals in order to see and understand the pattern and meaning of details. Approaching matters from the other direction, from the specialized study of the details in isolation (or as an interdisciplinary/integrated team), leads to confusion because the "parts" have no meaning except in relationship to the whole, which can never be seen from the perspective of the disciplines.

Second, to manage wholes at any level, we must define them in terms that relate our work properly to the greater and lesser wholes that make up our universe. This is possible because the basic principles that govern the ecosystem are universal and equally relevant at all levels.

The HRM model is simply a road map for putting these two points to work at the operational level. The last chapter mentioned holism in management as the first of four keys to effective resource management that led to the development of this model, and it is most manifest in the model's first two lines, goals and ecosystem foundation blocks. In a larger sense, however, the idea of holism accounts for the whole form of the model, why it consists of a few words on a page rather than a complicated computer program, and why only you can use it for the wholes you manage.

Powerful tools as they are in management for solving specific mechanical problems, computers cannot think holistically any better than the puppeteer could move his marionette more naturally with a hundred thousand strings. In particular they cannot evaluate emotions and human values, which are vital components of the whole. The human mind, by contrast, can see patterns and make decisions out of a deep, even unconscious sense of the whole, and given an awareness of the necessity and the mental crutch of a simple thought model, it can be brought about by the likes of you and me.

Because you are incorporated in the wholes you manage, only you and others directly involved in those wholes command the outward-looking perspective vital to your particular management needs.

Although still in the infancy of its development, the HRM model already enables us to look outward and choose from all the available knowledge and tools that which will promote our goals and ensure that the ecosystem can sustain them. It also lets us predict results ahead of time. After a little bit of training, almost anyone can use the model to solicit and direct the kind of advice specialists and interdisciplinary teams can constructively offer and judge when such advice does or does not serve the holistic view.

Frequently advice that appears perfectly sound from an economist's, agronomist's, engineer's, or any other's point of view proves unsound holistically in a particular situation at a particular time. This has spelled disaster, as Dorner's study predicted, for many a foreign aid project and national policy as well as family farms. As a culture we have acquired such an awe of experimental science that we have trained ourselves to simply phone any certified expert whenever adversity arises. Great difficulties lie ahead until a new generation can be trained to think holistically for itself and then weigh and select expertise that really fits the case.

The first section of this chapter distinguished between the list of mechanical problems that experimental science and management has handled well and those organic and multidimensional problems where it has failed. It is my belief that the unifying principles of the ecosystem that direct the model through the four ecosystem foundation blocks not only enable us to manage natural resources holistically but also carry beyond into economics, sociology, and politics to the extent that all those fields ultimately reflect the ecological vitality of our world.

It remains to be seen whether similar models might be found to enable us to tackle other such intractable questions as mass education, public health, and national rivalries. Surely, however, all must benefit from a clean, healthy, and productive environment.

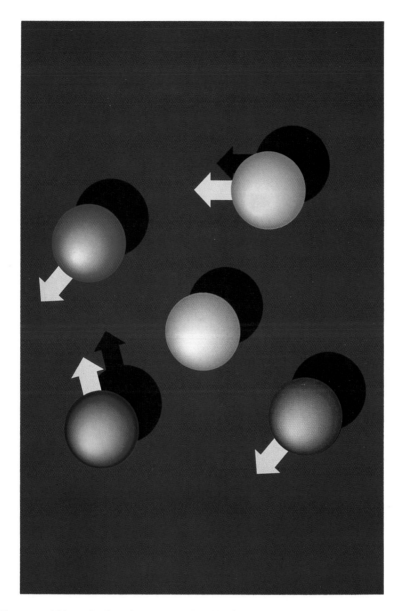

Plate 1. Although they have considerable knowledge of green, yellow, red, and blue, people in single, isolated disciplines are unable to manage gray (the "whole") of which they have no knowledge. Management is not even focused on gray, as the arrows indicate. This approach to management was generally recognized as a failure many years ago.

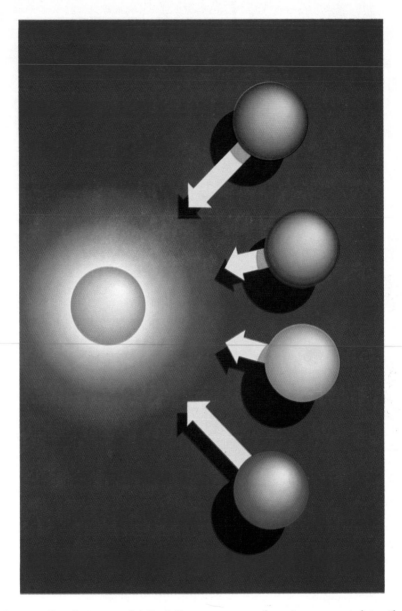

Plate 2. People in a multi-disciplinary team are focusing on gray from their perspective, as arrows indicate, but still with no knowledge of gray. Failures arising from this approach to management were attributed to poor communication owing to the jargon associated with the various disciplines, rather than a lack of knowledge.

Plate 3. To overcome communication problems, people trained in several disciplines form an interdisciplinary team which then focuses its attention on gray, as the arrows indicate. Knowledge of gray is still lacking, however. The failures arising from this approach to management have only recently been acknowledged.

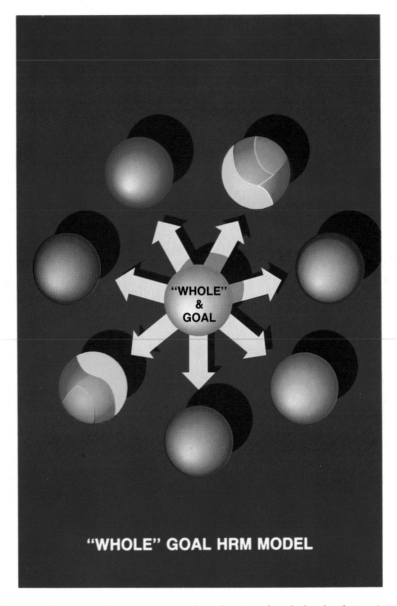

"WHOLE" GOAL HRM MODEL

Plate 4. The gray sphere represents the selection of a whole, the determination of the goal, and the application of the HRM model. Holistic management manages gray by looking outwardly from gray's perspectives at all available knowledge, as the arrows indicate. We now have knowledge of gray through selection of a management "whole" and the detailed formulation of a comprehensive goal in three parts combined with the use of a thought model to bring about that goal. Management now utilizes knowledge from all sources and disciplines.

5

Brittle and
Nonbrittle Environments

The next three keys helped to unravel the riddle of desertification, and are thus concerned mainly with the earth's vast and vital watersheds. Even if all croplands were managed on a sustainable basis today, they would still be vulnerable because in the end they are totally dependent on the health and stability of the watersheds surrounding them.

Generally stated, the second key is rejection of the comfortable belief that all environments in the ecosystem respond in the same manner to the same forces. They don't. The standard classifications of environments by vegetative features—desert, prairie, rain forest, etc.—accurately describe major variations within the ecosystem, as do climatic categories such as arid, semiarid, temperate, and so on. Nevertheless, new observations about such environments looking holistically at the question of why some environments desertify and others don't leads to a new way of classifying them.

More specifically then, the second key is the new principle that environments may be classified on a continuum from *brittle* to *nonbrittle*, according to the decay and successional processes present and the way they respond to certain forces. We have long recognized that some environments readily deteriorated under our agricultural practices. Herodotus, for example, described Libya in the fifth century B.C. as having deep, rich soils and an abundant supply of springs that provided a highly productive agricultural base for a large population. Today only desert remains. Those who chronicled this sort of deterioration believed that such regions were vulnerable to desertification because they were arid or semiarid.

The bulk of the world's arid and semiarid regions are in fact grasslands where livestock production has long been the chief occupation. When livestock management practices produce bare ground, a critical share of available moisture either evaporates or runs off. Springs dry up; silt chokes dams, rivers, and irrigation ditches; and less water remains for agriculture, industry, and people in nearby cities.

Going back even beyond Herodotus, common sense has always assumed that, once damaged, the best remedy for such land is to leave it undisturbed. But despite this wisdom and the fact that whole civilizations have been at stake, Libya and her neighbors have desertified anyway, as much of America is now doing.

The old assumption that rest will restore land damaged by grazing animals appears to satisfy the logic of cause and effect. Moreover, it does apply to the stable environments of northern Europe and the eastern United States, where modern agricultural science has its roots.

I worked under the old belief in my early game department days, but a unique experience led me to suspect a fundamental flaw in it. For many years, Zimbabwe had a practice of eradicating all game animals over vast areas in order to deny the tsetse fly a source of blood—its only source of nourishment. Once the tsetse fly was gone (and the fatal human and livestock diseases it carried), livestock could safely be introduced. As a research officer for both the Game Department and the Department of Tsetse Fly Control, I often worked in these areas.

I witnessed environmental damage I could not explain. The tsetse areas deteriorated seriously once the original game populations were decimated and the incidence of fires (to make the hunting easier) increased. On the other hand we *knew* that fire helped maintain grassland. The only other force we *knew* could cause such damage was overgrazing. However, neither game nor domestic animals were present. It was very puzzling.

Yet another experience added to the confusion. We had a massive build-up of animal numbers in a large game reserve known as the Tuli Circle, and as a result, thousands of animals starved to death. We all believed that with dramatically fewer animals living there the area would naturally recover, but it continued to deteriorate. Our scientists blamed drought, but in the year of worst so-called drought the records showed one of the best rainy seasons (in both total volume and distribution).

Another shock to my conviction that low rainfall and overgrazing inevitably produced desert came out of my first visit to northern Europe. There I saw areas that had as little as fifteen to twenty inches of rain per year that were not desertifying, despite hundreds of years of overgrazing and poor management. Areas in Africa that received as much as forty to fifty inches of rain annually, however, had desertified rapidly under the same practices. Even when we had greatly reduced the animal numbers in these areas, cleared the brush, and planted grass (at considerable expense) they continued to deteriorate. No matter how scientifically advanced we were, our knowledge still lacked a vital piece.

Finally in the vast and relatively unused lands of America I discovered what had eluded me in the highly populated and much used lands of Africa and in the different environments of Europe—that we had in fact two broad types of environment that had not been recognized. At their extremes, these react differently to management. Practices that benefited the one type of environment damaged the other. The names *brittle* and *nonbrittle* come from that insight.

No clear break exists between extremes of brittleness and nonbrittleness. On a scale that classifies true jungles as a one and true deserts as a ten, other environments fall on the scale somewhere in between, though a single vegetative category may cover a wide range of brittleness. Grasslands, for instance, may lie anywhere from one to nine or ten on the scale of brittleness. The degree of brittleness of a temperate forest could also be determined on this arbitrary scale.

Brittleness is not the same as fragility. Within many environmental classifications are areas that are very easily upset by a variety of forces and robust areas that withstand much more abuse. However, fragile areas may be nonbrittle (e.g., a delicate fern-dominated glade in a forest), and brittle areas may be nonfragile (e.g., the African savannahs and the American prairies).

Because the two extremes on our one-to-ten scale show such a clear correlation to total rainfall, it is easy to see in retrospect why we linked an environment's vulnerability to desertification to low rainfall. The degree of brittleness determines this, however, more than total precipitation. The closer we get to ten on the brittleness scale, even with high (thirty- to eighty-inch) rainfall, the faster the deterioration under modern agricultural practices. This is not to say that nonbrittle means nonvulnerable to deterioration, as the massive clearing of tropical rain forests makes clear.

The features that distinguish the two environments apparently derive not from total rainfall so much as from the distribution of precipitation and atmospheric humidity throughout the year. Brittle environments characteristically experience erratic distribution of moisture during the year. The pattern determines the degree of brittleness. A thirty- to fifty-inch rainfall area that typically has very dry periods in the middle of its growing season and a long dry season may be extremely brittle. Nonbrittle environments characteristically experience reliable moisture in the growing season. Even though total precipitation may seldom top twenty inches a year, during the remaining months of the year atmospheric humidity does not drop severely.

The distribution of the precipitation, as well as the elevation, temperature, and prevailing winds, clearly affects the day-to-day distribution of the atmospheric humidity and this links very closely to the degree of brittleness. The poorer the distribution of this humidity, particularly in the growing season, the more brittle the area tends to be, even though total rainfall may be high. Brittle environments commonly have a long period of nongrowth, which can be very arid.

The seasonal pattern of humidity appears to be the main factor in determining how quickly successional communities establish and maintain themselves on bare surfaces. It also largely dictates whether decay of old plant material will be biological, rapid, and taking place near ground level first—an essential trait of nonbrittle environments—or chemical (oxidation), physical (weathering), and slow and taking place from upper parts first, as it is in brittle environments.

As both the establishment, or reestablishment, of communities and the decay process are crucial to the health of the whole environment—soil, plant, and animal life, both above and below ground—determining the degree of brittleness becomes a prime factor in the management of any environment. Brittle and nonbrittle environments react very differently to many of the management tools we use daily, and yet we have generally treated them as though they reacted in exactly the same manner to all the tools we applied.

I could not have made this discovery had I not simultaneously arrived at the brink of articulating the other three missing keys. The full ramifications of the brittle/nonbrittle distinction do not become clear without them all.

At this point it suffices to say that the old belief that all land should be left undisturbed in order to reverse its deterioration has proven wrong. Only nonbrittle environments respond in this way. In brittle environments prolonged nondisturbance will lead to further deterioration and instability.

Once I had discovered the brittle and nonbrittle distinction and identified the charateristics, my puzzling observations of the past became clear. The Tuli Circle, where so much of the game had died off and where so much soil lay exposed, could not recover if left undisturbed because it was a brittle environment. It required some form of disturbance at the soil surface, similar to what the formerly large herds provided, in order to get more plants growing. In the tsetse fly areas I later realized that the increased use of fire had exposed soil, and though old grass plants remained healthy, nothing disturbed the soil sufficiently to allow establishment of new ones. Thus communities declined and soil became unstable.

Although it will not be fully understood until some of the following chapters have been covered, a look at figure 5-1 summarizes the differences in brittle and nonbrittle environments. At either end of the arbitrary one-to-ten scale the succession and decay processes are different in certain respects. Arising from this our actions tend to produce profoundly different effects on the land, depending where on the scale that land is. The items marked with an asterisk are standard management practice today and since over half of the earth's land surface leans toward the brittle end of the scale, it is no surprise that desertification is spreading at the rate it is.

All environments lie at some point along the scale of one to ten. The easiest way to determine where is to look at various sites and assess the decay process on old vegetation. At the nonbrittle extreme it is 100 percent

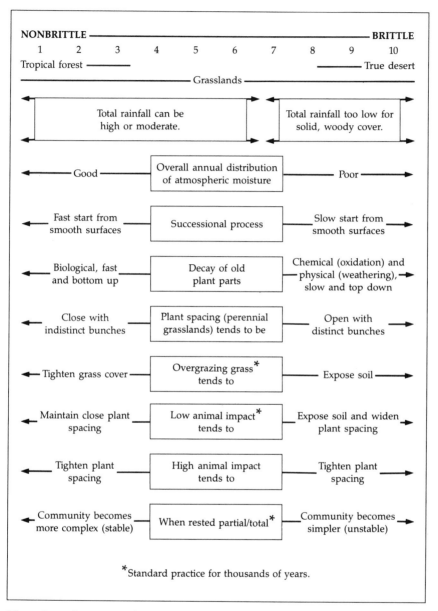

Figure 5-1. Summary of nonbrittle and brittle environments at the extreme ends of the spectrum.

biological. This decreases steadily as an environment moves toward brittleness when chemical and physical decay begins to appear and increases steadily with the degree of brittleness. It is the *net decay process* by year's end that should concern you. During the growing season in a high rainfall area of the tropics, decay might be predominantly biological. But in the long dry season that follows it is likely to be chemical and physical. In that case, the environment would lean toward the brittle end of the scale. Likewise, inspection of bare and smooth soil surfaces will indicate how the successional process progresses. If in a period of years such areas have not progressed beyond algae, lichens, and perhaps mosses, it suggests a degree of brittleness. Where lichens hang from trees and mosses grow freely on their trunks and branches, the environment is likely to be toward the nonbrittle end of the scale.

Taken by itself, the second key raises the practical question of how grazing animals might provide the disturbance necessary to the health of a brittle environment—without overgrazing it. This is crucial to watershed management throughout the world and fortunately the answer lies in the remaining two keys.

6

The Role of
Herding Animals and
Their Predators in
Brittle Environments

In my university training I learned, like all scientists of that era, that large animals such as domestic cattle could damage land. Only keeping numbers low and scattering stock widely would prevent the destructive trampling and intense grazing one could expect from livestock.

Once I left the university and went into the field as a biologist, my observations led me to question that dogma. I now defend the exact opposite conclusion. Relatively high numbers of heavy, herding animals, concentrated and moving as they naturally do in the presence of predators, support the health of the very lands we thought they destroyed.

This revelation came slowly and only after experience in a large variety of situations, because herding animals, like others, have more than one behavior pattern, and the effects on land are often delayed, subtle, and cumulative, not dramatic.

In the early years of Zimbabwe's tragic civil war I led a tracker unit and spent thousands of hours tracking people over all sorts of country, day after day. This discipline greatly sharpened my observational skills and also taught me much about the land in a context unencumbered by old prejudices about grazing herds. I doubt many scientists ever had such an opportunity for learning. I tracked people over game areas, tribal areas, European farms and ranches, and over all different soil and vegetation types in all rainfalls. Often I covered many different areas in a single day as I flew by helicopter from one trouble spot to the next. Everywhere I had to inspect plants and soils for the faintest sign of disturbance by people trying to leave no hint of their passage.

Gradually I realized that vast differences distinguished land where wildlife herded naturally, where people herded domestic stock, and where stock was fenced in by man and not herded at all. And compared to areas without any large animals (tsetse fly areas) the differences were startling indeed.

Most obvious was the fact that where animals were present, plants were green and growing. In areas without animals they were often grey and dying unless they had been burned (in which case the soil between plants was bare and eroding). When I compared areas heavily disturbed by animals (soil churned up and plants flattened), it became clear that the degree of disturbance had a proportionately positive impact on the health of plants and soils and thus the whole community.

I began to pay particular attention to the way animals behaved in different situations, as different patterns produced different effects. In tracking large buffalo herds, for instance, I noted that when feeding they tended to spread out, although not too far for fear of predation, and to walk gently and slowly. They placed their hooves beside coarse plants and not on top of them. They also placed their full weight on their hooves, compacting the soil below the surface but hardly disturbing the surface itself. While thus feeding they had remarkably little impact on the plants and the soil, other than the obvious removal of forage and the compaction.

Once feeding was over, however, and the herd began to move, or when predators threatened, the animals behaved differently. They suddenly bunched together and in their excitement kicked up quite a bit of dust. While bunched as a herd, each animal stepped recklessly, and even very coarse plants, containing much old material that would not be grazed, were trampled down. That provided cover for the soil surface. In addition, the trotting and galloping hooves left the soil chipped and broken as if a gardener had hoed it. Where the grazing herd had kept off the steep edges of gullies, it now beat down the edges to create a more gradual slope.

I became convinced that the disturbance created by the hooves of *herding* natural game populations was vital to the health of the land, and that mankind had lost this benefit when we domesticated cattle, horses, sheep, and goats and protected them from predators. Even where people herded livestock, as opposed to merely fencing them in, they did not behave as they would if naturally herding under threat of predation.

As the brittle environments evolved over millions of years, predators and their herding prey were the only things that could realistically have both created the necessary soil disturbance to provide a good seed bed for new plants and protected bare soil by trampling down old plant material. Both functions appear critical to the health of brittle environments, and indeed the world's large populations of herding animals appear to have evolved mainly in such areas.

My understanding of the tremendous significance of the herding animals to soils and plants itself evolved slowly. In Africa I dealt with large game herds and numerous predators. On more than one occasion I saw more than forty lions in a day's walk, which indicates the immense size of the herds that fed them. Not until I came to America, where predators no longer had significant impact on the wildlife population, did I realize how much they contributed to creating the kind of soil disturbance needed in brittle environments.

In America, massive destruction of predator populations and wild herds precipitated the decline in the environment we see today. We have only exacerbated it by spreading relatively few domestic animals over large areas. This explains why land deterioration has occurred more rapidly in America than in Africa.

In America the problem is compounded by the annual freezing and thawing, which creates air pockets in the soil. If the environment is brittle this means that not only must there be some agent of disturbance that will remove old oxidizing material from perennial grasses and chip soil surfaces, but that agent also has to provide soil compaction to increase grass seedling success.

I was not by any means the first to make the connection between the hooves of animals and the health of land. Many centuries ago Scottish shepherds referred to the "golden hooves" of sheep. The Navajo medicine men in America in the 1930s warned government officials who were drastically reducing their livestock numbers that a link existed between the hooves of the sheep and the health of the soil. In southern Africa the oldtimers of my childhood had a saying—"Hammer veld to sweeten it." They meant literally hammer the land with herds of livestock to improve forage quality. In the 1960s, André Voisin, a Frenchman who will figure in the next chapter, also mentioned often the connection between livestock and healthy plants and soil.

Unfortunately none of these earlier observations was fully understood because too many of us already *knew* that plants and soils needed protection from the damaging effects of animals. My own early observation of the vital relationship among natural herds, soils, and plants met violent rejection and ridicule from the international scientific community.

In the 1980s, thanks to some careful research done over a period of years on the herding wildlife populations in East Africa's brittle grasslands, a relationship between these animals and the plants they feed on was documented independently. Gradually scientists are becoming more comfortable with the idea. We hope further research will soon confirm beyond doubt the role of predators in the equation.

Acceptance of these insights will help reverse the millennia of damage mankind has inflicted on the land by trying to protect it from the effects of trampling that were perceived as evil. As bare ground increased and the environment deteriorated in response to the lack of *herd effect*, we attributed it to overgrazing, which we in turn blamed on too many animals. As a result, we decreased animal numbers and thus increased the bare ground and the deterioration.

That overgrazing is not in fact a function of animal numbers at all is the fourth missing key, as the next chapter will explain.

7

The Time Dimension in Soil, Plant, and Animal Relationships

In describing space, Einstein called time the fourth dimension, pointing out that where something is doesn't explain much unless you also know when it's there. This observation, so self-evident that every child can see it, opened the door to the theory of relativity and all that flowed from it.

The discovery of time as the fourth missing key to our understanding of ecological relationships did not come from the study of higher physics, but in retrospect it seems just as obvious as Einstein's fourth dimension. Its impact may also prove as revolutionary.

A fundamental belief, embraced throughout the world, holds that overgrazing, overtrampling, and the resultant destruction of land derives from the presence of too many animals. Despite massive and sophisticated research on plants, soils, and animals, virtually all land improvement schemes before now have rested on this very unsophisticated bit of common sense. They all include the recommendation to reduce animal numbers.

Until very recently no one truly explored the question of when animals are there as opposed to how many there are. My own experience illustrates how elusive an obvious principle can be.

As a child in Zimbabwe, I too learned of the destruction caused by too many animals when I accompanied my father into the native reserves. A civil engineer, he had the task of improving water distribution for the people and their stock. Overgrazing and overtrampling had devastated the areas surrounding the few existing water points, and the theory ran that creating more water points would scatter the stock and reduce the damage. The hot and dusty hours spent amid the rabble of cattle, goats, and donkeys on that barren land, together with what others told me, certainly convinced me that my father's work and the government policy that supported it made sense.

I did not question it for a decade or so, until as a young man I encountered historical records that showed what enormous herds of wild animals had existed on the land before man and his domestic stock replaced them. As pioneers made their way into the interior of South Africa they recorded herds of springbok (a pronghorn-sized antelope) so vast that when they migrated through settlements they trampled everything in their path, including yokes of oxen that couldn't be unhitched from wagons fast enough.

Such herds vastly outnumbered the cattle herds that came later and yet for millennia they had enjoyed an environment more abundant than anything the descendents of those pioneers can imagine. One sign of that former abundance is the names borne by villages and towns of today: Elands*fontein*, Spring*fontein*, and Buffels*fontein* from the Dutch word for fountain or spring. No hint of free-flowing water exists in those places today.

The weather, according to records, did not change, yet the "fountains" disappeared together with the healthy grasslands and the vast herds. As the memory of the wild herds also vanished, people blamed the disappearance of the water and the grasslands on the overgrazing and overtrampling of their own livestock, which were far fewer in number.

This riddle confused me, but I still could only conclude that overgrazing and overtrampling were related to animal numbers. The most obvious deterioration was occurring on the most heavily stocked tribal land and in certain national parks and game reserves where wildlife numbers were also high.

As a research officer in the Game Department I found myself recommending, despite my questions, a drastic culling of elephant and buffalo to arrest the damage. The decision was made in anguish because by this time I had already noted that removal of game (as in the tsetse fly areas) did not in fact bring improvement of the land. Overgrazing and overtrampling had to involve other factors besides mere numbers, but in the emergency I fell back on what I *knew*. Only later did I begin to penetrate the riddle.

I had observed that very large buffalo herds moved constantly and seldom occupied any area longer than two or three days, after which the land had an opportunity to recover. Could the time they stayed be an important factor? It also began to dawn on me that a lot of game confined to a small area—as happened in some of our newly forming game reserves surrounded by human settlement or tsetse fly areas—produced too many *herds* in too small an area. Though each herd moved frequently, plants and soil had little time to recover after being grazed or trampled. I did not yet see *time* as the crucial element, but I did realize that the reduced size of home ranges and territories on which the animals could move lay at the bottom of the problem.

I studied elephant herds. Did they shift location every few days? Did it matter? Did another herd move into areas only recently vacated? I decided to find out, but immediately struck an obstacle—I couldn't tell one herd from another. In those days before methods for marking animals were refined, I stalked unsuspecting elephants with homemade paint bombs, which I threw from close range. Such work, however, generated minimal enthusiasm among potential helpers, and I simply couldn't paint enough elephants single-handedly. I also lacked sufficient staff to conduct observations over enough area to support any conclusions.

For some time I had possessed a book entitled *Grass Productivity* by French researcher André Voisin. I had bought it because the title interested me, and I thought it might help clarify what was taking place in our wildlife areas. Voisin, however, had worked mainly on European cattle farms. After leafing through his book I could see no connection between dairy cows on lush French pastures and elephant and buffalo on dry African ranges. The book stayed unread on the shelf.

In the meantime I had begun, with some others, to promote what I called game ranching. If ranchers could substitute game for livestock, and if we could find ways to market the product effectively, perhaps we could save the game and the land. Ranchers would come to see wildlife as an asset (by custom they considered it vermin), and wildlife would not wreak nearly the damage of domestic stock, or so I thought.

Neither that idea nor the business of culling the buffalo and elephant proved very popular in the early '60s. I was forced out of my job by those not so subtle pressures bureaucracies apply to the dissenting. However, I turned to consulting as a livelihood and worked along similar lines with private landowners in Zimbabwe and other countries in southern Africa.

The many sophisticated schemes for preventing overgrazing on ranches always began by limiting livestock numbers. One of the most common sought to regulate numbers so that animals would not graze off more than half of certain "key indicator" plants in the community. Research indicated that many perennial grasses suffered from removal of more than 50 percent of their growing leaf area. If grazed beyond a certain point, the plant sacrificed root to provide energy for regrowth.

The theory, however, had to fail, as severe-grazing animals (both wild and domestic) don't bite off half the plants. Millions of years of evolution have given them jaw and teeth arrangements adapted to take significant mouthfuls. Fortunately the grasses, having sustained the same animals over the same eons of evolution, have developed growing points at their bases, out of harm's way.

As land continued to deteriorate under various attempts at take-half-leave-half management, government and research people began to doubt that the ranchers involved had tried seriously. Since my own clients were among them, I paid a visit to the research stations in Zimbabwe and South Africa where things were done "right" to learn what I could.

The research stations measured their success by the bulk of forage, the presence of a few species considered desirable, and the general appearance of the land at casual glance. By these criteria their plots had succeeded. By my own criteria, however, they had failed dismally. The soil between the plants was bare and eroding seriously—something not visible to the person who didn't get down on the ground and look for it. Plants were overgrazed severely in some patches while in others they had grown old, excessively fibrous, and, frequently, oxidized grey. The most shocking characteristic was the almost complete absence of new seedlings despite massive seed production on parent plants. Desirable species were indeed present, but very few other species.

The bulk produced by the "key indicator" species and the high production of a few individual animals had masked the evidence of degradation. Production per animal was high and increasing (along with supplementation costs) even as production per acre remained low and declining. For the first time I began to realize the extreme danger in considering short-term high production a measure of success. For the ranchers (and my country), blinded by such so-called success, I could only foresee ruination.

Continually seeking answers, I began reading the range management research from various countries, but they all appeared to follow the same thinking. Then one day while assisting a rancher in starting up a game ranching operation, I glanced at a South African farm magazine that lay on his coffee table. In it was an article on nonselective grazing by a man named John Acocks. Acocks proposed a grazing system he claimed would heal the land. It made more sense than anything I had read before, so I went to South Africa and tracked him down.

I found Acocks a delightful old botanist and very knowledgeable indeed about the extent of the land deterioration that had taken place in South Africa. He believed it came from the selective grazing of the livestock that had replaced the original large and diverse game populations. Livestock, he said, overgrazed the species they preferred until those species disappeared. They then overgrazed another until it too disappeared. Gradually only the poorest of species remained. Thus he explained how areas dominated two or three hundred years ago by perennial grasses had become the domain of desert shrubs. He had plotted the steady movement of these shrubs across southern Africa over the years as the desert spread.

Acocks saw that as overgrazing weakened or killed plants of a particular species, other species replaced them that appealed less to livestock and thus held an unfair advantage over the grazed plant in the competition for light, water, and nutrients. He concluded that the actual numbers of livestock mattered less than their repeated selection of species that were thus handicapped and eventually replaced in the community. The diverse game species of old, reasoned Acocks, used all plants equally because each selected a different diet. Thus, no plant type had an advantage over another, and many thrived side by side. Based on these observations and interpretations he made the remarkable statement that South Africa was "overgrazed and understocked."

His remedy called for concentrating livestock onto a small portion of land to force them to graze off all of the grasses. Once they had done this, they could be moved to another area to do the same thing. Each grazed area would then be rested so all the equally grazed plants could recover without unfair competition among them.

Acocks's theory did not answer all my concerns by any means—the deterioration of tsetse fly areas that had no grazing being one—but it had merit and offered a new direction. Before leaving he introduced me to a nearby farming couple who were practicing his ideas.

Len and Denise Howell had a deep concern for the land degradation occurring all over the country and were excited by the results of applying Acocks's idea. So was I. The Howells looked on in bewilderment as I fell to my knees and probed my fingers into the soil, pointing out excitedly what had happened where their stock had trodden in very high concentration for a short time in one corner of a paddock. The surface was broken, litter lay everywhere, water was soaking in rather than running off, aeration had improved, and new seedlings grew in abundance.

John Acocks had given me a vital piece of knowledge—that livestock could simulate the effects of wild herds on the soil. Here in one area was the heavy trampling I had seen following game but now done by livestock and without the damage to the land we had come to expect.

I rushed back to Zimbabwe eager to persuade some of my rancher clients to concentrate their livestock. The first one to do it rapidly produced the desired effects. Unfortunately, as fast as the land responded, his cattle fell off in condition. In fact they nearly died. Others who followed my advice reported the same results.

As disappointing as this was, I still believed we were at last approaching the answer, and much to their credit a handful of ranchers who loved their land decided to stick with me until we had it. We had no other allies in the quest. Under a barrage of criticism we confronted the new riddle of poor livestock performance.

The cattlemen and our government extension officers believed in scattering cattle so that they could select the grass species they needed to perform well. Acocks believed in concentrating the animals to keep those very grass species from getting selected out of existence. Both arguments had obvious merit and somewhere between them the clues to good cattle and land management had to lie. Now, indulging in the perfect vision of hindsight I can see that *time* was the factor staring us in the face and always overlooked.

As the problem now involved cattle, I once again dusted off André Voisin's book, and there it was. He had already found the missing key—*time*. He had proven that overgrazing bore little relationship to the number of animals but rather to the *time* plants were exposed to the animals. If animals remained in any one place for too long or if they returned to a place before plants had recovered, they overgrazed plants. The time of exposure was determined by the growth rate of the plants. Suddenly I could see how trampling also could be either good or bad. Time became the determining factor. The disturbance needed for the health of the soil became an evil if prolonged too much or repeated too soon.

I now went back to my clients and suggested that we combine the ideas of Acocks and Voisin, concentrating the animals but timing their exposure and reexposure to plants to the rate at which the plants grew. Again, we were very enthusiastic and this time certain of success. We did in fact improve animal performance somewhat, but in many important respects we fell flat on our faces once more.

Voisin had done his work in a nonbrittle environment, and we had not yet discovered the fundamental differences between brittle and nonbrittle. Thus, we did not immediately see how to fit our highly erratic growing conditions into his systematic accounting of time. Neither, of course, did we know then that the solution in our brittle region also depended on the actual behavior of the cattle—the herding behavior, not merely the concentration of animals. We also encountered variables that Voisin, managing planted, fertilized, and well-watered pastures, did not. Our rangelands had a tremendous variety of grasses, forbs, brush, and trees—all growing at different rates. We also had wildlife running with our stock, seriously affecting our time calculations. Whatever we suspected about time, we could not manage it effectively.

We would not unravel the whole mystery for a long time, but we knew at least that we had discovered the right path. In the years that followed, as our knowledge matured concerning the other missing keys—holism, the brittle-nonbrittle distinction, and the role of herding animals—the importance of the time dimension in nearly every aspect of our work became increasingly evident.

Politics as much as ecology forced us to learn. By the early 1970s Zimbabwe, then Rhodesia, had become a pariah among nations because the white-led government refused to give in to the demands of the black majority. The country had plunged into a protracted civil war, and to force an end to it the rest of the world raised economic sanctions against us. To survive under the embargo our ranchers and farmers had to greatly diversify their operations and manage great complexity and constant change on a day-to-day basis.

Livestock operations added new crops, and farmers, who had previously specialized in one or two cash crops, added many others and rotated crops and pastures to maintain livestock as well. To handle the difficulties inherent in such diversity, I developed a thorough but simple planning procedure based on military planning concepts I already knew. It proved successful, and within a few years it was being applied on more than one hundred farms and ranches throughout the country. The experience gathered from such varied situations gave birth to many new insights.

For one it showed us that John Acocks's statement that South Africa was overgrazed but understocked was true, but not for his reasons. Selection of the most palatable plant species by livestock and a consequent unfair competition against less handicapped ones did not explain the deterioration in southern Africa. Nor was the remedy to force livestock to eat off all plants equally. Wild herding animals select plants much as domestic ones do; they never graze all plants equally, and this has never been necessary.

The overgrazing Acocks observed reflected the *time* plants were exposed to livestock, not the low numbers of animals grazing selectively. The understocking he observed did not damage the land by allowing less palatable plants to escape punishment. In fact, lack of grazing allowed good plants to die from overrest in brittle environments as old material accumulated on them and blocked adequate sunlight from reaching their growing points. Understocking also meant that too few animals scattered too widely in an unexcited, nonherding manner failed to provide the disturbance so necessary in brittle environments.

We only discovered all this because the planning procedure allowed us to control the time dimension more subtly than ever before. We found we could minimize overgrazing and overtrampling while still allowing animals to select the plants and nutrients they required. We could also induce adequate disturbance on the soil surface so that new plants could establish. We were able to plan for crops and hay cuttings as well and manage habitat critical to wildlife in particular seasons. All this became possible once we had the missing key of *time* and a planning procedure.

We now realize that there is a time dimension in all that we do to the land, though time itself does not rank as a tool in the HRM model. It is, however, a factor that guides us in the use of all our tools. It not only affects grazing and animal impact, but also governs planting and harvesting and all the rhythms of agriculture. Even in applying the tool of technology, as in the case of chemical fertilization, we would time the applications to achieve the greatest reaction.

For most of history we considered plant, soil, and animal interrelationships a simple matter. If the land was overgrazed and overtrampled, reduce the animals. If the animals did not perform, give them more forage. If the herd did not breed, it had grown too large. If floods came, pray for less rain. If drought came, pray for more. If insects descended, poison them. If crops failed, add fertilizer. If that failed, genetically engineer new crops. A close look at the time dimension in all these things helps reveal by contrast how astoundingly complex the natural world really is.

In years to come we will look back on the time before the discovery of the four missing keys as truly the dark ages of agriculture and of mankind's whole attitude toward the ecosystem that sustains us. The time for change of course is now, lest ours go the way of other sophisticated civilizations that have bloomed and destroyed themselves in the brittle environments of the world.

As mentioned in Chapter 1, Einstein, remembered among other achievements for his insight about time, had a word of warning. Mankind, he said, cannot do anything meaningful without goals, which only mankind, and not science, can determine. Because the discovery of the four missing keys gives more power to science, the next chapter will address the question of goals.

PART III

Goals

8

Goals I:
Temporary Goals to
Get You Started

A short while ago I saw a sign that greatly appealed to me in front
of a fire station. It said, "Don't even *think* of parking here!" If I
rephrase that warning, it becomes very appropriate here:

DON'T EVEN THINK OF
MANAGING RESOURCES WITHOUT A GOAL

As obvious as the need for goals seems, for a number of reasons the
process of setting them has proven itself the hardest part of applying the
HRM model. First among these reasons is an ingrained human proclivity for
acting without clearly defined goals, or worse, simply reacting to events and
reaching for a quick fix. It is also just plain difficult to define an adequate
goal before thoroughly understanding the tools and guidelines in the model.

In practice you may have to set yourself a temporary goal and start
toward it, much as a military pilot might head generally toward the action
before knowing his precise destination. To wait on the ground for perfect
intelligence or to burn up fuel circling randomly would waste his chances,
his resources, or both. Like the pilot, as you obtain more information and
a clearer picture, you can refine your objectives so that by the time you know
the target, you are well on your way without having wasted time or fuel.

Though all living things, including humans, are totally interconnected,
to merely state one grand all-embracing goal is not practical when it comes
to actually managing the situation to achieve what we want. In managing
holistically we define a goal in three parts, all of them *essential*:

QUALITY OF LIFE: A well-thought-out statement of the quality of life
that the people involved want from the ecosystem. For example, a ranch
family might set out to "create a warm and stable environment for our family

55

and our staff that will encourage each of us to reach his or her potential; to ensure that our children will be adequately educated and that they will have the opportunity to return to the ranch when their schooling is over if they wish; to see our community revitalized; to enjoy life in the process of achieving our goals."

PRODUCTION: A description of the form or forms of production required from the ecosystem in order to deliver the quality of life sought. This may be profit, recreation, culture, aesthetics, or some other product. If profit is part of the production goal, the description will say whether from crops, water, livestock, game, timber, or other forms, but not the specific crop, species of livestock, game, or tree, as these could change to ensure the desired profit.

If some cultural aspect is contained in the production goal it would be spelled out in broad terms, such as "preserving a nomadic society" or "preserving rural American communities." Likewise an aesthetic production goal would be spelled out broadly—for instance, "preserving a wild area for recreational purposes."

Alongside "profitability from livestock," a ranch might simultaneously have cultural and aesthetic goals. Suppose the property contained some ancient Indian ruins or historic buildings from an original homestead. We would include "historic preservation" as a goal. If the river bottoms had a significant population of deer and waterfowl, we might want to keep the area as natural as possible and not have a lot of fencing, roads, or other hindrances that detract from the area's natural beauty. This would be an aesthetic goal.

Profit will not in fact always be a part of the production goal as many communities and societies seek cultural goals that do not depend on profit.

LANDSCAPE: A broad description of the landscape and how the four ecosystem processes must function to sustain indefinitely the production, which will, in turn, sustain the quality of life. Once we know what is to be produced and in what form, we can describe a landscape and how the four ecosystem processes must function within it to produce and sustain those products. In doing so, we dwell not on what we have today but on what we must have in the future.

In our ranch example we would describe the future landscape something like this: "Open grassland community at a high successional level with scattered trees and shrubs and a mosaic of brush thickets and grassland along the river bottoms giving us high successional complexity (including birds, insects, and other animals) and stability, a good mineral cycle, sound water cycle, and high energy flow." This would be adequate for a temporary goal. In Chapter 46 we look at more permanent goals.

The quality of life goal, too often merely assumed or taken for granted, has particular importance. Without it we risk pursuing production in ways that may destroy the quality of life we mean to sustain. Bear in mind also that in talking of quality of life we must go beyond ourselves as humans and consider all forms of life. Without them we would enjoy a very poor quality life.

Resolving conflicts among people using the same resources also demands agreement on goals starting with the quality of life each desires. The frequent bad feelings between ranchers and environmentalists makes this point. In most cases the conflict is actually over the means of production and the tools applied. When these people discuss their goals and start with the quality of life they all seek, they usually find a great deal of common ground and agreement. From there they can work toward producing and sustaining specific products and the necessary landscape goal that meets all their different needs as far as possible.

In much of the world agricultural goals are only production goals, with little thought for landscape or quality of life. Both have suffered drastically as a result and often that has wrecked production in the long run. The form of production must sustain that quality of life and be sustained by the landscape or it will fail.

The single most common mistake made in attempting to apply HRM is failure to put any effort into goal formation at all. Too often ranchers and government agencies start applying the grazing aspects of the model just to get on with things. Skipping this first and most vital step usually indicates poor understanding of the whole model and, inevitably, the cost is great down the line. On ranches we often encounter massive unnecessary financial outlays on things like fencing and other developments when a little patience and understanding could have produced greater profitability at the outset and generated the funds for development from the land base.

Another typical mistake is an owner's assumption that his family and staff share his goals. Time and again when a ranch or farm suffers financial loss we find it flows from lack of sharing or clarity on goals. This usually surprises the owner who didn't notice that the other people involved only agreed with him to escape the stress of argument on personal relationships, to avoid causing offense, or out of fear.

Government and international agencies responsible for resource management are particularly apt to set "nongoals," which I cover in Chapter 46 in more detail. Examples would be "eradication of brush," "eradication of grasshoppers," "preservation of a rare plant species," "flood control," and so on. These seem to be legitimate goals in a very narrow context, but appear quite different in the broad context of a three-part goal.

In the western states brush eradication has been a goal for fifty years, during which time enough new brush has grown to ensure a full century of similar effort. If your goal is to eradicate brush you will be eradicating brush the rest of your life. The cost in human and financial resources is staggering and will continue as long as brush eradication remains the goal.

In such cases one has to forget the problem itself for a while, as it is usually a symptom of something deeper, and determine the real goal in its three-part form. Brush may not present a problem at all after defining the production goal. If it is, then the landscape description will call for a level of succession where brush does not dominate. The tools and guidelines will determine the most economical and permanent way to produce that landscape, and a fortune is not squandered on attacking a problem that will remain as long as the underlying cause of it is not dealt with.

Remember, *without the goal, the model cannot be applied at all.*

As goal setting involves human values and collaboration, it demands great patience, sensitivity, and time. A year or two might do it. In the meantime you can set a temporary goal, a general heading toward the action, and start using the model. But don't let a temporary goal become like so many temporary things we build—a scruffy eyesore put up in haste that somehow becomes permanent!

Goals are never set in concrete. They are continually under review and subject to alteration. As a comprehensive knowledge of holism and the use of the HRM model is so vital to goal formation and achievement, I address the subject more fully in Chapter 46 after I've gone through the model in its entirety.

Whatever our goals, no matter where we are, they always rest upon the foundation of our ecosystem. Next we look at how our ecosystem has to function in order to achieve the goals we set.

PART IV

The Ecosystem

9
Introduction

There is only one ecosystem. As a whole in the holistic sense, it encompasses everything on our planet and in its surrounding atmosphere and probably more than that as well.

Much scientific literature today speaks of different ecosystems—riparian ecosystems, grassland ecosystems, jungle ecosystems, and so on. In deference to the fact that these elements exist only in dynamic relationship to each other and as members of a greater whole, I call them environments within one ecosystem. Missing this distinction leads to the frequent comment by ranchers and scientists that the HRM model might well apply in some places but probably not theirs.

To perceive the unity of our ecosystem requires no scientific training. The spread of acid rain across wide areas, the build-up of carbon dioxide and the breakdown of ozone in the atmosphere, the worldwide implications of a nuclear power plant disaster, all demonstrate that completely isolated environments don't exist. International monetery flows and counterflows reveal that the ecosystem includes a single global economy as well.

The HRM model derives from the nature of the ecosystem in its broadest sense and thus applies in all environments. Nevertheless, to comprehend and work with the complexity of our ecosystem we do have to break it up to some extent. The human brain, which can concentrate on very few things simultaneously, cannot embrace it otherwise. If, for example, I asked you to count the number of bicycles and cars racing past you, you might possibly give me an accurate count if you had a tally counter to aid you. If I added motorcycles to the group and asked you to count them as well, there is very little chance your count would be accurate. If our brains can't handle the complexity of thinking about three things simultaneously, what hope have we with dozens, hundreds, or thousands?

To aid our thinking and planning to achieve our desired goals, the HRM model divides the ecosystem into four basic building blocks. Each block represents a fundamental process at work in the ecosystem. In applying the model one need consciously modify only one or two of these blocks at a time while being aware that any change in one will change all in some way.

For example, if you decide to change the successional level to bring it closer to your goal, you will plan which tools to use and how to use them. But before going further, you also will have to think how these tools will affect each of the other processes. The model, properly used, will ensure that you do.

The next four chapters will cover the four ecosystem foundation blocks as if they were separate entities, though of course they are not. Much of the information in these chapters has appeared in basic textbooks over the last fifty years without having much of an impact on practice. Much is also new knowledge arising from the discovery of the four missing keys and from practical experience in applying the HRM model.

The general point, however, remains. There is only one ecosystem, and it serves as the foundation on which all our goals are built. The HRM model, based on that fact, applies to all environments within it.

10

Water Cycle

As far as we know there is a fixed amount of water on the planet that constantly cycles from the atmosphere to the surface and back to the atmosphere. Some becomes locked for vast periods of time underground or in polar icecaps before rejoining the cycle, but most remains constantly on the move, becoming now liquid, now ice, now vapor.

I have drawn the basic pattern of the water cycle in figure 10-1. It shows how precipitation goes various ways. Some evaporates straight away off soil and plant surfaces back into the atmosphere. Some runs off into streams, rivers, dams, lakes, and eventually the sea before evaporating. Some penetrates the soil and, of that, a portion sticks to soil particles. The rest flows on down to underground supplies. There it may remain for millennia or find its way back to the surface in river bank seepage, springs and sponges, or possibly through deep-rooted plants that pick it up and transpire it back into the air. Of water held by soil particles, a small portion remains tightly held, but the bulk is either attracted to drier particles or drawn away by plant roots and transpired. Thus, one way or another all the water eventually cycles between earth and air.

In an effective water cycle plants make maximum use of rainfall. Little evaporates directly off the soil. Any run-off causes no erosion and remains clear. A good air-to-water balance exists in the soil, enabling plant roots to absorb water readily. In a noneffective water cycle plants get minimal opportunity to use the full amount of precipitation received. Much is lost to surface evaporation or run-off and what soaks in is often not readily available to plants because air and water are not in balance.

In describing the landscape needed to achieve your goal you will state

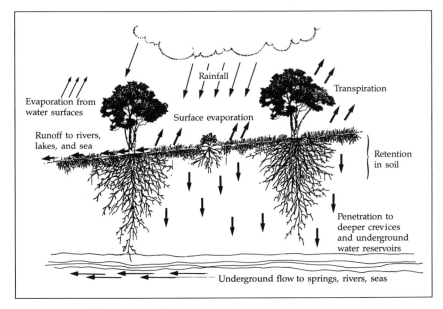

Figure 10-1.   The water cycle.

the general condition of the water cycle required. In most cases you will strive for an effective water cycle. Nevertheless, an aesthetic goal that involves the preservation of a rare semidesert plant or animal species might require a landscape produced by a less effective water cycle, and careful application of available tools and constant monitoring should produce this. Both cases require a deeper understanding of how a water cycle functions.

Effective Precipitation

Most people know the average rainfall their land receives and manage accordingly. Unfortunately, averages often mean little. In areas of erratic precipitation, as brittle environments are, the average seldom occurs. Nearly every year the amount of rain will be greater or less than average. When it is average the distribution can be very poor. If the water cycle is noneffective, then most years of below-average or poorly distributed rain become droughts, and the rainy times become flood years.

What really matters is the *effectiveness* of the precipitation. Effective rainfall is that which soaks in and becomes available to plant roots, insects, and microorganisms, or replenishes underground supplies, with very little subsequently evaporating from the soil surface.

Making precipitation as effective as possible means producing a cycle that directs most water either out to the atmosphere *through plants* or down to underground supplies. In all the arid and semiarid areas of the world where I have worked, rarely have I seen an effective water cycle. Typically, of, say, fourteen inches of rain received, only five or six inches were actually effective. In very rough figures, it takes approximately six hundred tons of water to produce one ton of vegetation, so one can't afford any waste.

For water to enter the soil, it first must penetrate the soil surface, and this depends on the rate at which it is applied and the porosity of the surface in particular. Tools that break up a sealed or "capped" surface, or increase the soil's organic content and crumb structure, speed penetration. Tools that create a surface that slows the flow of water slow the rate of application and allow more to soak in before running off. A loosened, rough surface or one covered by old, prone plant material achieves this.

Capping

From these remarks you can see that the nature of the soil surface is vital to the water cycle. On bare and exposed ground, the direct impact of rain-drops tends to destroy any crumb structure that is present. The amount of damage is actually governed by the size and velocity of the drop. Evidence of this shows up on bare ground under tall trees as large drops tend to come off the leaves and reach terminal velocity in about 22.5 feet of fall.

When raindrop impact breaks down surface crumb structure, it frees the organic and lightweight material to wash away while heavier fine particles settle and seal, or cap, the soil. The importance of crumb structure to water penetration is easily demonstrated by comparing a bowl of wheat grains and one of flour. Neither has a hard cap at the outset, but one has large particles, and the other has lost that structure. Pour a jug of water on each bowl and watch. Most of the water soaks into the grains but it seals the surface of the flour immediately and runs off.

Capping is not always obvious on sandy soils but it is almost always present. Some soils develop a cap so hard that only a sharp object can break it. Often you can actually tap a severely capped soil with your fingers and hear a hollow drum-like sound.

It is well-known that soil cover protects the soil surface from raindrops and thus preserves the crumb structure and prevents capping. Soil cover generally comes in two forms: erect growing plants, which intercept rainfall so that drops hit the ground with less energy; and dead, prone plant material that effectively slows the flow of water across the land. (Water can flow quite fast between plants where no litter impedes it.)

In nonbrittle environments, soil cover is seldom a problem since plants are spaced so closely that dead material stays in place. If bare areas do develop, they tend to recover rapidly because an active decay process causes surrounding plants to fall to the ground and provide the necessary litter in a short time. The successional process also advances so rapidly that the soil does not remain uncovered for long.

None of this happens in brittle environments. Old plant material only falls onto the soil surface after long delay because decay occurs mainly through oxidation and physical weathering. In addition, much wider plant spacings allow wind and water to carry litter away.

In both brittle and nonbrittle environments, once water penetrates the soil surface, it is strongly attracted to the soil particles. Each particle retains as much water as it can, and the rest flows on down. Gravity tends to keep excess water moving until particles capture it or it reaches an impenetrable layer of clay or rock or joins underground water supplies. It tends to remain there until extracted by plants, evaporated from the surface, or carried off into underground streams eventually to emerge in springs and rivers.

A small amount of rain may wet a few inches of soil. In covered soil such water can remain in position for a long time. Another soaking rain will flow through the wetted layer and wet the soil down deeper. In this manner cumulative light rains can slowly wet the soil to its full depth and begin to recharge underground reservoirs.

The porosity of soil below the surface matters too, as the faster water can move down, the faster it will be allowed in through a porous surface. Porosity at the surface and below is increased by organic material, which binds particles together into bigger structured pieces with bigger spaces between them, and by insects, worms, and small mammals, which create space by burrowing and tunneling. Plant roots also open up channels for water movement. One study conducted in Minnesota has shown that earthworms added to cornfields increased absorbtion rates thirty-five-fold over control fields. This tremendous response occurred over only a six-week period.[1]

To obtain an effective water cycle then, management tools must be applied so that soil acquires and maintains adequate organic content and animal activity. Unfortunately many agricultural experts ignore these attributes in their attempts to maintain high production with machinery and chemicals.

The fundamental interaction of water, soil, animals, and plants must be understood to explain how management practices affect the water cycle.

Water held by soil particles tends to move in two ways; upward through plant root systems or in any direction from wetter to drier particles.

Short of drying soil in the sun or an oven, it is hard to remove the final film of water from a soil particle. However, particles hold each added increment of water more feebly than the last. Conversely, as water is drawn away from a particle by any means, that particle tightens its hold on whatever remains, just as you, if mugged on the street with an armload of parcels, will defend the last one better than the first.

Water then will move slowly in any direction toward drier particles. This is why, after water has been in the ground for a while, no sharp edge between wet and dry soil remains, but rather a gradient from wetter to drier particles.

Plants absorb water, and essential nutrients dissolved in it, through root hairs. They can do this as long as their ability to draw water can overcome the grip on the water exercised by soil particles. As drying particles yield less and less water, the plant slows its growth rate. Eventually it begins to wilt in the heat of the day, or curl its leaves to conserve moisture, as its ability to obtain water from the soil is reduced.

Plants must have air as well as water. Given adequate temperatures, they grow best when soil particles have air spaces in between, so that the soil is saturated with water, but not oversaturated or waterlogged.

As a sugar cane farmer in Africa, I experienced firsthand just how critical proper aeration can be. I had my crops under overhead irrigation and was told by the local extension service to plant my cane in hollows between high ridges made with a ridging implement. I questioned this advice and sowed a test plot of cabbages said to produce two-pound heads.

I got the answer I sought very quickly but let the crop mature in order to sell it. Heads planted in the furrows averaged one pound. Those on flat ground averaged two pounds. Those planted on ridge tops averaged eight pounds! Clearly, several factors operate in such a situation, but most obvious was the fact that the soil in the ridges was never waterlogged and always well-aerated.

The aeration in the soil can be governed by a number of things, but the main ones again involve the structure of the soil itself and are:

1. Excessive compaction that reduces the air spaces between soil particles.

2. Lack of sufficient organic materal to maintain a crumb structure that provides air spaces.

3. An impervious layer of clay or rock under the soil, which inhibits the drainage of excess water and allows it to drive out air as it fills the spaces between particles.

4. A sealed or capped soil surface that reduces the soil's ability to breathe. A good crumb structure right to the surface provides spaces between particles large enough to allow carbon dioxide to get out and oxygen to get in readily.

Aeration is just as important on rangeland as on cropland. Lack of aeration tends to produce plant communities adapted through various mechanisms to prevent rapid passage of water. The narrow leaves, waxy skins, or cuticles seen in sedges and water lilies are charateristic. Such plants are likely to have slow growth rates. Good aeration with adequate water tends to favor broad-leaved grasses and other plants with rapid growth potential.

Conditions that stress plants affect the animal life that depends on them also. Livestock performance frequently drops in high rainfall years as well as in drought because of overwatering and poor aeration. Recent research also links insect damage to stressed plants.

Effective and Noneffective Water Cycles

How then do these basic relationships among plants, animals, water, and soil figure in the process of desertification? Imagine a brittle environment and a rainfall of one inch per month over the next three months. The land is level and light regular showers produce no run-off. In figure 10-2 we have an effective water cycle on the left. The soil is covered and plants have healthy roots and are plentiful. On the right we have a noneffective water cycle with exposed soil and fewer, less healthy plants.

Assume that the first inch of rain has fallen and all the water in both cases has soaked into the soil down to level A. We have an inch of water retained in the soil. Over the next month we receive no further rain and the

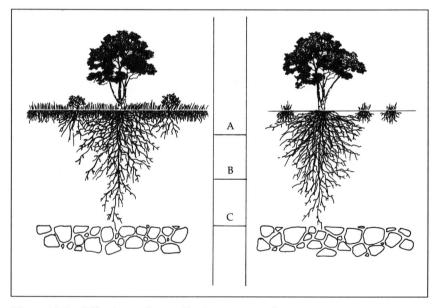

Figure 10-2. Effective and noneffective water cycles.

sun shines, temperatures are good, and plants grow. On the left they grow well, drawing out half an inch of water in the process. No further water losses take place, and by the end of the month half an inch of water still remains in the soil.

The plants on the right, which are poorly aerated due to the hard cap on the soil, have not been as productive but have grown as well as they could, using a quarter-inch of water. Theoretically then, three-quarters of an inch should remain at month's end. However, the soil surface is exposed, and the sun shines and the wind blows directly on it, thoroughly drying the surface soil particles. The surface particles, directly in contact with particles below, can take water from them, and they do. As sun and wind continue to dry them, they draw yet more water from the particles below, which in turn draw moisture from the next rank down. At month's end, most of the water that the plants on the right didn't use has evaporated.

Now comes the second inch of soaking rain. On the left it flows through particles already holding water and penetrates to level B, so we now have an inch and a half in the soil. During the next months the plants grow well again taking out half an inch, but by month's end an inch remains.

The water on the right has soaked in but the dry particles near the surface retained most of it, so it again only reaches level A. In the following month the plants again use a quarter-inch, and sun and wind dry up the rest as before.

When the same processes repeat after the third rain, the inch of precipitation will penetrate all the way to level C in the left hand picture, and there the excess trickles through larger decomposing rock fragments to join underground supplies.

The water on the right has still not pushed beyond level A. Ground water will receive no recharge at all this season. The soil has only an inch of water to carry plants through the long dry season to follow and all of that will be lost soon through plant use and surface evaporation. Growth could well end before reduced temperatures limit it. In the following season, when temperatures again rise, growth will have to await rainfall.

The soil on the left has almost two inches of water in it at the start of the dry season. Plants will continue to grow until temperatures fall. The following year they will still have enough moisture for an early start when the weather warms, even though rain may not fall for another month.

Noneffective water cycles like the one described here are evident over billions of acres in the world's brittle environments. As long as the soil surface is exposed, the water cycle will be less than optimum and the desertification process will continue.

Ignorance of these processes is widespread. In North America vast acreages of cropland are covered only briefly (by monoculture crops) during the year, and windbreaks are nonexistent. On the rangelands an incredibly

Zambezi River (which feeds the falls) I have no doubt that this is due to the damaged water cycle existing in those catchments.

Some years ago in Zimbabwe, a rancher who had just received an award for "The Best Managed Ranch of the Year" by the Natural Resources Board asked me for a second opinion as he wasn't sure that his ranch was really as good as the officials said. I ran a number of transects that showed that even on the best parts of the ranch, 97 percent of the soil surface between plants was bare, exposed, and visibly eroding to the naked eye!

In another instance I was asked to assist a rancher whose land was being expropriated by the Namibian government at what he thought was an unfair price. His land was being compared to a ranch that authorities said had no trace of erosion and in fact was managed to perfection. My transects and photographs on this so-called perfect ranch showed serious erosion on 95 percent of it.

These cases are not unusual. I believe we would find serious erosion in any brittle environment where land is managed under prolonged grazing with low numbers of widely scattered animals. What often appears as a sea of grass can fool the observer into thinking all is well. However, if one looks closely at the soil surface between the grass plants, the opposite is quite often found.

What would it be worth to you as a rancher or farmer or regional planner in an arid area to be able to double your rainfall? No doubt quite a lot. You can double your effective rainfall simply by applying the tools that will cover your soil and maintain crumb structure, and thus keep the water that does fall available for use. The HRM model will help you determine which tool or tools are most appropriate at any time.

The importance of water cycles does not apply only to rangelands, but to croplands, forests, fisheries, cities, industry, and all of mankind's activities dependent upon good healthy water supplies from healthy watersheds.

11

Succession

Succession is the name given to the process of change and development in communities of living organisms. Neither chaotic nor haphazard in any way, this process follows certain patterns and principles.

The very word "life" of course implies change—birth, growth, reproduction, death, decay. That taken for granted, however, we often fail to notice how change begets change, or how the succession of changes orders and defines the natural world. The basis of our own existence, and of the rest of the natural world as we know it, is the marvelous fact that succession, undefiled, tends to proceed toward more complex and more stable communities of living things. And in these living wholes the interplay of competition, interdependence, and adaptation never becomes static. It continually embraces the possibility of yet further advance.

I compare this upward tending characteristic of succession to a coiled spring, which, whenever pressed down by human intervention or natural catastrophe, will, by its nature, rebound as soon as the pressure is taken away. Thus grass reclaims old battlefields. Jungle climbs the slopes of dead volcanoes. And weeds invade fallow ground.

All management of land (watersheds or cropland) by definition affects succession. However, the full ramifications of the process in any given case remain so complex as to lie beyond the power of any science. In the words of American soil scientist Michael Crofoot, "Ecological processes are not only more complex than we think, they are more complex than we can ever think." On the other hand, our general understanding of succession has finally developed to the point where we can solve once baffling riddles.

The concept of succession entered the vocabulary of science through the work of plant ecologists who observed that disturbed areas revegetated in successional stages—e.g., from bare ground to algae/lichen/moss communities, to grasslands, brushlands, and forest. Later insight took account of the fact that plants cannot exist in isolation, and thus we now think of succession in terms of entire communities.

When I attended university in the mid-'50s, we studied succession strictly in terms of animal communities or plant communities. The separate disciplines of zoology and botany had successfully divorced the two obvious partners in the process. Soils were barely considered other than as a physical base.

We now know that the successional process includes all animals—from the most simple virus or unicellular organism to elephant and human. And it includes all plants—from the simplest fungus to the mightiest tree. It also includes the microscopic world within our soils where a complex web of life dwells among decomposing particles of rock, sand, clay, and "dead" organic material. Many complex and mutually dependent relationships exist among the various organisms to the extent that one cannot live without the other. And yet we know very little about them. We have no idea where one-third to two-thirds of the carbon dioxide in our soils is coming from. And we have yet to identify 90 percent of the organisms living in some of our soils.[1] Most of us still think of soil as inert material when in reality it is a living entity.

We still describe these whole communities by their general appearance— grassland, forest, etc.—for the obvious reason that vegetation is most visible. This unfortunately fosters the misconception that plants, and only certain plants at that, are more important than the whole. In reality a small fungus or rodent can be just as crucial to the survival of a forest as the trees themselves.

Change goes on continually in even the most highly developed successional communities—tropical rain forests or jungles. Individual populations fluctuate in numbers and individual animals and plants die and are replaced while the soil, a living part of this whole complex, continually develops. And beyond that, the community we talk of as a whole still does not stand on its own as an independent unit. Each in turn belongs to a greater community or whole whose changes follow the ordered patterns of succession.

Some scientists suggest with good evidence that our planet itself is in fact a living organism that modifies the atmosphere surrounding it through the successional process. The composition of earth's atmosphere, on which all life depends, can change gradually in conjunction with earth's life forms as the two—life and environment—influence each other. Billions of years ago the very earliest communities would have been suited to a totally different environment from that of today as there was no oxygen until it was formed by living organisms. We have remnants of these earliest communities in the anaerobic life forms (those that do not use oxygen), such as bacteria, that still exist. In ignorance we have overloaded our planet's respiratory system by greatly increasing our use of fire over what once occurred naturally, and consuming fossil fuels in massive amounts. Our planet's ability to balance the gasses in the air pocket surrounding it took billions of years to develop and we cannot expect it to adapt to the changed circumstances that arose in a few centuries.

The fundamental importance of dynamic change can too easily be overlooked. In range management we used to think an area good in terms of succession if we found the right high successional plants. Many of those areas, however, belonged at the other end of the scale. The microenvironment at the soil surface had deteriorated to the extent that the higher species, though still present, could only reproduce asexually through runners or stolons. The community had become static and was slowly losing its complexity as plants and other organisms died out. As a community moves successionally in one direction or another, any part that is altered affects the whole community, including the populations making up the community, the organic material, the structure of the soil and the microenvironment, and, ultimately, the atmosphere. We cannot clear an area of land and plant a single species without profound change.

The Successional Process

A simple understanding of the basic idea of succession is easy to grasp when one visualizes it in process on a tropical island lava flow.

After the lava has cooled and hardened, its surface remains a very harsh microenvironment. In rain it is very wet; minutes later it is extremely dry. At dawn it may be quite cold, but by midday too hot to touch. Only a few species can survive in such a place, and thus only a very simple community will establish there, while mobile species pass by.

Without soil, only algae, lichens, and minute organisms dependent on them will establish. The moment they do, however, the microenvironment becomes different. The meager collection of life will hold moisture a bit longer and reduce the daily temperature range ever so slightly, and moisture retained at the surface will now have time to begin dissolving the rock. When a few fine particles of dust catch on the algae and lichens, moss and other organisms can invade and the creation of simple soil has begun.

Gradually other organisms join the community as the microenvironment begins to favor them and their offspring. They further change the microenvironment. Succession accelerates. Moisture is retained longer. That breaks down the parent rock faster to join with living organisms in forming yet more soil. Anywhere physical weathering cracks the surface, the process speeds up in the environment of the crack, which in turn affects the immediate neighborhood.

Complexity, productivity, and stability increase, and the microenvironment changes as the successional process advances until something limits it, typically climate or some obstruction to further soil formation. Locally, conditions such as an impervious rock or clay layer under the surface can limit succession. Deep in the forest, grassland might appear over a rock layer that impedes soil development. Otherwise, the lava of the tropical volcano will eventually advance to a rain forest community complete with its soil and the millions of organisms forming the whole forest complex. Elsewhere dry seasons, hard winters, limited sunlight, and the pattern and volume of precipitation will define the kind of landscape unfettered succession can produce. But whether the outcome be jungle, desert, or savannah, the process itself never stops. The community remains dynamic, and constant death, decay, rebirth, and change continue within it.

The full implications of succession become clearer through an understanding of population dynamics at various successional levels—when do certain species thrive, in what numbers, and why?

Typically a particular population will begin to appear as its requirements for establishment are met. It will increase as conditions improve through the growth of the whole community and its environment. The community or whole will be made of many populations of different species, each with specific requirements for its survival and each with specific contributions to the community. Each population will tend to build in numbers as its requirements become optimized with the growth of the whole community and its environment. But as the community advances, a population may find its requirements for successful reproduction are no longer ideal. It will decline in numbers and may even disappear as the successional process advances beyond it.

Some general principles apply to this phenomenon. In the early stages of succession, communities usually contain few species in a microenvironment that can fluctuate widely in temperature and moisture over a short period. Such communities tend to be unstable in that wide fluctuations in numbers can occur within the species making up the community. A good spring rain may produce extraordinarily lush annual grassland on last year's barren desert. Another chance combination of circumstances may produce massive outbreaks of weeds, blights (viruses, fungi, bacteria), locusts, or grasshoppers.

As communities develop to higher levels they tend to contain more species and fewer numbers within them. Since one organism will depend on many others, and others will depend on it, none is likely to expand to a disruptive level. Thus stability is a function of complexity as figure 11-1 illustrates.

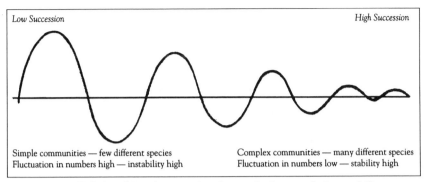

Figure 11-1. Relationship of successional complexity to relative stability.

The low successional situation on the left of the diagram supports few organisms, and the soil is barely developed. The moisture and temperature of the microenvironment fluctuate widely and thus create a vast variety of conditions in the course of time. Since the organisms characteristic of low successional communities frequently have very high reproductive rates and efficient dispersal mechanisms for their offspring, any one of them may explode into an outbreak when the right conditions occur.

The simplicity of low successional levels makes the problem worse. A grasshopper population confronted by some two hundred possible predators and parasites will less likely become a plague in a good breeding season than the same creature facing only half that opposition to the survival of its eggs and young. Thus chemical spraying, which simplifies a community, increases the possibility of further outbreaks, as Chapter 48 will explain.

Brittle environments are particularly vulnerable, as by definition they have erratic precipitation and wide swings in humidity. Here the relationship between succession and the other ecosystem foundation blocks becomes clear. A noneffective water cycle, for example, exacerbates fluctuations in the effectiveness of available moisture and that allied to a simple monoculture crop greatly increases instability.

As mentioned in earlier chapters, in Zimbabwe we eradicated big game from tsetse fly areas to deny the fly its source of blood food. To aid the hunters, we burned the brush. That exposed soil, damaged the water cycle, and greatly increased the fly's egg laying sites. With decreased blood supplies, but increased egg laying sites and reduced enemies, the tsetse flies advanced right through the hunting areas designed to stop them.

Similarly, for the grasshopper that lays its eggs in bare ground and requires a dry, warm soil for their survival, a damaged water cycle ensures higher breeding success than poor weather alone could. How many entomologists, however, consider the water cycle in their predictions? It is partly because this principle is not understood that insect damage to American crops has increased from 7 percent to 13 percent since the massive use of pesticides began in the late '40s.[2] The more chemicals are used, the simpler the community becomes and the greater the tendency for outbreaks of problem species. When a few fast breeding organisms develop an immunity to pesticides (or herbicides) the problem is made much worse. It is compounded further when the frequency of good breeding seasons is increased by the creation of a less effective water cycle.

In recent years a further principle has emerged from research—that some species may actively try to maintain their own ideal environment against the tendency of succession to advance.

Prairie dogs create open country around their towns to make their predators more visible. Some harvester termites maintain open ground (and thus a reduced water cycle and low successional community) around their mounds. Some grasses exude chemicals from their roots to prevent woody plants from establishing nearby, and some woody plants do the same. Of course we humans, who constantly modify our environment to maintain higher numbers of our own species, provide one of the best but least successful examples as we eventually destroy our environment, unlike other animals.

Other cases are more subtle and require more research to be properly understood. For example, algae, lichen, and moss communities in certain environments (commonly brittle, but not always) can retard the advance of the whole community for thousands of years once they populate and encrust soil surfaces. Breaking the crust allows other communities to establish and succession to resume. The fact that the crust does inhibit erosion somewhat in the short run, and on fairly flat ground, has produced hot debate in America. Does the risk of disturbing the algae offset the unrealized possibility of higher succession?

In several national parks and monuments in the western United States a number of signs are posted that inform the public of the value of these algal crusts. They explain that the crust protects the soil and provides rough surfaces on which grasses and other plants can establish. Despite the protection these areas have received (up to eighty years in some cases), it's the *lack* of grass plants and more complex communities that is most obvious. Illustration 11-1 shows this in Canyonlands National Park, Utah.

Officials in charge of such areas have attempted to aid grasses in establishing by placing a mulch encased in nylon netting over certain areas, as shown in illustration 11-2. The result after over a year is that the mulch is oxidizing (this is a very brittle environment) and the hoped-for grass communities have not even begun to develop, nor will they. To truly stabilize lands such as these in brittle environments we have to better understand succession. It will advance normally when the artificial manmade concept of rest is removed and the soils can be periodically disturbed and compacted. This will become clearer shortly as I discuss succession in brittle environments, and later in Chapter 20.

Illustration 11-1. Soil surface dominated by algae and lichens and roughened by freezing and thawing. Canyonlands, Utah.

It is important to remember that if you alter the community by any action aboveground, this will inevitably be followed by changes in the community underground. Likewise, if by excess compaction of the soil, exposure and capping of the soil, inadequate drainage, fertilization, or any other action, you alter the underground community, change will inevitably follow aboveground.

Succession in Brittle and Nonbrittle Environments

In very brittle environments the microenvironment on exposed soil surfaces is subject to such extremes that the successional process starts with the greatest of difficulty. On smooth surfaces that are steeply sloped or vertical, the process might never get beyond frail algal communities that are easily lost as a result of soil movement produced by rain, hail, wind, or animal action. This is why the walls of the Grand Canyon cannot really stabilize with higher communities although some plants and animals are always struggling to establish there.

Illustration 11-2. Unsuccessful attempt to get grass established with nylon netting and woodwool as litter. Dead sticks are holding down netting (not visible). Canyonlands, Utah.

In brittle environments the process starts more easily on soil covered by old material and on ground broken by weather (cracks) or by the physical impact of large animals or machinery, which chips the surface. In both cases a better microenvironment results, with two notable exceptions.

If fallen material all lies in one direction, as in the case of lodged wheat, it suppresses plant growth. The reason is not yet well-understood, though farmers have long known that a straw mulch has to be scattered to be effective. On brittle ranges snow and wind will lay old, moribund bunch grass in one direction, suppressing growth. Hail and animal impact tend to scatter it, encouraging growth.

The other exception concerns areas outside the tropics where certain soils become puffy and soft from alternate freezing and thawing. As illustration 11-1 shows they may have very broken and rough surfaces, and yet succession does not progress easily due to lack of compaction.

Illustration 11-3 shows broken, cracked, but very puffy soil, uncompacted by any physical disturbance. Old, dying grass clumps are obvious and the plants trying to establish are tap-rooted forbs (considered weeds). Not a single grass seedling can be found, although millions of seeds were produced locally.

Illustration 11-3.   Bare soil with only tap-rooted forbs establishing under partial rest. All seedlings (see arrow) are forbs. Laguna Pueblo, New Mexico.

Illustration 11-4 is the same soil on the same day five paces away, but across a fence where cattle have firmed up the ground somewhat, as can be seen by the absence of cracks. Thousands of new plants have sprouted, all of them perennial grasses, giving the ground a softer appearance. This is a low rainfall (nine-inch) brittle environment where nothing but grass could grow densely enough to stabilize the soil.

Such examples highlight the need for viewing the community as a whole. Managing plants or animals in isolation is meaningless and in most instances damaging.

The points above help reinforce the concept that the successional process is dynamic and forward-striving if not interfered with by mankind. Communities that evolved in brittle environments usually did so with herding animals and their predators. Rest, which implies removal of large herding animals and their predators as well as the prevention of natural fires, is not in any way natural and constitutes a manmade interference in this dynamic process. We will cover this in more detail in Chapter 18 where I will explain how the process regresses in brittle environments with the removal of essential components.

In completely nonbrittle environments the nature and distribution of temperature and humidity throughout the year allow the rapid advance of

the same difficulty developing and maintaining organic material and the community in the soil.

We must still strive for successional complexity and stability, because we can expect problems from any measures that promote a simpler successional community above or below ground. Herein lies the great danger of using chemicals to kill organisms on our crops or in our soils.

On rangeland and watersheds we have only just discovered the serious implications of the brittle/nonbrittle distinction. At this stage we do not know if our cropland has deteriorated more rapidly in one environment than the other. Civilizations that collapsed because of agricultural decline appear to have done so fastest in brittle environments, but of those I have studied, deteriorating watersheds rather than croplands did the main damage. We now see this in America.

On the other hand, if you inspect arable soils in the least brittle regions of America under conventional management and compare them to the soil in nearby forests, the obvious deterioration in so few years in such a young country may come as a shock. A short while ago I took a handful of soil from an uncleared forest in Pennsylvania. It was dark and alive and smelled like soil should. Placed on plowed ground nearby, the contrast was stark indeed, though management on that farm far surpassed most in the country. So much of the life and organic content had left the soil in the field.

Planting a field to crops in no way alters the fact that the successional process is still vital to all life above and below the surface. All organisms remain dependent on other populations in their community for their existence and stabilty.

Figure 11-2 illustrates simply successional complexity of populations both above and below ground as one complex interdependent whole. Each population is displayed as a single line, which curves upward as succession reaches a level at which it can establish, and then curves downward as succession advances beyond its tolerance.

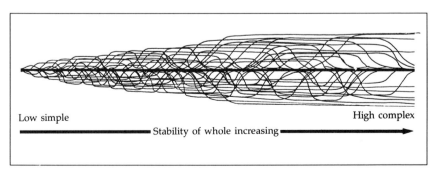

Low simple   High complex
◄━━━━━━━━━━ Stability of whole increasing ━━━━━━━━━━►

Figure 11-2.   Complex of millions of populations making up the whole.

Figure 11-3 illustrates what happens when succession is simplified with the planting of monoculture crops. Figure 11-4 illustrates what might happen when polycultures (mixed crops) are planted instead.

The remarkable achievements of the Japanese scientist Masanobu Fukuoka are noteworthy. He has produced grain yields equal to the best we can achieve with modern chemical agriculture and done it without damaging soils or the community as a whole. Behind his success lies a deep feeling for the successional process and the importance of complexity at all times. He realizes that even most crop rotations are dangerously simple, usually representing rotations of monocultures or near monocultures on the surface with adverse consequences underground.

Fukuoka truly appreciates that what we call weeds should not be blamed for stealing water and nutrients, but valued for the complexity they provide and the attendant protection against insects and disease. In fact, American scientists are just beginning to gather data indicating that complexity, as represented to a degree by weeds, can reduce insect damage in orchards previously reduced to a simplified community by keeping them clean.

Too often we reduce complexity in our croplands for no good reason. Illustration 11-6 portrays just such an example. The apple trees in this orchard are being irrigated and thus are not short of water. They are tap-rooted trees

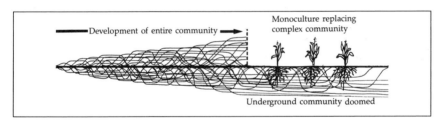

Figure 11-3. Disruption of whole to favor one population.

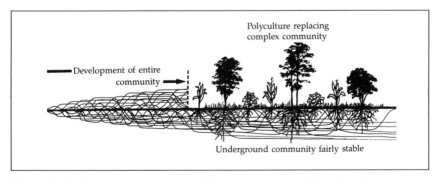

Figure 11-4. Improvement in population complexity with polycultures.

Illustration 11-6. A neat-looking orchard with newly mown grass. Pennsylvania.

with extensive, well-established root systems. Thus, the surrounding grasses and weeds cannot deprive them of water. The grasses and weeds provide ideal habitat for a multitude of insects and microorganisms, which help control apple pests and thus could do nothing but good in this orchard. Despite this, and at some expense in nonrenewable resources, the orchard has been mown and a host of habitat niches removed. This sort of thing is common practice throughout the world.

Farmers on the complex prairie soils of North America are farming soil communities that developed as a whole, which included herding ungulates and predators. Whether such soils can be maintained without animals in the farming system remains to be seen. I have serious doubts that they can.

Succession and Management

Obviously an understanding of succession opens all kinds of possibilities for better management of land, water, and all life. On the HRM model a dotted line surrounds both the ecosystem foundation block Succession and the tool Living Organisms to indicate that they are in fact the same thing. All life is successional and therefore all of our production and landscape goals revolve around succession. Our food comes from living organisms and so do our diseases. Our landscapes are composed of living organisms. But to date we have managed living organisms in ignorance of the successional process. If we continue to ignore it we will endanger all life.

If you seek profit from livestock, you may want a landscape that includes productive grassland. In one case that may mean advancing succession from desert scrub. In another it may mean preventing your pastures from returning to forest. Either way, certain plants, insects, predators, and other forms of life may become either allies or foes, depending on how you understand their place in succession.

If you wish to favor a species—game animal, plant, reptile, insect, or bird—then you must direct the movement of succession toward the optimum environment for that species. Not by automatically intervening with some technological tool, but by applying whatever tool, or tools, produce an environment in which that species thrives. Simply protecting the species, desirable as that might be, will not save it.

If you start with a landscape that contains problem numbers of undesirable species, your landscape goal will specify a level of succession that is less than ideal for that species and more suited to your production. Then you will manipulate the successional process through the appropriate tools to achieve it.

Along the way, however, one must not fall into the trap of seeking a monoculture of whatever plant appears most beneficial. Even if you want a less than maximum level of succession, as in the case of a pasture in a nonbrittle environment, you will probably need complexity. Most, but not all, production goals require stability, a direct function of complexity. To achieve a monoculture of your favorite perennial grass would quite probably require technological intervention on a scale that would reduce the soil communities to a successional level that would not allow your grass to reproduce without perennial technological support. Modern range science has given us many examples of this.

Your landscape goal, when you reach it, may still include the species you once considered pests, but in reduced numbers and likely as not in a beneficial role as they will contribute to complexity.

An exception to this would be a landscape goal preserving the aesthetics of badlands or a painted desert, or a production goal preserving an endangered lower successional community species. In either case the appropriate tools would be applied to create less effective water and mineral cycles and simplified communities.

These, however, are rare cases. A successful approach to management should rest on the concept of the coiled spring. By *nature* succession moves upward, as does the coiled spring, toward greater stability and complexity. All prolonged downward shifts, or compressions in the spring, that I have experienced (and they are many on three continents) could be traced to human intervention in the process by the purposeful or accidental application of one or other of the tools listed in the tools row of the HRM model. The moment we reduce or cease that pressure on the spring, it rebounds, and the community gradually returns to complexity and stability.

This is a *very* important principle as at present we spend billions of dollars annually worldwide on actions that compress the spring while chasing objectives that small advances in succession could produce. Attempts to eradicate a so-called pest plant or animal species with traps, guns, or poison generally symbolize our tendency to ignore the force of succession and deal only with its effects.

Theoretically these direct measures could work occasionally if our intervention did nothing to other species, but that rarely happens. Most intervention compresses the whole spring by damaging many species, when a real solution depends on letting the spring expand.

If the species we act against is for some reason itself a major predator, we risk greater consequences than if it had been a prey species, as the effects on the community become magnified. American biologist Robert Paine demonstrated this principle dramatically in a study he did in a seashore environment. When he removed the main predator—a certain species of starfish—from a population of fifteen species, things quickly changed. In the resulting competition for space, those species that could move left the area; those that couldn't simply died out. Within a year, the area was occupied by only eight of the original fifteen species. Paine speculated that in time even more species would be lost. His control area, which still contained the predatory starfish, over the same time remained a complex community where all species thrived.[3]

Some fluctuation of species is natural within the dynamic successional process, especially among short-lived organisms with high reproductive rates such as often characterize lower successional communities. Prolonged downward movement to lower successional levels of a whole community is unnatural, however, and, excepting the occasional natural catastrophe, virtually always betrays human intervention.

The cultivation of large areas of uniform crops is believed by modern agroeconomists to be the most efficient and most economical method of farming. This is a myth. Management is eased to the extent that larger machines save labor, but the amount of chemicals necessary to keep these monocultures productive leads to a dependency and financial commitment that becomes ever greater. Economists, who do not understand this, have promoted measures to reduce a farmer's hours of labor but caused him to lose the farm. Nature does not discern between a monoculture of mankind's chosen crops on one area and a monoculture of cheat grass on the watershed.

Both lead to severe disruption of the successional advance to stable communities.

The instability of monocultures expresses itself in many ways, the most obvious being blights, insect outbreaks, and soil destruction. These things in turn exact a very high social price in floods, droughts, unhealthy water, disease, starvation, political strife, and war. Our agricultural practices have already brought on enough of all that to make the point. When economists and politicians get a better grip on the principle of succession, they might still find a way out.

12

Mineral Cycle

L ike water, mineral nutrients follow a cyclical pattern as they are used and reused by living organisms. Nevertheless, because we don't see these nutrients so conspicuously in motion, we ignore the extent to which management methods can alter drastically the speed, efficiency, and complexity of their circular journey within the ecosystem.

A good mineral cycle implies a biologically active *living* soil with good aeration and energy to sustain an abundance of organisms, which are in continuous contact with nitrogen, oxygen, and carbon from the atmosphere. Because the organisms require energy derived from sunlight, but do not come to the surface to obtain it firsthand, they will rely on a continuous supply of decomposing plant and animal residues. A good mineral cycle cannot function in a dead soil, a fact often forgotten in our modern obsession with chemical fertilizers and other technology.

On farms, agricultural chemicals destroy many soil microorganisms and inhibit others, such as those that convert nitrogen from the air to a form that plants can use. Turning over soil speeds the breakdown of organic material, and the planting of monocultures means a less diverse root system and an environment that discourages diversity in microorganism species. All the same problems and possibilities nevertheless exist on rangeland as well.

To farm or ranch at low cost on a sustainable basis, soil and air should provide almost all the mineral nutrients required by plants and animals, including humans. Some minerals come directly from decomposing rocks.

Some come from the atmosphere via falling raindrops or organisms that convert gaseous substances such as nitrogen and carbon to usable form. For most goals involving crops, wildlife, livestock, and timber, we strive to keep nutrients from escaping the cycle and to steadily increase the volume of those cycling in the soil layers that sustain plants.

This concept of high and increasing volume of mineral nutrients cycling and available for use near the soil surface is easy to visualize (see figure 12-1). To achieve it, however, requires a grasp of the natural processes that produced healthy growing conditions for eons before anyone thought of chemical fertilizers or pesticides. These processes are incredibly complex, but here we will look at the basic principles we need to know to use the HRM model, remembering the mineral cycle itself is totally interconnected with the other three ecosystem foundation blocks; what we do to one affects them all.

In order to benefit humans, wildlife, and livestock, mineral nutrients have to be brought aboveground in living plants. To obtain maximum supplies in the active soil layers, minerals must be pumped up to the surface from deeper soil layers. Then they must be returned underground. And there they will be held in the active zones or lost back to greater depths.

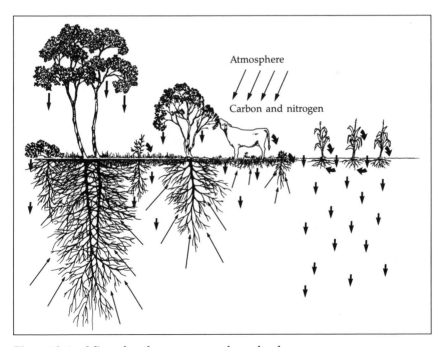

Figure 12-1. Mineral cycle on range and cropland.

Minerals to the Surface

Plant roots are the main agents for lifting mineral nutrients to the surface layers of soil or taking them aboveground. For a good mineral cycle then, we need deep, healthy root systems. In addition, we need a wide range of plant species. Just as you recognize plants aboveground by their appearance, so could you know them underground by the wide variety of rooting patterns. Some have abundant surface roots while others probe deep, sometimes reaching below the soil itself into rock crevices and cracks, to seek water and nutrients, which then move upward through the plant.

Even though your goal may rest primarily on shallow-rooted plants such as grass, corn, or wheat, some deep-rooted plants may be essential to the health of the whole community. Incredibly small amounts of many trace minerals are critical to plants and animals, including humans, and they may lie beyond reach of shallow roots. If you have ever noticed the many colors and textures in soil layers revealed by a highway cut, you have an idea of the variety of essential nutrients that might be found at widely varying depths.

Although plant roots are the main agents in mineral uplift, many small animals play an important role too. Earthworms are the obvious example, but in drier areas termites and other insects often help perform this function.

Aboveground to Surface

Plant material, having obtained nutrients from the soil and, in certain cases, air, finally returns to the soil surface in the form of crop residues, leaves, stems, bark, branches, seeds, and flowers. This may happen quickly, or over a period of many years in the case of some plant parts, though the activity of animals, birds, and other organisms may speed the process.

Returning plant material to the surface, however, does not necessarily make it available for reuse. For that, nutrients have to move underground, and this does not happen until they are broken down into finer particles by fire; chemical weathering (oxidation); mechanical forces such as rain, wind, and hail; or by biological activity.

Biological activity should play the lead role in both brittle and nonbrittle environments, though with one key difference. In nonbrittle situations, the microenvironment at the surface typically supports extremely active communities of small organisms throughout the year that will break down old plant material without any contribution from larger animals.

In brittle environments, conditions do not easily favor abundant or stable populations of small organisms. Only when the disturbance of large animals lays mulch and litter on the soil and breaks the surface so succession can be maintained can the proper microenvironment occur.

Without adequate large animal impact, plant spacings enlarge and soil becomes exposed, creating a harsh environment indeed. Some mobile organisms, like termites, will build their earth structures out over the bare soil to reach dung or leaf fall, but this activity alone cannot sustain a good mineral cycle. In an environment where plant spacings are wide and soil exposed, few forces exist to decompose old plant material or even hold it in place against the forces of wind and water.

Fire drastically alters material, of course, and this may not always be bad, though aside from other dangers its tendency to expose the soil surface can often be negative in a brittle environment.

The third force, weathering, also functions differently in brittle and nonbrittle environments. In the nonbrittle, where humidity tends to be higher and more consistent, weathering may play little part, as biological decay proceeds so rapidly. By contrast, in brittle environments, even those with high rainfall, most dead plant material breaks down through slow oxidation and weathering. This can create a bottleneck in the cycle as nutrients remain tied up aboveground for long periods in old material. Large accumulations of unrecycled plant parts suppress plant growth (especially in grasses where growth points are close to the ground) and reduce uptake of those nutrients that eventually do get below the soil.

In most brittle environments the same process can lead to the premature death of perennial grass plants, as sunlight is unable to penetrate the accumulated old growth to reach the plants' growing points.

In all brittle environments, therefore, animal activity in various forms speeds the breakdown and cycling of the plant material essential to building mineral supplies in the top layers of soil. Also, in contrast to fire, animal activity achieves this effect without exposing soil.

Surface to Underground

Once biological action, fire, oxidation, or weather has done its work, how do the critical nutrients move underground? Only two agents, water and animal life in the soil, can bring this about naturally. That explains why in applying the HRM model to enhance the mineral cycle you will tend most often to apply tools that encourage water penetration and animal activity.

One further danger remains, however. The same water that carries nutrients underground can carry them on down below the root zone of plant types you hope to encourage. This is called leaching. The main factor that impedes leaching is organic matter in the soil. The chemistry by which organic molecules bind mineral elements is extremely complex but derives from the same principles that allow organic matter to create the beneficial crumb structure referred to in Chapter 10. The less organic material (from dead plants and animals) and the less biological activity, the greater the tendency for leaching to occur.

Therein lies one of the great dangers of chemical herbicides, pesticides, and fertilizers to our soils. The more we apply, the more we destroy organic material and living organisms in the soil, and the more we decrease the soil's water-retaining capabilities, the more we increase the effects of leaching. This is why farmers who add soluble nitrogen in various forms to their land have to keep applying it in ever increasing amounts. By damaging the natural mineral cycle, they must spend increasing amounts to replace the nutrients that leach out of it. The leached minerals not only become unusable on that particular piece of ground, they may become highly dangerous pollutants as groundwater flow carries them to places they were never intended to be.

The Importance of the Soil Surface

The key to the health of the mineral cycle, like that of both succession and the water cycle, ultimately lies in the condition of the soil surface. An exposed surface, capped by the effects of rainfall, is a harsh microenvironment in which biological breakdown occurs slowly at best. Such a capped surface also limits air exchange between the soil and the atmosphere. As aeration decreases, so does life. As life decreases, so does organic material. As organic material decreases, so does soil structure. As soil structure decreases so does aeration. As this chain reaction ripples through the ecosystem, fewer plants produce less soil cover and more bare, capped soil.

Though this syndrome occurs seldom in nonbrittle environments, where new communities readily reestablish on bare soil surfaces, it is ever present in the desertification of brittle ones. In brittle environments too, the inter-connections among the four ecosystem foundation blocks, though present everywhere, show most clearly.

We have explored the relationships among water, soil structure, mineral availability, and the succession of living things from microorganisms to herds of large mammals and the plants they depend on. The next chapter will explore the flow of energy that animates them all.

13

Energy Flow

Three of the ecosystem foundation blocks, the water cycle, the mineral cycle, and succession, are dynamic processes that govern the ways in which all life on this planet relates as one whole. This chapter on the fourth block, energy flow, addresses the question of fuel to keep all processes and life functioning.

The energy flow in our ecosystem is sometimes referred to as the carbon cycle, because the storage of energy in living organisms always involves carbon. To focus on that, however, misses the point most relevant to the task of management: that the natural living world runs on solar power, and mankind's management decisions can drastically affect how much is captured and put to use.

The importance of this statement warrants a little reflection in this world of electronic marvels and drive-up burger joints. All living things, apart from a few such as rare organisms dwelling near thermal springs deep in the ocean, depend for food on the ability of green plants to capture the energy of sunlight and convert it to usable form.

Photovoltaic, hydroelectric, wind, and tidal power sources also convert energy, but not directly into edible forms. Nor do geothermal and nuclear power plants produce food directly. Fossil fuels, though they represent solar energy stored by green plants, are nonrenewable and inedible.

The Energy Pyramid

Traditionally the flow of sunlight is represented as an energy pyramid, as shown in figure 13-1. Of the sunlight striking land and water, some is re-

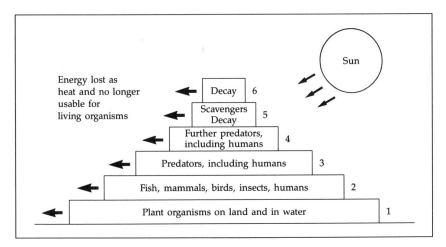

Figure 13-1.   Basic energy pyramid.

flected back immediately, some is absorbed as heat to be radiated back later. A very small portion is converted by green plants into food for their own growth and that of other organisms in the food chain. Thus green plants form the base, or level 1, of the energy pyramid and support almost all other forms of life, including, of course, humans.

Level 2 represents the energy stored by animals that eat the plants of level 1—fish, mammals, insects, birds, and humans. It is smaller by the amount of energy expended in the living process of the feeders.

Level 3, the realm of predators (again including humans), which eat the eaters of Level 1, is smaller still for the same reason.

At Level 4 we again find humans and some other predators dining on fish and the other predators that fed on level 2. Once more the living processes of the feeders have diminished the bulk of energy remaining in storage.

By level 5 humans drop out of the pyramid. Scavengers and organisms of decay reduce the bulk of stored energy yet further, and beyond that perhaps another level or two of decay organisms will consume the last remaining useful energy. The complicated organic molecules assembled by the original green plants will then have been broken down, having made energy from sunlight available to many organisms.

At all levels, of course, a portion of the energy passes straight on to decay levels through feces, urine, etc. in the animals and through microorganisms that feed on the plants. Thus in real life the energy pyramid is not exact or tidy. However, the concept of ever decreasing volume in usable energy holds throughout. None of this energy is actually destroyed or used up; its form merely changes to one that is nonusable as food for life.

Humanity's position in the pyramid covers three possible levels. One person can actually dine on all three in a good fish chowder, in which the potatoes represent level 1, the piece of grain-fed salt pork level 2, and the boiled cod level 3.

Where high human populations exist on restricted land, people tend to feed directly off level 1 rather than sacrifice the energy lost by first passing the food through the animals in Level 2. The animal protein they do consume probably comes from animals that do not compete with them. Fish or other animals may feed at the same level but off plants that humans cannot eat, or at higher levels from animal wastes, including humanity's.

The energy pyramid also extends belowground where the energy flow greatly affects the health of the other three ecosystem foundation blocks— mineral cycle, water cycle, and succession—as all three require a biologically active soil community, which in turn requires solar energy to be conveyed underground mainly by plant roots. This is depicted in figure 13-2.

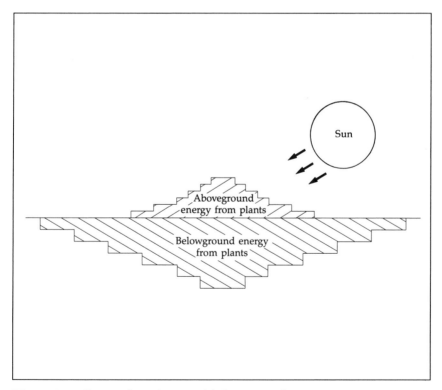

Figure 13-2. Energy flow above and below ground.

The Energy Tetrahedron

The discovery of the four missing keys has enabled us to see that the old two-dimensional pyramid diagram does not reveal the possibility of much sophistication in the management of energy flow.

Clearly, the broader the base of the pyramid, the larger the whole structure, and the more energy available for use at every level. The old two-dimensional view, however, suggests very few ways of broadening the base. On cropland we have done it by increasing acreage, producing better yielding crop strains, irrigating, planting two or more crops on the same land, and so on. On rangeland we have done it through various technologies such as brush clearing, range reseeding, and so on. In both cases, especially in industrialized countries, we accomplished this through heavy use of resources in a nonrenewable manner to fuel machinery and manufacture fertilizers and chemicals.

Even discounting the fact that many of these methods tend to damage natural water cycles, mineral cycles, and succession to the extent that only increasing outside energy input can compensate, most present technology quickly reaches the point of energy debt: Broadening the base requires more energy than it returns in captured sunlight. As long as fossil fuel remains abundant and cheap, and we ignore the long-term effects of our heavy consumption, this fact may appear academic. However, in countries where inputs are costly, it is already a question of life and death. It underlies much of the American farm crisis of the 1980s. And in the case of vast but minimally productive rangelands it already prices technical solutions far out of reach. The problems can only get worse until humanity understands and starts to manage energy flow as an integral part of succession, water, and mineral cycles.

With the application of the missing keys we have come to view the energy pyramid as multidimensional, above and below ground—i.e., as two tetrahedrons joined at their bases (figure 13-3). In applying this concept we now have opportunities for increasing the energy base greatly. The crucial bottom level now has three sides, which I call *time, volume,* and *area,* as indicated on the cross-section of the double tetrahedron shown in figure 13-4.

The right management can increase the volume of energy stored at level 1, not only by raising the *volume* of standing crop on a unit of ground, but also by lengthening the *time* during which that crop can grow, and by expanding the leaf *area* of individual plants to capture more energy.

Clearly, the more we can extend any of the three sides of the base, the more energy humans can harvest at levels 2, 3, and 4. On the other hand,

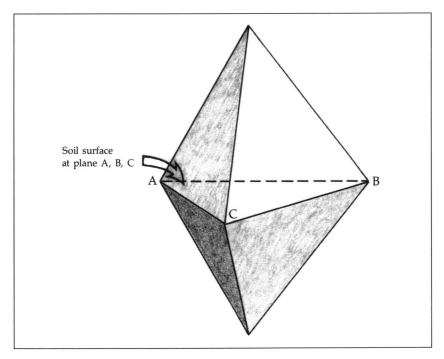

Soil surface
at plane A, B, C

A

B

C

Figure 13-3. Energy flow seen as two tetrahedrons.

shortening any single side cuts the amount of energy all the way up, and the same effect ripples underground.

Before going into detail about how this works in practice, one example should illustrate what attention to energy flow can mean in management.

Once while consulting on a ranch struck by a serious drought, I found that my lecturing on the importance of increasing energy flow appeared to bore the rancher to distraction. He wanted to discuss less theoretical questions like the hay he would have to buy and stock he would have to sell. But in fact his problem really *was* a matter of energy flow, and his exasperation forced me to state it in less theoretical terms.

I asked him to calculate the hay he would have to buy to replace the one extra ounce of grass that he could grow per square yard if he applied our knowledge of energy flow. Multiplied by the area of his land, that ounce represented fifteen million pounds of grass. We grew that, and more, at no extra cost by applying tools that increase energy flow, and it saved him thousands of dollars in hay purchases and herd reduction. Perceiving the full ramifications of energy flow nevertheless requires understanding by the practical rancher and farmer, so let us look at the three sides.

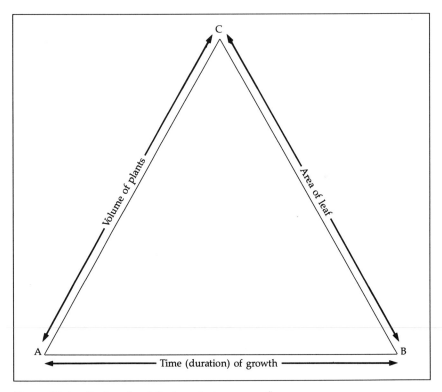

Figure 13-4. Surface level that controls energy flow.

Time (Duration) of Growth

The energy converted by plants when green and growing must support all life both above and below ground *throughout* the year. The longer the time when plants are growing, the more productive the ecosystem as a whole. We can increase the growing time (the time side of the base) by lengthening the growing season or by using the available growing time within the season more efficiently.

In practice, producing a better mineral cycle, water cycle, and higher successional complexity will extend growing time in both these ways. In the management of grasses, the growing time can also be used more efficiently if grazed or cut plants are not taken down too far. The less taken from a plant during its active growth, the faster it regrows, as it has more leaf area with which to convert sunlight immediately.

Earlier I described my frustrations in learning about time as a dimension in grazing on brittle rangelands and how we had to plan its manipulation to neither overgraze nor depress the performance of the animals. Later, under the guideline of time, we will see how to actually prevent severe grazers from reducing the energy flow on complex rangelands although they graze some plants severely within the first hour or so on the land as they select their diet.

Taking rangeland as an example, naturally anything that creates better growing conditions through improvements in water and mineral cycles will allow plants to make more efficient use of growing time. The role of the water cycle, however, deserves special attention. Under good management of the four ecosystem foundation blocks, moisture will remain available in the soil after falling temperatures and daylight hours end the growing season. As explained in Chapter 10, that enables plants to start growing the instant the new year restores those conditions. Given a noneffective water cycle, growth won't start until the first rain. Given a more effective water cycle, plants can also continue to grow for a much longer time during dry spells in the growing season since less moisture is lost through evaporation.

The opposite problem, too much water due to overirrigation or poor drainage and aeration, also occurs, cutting time out of the growing season. Every hour with adequate temperatures in which plants cannot grow at their best potential rate because of poor aeration means lost energy conversion on croplands under rainfall or irrigation as I illustrated with the example of the cabbages in Chapter 10.

Succession too has a fundamental relationship to growing time. The most obvious examples are rangelands that support both cool season and warm season grasses. A high and diverse level of succession will include enough of both to ensure that some part of the plant community will perform at peak capacity as long as any growth is possible. The annual grasslands produced by poor management, such as we find over most of California, illustrate this clearly. On these rangelands where the dominant grasses are now annuals there are prolonged good growth periods in every year in which no growth at all is taking place, as the perennial grasses that could and should be converting energy have for the most part disappeared.

Illustration 13-1 shows some of the few remnant patches of perennial grassland that yet survive on one California ranch today. Even as they continue to grow actively and convert energy to fuel the rest of the ecosystem, the annual grasses that have come to dominate the surrounding land have long since finished their cycle, dried off, and died. A change in management, now possible through the HRM model, could bring back the perennials that once covered the land and restore months of productivity to the area.

The same principles for extending time apply equally well on croplands and offer even more management opportunities. Illustration 13-2 shows the poor growth of plants in an overirrigated field in New Mexico alongside excellent growth in the same plants on the edge of the field where aeration

Illustration 13-1.   Remnant perennial grass patch in annual California grassland (courtesy Richard King).

is accidentally good. The plants on the edge reached cutting stage a month before the main crop. Similar photographs could show the difference in time efficiency rendered by applying nitrogen fertilizer in periodic light dressings as opposed to a single large dose. Good selection of heat- and cold-tolerant crops and planting dates can also extend effective growing seasons and, thus, the time base of the energy tetrahedron.

Volume (of Plants)

By volume, I am not referring to the simple bulk of the annual harvest, which of course we want to increase, but to the number of plants growing on each square yard of land. Ten plants growing on the average square yard of ground probably can convert more solar energy than three. Farmers have long recognized that the spaces between plants can greatly affect energy flow in their fields and have managed accordingly.

In nonbrittle rangelands the spacing between plants, which is close, is a reflection of climate more than physical disturbance of the soil. Management

Illustration 13-2.   Sparse growth of grass in overirrigated hay field with excellent growth on well-drained edge (foreground). Albuquerque, New Mexico.

can affect it, but plant spacing will be close with or without disturbance. By contrast, the more brittle the environment, the more plant spacings are affected by disturbance. Fire, animals, machines, or any combination of these over time can lead to close plant spacings. Incorrectly applied, any one of these can expand the bare spaces between plants.

Illustrations 13-3, 13-4, and 13-5, taken on the Barlite Ranch in west Texas, show the difference disturbance can make in a brittle environment. Illustration 13-3, taken in 1982, shows the bare spaces on a piece of land within the ranch boundaries that was fenced off and thus undisturbed for some years. A series of fixed-point photographs, including illustration 13-4 (taken in 1985), reveals that these plant spacings have widened continually as old plants stagnated from overrest and new seedlings failed to establish on the bare capped soil. Illustration 13-5, taken in 1984, shows nearby land where the rancher has planned the grazings and subjected the land to disturbance in the form of high animal impact. Its proximity to a livestock watering point intensifies the effect. Plant densities show a very positive correlation to disturbance by livestock. As animal impact increases closer to the water, the plants are more closely spaced. Clearly, more energy can be converted where more plants grow.

Illustration 13-3. View of long-rested land showing sparse grass and bare ground between plants, 1982. Barlite Ranch, Texas.

Traditionally people have believed that such plant spacings on arid rangelands were a function of climate and soil (which is correct in an extremely nonbrittle environment) and thus lay beyond their control, but management can be crucial as these photographs show. Chapter 18 describes animal impact and its management in more detail. Suffice it to say here that it does provide a means of increasing volume of plants per unit area of land significantly in brittle environments.

Area (of Leaf)

Plants adapt themselves in three major ways to suit growing conditions. Hydrophytic, or wet, plants thrive in soggy, poorly aerated ground. Mesophytic, or middle, plants grow best when air and water are balanced in the soil. Xerophytic, or dry, plants survive where water is poor, though the aeration may be good.

In some ways the wet and dry plants resemble each other more than they do the middle plants. Both often have cuticles or skins over their leaves,

Illustration 13-4. Identical view as illustration 13-3, taken three years later (1985). Grass has become more sparse and bare ground has increased under continued rest. Barlite Ranch, Texas.

and mechanisms around their breathing pores that enable them to pass little water through their systems. Both may have narrow leaves or leaf-stems (green stems that convert energy), which reduce the area exposed to sunlight. Some dry plants may have broader leaves, but they are tightly rolled for the same reason.

The wet-type plants, such as water lilies, bulrushes, cattails, many sedges, and some grasses, can be found in wet sites with poor drainage, but also where exposed, hard, and capped soil causes poor aeration. Likewise, dry plants such as cacti, euphorbias, and some grasses can be found in areas where moisture is minimal, and also where exposed, hard, and capped soil causes rapid loss of moisture either through run-off or evaporation. Among the dry-type plants, the perennial grasses often stand out clearly in the dormant season when they dry off to a white or very pale color.

Both wet- and dry-type plants tend to grow slowly and thus store a limited amount of solar energy in a given time.

The middle-type plants are very different. They produce generally open, flat, and broad leaves that only curl when wilting under moisture stress.

Illustration 13-5.   View of dense complex grassland growing right up to the watering point produced by heavy animal impact and grazing, 1984. (Bare ground on left is the waterpoint.) Barlite Ranch, Texas.

They do not have thick protective skins or well-developed mechanisms to shut off breathing pores. They also tend to grow rapidly when moisture and temperature are favorable. In contrast to their cousins in the dry category, many of the middle perennial grasses cure to red or gold in the dormant season, which happens also to reflect a far more nutritious dry forage for animals.

Old-timers in South Africa made the distinction between *witveld* and *rooiveld* (white range and red range). In America this difference can also be seen along many western highways. Protected from grazing and periodically disturbed by mowing, these roadside grasses often have a definite reddish or deep gold tinge when dormant. Yet, just over the fence, where overgrazing and insufficient animal impact have degraded the environment, the grasses show pale or dead white in color.

Obviously, to increase the area side of the energy tetrahedron on range- land you need to shift the community to the middle plant that spreads broad leaves to the sun and grows fast. As in the case of plant spacings, most people have always felt that plant type depended on soil type and lay beyond their control. Occasionally, something like an impervious layer of clay or rock below the surface can indeed kill any chance for the middle plant, but generally poor water-to-air balance results from sealed or capped soil and poor water cycles, which management can change.

In Zimbabwe I have seen, in the course of twelve years, a patch of 84 percent *Loudecia* grasses—known for their fibrousness, poor forage quality, and association with badly-drained ground—change to an 80 percent mix of productive middle grasses associated with good drainage. We had applied tools to minimize overgrazing and promote closer plant spacings. The change in species was an unexpected by-product and led to more observations of the same kind.

In addition to causing grass plants in brittle environments to grow closer together, animal impact and severe grazing (without overgrazing) causes many species to produce more leaves and less fiber, which in turn increases the flow of available energy to animals and humans.

Using Technology to Increase Energy Flow

We can also increase energy flow through direct use of technology in many forms—machinery, drainage, irrigation, chemicals, and genetic engineering, to name a few examples. However, in doing so we need to be particularly alert to the fact that such direct intervention in one of the ecosystem processes can be extremely dangerous because we are dealing with complex interrelationships of which we understand little. We must only intervene with technology in ways that allow for simultaneous development (and never damage) of the water cycle, mineral cycle, and successional process.

None of these ecosystem foundation blocks can safely be bolstered at the expense of the others. As I have mentioned, enhancing energy flow through heavy inputs of fossil fuel products (which damages succession, water, and mineral cycles) has been the cornerstone of American agriculture. But we are paying a heavy price for our ignorance—food and water riddled with life-threatening chemicals, rising rates of cancer and other diseases, accelerated erosion destroying millions of years of biological capital, millions in public funds spent yearly to kill insects and other increasingly resistant pests, and ultimately thousands of farmers and ranchers leaving the land followed by once healthy small businesses and rural communities.

Conclusion

Most of our goals involve a high quality of life and require the highest energy flow possible that doesn't damage the ecosystem, whether range, cropland, forest, or national park be our concern.

In most cropland situations we will strive to manage for a good water cycle, good mineral cycle, high successional complexity—above and below ground—and thus a high and sustainable energy flow. We will seek to maximize the *time* side of the energy tetrahedron's base by insuring good daily growth rates and lengthening the season through polyculture crops and two or more crops per year whenever possible. We will maximize *volume* by planting with close spacings. We will maximize the *area* of leaf open and exposed to sunlight by creating good drainage, crumb structure, and abundant organic matter in the soil and providing adequate soil cover. In the future we will be better able to manage our soils and increase the energy flow to the microorganisms that populate them by planting the perennial grain crops now under development.

In most rangeland situations we will increase energy flow by manipulating the tools of grazing and animal impact, with both livestock and wildlife, to produce and maintain the maximum *time, volume,* and *area* at the energy tetrahedron's base. The amount of energy we might have to buy from other producers on other land, to supplement what our own land does not provide, would be the measure of success or failure.

PART V

Tools to Manage Our Ecosystem

14

Introduction

Below the row of ecosystem foundation blocks in the HRM model stands the row of tools, but the word here gets a broad definition, not merely tools-of-the-trade but tools.

In the spirit of holism, tools include everything that gives humans the ability—which most organisms lack—to alter the ecosystem in order to achieve predetermined goals.

All tools available to humans—from stone age axes to genetic engineering—fall under one or another heading in the tools row. Be you politician, economist, engineer, sociologist, veterinarian, widget maker, or whatever, you will not find a tool that is not included within the general headings.

Human creativity and money and labor bracket the other tool headings in the model because both come into play in the use of any tool. We list money and labor together because the once simple combination of labor, creativity, and resources frequently operates through the agency of money—financial resources in bankers' jargon. The capitalist's investments, the labor of a tribal commune, or the unpaid children on a family farm all function according to similar principles to be covered in the Guidelines row of the model.

Short as it appears, the list of tools includes things that often fall outside an overspecialized perspective. A typical example is the civil engineer commissioned to stabilize an eroding watershed in order to save an important dam and irrigation project from silt.

The average engineer's toolkit contains only technology. Thus, the average engineer may contour all the slopes, build silt traps in all the valleys, and undertake great plantations of trees. But in a brittle environment that will only slow the process. Inevitably, the dam will silt up, as past civilizations have abundantly illustrated.

A look at tools other than technology may greatly expand the possibility of success. Brittle environments, for example, need some form of periodic disturbance over millions of acres to maintain productivity and stability and no technology can provide this. Within a short time the animal impact tool could lay mulch and litter, break the capping, and encourage new plants, thus eliminating the primary cause of the erosion.

Consider the veterinarian in Africa, paid to maintain cattle in an area where none ever grazed before. When the tick population builds up, he recommends a yearly dipping in a chemical pesticide. In time, however, that proves insufficient, so the dippings increase until weekly dipping becomes necessary although uneconomical. He tries a more powerful, and dangerous, pesticide. Eventually the ticks overwhelm that measure too, and other diseases accompanying environmental deterioration crop up as well.

Though the pesticide has killed a wide spectrum of organisms, including tick parasites, though poorly-managed grazing has accelerated the rádical simplification of the environment, that doesn't concern the vet. He only thinks about cattle health.

The problem is serious in Africa, but the average vet has only one tool—technology. When that fails, he will plead for research grants to finance his quest for some miracle that will protect cows in an ever deteriorating environment. A look at tools outside his profession would show that grazing and animal impact could improve cattle health by restoring ecosystem complexity. Costs, ticks, and disease would decrease and production would improve.

Sociologists, economists, and politicians can similarly move beyond the tools traditionally available to them within their professions.

The tools of the future will undoubtedly incorporate many technological wonders, but broad thinking might lead to others that break new ground. A small child in my own family, after watching a television program where Israel's Uri Geller bent iron with his mind and a light stroke of his fingers, picked up a steel nail file and did the same thing himself. He was of course too young to know, as we all do, that "you can't do that."

For most of us, such mind-over-matter phenomena fall completely outside the toolchest, and just reading the last paragraph makes us wince if we are respectable. Nevertheless, that is just the attitude we must avoid at all costs when looking at the Tools row of the HRM model, which may well be expanded in the future.

As holism is applied in management, all tools are equal. No tool is good or bad and no judgments should be made in isolation from the whole. Only when the three-part goal and the nature of the environment is known, together with all other factors having a bearing on the situation, is any tool finally judged suitable or unsuitable. Fire, for instance, is good when it keeps my hands warm on a cold morning, but it is bad when it is burning down my house.

We'll examine each of the tools in the following chapters in light of how they *tend* to affect each of the four ecosystem foundation blocks. Once those tendencies are acknowledged, a careful consideration of the guidelines helps us judge which tool, or tools, is best to apply. Even then we always assume that we could be wrong and we monitor our application of the tools to ensure that they take us toward our goals.

15

Money & Labor

Once upon a time people supported themselves by applying creativity and labor (brains and brawn) directly to the raw resources of the ecosystem. Many societies still do this, as do many farm and ranch families not actually paying for the labor of family members. We have used, and continue to use, our creativity to obtain the maximum effect with as little labor as possible.

Because money and labor are often linked (e.g., cash can be exchanged for labor), we group them together in the HRM model. Ideally, our natural tendency to economize on labor should apply equally to money. But money is a more complicated matter and this isn't often the case.

In 1985 I spoke to a group of economists from various universities and asked them to define wealth. To my surprise they grappled over that question for a long time and in the end only defined wealth as money. Well, once upon a time money probably did perfectly represent wealth, but that was a long time ago, and the fact that many experts still believe it is a disturbing aspect of modern times.

The distinction between wealth and money has taken a few millennia to develop. Humans in a primitive state organized around small family units had no money but they did have wealth. If we had bothered to measure that wealth, we would have tallied up the natural resources available for use in our group's home range or territory, our tools and weapons, the protective quality of our cave, and perhaps the closeness of our ties to one another.

There is some controversy over whether family groups evolved into urban societies after discovering how to domesticate certain plants and animals or after discovering excellent hunting grounds, which included sites rich in the resources needed for making tools and weapons. Whichever it was, at some point very early on human communities developed to the extent that individuals could share the tasks of survival and specialize in what they did best. Until this point was reached, there was no need for a medium of exchange.

Following settlement and specialization the need became urgent. If I had been crippled in the hunt but could make excellent spear points, and you were an excellent hunter, but not so good at making spear points, we could begin to trade spear points for meat or hides. If I grew a good crop but elephants flattened yours, we could do a trade this season. I would help feed your family in return for your doing the same for mine, should a similar fate befall me.

While our community was still very small such exchanges could be memorized or recorded as marks on a stick or bone. We would all know each other well and thus trust that our deals would be honored. As communities became larger, this might no longer apply. I might have become an expert sandal maker by this time who traded pairs of sandals for half a sheep or a basket of grain. However, I didn't always want the sheep or grain immediately and those needing the sandals might not be ready to slaughter or harvest. So they gave me a token representing the trade, which I would redeem later. This worked well until I needed a blanket from the man most expert at making them, but he needed no sandals. We overcame this impasse by creating money. I got my blanket by giving the blanket maker a token given to me by the grain farmer. The blanket maker then collected the basket of grain, which he did need. In fact he needed more than one basket of grain to feed his family and he got two more baskets by giving the grain farmer two blanket tokens, which he promised to honor before winter.

Such tokens would have been extremely convenient, as they still are, to carry and store or accumulate for later use, in exchange for some service (labor) or goods (grain, blanket, sandals).

Once such tokens were established as a trusted means of exchange, they inevitably began to be distributed through the population in an uneven manner. I might begin to accumulate more than my family required for services or goods. One day a close friend approaches me as he has cut his hand badly and is unable to make the hoes on which his family's livelihood depends. He is out of tokens and needs food. I know him and trust him and I realize he will be better soon and able to earn tokens in exchange for the excellent hoes he makes, so I lend him some tokens. However, for this favor we agree that he will return one more token than he borrowed. At this point my tokens (money) began earning me simple interest.

As our community grew, we established trade with a community in the next valley. Since we didn't always know the individuals, we were hesitant to exchange tokens in lieu of goods or services. Was this a token that I made and exchanged for grain a year ago, or has someone cleverly made it to look like mine?

In my Game Department days in Zambia I had the task of paying out a government bonus on bushpigs killed by villagers, over and above those my staff killed in control work. These bonuses were paid out on my behalf by the district commissioners in each district as the country was so large. Once a year I visited the district commissioners, counted the tails collected as tokens of payments made, and then reimbursed their department from mine. At one station I found that the district commissioner had paid out a very large sum to the local villagers. Indeed, he had an enormous pile of tails to prove the number of pigs killed and paid for. Much to his dismay, my game scouts and I sat down and inspected each tail carefully as we counted. Slowly we sorted out a small pile of genuine tails from a mountain of clever counterfeits. The villagers had economized on labor and found it paid better to spend their time making tails from parts of the hide, which they twisted, trimmed, and dried, than to actually hunt pigs.

I never did know who finally reimbursed the district commissioner for all the homemade tokens he had bought. I certainly didn't.

Those Zambian villagers weren't the first to make their own tokens. At some point in the past one source for making tokens in a way that made counterfeiting them difficult would have had to be agreed upon. Otherwise, we would not have retained our confidence in the value of tokens, or money as they had now officially become.

Once there was one source for the manufacture of money, there was also the possibility that more could be made and put into circulation than represented actual services or goods exchanged. Thus was primitive inflation born.

From here it was easy for one of us, who had accumulated money and was lending it periodically, to develop a safe place to keep it from thieves. Others might ask if they could also store their money with this person when they were away. Soon this storer-of-money would find that he could lend yours and earn interest as long as he had enough money available when you got back. In fact, he would increasingly find that he could do this even if you didn't go away, as long as we all had confidence in him and didn't ask for our money back at the same time. Thus was primitive banking born.

Now, you as a grain producer find that you want to build a larger house before winter and need several people to help you. Your grain won't be ready to harvest for several months, so you borrow the necessary money from the banker to pay for this labor. It's going to take more than he has in safekeeping and to allow for some who might come to get their money. He hasn't got enough to lend you but, at the same time, he does not want to lose this opportunty to earn interest. He is creative and agrees to let you have credit up to the amount you require. He will honor pieces of parchment with his mark on them up to this amount as and when your laborers present them to him. Now, not only can the central manufacturer of the money cause inflation, so can the lender of money.

Money has been the oil that has kept the wheels of society turning and has allowed the complexity of our present civilization to develop, but credit and the centralized creation of money have seriously destabilized the relationship between money and the goods and services, or wealth, it was meant to represent.

In my lifetime alone the distinction between wealth and money has probably become more blurred than at any time in history. Interest above 3 percent was usurious when I was a child; now that's seen as quaintly old-fashioned. Major banks move headquarters to states with more lenient usury laws and still retain customer confidence. Where it was once unacceptable for lenders to advertise or engage in aggressive promotion, it is now commonplace. The use of credit cards, compound interest, and the electronic speedup of monetary transactions (nationally and internationally) have blurred the distinction even further. Today fortunes can be made in corporate takeovers or through creative accounting, where real goods or services play little or no part.

It becomes easy as one stands in a plush, air-conditioned bank, humming with electronic activity, to lose sight of the underlying wealth in the financial resources we manage. Whatever the source of the money—real goods and services or corporate takeover—it all looks the same as we stare at the dollar bills or the computerized spreadsheet. Primitive societies did not make this mistake, as their wealth and reality were one and the same thing. But for us the *token*, which our ancestors created to facilitate the exchange of goods and labor, has become our *reality* today as those university economists so clearly demonstrated.

The urban life of most people seldom challenges this misconception as we fill all our basic and not so basic needs with cash or credit, and it doesn't seem to matter much where either comes from. As a rule, the bigger the institution, be it public or private, national or international, the farther it tends to depart from managing real wealth. Governments attempt to manage whole economies by manipulating the money supply but pay ever decreasing heed to the underlying sources of wealth.

Most of the goals we select in applying holistic resource management— whether they apply to us as individuals or to the nation as a whole—should involve a sustainable source of wealth, as the reality is more vital than the symbol. However, to manage wealth as it has become today, where a dollar— regardless of source—can purchase the same things as any other dollar, we must first understand the three most basic sources of wealth the dollar represents:

1. Human creativity combined with labor and raw resources (soil, timber, dung used as fuel, water, oil, coal, gas, gold, silver, uranium, etc.).

I call money derived from this first combination *mineral dollars*. Mineral dollar wealth has certain characteristics:

- The raw resources from which it is derived can be employed cyclically over prolonged time, as in the case of paper or metals that are recycled (with further input of energy, which itself involves mineral dollar wealth), or soil, timber, and dung that can be constantly regenerated with inputs of free solar energy.

Money so generated can be used to develop infrastructure for the generation of future wealth—e.g., education, buildings, factories, farms, railroads, highways, etc.

- The raw resources can be used noncyclically in a once only manner of consumption, e.g., soils in mainstream American agriculture, most oil and gas consumption, and underground water too polluted for reuse.

Energy derived from these raw resources can also produce by-products that are potentially destructive to the ecosystem. We have abundant evidence that the present consumption of coal, oil, gas, firewood, fire-dung, and uranium/plutonium may soon endanger life as we know it. Over billions of years our planet has evolved mechanisms for handling the tremendous changes in atmospheric gasses that take place slowly over a long period of time. It is now clear, however, that it cannot absorb the rapid changes thrust upon it by today's industries and transport systems, which belch fumes into the atmosphere at a phenomenal rate. The destruction of millions of acres of tropical forests (which once aided in purification) and the annual burning of millions of acres of rangelands worldwide, together with the vast areas of reduced vegetation on the world's desertifying watersheds, all hamper the planet's ability to cleanse itself.

2. Many of us acquire money through human creativity and labor alone. I refer to this source as *paper dollars*.

The beauty of such income is that it consumes no other resources. All we have to do is apply our creativity in thousands of different ways to the many avenues open for investment: speculation in futures markets, stocks, bonds, corporate takeovers, etc.

Various services also fall into this category. Service professions do not actually make anything or produce the kind of elemental wealth that supports life, though they do sustain lawyers, accountants, civil servants, etc., and may make life genuinely more comfortable.

The money generated has the fascinating characteristic of apparently instant and unlimited accessibility. Professional speakers, athletes, consultants, and lawyers can charge fees running into the thousands for an hour of labor or service rendered. They justify this correctly because of the time it took to accumulate skill and prepare for the job. At a cost of billions, large bureaucracies may sustain thousands of civil servants and soldiers who produce no useful form of wealth. We can make fortunes in a day with nothing but our creativity and minimal effort in the stock market, or by creating a scandal and selling the tale to a publisher or film maker. On the other hand, this money can vanish as quickly as it appeared.

Paper dollars are backed by confidence in the government and the banking system, rather than any substance.

3. Third, we can generate income from human creativity, labor, and constant sources of energy such as geothermal heat, wind, tides, wave action, falling water, and most of all the sun. Such energy as a source of wealth is noncyclical, but it is apparently inexhaustible (until our sun dies). A characteristic of wealth derived from this combination is that it tends not to damage our life support system or to endanger mankind as far as we know today (not long ago we thought the same of fossil energy and firewood).

A further characteristic is that it is the only form of wealth that can actually feed people. Unfortunately, this requires the conversion of solar energy through plants that depend on water and biologically active soils. Both fall into the first category, i.e., resources that can be mined in a consumptive manner or managed on a sustained basis, depending on the treatment.

I call this last class of money *solar dollars*.

Keeping the three categories of money in mind enables us to see the extent to which failure to do so governs our society now. Economists daily engage in juggling paper dollars, sublimely unaware of the realities of wealth. Farmers likewise (on the advice of "ag-biz" experts) diligently pursue mineral dollars while consumptively mining their soils to do so. The Soil Conservation Service calculates that u.s. farmers "export" two bushels of soil through erosion for every bushel of corn produced.

Sooner or later the underlying basis of a nation's, or an individual's, quality of life asserts its nature. A country rolling in oil revenue today must ask itself to what end the cash flows in. The nation that thrives by burning the oil must ask what that does to the ecosystem that sustains us all. What will happen to the nation's long-term quality of life, production, and landscape goals? If the wealth from oil goes to accumulating paper dollars and supports unproductive legions of bureaucrats, accountants, armed forces, and the thousands of people who consume and keep transactions going but do not create any new wealth besides paper dollars, is that sound?

Shouldn't some of the dollars from nonrenewable wealth go to develop ways to reap solar dollars? Can this be done?

As you use the HRM model in management, you will constantly assess the source of all money and the generation of new wealth. All forms of money will figure in your plans, but only the third form, the solar dollar, will sustain nations and humanity in the long run.

Whatever forms of wealth you control, success in achieving your goals depends on how creatively you use it. This is especially crucial for ranchers and farmers who must depend only on the solar wealth generated from their own land. How you do this will become clearer in the discussion in later chapters on the guidelines that apply to money and labor.

Success or failure, however, begins with *human creativity*, which we look at next.

16

Human Creativity

In *Meeting the Expectations of the Land* poet-farmer Wendell Berry noted that a whole generation of farmers has been brought up to use their heads to advertise others' products (on their caps) and to phone the extension service to be told what to do. The extension service in turn employs a generation of advisers trained in how to do rather than how to think.

A model for thought, such as the HRM model, is a foreign concept to many.

When the HRM model was in its infancy we needed a name for the reasoning and judgment attendant on any use of labor and resources. I first used brainpower but soon realized that that word didn't cover the ground. A man who adds up six-digit numbers in his head may have great brainpower but no common sense.

If all resource managers and, in particular, ranchers and farmers are to manage their resources and ensure their (and our) survival they need to go a step beyond the simple implications of IQ. They must create one of the few things humans can create, new ideas, custom-made to fit the situations at hand.

Every situation is in fact unique. No other individual, tribe, or nation has the same set of resources to manage in the same time frame or with the same people. Thus, every situation requires management that must be an original product of human imagination, and even that must evolve as the situation changes. Creativity, not brainpower, is the crucial element and it is needed constantly.

The idea that allows one person to attain maximum effect from his or her labor and money may not work for another. To ensure success, each person must think through a situation to discover whether the same management applies to his or her own unique set of goals and circumstances. If it does not, that person must create something different.

In my early years as a consultant I played the role of the extension agent and merely advised my clients what to do. When things went wrong I advised them to do something else. Using my head to design their management always produced imperfect advice because I was an outsider looking in at something very complex. Although superficially the results were good, depth and sustainability were lacking because I, not my clients, did the planning. Had I given them my knowledge first and then let them do the thinking for themselves, they could have developed management that was far superior and more holistic. My role should have been to bring in outside experience to stimulate their thinking. They would have known which bits of knowledge would fit their case and which wouldn't.

As it was, I did none of this. Many who became heavily dependent on me went seriously adrift when I suddenly had to flee my country as a political exile. Some of their mistakes had serious consequences for which I was really to blame.

Some years later I realized that any consultant or extension worker consistently has greater than a 90 percent chance of being wrong, no matter how knowledgeable or dedicated, because he or she is always an outsider looking in. To manage holistically, it has to be the other way around. To correct this, I subsequently only agreed to work with people who would first learn about holistic management and the use of the HRM model and how to plan for themselves. Then my counsel could become a matter of thinking through problems collaboratively. We could proceed from the client's point of view, not mine, using the HRM model to guide us.

The HRM model has been designed to help us assess the possible consequences, both good and bad (relative to our goals), of using any available tool. As many of the consequences are not quantifiable, this is not a task for a computer. Any human responsible for management will have certain feelings about it and will encounter the feelings of others. Love, fear, hopes, dreams, and interpersonal conflicts very much affect any management situation in ways no computer yet devised can understand.

The HRM model itself, however, is nothing more than a bit of software to help organize thinking and planning. Its successful application depends entirely on your ability to think and be creative. Fortunately, creativity is not simply a genetic endowment. It depends chiefly on one's own mental, emotional, and physical health, and one's environment.

Resources are rarely managed by one individual. More often a family, company, tribe, or nation has some kind of institutional responsibility. Relationships between the people involved can be at all points along a continuum from very stressful to very caring and loving, and the state of these relationships has a bearing on the creativity of each individual and the group as a whole. However, it's the person at the top—the owner, manager, chief, etc.—who sets the tone. His or her beliefs and behavior have the greatest impact on the creativity of the group whose actions ultimately affect the land.

The most vital responsibility any manager ever has is creating an environment that nurtures creativity. Research in the last thirty years or so has shown that the living and working *environment* is key to the release of creative potential—whether it be within a small family-run operation or in our largest corporations. Creativity of the group, regardless of its size, tends to be greatest when the leader's everyday actions display trust and confidence in his or her people, when the work is seen to be meaningful, when all feel free to express ideas, and when all feel valued.

Such a spirit cannot be faked. The person at the top really must value his or her employees as human beings and not mere tools for making profit. Corporations that saw profits rise when they treated employees as their prime resource saw them tumble when employees sensed they were merely being manipulated.

At present the majority of us take human creativity for granted and do not see it as something that must develop through the family, social, and work environment. We rarely see it as a tool that governs our success or failure. The male head of a small farming family leaving the land in America today, as hundreds of thousands are doing, no doubt blames the banks, the interest rates, the prices, the government, the weather and looks to society to help him and his family. It is difficult indeed for him to see that while he labored long and hard with his hands, using his head might have helped him survive.

Subconscious worries and stresses all too often completely sap our creative energies. Unfortunately, this is a common and subtle factor that affects many of us, but it is entirely within our control. Many of our stresses are allied to crisis management brought on by poor management of our time.

The stifling of creativity through poor time management, and the crisis management this leads to, has proven to be the weak link in many of the situations where I have consulted. Typically, a rancher would call on me to help stave off impending bankruptcy. Within a very short time I would realize that my talk of planning for the future was meaningless, because his mind was on the tractor clutch that was slipping badly, the pickup that needed new tires and wheel bearings, the boundary fence that was down, and the dam that had burst the night before.

In order to get himself out of the crisis he needed all the creativity he could muster to carefully plan the next crucial months. But his worries prevented him from planning his time or anything else.

Over many years I had perfected a good system for managing my time, which served me well and which I shared with clients in these sorts of cases. I would assist the rancher in plotting ahead and allocating his time for all the concerns that had piled up and were believed to be of equal importance (so much so that nothing at all was being done because everything, he thought, had to be done today). Once we established priorities (including family time and holidays) and allocated more than enough time over the next few months to complete them, there would always be many days left with nothing to do! The rancher would be immensely relieved. But the rancher inevitably did not follow through on the planning because he lacked the self-discipline, or so I thought. On reflection, I realized it was deeper than that. What was lacking was an established routine, or habit, and this could be learned.

Whatever time management system one uses, the keys to its success are *habit* and *trust*. A habitual procedure must be established whereby all the ideas that come to mind and all the commitments made are immediately recorded in one place, rather than on scattered scraps of paper, so that they can later be retrieved (and understood) and acted on. Once this habit is formed, then you cease to worry about commitments or ideas you might forget, i.e., you begin to *trust* the procedure and let go of your subconscious (or conscious) worries. This then frees the mind for creative thought.

Most of us complain that we just don't have enough time for creative thought, or in fact to do all that we want to do, and we marvel at those who seem to find it. Often we feel others have less to do while they actually achieve far more than we do. In truth, every person in the world has exactly the same amount of time. How we manage it makes the difference in the quality of our lives and in what we achieve through our creativity.

Human creativity will turn up in later chapters when we discuss the guidelines for creating a nurturing work environment in order to unleash the creativity inherent in us all. For the present, however, think of it as the key to using money, labor, and the other tools of management successfully and as being the *only* tool that can produce goals and plans.

17

Fire

Beware of the myth that any fire is natural and therefore safe to use. Although fire has existed ever since green plants began to render pure oxygen out of carbon dioxide in the earth's primordial atmosphere, manmade fires now wreak consequences on the land and in the atmosphere for which mankind alone must take responsibility.

Natural fires from lightning, spontaneous combustion, or volcanic activity occur infrequently in comparison to the number of manmade fires. In addition, most occur with rain and thus spread less. Although mankind has had the ability to make and use fire for the last eighty to one hundred thousand years (with some evidence that it might be over a million), booming populations and, more recently, matches have radically increased burning in modern times. On any given unit of land that is dry enough to burn, the frequency of fire has almost certainly undergone a recent, unnatural, and geometric increase against the background of the millions of years it took many communities to evolve.

It is my firm belief that increased frequency of fire in the last ten thousand years, when combined with a reduction in the disturbance to soil surfaces and vegetation caused by inadequate herding animals and predators in the last few centuries, is one of the prime factors leading to desertification in brittle environments. In discussing water cycles in Chapter 10, I mentioned the reported increased flow over the Victoria Falls in Africa since 1948. Scientists still puzzle over that, but in fact increased fire frequency and decreased large game populations are the only major changes that have taken place in that watershed in that period.

While I am very familiar with the tremendous use of fire by indigenous people in parts of Africa and its effects under different circumstances, we have lost much of the record of early Native American fire use. We do know that they used fire a great deal and that it was associated with areas that included free-roaming game populations and high levels of predation. It was that combination of factors—fire and animal impact—which produced the productivity found by early Europeans on the American prairies, not fire alone—a fact we easily lose sight of.

The emotionalism and myth attached to fire make it difficult for people to consider this tool objectively. This is not surprising as fire has played a vital role in human life for millennia, touching not only our hunting and agriculture, but also our religions and rituals. In parts of Africa it is now a belief that if some hills are not burned off each year, poor rains will follow. Visible damage to the water cycle at the source of many streams, and lack of any evidence that fire brings rain, make no difference to the belief.

A few years ago I encountered a similar absence of scientific curiosity at an American Soil Conservation Service training session on "prescribed burning" to eradicate woody vegetation. Discussion centered on such things as time of day to burn, wind velocities, temperatures, width of firebreaks. We learned how much warning to give neighbors in order to avoid litigation, argued whether the rancher or the civil servant should hold the match, and probed the legal fallout of fires that get out of hand.

Throughout the day not a word was uttered about effects on the eco-system processes or how burning might fit possible landscape goals. No one brought up the troublesome fact that fire invigorates many woody shrubs in the adult form. Every supporting argument rested either on ancient beliefs or research that had focused on plant species at the expense of the four ecosystem processes.

My own introduction, as a biologist in training, to the beliefs of game management was bouncing along in a pickup through Zambia's Kafue National Park while flicking lighted matches into the grass under instruction of a superior. We wanted the game to have green flushing grass but gave no thought at all to long-term consequences for the ecosystem's four fundamental processes or the wildlife we meant to help. In America, overreaction appears to be the controlling national trait in this matter. The majority is profire for a few years and then turns sharply against it for a few more.

The use of fire has so many ramifications that any one opinion either for or against it can seldom be right. Unfortunately, the effects of fire are so profound that both the dogmatic and the capricious attitude cause great damage.

Fire, like any other tool, can only be judged in the context of defined goals and the current state of the four ecosystem foundation blocks. To do that nevertheless requires an objective understanding of what it does and doesn't do and the effects it tends to produce on the four ecosystem foundation blocks.

First, and of primary importance, fire tends to expose soil surfaces. As soil surface management is central to the management of all four of the ecosystem foundation blocks; this trait must be kept in mind before all others. Bare ground is conspicuous right after a fire and until new growth appears. More critical, however, is the time required to build up the litter between plants. That depends on such things as the brittleness of the environment, amount of grazing or overgrazing, amount of rest, timing and degree of animal impact, and so on.

Soil exposure has the most impact where soil cover takes longest to form—the lower rainfall brittle environments. The lower rainfall produces less vegetation that might restore cover, but the fact that bare soil makes rain *less effective* compounds that effect. If fire is combined with either rest or low animal impact, soil cover accumulates even more slowly. (The guidelines for burning detailed in Chapter 38 discuss using other disturbances with fire instead of the unnatural two years' rest so commonly recommended.)

Fire affects plants in different ways. Some sensitive perennial grasses disappear if burned. The majority, at least as mature plants, thrive with fire as it removes all of the old material that prematurely kills grasses if allowed to accumulate through slow decay.

Some plants may even depend on periodic fire for survival. Many have specially adapted for establishing after fire. A number of grass seeds have awns (or tails) that actually twist and drill the seed into exposed soil when they become moist. As very few factors in nature except fire produce bare ground over vast areas, such adaptations likely evolved in response to it.

Woody plants may respond in many ways too. Some are extremely sensitive, others resilient. In many countries I have observed that anywhere up to 95 percent of the trees and shrubs considered problem species are resilient when past the seedling stage. They initially appear dead after burning, but then resprout more stems than before, as illustration 17-1 shows. This plant in the Arizona chaparral once had about six stems, but after burning has thickened up to a great many more.

A great many tree species are damaged by fire, yet some can still survive in the shrub form where burning is prolific. Mopane trees, common in the southern African tropics, once infested some land I wanted to irrigate for sugar cane. I easily cleared the forty-foot trees by building a small fire at the base of each tree and leaving it undisturbed for several days. The whole tree burned down, and as long as the fire was left undisturbed so that blow holes in the ash were not closed, the roots burned out far underground. Yet where frost and many past fires had kept the mopanes down to three-foot shrubs, the same trick failed, as they were completely fire-resistant, and a bulldozer had to pull out enormous root systems.

Fire that is not followed by any other soil disturbance tends to cause major changes in living communities, because any influence that creates

Illustration 17-1. Burned shrub that has resprouted with many new stems. Arizona.

essentially the same microenvironment over vast areas favors establishment of the few species of plants, insects, and other organisms adapted to it. In a community of mature organisms that survive the fire, the new species brought into the burned area usually add complexity initially. Frequent repetition, however, will provide a largely similar microenvironment over large areas for so long that complexity diminishes. Gradually the original community of diverse populations is replaced by those adapted to the fire-maintained uniform microenvironment. Thus, where a periodic fire can create greater diversity, frequent fires alone tend to do the opposite.

A uniform microenvironment leads to fewer species generally, and often a near monoculture of low stability. Test plots in both Zambia and Zimbabwe, which were burned annually for over forty years, were eventually dominated by one or two species of grass with self-drilling seeds adapted to charred, cracked, and bare ground.

A noteworthy corollary to this effect stems from the tendency of boundary areas to support particularly complex communities. Thus, a healthy diversity may thrive on the edges of burned areas, and the impact of fire that produces a mosaic of patches and tongues through unburned land may differ significantly from the effect of a uniform burn.

The HRM model has a guideline on burning that distinguishes hot and cool fires. Hot fires imply a lot of dry material that burns fiercely with large flames. Limited dry material produces a slow, creeping cool fire with small flames. The different immediate effect on certain plants sometimes obscures similar long-term effects.

Cool fires were used widely by foresters in Zimbabwe and Zambia to prevent hot fires later in the season. This policy appeared so successful in protecting large, mature trees that the impact of exposing the soil on the forest floor went unnoticed. The greatly altered microenvironment, resulting from the repeated exposure of the soil in that brittle environment, blocked the establishment of the very teak trees that had commercial value and which these national forests were formed to protect. Plenty of woody plants do grow there now, but of species adapted to a lower successional community. The slow destruction is now obvious over vast forest areas on the Kalahari sand soils of these countries.

Forestry provides many variations of this example. Experts have argued that the slow burning of "useless" dead wood on the ground cuts the risk of hot fires and allows nutrients to cycle faster as ash than they would through decay. In fact no one knows what the billions of organisms involved in that slow decay contribute to the health of the forest. Very likely we achieve little by trying to speed the process and treating the forest as a factory rather than the vital complex living organism it is.

Animals, like plants, also vary greatly in their response to fire. Many do not escape easily; many others do. Some are attracted to fires for the easy pickings of food from fleeing insects, etc. It is a myth to think the larger game animals of Africa always panic and flee from fire. Though men may drive them with flames and noise, they usually just get out of the way calmly. Once during a three-day battle against a grass fire in the Rukwa Valley of Tanzania, three companions and I barely escaped encirclement by plunging through a weak point. Only yards beyond the fire line we found a group of reedbuck who had just had the same experience and had lain down calmly on the warm ground to watch.

Some animals will seek out burned areas very soon after the passage of the fire, especially when the first green regrowth appears.

Throughout history we have made the mistake of noting only the immediate impact of fire on adult populations. The teak forests of the Kalahari sands were a case in point, but we tend to treat grass, trees, birds, reptiles, game, and other organisms in the same way. We only ask, were they hurt by fire, invigorated by it, or attracted to the green regrowth? Did food supplies increase? We have not watched and formed opinions on what happened to the ecosystem foundation blocks in terms of what these things we value need in order to reproduce over prolonged time.

A short-term benefit for adult populations can encourage further burnings that may destroy that population in the long run. I strongly suspect that the dwindling of roan antelope in Africa represents such ignorance.

For years I have watched totally protected herds decrease and die out wherever their ranges deteriorated from the complex higher successional grass and woodland communities they favored. Meanwhile, we concentrated on the actual diseases that affected them as being the cause. That seems a bit like citing pneumonia as the major cause of death among Russians left homeless by World War II, but the mistake is understandable. Roan antelope will come onto burned ground while logs still smoulder. Knowing they liked burns, we did our best to oblige, but our too frequent fires destroyed the very complexity necessary for the roans' survival.

Both the animals and the plants of grasslands provide many examples. A great many of our wildlife species are grassland community components, and their fate ultimately hangs on our more intelligent use of fire.

The above observations add up to debunk the old myth that fire maintains grassland. Like many myths it is easy to see how it arose, for superficial observation will find it borne out in the short term. However, the development and maintenance of the complex, stable, and highly productive grasslands of bygone days is much more complex than the myth implies, and particularly in semiarid, brittle environments, overdoses of fire can hurt.

Earlier I mentioned my first questioning of the beneficial fire myth when we used it to help us clear big game from tsetse fly areas in Africa. We had wiped out the large game herds, had not eliminated the tsetse fly, and not introduced cattle. Yet the grasslands, which looked lush enough from the window of a Land Rover traveling at fifty miles per hour, were deteriorating seriously, as a close consideration of the four ecosystem foundation blocks plainly showed. We were only using the tool of fire, having virtually eliminated grazing and animal impact. The temporary grassland we made masked a serious long-term desertification process, as time proved dramatically.

By the time the once complex and healthy grasslands were ready for occupation by people with cattle, they were in a bad state of degradation. Active erosion between plants had set in, seedlings had become scarce, monocultures of mature plants with poor age distribution abounded, and energy flow had dropped severely. While periodic fire in the past had contributed to the necessary disturbance of brittle environment grasslands, the animals had also played a major role in maintaining healthy communities. (Ironically, it is now my belief that the fires we used in the tsetse fly operations were probably one of the main causes of the tsetse fly's spread, as the fire-induced, less effective water cycles led to a dramatic increase in the breeding sites for this slow-breeding insect).

The extent of the destruction caused by fire alone is symbolized for me by the oil sump of a Land Rover. In 1959, while in charge of the burning and shooting operations in southeastern Zimbabwe, I drove out daily from my bush camp. After some months I was under the vehicle changing the oil and could not help noticing that the grass had polished the underside clean. In fact the front side of the brass sump plug had worn down so far and so smooth it would scarcely hold a wrench.

Six years later, because of the enduring fly, the area still lay largely unoccupied by large game, livestock, or people, though periodic burning had continued, so I made my old camp a base for training army trackers. After three months of continual driving over the same ground and remembering my past experience, I checked under all our vehicles and found the oil sumps caked with dusty grease.

On level ground the grasses persisted weakly, but on slopes and where soil had been shallow before, naked earth and exposed pebbles characterized the scene. Such profound changes, when gradual, escape notice unless an observation like this forces us to think.

When thinking of using fire as a tool, keep your goals in mind and apply the normal plan, monitor, control, and replan procedures entailed in the HRM model. Pay attention particularly to the soil surface microenvironment, asking if other tools could perform the task without exposing it. Remember that the viability of the whole population structure (as detailed in Chapter 37), *not* merely adult plants and animals, is critical.

To recap the basic tendencies of fire in the two extremes of brittle and nonbrittle environments:

Brittle Environments

Succession: Fire exposes soil. In low rainfall areas where plant spacings are wide, new cover develops very slowly. In the short term a fire increases diversity of species in grassland and woodland. Repeated fires reduce diversity.

Water cycle: Fire generally reduces the effectiveness of the water cycle as it exposes soil and destroys the litter that slows water flow and maintains crumb structure and aeration. The drier the area and the more frequent the fire, the greater this tendency.

Mineral cycle: Fire speeds the mineral cycle in the short term by converting dead material to ash. But because of soil exposure and damage to the microenvironment that supports decay, repeated fires tend to slow the mineral cycle in the long run. Once more, the drier the area and the more frequent the fire, the greater this tendency.

Energy flow: Fire may produce an immediate increase in energy flow by removing old material that hinders the growth of both grasses and brush. However, the consequent soil exposure leads to less effective mineral and water cycles, and successional changes that could reduce energy flow in the long term. The drier the area and the more frequent the fire, the greater this tendency.

Nonbrittle Environments

Succession: Fire appears to have a very brief short-term effect with little long-term consequence. The generally higher humidity inhibits fires in any case, and after a burn the return to complexity is typically rapid. The close plant spacing in nonbrittle grasslands helps minimize soil exposure.

Water cycle: Fire tends to damage the water cycle by exposing soil, but with the better annual distribution of humidity and the more rapid advance of succession on bare surfaces, the effect is temporary.

Mineral cycle: Fire appears to speed the cycling of nutrients, but this effect is often an illusion. Mineral cycles, however, appear to recover fast after a fire. For thousands of years fire was the main tool in so-called slash and burn agriculture. Although the fire freed many nutrients in the community for human use, again it was temporary. Such systems, sound as they were, broke down fast unless there was a twenty or more year rest between fire-use periods.

Energy flow: Fire again appears to favor energy flow in the short run, but this too is probably illusion. In any case, energy flow also recovers quickly after fire. In slash and burn agriculture, more energy is directed temporarily to human use.

This summary on the effects of fire in nonbrittle environments assumes one burning followed by rest. Rest allows such environments to recover quickly after any disturbance. Traditional slash and burn agriculture does set back the four ecosystem foundation blocks, but allows production of crops that convert more energy and nutrients for human use than a similar patch of forest. As once practiced with prolonged rests, the forest had time to recover, and did so.

As it is impossible to use fire as a tool without also using one of the other tools—*technology, rest, grazing,* or *animal impact*—these are discussed in the following chapters.

18
Rest

R est as a tool differs from the short, physiological rest a plant requires to recover from being severely bitten. The word rest here means rest from major physical disturbance and applies to the community as a whole.

Disturbance generally comes from large animals, domestic or wild, but particularly those that exhibit herding behavior, and from fire or machinery. Occasionally it is provided by hailstorms and natural catastrophes. A policy of withholding all of that completely for considerable time amounts to applying the tool of *total* rest. *Partial* rest, on the other hand, is applied in the presence of some livestock or large game, but so few and with such calm behavior in the absence of predators that a large proportion of plant life and soil surface remains undisturbed.

Applying partial rest is a widespread policy, and its effects are evident anywhere small numbers of livestock or large game animals are widely scattered and seldom agitated.

That rest in either form (total or partial) might function as a tool of the same order as a fire or a plow comes as a new concept. We considered rest natural until we registered the fact that brittle and nonbrittle environments react to it in very different ways, and that the major grazing areas of the world, in a state of pristine Nature, never experienced rest at all.

Once humans could light fires, fell trees, domesticate animals, and plant crops, they had to bear responsibility for their impact on Nature. The choice to give or withhold rest from a piece of land only amounts to another aspect of the powers we can exercise consciously. Our unconscious wielding of this tool, especially in combination with misguided use of other tools, has had the most devastating effect on the brittle environments of our probable origin. When humans first settled in permanent villages and thus drove wild herds from the surrounding area, they unintentionally but decisively subjected those lands to rest. We now intentionally rest land in the hope that it will recover from disturbance in the form of fire, overgrazing, and overtrampling. Though we justify this as leaving things to Nature, we have changed natural relationships no less than those first settlers did. To understand why, we must look at the different effects produced by rest in both nonbrittle and brittle environments.

Effects of Rest in Nonbrittle Environments

In nonbrittle environments plant material *by definition* decomposes quickly through biological decay, as opposed to weathering or other physical forces. Such rotting down starts close to the ground where the microenvironment supports the most organisms engaged in this process. This fact particularly suits the perennial grass plant, that great soil stabilizer, because its old leaves and stems weaken at the base and quickly fall aside allowing light to reach basal growing points and new growth to begin unimpeded.

Illustration 18-1 shows an example of this. Last season's leaves and stems have toppled, and new growth only awaits the right temperature and moisture.

This process allows nonbrittle communities under total rest to maintain a high degree of stability and complexity of species. Water, if it runs off at all, carries no booty of silt or other debris. Even very prolonged rest from fire or physical impact by machinery or large animals has little or no adverse effect on the water cycle, mineral cycle, succession, or energy flow in this nonbrittle environment.

Nonbrittle environments reduced to bare ground by some natural or manmade catastrophe respond rapidly to rest and return relatively quickly to their former complexity and stability, whether jungle, forest, or grassland. Desertification is seldom a danger.

Whether you use the tool of rest under these conditions depends entirely on your goals. Naturally, if your production goal includes livestock, game, or crops, you do not want total rest. Particularly if your landscape goal involves maintenance of stable grassland where you suspect natural succession proceeds toward forest, you will avoid rest. Any old-timer in such a place will explain how the fallow field goes first to weeds, then to briars, then to scrub, and finally to woods.

You could engineer a mosaic of grass and woodland by partially resting certain areas and not others, and if the environment could support solid jungle, you could get that too, through rest.

Illustration 18-1. Nonbrittle grassland showing last year's old growth already fallen (see arrow) and decaying and not choking new growth. Alaska.

That all this works so straightforwardly in nonbrittle situations has obscured the fact that it doesn't in brittle ones. Some of the greatest environmental tragedies in human history have ensued from the false assumption that all environments respond the same way to rest.

The Effects of Rest in Brittle Environments

In brittle environments *by definition* old plant material breaks down slowly, and succession advances slowly—at best—from bare soil. Most organisms of decay, especially at low successional levels, are scarce and only present intermittently when moisture is adequate. Thus, under conditions of rest, old plant material decomposes only gradually through oxidation and weathering. Being most exposed to the elements, the tips of leaves and stems break down first so that basal growth points often remain shaded and obstructed for years. Old material that lingers even through the next growing season weakens a grass plant, and several years' accumulation can actually kill it.

If, at the same time, the soil surface remains undisturbed, new plants do not easily replace the ones dying prematurely. Outside the tropics, prolonged rest allows freezing and thawing of the upper soil layers to create a puffiness that inhibits the establishment of young, fibrous-rooted grasses. The crust that often forms on rested soil offers poor opportunities to the germinating seed.

Brittle environments subjected to extended periods of rest (partial or total) characteristically have wide bare spaces between vestigial perennial grass plants. The remaining plants survive because light can reach the basal growing points around the edges of each plant, but the centers may already be dead. Illustration 18-2 illustrates these symptoms on totally rested perennial grass plants on the Sevilleta Wildlife Refuge, which lies in a brittle nine-inch-rainfall area of New Mexico. The only life shows around the edge of some clumps, and despite many years of seed production by these and other surrounding ungrazed plants, no seedlings at all have established on the bare, undisturbed surface nearby.

After a disturbance of the soil surface, closely-spaced perennial grass plants often do establish. If such land is then rested, however, the closely-

Illustration 18-2. United States Fish & Wildlife Service officials inspecting dying grassland with large, bare ground spaces opening between plants. Sevilleta Wildlife Refuge, New Mexico.

spaced plants kill one another off prematurely, as old growth shades even the edges of the neighboring clump. Illustration 18-3 shows such a grassland in a fifteen-inch-rainfall brittle environment in northern Mexico. Whole handfuls of dead grass can be pulled out by the roots with ease. Illustration 18-4 shows the same thing in a thirty-inch-rainfall brittle area of Zimbabwe.

If your landscape goal required a successional advance to woody plant species and the animal organisms associated with them, then you would consider continued rest for these lands if they received enough rainfall to support good stands of woody plants. The dead clumps of grass provide a good microenvironment for seed germination, and the dead roots lacing the soil make an excellent medium for penetration and establishment of the seedling's tap root.

Illustration 18-5, taken on the same ranch in Mexico as illustration 18-3, confirms that woody species (mesquite in this instance) have already found their niche as succession advances. (Note the correlation of mesquite and dead grass clumps).

If your goal does not involve this kind of change, don't apply either partial or total rest. Most of the brush and tree encroachment we consider

Illustration 18-3.   Brittle environment grassland, which had developed close spacing under animal impact, showing mass deaths under rest (all plants are grey and oxidizing). Coahuilla, Mexico.

Illustration 18-4. Perennial grasses dying under rest in a thirty-inch-rainfall brittle environment (all grasses are grey and oxidizing). Atlantica Ecological Research Station, Zimbabwe.

a problem today owes its existence to heavy doses of the tool of rest (total or partial).

Continued rest in low rainfall brittle environments can eventually destroy even the woody species, however. Once all remaining grass plants have oxidized and blown away, the bare surface becomes capped, and, lacking the old grass root systems, the once friable subsoil closes up. New seeds can only establish in cracks, if there are any, and growth proves difficult after that unless some form of disturbance is applied.

Illustration 18-6 shows a piece of Chaco Canyon National Monument in New Mexico, where a brittle environment has suffered rest for fifty years. Most grasses are dead. The shrubs, too, are dying now, and the soil is bare and eroding severely.

In summary, total or partial rest in brittle environments generally subverts most goals and ensures that deserts will keep expanding. This would definitely occur in environments falling between 5 and 10 on the arbitrary scale depicted in Chapter 5 (figure 5-1). In many cases where we hoped rest would cure problems it has only exacerbated them.

Cartoonist Ace Reid summed up this paradox some years ago without realizing he had stumbled onto something vital (illustration 18-7).

Illustration 18-5.   Successional shift from grassland to dense forbs and mesquite has occurred in rested patch, while overgrazed patch in foreground erodes. Coahuilla, Mexico.

Effects of Rest in Semibrittle Environments

Many environments naturally lie somewhere in the middle of the 1 to 10 scale from extremely nonbrittle to brittle. In the main, rest does adversely affect environments that exhibit a degree of brittleness (5 or 6 on the scale), but the symptoms develop more slowly than in more extreme cases.

The evidence is easier to show photographically in grassland than forest. Illustration 18-8, from the Crescent Lake Wildlife Refuge in Nebraska, shows land that had been rested for twelve years. Close inspection revealed weakened grasses and an invasion of tap-rooted plants into what once was grassland. All four ecosystem foundation blocks show early signs of adverse change.

Illustration 18-9 shows nearby land on the same refuge rested fifty years. By this stage all four ecosystem foundation blocks have visibly suffered. Grasses, which earlier provided ground cover and thus a healthy environment, are clearly dying and many are dead. All new plants are what many would consider weeds. A large proportion of the ground has become bare, and once the dead grass litter breaks down, this area will expand.

Treated by the tool of total rest, this environment is too brittle to sustain

Illustration 18-6.   Fifty years of rest in a low rainfall brittle environment. Most grass dead, bare ground and erosion extensive, and many shrubs dying. Chaco Canyon, New Mexico.

a more complex successional level, effective water and mineral cycles, and energy flow. Partial rest with low numbers of livestock or game would only have masked this clear and dramatic effect for many years by slowing down the process.

Since probably over 50 percent of the earth's land surface is brittle to varying degrees, and since the dawn of history it has carried livestock under management that paradoxically produces *both* partial rest and overgrazing of plants, the remorseless growth of deserts is no mystery.

Some brittle grasslands rested long enough to produce woodlands do maintain stability — the Brachystegia woodlands that abound in Central Africa are a good example. Almost invariably such areas have moderate to high rainfall, which is very seasonal. I've also seen places where tap-rooted woody plants achieved the same stability because of subterranean moisture.

The typical example of the latter situation occurs along riparian (riverine) strips. If rested for prolonged periods, such environments tend to pass on to very stable woodlands. But don't let this fool you into believing all riparian areas need rest for all goals. Some riparian areas lack sufficient subterranean moisture to maintain dense, woody cover. In addition, even though the area

Illustration 18-7.   (Courtesy Ace Reid)

adjacent to the stream or river may be nonbrittle, it may be surrounded by very brittle catchments, and since the health of the stream is entirely dependent on its catchments, or watersheds, management has to cater for this larger whole. The serious death of vegetation apparent in illustration 18-6 is in the low-lying riparian area of a brittle environment.

Delayed Effect of Rest in Brittle Environments

Failure to note the distinction between rest as a long-term tool and rest as the time it takes a damaged plant to rebuild a root system has thrown desertification research off the scent for several thousand years. We correctly observed that animals in certain circumstances overgraze and damage plants. We removed the animals and witnessed an immediate and dramatic recovery. In fact, we had stopped two animal-produced effects, one negative and one positive. The result was that the positive and immediate effect of allowing overgrazed plants to recover colors our ability to determine and even see eventual damage we create by eliminating beneficial animal impact.

Hooved animals, continuously run in the same brittle environment for

Illustration 18-8.   Twelve years of rest. A high proportion of these grasses are now grey and dead. Crescent Lake Wildlife Refuge, Nebraska.

years in succession, overgraze a great many plants, and vulnerable species die out. Nevertheless, because the animals do have a physical impact while grazing, many plants also establish, and vegetation persists, even as water and mineral cycles, energy flow, and succession gradually deteriorate. For generations untold we have seen the decline and advocated cutting the animal numbers and resting the land.

More often than not, society lacked the willpower to actually take on such a measure. To demonstrate the advantages of total destocking (rest) the u.s. government in the 1930s fenced off plots throughout the western states. The same was done in parts of Africa and elsewhere.

Once protected from overgrazing and unimpeded by old growth, the plots indeed grew lush and became the justification for often draconian campaigns to reduce stock. Illustration 18-10 and the accompanying caption show an example from Arizona after three years of rest. The photograph really only shows the favorable response to an end of overgrazing. We cannot see the detail within each plant, but, knowing that old growth in that area does not decay fast enough for the health of the grasses, we can bet that after three years enough has accumulated to start to weaken them.

Illustration 18-11 shows grassland in the same area in 1985 after fifty

Illustration 18-9.   Fifty years of rest. Crescent Lake Wildlife Refuge, Nebraska.

years of rest. Wide spaces have opened among the tufts, and new seedlings are few and far between. In this case a few antelope have broken the regime of total rest. Even so damage to all four ecosystem foundation blocks stands out.

Another example shows how old myths persist in human (and scientific!) dogma. Illustration 18-12 shows an exclosure (to keep livestock out) set up and photographed during the 1930s in the Rio Puerco Basin of New Mexico — a very brittle environment. It appeared in the Council for Environmental Quality's report on *Desertification in the United States*, published in 1981. Although the photograph lacks detail within the exclosure, we can see a good stand of vigorous grass, freed from the overgrazing evident on the other side of the fence. There we see a tightly-spaced community of over-grazed grasses typical of land under continuous grazing and high levels of disturbance. The caption reads, "Range improvement in the Rio Puerco Valley, Sandoval County, New Mexico. Grass on the left is protected from overgrazing (Soil Conservation Service)."[1]

Though the report was written in 1981, a 1930s photograph was used — one that illustrates the immediate benefits of plant recovery from overgrazing in a community still benefiting from the residual effect of the animal impact. In fact, the remaining exclosures in the Rio Puerco in 1981 all looked like

Illustration 18-10. The caption accompanying this photograph, which appeared in *Along the Beale Trail*, a u.s. Office of Indian Affairs booklet published in 1938, reads: "Protected for three years by the National Park Service, this area in the Petrified Forest, for years overgrazed, proves that protection will speed recovery." Arizona.

what you see in illustration 18-13. The report writers, knowing the world to be flat, had felt no urge to check up on the current status of the exclosures. Had a 1980s photograph of any one of the exclosures been used, instead of a 1930s one, a very different conclusion would have been reached. This totally rested land is desertifying as badly as anything I have experienced in Africa or the Middle East. The authors were not being dishonest, just human. Why question what is already known?

Initiation of Crisis Management of Land under Rest

Misunderstanding of what rest does to brittle environments often leads to crisis management of land that people intend to preserve in pristine condition.

I have seen more than one environmental organization acquire badly-

Illustration 18-11.   View of the grassland in Petrified Forest National Park in 1985 after forty years of partial rest. Arizona.

damaged brittle land and slowly change their management of it from a dogmatic hands-off, leave-it-to-Nature approach to application of the most drastic techniques available. It happens in a predictable sequence.

After years of partial rest and simultaneous overgrazing of certain plants by livestock, the land responds vigorously to rest and all looks good. The increase in volume and cover benefits many creatures and complexity builds up. Progress under Nature toward all goals appears on target and no one dissents. Sometimes official transects and measurements record the advance, as has happened on the Audubon Society's Appleton-Whittel Biological Research Station in southeastern Arizona. Lists of small mammals, birds, and insects become impressive as more species reap the new bounty.

Gradually, however, the measurements note the first signs of adverse change. Moribund grasses turn up in the log books, various weedy plants increase in number, and bare spots begin to open up. None of this is expected, and for a year or so it proceeds while people hope the problem goes away.

Inevitably the managers conclude that fire should be used as "fire is natural and it maintained grassland in the past." The first unnatural means of returning the land to Nature has led to another. As argued earlier, man-made fires are unnatural in the strict sense. In a brittle environment fire

Illustration 18-12. A 1930s photograph of an exclosure in the Rio Puerco Valley used in 1981 in the Council on Environmental Quality report on *Desertification of the United States.* Note Cabezon Peak, which appears in the background. New Mexico.

Illustration 18-13. A 1987 photograph of one of the remaining exclosures in the Rio Puerco Valley. Cabezon Peak again appears in the background. New Mexico.

invigorates mature grasses but threatens all four of the ecosystem foundation blocks by exposing soil. Given that rest also tends to expose soil, and that the cause of the old vegetation accumulating has not been removed, the situation predictably worsens as fire use becomes too frequent.

Technology often comes next—seedings, plowings, plantings, check dams, ditching, and the like. However, the problem remains insoluble until the managers understand the implications of rest in brittle environments.

When confronted by the argument for reintroducing animal impact as a natural influence, such managers typically respond, "But no buffalo ever roamed here." Well, no doubt they have a point, but when trying to attain a particular landscape goal one must employ the tools at hand today. Not only bison but also deer, elk, pronghorn, bighorn sheep, and other animals may break a period of rest, and so little is known about the actual number and distribution of these animals, even a century ago, that debates about them tend to be academic. In some parts of the Southwest, where people insist that large herds never occurred, we now have evidence that hunting peoples once thrived. In fact, aerial inspections have revealed a remarkable density of not so ancient pronghorn traps.

If a pocket of land now isolated by ranches, roads, and international borders once supported a teeming grassland, then with very few exceptions animal impact of some sort *by definition* helped maintain it. And even if no wild population exists that could conceivably do that now, to rule out domestic stock as a less natural tool than fires and bulldozers for producing pristine habitat makes little sense.

Illustration 18-2 showed one more case of a brittle area returned to Nature through unnatural rest. Fifteen years prior, the Sevilleta Refuge was willed to the Nature Conservancy and put under management of the u.s. Fish and Wildlife Service. Unfortunately, New Mexico no longer has wolf packs that chase large, free-roaming herds, and small groups of undisturbed deer and pronghorn don't mitigate the regime of rest imposed on the refuge. All the symptoms of desertification that the donor of the land sought to avert have appeared.

Invariably, some people at this point close their minds because grassland does exist in parts of America, Australia, and Argentina without any evidence of help from herding animals in the recent past. In my experience a grassland will always reflect the degree of its brittleness and the net result of the amount of rest or disturbance it has received. This will reflect in its complexity, plant spacings, and overall energy flow. If plant spacings are close and age structure good in the absence of disturbance (by fire or animals), then the environment is not likely to be very brittle. If plant spacings are wide, age structure poor (and reproduction predominantly asexual) in the absence of disturbance, then the environment is likely to be very brittle. If we were to discover a grassland that lay on the brittle end of the scale and that had developed great complexity, stability, and closely-spaced plants with no disturbance, we would have discovered a distinct new environment with rules of its own, and the concept of brittleness would have to be revised.

Brittle grasslands that do persist under prolonged rest contain plants adapted to do better without it, and close inspection finds them highly unstable and typified by wide plant spacings, sparse asexual reproduction (from above and below ground runners that establish new plants without genetic diversity), and low productivity. Especially where freezing and thawing creates puffy soil, such grassland almost never develops on the steeper slopes of canyon and gully walls.

Such cases raise again and again the philosophical question, "What is natural?"

Eons ago, before mankind controlled fire, livestock, and technology, there was an Eden to which we can no longer return. Logic tells us that all plant and animal life was an indivisible part of the successional development of wholes (microenvironment, community, and climate)—whole atoms, whole molecules, whole cells, whole organs, whole plants and animals, and whole populations in whole communities on a whole planet in a whole system beyond our comprehension. There must have been brittle and non-brittle environments and all the grades in between for millions of years. The extraordinary expansion of deserts within the last few thousand years can only be the work of humans.

We go to great lengths to avoid this conclusion. The archaeologists delving the secrets of ancient ruins in New Mexico conjecture that the climate changed, that overpopulation led to a collapse of agriculture in fragile bottomland, that war destroyed the social fabric. They point to ancient tree rings that indicate prolonged drought. They do not consider that even a primitive population, by hunting, by driving game with fire, by setting accidental fires, might have upset the water cycle enough to affect tree growth more than any drought could.

To regain any part of Eden now means reproducing as closely as possible the conditions under which various successional communities, microenvironments, and climates developed. Wherever we manage to do that, the life that flourishes will be natural whether or not it represents what existed in that place at any given moment during the history of "unnatural" human influence.

The high desert of Oregon provided a perfect background when a group of environmentalists discussed that idea with me at a conference near the small town of Brothers. The area is often cited as an example of stability under conditions of rest, for even the earliest records note the scarcity of large game. Near the town, where cattle have run for fifty years, conferees had difficulty stepping without touching some living plant. Though many plants showed signs of overgrazing, many did not, and new seedlings had sprouted everywhere.

Not far away, however, where lack of water and a federal jurisdiction thwarted the presence of grazing animals, the people easily found enough bare ground to sit on. They found no overgrazed plants but many weak and dead ones and very few new sprouts, and erosion proceeded apace.

The second area may well have been natural in light of known history. It had definitely had time to reach its full potential under rest-is-better management, and indeed many a range scientist, citing its history of rest, would use it as a standard for judging the condition of surrounding land.

Yet the same land, the same climate, the same plants obviously will develop into a richer, more complex, and more stable environment without rest, and that, too, would be natural in terms of natural potential if not written history.

The choice ultimately falls to human management in the context of human goals. Canyonlands National Park in Utah contains a site called Virginia Park surrounded on all sides by perpendicular cliffs that have excluded large animals for a long tick of geological time. The grass cover is unstable and very fragile. It needs the tool of rest because the American people quite rightly have chosen to preserve a landscape created some eons ago. But Virginia Park does not represent what more accessible places once were or might become in brittle environments.

The visitor's center at the nearby Arches National Monument passes out literature that describes the grassland that existed at the time the monument was set aside for preservation. The rest that has been imposed since then has resulted in a dying grassland where widening bare patches are obvious. Even if one is unobservant, your attention is drawn to areas where nylon mesh holds mulch to the ground (mentioned in Chapter 11) in an attempt to get grasses growing again. Personally, although I once detested herds of cattle like so many environmentalists, I find them more natural over vast areas than nylon netting.

In summary, the effects of rest on the ecosystem foundation blocks are as follows.

Nonbrittle Environments

Succession develops great diversity and stability in the community as a whole.

Water and mineral cycles build and maintain high levels of effectiveness.

Energy flow reaches a high level.

Brittle Environments

Succession declines and greater simplicity and instability ensue.

Water and mineral cycles become less effective.

Energy flow declines significantly.

Between the two extremes we find all gradations of these tendencies as they merge into one another. Because rest has such clearly different tendencies at the extremes, the condition of rested sites generally indicates the underlying brittleness of any area and thus helps determine what tools will best achieve a given goal.

Rest is in many ways the flip side of grazing and animal impact. Its full implications will become clearer as we turn to them next.

19

Grazing

This chapter undertakes the debunking of myths about grazing that have confounded all our efforts to halt the spread of deserts and subverted a good deal of our watershed management generally.

That severe grazing is bad, that overgrazing comes from the presence of too many animals, that selective grazing destroys beneficial plants, even that whole ranges can be overgrazed are all fictions that science has consistently embraced as gospel. In their place belong facts that have made little headway against the weight of tradition and beliefs based upon knowledge that was unquestionable.

Grazing ranks as a tool alongside fire and rest because management can manipulate it. But, like the others, it has natural aspects in that mankind did not design the mouths of livestock and game, teach them how and what to eat, or how to behave. Here we will consider the ramifications of grazing as if animals floated over the ground without dunging, urinating, salivating, or trampling as they fed.

Though grazing never occurs apart from these things, as a tool it has a quite different impact from the other physical effects of the animal. Proper grazing may tend to advance succession even while low animal impact (partial rest) tends to push it backward. Overgrazing may shift succession toward simplicity even as high animal impact (disturbance) promotes complexity. While grazing and adequate disturbance can maintain healthy brittle watersheds, overgrazing of plants and partial rest can cause them to desertify.

The ability to analyze the effect of both tools independently allows one to unravel such questions as how Western scientists and ranchers damaged parts of Africa, Australia, and the Americas more in three hundred years

151

than nomads and their flocks managed to do in five thousand years in other parts of the world.

A thorough discussion of grazing by itself first of all requires a working definition of the terms grazing and overgrazing.

To grasp the difference, consider a clump of perennial grass in a brittle environment. The fate of perennial grasses symbolizes the issue of desertification, for the most seriously deteriorating parts of the world do not have the rainfall to support any other kind of stable soil cover. Annual grass populations fluctuate greatly from season to season and may leave ground bare for months and sometimes fail to grow at all.

In a very direct sense, perennial bunch grass underpins the fortunes of the politicians, bankers, businessmen, ranchers, tribespeople, and citizens who have a stake in over 50 percent of the earth's surface, which I estimate is brittle environment and serves as our watersheds.

Picture a healthy plant and imagine that a large animal appears and bites all stem and leaf down to an inch or two. That is severe grazing, but not unusual or bad in that certain animals evolved to graze in such a manner in harmony with such grasses over millions of years. In the growing season the plant receives a short-term setback, but a long-term boost. The bitten plant demands time for recovery but it may still finish the season better off and less encumbered than its neighbors. The growth points at the base remain intact, and no old growth of the previous year stands in the way of regeneration.

If the bite comes in the dormant season, when the plant *has no use for the leaves and stems of the past season*, it loses nothing and gains an uncluttered start on the new season. On balance, severe grazing benefits the grazed plant.

Overgrazing occurs when a plant bitten severely *in the growing season* gets severely bitten again before it completely recovers from the first bite. This can happen because the plant is exposed to the animals for too long or because they move off but return too soon.

That second bite has serious consequences because of the way grasses use and store energy. At the end of the growing season, most perennial grasses transfer energy and protein from leaves and stems to stem bases and/or roots. This reserve carries the plant through the dormant period and supports the next year's first growth.

If bitten during the growing season, however, when such reserves have been used up in early-season growth, grasses can only take energy from growing roots, allowing them to die back in the interest of putting out new shoots. Some scientists argue that energy for new growth is taken from what leaves and stems remain on the grazed plant and in the process some roots die to maintain root-to-leaf balance. Whichever theory you subscribe to, repeated severe defoliation kills roots and, eventually, most plants.

The organic material in the sacrificed root benefits the organisms living within the soil, adds to soil structure, and provides a medium for regrowth, so all goes well if the root has time to regrow once the new leaf can supply adequate energy. A second bite before root regrowth, however, requires the sacrifice of yet more root. That is overgrazing. Subsequent bites without root regeneration may demand sacrifices to the point of death.

Overgrazing tends to be damaging because it reduces the yield of the plant and reduces its root volume. If the aboveground part of the plant grows less, it provides less material to feed the animals and cover soil. If the root is reduced, then less energy and organic material is available for soil life; soil also settles and compacts, thus hampering aeration.

Severe grazing tends to maintain plant vigor, soil cover, and soil life. From here on, I will refer to this simply as grazing, since most grazing animals (including domesticated ones) are severe grazers—grazing by the mouthful rather than by the leaf.

Light grazing, as it leaves so much leaf and stem to become old and choke the plant (in brittle environments), tends to damage the plant slowly and lead to a shift in succession.

A look at the impact of grazing and overgrazing on the four ecosystem foundation blocks in extremes of nonbrittle and brittle environments gives a rough indication of the implications for management.

Nonbrittle Environments

Succession: Grazing tends to maintain grass root vigor at a high level. If the area would normally progress toward woody communities, grazing will impede this shift or halt it at a grassland level of great complexity, probably including many legumes and other broad-leaved plants.

Overgrazing will damage root vigor but not expose soil, as it leads to the formation of a solid mat of grass. Some species may disappear, leading to a more unstable community. Given conducive climate and surface conditions, it may produce a shift towards woody communities, as the damaged grass roots allow easy establishment of tap-rooted species.

Water and mineral cycles: Grazing will not expose soil but rather cause even denser cover and thus probably enhance these cycles in a grassland. Where human intervention has reduced a natural forest or jungle to grassland and maintained it at that level by grazing, water and mineral cycles probably will never reach their former levels.

In either natural or manmade pasture, grass root reduction and compaction stemming from overgrazing adversely affects the cycling of both water and minerals. If continued overgrazing allows succession to produce stable woody communities, as it will given enough rainfall, water and mineral cycles benefit accordingly.

Energy flow: Grazing increases energy flow both above and below ground in natural grassland or pastures. Where rest would produce woods or jungle, grazing, which holds succession at the grassland level, keeps energy flow down but available for our purposes.

Overgrazing reduces energy flow in grassland or pasture. Only where it produces a shift to woody communities, which the climate can sustain, does it do otherwise.

Brittle Environments

Succession: Grazing tends to maintain grassland communities, increase their diversity, cover soil, and retard shifts toward woody species.

Overgrazing, by reducing litter and soil cover even as it damages roots, fosters shifts away from grassland and woody communities toward forbs (or weeds*). It also promotes monocultures with reduced numbers of grass species.

Water and mineral cycles: Grazing enhances both of these through healthier and more stable root systems.

Overgrazing reduces water and mineral cycling by exposing soil and limiting litter production while decreasing soil structure, porosity, and organic content.

Energy flow: Grazing increases energy flow by preventing old oxidizing blockages of material and promoting vigorous leaf growth. Healthier root systems also support millions of microorganisms underground.

Overgrazing cuts energy flow through both root reduction and surface exposure of the soil.

These are the straightforward tendencies that guide us in management. In practice they proceed in concert with so many other forces that one cannot always predict how significantly they will influence a given case. The plan, monitor, control, and replan routine of the HRM model generally leads to that knowledge. Nevertheless, a deeper understanding of the adaptations that allow severe grazers and grass to coexist, and the situations that lead to overgrazing, makes the job easier.

The perennial grass plants and severe grazers developed a mutually advantageous relationship over the eons of the past. They never required human intervention or opinion as to whether it was good or bad.

The previous chapter explained how accumulations of old growth can choke a growing plant to death in a brittle environment. Nothing addresses this problem better than the grazing and social behavior of herding animals. Why then do the experts so often recommend cutting the animal numbers and burning the ungrazed grass? No animal ever defoliated plants as completely as a fire.

---

*I prefer to use the term forbs when referring to the smaller tap-rooted (or dicotyledenous) plants. The term weeds is almost always used in a negative sense and can apply to a tap-rooted or fibrous-rooted (grass) plant.

Illustration 19-1. Ranch, stocked at conventional stocking rate, showing tendency to overgraze areas (light patches) and overrest other areas (darker patches). Coahuilla, Mexico.

The prejudice against severe grazers persists because only recently has anyone considered regulating the timing of an animal's bite or tried to link the known behavior of animals in the wild to the problem of maintaining the vitality of grass.

The cow takes a mouthful from a particular plant, then moves on a step or two, leaving other plants of the same or different species untouched. The grazed plant should benefit from the bite, but frequently doesn't because its regrowth, offering more protein and energy and less fiber, will attract a second bite some days later if the cow remains in the area. Thus, one plant gets overgrazed while its neighbors rest, and one cow may actually kill a few plants while a great many rest. More cows can kill more plants while somewhat fewer rest.

This process accounts for the apparent paradox that animals grazing continuously under the management most commonly practiced in America usually produce both overgrazed and overrested plants in the same area. Sometimes this may manifest itself as a startling mosaic of ungrazed and overgrazed patches, or it may be so dispersed among a variety of plants and species as to escape the casual glance. .

Illustration 19-1 gives an aerial view of a "conventionally well-run ranch" with a so-called correct (light) stocking rate. Obviously, over large areas nearly all plants have suffered overgrazing, as the ground-level close-up

Illustration 19-2.   Ground view of the same ranch as in illustration 19-1, showing close-up of overrested and overgrazed sites. Coahuilla, Mexico.

Illustration 19-3.   Large-scale death of perennial grasses taking place in over-rested site on the same ranch as in illustrations 19-1 and 19-2. Coahuilla, Mexico.

(illustration 19-2) makes painfully clear. The other areas contain a great quantity of overrested and dying grass plants, as illustration 19-3 shows in detail. Changing the numbers will only alter the proportions of overrested and overgrazed plants, as the physical structure of the animal's mouth, and thus the way it feeds, is not altered by stocking rate.

Playing the numbers game cannot alter the fact of overgrazing, and very often the overrested sites, as mentioned, shift to woody plant communities. This underlies the invasion of problem woody species into millions of acres of American grassland. Vast sums have gone for research, chemicals, machinery, and publicity in the attempt to eradicate plants that never caused a problem until our misunderstanding of overgrazing allowed them to become one.

The French scientist André Voisin was the first to look at this well-documented syndrome from the standpoint of a single plant. He concluded that overgrazing had nothing to do with the number of animals in the pasture. The plant that got bitten by the single cow stood a good chance of damage or death if the cow hung around very long. On the other hand, a thousand cows that moved on after a day posed no threat at all. More plants in the pasture got bitten, but none was bitten while trying to regrow.

Time, said Voisin, not the number of animals, controls overgrazing. Because of this conclusion, the HRM model focuses considerable attention on managing the time plants are exposed and reexposed to the animals, but wild animals don't wear watches. How then does Nature maintain the harmonious rhythm of growth and grazing?

Once upon a time cattle no doubt behaved like American bison or African buffalo. Even when feeding, those animals remained fairly close together, and they moved frequently.

Some believe that this habit of concentration and movement represented an instinctive sense that perennial grasses became more nutritious and tillered more when grazed intensely and then rested. I hold to the theory that fear of predators, and a certain amount of parental instinct, caused certain animals to herd closely and coincidentally concentrate dung and urine wherever they grazed. As Voisin observed in cattle, and I in wild herds, grazing animals do not like to feed over ground they have fouled. They keep moving to fresh ground and don't normally return until the dung has decomposed, usually long enough for plants to regrow (in growing seasons), thus avoiding overgrazing.

When bison, pronghorn, springbok, wildebeest, or buffalo sense no danger from predators (including man, who was a major predator), they do change behavior and overgrazing increases. The herd remains spread for longer and longer periods, and even females with calves will graze and lie

Illustration 19-4. Paddock grazed by three horses for one year, showing dung-free grazing area in the foreground. Longer grass in background contains much dung. New Mexico.

Illustration 19-5. Chaco Canyon boundary looking through the fence to land where almost all plants have been heavily overgrazed for the last fifty years. New Mexico.

well away from others. Then they scatter dung so widely it no longer inhibits feeding nor induces movement and the same animals remain on the same ground day after day.

This theme has several variations. Cattle at low density, especially on nonbrittle land, often avoid dung sites long after the dung has decomposed, but this probably indicates that the rest allowed plants at the site to become too rank and fibrous. Many animals, and especially horses, will dung only in one area of a pasture and graze elsewhere.

Illustration 19-4 shows a pasture in which three horses have done this for a year. They have returned almost daily to a severely grazed patch where they do not dung, while other areas where they do have grown up in longer, ranker grass, which will only be grazed under extreme stress. As inevitably happens when animals remain on the same ground, the grazed patch becomes overgrazed because regrowing plants offering more protein and energy and less fiber, and a more convenient grazing height, get bitten again and again, while the older, more fibrous plants elsewhere subside into stagnation for lack of use.

Supporters of nonselective or mob grazing argue that a tight, moving herd does not graze as selectively as scattered animals and they advocate concentrating stock as a means of forcing greater utilization of forage and limiting overgrazing. Another school advocates monitoring key indicator species and limiting stock until they take only 50 percent of the forage from those plants. Both theories miss the point.

As far as we know, all grazing and browsing animals have to select their diets carefully to function well. We do not understand how they do this. The small amount of existing research shows it to be more complex than the simple senses of taste, sight, scent, and smell. Concentrating animals greatly in order to force them to graze off all plants uniformly, as I did in my early work, merely results in poor weight gains, low breeding success, and other signs of stressed animals, as by nature they do not feed in that way.

Granting that severe grazing, by removing old moribund material, actually stimulates plants, then of course allowing selection should increase, not reduce, the favored ones. In very brittle environments even gross overgrazing can maintain a grassland community longer than total rest. Illustration 18-6 showed the extreme damage in the Chaco Canyon National Monument following fifty years of rest with no grazing or overgrazing. Perennial grass has largely disappeared and there are large patches of bare dying soil. Illustration 19-5 shows the land two hundred yards away on the same day where overgrazing at a high level has continued for those same fifty years. Although every plant shows signs of being overgrazed, and a near monoculture has been formed, it is hard to place a foot on bare ground without touching a green and growing plant.

The idea of removing 50 percent of the leaf from key species proves

Illustration 19-6. A severely distorted perennial grass, which has sent out a seed stalk flat along the ground. Zimbabwe.

unworkable for a number of reasons. Severe grazers don't slowly nibble all the members of a given species until half the leaves are taken from each plant. They tend to take one plant all the way down and leave the next. They avoid feeding on plants near their own dung. They select younger plants of a species over older ones and avoid those clogged by last year's dead growth. Many animals are genetically made up to select their diets at a high level, but *by the mouthful* (not by the leaf), which means that only plants of a certain physical form readily provide for their needs.

The concept also assumes that everything less important than the key species may go, but if that really happened the community would soon have changed so much that the key species might no longer be key.

In any case, as stated before, stocking rate has little bearing on what happens to any individual plant. One should discuss overgrazing only in regard to individual plants. Applying the word to a whole area falls into the same irrelevancies as trying to define 50 percent grazing of key species. One example illustrates the point.

Near Albuquerque, New Mexico, the Sandia Indians have run livestock on a piece of land for over three hundred years, one of the oldest examples of continuous grazing of domestic stock in the New World. In recent decades they have run a low number of cattle scattered thinly over the range in the common American way, and all the while the u.s. Bureau of Indian Affairs has complained bitterly of watershed damage from "overgrazing and overstocking."

On inspection, the site contained many plants matted with old, oxidizing leaves and stems and dying prematurely from overrest. Other plants, however, thrived, as cattle had removed the obstructing matter. Others were weak from overgrazing. Some new plants grew where physical trampling had created the right conditions. Elsewhere rain impact had recapped old disturbance, and many areas had seen no disturbance for so long that little grew there at all. Generally litter and ground cover were scarce, due to both the overgrazing of plants and the simultaneous partial rest of the whole.

Amid such a variety of symptoms, the blanket label overgrazed means nothing and offers no guide to a solution. The presence of so many overrested plants belies the description overstocked altogether.

On rangelands in Africa, South America, Central America, North America, and the Middle East, I have seen and heard the same things, but apart from one artificial simulation, I have never seen prolonged land deterioration caused by overstocking. Almost all sites commonly called overstocked do contain a high number of overgrazed plants, but virtually always a very

Illustration 19-7.   Severe distortion of a normally erect perennial grass, which has been overgrazed. The knife indicates how close and flat the leaves are to the ground. Zimbabwe.

significant quantity of overrested ones, along with much bare ground due to partial rest. As the last chapter explained, partial rest in a brittle environment leads to the same or greater increase in bare ground as can be produced by overgrazing. The two influences compound each other, but the blame always falls on overstocking.

Overgrazing is by no means an entirely human invention. Although wild herds, at least under threat of predation, follow rather constructive patterns of grazing, they often do overgraze. If they didn't, plants would not have developed such ingenious defenses against it, and our ignorance would have done more damage than it has.

On my own game reserve and research station in Zimbabwe, it was a common experience to see a buffalo herd concentrate for two or three days on a site and then move off the fouled ground. Not uncommonly a herd of zebra, wildebeest, eland, tsessebe, gemsbok, sable, roan, or some other species would follow them, apparently not bothered by the droppings of another species. Although in complex wildlife populations, different animals may favor different plants and feed at different levels, from the rooting wart hog to the tree-nibbling giraffe, overlap is considerable. Plants severely grazed by one herd often get overgrazed by another following close behind.

Some grass species cannot stand much overgrazing and, after several consecutive root sacrifices, die out except where protected by thorny bushes and cracks in rocks. Others take evasive or defensive action. Some sacrifice the center of the clump but continue to hang onto life around the edges. Some distort their leaf and stem growth flat along the ground below the grazing height of the animals (illustrations 19-6 and 19-7). Other species develop a tight, round, spiny ball like a rolled-up hedgehog. The prickly aspect comes from old stem remains, amongst which small leaves persist (illustration 19-8).

A few species use more than one of the adaptations, as you see in illustration 19-6 where a plant that normally would have grown two to three feet high has sacrificed the center of its clump and sent leaves out flat about half an inch above the ground.

In extreme cases of overgrazing whole communities may shift toward a solid mat of runner-type grasses, which maintain leaf growth more easily below the grazing height of animals. One such community I know of continued to thrive under heavy daily cattle pressure but perished quickly under an onslaught of geese, which grazed at a much lower level.

In all countries I have observed, perennial grasses appear remarkably resilient to overgrazing, with one notable exception. For some reason not yet fully understood or explained by anyone, they seem particularly vulnerable in Mediterranean climates, such as predominate in the southern tip of Africa and along the California coast. These places contain vast areas that have lost almost every perennial grass after years of overgrazing.

Illustration 19-8. Long overgrazed, this normally matted perennial grass is surviving by forming a hedged ball. Baluchistan Province, Pakistan.

Fortunately, although we do not yet understand their extreme sensitivity, they do return when both overgrazing and partial rest are stopped.

The grazing styles of various animals do affect management decisions to the extent that if production goals include a certain kind of livestock or wildlife, one would use grazing as one tool for achieving the mix of food and cover plants it required. However, a few false myths linger in this area as well.

Grazing styles fall into three categories. Nibblers, endowed with narrow mouths, nip a leaf here and there off a plant. The duiker and steenbok and some other small African antelope belong to this group. Most of them are solitary, nonherding animals, with self-regulating populations (which we do not yet understand), and none has domestic relatives.

A second, broad-mouthed group feeds by the mouthful. Buffalo, bison, zebra, horses, cattle, and hippo do this. Most are gregarious members of nonself-regulating populations, and tend to defoliate plants severely. Elephants, which pull up grasses by the trunkful, also belong in this group.

Somewhere between these two extremes come animals capable of nipping an isolated leaf but habitually given to taking several at a time and concentrating on the same plant to such a degree that they have to be managed as severe grazers/browsers. Among them would be sheep, goats, deer, pronghorn, impala, and other herding antelope. Again, they are gregarious and nonself-regulating and represented amongst domestic stock.

Illustration 19-9.   Overbrowsed and hedged perennial shrub of great age. North Yemen.

The distinction between self-regulating and nonself-regulating populations is an important one, which I will return to in Chapter 37. We suspect that the solitary, self-regulating nibblers (which generally do not overgraze) control their population by some form of breeding inhibition allied to social stress above certain densities. The nonself-regulating severe grazers/browsers (which can and do overgraze) are heavily dependent for their survival on a high rate of annual loss to accidents, predation, and eventually parasitism, disease, or starvation if predation is inadequate. All of these predator-dependent species also herd.

The presence of a wide diversity of animals on a piece of land often means more thorough utilization of available feed, as becomes evident where combinations of sheep, cattle, goats, and horses run together. It nevertheless does not change the basic dynamics of overgrazing, and the grazing aspects of planning for most kinds of domestic stock are remarkably similar.

So far we have considered grazing and grazing animals, but what of browsers and browsing? Among wild species (and among our domestic animals), we have many that browse woody plants and forbs more than they graze, and some that purely browse, some that browse forbs in open grasslands and some that subsist entirely on trees. Do the same principles apply? In general, yes.

Illustration 19-10. New stems growing below the old browseline once the overbrowsing has stopped. Namibia.

Though not nearly as much research has concentrated on browsing as on grazing, all results seem to point in the same direction. Woody plants can withstand heavy browsing, which removes all of the green leaf as long as the plants get adequate time in which to recover afterward. They can also withstand continuous severe browsing as long as sufficient foliage remains out of reach of the animals. A few very sensitive species, lacking an effective defense mechanism, become conspicuous by their absence when under continuous pressure.

The most common response to overbrowsing by resilient plants is hedging. Plants develop the look of a clipped garden hedge in which short, tightly-spaced stems protect leaves crowded in amongst them. Illustration 19-9 shows a heavily hedged plant growing in the biblical lands where heavy browsing goes back at least two thousand years. There is no knowing how old this plant is. Plants that do hedge can withstand overbrowsing for such prolonged periods that they well may live a normal lifespan, although I have seen elephants reach through their defenses and browse to death trees that had hedged successfully against lesser animals for years.

Other plants do not hedge, but larger individuals develop a browseline below which the animals take everything, while the plant continues to grow. Illustration 19-10 shows a browseline on the underside of a tree, but you can also see normal growth resuming, thanks to introduction of a grazing plan that eliminated overbrowsing.

Illustration 19-11.   Close-cropped, matted leaves along the trunk of a tree suffering from severe overbrowsing. Cape Province, South Africa.

Some species, when overbrowsed, develop very heavy root systems and straggly aboveground parts. This, however, can also result from frequent fire or regular frosting in the tropics, both of which remove leaf and damage stems routinely.

An occasional species grows small, matted leaves along the main stems, as seen in illustration 19-11.

Unfortunately, the survival techniques do not usually work for seedlings. Overbrowsing may eliminate young plants absolutely, even when the adults hold on for centuries. Without replacements, however, the population gradually declines.

Browsing enhances the productivity of forbs and woody plants and thus, like the perennial grasses, they share an interdependence with the animals that feed on them that we don't understand very well at this point.

As in the case of grasses, overbrowsing bears no relationship to the number of animals, only to the proportion of leaf removed and the time that a plant has to regenerate. Illustration 19-12 shows a browseline on trees in the Navajo-Hopi Joint Use Area in Arizona. A 90 percent reduction in livestock has not affected the overbrowsing at all, as the trees are continually exposed to the remaining few animals.

On the other hand, illustrations 19-13 and 19-14 show what can happen

Illustration 19-12.   Browseline clearly showing on trees, despite a massive stock reduction. Arizona.

even under doubled stocking rates when the animals are concentrated and their grazing (and browsing) times planned. Illustration 19-13 shows a highly nutritious but severely overbrowsed plant in Arizona called winterfat. Every single plant we found on this particular ranch had suffered to the extent of having no observable seed or seedling production.

Illustration 19-14 shows the same area after two years of planned grazing with greatly increased and concentrated livestock. Far more leaf, stem, wild-life cover, and seed had appeared. A year after that we saw seedlings as well.

Illustration 19-15 gives a view of the Karroo area of South Africa during a drought. It gets about nine inches of annual rainfall, and overgrazing and overbrowsing with partial rest have gone on for more than three hundred years. The highly nutritious and long-overbrowsed plant in the foreground has assumed an extremely hedged form. Illustration 19-16 is a close-up of the same plant. A management plan that doubled the animal numbers, but concentrated them and planned the time of grazing, accounts for the new, free-flowering, and seeding growth.

The role of the concentrated herd in these examples will become clearer in the following chapter on animal impact. Suffice it to say that good management can have the same positive impact on browse plants as on grasses, and the number of animals is not as crucial as the time the plants are exposed and then reexposed to the animals.

Where fouled ground induced movement in concentrated grazers, it also does so with those browsers that feed on forbs at ground level. Those

Illustration 19-13.   Severely overbrowsed stub of a bush. Arizona.

animals that do their browsing at higher levels of course are not to the same degree feeding on fouled ground, as their noses and mouths are well above it. We may never know, now that we have lost natural populations to research in most parts of the world, but I strongly suspect that these species were heavily dependent on certain predators to induce movement. These predators typically would have hunted in bands or packs, such as humans once did, and wolves, wild dogs, and hyenas still do in some places.

My personal feelings about all of these issues are haunted by the fate of a place in the lower Zambezi Valley of Zimbabwe where I began to wrestle seriously with the problem of desertification. It was among the finest big game areas in the world and in those days very wild. I began working there in 1959 just after the human population had been moved out because of the dreaded sleeping sickness, and it had become purely a game area to be managed as such. It later became a fine national park called Mana Pools.

I researched and reported on the terrible destruction of the alluvial river plains that was becoming apparent under heavy populations of elephant, buffalo, impala, waterbuck, and several other species. The reedbeds were destroyed, rambling shrub thickets wiped out. Once plentiful bushbuck and reedbuck were becoming rare. Large parklands of highly productive and beautiful trees were being heavily overbrowsed. And though seedlings ger-

Illustration 19-14. Typical bush, on the same ranch as in illustration 19-13, growing out well with grazing/browsing planned and livestock numbers doubled. Arizona.

minated freely, over many square miles not a single one survived. Day and night large chunks of riverbank toppled into the river.

I recommended heavy culling of the elephants and buffalo in particular, as it was so obvious to me, and all of the scientists who visited the area, that there were simply too many. Illustration 19-17 shows a general view of the river area in 1960.

Much later my recommendations became policy, and the heavy culling still goes on. Numbers have been reduced, and all should now be well. When I went back in 1985, however, I found the damage as bad as ever. Trees germinate but none survive to fill the thinning ranks of those I knew. The few elephants and other animals that remain continue to overbrowse. Much more bark is now being ripped off remaining large trees, speeding their demise. Illustration 19-18 is a view of the general area in 1985. I, like others involved, had also missed the full significance of man's role as a key predator. Elephants, although being culled at a high rate, do not know that humans are doing it and are thus unafraid. This deception is considered necessary as it is a national park and tourists require tame elephants. (The elephants that I walked amongst in 1985 were very different in their response to human

Illustration 19-15. During a very dry year, livestock numbers were doubled on this severely depleted rangeland, while the livestock moves were planned to avoid further overbrowsing/overgrazing. Illustration 19-16 is a close-up view of the plant in the lower right (see arrow). Karroo, South Africa.

scent than they were when wilder in 1959.) Unfortunately, tame elephants, or any other game interdependent with predators, including man, are not natural and therefore lose their natural relationship with the plants in their community. Basically they dally too often and too long in the most favored areas and thus overbrowse.

The answers are not simple, certainly not as simple as just deciding to regulate or not regulate the number of animals. The proper stocking rate is important, particularly in order to leave enough forage to carry animals through the nongrowing season. But other factors enter the equation.

Wildlife management in particular poses many questions. Since we can't stop overgrazing by controlling numbers, how do we control time? How do we determine what the land may carry? We must consider what else the animals do on the land—dunging, trampling, picking up litter, and so on. We must look at the relationship of different animals to one another. If herds are to move, where will they move to? What territories and home ranges and migration routes do they require? What will induce and maintain the necessary movement? How does population size regulate territory and this, in turn, regulate the time plants are exposed to herds?

In national parks, which we know have limits, we cannot establish

Illustration 19-16.   Once no longer overbrowsed, this plant is flowering and seeding heavily despite the drought and increased livestock numbers. Karroo, South Africa.

stocking rates by simply keeping numbers low enough to avoid a heavy die off in dry years, as the famous Kruger National Park in South Africa does. In average and good years that leads to overrest and shifts in succession to woody plants, which in turn encourages too frequent use of fire and technology in what becomes crisis management—reaction to unexpected developments.

Some of the answers lie in the planning of time, others in the biological planning described in later chapters. Much can also be done with the tool of animal impact, discussed in the next chapter.

Illustration 19-17.   Severe overbrowsing under very high numbers of large game. Rambling shrub thickets have been wiped out. Mana Pools Non-Hunting Area, Zambezi Valley, 1960. Zimbabwe.

Illustration 19-18.   Severe overbrowsing under reduced numbers of large game, following heavy culling. The majority of the trees have been heavily browsed to the height elephants can reach. Mana Pools National Park, Zambezi Valley, 1985. Zimbabwe.

20

Animal Impact

A nimal impact refers to all the things grazing animals do besides eat. Instinctively we have considered the dunging, urinating, salivating, rubbing, and trampling of large animals as generally inconvenient conditions of their presence. Especially since fertilizer has become an item sprayed from tanks or poured out of sacks, few people even think of the more pungent aspects of livestock except when downwind of them.

Fortunately Nature has not been so shortsighted, and we have recently discovered in the lumbering, smelly, but powerful behavior of grazing animals a tool of enormous significance for better management of watersheds, some croplands, wildlife, and forests.

The theory and practice of holistic resource management grew from the discovery of the four keys described in earlier chapters, and two of them (the fundamental differences between brittle and nonbrittle environments and the role of herding animals and their predators in maintaining brittle ones) led to recognition of animal impact as a tool.

The following examples give an idea of the power and versatility of this tool. Though critical to the maintenance of brittle environments and most often called for in those conditions, it is useful in nonbrittle areas as well.

— In a brittle environment, overrest has allowed plants to accumulate several years of old material. Roots have suffered severe damage, and succession has started the shift to forbs, shrubs, and trees, mocking our landscape goal of open grassland. Fire would expose soil and invigorate many of the woody plants. Chemicals or machinery might clear the ground but could not guarantee that grass would establish or persist if the soil was insufficiently compacted.

Periodic high animal impact applied at minimal or no cost, together with grazing (but not overgrazing), could remove old material, invigorate existing plants without exposing soil, create conditions for new plants to establish, and move succession away from forbs and woody plants. Low animal impact for prolonged time, as much observation and research data has shown, does not do so.

— We need a firebreak through a strip of brush and scrub. A fine spray of very dilute molasses or saline (salt solution) will excite a herd of cattle enough to make a firebreak through almost any kind of country at minimal expense without exposing soil or setting off erosion.

— Bare eroding ground, which we once might have fenced off and seeded at great expense, we can now subject to periodic heavy impact, by giving a large herd a few bales of hay, and thus advance succession at no cost or lost production.

— Erosion gullies, whose steep banks grant no foothold to plants, spread across the land. Why pay for a bulldozer to slope the banks and chew up more land, when a herd of livestock or wildlife attracted to the gully can break down the banks and create the conditions for natural succession to heal them? This high animal impact, while curing the gully, also tends to correct the water cycle that caused the damage in the first place. Once again, research data have shown that low animal impact, especially for prolonged time, leads to less effective water cycles.

— Impenetrable brush clogs potential grassland. Although low densities of calm cattle will not touch it, a large herd, set on by means discussed in Chapter 26, will penetrate and break it down. As the thick-skinned, excited animals open the thicket, sunlight penetrates and grass can flourish. As grass flourishes with healthy roots, new woody plants establish with difficulty.

— Fish management often requires steep, vegetated banks rather than steep eroding ones, as shown in figure 20-1. Very high animal impact for very short periods can promote this, as the well-vegetated river bank in illustration 20-1 shows.

— Stock trails to water or down a hillside threaten to wash out. Though it may seem strange that damage caused by trampling can be cured by trampling, the treatment works because of the vast difference between the effect of prolonged, one-way trailing and the milling of excited animals for very short periods.

— Coarse, fibrous grass has come to dominate a bottomland where low stocking rates have prevailed. Traditionally fire would be used to keep the grass palatable. But this exposes soil and, combined with low animal impact, leads to wider plant spacing and more fibrous plants. A dose of high animal impact removes plant tops and covers the soil, thus favoring more lateral growth, closer plant spacing, and less fibrous plants. Once again this tool removes the cause while curing the problem.

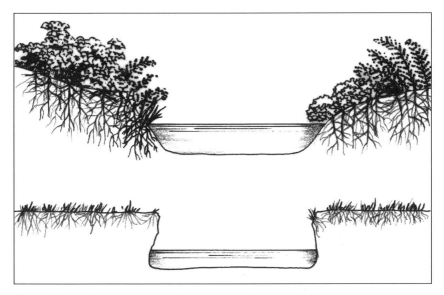

Figure 20-1.   Steep stream banks—vegetated and eroded.

Illustration 20-1.   Vegetated river bank produced with cattle trampling and well-planned grazing. Zimbabwe (courtesy R. H. Vaughan-Evans).

— Desert soils have remained hard capped from lack of disturbance for over three thousand years. Nomads periodically herd their cattle and sheep over the land overgrazing the few remaining plants. Occasionally a new grass establishes where a cow has broken the hard surface. A herd is concentrated and excited for a brief moment and the desert starts to make its recovery at last. Remember, the coiled spring will always expand when the weight is removed—the weight of years of partial rest in this case.

All the above are common situations where animal impact is the most practical tool available. Animal impact is indeed such a versatile tool that we run the danger of prescribing it reflexively as some now hand out knee-jerk technology fixes; the HRM model has guidelines to prevent that.

The discovery that brittle environments need periodic disturbance to maintain stable soil cover nevertheless leads us to recognize animal impact as perhaps the *only* practical tool that can realistically halt the advance of deserts over billions of acres of rough country. Here and there other tools can help, but what other way exists to treat millions of square miles of often rugged country each year without consuming fossil fuel, without pollution, and by a means millions of even illiterate people can employ, even while it feeds them?

On the other hand, no other aspect of HRM has caused as much controversy as this tool has. That trampling by livestock damages both plants and soils *is a deeply held belief throughout the world* supported by overwhelming superficial evidence. By some tragic irony, some of our most serious academics have rejected the one idea that has more promise of solving the riddle of desertification than any other. Meanwhile, imprinters and other machines of extraordinary size and cost have been developed to provide mechanical impact toward the same end (illustration 20-2).

Objectively speaking, few would question the three salient aspects of animal impact.

1. Hooved animals tend to compact the soil, as at every step they concentrate a big weight on a small foot. The sheep's foot rollers of modern civil engineering memorialize the herds used to compact road beds and earthworks not even a century ago.

2. When animals trample the land, they tend to cause breaks and irregularities on the surface, as anyone who has tracked game knows.

3. Such animals tend to speed the return of plant material to the soil surface through their dung, urine, and the litter they trample down, faster than it would return if they were not on the land.

Whether any of these tendencies works for good or ill on the land depends entirely on management, not on their intrinsic nature.

I myself, of course, did not overcome my old biases without considerable effort, doubt, and false beginnings. Early on I entertained the hypothesis

Illustration 20-2. The Dixon Land Imprinter designed to rehabilitate poor rangelands (courtesy Robert M. Dixon).

that animal impact had some important function, but I could not articulate it well until I saw the distinction between brittle and nonbrittle environments and understood the importance of time.

The following example illustrates once again how timing may fundamentally change the quality of an event. Suppose you have a small house on a hill and you and your donkey fetch water daily from the stream below. After one year of trodding the same path day after day a substantial gully forms, and the bank where you load the water cans becomes a trampled-out bog, which threatens to wash away entirely. Doubtless the force of 365 donkey-days of trampling per year could have this effect.

And yet they might not. Suppose you took a train of 365 donkeys down the hill and hauled a year's worth of water in one morning. Though a passer-by that afternoon would remark on severe trailing and trampling of the bank, those wounds would have 364 days to heal before you had to come back. When you did, you could expect to find both the trail and the loading place completely overrun by new growth. In fact both might well be greener and healthier than before with the old grass removed and the dung and urine deposited, though they had still borne 365 donkey-days of traffic per year.

For thousands of years we simply overlooked that timing governs whether animal impact acted favorably or adversely on land, and we did not distinguish between brittle and nonbrittle land.

One other observation has escaped many scholars of this subject, and poor appreciation of it continues to bias research at many levels. The herding animals that contribute most to the maintenance of brittle environments behave in a variety of ways that produce different effects.

Normally we use two guidelines in applying animal impact to land—stock density and herd effect. While stocking rate describes the number of animals continuously supported by a given unit of land, stock density reflects the concentration of animals on the unit of land where they actually are at a given moment. Neither describes whether the animals are feeding placidly or milling around at the smell of predators, and that makes a critical difference to the land.

We apply the term herd effect to the excited movement of crowded, hooved animals when under threat or attack by predators, in full migration, being driven, or competing for food as livestock do when turned on to hay or supplements. Herd effect is difficult to quantify but easy to identify. Normally, grazing or walking animals place their hooves carefully, avoiding coarse plants and barely breaking the soil surface, but still compacting the soil to a degree. When herd effect occurs, the same animals break down coarse plants, raise dust, chip soil surfaces, and open the soil to aeration.

My observations of how these different modes of behavior affect plants and soils led eventually to the definition of partial rest, mentioned in Chapter 18. Land sustains partial rest when animals, either domestic or wild, are present but never have cause to produce herd effect. They may slightly disturb the soil cover of algae, lichens, or mosses, but seldom can stimulate a successional shift to more complex communities and stability. The millions of acres in America deteriorating under the combination of partial rest and overgrazing support this conclusion.

Traditional American range management favors protecting algal crust because it does inhibit erosion to a degree. Standard doctrine therefore disparages any kind of trampling because breaking the crust obviously increases erosion in the short run. It takes a much deeper, long-term observation to see that a really heavy trampling over a short period leads to establishment of plants that protect the soil better than algae ever can.

Illustration 20-3 shows one of the most dramatic examples I have ever seen of land deteriorating badly under a little overgrazing and low animal impact (partial rest). This ranch, in a very brittle nine-inch-rainfall area of Namibia, once supported a commercial dairy operation, so nutritious and abundant was the forage. By the time we started applying some of the tools that later became part of the HRM model, it looked as you see on the left of the fence—real desert.

We could find some overgrazed plants, but more bare ground than

Illustration 20-3. Heavy animal impact has led to the immediate response in plant growth seen to the right of this fence on badly desertified rangeland. Namibia.

anything else. As can be seen, the level of animal trampling had destroyed algal communities but not stimulated the successional process enough to maintain grassland. Long-rested sites in the area had an algal crust hard enough to ring like a drum head when tapped.

The first year we greatly concentrated the sheep (the only type of domestic stock they could still profitably run) and planned the grazing to minimize overgrazing. The area to the right of the fence in illustration 20-3, which got high animal impact, shows how succession clearly started to move forward again without any assistance in the way of reseeding. Animal impact definitely accounts for the immediate change, as just minimizing overgrazing (when you're down to bare ground) takes much longer to show results. Forbs dominated the first successional advance, but grasses soon took over.

Trampling, carried to extremes, can cause temporary or even long-lasting damage to the ecosystem foundation blocks, but when the time factor is controlled, most environments have astounding resilience. Some two thousand cattle concentrating at a fence corner during a heavy downpour of rain created the scene in illustration 20-4. The first time a rancher called me out

Illustration 20-4. Extreme trampling resulting from two thousand head of cattle concentrating during a storm. Chaco, Paraguay.

to inspect damage caused by a herd in a storm we photographed and discussed the resulting quagmire at great length, but finally decided to ignore it and keep on with the concentration and movement as planned. About eighteen months later we recalled the incident but could no longer determine where it had happened as all paddocks looked much the same. In many cases I have seen the temporarily overtrampled area look much better after a season.

The continuous trampling we see so often around gates, water points, and feed troughs does not allow recovery to take place, but such examples often figure in arguments against trampling in general. Even sophisticated time management may not eliminate all such cases, but usually the area involved is insignificant.

To date, most of our experience with animal impact as a tool has involved domestic stock. On the game reserve I once owned, I frequently noted its benefits but had little reason to create it artificially, as the big game enjoyed extremely natural circumstances that included a good level of predation by lions, leopards, hyena, cheetah, and wild dogs. I also hunted periodically myself and made no attempt to tame animals. The same species behaved quite differently on ranches where predators (including humans) had been eliminated. The animals had become more localized and calm. Where baboons in my game reserve thrived in the community but ran at the sight of people, in the nearby national parks they sat on cars and had to be destroyed as a nuisance.

We are in our infancy in understanding the control of time and the relationship of herds, home ranges, territories, and predation in wild populations.

Likewise, we have much to learn about how animal impact might serve our goals on crop land. The concept of brittle and nonbrittle environments has not yet entered the thinking of most farmers, but we do suspect that cropland in brittle areas deteriorates fastest under our conventional row-cropping practices. The American Dust Bowl of the 1930s became a legendary monument to that discovery. Perhaps the problems are related to those arising on brittle rangeland from the difficulty of maintaining organic soil components and adequate ground cover.

In this context, work underway in the United States at The Land Institute and the Rodale Institute on developing perennial grain crops could open up enormous possibilities. Success in these efforts would go a long way toward solving two major problems in agriculture—high production costs and soil destruction—brought about by our vast commitment to annual grain monocultures.

Like rangeland, perennial grain fields will require the removal and recycling of the old material that does not decay fast in brittle conditions. Animal impact may provide the answer. Where surface crumb structure and porosity are vital on croplands, livestock could be introduced in high concentrations for very short periods to speed cycling and decay of crop residues.

The greatest immediate benefit from animal impact can be in the restoration and maintenance of brittle watersheds. I have mentioned elsewhere that irrigable and arable land accounts for only about 10 percent of my country, Zimbabwe. The water on which all cities, mining, irrigation, and industry depend comes from the largely brittle land that comprises nearly all the rest. No mechanical or other technological means exists that could replace animal impact across all the ranches, farms, tribal lands, national parks, and forests that cover the great bulk of the country.

On a world scale the figures don't look much better. As mentioned in previous chapters, land that falls at the brittle end of the scale accounts for more than half the land on earth, and our civilization depends heavily on water from that land.

The effects of animal impact on brittle and nonbrittle environments are in summary:

Brittle Environments

Succession: Periodic high animal impact promotes the successional process on bare, gullied, and eroding ground. On dense grassland, high impact retards the process at the grassland level, preventing a shift to woody communities.

Low animal impact tends to produce bare ground, as it disturbs algal communities but does not advance succession. It allows plant spacings to increase, but does not reverse succession as decisively as total, prolonged rest.

Under low impact, dense grassland with close spacings may proceed toward woody communities and forbs, but these will give way to a landscape of scattered shrubs or trees and much bare or algae-covered ground unless rainfall suffices to sustain a full woody cover.

Mineral and water cycles: Periodic high animal impact generally improves water and mineral cycles. Few other tools approach it for achieving this goal. It tends to be much more effective than the traditional tools—fire and machinery.

Low animal impact, usually associated with partial rest, reduces mineral and water cycles below the land's potential. Where significant overgrazing of plants accompanies this, the effects are compounded.

Energy flow: As periodic high impact tends to advance succession and improve water and mineral cycles, energy flow also tends to improve. A possible exception would be certain tropical areas, which, though brittle, have enough rainfall to support a solid woodland canopy. Even then, periodic high impact could keep the land in grass with scattered trees, which might make more energy available for human use through livestock and game.

Low impact generally reduces energy flow below its potential. The shortfall often becomes severe if compounded by overgrazing, and unfortunately this is the most pervasive situation worldwide. It is endemic in the management of national parks like the famous Kruger Park mentioned earlier, where game numbers are kept deliberately low to avoid die off in dry years. The resulting accumulation of old material and threat of successional shifts to woody communities leads to repeated use of fire, which adds yet another debilitating force.

Nonbrittle Environments

Succession: Periodic high impact, by maintaining grass root vigor while discouraging the establishment of new woody plants, slows successional shifts to woody communities. In cases of grassland in potential forest this alone may not, however, entirely halt the successional shift back to forest.

Nonbrittle grassland, which cannot advance to forest because of shallow soil, elevation, annual frosting, etc., increases in complexity under periodic high animal impact.

Low animal impact has little effect on succession and woodland will develop if it can. Wherever it can't for the above reasons, low impact will not set succession back. Even combined with overgrazing it will seldom produce bare ground in extremely nonbrittle areas. This tendency to bare ground with low impact becomes a danger as one goes along the scale toward brittleness.

Mineral and water cycles: High animal impact tends to improve both water and mineral cycles, except where it is used to maintain grassland when natural succession would lead to woods. Low animal impact has little effect.

Energy flow: Periodic high animal impact tends to increase energy flow, though again, when used to maintain grassland in lieu of woods, energy flow will never reach the full potential of the land. Low animal impact has little effect.

Like rest and grazing, animal impact is a natural phenomenon that we choose to call a tool because we manipulate it to serve our ends. That distinction becomes even less distinct in regard to the next tool, *living organisms*, though they are our most vital allies in achieving our production and landscape goals.

21

Living Organisms

The phrase living organisms may seem an ambitiously broad way to define a tool, and it is. Plants and animals sounds earthier but doesn't force us to consider the utility of bacilli and viruses in the same breath as wheat and cattle, and we must. All living things share the power to change their microenvironment by their mere presence, and that must concern anyone whose goals depend on land.

The two previously discussed tools, grazing and animal impact, of course involve the use of living creatures in the service of management goals, and technically this tool does encompass those also.

It stands apart for two practical reasons. A separate heading forces us to weigh possible biological solutions to a problem against technological ones—successional complexity against pesticide and herbicide, crop poly-cultures and rotations against chemical fertilizers. Also, it makes us treat the whole complex of life in an environment as a whole rather than a menu of pesky or beneficial artifacts that we may kill or husband at will.

Failure to think along these two lines accounts for much of the environmental damage humans have wrought. The human race has only recently even considered that the current rate of extinction of other species might have highly dangerous consequences aside from the sheer horror of our destruction of other life. Many people still do not realize that a few hundred acres of tropical forest may contain more different living organisms than any state in America or any country in Europe. Considering that something as powerful as penicillin came from a simple mold, the losses implicit in our reckless clearing of jungle lie beyond any estimation.

The living organisms tool, because it involves all life, embodies both landscape and production goals. Where technology, fire, grazing, and animal impact act on the environment to achieve these goals, living organisms describe the goal itself.

Virtually all mankind's resource management goals depend on living organisms, possibly excepting some mineral extraction. Even there a sophist could argue that organic activity accounts for all hydrocarbons and even for the precipitation of uranium and some other minerals into ore. Thus, nearly all our material wealth derives from the underlying successional process of our ecosystem. Economists, particularly agricultural economists, hunched over their financial models as they tally capital and operating costs against cash prices, characteristically ignore this pillar that undergirds all their reckoning.

In the HRM model, a broken line surrounds both the living organisms tool and the ecosystem foundation block of succession because they merely represent two aspects of the same thing. Succession is a process manifested in living organisms. They in turn are the tools, the factories if you will, of most wealth and human sustenance.

The relationship of this tool to the others in the tools row looks a bit clearer from the viewpoint of the earliest cave dwellers. Assuming they could have analyzed their situation through the HRM model, they would have seen that they required a certain landscape from which they could produce the food, cover, and water necessary to maintain their quality of life. They would have recognized that all this depended on the same four ecosystem processes that sustain us. But their tools row was nearly empty. They had no fire, no livestock, and no technology. They knew implicitly that the dynamics of succession (living organisms) controlled them absolutely and defined what they could do in their environment.

We have not escaped that relationship as much as we tend to believe. Yet, to the extent that we understand it, we can use it to our advantage, as a tool, and the breadth of our options is remarkable, as the following examples illustrate.

In 1978 the Chinese, noting that the Gobi Desert annexed to itself over six hundred square miles annually, began planting green belts of trees, an overt case of enlisting living organisms as tools in their struggle against the advancing sand. By 1985 they had hand planted some 14.8 million acres. The success or failure of this stupendous effort to establish an advanced level of succession by main force depends on many factors. Later discussion of the guidelines in the HRM model explains in detail how to figure odds on the trees' survival and success in halting the desert's advance.

In simple terms, however, trees planted in the desert, effective as they may be as wind breaks, cannot grow and reproduce independent of the successional level of the total environment. Even if trees once did flourish on the edge of the Gobi, whatever distortion of succession killed them, if still active, will prevent the new plantings from establishing young and sustaining themselves.

By contrast, the Japanese scientist Fukuoka, mentioned earlier, undertook to use succession and the organisms associated with particular levels to produce high yields of small grain crops without fertilizers, compost, chemicals, soil disturbance, or weeding. He succeeded because his profound feeling for succession allowed him to enlist a great number of plants, insects, birds, and microorganisms in creating an environment where his grain thrived.

I recently saw a less complex but equally dramatic example on a Mexican ranch where the owner had built a small concrete ramp up the outside and down into a water tank. One night, while camped nearby, a terrific noise aroused us, and we discovered a massive mating of toads in the tank. By dawn they had dispersed to resume their pursuit of bugs and flies around the ranch. The ramp in fact enabled a great variety of insects, birds, rodents, etc. to survive and contribute to the complexity and stability of the whole area. The rancher needed that for his recreational and aesthetic goals, which for him included big game too—black bear, deer, turkey, and javelina.

Illustration 21-1 shows a leaking water pipe on a Namibian ranch. There, water pipes run along the fences to frustrate the local porcupines' appetite for plastic. For years the rancher struggled to control minor leaks. Then, when he articulated for himself production and landscape goals involving complex living communities, he saw opportunity in the leaks. Half-drums below them created additional watering points for thousands of birds, insects, and small mammals.

Previously this rancher had thought such creatures had no connection to cattle ranching. Now he jokingly talks about his enormous unpaid force of millions of "little people" all busily working for his family. Incidentally, this rancher's costs have decreased, while production and stability have increased dramatically.

When we nurture crops and domestic animals, and even when we produce wild animals on game ranches or cultivate fish, we tend to proceed as if Earth were more a machine than a living thing. Whatever we produce in this way does represent the use of living organisms as a tool for our survival, but we typically fail to see them in the context of succession. The hope that technology will enable us to completely protect our harvests from predators, competitors, and diseases, and thus reap a bounty independent of natural succession, has always proven false.

The so-called Green Revolution of extravagantly productive hybrid crops has foundered on this fact. The high-yielding strains owed their productivity to extreme uniformity and an engineered ability to make good use of fertilizer, but they required lavish protection from insects and disease. The combination of chemicals damaged the living soil, polluted our environment, increased

Illustration 21-1.   Leaking waterline turned into a waterpoint for birds, small animals, and insects. Namibia (courtesy Argo Rust).

insect damage, and generated resistant pests, and resulted in such escalating costs that thousands of American farmers are leaving their land and homes of generations. Some countries (e.g., Indonesia and West Germany) are already starting to ban chemical farming either because of pollution or increased insect damage.

The arrogant assumption that technology can supplant succession has embedded itself deeply enough in our culture to distort scientific reasoning. A booklet, "New Mexico Range Plants," issued in 1980 by the Cooperative Extension Service of New Mexico State University, makes the following statement about Hall's panic grass (*Panicum hallii Vasey*):

> Growing Hall's panic grass is highly palatable for all livestock. It retains this quality after curing, because some leaves remain green most of the year. Palatability causes the grass to decrease quickly under grazing, even when associated grasses are properly utilized. *Therefore, this species can be maintained only on areas reseeded as pure stands* [emphasis added].[1]

Here we have a valuable plant, which has maintained itself for millions of years as part of a complex community, while countless billions of antelope, buffalo, elk, and other species have prized it as much as domestic stock. Yet, the booklet tells us it needs the technology of modern wheat farming to survive at all. We have failed to sustain pure stands of any plant without massive injections of capital in fertilizers, herbicides, and pesticides. I doubt that it ever occurred to the authors that one might reap the benefits of Hall's panic grass by respecting its place in natural succession.

The use of biological controls in lieu of chemicals represents a generally more positive marriage of modern science and succession. Clear examples are the breeding of ladybugs to prey on aphids and the nurturing of certain bugs that eat problem plants. Parasites that attack fly larvae can decimate the fly population in feedyards and other mass breeding sites. Screw worms have been controlled so far through the use of sterile males. When they mate, the female dies without reproducing. When prickly pear cacti were introduced to Australia in the early 1920s they thrived, so much so that vast acres were so heavily infested that the land was considered useless. The cost of removing the cacti mechanically or poisoning them with chemicals was more than the land itself was worth, so entomologists ransacked their American homeland to find an insect that might help control the pest. They found it in the larvae of a small moth, which proved to be voracious eaters of the cacti. Within five years after being released in Australia, the moth had done a spectacular job of destroying the vast majority of the cacti.[2]

Though not without risk, such measures have usually proven less damaging to ecosystem processes than direct use of chemical poisons.

Modern breakthroughs in genetic engineering open the door to tremendous possibilities, but to equal temptations and dangers as well. Civilization might have spared itself some grief if it had gained more wisdom about ecosystem processes before acquiring this new power to intervene.

The new genii have escaped the test tube, however, so we must do the best we can to avoid embarking on a new Green Revolution as faulty as the last. A fundamental understanding of our massive agricultural failures and the customs and practices that cause the bedeviling spread of desert should undergird the creation of new forms of life.

The problems are not altogether unfamiliar. Traditional breeding techniques have produced species such as corn (maize) that have departed so far from their wild ancestry that we can no longer trace the link. They now depend totally on human cultivation. Genetic engineering merely shortens this process by several thousand years, but the new forms do not escape the laws of succession any more than corn, sheep, or white leghorn chickens. *Every organism, including man, has to take its place in succession, and cannot fly in defiance of this process.*

The current attempts to escape succession by creating crop plants that survive herbicides used against their competitors represent the wrong kind of thinking and will not solve any of the world's problems. It considers soil as simply a medium for holding plants upright while man feeds and nurtures them in an artificial, hydroponics-type situation. Agricultural scientists who have lost their connection with the land and have little or no feeling for the human quality of life may dream that success lies in that direction, but reality dictates that living soil must do far more than support plants physically if mankind is to survive in intelligent form.

It is my belief that genetic engineering will become a powerful tool for good if handled with wisdom. I hope that the HRM model will play a role in assisting us to that wisdom. I do not believe that we are going to see any successful quick fix solutions from such genetic work, marvelous as it is.

Looking to the future of science and management of resources, it is clear that we must turn far more to studying function, population and community health, and underlying principles and relationships—to prevention rather than cure, cure, cure, and recure while destroying our life-supporting ecosystem. Agriculture suffers no less from our myopia than the fields of human medicine, mental health, and veterinary science. As Chapter 17 mentioned in reference to using fire, we concentrate our efforts on fixing adults, without consideration of the environment in which our children grow, the context that made us what we are.

Isolated people and organizations have thought more holistically, but for several hundred years the mainstream has flowed in other channels. To change that will require more humility than past generations have shown and a greater acceptance that the unknowns in Nature (and science) still far outweigh the knowns. In addition, it will demand clarity of goals and the will to plan, monitor, control, and replan. The guidelines discussed in later chapters tackle this challenge, but first we must consider that most powerful and inscrutable tool of all, *technology.*

22

Technology

How many times have we heard it said that technology, the hallmark of modern man, holds the key to the future? It will feed us better. It will provide lightning-speed transportation and communications. It will heal our wounds and cure our diseases. As a tool for modifying the ecosystem, we have not seen the beginning of its potential.

The twentieth century has provided a constant stream of wonders that have generated this faith, but only recently have we had to entertain the possibility that technology does more than simply produce better and better mousetraps. It now forces humanity to make choices not imagined since the beginning of time.

Two events, the atom bomb and the landing of men on the moon, symbolize our dilemma. The bomb dramatically demonstrated that humanity does have the power to destroy itself, while the moon landing, which far surpassed the legendary tower of Babel in its vision, dares us to set no limits to our endeavors. Over forty years after Hiroshima we finally begin to understand that atomic power is not the *only* invention that can destroy us, that the arrogant pursuit of technological triumph may have dire consequences, and that the laws of Nature are still binding. Agriculture and other natural resource fields, no less than military science, have reached this crossroads a little ahead of the rest of society, and therefore must accept the challenge of leadership.

We cannot go back, of course, to rudimentary living and agriculture. However, recognition that going forward will demand wisdom and humility is a breakthrough in thinking more significant in its way than the notion of manned space travel. The HRM model represents a Wright Brothers-level attempt to analyze our technological power constructively in the context of what we now understand about the natural universe.

We do need some kind of schematic thought model that Everyman can use, because the human mind does not enjoy "simultaneous perception" of anything like the number of variables relevant to most common technological decisions. The technology of artificial intelligence may someday manage the mathematical ramifications of such a challenge, but few people will ever trust their deeper values and feelings to the whim of some software wizard, even in developed countries.

We must learn how to weigh technological tools against likely consequences and possible alternatives. Most of our most hazardous inventions have existed less than fifty years, and we must consider the evidence that mankind did remarkably well for many thousands of years using other tools for many of the same tasks. Though the HRM model occasionally may lead us to solve a short-term problem (out of urgent necessity) in a way that has adverse long-term effects, it will force us to act so that the situation won't arise again. In other cases it will justify the courage to forgo ephemeral gratification in lieu of lasting gain.

Our current use of technology expresses a prebomb state of mind that considers only the problem at hand without thought of larger implications. Thus, many of our inventions characteristically produce immediate reward but at a cumulative social cost that an innocent public may not even connect to the original problem. The principle known as "The Tragedy of the Commons"[1] compounds this syndrome.

Most societies long ago encountered the paradox of common land. If people may freely graze cattle on common ground, then individual operators reap all the profit from an extra cow, and the cost, divided among all the users, appears minimal. Thus, everyone has a strong incentive to run more stock until the land collapses, and everyone starves. Technology tempts us into the commons tragedy on a far grander scale, and the recent outcry over acid rain, water and air pollution, and toxic waste shows that we haven't developed a sense of collective responsibility yet.

I do not know a more serious or complete example of the pitfalls of quick fix, quick profit technological solutions leading to disaster than the current American agricultural crisis. A cash estimate of the annual cost to the nation in family tragedy, withered towns and businesses, soil damage and loss, advancing desertification, chemically tainted food, deterioration of water quality and quantity, and loss of wildlife goes beyond calculation. And worse will come before the public and its scholars, politicians, and bureaucrats confront the causes. Still committed to our present course, we export our so-called solutions to developing countries through the World Bank, foreign aid programs, consultants, and education as do other developed nations.

The testing guidelines in the HRM model help expose nonsolutions among technological remedies. Many of the same guidelines also apply to other tools such as fire and living organisms because they, too, often present the same questions of immediate gain versus long-term or collective loss. Nevertheless, that problem and the related tendency of short-term fixes to become addictive haunt technology most of all.

Much technology stems from our desire to dominate Nature, a desire that goes back a long way and which has generated its own philosophical justifications and patterns of thought. In resource management, agriculture, health care, and many other fields, all but a few professionals define their work entirely in terms of their technological tools. Their education and traditions do not even consider the broader principles that govern the ecosystem. Such people naturally devote their best energy to quick, unnatural answers, and often achieve immediate, dramatic, popular, and profitable results. To doubters, they can answer, on the way to the bank, "I won't be around to hear the music stop," "Science will find a way when the time comes," or "Let them handle it" (meaning our children).

Consider the following examples of how we exercise our misplaced technological faith on the four ecosystem foundation blocks.

- We often want to change the successional level of a piece of land. On unproductive rangeland, machines or herbicides will clear the brush and scrub, and we can drill in seed. Where a mixed forest makes logging inconvenient, we can rip out the native trees and plant uniform stands of faster-growing species that permit mass processing. When our chosen plants falter we can kill their enemies and fertilize their soil. We even predict total control in the form of plants genetically engineered to thrive in an artificially fertilized environment chemically rendered lethal to *everything* else. All these actions conflict with how the successional process functions. Successful as they appear, in the end they fail, often generating new, more severe problems.

- When water cycles begin to lose efficiency we dispatch large yellow machines to scour out contour and drainage ditches, deep rippers to reverse the compaction caused by heavy wheels, and irrigation pumps to put water back where it came from. Again, we show little understanding of how water cycles function and our immediate successes turn to long-term failure.

- We need more mineral cycling. Well, the local agrichemical dealer can supply anything our land lacks and change the soil pH to suit any crop, and on the strength of some diesel fuel, the old John Deere can plow it in. In implementing these measures we have so damaged soils (loss of crumb structure and soil organisms) that the natural cycling of minerals has been greatly impaired. Thus the treatments need repeating in ever stronger doses.

• We want more energy flowing into cash crops, so we look to jungles, marshes, and forests, believing that we can cut, bulldoze, drain, irrigate, spray, or dope them into any form we imagine suits that end. As the face of the earth changes, so too do its atmospheric gases, thus in implementing these measures we risk damaging all life.

Such thinking overlooks two important attributes of Nature. The ecosystem is not a machine but a living thing that energetically moves and reproduces itself according to its own principles, and it sometimes fights back. Second, the life that we artificially suppress may have contributed to our own survival. To ignore these facts triggers the same mechanisms of dependency familiar from cases of drug and alcohol abuse.

The parallel is striking. The clinical stages of alcohol or heroin addiction—becoming hooked, denial, degradation, skid row, death—occur routinely now in agriculture. Farmers get pulled in by sales pitches on the wonders of fertilizers and pesticides. The pushers themselves get hooked on research grants and government policies, and everybody feels great.

However, rapidly-breeding microorganisms and insects adapt far faster to new conditions than do humans or many of the predators that once provided natural control. Once the array of chemicals we use shows signs of failure, we do not review our reasoning. We simply increase the strength and quantity of our attack and/or attempt to isolate new compounds.

We now have some forty-five thousand chemical pesticides on the market, most of them inadequately tested for human safety, and virtually none for their impact on the ecosystem as a whole.[2] Crop damage continues to increase, even as evidence mounts that we are now poisoning ourselves and other slow-breeding creatures while strengthening the pests we set out to kill. Statistics on condemned water sources and sales of bottled water alone confirm this.

We now have reached the denial stage. Government and industry point fingers every which way but at the real problem. Some policy makers cynically seek a resolution in letting enough farmers go broke to silence the outcry. Sympathetic people and organizations offer stress counseling for potential suicides and ease relocation from countryside to city.

No one wants to talk about a debilitating dependency because we can no longer conceive of life without it. Perpetual monocultures, inadequate rotations of monocultures, chemical treatments, and heavy machinery have become standard practice, but have so simplified soil communities and structure that, like a junkie's worn-out body, our land demands even harsher stimulation to produce the same high.

The habit quickly becomes expensive: 53.3 kg of corn bought 100 kg of manufactured nitrogen in 1973, but it took 527 kg of corn to buy it in 1983, and many cornfields now demand a bigger injection than before.[3] Not surprisingly, many corn growers become desperate raising money for that fix, but their cash flow can't stand a cold turkey withdrawal either. The dying soil won't grow enough to pay last year's debt.

The basic fallacy, straight from the mouth of the local crack dealer, goes, "One little puff won't hurt you." Right now Zimbabwe justifies the use of DDT (banned in the United States) against the tsetse fly over a wide area with the argument that "only low dosages are being applied in specific sites." Such pronouncements have calmed public doubt, yet in the same areas excessive levels of DDT have already turned up in human milk.

Entomologists contend that the slow-breeding tsetse will not likely develop DDT tolerance. However, malaria mosquitoes and myriad agricultural pests present a far greater threat to Africa then the tsetse, and low dosage spraying is a doctor's prescription for enhancing their resistance. We cannot apply any pesticide to just one target organism; thousands are affected.

Having been a farmer and householder myself I understand the frustrations, pressures, and urge for quick fixes. "They are eating my crops! What else can I do?" "Last night I went to the kitchen and you should have seen all the cockroaches when I turned on the light!" "If my house is on fire, you surely don't expect me just to watch it burn!" No, of course not, but mind you don't throw kerosene on it instead of water. The flames will gutter only an instant before they explode.

That happens sometimes. Recently over a million Ethiopians died because misguided technology had damaged the four ecosystem foundation blocks and crippled the capacity of their country to support its population through a dry period. *Homo sapiens*, thanks to a flair for technology, is the only creature that occasionally starves itself before its population reaches the potential carrying capacity of its territory.

On the other hand, we can never hope to feed future generations without technology, and we certainly can apply it in ways that don't become pathological. Even the most ardent campaigners against drug abuse seldom forgo a bit of Novocaine when their dentist unlimbers his drill. Research into biological pest control, machinery for handling intersown crops, cultivation techniques that don't excessively compact soil, and even better mousetraps in place of stronger poisons represent a healthier direction for development.

A questioning attitude may also lead to surprisingly simple ways to supplant destructive practices. My family once had to draw water from an irrigation canal infested with parasites that cause bilharzia, a major scourge of Africa. The market offered various chemical treatments, but for economic and health reasons we sought remedy in the fact that the parasite had to find a human host within twenty-four hours after leaving a certain snail that carried it. By keeping our water in a holding tank for forty-eight hours before letting it into our main cistern, we imbibed only parasites that had suffered a natural death, and no chemicals.

Such efforts add up. Householders, builders, and appliance manufacturers can dent the stocking rate of kitchen vermin significantly by sealing cracks behind refrigerators and stoves to deny them a sanctuary. Physical traps for cockroaches (and mice) cut populations without cumulative damage. The state of California alone spends millions annually poisoning Californians unlucky enough to share their environment with roaches. Since the bugs have survived from the age of the trilobites, smart money says this will give them an even greater long-term edge over humans than they enjoyed before.

The HRM model offers us a way to assess technology and foresee where it leads to crisis. It is hoped that it will contribute to a new political attitude toward technology that embraces everyone from the householder who poisons roaches to multinational cartels that dam rivers and chainsaw jungles. Yet despite the best efforts of individuals, that will not happen until nations develop a consensus on landscape and production goals broad enough to parallel the extraordinary interdependence of our ecosystem.

At present we have no traditional land ethic or collective sense of conscience and responsibility, either to our fellow humans or other life. Private virtue will not suffice. I would like to know for certain, for example, that the pages of this book do not reflect profiteering on bad forestry, destruction of land, air and water pollution, and exploitation of people. They could as easily represent solar wealth and a stable community in an ever vital landscape where the hunting is good now and will be better. Technology can achieve that, but only a public will can assure it.

On the other hand, all great journeys start by putting one foot forward. The guidelines in the chapters that follow will help direct us step by step toward our goals.

PART VI

The Guidelines

23
Introduction

U p to now this book has concentrated on the broad theme of holistic management and the structure of the thought model used to bring it about: the essential goal setting, the four fundamental ecosystem processes, or foundation blocks, on which all human goals ultimately rest, the six headings under which all the tools available to mankind fall, and the agencies of their application (money and labor and human creativity). Now comes the practical side, the guidelines for determining which tool to apply when and how, to ensure that goals are achieved in a holistically-sound manner.

On first exposure, the guidelines appear a bit confusing. Some titles seem absurdly abstract and others narrowly concrete. That comes, however, from the nature of their origin and the manner of their use. Unlike the broad principles discussed earlier, they were not born out of systematic theoretical analysis, but from the day-to-day demands of connecting neat theories to the messy realities of practical life.

Holism as a fine idea has languished a long time because it proved difficult to translate into dollars, acres, work schedules, and daily management. All of the guidelines in the HRM model have crystallized out of our struggle to do that. Thus they represent the cutting edge of holistic management, the area of most creativity and change. Research and experience continually add new guidelines and refine old ones.

The main thrust of our work to date has been in the fields of game and livestock ranching, farming, and wildlife management, with an eye to stabilizing the watersheds that cover the bulk of the earth's land surface. As we expand into all fields of resource management new guidelines will surely develop.

We can already foresee a need for submodels in the place of some of today's guidelines to handle today's highly complex economic systems. Most of the sophisticated economic modeling now evolving does not proceed from a goal-oriented, holistic viewpoint and does not seriously consider basic ecosystem processes, the foundation of sustainable economies. We must try to fill that void, and we hope that the same constant criticism and learning from mistakes that have brought us this far will keep our efforts in that direction sound.

Meanwhile the present model is simple enough for most people to understand and use, and we at the Center for Holistic Resource Management believe strongly that we must keep it simple. Reversing desertification and the attendant decline of our agriculture, watersheds, forests, and wildlife will demand the participation of millions of people who do not possess or need college degrees.

The present guidelines are grouped in the model by category. The first seven are the "testing guidelines." Through these we determine whether or not a tool should be used. The remaining ten are the "management guide-lines," which assist in using the tools in the right way. Some people think of the two categories as the "whether to" and the "how to" guidelines.

Testing Guidelines

Ideally, every tool should be passed through each testing guideline before it is used. Only then can a tool be seen as appropriate or inappropriate in relation to the goal at any time. If a tool fails to pass any test it isn't ruled out automatically, as there may be no alternative at that moment. However, if you do apply that tool you know you will ultimately fail to reach your goal unless you find a better way. The application of the HRM model in a "research orientation" mode (Chapter 50) can help in the search.

Although this testing process is thorough, and better than anything we've had before, it is far from foolproof. To cater for human fallibility, the whims of nature, and the complexity of holism, we constantly monitor and control our application of the tools through the management guidelines.

Management Guidelines

Some of these guidelines apply to only one tool. Burning, for example, applies only to the tool of fire; organization and personal growth apply only to human creativity. Others apply to more than one tool or to all of the tools.

Some may govern daily management situations, while others may come into play once in a lifetime or only in emergencies. Some apply in conjunction with one or more of the other management guidelines. Time, stock density, and herd effect, for instance, all relate to the use of animal impact and grazing and interrelate with one another.

Most of the principles reflected in the guidelines are plain old-fashioned common sense. Others stem from new understanding about the time dimension in resource management, the different decay processes and functioning of succession in brittle and nonbrittle environments, and the roles that herding animals and their predators play in brittle environments. These we consider most critical to our hopes of halting and reversing desertification.

In practice we use the testing guidelines first, for if a tool does not pass these tests we usually need go no further with that tool but have to consider and test another. In the following chapters, however, we will go through some of the management guidelines first, as knowledge gleaned from them enlightens the testing process. I will follow the easiest learning order beginning with time, which, because of its scope, necessitates four chapters. After that I'll cover the other management guidelines most involved in the new discoveries, the testing guidelines, and then finally the remaining management guidelines.

24

Time in Cropping, Grazing, Browsing, and Trampling

The remorseless march of seasons by and large makes farmers servants of time. They must race to plant, harvest, and replant before life's ever ticking clock sends frost, or monsoon, or dries out the mother ditch. By contrast, ranchers can control time and use it to their advantage. They choose when calves will drop or when they will move to new ground or when to build a fence.

This guideline of the HRM model, as covered in this and the next three chapters, should enable you to analyze how time functions in a number of rather different circumstances. The companion volume contains specific details on how to put these points into practice. In reading this and the following three chapters try to absorb the underlying principles rather than the detail that might apply specifically to your own situation.

Characteristically, holistic management implies no systematic dogma for managing time and suggests no limit to the situations where time demands creative consideration. Consider the case of a rancher I knew in Africa who decided to construct fencing and handling facilities far from major supply points. To save time he paid dearly for large trucks to ferry supplies. His habit of mind led him to see only that time is money in the narrowest sense.

He failed to notice the true value of time in an economy that imported both trucks and fuel against an adverse trade balance. He had no frost or monsoon to beat, and an unlimited supply of labor and oxen surrounded him. By forward planning he could have mobilized the local people working with him months in advance and moved his material far more cheaply, lifted by the thought that while trucks depreciate and drink foreign exchange, oxen gain value, put local people to work, and run on home grown energy.

I have heard American ranchers say, "Oh but that doesn't apply here in the land of the minimum wage. We'd have to go with the big truck." But they too did not assess carefully the value of time in their own personal economy. They would send empty pickups to a building site day after day for mundane tasks, then fork over scarce cash for a diesel rig to carry supplies in from headquarters at the last minute.

Even in crop farming, original thinking can lead to more control over time and thus production and costs. Starting crops early and double-cropping a field in one season are well-known ways to use time efficiently. Irrigation helps in this by assuring proper moisture at the very threshold of the growing season, but are you powerless without it? Native American farmers in the Southwest often pregerminate corn seed before planting, plant several seeds in a single hole, and hand carry enough water to maintain growth until more reliable rains come in July. Farmers in Zimbabwe developed a similar technique called water planting that was half mechanized and half labor, but could be mechanized entirely or done by labor only. It spared many a farm the cost of replanting an early seeding that failed, and it made good use of potential growing time denied by a limitation of water early in the season.

Early starting of seedlings in greenhouses or shielding them in the field from frost represent similar efforts to manipulate growing time rather than be controlled by it, but the subtleties of timing in multicrop situations offer many unexplored possibilities. The Japanese scientist Fukuoka, mentioned in earlier chapters, has made timing a major part of his farming operation to increase yields and decrease predation. His writings give an indication of how much more scientific Western agriculture might become through increased research on time management of crops, especially mixed crops.

This crucial matter of time management in mixed crops is little understood and studied at present but in future editions of this book it will be necessary to expand greatly in this area.

In this chapter we mainly discuss progress so far in understanding the ramifications of timing in managing plants that are grazed and browsed. In the next three we'll discuss how time can be manipulated to increase the energy that flows through the ecosystem; how time can be manipulated to improve the nutritive value of plants in order to improve the condition of the animals that feed on them; and last, the importance of the time dimension in managing the wild herding ungulates that roam our national parks and preserves.

Time and Overgrazing/Overbrowsing

Most goals that involve grazing animals for any reason require maximum functioning of all four ecosystem processes. This means that overgrazing and overbrowsing will need to be minimized. Earlier chapters have reiterated the finding of André Voisin that overgrazing is linked to the time plants are exposed to animals rather than to the number of animals. But how do we time the exposure and reexposure of plants to animals?

Should we monitor key indicator plants, set arbitrary grazing or recovery periods, or follow some aspect of animal performance? Should timing reflect the growth rates of plants, and if so which of the millions in the community? Do we choose individuals of a particular species or a random selection? What about the time animals are exposed to poisonous plants? What about wildlife and other land uses? Should animals be allowed to select, or should they be forced to eat everything in a short time?

Voisin's outstanding work in pastures in nonbrittle environments answered only a few of these questions for me when, back in the 1960s, I first saw that timing mattered on the rangelands of Africa and began to look for ways to manipulate it successfully.

Healthy rangeland communities include a mind-boggling diversity of plant species from the simplest algae-like forms to a variety of trees. Animal life ranges from billions of microorganisms to a vast complexity of birds and animals, small and large. The greater mass of both flora and fauna is hidden amongst the plants or underground, and even if one could see it all, activity differs greatly from day to night. The more one dwells on the idea of holism, the more one sees a scintillating interdependence that constitutes a single living whole. It is a whole, without parts in the mechanical sense, and a change in any component of the community changes the whole to some degree.

Range science, limiting its view to the direct needs of relatively few species, habitually considers some species more important than others. However, if we decide that a particular grass population can be sacrificed to overgrazing we unleash consequences beyond human ability to even understand, let alone manage. Other species depend on species that depend on species that depend on those we have sacrificed, and on and on. As but one simple example, there are some nine hundred species of figs and each apparently has a particular species of wasp that fertilizes it and the wasp in turn depends on that fig for its life cycle.[1] A great many other insects, birds, reptiles, etc. will be dependent upon that species of fig and thus dependent on its specific wasp, which could be poisoned in an agricultural spraying program.

We cannot play God and in good conscience eliminate anything. Since most of our goals do involve maintaining the complex integrity of the whole, we hope to minimize overgrazing on every plant we possibly can. To the best of our ability we base the time of exposure on the severely grazed plants, wherever they are and whatever species they are. Even when dealing with a monoculture of one species, we would, in principle, base the timing on the first plant bitten severely.

The Reverend Martin Niemöller, imprisoned at the Dachau concentration camp by the Nazis for resistance, captured the idea precisely and gave the best description of how overgrazing occurs when he wrote, "In Germany, the Nazis first came for the Communists, and I didn't speak up because I wasn't a Communist. Then they came for the Jews, and I didn't speak up because I wasn't a Jew. Then they came for the trade unionists, and I didn't speak up because I wasn't a trade unionist. Then they came for the Catholics, and I didn't speak up because I was a Protestant. Then they came for me, and by that time no one was left to speak up for me."

I will return to this famous saying many times. Again, in this context it means we ideally should time grazing according to the needs of the first severely grazed plant, or as Rev. Niemöller would say, we should protest when the first person of any persuasion is taken.

Time Manipulation Based upon the Perennial Grass Component

Reality of course puts some severe difficulties in the way of the ideal. Grazing animals select different plants and different parts of plants in different seasons, and different plants recover at different rates. When I first began wrestling with this problem, I had to make a practical compromise, pursue it, monitor the results, and modify if necessary. I chose to watch the perennial grass plants as the group most vital to the stability of the whole.

We did not then recognize the distinction between brittle and nonbrittle environments, but experience has borne out the hypothesis that particularly in low rainfall brittle environments grass stability in fact contributes to the health of the whole more than any other factor. Perennial grass often provides the main source of soil cover required for the stability of everything else. As over half the world's land surface leans to the brittle end of the scale, and little of that enjoys enough rainfall to support a full tree cover, the health of perennial grass acquires enormous significance.

In choosing to consider perennial grass first, we risk violating the guideline in two important ways. A tree or shrub species might suffer severe defoliation before animals start on the grass. Also, time allowed for recovery of a severely bitten grass plant might not suffice for a severely browsed shrub or tree. This potential problem had to be worked out, and I will return to it later in a way that still justifies the practical guideline: *to reach the richest level of succession in brittle environments, time grazings according to the needs of perennial grasses.*

In nonbrittle environments where the landscape and production goals require the maintenance of grassland, the same guideline applies of minimizing overgrazing through regulating the time of exposure of the grass plants to the animals. Differences of some importance here are that long-rested grass plants can maintain themselves, and where biological decay is rapid grasslands can survive where some soil or climatic factor limits successional movement to woody communities and their associated animal life. Even with considerable overgrazing of plants, such environments remain remarkably stable as little or no soil exposure occurs. As we often are unable to distinguish individual grass plants in a nonbrittle environment pasture, timing is based on grass volume. But whenever we monitor volume, rather than severely grazed individuals, we can expect a reduction in species composition, which may be acceptable in pastures.

Time and Trampling

From over thirty years of observation and practice during the development of the HRM model, I concluded that the consequence of trampling is also a function of the time soil and plants are exposed to animals rather than to the absolute number of animals.

Prolonged trampling has largely adverse effects—pulverization of the soil surface, excessive underground compaction and injury to plants. Chapter 20 on animal impact gave the example of 365 successive donkey-days of traffic producing a beaten out track between a house and a water hole.

On the other hand, the same traffic produced by 365 donkeys on a single day, followed by 364 days of recovery time, would produce a far different result. The plants and the whole soil community could recover from the damaging component of the trampling and benefit from the intense deposition of dung and urine. Time, rather than numbers, governs the ultimate impact.

In the donkey analogy every animal would tramp on exactly the same piece of ground, thus maximizing the damage on the day it occurred. In reality that seldom happens—even on trails, as animals follow multiple routes—but the principle remains the same. Maximum impact over minimum time followed by a sufficient recovery period makes trampling an extremely effective tool for maintaining brittle rangelands and watersheds as well as cropland soils. To maintain healthy, productive, diverse perennial grassland in brittle environments, some factor is essential that will remove old oxidizing plant parts periodically and scatter them on the ground, break soil surface capping (the crust that develops on exposed soils) and algal communities between plants, and provide some compaction to the soil to enable grass seedlings to establish.

For millions of years only herding animals and their predators could do this as weather, hail, fire, birds, insects, and small mammals cannot. Some factors, like hail, can perform all the necessary functions but not with the frequency required over millions of acres. Fire, birds, insects, or small mammals can remove the old material, but do not break the surface adequately or compact soils enough over millions of acres.

Whenever you consider using animal impact as a tool, the following general guidelines apply:

Where production and landscape goals require high successional complexity, good mineral and water cycles, and high energy flows

- little if any animal impact will be needed in nonbrittle environments.
- in brittle environments use the highest possible impact for the shortest possible time as a rough rule of thumb.

Where the landscape goal calls for low successional diversity, poor mineral and water cycle, and low energy flow in a brittle environment, as it might for aesthetic reasons or the preservation of some unique plant or animal, either use no animal impact, or prolonged light impact and monitor the attendant overgrazing. If overgrazing must also be limited, then apply low impact and control the time the plants are exposed to the animals.

Grazing and Recovery Periods Are Linked to One Another

Where grazing times are regulated by moving animals from one division of land to another until a whole area is covered, longer recovery periods require longer grazing periods. The dynamics of this relationship are simple but easy to overlook.

Assume that the top drawing in figure 24-1 represents a piece of land divided into six paddocks to be grazed by livestock, and that animals graze in each one for four days. From the time they leave a paddock until they return to it will then take twenty days—four days in each of five paddocks (six paddocks minus the one they are in). Each paddock will get four days of grazing and twenty days to recover.

If on leaving paddock 1 you decided it would require forty days for a severely grazed plant to recover, you would have to add twenty more days somewhere in the other five paddocks as the middle drawing shows.

Therein lies the rub. Any change in recovery time in one paddock will change the grazing times in many paddocks that follow. In the bottom drawing the operator planned a forty-day recovery period for each paddock and thus eight-day grazings. But after five days of grazing, paddock 3 looked a bit sparse, so he moved on. He thereby cut the recovery time in all paddocks back to thirty-seven days. Each paddock that was grazed for fewer days than planned would reduce recovery times accordingly in all paddocks. Conversely, each day that stock are held longer in a paddock adds a day of recovery to all remaining paddocks.

1	2	3
4 Days	4 Days	4 Days
4	5	6
4 Days	4 Days	4 Days

Paddock 1, recovery period 20 days

1	2	3
4 Days	10 Days	6 Days
4	5	6
8 Days	7 Days	9 Days

Paddock 1, recovery period 40 days

1	2	3
4 Days	8 Days	5 Days
4	5	6
8 Days	8 Days	8 Days

Paddock 1, recovery period 37 days

Figure 24-1.   Relationship of grazing periods to recovery periods.

Again—*as long as a herd of livestock remains on the land and moves through a series of subdivisions, the grazing periods will be inextricably linked to the recovery periods.*

An important corollary to this axiom holds that maintaining adequate recovery periods requires forward planning and a certain discipline, because they must be built up or reduced through shortening or lengthening grazing periods in several or all paddocks. Conversely, grazing periods can be changed on impulse by simply opening a gate, **but** *such changes have a cumulative effect on recovery periods.*

An error in either direction can cause overgrazing, which happens when animals bite off a regrowing plant before it has restored its sacrificed roots. This will occur if animals stay in one area long enough to catch a regrowing plant, *or* if they come back to that place before the severely grazed plant has recovered. (If severely grazed during dormancy, plants are unlikely to be overgrazed as they have translocated energy to stem bases and roots and are not trying to grow.)

In light of the above argument we go by this rule: *Plan grazing periods on the basis of desired recovery periods rather than vice versa.*

Computing Grazing Periods from a Preselected Recovery Period

Land managed as a unit for grazing we call a grazing cell, and the timing of herd moves within the cell naturally depends on the number of subdivisions per herd. We call fenced divisions paddocks, and unfenced ones where herders concentrate animals according to their own marks grazing areas. Because both terms have precisely the same implications for the present discussion, I'll refer only to paddocks.

Later I will describe how the duration of recovery periods is decided, but for the moment assume we have selected a recovery period that we believe will minimize overgrazing during the growing season. In reality the situation will be more complex as growth rates vary and various recovery periods will be necessary (as will be covered) but the simple case will illustrate the principle first.

Domestic stock, being severe grazers, will predictably defoliate some plants severely soon after entering a paddock, regardless of how few animals there are. Illustration 24-1 shows what one horse did in one hour to one plant among thousands of others. Remembering Niemöller's mistake, "They came for the Communists, but I wasn't a Communist . . ." we must try to minimize the chance that that first severely grazed plant will get overgrazed.

Perennial grass plants in the Rio Grande Valley of New Mexico where this photograph was taken might need a recovery period of sixty days in

Illustration 24-1. The arrow marks a severely grazed plant after one horse had grazed for one hour. New Mexico.

slow growth. If, in our simple case, the grazing cell contains nine equal paddocks, then a sixty-day recovery period will require a 7.5-day grazing period in each paddock. The reasoning goes thus: After leaving any one of the nine paddocks, the horse will have to pass through the eight others before coming back. A sixty-day recovery period, divided by eight paddocks, yields 7.5 days of grazing in each paddock. The algebraic formula, which Voisin gave us, is:

Grazing Period = Recovery Period ÷ (Number of Paddocks − 1)

In contrast to this method, seat-of-the-pants management would tend to eyeball each paddock after stock had been in it awhile and then decide when they should move. It might work, but it more likely wouldn't because it leaves to chance the really crucial time, the recovery period.

As the number of paddocks increases, naturally the length of the grazing period decreases because the same recovery period gets divided by a larger number. This is because a severely grazed plant takes a certain time to recover no matter how many paddocks there are. A few academics have argued that a grazing cell should not contain more than eight paddocks. This bizarre contention perhaps stems from publicity twenty years ago about cells that did chance to have eight paddocks, or to the fact that it happens to be the easiest configuration to draw on a blackboard during lectures. Both scientific theory and practical evidence show that tremendous advantages flow from having many paddocks in a cell, as later discussion will demonstrate. More paddocks in no way frustrate the freedom to plan or provide a given recovery period for the grass plant that an animal bit off on the first day.

The Role of Time in Measuring Forage Consumption

Given unfettered access to good grazing, animals will eat a predictable amount in a day, depending on their size, weight, reproductive status, etc. In feedlots and confined situations we easily compute the amount of feed needed to carry a given number of animals for a given number of days. This obvious relationship is roughly paralleled in the common American practice of basing grazing fees on Animal Unit Months (AUMs).

The AUM, however, is too crude a figure to use in detailed and well-planned grazing. Instead of the Animal Month, we use the Animal Day. The animal day can be based on any animal you choose—cow, sheep, donkey,

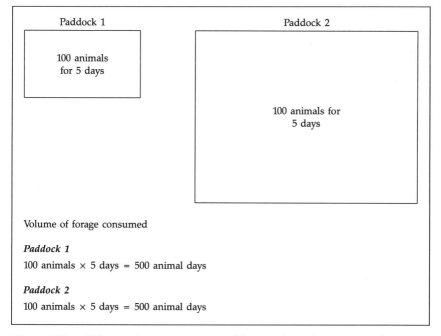

Paddock 1

100 animals
for 5 days

Paddock 2

100 animals for
5 days

Volume of forage consumed

Paddock 1
100 animals × 5 days = 500 animal days

Paddock 2
100 animals × 5 days = 500 animal days

Figure 24-2. Volume of grazing governed by number of animals and time on the land.

etc. (In the companion volume we deal with more accurate measurements, called Standard Animal Units, where we attempt to allow for the weight and growth rate required, or breeding state of the animals). You can think of an Animal Day as the forage an animal harvests in a day. Ignoring the volume of forage present, the amount the animals take from a given paddock depends on two factors:

1. The number of animals.
2. The number of days of grazing.

As figure 24-2 shows, given adequate and similar forage an equal number of animals will harvest the same amount in the same time regardless of paddock size—five hundred animal days in this case.

Naturally such equal treatment depletes the smaller paddock more than the larger one, and one can even the score by grazing the bigger one longer or stocking it more heavily. To see how even or uneven they are we need only divide the animal days by the area of each paddock as in figure 24-3.

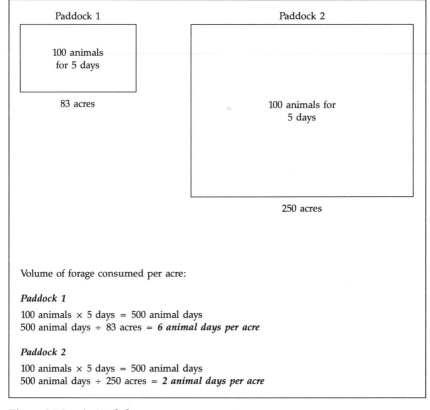

Figure 24-3. Animal days per acre concept.

That leads to a need for a way to measure the harvest from a unit of land over time. The Animal Days per Acre (ADA), which is the animal days harvested divided by the number of acres in the paddock, shows the amount of forage that each acre of land will have to render on average.

Figure 24-3 reckons the ADA values for the example given in figure 24-2. Though animals harvested an equal amount of forage from both paddocks, each average acre of the smaller one supplied six Animal Days, while each average acre in the large paddock supplied only two.

The grazing aspects of holistic management require a thorough understanding of ADA and how to use them. Since André Voisin first developed the concept in his pasture work we have found ways to apply it in many other contexts: to plan drought reserves, stocking rates, reduce competition with wildlife, and so on. Obviously it enables us to relate past grazing pressure to present condition of the forage. Its most powerful application, however, comes in planning future operations in complex situations.

In the biological planning that will be explained in Chapter 40, computing the ADA will allow us to foresee more accurately the grazing needs at all times of the year and decide which paddocks will supply it. We can then know in advance if the land can provide the forage needed. We can plan for enough margin to feed wildlife and buffer the risk of drought. We can

Cell size 2000 ac, herd size 300 head, recovery period in use 60 days					
Number of paddocks	Average paddock size	Recovery period	Average grazing period	$\dfrac{\text{Animals} \times \text{days}}{\text{area}}$	Animal days per acre
6	333.3	60	12	$\dfrac{300 \times 12}{333.3}$	10.8
11	181.8	60	6	$\dfrac{300 \times 6}{181.8}$	9.9
31	64.5	60	2	$\dfrac{300 \times 2}{64.5}$	9.3
61	32.8	60	1	$\dfrac{300 \times 1}{32.8}$	9.1
		Grazing days drastic decrease		Forage consumption no real change	

Figure 24-4.   Effect of increasing number of paddocks and decreasing paddock size on grazing pressure in a cell.

plan, and later evaluate, the performance of every paddock and make allowances for conflicting uses, poison plant seasons, winter cover, and many other considerations related to production and landscape goals.

Increasing the number of paddocks does not change the grazing pressure on a grazing cell at all. In general, *only a change in the number of animals or in the time they spend in a cell will change the amount of forage they will harvest.* Figure 24-4 shows the relationship between numbers of paddocks and grazing periods in a two-thousand-acre cell managed for a sixty-day recovery period.

The final column in figure 24-4 shows the ADA taken from each paddock during one cycle. They are not exactly the same, because with six paddocks a cycle takes seventy-two days, and with sixty-one paddocks sixty-one days. In an equal overall time, the stock will consume precisely the same amounts from the cell as a whole. This means that, contrary to an often-published opinion, more paddocks do not force a greater consumption or put more pressure on animals to eat plants they would not normally select. *Animals should never be forced to graze nonselectively unless you deliberately want lower performance from them.*

Confusion on this point derives from another effect. As paddock size decreases, given a constant herd size, the *proportion* of plants grazed increases. This does not, however, mean less dietary selection as the time in the paddock is decreased and thus the same volume of forage essentially is taken. However, what we do tend to find is that as the animals select a diet balanced for levels of protein, energy, fiber, and other nutrients, they tend to feed over a higher proportion of the plants available. This has the marked tendency to keep a higher proportion of the leaves and stems on the plants fresh and young. With the commonly practiced low density grazing there is a marked tendency for the animals to feed off a lower proportion of the available plants and thus allow a higher proportion to become cluttered with old stems and leaves of low nutritive value. Also the effects of trampling, dunging, and urinating will tend to be more uniform at higher densities.

Chapter 28 on Stock Density will explain further how to manage these generally beneficial aspects of small paddocks. Nevertheless, reducing paddock size has one other effect that falls under the heading of time management. As figure 24-5 shows, in a six-paddock cell, 0.9 animals take their rations from one acre each day. Said another way, for each day the herd remains in a paddock, 0.9 Animal Days (of forage) per Acre are consumed (0.9 ADA/day). In a sixty-one-paddock cell, however, although no more forage is taken in a grazing period, 9.1 ADA are taken for each day the herd stays in a paddock (9.1 ADA/day). *One extra day in the smaller paddock therefore takes ten times as much from each acre as an extra day in the bigger paddock.* A twenty-four-hour mistake could mean extreme depletion of forage in a given paddock, loss of selectivity, and a drop in animal performance, so management

Cell size 2000 ac, herd size 300 head, recovery period in use 60 days

Number of paddocks	Average paddock size	Recovery period	Average grazing period	Animal days per acre	$\dfrac{\text{Animals}}{\text{acres}}$	Animals per acre (stock density)
6	333.3	60	12	10.8	$\dfrac{300}{333.3}$	0.90
11	181.8	60	6	9.9	$\dfrac{300}{181.8}$	1.6
31	64.5	60	2	9.3	$\dfrac{300}{64.5}$	4.6
61	32.8	60	1	9.1	$\dfrac{300}{32.8}$	9.1

Grazing day decrease ⬆

Stock density rises dramatically ⬆

Figure 24-5. Effect of increasing number of paddocks and decreasing paddock size on number of animals per acre (stock density).

becomes more critical as paddock sizes drop. Fortunately it is easy to remember that stock density (animals per acre) always equals the amount of additional ADA that are taken with each day the animals are left in a paddock.

Some, on considering that possibility, have decided that more paddocks mean more *risk*. As the word risk implies chance beyond management control, I would rather say that more paddocks simply increase the *penalty* for poor management (e.g., leaving crucial stock moves to untrained cowboys).

Decreasing Risk with Increasing Paddocks and Control of Time

As the discussion so far has explained, as paddock numbers increase, time in each paddock decreases, stock density increases (causing better distribution of dung, urine, and trampling), and more plants are grazed.

All of these things take place while total forage consumption remains the same as at low paddock numbers. That, remember, depends only on the number of animals and the time they spend in the whole cell. Overall, the fact that animals—though consuming no more—move more frequently onto fresh, unfouled ground means that they receive a better plane of nutrition and reduced danger of parasite infection and build-up. In addition, the reduced overgrazing leads to more production from the whole complex of plants, soil, microorganisms, and all that contributes to energy flow. The better distribution of animal impact for shorter time periods also benefits water and mineral cycles, as earlier chapters discussed.

As more paddocks bring about all those positive developments, risk from all other natural (as opposed to market) threats to ranching also decreases. Damage from drought, flood, insect outbreaks, disease, parasitism, poor nutrition, and costly feed supplementation has an inverse relationship to the number of paddocks. This is because as paddock numbers rise, so generally does stock density and animal impact, while time on the land decreases. A better water cycle reduces both the severity and frequency of doughts. Higher energy flow and better mineral cycles lead to better nutrition and less parasitism, disease, and need for supplementation. The combination of more uniform animal impact and minimum overgrazing promotes a level of succession that discourages radical outbreaks of weeds or pests.

Even the risk of lightning does not increase with more animals concentrated in smaller paddocks. I once feared the contrary, because in the best of times in Zimbabwe lightning kills some one hundred people and many animals every year. However, we soon realized that regardless of density in a paddock, cattle still tended to gather in small bunches under trees. They did not crowd into a large herd. One strike into a paddock hit no more animals than it would otherwise, and 90 percent of the land over which a storm passed had no animals on it.

The Dangers of Inflexible Schedules (Rotational Grazing)

At the crudest level, recovery periods and the grazing periods derived from them must reflect the size and quality of paddocks, so that all paddocks, regardless of size, will have to yield appropriate Animal Days of forage per Acre (ADA). A couple of years ago I inspected a research station that claimed to be testing my ideas on their land and cattle. Their breeding cow herd was being rotated through several paddocks in a short duration grazing system. I merely asked the man in charge which was his best and which his worst paddock and then did some simple ADA calculations. On each rotation the herd consumed five times more ADA from the worst paddock than from the best!

One would not have to await publication of the research to know that cattle that hit several days of short rations two or three times during breeding do not cycle reliably, conceive as well, or produce calves as heavy as a control group will.

A subtler kind of damage also arises from inflexible rotations. As discussed before, overgrazing occurs when perennial plants are bitten while growing on energy from sacrificed roots, and it can happen in two ways. The first is when animals remain in an area long enough to rebite a regrowing plant. *The second occurs when animals move off but return before severely bitten plants recover.*

Up to this point, for the sake of simplicity, I have mentioned only the need to select a suitable recovery period. In fact, unless you have a great many paddocks, no single recovery period will suit all conditions *because the daily growth rate of plants, especially in brittle environments, keeps changing during the growing season.* This is one of the several serious pitfalls of the rotational grazing systems practiced by many people.

Figure 24-6 lays out this problem graphically. The first row shows what happens in an eight-paddock cell scheduled for a thirty-day recovery period, which in this example we assume is sufficient time for recovery when good growth conditions prevail. Looking to the right under the Fast Daily Growth Rate heading, both grazing and recovery periods appear satisfactory. Plants will probably not grow fast enough to suffer a second defoliation during the four-day grazing period, and will regain lost ground by the time stock return.

All will go well *as long as the growth rate remains fast.* However, the outlook darkens drastically if soil dries out a bit or temperature changes enough to slow down daily growth.

The Slow Daily Growth Rate column shows what happens then. The four-day grazing period remains benign, because slow growth further reduces the chance that once-grazed plants will regrow in time to offer a second bite. On the other hand, under the changed conditions, severely grazed plants may not recover within thirty days and *stand in real danger of overgrazing.*

Given that such a fast move will lead to overgrazing when growth slows down, why not simply lock into a long rest period as outlined in row two of the chart? There it appears that a cell divided into eight equal paddocks will require, on average, thirteen-day grazing periods to yield ninety-day recovery periods. This works well during slow growth, because plants grazed on the first day in a paddock are unlikely to recover enough in thirteen days to tempt that second bite, while three months of recovery time should restore vigor.

If rapid growth returns, however, thirteen-day grazing periods may allow extreme overgrazing, because rapidly growing plants may get bitten two or more times before stock move on. In brittle environments where 90 percent of a whole year's forage may grow in a few weeks of prime conditions, such an error could devastate the production of several paddocks.

Because inflexible adherence to either slow or fast rotation schedules inevitably leads to overgrazing at low paddock numbers, practitioners of holistic resource management talk about *planned grazing,* never rotational grazing or short duration grazing, terms which have become associated with the kind of inflexible time schedules just described. Planning of course takes

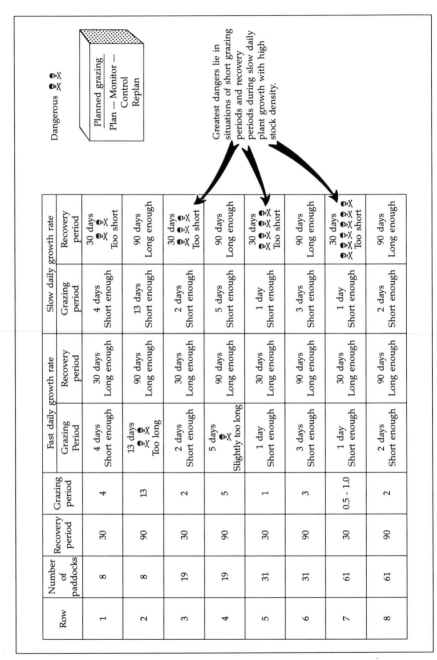

Dangerous X⊕ X⊕

Planned grazing
————————————
Plan – Monitor –
   Control
   Replan

Greatest dangers lie in situations of short grazing periods and recovery periods during slow daily plant growth with high stock density.

| | | | | Fast daily growth rate | | Slow daily growth rate | |
Row	Number of paddocks	Recovery period	Grazing period	Grazing Period	Recovery period	Grazing period	Recovery period
1	8	30	4	4 days Short enough	30 days Long enough	4 days Short enough	30 days ⊕X ⊕X Too short
2	8	90	13	13 days ⊕X ⊕X Too long	90 days Long enough	13 days Short enough	90 days Long enough
3	19	30	2	2 days Short enough	30 days Long enough	2 days Short enough	30 days ⊕X ⊕X Too short
4	19	90	5	5 days ⊕X Slightly too long	90 days Long enough	5 days Short enough	90 days Long enough
5	31	30	1	1 day Short enough	30 days Long enough	1 day Short enough	30 days ⊕X ⊕X ⊕X Too short
6	31	90	3	3 days Short enough	90 days Long enough	3 days Short enough	90 days Long enough
7	61	30	0.5 - 1.0	1 day Short enough	30 days Long enough	1 day Short enough	30 days ⊕X ⊕X ⊕X ⊕X Too short
8	61	90	2	2 days Short enough	90 days Long enough	2 days Short enough	90 days Long enough

Figure 24-6. Necessity for planned grazing to minimize overgrazing at low paddock numbers.

into account other subtleties such as paddocks of unequal size and productivity, cover, poison plants, seasonal and handling factors, differing growth rates and production of goals, and thus deserves a chapter of its own (Chapter 40).

Now, assuming equal, homogeneous paddocks, consider what happens as their number increases. In rows three through eight of the table you will see how the picture changes. Forgetting livestock performance for the moment, what happens to our efforts to minimize overgrazing? At about the level of nineteen paddocks, grazing periods have become short enough to practically eliminate the danger from slow rotation without full planning. However, the danger during fast rotation has increased. As paddocks increase to fifty or sixty this pattern continues with less risk from slower rotation and more from fast rotation.

The danger at high paddock numbers derives from high stock density. As said earlier, increasing stock density increases the proportion of plants used. In Chapter 19 we noted that a major part of the destructiveness of overgrazing stems from the inability of plants to satisfy extreme forage demands *and furnish litter to cover the soil*, the key to full functioning of all four ecosystem processes.

Going back again to Rev. Niemöller, if overgrazing occurs at low paddock numbers, his saying goes, "They came for the Communists, and I did not notice as plenty of Jews, trade unionists, and Catholics provided feed and litter cover." In addition, higher animal impact and shorter trampling time on soils often have enough favorable impact on water and mineral cycles and energy flow to strongly mitigate the adverse effects of overgrazing. Next year the livestock might "come for the Jews" as succession continues to shift toward a less stable monoculture, but it wouldn't show without careful monitoring. There are many grazing cells in America under rotational grazing systems that produce enough bulk forage to entirely satisfy ranchers and researchers, but which are likely to be developing toward monocultures in the long run.

At higher paddock numbers, however, Niemöller's saying goes, "They came for the Communists, Jews, trade unionists, Catholics, and me all at once, and left nothing to provide forage, not to mention litter." When overgrazing is allowed to happen at high paddock levels and high stock density, it strikes a great many plants and exposes soil simultaneously, and collapse is rapid and dramatic.

The dangers of inadequately planned rotational grazings are thus extreme, particularly in brittle areas where erratic growth rates throughout most seasons are a fact of life. Many Americans in the West have developed grazing systems directly from my work or from New Zealanders who adapted them from André Voisin. However, France and New Zealand epitomize nonbrittle conditions where growth rates are not as erratic and overgrazing

Illustration 24-2. Dense and vigorous grass growth after eight years of planned grazing. Igava Ranch, Zimbabwe.

has far less drastic consequences because it does not result in bare ground. Both Voisin's warnings about growth rates and my own about planned grazing to deal with brittle environments have generally been ignored.

The two most advanced grazing cells that my clients developed in Zimbabwe had, respectively, thirty and forty-one paddocks. Both were in brittle environments, the former with a twelve-inch average rainfall, the latter with thirty-five. Both ran at far higher than conventional stocking rates on planned grazings such as Chapter 40 will describe. Our work continued for more than ten years with good results and much learning. Illustration 24-2 shows the growth of grass up close to the watering point in the thirty-five-inch rainfall cell after some eight years of planned grazings.

I had to flee Zimbabwe as a political exile toward the end of the long civil war, and thus all contact with these ranchers stopped abruptly. Left on their own they first dropped the planning process. They had never liked it and we often joked about only doing it to stop my nagging! After all, there seemed no need for planning after things had gone so smoothly for so many years.

After my departure, they continued for four more years, rotating their livestock every one to two days while keeping an eye on the abundance of forage and cattle performance—but not the daily growth rate of the plants.

Unfortunately, at high stock density on brittle ranges where growth occurs sporadically, this courts disaster. The rotations were too fast at times

Illustration 24-3.   Severe overgrazing on the same ground as seen in illustration 24-2 after four years of short duration grazing rotation. Igava Ranch, Zimbabwe.

of slow growth. Each time this happened, overgrazing took place on a large scale, and damage progressed rapidly. When serious drought hit, destruction was nearly total.

Illustration 24-3 shows the same part of the same grazing cell as illustration 24-2 after four years of short duration rotation. It was a dry year, when shorter than normal grass could be expected, but inspection showed the lack of growth due to severely overgrazed plants and poor water cycle rather than drought. Illustration 24-4 is a close-up of a typical plant in the foreground of the previous scene. This plant, which even in a dry year should have grown two or three feet tall, has assumed a low, creeping form, half an inch above the ground. Such distortion did not come from a single drought, but from four years of periodic heavy overgrazing.

Illustration 24-5 is a view of the twelve-inch-rainfall grazing cell close to the watering point after about eight years of operation on the basis of planned grazings. Illustration 24-6 is a view of the same grazing cell after it had been run for four years as a short duration grazing system, similar to the first. In this case the overgrazing was so heavy that there were no animals left on the land. This picture was taken in the growing season and in a very dry year, but the overgrazed form of the remaining plants and the lack of

Illustration 24-4. Severely overgrazed plant in the foreground of illustration 24-3. Normally this plant would grow to a height of three feet or more. Igava Ranch, Zimbabwe.

all litter, together with the capped soil, indicated that overgrazing of a high proportion of the plants was a greater cause of collapse than the dry year.

The biological planning guideline that enables us to minimize overgrazing while achieving landscape and production goals is very simple as Chapter 40 will show. A tragic common fault I have found with ranchers is that it is so simple and produces such good results that after a few years of good results they forget that planning did that and drop the planning. It is exactly like your going on an exercise program to become fit. You dislike doing the exercises but do get very fit doing them. After a couple of years you are so fit that you see no further need to continue such an unpleasant task with any regularity. No matter how fit you were it is but a short time before your muscles go soft and your lungs strain on exertion.

The Fate of Woody Plants When Time Management is Based on Perennial Grasses

Earlier I promised to return to the question of possible discrimination against woody plants when grazing is timed to the needs of perennial grasses. Three real life examples illustrate how this apparent dilemma generally works out in practice.

Illustration 24-5.   Perennial grassland at the watering point in a twelve-inch-rainfall brittle environment after eight years of planned grazing. Liebig's Ranch, Zimbabwe.

The Karroo area of South Africa has seen some three hundred years of overgrazing of plants and partial rest of ranges over a vast expanse of low rainfall brittle environment. Some of the ranches where I worked had long ago declined to bare soil and scattered small desert bushes, which had replaced what used to be grassland under the game populations of old. In the nearly total absence of any alternative, these desert bushes had become the main feed for all livestock and were consequently highly prized by ranchers and range management professionals alike.

Given a landscape goal of establishing perennial grassland once more, I advised application of time management that would promote perennial grass plants. To many academics this seemed illogical, as for all practical purposes perennial grasses no longer existed. They claimed, as did many ranchers, that severely defoliated desert brush could not recover in the short times my planning allotted. Available research showed that the plants in question required anything from a year to eighteen months to recover after severe browsing. Pressure grew to make recovery periods reflect this finding.

The ranchers had between five and sixteen paddocks available. To schedule a 450-day recovery period in a nine-paddock cell means grazing periods

Illustration 24-6. View looking toward the same watering point shown in illustration 24-5 after four years of short duration grazing rotation. Liebig's Ranch, Zimbabwe.

of fixty-six days. Even in a sixteen-paddock cell a 450-day recovery period means a grazing period of thirty days at a high stock density. Such grazing periods would guarantee overgrazing of any perennial grass plant that might try to establish. In addition, such grazing pressure would severely defoliate the desert shrubs thus probably causing them to require the very long recovery period. At the same time it would put extraordinary nutritional stress on the livestock and could lead to damage from overtrampling in some areas.

It would, in other words, make a landscape goal of perennial grassland unlikely to be achieved as well as a production goal of profit necessitating good animal performance.

Sixty-day recovery periods at the nine-paddock level mean 7.5-day average grazing periods. Sixteen paddocks lowers this to four days. Such a regime reduces stress on animals, cuts trampling time, and ensures a good chance of achieving a grassland landscape. Also, it does not in fact expose bushes to the kind of heavy and prolonged browsing that necessitates long rest. Bushes do not regrow from basal growth points like grasses, or from sacrificed root, but rather from remaining leaf. Thus, the kind that had already survived under the conditions described were not likely to die out from a little overbrowsing, even if returned to prematurely. Even their seedlings, once complexity returned, would have more chance of survival.

In this case perennial grass and many other plants, vestiges of which had in fact persisted, did increase, lowering the pressure on the shrubs still further. As the grass began to provide soil cover, better water and mineral cycles and energy flow supported increasingly rapid change (illustration 24-7).

A similar progression of events took place more recently in Arizona chaparral country where a researcher established a cell for goats. His goal was to return an area containing alarming proportions of bare ground and woody scrub to the shrub-flecked grassland recorded long before and still to be found in remnant areas.

He had built the cell and completed the biological planning when I arrived, but I found the grazing and recovery periods much too long for perennial grass in such a climate. He reiterated the argument I had heard in Africa, that perennial grass no longer existed in the area. In addition he said that since goats elect to browse, not graze, he actually intended to overbrowse the scrub while grass established.

I answered that from my experience, goats certainly do graze, and under stress, which he had built into his plan, they take a wide range of plants. Even granted his claim that perennial grass had vanished absolutely, I was concerned that none ever would reappear if the timing ensured overgrazing of the first plant to try to establish.

Out on the land, we stopped at a random spot in the first paddock, and within ten yards of the vehicle I found the first perennial grass plant—an overrested, almost dead, remnant. After that the researcher and I found one

Illustration 24-7. Complexity of community increasing on what had been essentially desert bushes and bare ground. Karroo, South Africa.

after another. Together we found hundreds, among rocks, under bushes, half dead in the open. We even found one growing on level ground, still green and seriously overgrazed!

The lesson is, be careful, not only of your observations, but also of common assumptions. This man's statement about goats was typical. I can remember years ago in my Game Department days, I often heard that elephants were browsing animals. Old hands looked sideways when I asked if they grazed. Later I would analyze stomach contents of many elephants and found they quite commonly graze, given access to healthy grassland. I found much the same with impala, said to be committed browsers. On healthy range with a still-good grass component each stomach contained up to 60 percent grass.

Goats of course, though famous for their ability to survive in low successional environments by eating nearly anything, aren't at all snooty about grass.

You may still feel deeply concerned about some particularly attractive and heavily selected woody species in the community, and not feel confident that it will thrive when timing favors severely-grazed grasses. By all means monitor such situations, but do not reject this guideline before trying it.

In Chapter 19 I gave the example of the very desirable winterfat plants that greatly increased production on an Arizona ranch under higher animal numbers but with planned grazings. Within three years we began to find new young seedlings of this valued plant in the community where it had not seeded for years. As Chapter 37 on Population Management will emphasize, the recruitment of new plants is more crucial than the mere survival of established old ones.

In this case, timing that advanced perennial grasses lessened severe browsing and allowed a critical amount of regrowth. Furthermore it provided a healthier grass community that probably lessened the tendency to select winterfat, and obvious improvement in the microenvironment at the soil surface permitted seeds to establish where they couldn't before.

All this argument that woody plants can also thrive when the timing of grazing is designed for the benefit of grass may seem paradoxical in light of many statements about shifting succession away from woody plants and toward grassland. The timing and the degree and nature of animal impact, however, can be manipulated either to advance the successional process to more diversity or to retard it from proceeding to heavy woody communities.

So far we've concerned ourselves mainly with the role of time in overgrazing and overbrowsing. We'll now look at how time can be manipulated to increase energy flow and thus the productivity of the entire community.

25

Time and Energy Flow

In Chapter 13 I mentioned that we could increase the time base of the energy tetrahedron through better management of time. Indirectly that occurs if better timing of grazing and application of animal impact allows succession to develop a mix of cool and warm season plants that effectively lengthen the productive growing season. Directly, however, proper timing generally will speed the recovery of plants after grazing, thus allowing them to convert more sunlight energy over a shorter period of time. The dynamics of this process are somewhat complex and again involve the matter of stock density as well as time.

Much research in several countries has shown that during the growing season, the amount of green leaf removed greatly affects the rate at which plants regrow after being grazed. Figure 25-1 shows two equal perennial grass plants. Both had almost all of their old leaf and stem material removed in the previous year and began growth as equals in this season. Early on some animal severely defoliates A removing some 90 percent of the leaf but takes only about 40 percent of B. The two plants then recover at very different rates. B must sacrifice little or no root and starts regrowth immediately. Over the next two weeks it produces much more volume of leaf and stem than A. At some point, however, it slows down, and A will catch up.

The higher the proportion of less severely grazed plants compared to severely grazed plants, the more total forage produced in a given recovery period. In brittle environments, as one never knows when rain and growth for the season will end, it is important to try to have as many plants as possible in all paddocks grazed down as little as possible during growth. The result is more production from higher energy flow.

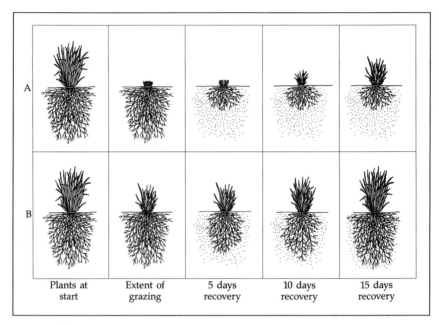

| | Plants at start | Extent of grazing | 5 days recovery | 10 days recovery | 15 days recovery |

Figure 25-1.   Rate of immediate regrowth as affected by amount of leaf removed by grazing.

Most perennial grasses in brittle rangelands would flourish if all the old material were grazed or trampled off in the dormant season and they enjoyed a full, uninterrupted growing season. But what might be ideal for an adult plant is not always best for its young, the community, or the goals. If too many plants rest through the full growing season, the energy flow can be substantially less than it would have been with some grazing and regrowth. In addition, plants that age and increase in proportion of fiber can depress animal performance.

Where the environment is brittle and interplant spaces require distur-bance to maintain high levels of seedling success, you may want animals to break and aerate these bare spaces—which seal over with each rainfall—and to lay down litter, dung, and urine. Where such brittle environments are subject to severe freezing and thawing and thus a degree of soil puffiness that deters seedling establishment, the compaction provided by animal hooves in the growing season can make a great difference as to whether grasses reproduce sexually through seedlings, asexually through runners, or not at all.

In nonbrittle environments disturbance in the growing season is gen-erally unnecessary as plant spacing is so close and succession so speedy, even in rested conditions. However, energy flow (to human use) will still increase with growing season grazing.

As our domesticated animals rank among the severe grazers, one might well wonder how decreasing paddock size and time could cause them not to severely graze a large proportion of plants. As mentioned earlier, animals such as the cow and buffalo feed by the mouthful (or several leaves at a time), which results in severe defoliation of some. This happens especially when only a few plants are free of old material and thus capable of providing a high protein and energy and low fiber diet by the mouthful.

Severe grazers defoliate severely not for sport, but because by nature they try to balance their diet by the mouthful. I have observed that as more plants become cleaner (less dead, grey, oxidizing material or excessive old fiber) animals often take their mouthfuls off the tops of more plants without having to take down severely a smaller number of relatively cleaner plants. I have also noticed that the longer we hold any number of animals in any paddock, the higher the proportion of plants becomes that do get severely grazed. These remarks cover general principles on which we have to manage practically most of the time. Periodically you can observe divergence, such as animals grazing off seedheads before leaf, or even managing to graze off leaf by the mouthful and leave seedheads.

In practice, the more paddocks, the better the distribution of the grazing on the plants, the fewer severely grazed plants, and the greater proportion of plants able to recover quickly from grazing, thus an increased energy flow is what we observe in well managed grazing.[1]

For a time in the early days I reasoned that we could capitalize further on this happy chain of effects and reduce recovery periods. This in turn would reduce grazing periods (remember, they are linked) and produce a snowball effect. But, "they came for the Jews." In other words, where the theory appeared sound, in reality some animals always did graze some plants severely. As the recovery periods shortened, these plants did not recover and were overgrazed. As they weakened and vanished the same fate befell others.

In Africa I noticed this first around anthills (termite mounds) where cattle tended to linger and thus graze more plants severely. When I shortened grazing and recovery periods, plants in these areas began to show visible signs of overgrazing when all should have been well. We had to go back to basing the timing on the most severely grazed plants and rest content with what higher energy flow we still got from the bulk of the plants.

The Problem of Ungrazed Plants in the Community

When you plan grazing along the lines developed here, it is common to have plants that remain ungrazed throughout the growing season. This is inevitable, even at fairly high stock densities, because time management looks to the severely grazed plants. If high energy flow and profitability are part of your goal, you'll have to watch carefully that these plants don't remain ungrazed throughout the rest of the year as this can result in a variety of management problems.

This phenomenon has particularly serious ramifications in nonbrittle environments with high rainfall. The leached soils that can characterize such places cause older plants to lose nutritional value and increase in proportion of fiber to the extent that performance can decline severely as the animals face more such plants in their diet. In addition, the old ungrazed plants rapidly encourage shifts in the community to woody plants. We have not yet found a better remedy for this other than using very high stock densities in a fairly high number of paddocks right from the start. This greatly increases the proportion of plants grazed, reduces the percentage of those that become excessively fibrous, and keeps the animals moving frequently to fresh grazing from which they can select at a high level.

Much the same problem arises in brittle environments with high rainfall and very coarse fibrous grasses, and the same solution applies. In both cases, if the problem is not corrected within a year or two, then in addition to very poor animal performance, we can anticipate a successional shift to woody communities, which may not fit the landscape goal.

In low rainfall brittle environments, if plants continue ungrazed through the growing season livestock suffer little, if at all. In addition we have more time in which to have these plants either trampled or grazed before we risk successional shift. In nonbrittle or brittle high rainfall areas where soil is highly leached, old grass does not tend to cure well and rapidly loses nutritional value. In such areas old unused grass is often a liability to animal performance.

The more highly mineralized soils in drier areas, however, produce grass that remains an asset as good forage long into the dormant season or even beyond. I've seen animals live on forage two years old or older in such areas. The same animals in higher rainfall areas could starve on coarse grass of the year. Thus in drier areas old grass can be grazed out through the dormant season without a drop in animal performance, and often without any supplementation.

The connection between animal production and soils is far more complicated than we realize. On certain soils it is hard not to achieve good individual animal production even under bad management. On other soils it is hard to achieve that production even under the best of management measures. On those soils that are poor for animal production there has been a tendency to mask the situation with high inputs of supplements but at high cost. One low cost essential step we have discovered is to build up to very high stock densities on such soils quickly and allow very frequent moves to fresh grazing.

In any case, remember that prolonged rest does not generally benefit perennial grass plants. At some point we must plan to remove the upper parts and return them to the soil by one of the tools at our disposal: Grazing, Animal Impact, Fire, Living Organisms, or Technology. For energy to flow, the processes of life and decay must proceed smoothly.

Drought Reserve of Grazing Held as "Time" and not "Area"

How you plan for drought reserves of forage can influence the energy flow on a ranch enormously. Typically, prudent ranchers withdraw certain areas from grazing as a drought reserve to give themselves a margin of time should poor growth conditions lead to depletion of forage elsewhere. However, since all forage can be measured in Animal Days, no rule says *where* they must be reserved. You only really need to know *when* they will be necessary.

This means that instead of reasoning that your animals will use a major portion of your land in average years but in drought years require the whole spread, you will think thusly: "My whole spread has X number of Animal Days of forage. Normally I will need Y, so I will have X - Y Animal Days of reserve." This reflects the fact that we also measure drought in days—days until the rain comes, days until growth starts. Your banker doesn't ask, "How many acres do you have in reserve?" but simply, "How long can you hold out?"

Figure 25-2 shows a ten-paddock cell. Assume that in a drought-prone area a traditional rancher withdraws two paddocks from grazing as a reserve should the dormant or dry season last longer than expected (A). This leaves eight paddocks. Given an average recovery period of sixty days, this means 8.5-day average grazing periods as opposed to 6.6 days if all ten paddocks had been grazed.

The shorter grazing periods for the fully utilized cell (B) would have meant greater energy flow with better livestock performance, better plant growth, and less pressure on the land that was grazed (3.3 vs. 4.3 Animal Days Per Acre). Thus, even before the drought ever occurs, the area reserve approach usually means a production loss. Quite likely the growth in the two rested paddocks didn't offset the amount *not* grown in the other eight. In addition, the two long rested paddocks may have suffered from the lack of animal impact and the forage itself become stale, excessively fibrous, and low in protein and energy.

The problem continues into the dormant season, as the livestock continue to move through fewer paddocks, meaning longer grazing periods and more grazing on fouled ground. Fire risk also increases as all the eggs now rest in only two paddocks.

Finally, considering that over half the time the growing season begins

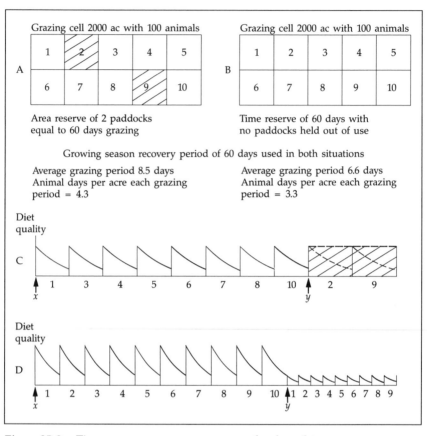

Figure 25-2. Time reserve versus area reserve for droughts.

on schedule, the ungrazed paddocks may become a liability unless this occurs in a low rainfall area with low-fiber grass. What do you do with all that old grass? In many environments it will encourage successional shifts toward woody brush that you do not want.

The dormant season pattern appears in the sketches at the bottom of figure 25-2. C represents the pattern with two paddocks withdrawn as an area reserve. At the start of the dormant season (point X) the area reserve cell has less forage in each of the grazed paddocks than the time reserve cell does because the same number of Animal Days of forage have been taken from less land and over a longer grazing period. In addition, the stock start off in worse condition due to longer grazing periods during the months of most promising gain.

By point Y, where the next growing season should begin, all eight paddocks in use will be grazed down to scratch. If new growth doesn't start then, the reserve paddocks will carry the herd another two months. However, the animals have only one move and stay on fouled ground for a prolonged time without any stimulation from moving. If new growth does begin, then the old growth in the rested paddocks (shaded areas) will remain a problem, because stock won't select it over fresh green leaves.

D shows the pattern in the time reserve cell. All paddocks and animals start the dormant season in better condition due to faster moves previously made over more ground. All ten paddocks can be grazed to point Y with shorter grazing periods and less time on fouled ground. If new growth does not start at point Y, the ten paddocks still contain a total of sixty *days* of forage that will carry the herd for the next two months. The animals reached point Y in better condition and now have frequent stimulating moves onto fresh ground, as they go through ten paddocks. If new growth does commence on schedule, then little or no excessive old grass remains as a problem in any paddock.

In practice, the paddocks could be grazed in a number of different ways, depending on the planning, but the underlying principles remain. *Think twice and again before you continue with old-fashioned drought reserves.*

So far we have looked mainly at plants. Now let's look in more detail at how time management guidelines also enable animals to perform well.

26

Time and
Livestock Nutrition

Over many years we have developed ways to optimize the relationship between what livestock do to vegetation and landscape production in a grazing cell and what they actually need by way of nutrition. Considering that the wax and wane of seasons and the demands of breeding, lactating, and growing animals, not to mention the needs of wildlife and the landscape goal to be produced, represent another formidable knot of complexity, this is no mean feat.

Further chapters on planning and much of the companion volume will address many aspects of this problem. The controlling principles, however, once again involve timing and stock density, particularly the former, but much also depends on the eating habits of animals.

Over many years we have observed livestock feeding as they move to new paddocks. In addition, fistulated animals, which wear a device that samples intake, have taught us much, and we have had opportunity to record the supplements that animals select on a free choice basis as they move from paddock to paddock. All this evidence combines to show that animals have a remarkable ability to balance their diets and by and large know what their bodies require. The task of management then is not to preplan or force any particular diet but to anticipate times of varying need and ensure that the animals are able to select to the best of their ability.

How animals sense their own needs remains somewhat a mystery. Obviously it involves some combination of taste, smell, and sight, but a deeper instinct also comes into play that science has not explained. People have this power to some extent. If circumstances ever force you onto a deficient diet for a long period, you will start to crave certain things and even dream of foods you have not seen, smelled, or tasted for months and may not habitually eat. The craving of some pregnant women for lime off walls or pickles and ice cream represents the same thing, but apparently grazing animals have developed this primordial wisdom to a high degree.

In the main, animals select from pasture or range a diet with a balance of protein, energy, and fiber to the extent that the forage available will permit. More puzzling is the evidence that a cow can accurately select for minute amounts of trace minerals, given a smorgasbord to choose from. In tropical Africa I have observed cattle moved through the radial paddocks of a grazing cell that covered two soil types, granitic sand and red laterite. Where all the paddocks met at the center, stock could freely select from a number of minerals and trace elements in separate containers. Palatability was hardly a factor as any of the cows could have demolished the total amount of any item that had a pleasant taste.

As the cattle moved through the paddocks it soon became obvious that they consumed a certain pattern of minerals when on the granite soil and changed to a different pattern within twenty-four hours of entering a red soil paddock. The new pattern continued until they returned to the granite soil, when they would switch back within a day. Clearly some sense beyond a crude concern for protein, energy, and fiber informed them.

Animals moving into a fresh paddock may graze almost everywhere, as they encounter no fouling. They will easily take in a good volume of a well-balanced diet. Most often, they select for high protein and energy and low fiber. One can watch them take mouthfuls of the most leafy material available. During the first day, they tend to select what is readily available, while at the same time dunging, trampling, and urinating over much of the paddock.

They do the same the following day, but find it not quite so easy, because less leafy material remains and they try to avoid grazing on their own fouling of the previous day. Consequently, the second day the animals may experience a lower quality diet. Quality drops again the third day, and so on.

The pattern continues until the animals go to a new paddock. If they ever stay in a paddock until all forage is depleted, the consequent severe drop in nutrition inevitably results in poor performance. Though common sense and long experience in Africa affirm the truth of this scenario, many American researchers supposedly investigating my work put cattle in cells laid out in radial paddocks and moved them "from pasture to pasture as the forage was depleted."[1] Needless to say they published a finding of poor cattle performance, putting many people off, though planned grazing as described here would never have led to that trap and its obvious result.

Sketch A in figure 26-1 shows the pattern of intake of quality and volume of diet as a herd moves through six equal-sized (but not equal quality) paddocks on a schedule of six-day grazing periods and thirty-day recovery

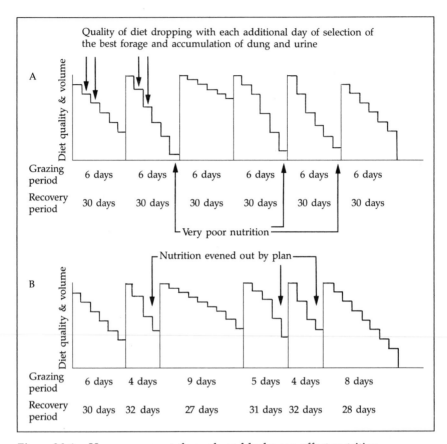

Figure 26-1. How movement through paddocks can affect nutrition.

periods. In each paddock the diet starts off at a high level only to drop daily until the animals move. As paddocks 2, 4, and 5 have poorer quality forage in them with less leafy material, the diet drops lower than in the remaining paddocks. The herd would have three days (heavy arrows) on which nutrition fell to a particularly low level.

The rapidity of falloff in diet quality depends on two factors—stock density, and volume and quality of forage.

The more Animal Days per Acre taken from a paddock each day, the faster the decline, both because of the actual amount eaten and the distribution of the fouling. Given little fresh leafy material at the start, however, we can expect a drop even with low stock density and minimal fouling.

With a bit of planning we could improve on sketch A, which for breeding and lactating animals obviously would lead to lower conception rates and calf/lamb/kid weights. Sketch B in the same figure shows how an adjustment in the planned grazings might look. The six days in poor paddock 2 are cut to four, and paddocks 4 and 5 drop to five and four days, respectively. At the same time paddocks 3 and 6 get grazing periods of nine and eight days. Now, on no day does the plane of nutrition fall badly.

The recovery periods still average thirty days and the grazings six; however, each paddock's recovery period has changed. Recovery time in poor paddocks has now increased to thirty-one and thirty-two days and fallen to twenty-seven and twenty-eight days in good paddocks. As the better paddocks also have had the grazing periods lengthened, plants in them are in greater danger of being overgrazed. In the immediate future, one would intensify monitoring for signs of damage. In the long run, one would want to divide the better paddocks to reduce the danger. When to act on that, however, would depend on holistically-sound financial and long-term land planning, such as Chapters 39 and 44 and much of the companion volume will cover.

If you make adjustments in a six-paddock cell like the previous example, of course you will have to plan different grazing and recovery periods for slow and fast growth. That may seem daunting at this point, but the techniques of biological planning described in Chapter 40 will make it easy.

Advantage of Many Paddocks or of Herded Animals in Many Grazing Areas

Assume that you now have one hundred paddocks available for a large herd. If you use herding instead of fences and have the good control most herders do, consider you have marked out one hundred grazing areas. Given the high cost of fencing and the many disadvantages of it to wildlife and other users of the land, herding has much to recommend it.

In a brittle environment with a 140- to a 180-day growing season and a similar nongrowing season, you can plan around a single rest period of two hundred days for the growing season, as all grazing periods will be short—in this case an average of two days. Whatever the growth rate, fast or slow, such grazing periods do not allow overgrazing of even the most severely bitten plant, and recovery time is adequate even in quite poor years. Animals move so frequently that they enjoy good nutrition throughout the growing season, and by constantly moving to fresh ground suffer little parasitism or disease. (In America a number of ranchers report fewer flies on cattle moving that often, as the majority of flies hatch in the dung in vacated paddocks.)

In addition to the advantages above, the stock density in this example is high and herd effect can be applied also with ease causing excellent animal impact, which can stimulate succession, water and mineral cycles, as well as energy flow. Chapter 20 explained how high impact causes the grass component of a community to become less fibrous. At the one-hundred-paddock level, worry about depressed performance due to fibrous plants decreases markedly. Illustration 26-1 shows excellent, lush, leafy growth right up to the watering point on the Barlite Ranch in Texas which, thanks to 101 paddocks, carried cattle at twice the traditional stocking rate through one of the worst dry years in recorded history, 1983–84, and even increased cattle numbers. No other ranch in Texas to my knowledge managed to do that. In addition, through planning the selections, as we will discuss next, they actually cut their supplementary feed bill during the drought in half— a savings of $26,000.

The results were dramatic, but predictable from what we now know about the functioning of the ecosystem and animal grazing.

Moving livestock at high densities through many paddocks with very short grazing periods is the best that we can do to get high performance off the natural vegetation and soil. This will still give very different results on different soils. On those soils that are inherently not good livestock producing soils, it has been my experience that allowing the livestock to select trace and other minerals on what is called a free choice basis (i.e., each mineral

Illustration 26-1.   Dense, lush, and leafy growth in a complex community produced by very high animal impact from cattle moving through 101 paddocks on planned grazing. Barlite Ranch, Texas.

is held in a separate container and animals are allowed to choose what they want in the quantities they want), leads to much better individual animal performance, sometimes dramatically so. Many animal nutritionists refute the grazing animal's ability to balance its diet naturally, given a full and unimpeded opportunity, and have proven their point in countless trials in controlled circumstances. On my own ranch, after reading all of the research I could of many countries and observing livestock on many ranches I left selection to the animals and planned grazings so that selection could be at the highest level possible.

Time Management and Control of Number of Selections

So far we have looked at managing time to minimize overgrazing and improve livestock performance during the growing season. What about time management during the periods when perennial grasses become dormant and livestock are normally supplemented—usually at high cost?

Even then of course animals eat and have a physical impact on soil and plants, so many of the same considerations govern the situation as before. Stock will avoid ground fouled by dung and urine, and parasites and infection will usually increase when herds linger in the same area. Hooves will continue to trample. The timing must still assure that these factors contribute to the health of the soil surface microenvironment and good performance of animals, both wild and domestic.

Dormant periods are the most critical times of year for wildlife as their food will depend entirely on the grazing plan for livestock. If stock simply rotate through the paddocks on an arbitrary schedule, as is tragically so common, it can devastate wildlife. In addition, such rotational grazing commonly results in very high supplemental feed costs because domestic animals will suffer from the same decreasing plane of nutrition inflicted on the wild ones.

From what we currently know, animals select their diet in the same way, regardless of season. The pattern in figure 26-1 continues. Each time stock enter a fresh paddock, they balance their diets as best they can. If they enter the same paddock a second time during dormancy, it will not have regrown any new leaf. However, the effect will not be the same as a single prolonged stay. An intervening rest will allow fouling to wear off and the mere act of moving onto fresh forage, even when depleted, seems to stimulate livestock in ways we do not properly understand. And yet the selection from the forage remaining the second time around will certainly contain less protein and energy and more fiber than before. By manipulating recovery periods and the related grazing periods we can control the number of times animals select from a paddock in dormancy.

In America, government advisors and private consultants commonly recommend putting stock on a short duration grazing system in an eight-paddock cell. Figure 26-2 shows what happens to the plane of nutrition in one paddock when the rotation makes four cycles during the dormant season. The first cycle provides relatively good feed, but its value drops drastically in each successive cycle. When, toward the end of the season, the gap between supplies and needs becomes excessive, a well-capitalized rancher can buy supplements to make up the difference. Wild animals, even if mobile, often just starve.

Having coined the term short duration grazing myself, it is a personal tragedy that it stuck to a practice that still destroys budgets and animals many years after we found it flawed.

Given only eight paddocks, we might do a little better by lengthening recovery and grazing periods to reduce the number of selections. Figure 26-3 shows the result of two selections and a recovery period of fifty days. Nutrition still drops enough to require supplementation for top livestock performance, but wildlife would have a better chance than before. Although the same amount of forage has been taken by the livestock, the distribution is such that at the critical time of the year there is likely to be more for wildlife, particularly if the rains and growth do come early. If new growth

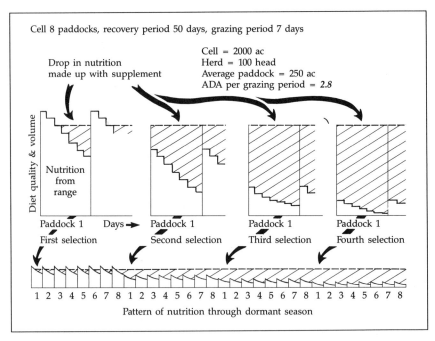

Figure 26-2. Four selections from each paddock.

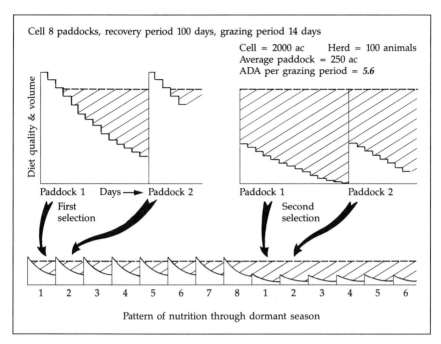

Figure 26-3. Two selections from each paddock.

is late then ultimately they aren't any better off because of the bottleneck principle we will discuss in Chapter 37.

Figure 26-4 shows one selection from each paddock with recovery periods lengthened to two hundred days to ensure that each paddock is only grazed once in this time. Obviously nutrition drops seriously toward the end of each grazing period and animals would require costly supplementation to maintain the rumenal flora populations essential to their digestion. (The rumens, or stomachs, of cud-chewing animals such as cattle, sheep, goats, and deer cannot achieve digestion without these microorganisms). From a wildlife point of view, with no supplementation, mobile animals could obtain a reasonable plane of nutrition in various paddocks through the season. Toward the end, they would obtain most feed in the remaining ungrazed paddocks, but commonly a new flush of growth would start appearing in all paddocks by then. Fences allowing fairly free wildlife movement (which will be discussed later) would allow them access to it.

Obviously, however, low paddock numbers do not offer a perfect solution. More paddocks or grazing areas once more provide an answer. Figure 26-5 helps illustrate why. The same cell of previous examples now has one hundred paddocks and to give stock one selection from each, they will move, on the average, every second day. Thus, throughout the nongrowing season,

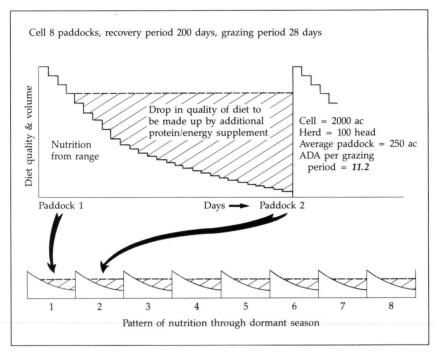

Cell 8 paddocks, recovery period 200 days, grazing period 28 days

Drop in quality of diet to
be made up by additional
protein/energy supplement

Nutrition
from range

Cell = 2000 ac
Herd = 100 head
Average paddock = 250 ac
ADA per grazing
period = 11.2

Diet quality & volume

Paddock 1   Days ➞   Paddock 2

1   2   3   4   5   6   7   8

Pattern of nutrition through dormant season

Figure 26-4.   Single selection from each paddock, with few paddocks.

they will move to fresh ground constantly, and on the last day will enjoy a reasonable plane of nutrition and a quick move. Both cover and forage conditions for wildlife will improve considerably, as we have found. But the high amount of fencing, which inhibits free movement, counters this to some extent. If herding can be substituted for fencing not only does the wildlife benefit but the landscape is far more pleasing to the eye.

On first analysis, the above claim may look fishy. After all, cutting a cell into eight paddocks or a hundred makes absolutely no difference to the amount of standing forage at the onset of the dormant season, and livestock will eat exactly the same amount in the same time in either case. A parallel example from the mining industry explains perhaps better what happens.

Most mines contain various grades of ore. For maximum immediate profit an operator may elect to high grade, only mining and selling the best. If he does this, however, he will eventually have only low grade ore left, which he cannot sell at all. Thousands of shafts abandoned for this reason dot the western United States. On the other hand, the same operator could have mixed the ore, keeping the aggregate just rich enough to produce an acceptable profit. In that way he could have extracted a vastly larger proportion of the original ore body at far greater total profit.

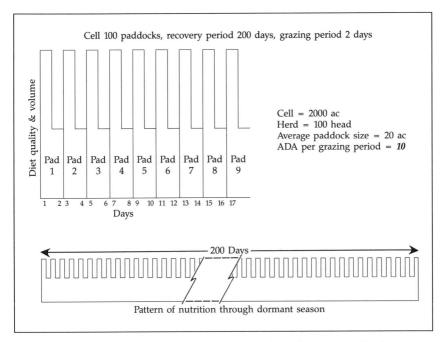

Figure 26-5. Single selection from each paddock, with many paddocks.

Stimulaton From Frequent Moves

Earlier I mentioned that moving onto fresh grazing stimulates livestock in a way not entirely accounted for by nutrition or any other explanation. Voisin noticed this phenomenon, and, like me, could not entirely explain it.

The fact remains, however, that livestock moved frequently onto fresh, unfouled ground will fare better in adverse circumstances than they would under more static management. I experienced a really dramatic demonstration of this years ago in Africa and have seen many lesser examples since.

At the time I had a ranch of my own in the Kezi area of Zimbabwe and was assisting two young brothers and their families who ranched nearby. Widespread damage to the water cycle sharpened risk in this drought-prone area, and the brothers' ranches were in a bad state after many years of overgrazing and low animal impact. They had lost animals to actual starvation in years past.

In the first year of my consulting I persuaded them to put in some more fences, and we planned the grazings. They also substantially increased both total numbers and stock density in order to advance succession through animal impact and grazing. Hardly had we begun before a truly terrible drought developed, on top of which came a severe outbreak of army worm. This small caterpillar travels in bands that devastate absolutely all leafy vegetation in their way. They, like the exacerbated drought, were just another result of the low state of succession on the land.

My visits to the two families became frequent as we planned our way ahead under the curling wave of tragedy. First I advised against spraying caterpillars, as that wasted money and would increase the chance of other outbreaks by simplifying the community. To reduce the livestock would cost dearly because the market had collapsed and we needed animal impact. Even though plant growth had stopped, more fences seemed a better investment than supplements. Last, we ruthlessly amalgamated several small herds from both families and planned grazing as if the two ranches were one huge cell with many paddocks.

The lack of forage was appalling. The cattle literally seemed to exist on a daily ration of whatever leaves and twigs fell from the trees, and we joked about a new breed that could live on stones, as they appeared to have little else. Over vast areas the caterpillars had not missed a single leaf.

The cattle became desperately thin, but the stimulation of the frequent moves onto largely bare but fresh ground was little short of a miracle. Nothing but the moves could explain why we did not lose one animal to starvation. Under continuous grazing without moves, lesser droughts—unassisted by the army worm or a higher stocking rate—had always taken their toll.

No research explains what really happened, but I have seen many other cases since and derived a practical rule of thumb. In a serious drought, do not scatter animals but concentrate them ruthlessly, and keep them moving. The results will surprise you, though one qualification does exist. The above case occurred on highly mineralized soil. In higher rainfall areas with leached soils, animals can be lost to malnutrition even amid a substantial amount of standing forage. Despite this you will, I believe, still stand more chance in severe droughts with continually moving stock in all areas.

Good Land Planning, Animal Training, and Habit Necessary to Reduce the Stress of Frequent Moves

When livestock move frequently, the stress of movement will hurt performance unless they learn to move themselves calmly. As a general guideline you should train them to move themselves, when allowed to, without your intervention. If you have to drive them, you can anticipate less than maximum performance.

A good land plan is key, as fencing or land divisions should permit an easy, unconfused flow. Good planning of the actual moves should support this so that, for instance, during calving, lambing, and kidding, herds move to adjacent ground. Later chapters and the companion volume will cover the ins and outs of this. Fortunately, however, the native intelligence of livestock will overcome many obstacles.

Animals, like humans, are creatures of habit and train easily. Nothing justifies spending $200 an hour for helicopters to flush steers out of heavy brush, as some American ranchers do, when a fifty-cent plastic whistle will do the same job more quickly and with less stress. I once heard a New Mexico rancher tell how three generations of experience proved that it took four mounted cowboys a day to gather a particularly brushy bull pasture. A new hand present, who had no cattle experience whatever, nevertheless bought himself a whistle on the strength of my anecdotes about training. Four days later they sent him, probably with a few knowing grins, to round up the bulls. He did it alone in twenty minutes and on foot.

To this point we have mainly considered livestock in our time management. What of large game populations that either coexist with livestock or run freely in our national parks and refuges?

27

Time and Game Management

Chapter 19 described the destruction of vegetation and soil communities in the Mana Pools National Park in Zimbabwe despite a heavy culling of elephants. Since the policy stems from some false assumptions I myself made in the 1960s, I have it ever on my conscience as abiding proof that timing of the exposure of plants to animals means more than animal numbers.

In Mana Pools the culling theoretically would reduce environmental damage. However, because tourists want to see tame elephants, the mass killing was done in a way the elephants did not link to humans. Today, fewer, unnatural (semitame) elephants without fear of man do as much damage as many more natural wild ones did before. The tame animals simply feed on the same ground day after day, continuously grazing and browsing the same plants.

Exactly the same principles that apply to livestock govern wild grazing and herding animals, however much the details of practice may differ. Trampled litter and soil do not distinguish between buffalo and cow. The health of the community in brittle environments demands some trampling but any number of species can provide it either in a beneficial way, or too long and too often.

In the case of livestock we can easily distinguish between time and numbers, as no matter what the numbers we can control the time through fencing or herding. Wild animals do not submit to the same kind of control, and the distinction blurs, especially *because in their case numbers can influence time.* The social behavior of large unrestricted herds on home ranges bears little resemblance to that of small bands moving randomly in a limited area.

In addition, predators, including man, have a very decided effect on the time their prey spends in the proximity of any plant.

Where heavy predation, accident, and disease control numbers, size of a herd's territory or home range tends to regulate the frequency of return to feeding areas. The concentrated fouling of animals bunched for self-protection will ensure short periods of grazing on the same ground. If lack of predation and other deaths allows numbers to rise, home ranges and territories appear to become smaller as more herds occupy the same area and herds return to past feeding ground sooner. This starts a snowballing breakdown of the ecosystem processes, including the loss of many nongame species.

I thought through the logic of all of this years ago when doing my early work in the Luangwa and Zambezi Valleys of Zambia and Zimbabwe. However, one bit of evidence did not fit and appeared to disprove the theory.

Both the areas in question had very heavy natural predation, which should have provided both population control and reinforced herding instincts. The Luangwa in particular had the highest known concentrations of lions in the world. Why were the ecosystem processes breaking down so badly?

One thing both areas had in common was the removal of man as a predator. Did Man the Hunter have a niche that nothing else could fill? Nearby areas where human hunters and game still coexisted were nevertheless breaking down too, so perhaps humans were not a vital predator.

A closer look at hunted and protected areas, however, revealed another difference. *Where humans still held rank among natural predators, the deterioration could clearly be linked to soil exposure through frequent fire.* In the protected areas *soil exposure clearly came more from overgrazing and consequent destruction of vegetation.* The evidence was striking in the '50s and early '60s when the Zambian side of the Zambezi had predation from humans and the Zimbabwean side didn't.

I had the luck to work in the game departments of both countries, but it took me a long time to put all the pieces together. It would take even longer to document it, and many opportunities have now vanished, along with most major natural game populations, even in national parks. My own observations nonetheless convinced me that modern man and his predecessors have been a major natural predator of most big game for many millions of years. Some larger game animals have few predators but man.

Current research does document the drastic consequences to a community that can follow removal of one main predator, as mentioned in Chapter 11. It should come as no surprise, therefore, that man's changing roles might upset natural relationships worldwide. Where, as principle predator, we once ensured constant movement and had no ability to light fires, we now have taken the part of protector and friend, stopping movement and reducing other predators while increasing the frequency of fire world-wide. Successional communities that evolved over millions of years could compensate no better if wolves and lions donned business suits, moved to the suburbs, and sent their agents out to burn the forage and expose soil.

Our concept of national parks set aside for large game has got to change, and, fortunately, circumstances are compelling scientists in many disciplines to rethink old concepts. In Africa in particular, home of most of the large game national parks, the sense of urgency to increase understanding has grown dramatically.

Much new work will be needed to find ways of inducing movement in game populations again and to maintain concentrations in brittle environments. Management schemes now commonly call for cutting off water periodically to force herds to move to other sources. To an extent, this causes movement. However, it does not cause concentration. It does not cause frequent enough movement. It may let nonmobile species die of thirst, thus hindering the build-up of complex communities. I have seen many attempts to use this technique but I've never seen it work as a realistic means of managing the crucial time factor.

Attractants such as we use with livestock (which will be discussed at greater length in Chapter 29) need more research. I started some work in my own game reserve, with encouraging signs, but when the government expropriated the land to form a national park they did not continue the work.

In the 1950s a man by the name of Vesey-Fitzgerald working in the Rukwa valley of Tanzania observed what he called "grazing succession," which might give a clue to the use of livestock herds to induce movement in other species. In each wet season most big game moved out of the valley and vegetation became very rank. At the onset of the dry months, the game returned in a definite pattern. Those that could handle and digest very coarse, tall, fibrous grass, like elephants, returned first. Next came others that could handle coarse forage opened up to some extent by the elephants. This group included zebra (with teeth on both jaws) and buffalo. Finally smaller species requiring more opened forage came in.

We have observed a similar pattern when handling large herds of cattle in areas of significant game. Here the game shadowed the cattle herd, feeding some days behind it in the growing season. This opens up real possibilities for better control of time for all grazing animals.

It is common in Africa to travel miles and see nothing, then one type of animal is seen and immediately several others. Different species of grazing animals do associate to varying degrees, including game and domestic stock. We first picked this up on a Zimbabwean ranch that ran sixty thousand cattle and a game ranching operation on one and a quarter million acres. We had a test project on four thousand acres in which we used for the first time a central watering point and a radial layout of thirty paddocks divided by simple fences that allowed most game to move.

We trebled the stocking rate of the cattle to test the new design under very high pressure and planned grazings, all of which attracted total condemnation from all the experts in the wings. Game harvesters hunting in the same area soon discovered that wild animals (mainly zebra, kudu, wildebeest, giraffe, and impala) routinely turned up in paddocks two moves behind the large herd of cattle. Depending on plant growth rate and speed of cattle move, they thus chose to feed two to four days later.

Investigation on other ranches confirmed a similar link between livestock movement and game. Sometimes the game followed cattle or sheep and at other times moved with them in what amounted to a mixed herd, although the game might stay slightly off to one side. The game tended to avoid heavy human disturbance and sometimes only joined the livestock at night. On one Texas ranch the manager, after long observation, reported no link between cattle and pronghorn, but I, rising a bit earlier, found them together at dawn. As the clamor of the ranch headquarters coming to life wafted over the range, the antelope left.

Wherever association occurs or can be encouraged, it eases time management greatly because control of the livestock will carry over to the game to some degree. The plants do not care what kind of animal eats them, only that they aren't bitten again until they've had time to recover.

In the case of our test project in Zimbabwe, the coming of the game only a few days after the stock lengthened the grazing period. Even when the cattle moved every day, plants were exposed for three days (a single intervening day between the cattle and the game was not enough time for grazed plants to recover). In the same way, the recovery period extended from the time the game left until the cattle returned.

At this stage you may feel that even a superhuman time manager could not simultaneously restore the most severely bitten plant, defend the "Communists," and think about game tagging along behind his cattle. Fortunately time factors do not stand alone, and perfection is not necessary. Other influences such as animal impact go on simultaneously in the whole and you will not have to reach your goal solely through time management and grazing.

You will do your best, through careful planning of time, to minimize overgrazing, but between the livestock and the game, some will occur nonetheless. Yet, even as it tends to push succession backwards, high animal impact at the same time can overwhelm that tendency and keep it moving forward. Today's alarming degree of overgrazing came about under low animal impact, which in turn provided less than ideal conditions for the establishment of young plants in brittle environments. If seeds and sprouts can establish, losses to overgrazing matter far less, as eons of evolutionary history show.

Conclusion

It has been necessary to devote considerable space to the concept of time as it relates to our management of plants, soils, livestock, and wildlife as it is so new to us. Experience in many contexts in many countries is now showing clearly that planned grazings with time management will be important in maintaining the health of rangelands and watersheds and halting the advance of deserts throughout the world. I feel sure we have by no means yet seen the full implications.

Nevertheless, if you will sit down with pencil and paper and work through simple calculations of time, as we will discuss in detail in later chapters and the companion volume, you will reap an enormous return.

Let's now proceed to those guidelines that cover animal impact, the other aspect of livestock grazing.

28

Stock Density

Stock density is an important consideration in the application of the two management tools, grazing and animal impact. As the previous chapters made clear, it has a strong relationship to many of the time guidelines just covered, but deserves some discussion in its own right.

Crudely defined, stock density means the concentration of animals in any paddock on a given day and is a function of paddock size and stock numbers, usually expressed as animals per acre (number of head divided by acres). Thus two hundred cows in a one-hundred-acre paddock is a stock density of two cows per acre (2:1). A hundred cows in a two-hundred-acre paddock give a density of 0.5 cows per acre (0.5:1).

Because of the old human prejudice that hooves in any context damage soils and plants, low stock density has usually characterized management of livestock on croplands, rangelands, and watersheds. Our traditional bias, however, made us attribute the many damaging side effects of this policy to other causes.

Low density, not overgrazing or overstocking, should bear the blame for many serious range and production problems, including severe trailing, successional shifts toward brush and weeds, grasshopper outbreaks, poor animal performance and high supplemental feed costs, excessive use of fire to even out grazing and suppress brush, and the development of mosaics of grazed out patches and unpalatable brush on rangelands and pastures.

A high degree of patchiness and trailing is a hallmark of low density, the grazed patches commonly ending sharply where ungrazed plants—often of the same species—begin, as if a gardener had laid them out. Many people talk of patch grazing or spot grazing. When I first recognized it, I called it

251

hippo grazing because hippos move over grassland like a lawnmower, their wide flat mouths taking everything and leaving a sharp edge where they stop. The term low density grazing serves better than any of these names because it describes the process and suggests a solution.

Chapter 24 made an ample case for developing many paddocks and described how, as this proceeds, certain things follow automatically. Time in paddocks gets shorter, stock densities get higher, and animals move faster to fresh ground without consuming more feed. However, aside from these effects, some circumstances require increasing stock density for its own sake, without consideration of timing.

As we saw, as paddock numbers go up, the advantages of shorter grazing periods extend over the whole cell. A new fence dividing one paddock can change the grazing period in all paddocks. However, stock density only increases in the divided paddock. Figure 28-1 illustrates this. The drawing shows a cell of two thousand acres carrying four hundred head with an average recovery period of sixty days. Thus, the equal-sized paddocks have a stock density of 1.2 animals per acre, and average grazing periods run twelve days. Now assume that income generated from the cell allows us to add a new fence, which splits paddock 6, creating a paddock 7.

The recovery periods remain sixty days on average, and the average grazing period for *all* paddocks drops to ten days. However, the density remains 1.2 animals per acre in all paddocks except 6 and 7. They now both

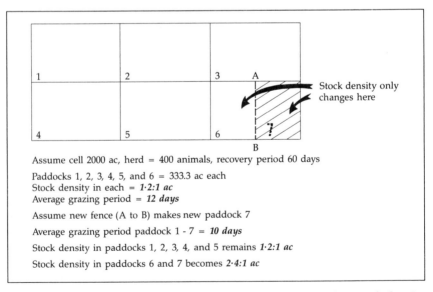

Figure 28-1. With a new fence, time can change everywhere but stock density only changes where paddock size changes.

have 2.4 animals per acre. As the division of the cell continues this principle always holds—timing can change in any of the paddocks as a consequence of increased paddock numbers, but stock density can only change in the new paddocks of altered size. If forage and other conditions were absolutely even and if a rigid rotation were applied, the timing too would tend to change only where the paddock size changed. In practice this is seldom the case. Thus we work with a decreasing average grazing period as paddock numbers rise, and take advantage of the decreased grazing period at any point on the land where the planning calls for it. Theoretically the average stock density also changes when any paddock is split to create another, but in practice we cannot transfer that advantage elsewhere. Thus no matter what we do with the change of time in any paddock, the stock density can only change where we actually changed the paddock size.

Why we might choose to raise density on some parts of the land and not others goes back to both production and landscape goals. Stock density can have profound effects on both animals and land.

As stock density rises and grazing periods shorten on average, the following things occur:

- Distribution of grazing, dung, and urine tends to become more even.
- The proportion of plants grazed severely shrinks as grazing is spread over more plants with no greater consumption.
- A tighter plant community tends to develop with more leaf and less fiber in the plants (this can often be seen on ranches where animals are crowded in pens once or twice a year).
- Animal performance improves (as long as grazings are correctly planned).

Any of these reasons could justify raising stock density in many situations, but animal performance commonly ranks first among them. Usually we target areas where the grass has become too fibrous for a particular type of livestock to perform well. Such problems commonly develop in high rainfall areas or on sandy soils where available precipitation is very effective.

When planning grazing cells for such areas, prior knowledge of the area helps considerably. In a grassland that has the potential of becoming one that is dominated by a high proportion of tall and fibrous plants, and thus requires high stock density, cell sizes will need to be smaller than one might anticipate initially. Ranchers who have failed to plan radial cells properly in these situations have divided and redivided paddocks in an attempt to increase stock density and have ended up with a hopeless mess of paddocks that converged into long, narrow corridors as they approached the center. Chapter 39 will discuss how to avoid this trap.

The apparent paradox of lush, improving plant communities and falling animal performance plagued my early work. It haunted all our various grazing systems and rotations. Though careful monitoring clearly documented the improvement of plant communities and soils, no class of livestock performed as well as the same animals continuously grazing a deteriorating control area. On stable irrigated pastures, André Voisin's work guided us to success, but large concentrated herds on rangelands did not thrive.

For eight years I carried the albatross of almost continuous poor animal performance while many critics rubbed their hands and snickered. I never questioned the conventional wisdom that cattle select certain species of tastier grasses and reject others. Academic articles had belabored the subject ad nauseum and allayed any doubt.

One day while discussing the problem of poor performance with a ranch manager in Swaziland as we walked over his land, a pair of grass plants of the same species caught my eye, and the pieces of the puzzle began to fall into place.

Range scientists considered this species less desirable, and indeed one plant stood untouched in a rank clump, but another, right next to it, had been eaten right down. I had noticed such things before but had never paid them much attention, so I just sat down and thought for a long time.

I asked myself, "Why would two plants of the same kind, enjoying the same weather, soil, moisture, and exposure to cattle, come to such different ends?" After a while I startled the already bewildered manager by blurting out the observation that "cattle don't select species, they don't even know the Latin name of this plant."

It had taken me years to register that although cattle carefully and intelligently select their diet, they do it by what they actually sense in front of them, not by choosing from a Linnaean menu of desirable and undesirable species as common knowledge would have us believe. In many cases, perhaps even most cases, the physical and chemical condition of separate plants determines desirability more than family reputation does. The point was controversial in Africa at the time. A similar observation about mankind would get me into even deeper hot water politically later. One should judge individuals, not races. Bovine logic knows less prejudice. If fresh tender leaves of undesirable brand X go down better than old, stale leaves of desirable brand Y, eat them.

I immediately determined to approach my old dilemma from a new tack. This meant planning grazings and animal impact so as to produce abundant leafy material of all species, and not simply consider absolute bulk or worry about the abundance of species considered desirable by range scientists and ranchers. I now use the following analogy in training courses.

Assume I asked you to visit for a year. As a good host I ask you for a list of your favorite foods (your most desired species), and on your arrival you find a smorgasbord of every one of your selections, from which you choose a substantial meal but of course leave many items untouched or only nibbled.

While you rest, I replace exactly what you ate, leaving everything else as before. At the next meal you choose again, and I replace that.

After a few months, you will only dare eat things I replaced in the last day or so, despite the fact that everything on the table started out as a "desirable species." Some of the most delectable dishes now reek from mold and decay. If I suddenly stopped replacing your daily selection, your performance would take a nasty drop. The problem was, of course, low density feeding! Had I invited enough people to constitute a real "Clean Plate Club," and replaced everything in the same way, every meal would have been as good as the last.

As soon as we made stock density a factor in grazing planning, my clients began to notice better and better animal performance. Higher stock densities led to a higher proportion of plants being grazed. This boosted my spirits for a while, but soon the results became spotty again. But now, having hundreds of planned grazing cells in five countries under my eye, ample evidence led to a diagnosis.

Livestock performance appeared to have been maintained in the past for prolonged times with low density grazing. But this was only an illusion. Individuals did perform better but herd sizes were steadily dropping and supplement costs rising. That conclusion eliminated any further need to compare the cells to traditional practices. Clearly a new problem, unique to the cells, was developing over time, and it definitely affected animals in high rainfall areas most.

Continuing the smorgasbord analogy, the reason evidently lay in the existence of different kitchens supplying the food. One cuisine might go stale much faster than the next. On the range, low rainfall and highly mineralized soils proved most forgiving. These areas supported grass populations that had less fiber, shorter height, and better curing properties. Higher mineralization in the plants most likely kept rumenal microflora populations high in the animals, thus maximizing digestive efficiency and leading to better performance, even on old forage. Higher rainfall areas, characterized by leached soils, produced generally taller, tougher grasses of much higher fiber content. Older specimens had little or no feed value compared to plants of similar age in highly mineralized soils. Without heavy protein and energy supplementation rumenal microflora most likely decreased and thus livestock performance fell badly.

Higher stock density should have mitigated the problem and appeared to on some ranches but not others. Why? I suspected timing made a difference, but did not at first know how.

A look at the planning sheets from many grazing cells, as well as the stock densities and the state of the forage, led to the conclusion that the poorest results came from the poorest planning and the poorest monitoring of plant growth and livestock condition. Some operations it turned out had let planning develop into a rigid scheduling that *had* to be followed at all cost. Although technically they had done the planning I asked for, on the ground they in fact carried out a rigid grazing rotation. I called it planned rigidity and eventually had to drop a very sophisticated planning procedure as I discovered that the more work a rancher put into it, the more inflexibly he stuck to it regardless of what monitoring might show.

Using the smorgasbord analogy once more, people suddenly found they didn't have time to eat all they actually could have. The butler moved them on half-way through the main course. The food that was eaten got replaced according to standard practice, but the rest grew a little staler. When again the next day they had only ten minutes to clean up, the stale got staler. Once again, when matters progressed until they had to eat stale food, performance dropped. Technically we had enough people (density) at the table to keep the food fresh, but without enough time to clean their plates, much of the food grew stale anyway.

On the land, the problem is compounded by varying daily growth rates and varying degrees of fiber and mineral content in the plants.

Illustration 28-1 is an aerial view of a ranch that has seen many years of low density grazing. The mosaic of heavily overgrazed and seriously overrested patches shows clearly. This situation developed at the old correct

Illustration 28-1. Low density grazing pattern seen from the air with two different stocking rates. Coahuilla, Mexico.

stocking rate and under prolonged grazing periods. When I've shown similar pictures before, some viewers have insisted that the pattern was due to soil differences and not grazing at low densities. So I've taken this picture at the fence between two paddocks that were grazed at different densities. The land in the foreground, grazed at very low density, shows less of the light-colored patches where plants are heavily overgrazed and thus shows clearly that the mosaic seen is due to grazing patterns and not soil.

Sketch A in figure 28-2 shows such an area on which a rancher intends to make an eight-paddock radial grazing cell so he can graze his animals on a rapid, but fixed, rotation (i.e., move the animals every few days regardless of growth rates). The old, stale material will affect the animals adversely as he starts to move them at higher concentration. Where previously they could scatter over the whole area, seeking out fresh, leafy feed, they can now get to only an eighth of the land, where most of the forage has already gone stale.

At this point the rancher has to make some management choices. He

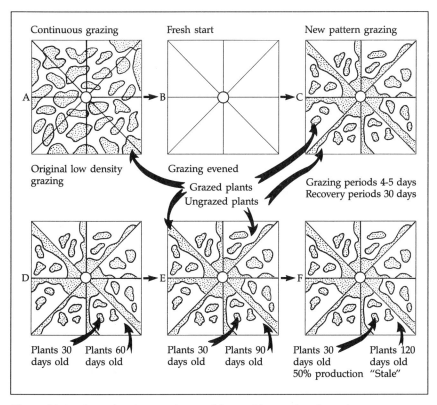

Figure 28-2. Low density grazing problem with rotational grazing.

can either burn the range to even up the forage as tradition would indicate, or he can select another tool to eliminate the old material. He could use animal impact in the form of herd effect, which we will cover in the next chapter, or he could mow the old grass (technology). He could supplement at a higher level, or he could bite the bullet and accept the performance loss during the first few cycles, recognizing it as a legacy of the past.

In this situation the guidelines of the model will always enable you to choose the answer that fits your goals and position. Assume in this case the rancher burns the stale patches and his herd starts off on completely fresh forage (B), a thirty-day recovery period and four- or five-day grazings. He lucks into good rapid growth following the burn and the animals eat all they can in each paddock. Sketch C shows how they have grazed certain areas and left others, as is normal with short grazing periods and fast growth. They physically could not have eaten more.

The next time around (D) the cattle get most of their diet from the thirty-day growth in the patches they grazed before, leaving much of the grass untouched a second time. This may happen again the following time (E), creating ninety-day-old islands of old feed. Still the cattle may do well enough, unless, as will happen sooner or later, general growth slows down and plants then get overgrazed. The grazed patches will not have produced enough in thirty days, and the animals will be forced to eat the 120-day-old material next time around (F).

In an area of low rainfall and high mineralization, performance may drop too little to draw immediate attention. In high rainfall areas the old grass will have so little nutritional value that serious hunger appears almost at once. The operator then has four choices: speed up his rotation, slow it down, forge ahead on the old rotation, or reduce animal numbers. In every case I have ever seen where the rancher relied on tradition and intuition without benefit of training in HRM, he has stuck to his old schedule, sped up the rotation, or reduced animal numbers.

A more rapid rotation in that situation will lead to a short-term benefit to the cattle as they move onto new ground, albeit limited by the rank patches in all paddocks. However, the quicker moves cut the recovery time for the heavily grazed patches at a time of slow growth, assuring overgrazing and increased problems. Simply keeping the old schedule or reducing numbers does not address the problem of overgrazing of some plants and overresting of others and, thus, when these choices are made difficulties increase as well.

As Chapter 26 explained, two factors govern the *rate* of drop-off in nutrition in a paddock—the quality and volume of forage at the start and the stock density. The higher the density and the poorer the forage, the quicker the decline. If patches of overrested grass limit the amount of ground actually in use, a more rapid fall will ensue because although the paddocks remain the same size, the area of land actually usable decreases.

Grazing on fixed rotations leads to other problems worth mentioning here as well. If animals always move to an adjacent paddock on a predictable schedule, they quickly learn the routine and tend to feed mostly on the side of each paddock nearest the fence they know they will cross next. In some cases, by milling around the gates, cattle have trained ranchers to speed up the rotation against their better judgment. No logic says that moves have to follow a circular pattern. Many reasons may dictate otherwise and should be taken into account in well-planned grazing.

In the last example proper planning and monitoring of daily growth rates would have produced the patterns shown in diagram 28-3. During fast growth (A), short grazing periods—allowing low animal days of consumption—would have led to fewer severely grazed plants, as before. Each time in a paddock, stock would have taken only 6.4 Animal Days per Acre (ADA). When monitoring detected slowing growth rates, moves would slow down, and the herd could take up to 20.8 ADA from each paddock in each grazing period, as shown in B, and graze a larger proportion of plants. By moving the animals according to plant growth rates, both overgrazing and over-resting are thus minimized and the plants more evenly used. This helps keep the performance of land and livestock higher over time.

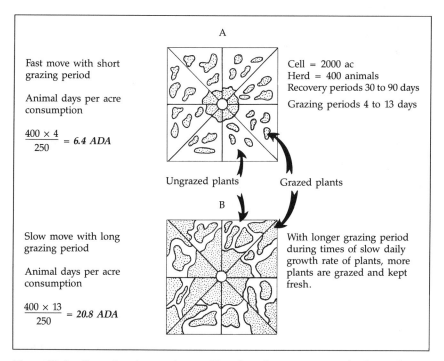

A

Fast move with short grazing period

Animal days per acre consumption

$$\frac{400 \times 4}{250} = 6.4\ ADA$$

Cell = 2000 ac
Herd = 400 animals
Recovery periods 30 to 90 days
Grazing periods 4 to 13 days

Ungrazed plants   Grazed plants

B

Slow move with long grazing period

Animal days per acre consumption

$$\frac{400 \times 13}{250} = 20.8\ ADA$$

With longer grazing period during times of slow daily growth rate of plants, more plants are grazed and kept fresh.

Figure 28-3.   Low density grazing problem largely overcome with planned grazing (plan-monitor-control-replan).

Whenever livestock moves have to be slowed down with slower daily growth rates, individual animal performance is likely to be less than it would have been on continued fast moves. However, as we have just learned, where continued fast moves benefit the animals in the short term they damage both land and animals in the long term.

Where fiber is low and mineralization high, an accumulation of old grass will affect performance little, if at all. In such areas, cells with as few as eight paddocks typically show the patchiness of low density grazing at the beginning of the dormant season, but by the end, stock and wildlife have cleaned up the previously ungrazed plants with no drop in performance.

In areas of high rainfall and leached soils, however, animal performance almost always suffers when paddocks are few. During rapid growth, short grazing periods do not allow them to graze a high proportion of plants, so the bulk of the plants may become too rank. During slow growth, the long grazing periods force them to take old material that has lost much of its value and become fibrous.

This dilemma can be overcome when paddock numbers reach as high as eighty to one hundred or where animals are herded within a similar number of grazing areas. In these cases animals can move every day or two to fresh grazing without worry of overgrazing because they wouldn't return to any one paddock before eighty to two hundred days. This would almost always be adequate time for plants to recover in the growing season whether growth was fast or slow and as stock density is great, feeding is spread over more plants keeping them fresh.

In the days before I understood the full implications of stock density and time, I cost my long-suffering clients many thousands of dollars in poor animal performance by trying to obtain high animal performance at low paddock numbers in high rainfall leached-soil areas.[1] In my ignorance I had started some of them off on eight- to ten-paddock cells in one-hundred-inch rainfall areas. Now, assuming a production goal of high animal performance, in that situation I would never dream of suggesting anything less than forty paddocks right at the beginning. That would allow enough density to ensure that animals would graze or trample a high proportion of plants in each paddock during each grazing period, keeping them fresh and nutritious. Though range experts continually confuse the point, that is not at all the same as increasing utilization by forcing stock to deplete the forage.

Many people are so locked into the belief that increasing stock density means grazing off all plants severely that they are blind to other possibilities, such as the effects produced when grazing *time* is simultaneously reduced. Illustration 28-2 is a view of the boundary between two ranches in a fifty-inch rainfall area in Zimbabwe. Both ranchers were clients of mine in the early days. One client was wealthy and quickly developed to forty paddocks per herd. The other client was deep in debt and was only able to develop six paddocks per herd in the same period.

Illustration 28-2.   Two ranches at different levels of paddocking and stock density. Six paddocks per herd on the left and forty paddocks per herd on the right. Grass plants on the right are more closely spaced and more vigorous. Chipinge, Zimbabwe.

Both of these clients were using the biological planning described in Chapter 40 and in the companion volume and doing a good job of it, but the contrast in their results is striking. Where we had forty paddocks per herd, and thus higher stock density and shorter grazing periods, the forage had grown denser, leafier, and less fibrous. Livestock performance was also much higher.

High paddock numbers, however, demand careful management and monitoring. In Chapter 24 I discussed the acute overgrazing in a forty-one-paddock cell that ran for four years on an inflexible rotation. Illustration 28-3 shows that overrest also resulted from this practice and has killed whole mats of plants. The overrest came from a series of fast moves that were made regardless of growth rate. This permitted some plants to become so stale that they could never again be grazed.

Virtually all of the ungrazed plants belonged to highly desirable species, but on that granite soil in that climate (thirty-five-inch rainfall) anything that went untouched through two seasons became so inedible that nothing short of death would force a cow to try it. Planning and monitoring could have prevented the situation completely, and even at a late and dangerous stage,

Illustration 28-3. Severe overrest resulting from rotational grazing has killed large areas of grass in the right-hand paddock. These plants are grey, oxidizing, and dying and are thus ungrazed. Plants on the left are green, growing, and grazed. Igava Ranch, Zimbabwe.

herd effect (as covered in the next chapter) could have rectified it before animal performance dropped. Even at high stock densities, planning is abandoned at your own peril.

Livestock, even at remarkably high densities, place their hooves carefully and do not as a rule trample coarse old plants or break soil surfaces. Nor do they trample steep eroding soil banks or dense brush and thus we need to alter their behavior at times as fear of predation once did. Where stock density is applied mainly to enhance animal performance, herd effect is applied mainly to create or maintain stable grassland communities in brittle environments.

29

Herd Effect

Herd effect is that aspect of animal impact that occurs when many animals move together or mill around on the land in an excited manner, treading down old, coarse plant material, raising dust at times, and chipping the soil surface.

Though such behavior strongly affects grassland succession, and wild herds in truly wild conditions exhibit it frequently, neither herding game nor livestock produce much herd effect without outside stimulus. Inducing herd effect thus comprises one of the biggest challenges in the management of brittle environment grasslands and the difficulty of inducing it enough is a weakness that future management might confront.

Without question, the large herding animals, their predators, the grassland soils, and biotic communities developed together. It now appears to us that the predators played a major role in producing herd effect by causing their prey to bunch together for protection. Many excellent television documentaries show how hard great cats and wolves must work to beat that defense and isolate the weak calf or the aging bull in order to bring it down.

While the carnivores do their job, ungulates in the milling herd, concentrated for protection, do not respect the grass and brush beneath their hooves as they do when grazing unmolested. Free from fear of fang, claw, and spear, even instinctively timid wild animals soon lose the habit of vigilance, scatter widely when grazing, and avoid stepping on anything as uncomfortable as a tussock of old grass or spiny shrub.

Starting in my game department days I gradually built on the observation that wherever predators caused bunching, the concentrated dung and urine of the herd also induced movement, and this in turn regulated the overgrazing of plants by governing their time of exposure and reexposure to animals. Wherever the predators and their large prey were not present for any reason over prolonged periods, the grassland became much more fragile, plant spacing widened, and more algae flourished on ground that became bare between plants. Rhizomes, runners, and stolons, rather than seeds, became the main agent of grass propagation.

That said, however, researchers and ranchers may take heart from the fact that herd effect does not arise only from fear of predation. Many examples can be seen of animals bunching in an eager or playful manner and having the same impact.

I first began to observe herd effect without realizing its vital role in the desertification problem. During a period of my life I lived close to large buffalo herds followed by a varied host of predators. At times I would pick up tracks several days old and follow them to find a herd. In places even an inexperienced tracker could follow the spoor at a trot. Elsewhere the trail would dissipate almost entirely though the country did not change. That happened whenever the animals calmed down and fed. At such times their hooves avoided coarse plants and did not break soil surfaces as much, nor did they trample old plant material, as they did when bunched and excited.

Since then I have observed the same differences among all herding animals and even humans. When tracking men, as I did often during Zimbabwe's long civil war, one learns much about the mental and physical state of the quarry by noting the way he places his feet. Individuals in an excited group, walking and talking, leave a very different trail than the same people walking quietly alone. Nor does a panicking person place his feet like a calmer man.

Without predators, and not forgetting man who has stalked big game for millennia beyond number, most ungulates acquire behavior characterized by nearly unbroken calm. Now, several million years of predator-induced herd effect has given way to manmade protection in the last second of time. We generally fail to grasp what that means to a piece of ground and the community living on it in a brittle environment.

The vast scale of desertification in the world today attests to the enormous impact. We would understand instinctively devastation caused by witholding rain showers that had occurred for eons, but the damage to water cycles caused by eliminating herd effect has in reality done that very thing.

Tragically, in the brittle environments of most continents only pitiful remnants of once prolific wild herds and predators still survive. To simulate their presence on the land and try to restore communities and water cycles, we now realistically have only livestock at our disposal. This realization changed me from a passionate foe of the livestock industry to a collaborator in search of better management. The alternative of continued deterioration of the land that ultimately had to support all life was unacceptable.

In the last chapter we defined stock density as a function of paddock size and number of animals. Herd effect, on the other hand, results from animal behavior regardless of paddock size. Long ago the world's most productive brittle grasslands, such as those in North America and Africa, had extremely low stock density, as the paddock was a whole continent. However, as herds were so vast and wolves, cats, hyenas, wild dogs, and hunting tribes so prevalent, herd effect was great and applied somewhere most of the time.

Chapter 20 explained that the tool of animal impact is applied through the guidelines of stock density and herd effect. A situation may call for one or the other or both for maximum effect. A number of researchers have published papers concluding that animal impact does not produce the sort of changes in succession, water and mineral cycles, and energy flow that I describe in my work. In fact, they designed their projects without really understanding the totally new concept of herd effect and made no effort to apply it. Thus they effectively proved that *stock density* does not do what I claim *herd effect* does. In two of the research projects that I have in mind, high stock density was applied to brittle environment communities that really needed herd effect. The herds, in fact, were minute—in one case consisting of two steers, which could not have done much even if the researchers had excited them.[1]

Why researchers studying animal impact have consistently ignored herd effect is not easy to understand. While it cannot be isolated for research, herd effect can easily be observed and monitored in the field. Grazing too cannot be isolated but many researchers have still studied it and given us many insights. Perhaps our belief that heavy trampling is damaging is so deep that we cannot bring ourselves to investigate a *known* fact.

In practice herd effect requires two factors:

1. Large herds—the larger the herd the greater the effect. A herd of several thousand animals has a vastly different impact than two steers.

2. Excited behavior—even vast herds, when scattered and unexcited, produce no herd effect and thus little animal impact (the soil surface may not even appear disturbed).

When we domesticated livestock and protected them, we removed much of the tendency to produce herd effect. This holds true for the American rancher as well as the Andalusian shepherd and African nomad. Fencing and grazing systems designed to spread livestock evenly over the land in a totally unnatural manner have exacerbated the problem, severely disrupting the evolutionary interdependence of animals, plants, and soils that has come down from creation.

When we drive animals in herds we do produce herd effect of course, but too often they go over the same ground and generally in the same direction. The severe trailing this causes has reinforced our fear of animal impact.

Unfortunately, even though we can now define a positive application of herd effect, actually generating it remains a problem. Obviously wolves and lions enlisted in the management of domestic sheep and cattle might eat into profit. Many people, however, do not see that the same problem arises in the management of wild animals even in our national parks. In many of these, predators are low and are kept low by man, and typically subsistence hunting by indigenous human populations—a vital feature for millions of years—is now rarely permitted. Frequently a limited land base will not allow a herd size large enough to provide adequate trampling or sufficient to sustain enough predators.

Now we must learn how to simulate the predator-induced behavior, about which we have learned much over the past twenty-five years. The most successful methods so far involve a combination of training and attracting to any reward that induces excitement and is consumed quickly. Supplemental feed cubes (cake to many American ranchers), a bale of hay, or a few handfuls of granular salt for animals purposely deprived of salt will work.

Long-lasting blocks of supplement, molasses/urea liquid licks, or salt blocks do not. They do not generally excite the animals, which come for them a few at a time and linger too long in the vicinity, pulverizing the surface and excessively compacting the soil. In contrast, proper herd effect chips bare surfaces, allowing the soil to breathe, and produces only slight compaction below the surface in most circumstances.

The discovery that salt in granular form did excite cattle represents the kind of creative breakthrough that affirms again the difficulty in seeing beyond habit. Salt blocks are simply a part of the landscape on most ranches. It took one rancher, Ron Moll, to ask himself if cattle needed continual access to salt. When they got it as a treat, he found they became as excited as they would for hay. In granular form he could spread it easily, and a large herd consumed it quickly enough to eliminate the danger of overtrampling.

Training cattle is another simple solution. It requires only a small whistle and constant reward as the livestock respond. If you have a constantly changing herd, as ranchers running steers often do, it helps to hold back a few trained animals so the new group learns faster. Once they learn to respond, however, a herd can be drawn in an excited bunch to any spot on the land where herd effect is called for to build toward the landscape goal required.

Illustration 29-1 shows part of a herd of two thousand animals on a Texas ranch. The herd has no fear of predators and is spread out in the fashion typical today. Even young animals lie in the grass away from others, fearless and safe. Illustration 29-2 is a close-up view of the ground itself under the influence of this large herd. The soil is barely impacted, and a slick of algae covers the surface despite three years of high stock density. Succession does not move easily on it and soil respiration is badly impeded.

Illustration 29-1.   Part of a herd of two thousand animals widely scattered and calm although at high stock density on the range. Barlite Ranch, Texas.

Illustration 29-2.   Close-up of the soil surface between grasses in illustration 29-1. The soil is hard capped and unable to breathe.

Illustration 29-3.   The herd being attracted and excited to cause herd effect on the soil.

In illustration 29-3 the herd has been attracted to the area shown in illustration 29-2. Illustration 29-4 shows the excited hoof action as the cattle concentrate; their hooves kick up dust. Illustration 29-5 shows the same piece of ground about three minutes later. Soil respiration is improved, water can penetrate faster, and succession can move forward more quickly. Any knowledgeable gardener, going back several thousand years, would read the ground that way. The only novelty is the realization that livestock can do the same job periodically over billions of acres of the world's watersheds, which once had the benefit of herding game.

Occasionally situations arise that allow use of animal impact as a tool without a concern for keeping the time short. Opening a firebreak through very dense brush would, for example. In such cases attractants can be used that hold animals for longer periods, such as a dilute molasses or saline spray over the vegetation, or supplementary blocks. I have seen a mobile trailer with all of the separate minerals (free choice or cafeteria system) used to move animal impact around, as shown in illustration 29-6. This does hold the animals too long, but is still better than static minerals or liquid feed.

The Type of Livestock Matters

While any herd effect is better than none for water cycle management on most brittle watersheds, the type of animal is important on some. Almost any livestock—sheep, goats, cattle, or horses—can produce adequate impact on sandy soil. However, on clay soils that compact badly at the surface, sheep and goats have limited effect. Cattle or horses are required to really move succession and improve respiration. On some soils, horses have a much better impact than cattle, but unfortunately we seldom have very large horse herds, so cattle must suffice.

Illustration 29-4.   Excited animals place their hooves carelessly and raise dust.

Illustration 29-5.   Close-up of the soil surface after applying herd effect. The soil is chipped and able to breathe and succession can move forward once more.

Illustration 29-6. Mobile mineral wagon with a full spectrum of trace and macrominerals. Transvaal, South Africa.

The vegetation also makes a difference to the type of animal you select. Where sheep and goats in animated herds can trample short vegetation, very tall old grass clumps escape. The small stock simply flows around them. For such situations and for opening up very dense brush to let in light and increase grass growth, only larger animals such as cattle will serve.

Herd Size Matters

When seeking to apply herd effect, the small area actually impacted in the manner shown in illustration 29-3 will often disappoint you. Two thousand head will seriously affect an area only about fifty yards across each time they are attracted, though somewhat lesser impact grades out from there.

Deeply rooted emotion and myth surround the question of cattle herd size in particular. Prominent cattlemen heavily condemned me for even suggesting that herds of two hundred cows could be run and still breed well. Beyond one hundred forty cows lay the edge of the world and a long fall to disaster. Nevertheless, we have gradually increased herd sizes without encountering any problems. To date we have not yet had one scrap of evidence that conception rate or weaner weight in breeding herds depends on anything outside quality of handling, health, and nutrition. We have no evidence yet of any drop in performance in any large herd, handled well in adequate facilities on well-planned grazing.

Having worked with vast buffalo herds as well as cattle herds of up to five thousand, I have no doubt in my own mind that for watershed management in brittle environments the larger the herd the better. Herds of two to five thousand head followed by longer recovery produce far better results than small ones of two to five hundred followed by shorter recovery periods. Unfortunately land is now so divided and attitudes so entrenched that we often have to make do with small herds and poor ratios of grazing/trampling to recovery.

In the future, as knowledge increases and attitudes change, I believe that fewer, larger herds will become the principal tool in watershed management on the public lands of America and many of the desert fringes of the world. Today, fear that vast herds will destroy land, especially along streams and rivers, dominates many policy decisions. The streams of America were nevertheless in generally superb condition in days gone by when subjected to periodic very large herd effect. Now subjected to a few animals continually overgrazing and trampling, they have reached a deplorable state. Attitudes will not change until people actually witness what can be done.

Remember the donkey analogy. It was easy to imagine that land subjected to three hundred sixty-five donkeys for one day might be in good condition a year later. A herd of five thousand animals would normally give a particular piece of ground *five minutes* of concentrated impact in many months or even years.

The truth of this becomes clear as you plan for herd effect. You will think at first that it is an easy matter. When you actually compute how small the impacted areas usually are and how few times animals come into a paddock in a year you will be hard put to treat country that has suffered from a century or two of low density grazing and partial rest.

We do not yet in fact know if we can simulate the herd effect of old sufficiently. The past herds were of many different species and vulnerable to predation day and night, year-round. In the millions of years past, an area might have been home range to herds of many different animals, each bunched for about sixteen hours a day while not feeding. Nothing like that exists today. We typically have one species, usually cattle or sheep, feeding or resting unbunched for over twenty-three hours a day and concentrated on a smidgen of land for only five or ten minutes.

We don't yet know if that will prove enough, but results are encouraging where a conscientious effort is made to greatly increase herd size and apply herd effect, as was illustrated in Chapter 13 (illustrations 13-3, 13-4, and 13-5).

The guideline of herd effect has concerned a tool new to us and of great power. We had to have a basic understanding of the guidelines concerning time, grazing, and animal impact before all of the guidelines we use in the testing process could make sense. We turn to them now.

30

Whole Ecosystem

The whole ecosystem guideline is the first of the "whether to" or testing guidelines, those that will help you determine whether or not to use a given tool at all as opposed to helping you use it correctly.

Simply stated, this one requires you to consider how any tool affects *all* elements and ecosystem processes in the whole you wish to manage, not just what it does to the thing that interests you most. If you manage for the health of the whole, then various species tend to take care of themselves and thrive within their community. When we manage for a particular species, or "part," with little regard for the whole, we find that the object of our effort all too often dwindles like sand between our fingers.

Unfortunately, most human management now as in the past has the narrow goal of maximizing the number of humans, forgetting that like all living creatures, human numbers shrink when our environment deteriorates. *From our knowledge of ecology and holism, we can predict without any fear of informed contradiction that by single-mindedly managing for mankind we will destroy ourselves.* The thin populations that hang on today amid the ruins of empires now lost to desert attest to this fact.

Among committed environmentalists one would not expect to have to argue this principle. The environmental movement developed specifically to refute the notion that short-term profit to immediate investors justified pollution and disruption of Nature on a vast scale. As a practical matter, however, environmentalists all too frequently succumb to narrowly conceived appeals to save this or that endangered species, to fund some reclamation scheme, or back a piece of legislation when true solutions demand a broader view.

Many people dedicated to saving a particular species find this thinking surprisingly difficult to translate into action, as many of our various laws and programs for saving the ferret, the eagle, the wild mustang, the condor, the local trout, etc. show. How many commit enormous resources into protection, often to the detriment of other species, and little into regeneration of the whole?

No amount of captive breeding, plantings, culling of predators, poisoning of competitors, or other narrowly focused actions will bring back a creature that has lost its niche. The only way to truly save any species is to manage for a healthy, whole ecosystem.

In applying the HRM model to any situation, you will have defined the whole encompassed by your management and the three-part goal you hope to achieve within it. In planning which tools to apply to reach your goal, this guideline then asks, "Will the tool under consideration move the whole toward the goal?"

The tool of fire is commonly abused and makes a good example of how to tackle this question. Because fire invigorates mature grass and visibly consumes brush, people frequently burn to promote grass and reduce brush, especially if their production goals favor wild or domestic grazers.

If your goals involve an open grassland in order to meet production and quality of life needs, and certain areas are moving toward dense brushland, you might consider applying fire, but you would review the effects of fire on the four ecosystem processes.

- *Succession:* Will fire actually kill the brush in question or merely damage the aboveground parts temporarily? What other fire-sensitive species are present that you do not want to kill? How will other species and their young fare in the microenvironment that fire creates at the surface? What species will find opportunity in the bare soil exposed by the flame? How often will fire be necessary?
- *Water cycle:* Fire will damage it some. How much damage can the land stand? What loss in soil structure and aeration quality can the land afford?
- *Mineral cycle:* How well is this functioning now? When the fire exposes the surface and reduces its population of microorganisms, how long will it take to build them back to levels that cycle minerals efficiently? Do you have ways to cope without burning again before that?
- *Energy flow:* How much of the present energy flow enhances production goals? Would this be increased or reduced by fire?

If many of these answers turn up negative, you should consider another tool to stop the brush. Ideally that would be one that would maintain grass root vigor without exposing the soil between plants or aggravating the brush problem by causing more stems to emerge. You might well decide in this particular case to use very high animal impact (herd effect) and apply limited doses of herbicide (technology) in the worst places, but again only if this passed the same testing.

The world abounds in examples of failures stemming from failure to look at the broad picture. I think back to Zimbabwe, where early in this century vast ranches in the southern part of the country had high populations of sable and roan antelope alongside significant herds of wildebeest and zebra. As the ranchers regarded the latter as serious competitors, they shot them on sight by the thousands, while the majestic sable and roan, valued by the government as royal game, enjoyed complete protection from hunters.

Nevertheless, within about thirty years the roan and sable disappeared completely, while the shooting of zebra and wildebeest continues, now for the commercial market. During this time the four ecosystem processes in the area have changed profoundly. Succession is simple and suppressed, water and mineral cycles are badly damaged, and energy flow has declined to a fraction of its potential as the land desertifies, and this, not hunting policy, explains what happened to the game.

Zebra and wildebeest survive over a wide range of successional communities, while the sable and roan thrive only in a much narrower range that is higher in succession. Figure 30-1 shows what happened. European colonists found wonderfully productive cattle country in condition A, but by the 1950s they had reduced it to condition B through their manner of applying the management tools. Overgrazing of plants, prolonged low impact of cattle, fencing that impeded game movement, killing of predators that had promoted game concentration and movement, and increased use of fire caused succession to slip below the level that supports roan and sable.

Besides the roan and sable, other doomed species included the fish that

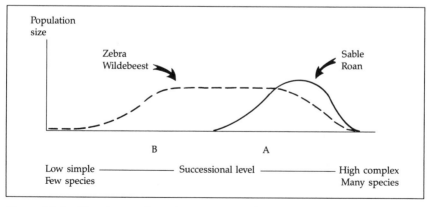

Figure 30-1. The destruction of two species of protected game animals under conventional grazing practices.

once lived in perennial streams and the fish eagles and kingfishers that fed on them, plus thousands of creatures too small to notice but which played a crucial role in overall stability.

Typical policies toward predators present another example of deeply ingrained blindness that the whole ecosystem guideline might enlighten. We need much more research into the role of predators, but we at last sense how the relationship between predators and herding animals keeps brittle environments vital. We can only guess at the number of other situations where our uninformed destruction of predators has cost us dearly.

Livestock owners the world over have tended to regard all predators as enemies. Nowhere has this aversion led to worse extremes than the United States where ranchers and government go to incredible lengths to kill predators while making little genuine effort to live with them or protect livestock by other simple means.

I have worked with ranchers who went out of business killing predators while not making the slightest effort to protect their stock. In one case the rancher had access to at least half a dozen well-known and tested methods to eliminate losses to coyotes without killing a single one, yet he kept killing coyotes until he went broke. That his war on the coyote did not save him was not surprising. Typically, the predators that take on man and his livestock are particular individuals that become increasingly cunning as attempts to get them fail.

Killing coyotes does little good, if you fail to get the one that is killing your stock. No matter how many you kill that haven't acquired the habit, the killer remains, becomes ever more clever, and will in time educate others. If you doubt that hunting animals do learn destructive habits from each other, consider how quickly a cow that breaks through fences can pass on the trick.

With man-eating lions, tigers, and leopards as well as problem hippo, elephants, bears, etc., we have long known that one must deal with the particular animal, not all of them. We have the same principle when one of our own kind becomes a murderer. Killing people at random is no response. We have to try, no matter how hard, to catch the murderer.

Some years ago in Zimbabwe, a nasty-tempered elephant had brought railroad maintenance to a virtual halt on an important section of a much used line. Each night he harrassed the workers as they slept and so terrified them that they refused to turn out the next day. Several bulls were shot in the vicinity, but each time the section camp turned in in peace it woke in terror. By the time I arrived the rogue had acquired a definite style. I waited on the edge of the camp at night and when an elephant singled me out for attack I knew I had the culprit. After that, despite many elephants in the area, the camp slept in peace.

In Chapter 11 I referred to a research study in which only one species of predator was removed from a community. With no other disturbance, as we saw, within one year the fifteen common species in that community had been reduced to eight. Few simple studies have illustrated so clearly the vital stabilizing role of predators in communities. Unfortunately in many areas, particularly those now set aside as national parks, man was the main predator who kept animals healthy and wild, but today's sightseeing crowds want tame animals.

Many years ago Charles Elton, one of the earliest animal ecologists (as they were then called), described the Eltonian pyramid of numbers. In concept it resembles the energy pyramid shown in Chapter 13 (figure 13-2). While we normally see the relationship in terms of the number of lower animals it takes to support one predator, if predation plays the crucial role we suspect it does, the pyramid also shows how many prey animals depend on a single species of predator.

Having been a rancher, I understand the frustration when a wild hunter turns to man's domestic stock, but it does not excuse the wholesale slaughter of innocent predators that play a vital part in balancing populations, including many that are agricultural pests.

Certainly as I think back on the many years that I have worked with croplands, rangelands, livestock, and game populations, the healthiest situations contained high levels of predators. Conversely, the most unhealthy situations for the land, crops, wildlife, and stock have always had a history of predator persecution. I don't believe this is coincidence. Clearly we have much to learn and many attitudes to change before we will see intelligent and wise management of our ecosystem as a whole.

The whole ecosystem guideline also has particular importance in assessing the policies of the so-called Green Revolution, that era when we had supreme confidence that modern high-tech agriculture could feed the world without any problem. As a result we now use without question fertilizers, herbicides, pesticides, extraordinary machines, and other tools under the heading of Technology. These have encouraged monoculture plantings of annual crops, another practice rarely doubted as sound. However, abundant evidence now indicates the likely damage to all four of the ecosystem processes that sustain us.

When phasing farms from Green Revolution agriculture to more scientifically (and holistically) sound practices we'll most likely have to use measures that fail the Whole Ecosystem test, just to stay solvent. However, this is not done in ignorance. Knowing that a measure is unsound allows you to start shifting your management in the time bought by its use and find a way back to sustainable agricultural practices.

In the past we have grown accustomed to judging the various management options at hand only on whether or not they are cost effective or cash flow well. Giving other tests prior importance comes hard at first. Before the long-term returns come in it may take a bit of faith to abandon a seemingly profitable course, but the payoff does come.

In practice, when using the model in any of its modes, you will not have to go through the testing guidelines in any particular order, but you should go through them all unless a tool fails one or more outright. In time you will develop a feel for which of them a tool is least likely to pass and so consider that first.

This particular guideline serves to remind us that the whole is the only reality in nature and thus the only unit that we can manage. In the long run we cannot manage any species, be it humans, a rare bird, or a field of potatoes, without doing so through the management of the whole. Management of a rare species without regard to the whole will doom that species. Management of a monoculture crop will also fail eventually, as it damages the whole.

As one of the "whether to" tests, the whole ecosystem guideline assures that all tools are evaluated for their likely effects on all four ecosystem processes in terms of our goals. Next we'll look at the guideline for finding the weak links that hamper progress.

31

Weak Link

A chain stretched to breaking will fail, by definition, at the weakest link. At any moment in time every chain has one and only one weakest link that alone accounts for the strength of the entire chain, regardless of how strong other links might be.

To strengthen a chain when resources are limited one must always attend only to the weakest link. Other links, no matter how frail they appear, are nonproblems until weaker links are fixed. If $100 would correct the weakest link, and we spent $200 to make sure, we would have theoretically squandered $100, because after the first $100 repair, the chain has a different weak link on which the second $100 should have been spent.

The ecosystem, our only source of true wealth, functions as a chain of processes, and we cannot afford to waste the wealth it generates by investing in any but the weakest of them. The same applies to man-hours of endeavor. Unless an undertaking affords us actual pleasure as a quality of life goal, we normally try to spend our working time on the most critical obstacle between us and our goal.

The undetected weak link can cause mighty undertakings to fail outright or suffer continual setbacks. Thus, we have a guideline that compels us to check our operations and knowledge constantly for the weak link at any moment that impedes progress toward our goals.

To identify the weak link you will find it helpful to divide your resources into biological, human, and financial categories, and consider each one separately.

Biological Resources

The weak link guideline almost always applies in the testing of tools that influence the successional process, typically for the purpose of increasing or decreasing the success of a certain population in the community.

Every organism in its life cycle has a point of greatest vulnerability, a weakest link. Recognize this, and you can apply tools quite efficiently to the four ecosystem foundation blocks to increase or decrease that species' ability to recruit new members to its population. If we mean to prevent a grassland from shifting toward woody plants or problem forbs (weeds), then it becomes vital to find the weak link in their life cycle.

Generally plants are most vulnerable during their initial establishment when the seed has germinated, and root and leaf must find sustaining conditions in a limited time. If seeds, once sprouted, do not encounter the right soil, moisture, temperature, and sunlight for long enough to establish, it makes no difference how many seeds are produced or spread. None will survive.

Understanding this concept enables us at minimal cost to manage and control encroachment by undesirable forbs, brush, grasses, insects, and so on. Otherwise we tend to combat the population as a whole, often committing expensive and dangerous technologies to attack mature, resistant pests, that new, unscathed recruits immediately replace. The next chapter on cause and effect will develop this theme further.

The same principle works in reverse when the goal calls for advancing the successional process from a low level. Where complexity has been severely reduced, advance depends on every organism present. In some areas where several centuries of overgrazing and inadequate animal impact (partial rest) have eliminated perennial grasses entirely, the weak link would be establishment of that first plant. Without it there can be no others. After it, the population increases geometrically.

The survival of that first plant is far more crucial than the establishment of those that follow. The old anecdote about the penny that doubles every day illustrates why. If I agree to give you a penny today and then double the money daily, you would have over $10 million by month's end. However, if I didn't happen to have a penny that first day and waited until the second, by the thirty-first you would only have $5 million. By contrast, if I came up one penny short on the sixteenth day you would only lose $16. Obviously each penny, or seed plant, has tremendous impact at the outset, but less as the geometric progression advances.

In practice, this point is often overlooked. The rancher who wants to advance his annual cheat grass range to perennial species may allow, for instance, a couple of horses free rein of the place throughout the year. When this happens, the first perennial grasses that try to establish are exposed to 2 x 365 = 730 horse-days of grazing, most of them when the cheat grass has dried off, and the horses have every incentive to scavenge remorselessly for every blade of green.

Correcting the weak link in this case means changing the management of the horses. The same 730 horse-days of grazing done by 365 horses in two days of the year would of course give perennials plenty of time to establish and the intense animal impact would in fact help their cause immensely. Later, after the first perennials have multiplied into millions, two continually grazing horses, though damaging, are probably no longer the weak link.

Maybe you're too impatient to await the arrival of that first plant, and you decide to reseed on a grand scale. This seldom pays, because you are attempting to introduce a higher successional species into a low successional environment where it will encounter great difficulties, but even if that is not the case it violates the principle of the weakest link. If higher successional grasses can germinate and survive, then by the doubling penny principle, you can correct the weak link to dramatic effect with only a few seeding nuclei.

Acres of seeding are simply gilding the lily. Yank a few seeding plants, roots, dirt, and all, from other areas, and cast them about in spots where you believe they may flourish. Make this a rainy day job, when other work has been halted and the pickup happens to pass through an area where a pocket of higher successional grasses remains, rather than one that involves additional time or effort.

On my own ranch I used this technique successfully to recover large patches of bare, eroding ground. Without any favored treatment, the seeding nuclei expanded and did the job within a couple of seasons under the same grazing and animal impact as the surrounding land.

Human Resources

When management makes no progress and projects constantly have to be restarted, look to weakness in one of three areas: the top administrator or owner, the structure and function of the organization (which usually reflects the attitudes and beliefs of the boss), or the basic knowledge that supports decisions.

Poor leadership at the top—not incompetent staff, bad markets, government policy, droughts, or any of many other forces often cited—is the common cause of failure in agriculture. If the top person in an operation acknowledges shortcomings, a cure often presents little difficulty, and management will improve steadily. However, when leadership cannot recognize or admit how certain beliefs, attitudes, and practices limit and undermine the best of intentions, then little can be done.

The stubborn denial associated with a chemical dependency such as alcoholism, a regrettably common disease, makes for particularly difficult cases. Whatever the reasons, however, when a weak link at the top will not see the problem and face it, the loss of the farm or business is almost inevitable, though everything else under the sun inevitably gets the blame.

In many situations the organization itself constitutes the weak link. The best people in the world can achieve little if ideas and actions hang up in the gears of an organization. Unfortunately the structure longest and best known to us—the autocratic hierarchy—also functions worst in the management of resources, because it stifles the creativity demanded by the complexity of the task. Chapter 42 will take on this question in detail, but it suffices to say here that we can credit a great deal of the mismanagement of our resources to the hierarchical structures that unfortunately entrap government agencies, universities, and many private enterprises.

However, even under the best of structures, the best laid schemes of the best mice and men can still founder on sheer lack of knowledge. Our past failure to halt the spread of deserts is an excellent example. Without an understanding of the four missing keys, most advances in this area resemble attempts to reach the moon by climbing taller and taller trees. It simply can't be done. And more often than we like to admit, we cannot advance without learning, thinking, discovering, and inventing. When that is the case, education, training, open-mindedness, and an atmosphere in the organization that nurtures creativity are the remedies of the hour.

Financial Resources

Every ranch or farm attempts to derive wealth from the conversion of sunlight energy into a usable form through a chain of processes from the growing of plants to the marketing of a product. Obviously whenever strengthening this chain requires money, all proposed investments must pass the weak link test.

Three links generally span the distance from sunshine to cash (as seen in figure 31-2). These are energy conversion, in which sunlight energy becomes useful plant material; product conversion, in which plants are rendered into a marketable form (crops for humans, fodder for livestock, wildlife, fish, etc.); and marketing, in which the product returns the kind of cash we referred to as solar dollars in Chapter 15 because they derive from sunlight captured at the first link.

According to the guideline, only investment in the weak link will result in more wealth at the end. For example, no amount of advertising (market link) expense will profit an operation that turns out a poor product. Nor will a better breed of cattle (product conversion link) help in cases where grass to feed them is lacking.

In practice, however, these fairly obvious distinctions seldom look so clear. Figure 31-1 represents a twenty-thousand-acre ranch in a brittle environment blessed by fifteen inches of rainfall. The ranch has carried a conventional stocking rate for many years on the basis of key indicator plants and a take-half-leave-half policy on grazing of forage. Existing fences divide the ranch into five grazing areas. Serious erosion, soil exposure, and brush encroachment have caused some severe gullying and nearly constant drought symptoms (an impaired water cycle). The debt on the land and its interest payments are crushing, but you intend to survive.

Enter your local extension agent. He says you need to eradicate the brush and cure the gullies right away, and furthermore he offers you a 50 percent cost-sharing program to make it easy. He demonstrates on paper that it will be cost-effective by growing enough extra grass to feed enough extra cattle to return the investment in a moderate number of years. With the government paying half, cash flow planning shows that you theoretically will have the money to pay your share when it comes due.

You are tempted, not only because the terms look good, but because the worn-out land hurts your conscience. You want that dense grassland in

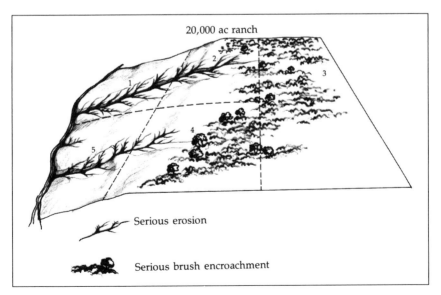

Figure 31-1. Theoretical ranch.

your landscape goal sooner rather than later, and the mechanical operations the agent proposes appear to pass the whole ecosystem test. And yet, after carefully considering the weak link in your ranching, you turn down the offer and buy cattle, yearling stockers perhaps.

Figure 31-2 represents the ranch and the chain from sunlight to solar dollar. You invested mineral or paper dollars when you bought the land. Now you must service that debt and meet your family's quality of life goals with solar dollars from selling livestock. Why shouldn't you put whatever is left into the government's cost-sharing plan?

At your present stocking rate and take-half-leave-half grazing strategy, you are not using approximately 50 percent of the available forage each year. In other words, despite the erosion and brush, you aren't short of forage or energy conversion. The weak link is product conversion. You aren't converting all the grass you already have into a marketable product. Your range condition, though poor, is a nonproblem for you at this point. Money spent increasing grass (to convert more energy) would go to waste since you have no cattle (product) through which to market it.

The land you already have will allow you to plan grazing, increase animal impact, and reduce overgrazing enough to reverse the downward trend in the energy conversion link, so your conscience need not suffer for the land, even though you won't see the rapid improvement you might wish.

Sooner or later, another agent or a fence salesman will come along and

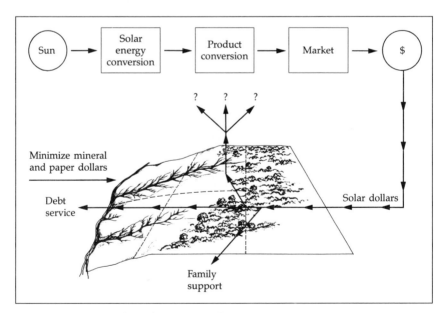

Figure 31-2.   Annual reinvestment cycle.

advise you to cut your five pastures into a hundred little paddocks. You will again decline, however, until you know for sure that forage (energy conversion) is the weak link. Any number of people attending HRM training courses have failed to grasp this point because the prospect of radically improving their landscape through high animal impact and long recovery periods tends to short-circuit clear thinking.

It is important to realize that the level of government cost-sharing has no bearing on the logic of your decision. Even if you got a 90 percent subsidy, the 10 percent you invested would return less than nothing, because of the opportunity cost in not putting it where it would directly increase your yield of solar dollars.

A farming example would follow the same principles. You should not put money into growing a bigger crop, either by increasing acreage or nutrients, if you cannot market what you already produce, or if you could increase the price through better marketing. You should not invest in a bigger and better harvester if your average yield doesn't justify it, and so on. Much of this is just common sense and a cautious, sensible farmer does it without even thinking in terms of the chain.

In a ranching context weakness in the energy conversion link shows up as a shortage of forage for livestock and/or wildlife. In farming, poor crop yields naturally indicate poor energy conversion, but in this era of mechanized, chemical agriculture, exorbitant input costs are a more common symptom. If you must expend vast amounts of petrochemical energy to capture solar energy you will net less in solar wealth.

Many farms go under because the expense of overcoming a damaged natural energy flow keeps climbing. Low prices, high interest rates, and overproduction may be blamed, but no relief there will save a farmer who must import all his fertility from fossil energy to create solar dollars. Once he sees energy conversion as the weak link, he can begin to recover by decreasing the amount of hard-earned solar dollars he invests in fossil energy inputs that do what a healthy soil community does for free.

Where ranchers can detect a weak product conversion link when their animals cannot use available forage, the farmer can spot it when he can produce a solar energy crop (one requiring minimal fossil energy inputs) but can't market it well due to transport or storage costs or inability to harvest completely.

In both ranching and farming, and virtually every other business, the product and market links are closely related. Marketing is usually the weak link when the producer fails to meet the needs of his or her market, such as the manufacturer who continues to build chrome and horsepower into automobiles when consumers want durability and fuel economy, or the cattleman who raises fatty, chemically-tainted beef when buyers want it lean and clean.

Marketing is also the weak link whenever available markets remain untapped because they are not researched, because the product is poorly presented or badly promoted, or because the supply is erratic or out of sync with peak demand. One client of mine did exceptionally well year after year in a market where other onion farmers continually failed. He merely perfected his storage system and released his crop whenever supplies ran low in the local market.

Not all enterprises involve all the links. Hay sold from the field, for example, does not undergo much product conversion compared to boxed beef or frozen orange juice. Yet, one always must consider where value may be added to a calorie of solar energy.

At times the final marketing and solar dollar links become obscure as when the product goes directly to a family or community without a formal market. One can reckon of course what the same thing would cost if purchased.

In some resource management situations the links may be difficult to discern at all. What is going on for instance when your product is a guided elk hunt, and the hunters buy gas at your brother-in-law's gas station, stay in your cousin's motel, and shoot your neighbor's prize bull?

Many cases where production goals are aesthetic, recreational, scientific, or educational may require considerable analysis, and yet the weak link test inevitably applies, even though you cannot always attach precise figures. In an earlier example I talked of misspending exactly $100, but real life never allows that kind of accuracy. Being consistently right with the vast majority of your dollars is what matters.

On the other hand the weak link guideline requires that once the weak link has been discovered it *has* to be dealt with. It is not merely desirable or important to do so. And yet any actions or investments must pass other tests as well to assure that they really do address the situation. Just as perceived problems that don't represent the weak link are nonproblems, so remedies that don't correct primary causes are nonsolutions.

The next chapter on the cause and effect guideline helps refine further decisions about what to do and when to do it.

32

Cause and Effect

The cause and effect guideline winnows out tools and policies that only suppress symptoms of a problem when we should correct the cause. Just as the weak link guideline requires us to eliminate nonproblems from our thinking, so this one exposes nonsolutions.

The logic of going to the root of a situation presents no difficulty to the simplest mind, yet political and economic expediency so often subvert that course that we have developed a culturally programmed habit of doing just the opposite. I don't apologize therefore for using the most simple-minded metaphor to illustrate the point.

If I followed you around and periodically bashed your head with a hammer, you would acquire a headache sooner or later. You might start taking aspirin and then even more powerful pain killers, adding yet more treatments for the side effects. Or you might try to stop my hammering.

Real life presents situations of more deviously related cause and effect. Many symptoms result from multiple causes. Cause and effect is never a simple chain but a mesh extending infinitely in all directions (figure 32-1). Nevertheless, the lesson of the aspirin and the hammer still holds, and as a practical matter we can usually see how cause A leads to B without necessarily knowing why A happened or what will follow B. In other words, *why* I am hitting you on the head should not blind you to the fact that the blows are causing your headache. We can act effectively on that insight (i.e., stop the blows rather than take the aspirin) without untangling the infinite ramifications that qualify it.

The real problem is the temptation of quick fixes, sweetened immensely by the power of modern science to conjure up spectacular ones at the drop

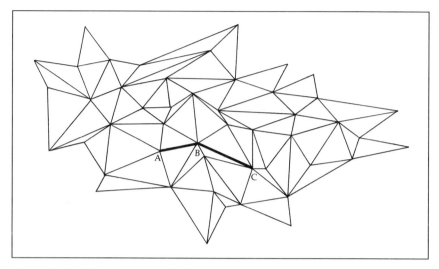

Figure 32-1.   Simple cause and effect.

of a hat. This seduction has weakened mankind's endeavors in all areas, from economics to human and veterinary medicine to the conduct of war and diplomacy, education, governance, and of course the management of natural resources. Instead of fixing what's really broken or finding a fundamentally different path, we print more money, invent a new drug, make a bigger bomb, suppress or buy off dissent, or build a dam.

Because it obsesses so many managers of land, I will make once again the brush encroachment phenomenon exhibit A in the case of desertification. When I first visited America on an eight-state lecture tour, everyone held it up to me as the big problem of the hour. I saw where literally millions of dollars had gone toward both eradication research and actual control to no avail. Nobody, however, discussed the cause seriously, and when I asked the question a chorus answered in unison, "Overgrazing. And livestock spread the seeds."

In fact, as the previous chapter on the weak link guideline argued, brush is almost always a nonproblem in the initial stages of holistic management. Many managers who *know* what it has done to them instantly recognize their mistake from an airplane, when they look down as the sun does and see the more serious problem of the bare ground. From a pickup, they only see brush. Nevertheless, that only makes the rage to exterminate brush without deeply considering its causes yet more lamentable.

The simple overgrazing explanation does not stand up to any serious test. Even ranchers and experts who have never heard of the four missing keys and do not believe that animal impact or timing relate to the problem at all recognize that brush *also* invades areas under total rest and moves *less* rapidly into areas of truly heavy overgrazing.

Under pressure to do something about the brush and unable (without the four keys) to explain fully why the brush has come, most people just stop asking the question and look around for ways to kill it. John Deere, Caterpillar, Dow Chemical, Monsanto accept the challenge. A whole new industry arises out of the ensuing competition, complete with research grants predicated on *not* asking the main question and advertising to make it appear irrelevant in the light of so-called technological success.

Under those circumstances, returning to the basic question of what causes brush encroachment demands no little courage, perseverance, and willingness to entertain new ideas, as everyone rapidly discovers who applies this guideline to the host of situations that arise in everyday management. When you can actually hear the grasshoppers stripping your irrigated pasture, can you stop and say to yourself, "I'm not going to spray until I know what I can do to cut the chance of grasshoppers becoming so thick again"?

In resource management situations, knowledge of the four missing keys helps a great deal. It does unravel the brush encroachment dilemma, for example.

Almost all problem plants, from noxious forbs to trees, are tap-rooted. All grasses have fibrous roots. A brush invasion represents a shift to tap-rooted plants. As discussed in the last chapter, the weak link in the establishment of most plants comes between germination and establishment. Because of the doubling penny phenomenon, the number of seeds or how they are spread matters little compared to conditions for establishment.

For a shift from grassland to tap-rooted plants to occur, *two factors must coincide*: good germinating conditions, and porous or easily penetrated soil, which happens to be typical of areas where dead fibrous roots remain in the soil. *Only one* of the tools listed in the HRM model can produce such conditions simultaneously over millions of acres, and that is rest, either total or partial (with scattered, unexcited animals on the land).

Overgrazing does damage grass roots, but it also tends to lead to soil compaction and exposed surfaces. Compacted soils, unless they crack, don't favor penetration by infantile tap roots growing on the small store of energy in a seed. Exposed surfaces generally are not conducive to mass germination, especially of those species associated with higher successional communities containing trees and brush, though disturbed and cracked surfaces may permit widespread establishment of lower successional communities containing forbs, such as Russian thistle, ragweed, etc.

By contrast, rested sites in brittle or nonbrittle environments tend to provide good germinating conditions for many higher successional woody plants due to less temperature fluctuation and more moisture. Such sites commonly have good soil porosity. In brittle environments where slow decay processes allow old growth to clog perennial grass plants, the stagnant root systems abet the tap-rooted invader.

Illustration 32-1 is a fairly typical view of a range site in Texas where partial rest has caused a shift from grass to mesquite. Conservative stocking, well-dispersed by water distribution and fencing, produced the familiar combination of heavily overgrazed plants among others untouched for many seasons. This has led to two situations developing all over the range— overgrazed areas with seriously compacted bare soil and overrested sites where dying grass has provided soft, porous soil, and some surface protection. The photograph shows both conditions. The overgrazed sites are eroding badly and show a slight shift to forbs. The overrested sites show a massive shift to forbs and mesquite.

I have seen the same thing throughout the world. Only the Latin names of the plants differed. Clearing the brush with aspirin (or more potent remedies) is a costly nonsolution as long as the hammering (from overrest) continues. In this case the real solution, ending overgrazing and overrest, will probably make money rather than cost it.

Illustration 32-2 shows from the air an area that demonstrates the point. On the left of the fence we ignored the dense acacia encroachment and

Illustration 32-1.   Mesquite trees have been cleared three times already on this rangeland showing both overgrazing and overresting. West Texas.

increased (doubled) the livestock numbers while stopping the overgrazing and overresting through biological planning (Chapter 40). The woody plants dotting the grassland, which developed in a few years, were a definite asset. On the right, the government concerned still recommended stock reduction, reseeding, and brush clearing—three costly forms of aspirin doomed to fail.

The search for causes requires constant questioning, probing, and doubting. Once in Zimbabwe I attended a field day where an agricultural extension officer addressed the problem of extensive tree cover on ranches in the district. We gathered in the shade of the offending canopy as he wielded his pointer over the flip chart and laid out decimal-studded statistics. His argument, supported by findings from three research stations, had no flaw. The trees had to go as they were destroying the grass and stealing the water.

Now, the HRM model would enable me to spot several fallacies at once. At the time, however, only a vague distaste for cutting down trees that had taken a long time growing kept my skepticism aglow. Up to now we had looked only at the ground where beleaguered remnants of grass certainly indicted the trees. Then, looking up, I noticed blackened limbs twenty to thirty feet above the ground. "What," I wondered aloud, "did that?"

Illustration 32-2.   View of effective management on the left of the fence producing dense perennial grassland despite the density of the acacia trees and shrubs. Lebowa, South Africa.

The trees, unlike American conifers, were not particularly flammable, so it took very little discussion for us all to conclude that nothing but a vigorous grass fire could have burned those limbs. Thus grass had once grown rank under the tress, and something else caused its demise.

The grass had suffered a high level of overgrazing by animals that congregated under the trees for two reasons. They sought both shade and a better mineral cycle. A twenty-inch rainfall on a granitic soil leached nutrients that the deeply-rooted trees returned to the surface, and its grasses, through leaf fall. Also, once denuded, the soil under the trees became extremely compacted from the enlarged raindrops that collected and fell from the canopy.

This conclusion fascinated the extension agent, and together we engaged the ranch owners in trying for themselves to find out what applying animal impact and stopping overgrazing would do. One year later we took the photograph in illustration 32-3.

The dipping of cattle for ticks in Africa, referred to previously in Chapter 14, provides another example of unappreciated cause and effect relationships. In my game department days I watched the tragedy repeated often.

The law required weekly dips whether or not cattle had ticks. That poisoned many ticks but also virtually all of the oxpecker birds that ate ticks. Different species of oxpecker accompany different types of animal, spending most of the day running all over them, even hanging upside down on their

Illustration 32-3.   Dense growth of new perennial grasses under the trees where the ground cover had been sparse the year before. Kwe Kwe, Zimbabwe.

bellies and probing their ears and under their tails. A healthy bird population, as well as other tick parasites and predators, can keep game animals incredibly clean. I also suspect some repellent action from a healthy animal's hair and skin, because a sick animal away from the herd will begin to accumulate ticks.

Once chemical dipping kills off the oxpeckers, however, the tick problem rapidly gets out of hand, requiring ever stronger chemicals. In addition, nearby game, undipped, becomes badly infested once the oxpeckers have gone. I used to joke, half seriously, that the veterinary service and its power over politicians were the greatest cause of tick-borne diseases in Africa.

One must take tick-borne diseases seriously, of course, but not by killing their most potent predator. If ticks are in fact increasing, one must look at the current application of the tools to determine which of them is simplifying the successional process. All too often in a livestock economy, it is the same two factors that increase brush, grasshopper outbreaks, flash floods, and drought—overgrazing of plants and low animal impact (partial rest).

The repeated spraying of grasshoppers on American rangelands represents a similar case of continually attacking the symptom at ever increasing cost without thought for the cause. The cost not only extends to the amount and price of the poison and many ecological side effects; it also shows up in the price we pay for water to drink. Pesticides, together with other agricultural and industrial pollutants, account for much of the $1.5 billion Americans pay for bottled drinking water. A gallon in many places now costs more than a gallon of gasoline.

Massive monocultures in farming have spawned a whole cluster of spiraling problems characterized by public unwillingness to question the root cause. Rather than admit the inherent instability of monocultures, we try to keep them viable through chemistry, machinery, genetic engineering, and ultimately cash subsidy. More often than not, however, the side effects of these fixes exacerbate the problems.

Though few farmers in the world enjoy higher product prices or cheaper input costs in vehicles, fertilizers, etc., we still have broke farmers blaming overproduction, low prices, and high costs. If those really are the causes, one might wonder why the Amish and many other farmers who approach agriculture with different assumptions remain profitable.

I myself once farmed and stood ready to kill weeds by any means necessary in the interest of perfectly clean fields. I now see that such unqualified zeal was a nongoal beset by nonproblems for which I exercised nonsolutions. Even Justus von Liebig, the father of inorganic chemistry who first proposed in the 1800s the "chemical alteration of soils" through the use of fertilizers, had second thoughts. Toward the end of his life he wrote, "I had sinned against the wisdom of the Creator, and received my righteous punishment. I wished to improve his work, and in my blindness believed that, in the marvelous chain of laws binding life on earth's surface and keeping it always new, a link had been forgotten which I, weak and powerless worm, must supply."

So reads the quote in the 1899 *Encylopaedia Britannica*, according to John Hamaker and Donald A. Weaver in their book *The Survival of Civilization.*[1] Today such an opinion, though it may enable us to see real causes of real problems, amounts to heresy in some quarters, and doesn't appear in modern encyclopedias.

Politicians, more than those in any other profession, have most difficulty in overcoming the temptation to ignore cause and effect. Pork barrel legislation is only the most mundane example. The worldwide response to desertification shows how people may fall into the same trap without the slightest trace of cynicism.

We've fed starving people, reduced livestock herds, settled nomads, imposed grazing systems, installed mighty irrigation works, and done a host of other things time and again. Apparently ancient Hebrew texts mention many of the same measures, including settling the nomads, yet the deserts grow because none of the above tackles the cause.

In this sad tradition, the head of the United Nations Environmental Program called in 1984 for the annual expenditure of $4.5 billion on quick fixes for the symptoms of desertification.[2] To point out that none of the proposals he has in mind has ever reversed the decline of any land anywhere offends certain diplomatic and political sensibilities, however honest the intent.

When leaders face a problem and have money, they come under great pressure to act somehow, anyhow. Nevertheless, a field look at the effects of some of the many well-intentioned programs makes it easier to justify holding off some remedies until the real causes are known, even in rather dire situations.

While spending time in Zimbabwe in 1986 I came across an excellent example of one such program. After many years of overgrazing, the sandy granitic soil in the Buhera district was eroding badly under twenty inches of tropical rain. Silt clogged irrigation ditches there and on down the Sabi River Valley. Recently, one of the major conservation awards of the year went to the local community and its agricultural extension officer for outstanding management of their portion of the vital watershed.

However, the extension officer had just completed six months of intensive training at the Center for HRM and could now point out the futility of the project.

This portion of the watershed has been fenced in completely and destocked. Concrete check dams now block the worst gullies. Eucalyptus trees have been planted and termites that consumed the eucalyptus and allegedly caused bare ground were sprayed. The "improvement" pleased everyone, as the first stages of quick fixes usually do.

Illustration 32-4. Extension officer with his foot on one of the unpoisoned termite mounds that is surrounded by lush, perennial grass growth.

However, degeneration had already set in when I saw it. A hard algal cap had sealed 80 percent of the soil surface. Established grasses, though lush now without the burden of overgrazing, had not started a new generation, and the choking effect of old growth had begun. It would not be long before a deteriorating water cycle silted up the check dams and washed them out. And the termites, despite the spraying, would soon explode on the abundance of standing dead grass. Ironically the best grass grew in association with mounds of one species of termite, as seen in illustration 32-4.

The eucalyptus trees were supposed to hold soil and improve water retention. However, having occasionally recommended them as a means of draining soil, I know their renowned ability to rapidly transpire enormous amounts of water, the intended end product of the project. Illustration 32-5 shows a new tree surrounded by its hard, capped soil. The eucalyptus trees, foreign to that environment, were also the only plants showing insect damage.

Finally, how long could any nation—not to mention a struggling African country where people clamor for land—fence out and protect a significant part of a major valley without touching off rebellion?

One cannot fault the people in any of the above examples for trying to

Illustration 32-5. Young, newly planted eucalyptus trees surrounded by hard capped soil, which has produced a noneffective water cycle. Buhera, Zimbabwe.

do what they thought they had to do, but the four keys and the HRM model make their situation infinitely clearer. In the Zimbabwean case, they only had to determine their desired landscape goal (which involved stable grassland) and implement the biological planning to achieve it. There was no need to rest the land—partial rest, together with overgrazing, had in fact led to the poor state of the water cycle.

In general the cause and effect guideline dictates that you not apply a tool unless you feel sure that the tool addresses the cause rather than the symptom. In an emergency you may proceed, but only with full knowledge of the dangers and only to buy time to rectify the cause. *To repeat the application of a faulty tool is never wise.*

It can be argued that it is sensible at times to remove a cause and treat the symptom simultaneously. In practice, however, this too often results in draining resources from the most efficient response and represents not effective policy, but a response to advertising or political pressure. From years of practice I have found it wisest to remove the cause first and see what happens. Most often the symptom disappears at no cost.

Illustrations 32-6 and 32-7 show another case. These are fixed point photographs taken a few years apart. Illustration 32-6 shows a high infes-

Illustration 32-6. A heavy locoweed population in 1981 after years of over-grazing and partial rest had been practiced. Barlite Ranch, Texas.

Illustration 32-7. A 1985 photograph of the identical area seen in illustration 32-6, showing the absence of locoweed following planned grazing with heavy animal impact. Barlite Ranch, Texas.

tation of locoweed, a plant that is said to kill horses outright and seriously affects ruminants as well. Illustration 32-7 shows the same spot after stopping overgrazing had increased grass root vigor. In other areas where the landowner sprayed the plants but did not eliminate the overgrazing, the infestation continued through the same seasons.

Like the other "whether to" tests, the cause and effect guideline should be applied year after year, because the time may come when a tool that failed one or more tests last year passes all of them now. Chapter 31 argued that the famous brush clearing example seldom passed the weak link guideline initially, because where much bare ground exists, brush is a nonproblem until the bare ground is covered. This chapter showed that brush clearing fails the cause and effect guideline until the cause of the encroachment has been discovered and eliminated.

At some time, however, when grass grows among the purple sage and you have mastered the subtleties of herd effect, stock density, and timing, brush clearing (by methods that don't damage the whole ecosystem of course) might pass. Then you might consider the next guideline—marginal reaction—to see if it promotes the most rapid attainment of goals at minimal investment of resources.

33

Marginal Reaction

The marginal reaction guideline assures that your commitment of time, effort, and wealth provides the maximum possible thrust toward your three-part goal at any moment. It thus parallels the tests for the weak link and cause and effect but differs in some significant ways.

Many people summarize the marginal reaction guideline with the phrase "getting the biggest bang for the buck," and the example I generally use to illustrate the principle involves just that. This guideline, however, should become a habit of thought that we apply continually in many less tangible situations, including the mundane dilemmas of everyday life.

I do not know of any management situation, right down to the family budget, where the marginal reaction guideline would not be of great benefit. Governments are notorious for their lack of use of such a principle, which reflects in unbalanced budgets and high costs.

In applying it one asks, "How should *each additional unit* of time, money, and/or labor be invested to provide the greatest return *in terms of my goal?*" The following hypothetical example, which people in HRM training come to know as the "Bank A and Bank B Case," shows this principle in dollars and cents.

Suppose you have $20,000 and must invest it in two banks under a peculiar set of rules. You may only open one account in each bank, and the interest earned on each additional deposit declines.

Bank A pays 5 percent on the first $5,000 but on each additional $1,000 it gives you 1 percent less; i.e., extra deposits up to $6,000 pay only 4 percent, the next $1,000 brings only 3 percent, etc.

Bank B pays 4.5 percent on the first $7,000, but the rate declines 0.75 percent on each additional $1,000.

In practice such rules would discourage saving, but you can get the best possible yield from your capital only by following the marginal reaction guideline. Think about it and then look at figure 33-1 to see how the investment would take place.

As you discover, you wind up investing $9,000 in Bank A and $11,000 in Bank B. No other combination except opening four accounts in Bank A (a violation of the rules) will yield more interest. Figure 33-1 was worked out by taking each dollar and asking where it would earn the highest interest. The first $5,000 earned 5 percent in Bank A, but Bank A would pay only 4 percent on the very next dollar instead of the 4.5 percent offered by Bank B. The next $7,000 would thus go to Bank B, but the $1,000 after that would go to Bank A because its 4 percent now beats Bank B's 3.75 percent. Similar thinking for each of the remaining $1,000 deposits determines the final outcome.

Such neat examples rarely occur in management, but the real life situations that we cannot quantify are no less real. Nowhere does the marginal reaction guideline apply more than in our allocation of time. We have only a fixed amount, and it ticks by day and night. To achieve the quality of life we desire, we choose how to spend it. Constant awareness of the marginal reaction in investments of time frees time to do things we love, and the

Bank A	Bank B	Interest %	Balance	Interest earned
5,000	—	5.00	15,000	250.00
—	7,000	4.50	8,000	315.00
1,000	—	4.00	7,000	40.00
—	1,000	3.75	6,000	37.50
1,000	1,000	3.00	4,000	60.00
—	1,000	2.25	3,000	22.50
1,000	—	2.00	2,000	20.00
—	1,000	1.25	1,000	12.50
1,000	—	1.00	0	10.00
9,000	11,000	—	20,000	542.50

Figure 33-1. Twenty thousand dollars to invest on basis of highest return on each additional dollar invested.

emergencies and crisis management we thereby avoid saves the money to pay for them.

I recently visited a tobacco farm where near panic reigned as harvest had to start in ten days, and yet the curing barns still had no roofs. Somewhere in the prior year the owner had spent time in the coffee house or fixing a tractor when he might have worked out a construction schedule. Now he was paying heavily in extra labor, rushed transport, and high blood pressure, not to mention the probability of getting shoddy work and losing part of his crop anyway.

I learned my lesson years ago as a struggling sugar farmer. Along with twelve neighbors, I purchased tracts of raw bush in Zimbabwe and developed farms for sugar cane under irrigation. We cooperated with one another and often compared costs to see how we were each doing against our average. My neighbors each bought one new tractor and set of implements and contracted with heavy equipment operators to have the large trees and brush cleared to the point where a wheeled tractor could take over land preparation. Being very hard up I bought a twenty-year-old tractor and implements as well as two twenty-year-old bulldozers from a deceased estate. After overhauling them in the bush and then getting them to my farm I did almost all of my own work.

The cost comparison was very enlightening. Despite doing the heavy work and running three old machines, my machinery maintenance costs ran at half the average of my twelve neighbors who each ran one new machine which performed no heavy work. My neighbors were all more experienced farmers than I—but I was desperately short of money and frantically using my head to survive. Where they merely had their damaged machines repaired I, doing my own work, thought about the chain of events leading to each breakdown (cause and effect) and ways to prevent a recurrence. It was this time that yielded me such a high return in lower maintenance costs.

We did not have comparisons of the time that we each spent with pencil and paper plotting and planning, but I would guess I must have spent ten hours to their one. Watch marginal reaction per hour as much as per dollar!

That said, consider the brush clearing example discussed in previous chapters in the context of the marginal reaction guideline. Assume that in this year's analysis brush clearing passes the weak link guideline. Shortage of forage (energy conversion) has become the limiting factor in the chain of events from sunlight to solar dollar. Furthermore, you have followed the cause and effect guideline and ended the practices that caused the invasion, and yet the previously established brush remains. So, why not buy a used bulldozer at auction and root out the brush?

Before doing that, the marginal reaction guideline requires you to look at all possible alternatives for increasing energy conversion. This comparison will not be quantifiable like the Bank A/Bank B example, therefore it demands

even more careful thought. *Achieving your three-part goal depends on consistently putting the majority of your resources behind the right decision.*
Ways to increase energy conversion on your ranch might include:

• Combining smaller herds into larger ones or subdividing grazing areas and paddocks through different herding routines or fences. This would increase stock density and thus animal impact, and it would improve the ratio between grazing and recovery periods as more animals spend less time on each unit of land.
• Increasing animal impact by inducing herd effect with attractants even at times when you would not normally feed supplements.
• Improving biological planning.
• Improving drainage and/or aeration.
• Buying or leasing more land.

These are but a few of the more obvious measures that could increase the volume of solar energy converted through forage, but for simplicity's sake, and also because many situations in fact boil down to this choice, compare brush clearing to the case for more fencing.

What does brush clearing (Bank A) offer on the land discussed earlier in Chapter 31 and depicted there in figure 31-1?

1. Clearing brush from paddock 2 will allow more grass to grow by letting in more light to a wider area, and the disturbance created by the tractors and chains may increase soil respiration and water penetration. Dead roots left underground will provide a mass of organic matter, which will enhance water retention, mineral cycling, and soil structure for some years.

2. In addition, thanks to the time dimension in our biological planning, improving one paddock will affect all. Without more paddocks we cannot move animals faster, but more forage in the cleared paddock may allow us to hold animals there a day or two longer, and that means more recovery time elsewhere. The cost of brush clearing will be $30,000.

On the other hand, at $300 a mile, I could build two miles of fence, split paddocks 3 and 4 for a cost of $600, and anticipate the following benefits.

1. Halving the size of two paddocks will double the stock density in the divided areas during each use. Although stock density does not provide as great an impact as does herd effect, it does increase it significantly. This will improve the distribution of dung and urine in the four new paddocks. Forage production will also improve geometrically in these paddocks for many years to come.

2. With two additional paddocks and the same average recovery periods now planned, grazing periods will decrease on average in every paddock on the ranch in every growing season over the fifty-year life of the fences. (Although mathematically it appears that the grazing period decreases only in the area of the new paddocks, in practice, as the biological planning is

used, you have the ability to decrease the grazing period anywhere you choose and thus we work on the assumption of average grazing period decreasing as paddock numbers increase.)

3. Disease risks are reduced because animals receive a higher plane of nutrition and spend shorter times on fouled ground.

4. Biological planning becomes easier, thanks to the versatility of having more paddocks to use. In addition, increasing paddocks now brings the possibility of cutting supplements by more efficient use of forage in dormant seasons.

Clearly, even if any case still remained for putting $30,000 into brush clearing, diverting 2 percent of that for a bit of fence makes a lot of sense.

Although we cannot quantify perfectly the comparison of brush clearing and fence building as ways to increase energy flow, if they both offered

A single investment of $16,000 being tested	
Bank A Herbicide Spraying	**Bank B** Fencing and Biological Planning
Return estimated up to 5% = *$800*	
Problem remains as cause not treated only symptom	1. Will be able to carry 300 extra cows = 600
Herbicide added to pollution of ecosystem and water supplies	2. Assume able to gain 0.5 lbs. per day extra on each animal over at least 100 days/year. Life of fence 50 years
	0.5 × 100 × 50 × 600 = 1,500,000 lbs. @ 50 cents = *$750,000*
	3. Present supplement $50/cow/yr can be lowered to $25/cow/yr over 600 cows = *$750,000*
	4. Many other advantages — better control and management, less disease, improved land, development towards goal, no damage to water and ecosystem
	5. Problem cured by removal of cause
	Approximate return *$1,500,000*

Figure 33-2. Grazing area of four thousand acres carrying three hundred cows with severe invasion of locoweed.

approximately the same gains, the fence would beat the bush hog through the marginal reaction guideline by 200 percent. Therefore, I would not recommend brush clearing *yet*. *Only when a year arrives when solar dollars invested in brush clearing will bring us closer to our three-part goal than any other alternative is it justified.*

A few years ago I was called in to advise a rancher worried about a bad infestation of locoweed. He ran three hundred cows on four thousand acres in a brittle environment and had been advised by his extension agent to poison the loco at a cost of $16,000. The extension agent had provided the figures to show that this would be cost-effective and the rancher's cash flow plan showed that the cost was acceptable.

At the time the ranch, in effect, was one large paddock, which exhibited the classical symptoms resulting from continuous low density grazing—large overgrazed areas and large overrested sites and locoweed throughout. The rancher was concerned about the overgrazing, and thought it might be curbed if he could build more fence. But he was convinced that the weeds had to go first and that's where his money would go this year. I suggested we run both actions through the marginal reaction guideline: herbicide spraying (Bank A) versus fencing (Bank B).

Like most practical situations, this one was not easily quantifiable. In

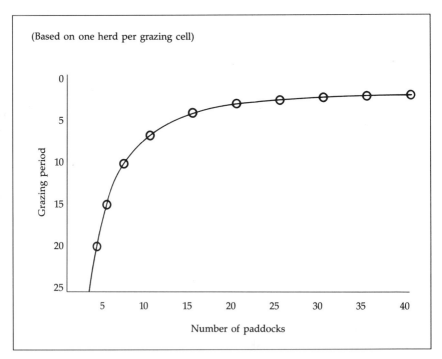

Figure 33-3.   Fencing curve of diminishing marginal reaction per dollar.

deciding where to invest money that year we'd have to rely on best guesses and quite a few assumptions. Figure 33-2 lays out the situation. Looking at the herbicide we realized that the return in solar dollars was negligible. The herbicide would kill most of the adult loco plants and thus his cattle wouldn't eat them. Approximately 10 percent of the herd was "locoed" (addicted to the plant) each season and gained less weight during the growing season— aproximately 0.5 pound less per day. Thus, if we took that into account, we could figure a return of $750 on our money over the one-hundred-day grow-ing season (0.5 pound @ $.50 per pound × thirty animals × one hundred days). This was offset, however, by the knowledge that the spraying would poison more than just the loco, thus simplifying the community when we wanted it more complex. And it would not be tackling the cause of the loco being there in the first place. In fact we'd probably be faced with the same decision again next year.

What of Bank B fencing (and thus better biological planning)? The $16,000 would give him twenty-six paddocks with permanent electric fencing (costs at the time of this case). This would allow him to plan his grazings to stop overgrazing immediately and begin to get rid of the overrested areas. He could now double his stocking rate while improving the land and removing the cause of the shift to locoweed. He would not risk simplifying the com-munity as the poison would have done.

In our calculations, we did not include the cost of purchasing three hundred extra cows because he was short of money and would have to run

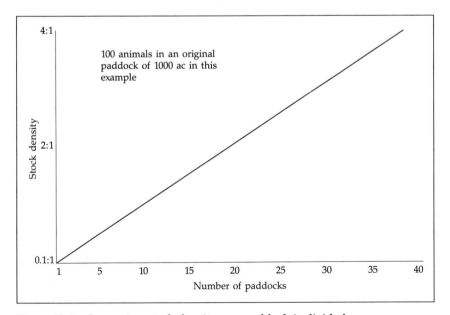

Figure 33-4. Increasing stock density as a paddock is divided.

someone else's (for which he would be paid according to pounds gained). With his present ability to plan the grazings thoroughly, he could move the cows every few days to fresh ground and we could expect weight gains of 0.5 pound more per day on each calf. We could also expect higher calving rates but we left that out to keep the exercise simple. With approximately six hundred calves gaining 0.5 pound per day extra (at .50/pound) over one hundred days in each season for the life of the fence (fifty years), he would get an additional return of about $750,000.

In addition, his cows were being supplemented at a cost of $50 per head per year and with the ability to plan the grazings (because of the fencing), we figured (conservatively) that we could reduce the supplement by half, a savings of $25 per cow per year. This provided an additional return on fencing of $750,000 over the next fifty years.

There were a number of other advantages to be gained by the fencing. Because the herd would now be concentrated in a much smaller area, he would see them all every day. Handling would be easier and calmer, calf mortality lower, the risks of parasitism and disease less, etc. But we did not put dollar values to this because we had seen enough to make a decision. In terms of the rancher's goals this year his investment would be in fencing (and planning) rather than herbicide, as the marginal reaction per dollar was clearly greater.

Having given two ranching examples using fencing I must warn you that if you do invest in fencing, remember that like many other investments, the law of diminishing returns sets in at some point. Figure 33-3 shows how the effect on grazing periods flattens as paddock numbers increase. Though in fact a similar graph of stock density (figure 33-4) continues to climb at a constant rate, other factors such as handling, maintenance, and aesthetics obviously limit the appeal of more fence at some point.

You should use the marginal reaction guideline to challenge routine costs that you may have given little thought to previously. Take for example the very high supplementary feed costs on ranches that have little or no snow over the winter months. Cows are made to calve very early in the year and expected to breed back at a time when forage value is at its lowest. This policy was established years ago to avoid excessive calf mortality from screw worms, which posed no threat in the early months. The supplement costs may have been justified then. Although the screwworm is no longer the problem it was, many ranchers continue the same policy. Various grazing systems also affect the need for supplement, depending on the quality of the forage they produce at the time cows are lactating.

Though actual months and breeding times vary in different parts of the world, figures 33-5 and 33-6 show the principle. The first (figure 33-5) represents a cycle typical of the American Southwest. As can be seen, cows have their highest nutritional demand at the worst time of the year when

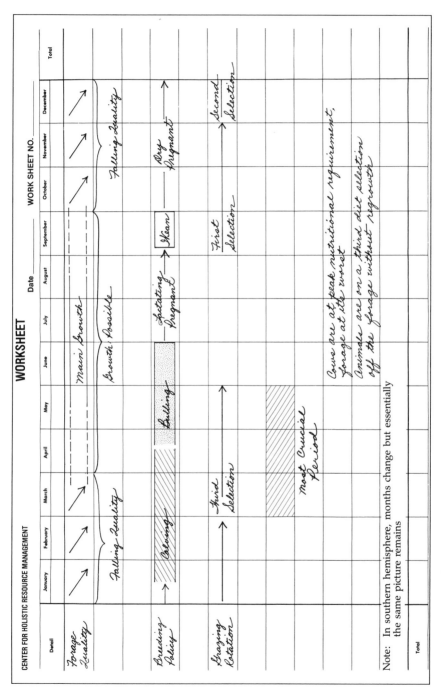

Figure 33-5. Conventional cattle production in many areas.

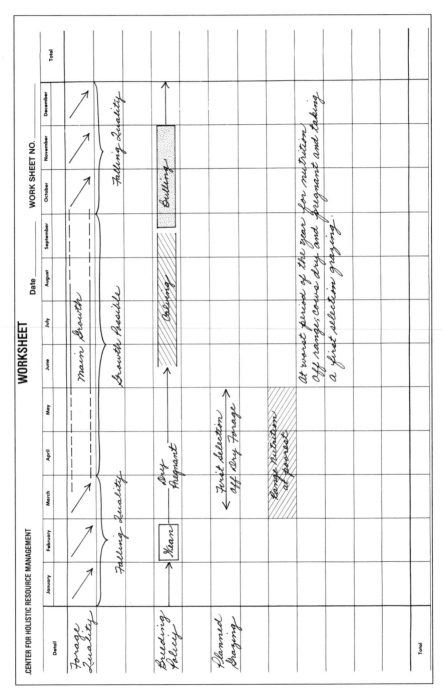

Figure 33-6. Example of cattle production planned to lower annual production costs.

selecting off the land for the third time. Only heavy supplementation in many cases enables the cows to do well but at very high annual cost.

Figure 33-6 shows a different policy brought about by a shift in the time of breeding and biological planning with many more paddocks. In this case the cows are at their toughest with lowest nutritional needs and selecting off land for the first time at the worst time of the year. In such cases the annual supplementary feed cost can be drastically lowered. However, such a change could not be brought about in one year without loss and it would necessitate careful planning over a few seasons as dollars are shifted from supplementation to fencing to give a higher marginal reaction in the long run.

While many good arguments against such a program might turn up, my point is that a management team must keep challenging the old ideas and dogma constantly in seeking to find the best marginal reaction per dollar. Much can be done on almost all farms, ranches, forests, game reserves, etc. to reduce the high costs of routine management, if the people in charge give constant thought to this guideline.

Once we have established where we think our dollars will give the highest return at this moment in the context of our goal, we should proceed. Before moving, however, we need to remind ourselves that our goal is always a trinity, and too often we neglect the quality of life part. I may determine that this year at last $30,000 really should go to clearing that brush that has bothered me so long. But while conditions have evolved so it passes all the tests covered so far, my children have also grown, and my daughter's college education now takes priority. The brush can wait a year or so more, especially as it has never yet accounted for any loss of income.

That would not be a difficult decision, but unfortunately the question of how and where to invest resources in the various possible production enterprises on a farm or ranch can be complex. Having the potential to convert a certain amount of energy will not suffice if we cannot find the best way to arrive at a marketable product. The next guideline, gross margin analysis, helps do that.

34

Gross Margin Analysis

If profit is an essential part of your goal, then you need to apply the gross margin analysis guideline frequently. It assists in determining the strongest possible links of product conversion and marketing in the chain from sunlight energy to solar dollar.

On most farms and ranches money is tied up unproductively in fixed costs, what we would normally call overhead—cost of the land, salaries, family withdrawings, vehicles, machinery, and so on. None of these actually creates new wealth and thus the income to keep the place going. That is only done by the various activities that actually lead to a saleable product. To be most profitable we need to find that enterprise or combination of enterprises that brings in the most for the least additional cost each year.

Various procedures exist to help you do this, but I find most of them too complex, confusing, and impractical for widespread use. This guideline, derived from the work of a Cambridge University agricultural economist named David Wallace, also has flaws, but provides a clear and simple way to approach the problem.

Wallace originally used the term gross profit, because, for example, when he compared the advisability of a wheat crop versus pasture, he ignored the overheads and looked only at the direct costs involved. Although Wallace realized that net profit, which includes these overhead costs, is quite a different animal, the struggling British farmers who read his work found it confusing to compute positive profits of any kind when their actual bottom line was bright red.

Therefore Wallace invented the term gross margin, which has little intrinsic meaning but helps distinguish his analysis from the more familiar profit and loss statement. Since he deserves credit for the work, we have kept his name for it.

The key to gross margin analysis is the careful distinction of fixed (overhead) and variable (direct) costs at a given moment in time. Wallace divides all farm costs into these two categories. Fixed costs exist no matter what or how much is produced. Variable costs are a function of volume of production.

When you plan wheat production, for example, seed and gasoline for the machinery during sowing and harvesting are variable costs. You only incur them if you grow wheat, and you compute the amount from the acreage you intend to plant. Payments on the combine that you already own, however, are fixed costs because *even though you use it exclusively for wheat*, you must make the payments whether or not you actually grow wheat.

Many kinds of analysis conducted in America and elsewhere do not make a clear distinction between fixed and variable costs, and try to allocate part of the former to various enterprises. In the case above, all combine expenses would be charged against the wheat, and the tractor perhaps half to wheat and half to something else. Labor costs might wind up apportioned under many headings.

Figure 34-1 compares income and expense projections for two enterprises where fixed costs are apportioned. I have used A and B to represent any

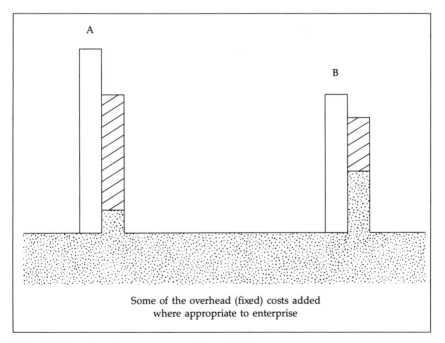

Figure 34-1. American gross margin analysis.

two alternatives on that land—growing wheat versus hay, for example. Note that A and B show the same 20 percent margin of profit.

The gross margin analysis in figure 34-2, however, tells a very different story. Since most of the expense allocated to enterprise B would have to be paid anyway, clearly enterprise B contributes far more toward covering overall farm expenses (fixed costs) than enterprise A. If the farmer needed an operating loan to cover variable costs, obviously B would take far less than A.

As usual, however, reality raises many other questions that often demand a lot of thought. Many find the matter of sorting out fixed and variable costs in itself confusing. No formula or list can do this because in fact any item could be either fixed or variable depending on the situation and the time frame under consideration. The following observations help me visualize the problem:

1. In the very long term all costs are variable, and in the very short term all costs are fixed. If forgoing wheat production opens the possibility of selling the farm, then taxes and mortgage payments are indeed variable costs assignable to wheat. On the other hand, if a sudden price drop causes you to reconsider wheat the day after you took delivery of the seed, the seed

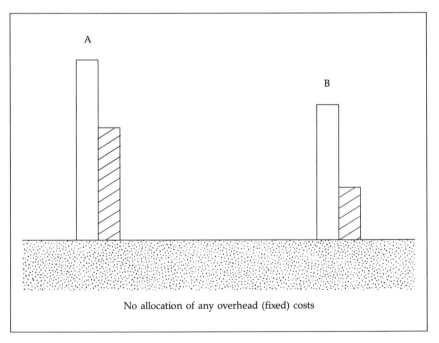

No allocation of any overhead (fixed) costs

Figure 34-2. David Wallace's gross margin analysis.

itself is a fixed cost because you must pay for it whether or not you do so by raising wheat.

2. In light of the above, I picture myself standing on a bridge looking upstream. Any water (cost) that has passed under my feet is fixed and any (cost) upstream is still variable.

Of course, in doing this one should also make sure variable purchases really are necessary. In ranching, the provision of supplemental feed and salt—expenses routinely computed from the number of livestock on the ranch—may have no justification at all, because the same funds invested elsewhere would give a higher marginal reaction. No matter how sound the use of a supplement and no matter what comes up in a gross margin analysis and cash flow, supplements seldom pass the marginal reaction guideline when compared to fencing until paddock levels reach thirty or more per herd, if good biological planning is in place.

Gross margin analysis allows comparison of very different enterprises. How, for instance, does putting land into crops stand up against using the same land for livestock or various forms of recreational, income-bearing activities? You can compare various different crops, mixtures of crops and livestock, or other enterprises to find the best strategy for covering those fixed overheads and making a profit at minimum risk. A single enterprise such as livestock production can be broken into components and checked for weaknesses. Maybe replacement stock should be bought, not bred. Maybe hay and silage for winter bulk feeding should be bought, not grown, in order to free more land for livestock and thus decrease the capital tied up per animal unit.

In order to compare very dissimilar enterprises, the gross margin analysis must be computed in the same units. When land represents the major commitment of capital, gross margin per acre per year shows best how to put the land to use. In other cases gross margin per dollar of capital or per man-hour of labor makes more sense.

Enterprises on the average farm or ranch benefit from gross margin analysis at least three times during the year:

1. at the point of initial interest in a new enterprise or as human needs and markets affecting an old one shift;

2. at the annual financial planning stage when the main strategy for the whole operation takes shape (Chapter 44 covers this in detail); and

3. at year's end when results are apparent.

The advance application of gross margin analysis must take into account the major variables that define risk. What yields will we really achieve? What will prices really be? To see the implications, one has to project worst, average, and best cases, starting with the variable *least* within our control. For example, for a dry farmer of pinto beans in the American Southwest, weather might be the most critical factor. For irrigated beans, price might be. The dry farmer would therefore pick an average price and compute his gross margin for low, average, and high yields. For the irrigated farm a comparison of low, average, and high prices would mean more. Obviously one could add infinite levels of sophistication to this process, given a computer and a bit of time.

Having decided on an enterprise, or a combination of enterprises, through an analysis of various levels of risk, you still don't know if you can make a *net* profit. The annual planning, however, which Chapter 44 and the companion workbook describe in some detail, will show whether or not your strategy adds up to black ink. If it doesn't, another rigorous comparison of gross margins will help find a way.

The third application of gross margin analysis will show actual performance, which will then bear on future plans and reactions to shifting markets, etc.

In spite of all its benefits, gross margin analysis has some serious shortcomings, some of which show up in the context of other guidelines and some in the light of common sense.

In the theoretical cases portrayed in figures 34-1 and 34-2, enterprise B turns out so far ahead of enterprise A that one could easily argue for committing the entire farm to it. In practice, however, that could be very unwise. First of all the advantages of B derived from being able to use assets already on hand and accounted for as fixed costs. If, however, doubling enterprise B meant paying for more land, equipment, or labor, those would be variable costs, and might lead to a very different conclusion.

More important, gross margin analysis takes no account of the ecosystem processes or many less tangible considerations. In farming it quite frequently shows a complete and chemically-enhanced monoculture as the most profitable strategy, and yet we know that:

1. High fertilizer application damages the soil's natural ability to convert nitrogen, reduces organic matter, and degrades soil structure.

2. Once initiated, such damage leads to a spiraling chemical dependency and rising costs.

3. Insect damage, aggravated by the presence of only one plant for food, may require short-term control with pesticides that create a long-term problem.

4. Down the road my community and I will have to pay the bill for polluted air and water.

Despite the problems, however, the technique still throws light on many situations and other guidelines usually call attention to its limitations. *The ideal is to find the best enterprise or combination in which all the technology and other tools pass all guideline tests. At that point, to the best of our knowledge, you have a holistically sound chain of events from sunlight to solar dollar produced.*

35

Energy/Wealth Source and Use

The last chapter explained how gross margin analysis helps decide the most profitable form of production, but it ended on a note of warning. The means to profit may not be holistically sound. Not only the enterprise itself, but also the secondary inputs that support it, must pass all the other testing guidelines as well.

Does the production strategy involve an unstable monoculture? Will it require chemicals that damage the whole ecosystem? Will profit depend on suppressing symptoms rather than addressing causes? Do some inputs pass all those tests but then fail to represent the best marginal reaction for re-investing the wealth the land generates?

In the spirit of holism, all these questions help put any management decision in the context of the whole. Rather late in the development of the HRM model, however, it became evident that one must press that line of testing yet one level deeper and examine both the sources and patterns of use of the energy and wealth that are involved in production.

Chapter 15 differentiated solar, mineral, and paper dollars and distinguished consumptive versus cyclical use of biological and mineral resources. This guideline uses those insights to ask two questions: First, is the resource from which we have derived wealth, or are intending to do so, being used sensibly for the good of humanity? Second, if we are planning to use any resource in a dangerous way, as in the case of nuclear power, or consumptively, as in the case of fossil fuels, are we doing so as sparingly as possible while trying to build toward less damaging methods? These tests particularly apply to all tools under the heading of technology.

The lumping together of wealth and energy may appear confusing, but closer scrutiny shows them indivisible in terms of this guideline. Wealth, other than the paper dollars described in Chapter 15, derives mainly from mineral and biological resources, but always involves energy in some form. The production of usable energy from fossil fuels, nuclear fission, or any other source also itself represents wealth. As energy is both wealth in its own right and also contributes to other forms of wealth, we cannot separate them. At the same time, we cannot quite regard them as one.

Energy Sources and Use

When a society chooses between oxen and tractors (solar versus fossil energy) for the work of its food production, how does it decide? Unfortunately, you as an individual seldom have this choice. Normally communities or governments decide the form in which energy is made available. Ideally they should consider the long-term health of nations, but their track record is poor for two reasons that sooner or later (and, one hopes, the former) most societies will have to question.

First is the belief that the planet will always have the ability to cleanse itself of waste and toxic products produced by humanity. Though we understand the danger now, our social and economic structure, based on high consumption rates of firewood, fossil, and now nuclear energy, still runs on tracks laid down long ago when humanity could more easily ignore its impact on Nature.

The Industrial Revolution that set us on this course did not occur painlessly, and neither will the changes that put us on a new path.

Second, even though we can see the danger ahead now, the destruction of shared resources is a typical "Tragedy of the Commons," the sort of problem that lies in the nature of governments and individuals to aggravate. While governments are supposed to regulate the commons, they in fact, because of short-term vision and planning combined with responsiveness to interest group lobbying and bureaucratic ineptitude, usually fail in this task. When individual exploiters enjoy the gross return from their acts but only bear their small share of the common cost, an unalloyed profit motive will drive exploitation until the common resource disappears—a car driven and owned by many people seldom lasts as well as when driven and owned by any one of those people. Few citizens demand sensible energy use planning, while many demand immediate personal gain.

The energy from which we generate new wealth or that we employ in the conversion of other resources into usable form falls into two categories. Nuclear, fossil, and firewood directly and unavoidably cause damage at high rates of consumption. On the other hand, constant sources—solar, tidal, wind, etc.—are intrinsically neutral (as far as we know), though the mechanism used to harness and distribute such energy may be harmful. A large hydroelectric dam, for instance, may seriously upset the ecosystem as a whole where any number of mill wheels and smaller projects along the same stream might not.

Most individuals have only limited power to control the source of energy they use, though as a citizen one can speak out for better policies, planning, and regulation. You can also let conscience enter your own decisions to flip a switch, design a building, or raise a crop. The greatest floods start from trickles, and we have some serious habits to confront in the United States. In the three months of summer American air conditioners alone suck up more kilowatt hours of electric power than all of China, with four times our population, uses in an entire year for all purposes.[1]

The energy source and use guideline asks you to use inputs in your production that involve the least destructive forms of energy and apply it in the most constructive manner possible.

Wealth Sources and Use

Just as this guideline requires that energy comes from the least damaging sources and goes to the most sustainable and constructive ends, so we must also review our treatment of the other resources from which we generate wealth.

The whole ecosystem guideline, by forcing us to review our impact on the four ecosystem processes, in effect eliminates most destructive practices, so in some sense another test is redundant. Nevertheless, a look at our impact on specific resources as well as underlying processes throws more light on how our activity fits into the larger picture. We commonly speak of renewable and nonrenewable resources, but all too often we destroy the distinction by treating soils, forests, fisheries, and other potentially self-perpetuating assets so badly that they never recover. Careful examination of the sources and uses of the wealth that passes through our hands helps avoid this.

Though this book repeatedly raises the case of soil destruction—the proclivity of our civilization to treat living soil as a thing to mine and consume like coal—it deserves yet another review here as a prime example of what the wealth source and use guideline attempts to counter.

The survival of the human race depends entirely on healthy, stable, "living" soil. From it come the plants that nourish us and the other organisms we eat and that feed on us and our wastes. It supplies the timber that shelters us, warms us, and purifies the air we breathe. Plentiful, stable water supplies, a fundamental requirement for all natural life as well for the irrigated fields and urban extravagance of civilizations, also depend on healthy soils.

America, however, loses two bushels of soil from its croplands for every bushel of corn it exports. The u.s. Department of Agriculture says this amounts to a train of loaded hopper cars 117 miles long *every day*! The National Wildlife Federation reports that agriculture accounts for 57 percent of the lakes in America polluted by run-off, and total damage from erosion off the farm costs the nation between $4 billion and $16 billion a year. The bill for dredging silt out of rivers and reservoirs alone is shocking.[2]

More alarming still are the u.s. Department of Agriculture's published figures on the amount of soil loss off the farm that is viewed as acceptable. Any nation serious about its long-term survival, and the quality of life of its citizens, should not accept any loss at all. We should be striving to build up agricultural soils, rather than accept their breakdown.

Soil damage on rangeland has also reached catastrophic proportions but often goes unrecognized. In May 1987 the United Nations Environment Program, headquartered in Kenya, reported that North America's rangelands were improving in all ways (including soil erosion) but one. Ground water supplies still showed a decline.[3] No figures supported this claim, and although some might be found, I've not seen this so-called improvement on the ground. Monitoring of the rangeland watersheds on many ranches and public lands by myself, our staff, and HRM practitioners in North America consistently shows exposed and eroding soils between plants accounting for 50 percent to 90 percent of surface area over vast regions. Even gullies, the most obvious signs of deterioration, are visible mile after mile from the roadside or a light plane. Large numbers of check dams and other conservation works, most dating back to public works projects of the 1930s, and most overcome by silt, dot the land, but few recent efforts are visible.

So America's most vital resource, her soil, goes down the gullet of mainstream agriculture as a nonrenewable resource just as if we intentionally mined it, loaded it in those hopper cars, hauled it away, and dumped it into the sea. Because we consider soil expendable, we don't hesitate to pour on chemicals that kill the billions of living organisms that give it life. In their place we substitute fossil fuel-based fertilizers in ever increasing quantity, aggravating the damage.

Every operator on the land must take responsibility for the consumption of vital resources, especially soils. Individuals can do much by questioning every practice before implementation. Does a particular technology involve wealth and energy? How does that proposed wealth and energy use show up against the guideline? Will the resources in question recycle or see only one-time use, and if the latter, what lasting infrastructure will they build? If potentially renewable, will renewal occur in fact? If not renewable, are you using them sparingly or in a cyclical manner? What waste could you eliminate? If the resources can recycle, what form of energy does that require and what does that manner of energy use do to our ecosystem? Are you consuming fossil-based energy or firewood at the lowest possible rate?

That all boils down to the general question, "Am I contributing to unwise consumptive use of resources or to a better future?" If you have doubts, then look for alternatives. Individual actions count and do pressure governments into taking more responsibility for their own role in the abuse of a nation's natural wealth.

This doesn't mean avoiding fossil fuels and firewood altogether. It is not their consumption alone but the high *rate* of consumption that endangers the planet. Governments could curb this by taxation or other means. I will return to the individual's role in Chapter 44, where I discuss the annual financial planning and the generation of wealth.

For now there remains one more testing guideline under which we question the possible effects of any tool on the quality of life at a personal level and in the larger context of society and culture as a whole.

36

Society and Culture

This guideline tests all actions and their associated tools for how they serve the quality of life goal. Production and landscape goals and all the rest of holistic management are aimed at that, so this guideline governs holistic management in its broadest sense. Will an action really lead to the quality of life we seek, and what will it do to that of others?

Without a doubt that is the most fundamental of questions. None deserves more research and reflection, and typically none gets less. But we must think not only of our quality of life as individuals or families, but also as members of society and the many cultures it embraces. Healthier individuals and families promote a healthier society.

The difficulties we encounter in applying this guideline come in many forms, some of which have been discussed in other contexts. Tradition, custom, specialization, and unquestioned pursuit of progress impart a short view of how things are supposed to be.

Ranchers concentrate on profit from livestock. Environmentalists worry about growing trees. Loggers concentrate on cutting trees. Generals fixate on counting bodies and missionaries on counting souls. Few of us stop often enough to notice when we shoot down our own dreams and those of others in the name of how it's supposed to be. The matter of ethics enters here. The most important assumptions about the processes and organisms of the ecosystem I extend to human society and culture as well. The biological principle that in complexity lies stability holds true as a sociological principle.

It is in our best interests to maintain cultural complexity within society as a whole. Ideas, enterprises, and relationships flourish according to a succession not unlike the patterns of Nature and can be advanced or set back in parallel ways. Religion and the life of the spirit, being part of any culture, has a place in the quality of life goal, and in this testing guideline, but never as a justification for force or compulsion of any kind.

On first exposure to this guideline, many people in developed countries immediately conclude that it applies particularly to people in undeveloped countries. They think of modern technology, for example, and see that it might damage a so-called primitive culture. Apart from developed and undeveloped being poor descriptions when looked at holistically, this misses the point. The question is never, "What will it do to these people and their culture?" for the simple reason that *we can never apply holistic management* **to** *"other people."* Though outsiders can assist in training, the people on the ground must apply holistic management themselves, as individuals and as part of a greater society, based on their knowledge of themselves and their communities.

In many respects the developed countries are in as bad a state as the undeveloped ones because they haven't seen the importance of asking the fundamental questions of themselves. It is important that a quality of life goal spell out cultural values, including religious and spiritual ones, as explictly as everyone involved finds necessary. Individuals or families managing private land have no less need to do this than others.

Suppose you have a farm and you contemplate building a dam. Your production and landscape goals foresee establishment of duck and fish breeding habitat for recreational use and to supply food for your household and labor. In each of the last five years the $30,000 required to build the dam has failed to pass some other testing guidelines, and you have spent your money elsewhere to achieve your goals faster. Now at last, however, dam construction passes them all, and you look at it in the context of personal quality of life as well as society and culture.

As you think about your life, you realize that putting the final touch on your landscape goal may not justify forgoing certain aspects of quality of life needing attention. In the ensuing years while you have been building toward your goals, your and your neighbor's children are now five years older. For various reasons you may now decide that building a tennis court, or a rodeo arena, will contribute more to your lives and the community than building that dam this year could do. After all, the goal was a high quality of life with healthy families and community and not dam building.

When land is held publicly or communally, the question is posed against the quality of life goals that the broader community has established for itself. Suppose you made a living cutting timber in a national forest and had participated with local ranchers, hunters, and environmentalists in establishing the three-part goal. Production includes profitability from timber and livestock, aesthetic value for hikers and hunters, and fly fishing from clear waters. In planning how you'll extract the timber, you see the highest profit in grading roads capable of handling heavy equipment. However, you know that this will not pass the quality of life tests that stem in large measure from the other users of the forest. Your road grading would wash into the trout streams, and your equipment and the recreational vehicles and poachers that followed it would upset the wildlife, livestock, and the aesthetics of the area in general.

Do you lobby for special treatment or fold up your business? Such dilemmas are agonizing, but rarely do we face only two choices, given a little human creativity. In this case skidding logs with mule teams or elephants (depending on the continent) might satisfy all parties, including your banker.

Private operators, more often than most like to believe, must exercise similar sensitivity to the society around them. Even in America where private rights have long standing, the Anglo, ranching land severed deviously generations ago from a Spanish land grant, ignores local opinion at his peril. So do those who lease Native American land or move on a grand scale into any long-established local culture.

Under such circumstances, pleasing everybody may seem impossible, but one goes a long way by vigorously embracing the holistic principle that the health of your particular interest is not distinct from the health of the whole. Even where resentments lie impacted in centuries of abuse, more people than not respond to good will and an open mind.

The planning of communal land, either tribal or public, obviously requires particular attention to the society and culture guideline. Using techniques discussed in Chapter 39 (and in more detail in the companion workbook), one attempts to settle on a plan that advances quality of life in both the short and long term without conflicting with traditional cultural practices and values.

If for instance you set out to help a small African village halt the overgrazing caused by livestock, you would naturally work with the villagers on planning land and grazing, but you could not proceed toward a realistic plan without a full understanding of their quality of life goals, including many areas beyond the health of the range. Through many conversations and discussions you might discover that the women traditionally milk cows daily at the village in addition to tilling the fields, while the men are away at the local mine. Currently the children herd the cattle, mainly to keep them out of the fields, but the village would much rather see the children in school instead.

Within these limits it is possible to make a land plan that meets all these needs in addition to advancing the production and landscape parts of the goal. Fencing could cut the need for herders, allowing the children to go to school, and if the fences radiated from the village, the women would not have to trudge to a distant paddock for milking after a weary day of hoeing sorghum.

This thinking applies equally to nomadic societies. Many governments now forcibly settle them in villages in the hope that they will turn to farming rather than graze livestock in an ever deteriorating environment. And yet plans could be devised that would allow them to graze their animals in an ever improving environment while safeguarding their cultural heritage.

The lack of attention to the quality of life factor in our national goals has resulted in numerous tragedies, one of the most obvious being the state of American agriculture. The American government, with the acquiescence of many in the industry, undertook to increase production, solely in terms of quantity. From government and universities and industry leaders the message was put over powerfully—get big or get out. Production, production, production with only minimal quantifiable costs considered. Sufficient attention was not paid to those who would be displaced as big farms swallowed smaller ones and more powerful machinery supplanted labor.

Production boomed, but at the cost of a polluted environment, massive soil erosion, and enormous social dislocation. Thousands of family farms vanished, dissipating generations of practical knowledge. The dispossessed have drifted to urban centers and struggled to adjust to an alien culture. The churches, small businesses, and cultural centers in the small towns that served those people have withered away also.

Hindsight gives us perfect vision. What if we had used this guideline test before so optimistically turning agriculture into a mechanized, capital-intense industry? With its once vast and fertile prairie soils, the likes of which no nation had ever enjoyed, America still would most likely have become the world's greatest agricultural producer, while maintaining its healthy rural populations, the villages and towns that served them, and vast, diversified markets. Some people, such as the Amish mentioned earlier, did not ignore the quality of life factor in establishing their goals. It was and still remains paramount. Yet while more so-called progressive, production-oriented farmers flounder, they continue to flourish.

In summary then, the society and culture guideline holds a prime place in resource management at all levels. If you can foresee that any tool or action could affect your quality of life adversely, or that of your community or society as a whole, seek alternatives. If money you consider putting to work in one direction could yield a higher marginal reaction toward the quality of life you seek, then take heed and act accordingly.

Testing in Summary

We have now covered all of the testing guidelines developed to date. If you have considered each of these guidelines in the evaluation of any tool, you will have gone far in preventing costly and unsound decisions. Ideally all tools should pass all the tests. Those that do almost certainly will give holistically sound results right now. And tools that fail this year may pass later as management takes effect and the whole situation changes.

Before leaving the subject I'll cite again the matter of brush clearing that so obsesses American extension service people and the ranchers they serve. So many succumb to the enormous pressure to clear brush immediately, no matter what the situation, that I have emphasized all the cases where it makes no sense. Year after year, the clearing of brush may well fail one or more of the tests, and money and effort are put where the testing guidelines indicate they will advance all goals more quickly. Nevertheless, as you move closer to your goals, there may well come a time when the clearing of that brush and the method proposed does pass all the tests. Then, of course, do it.

Only after all the testing guidelines have been considered are you ready to pass on to the management guidelines. At no time is it sound to go directly to the mangement guidelines, as they only tell you how to use a tool, not when to use it. Once you know that action involving any tool is safe, you can look at how to apply it.

37

Population Management

Earlier we looked at management guidelines derived from the missing keys—time as it governs the application of grazing, and herd effect and stock density as critical factors determining the effect of the animal impact tool. That was a digression justified as a prerequisite for understanding the separate group of guidelines that test whether or not a tool should be used at all. We can now return to the questions of management.

The population management guideline bears on the "tool" of living organisms and thus figures in every conceivable management goal. All involve living organisms. We humans ourselves are such. Also we frequently define our desires, good or bad, in terms of populations of plants and animals. We want more corn or cattle, more timber, fewer fruit flies and mosquitoes, more of our team, and less of theirs.

Unfortunately from conventional wisdom and habit we often pursue these desires without any subtlety at all, considering only the raw numbers of whatever interests us at the moment. In the livestock business the question goes, "What is your stocking rate?" Game enthusiasts ask, "What is the deer count?" Farmers ask, "How many bushels?" Economic development specialists talk about people per square mile, consumption per capita, and growth of GNP. All of these questions are important, but in addition, or even ahead of them, this guideline raises other considerations that clarify the management of populations in the context of whole communities.

One example shows both how much this broader approach can contribute to the solution of some of our most urgent problems, and how easily the best of minds can fall into the old rut.

A few years ago a consulting assignment from the United Nations Food and Agriculture Organization took me to Pakistan's Baluchistan Province. Having been charged with reporting on the overall status of resource management in this province, I had read numerous reports previously prepared by other consultants and government officials. These all cited one problem that overshadowed most others: the overharvesting of desert brush for fuel. Villagers were scavenging an ever expanding area for them and didn't just lop off branches; they took roots and all, leaving the ground bare. An ever widening circle of bare ground extended around most settlements. What would hold the soil, and how would the villagers cook in the long run?

All the reports had concluded that alternative stoves and fuel had to be found, but no one had an idea the villagers could afford. The report writers, however, looked only at the number of bushes available and the rate of harvesting, ignoring all other aspects of population growth and maintenance. None seized on the fact that there were no young bushes, even though new growth, lacking fuel value, did not interest wood gatherers.

Without any harvesting at all, a population that does not reproduce will disappear. Bushes that reseed themselves will provide a source of fuel that satisfies a good share of the village demand forever, regardless of total demand. The rate of consumption of mature bushes was therefore irrelevant. The challenge lay in determining why none of the millions of seeds produced annually by the remaining mature bushes survived.

We'll return to this case later. The point I wish to make now, which this case highlights so well, is that there is a need for two kinds of knowledge in managing a living population. First, one must be able to assess its health and stability. Then one must pinpoint the cause of its condition. The population management guideline addresses these questions on the basis of some rather obvious principles that modern production systems have increasingly obscured.

In crop farming particularly, we have come to think in terms of annual or short-term monocultures where we plant an entire population, nurture it artificially, then harvest it completely. The same logic extends to the clear cutting and reseeding of timber. We even rip up fruit orchards at a certain age and replant them because it suits our mechanized handling techniques to have everything the same age and on the same schedule. All of that, however, does violence to the natural dynamics of populations in whole communities and inevitably leads to instability and failure.

Self-Regulating and Nonself-Regulating Populations

Amongst animal populations these are the two fundamental types. We don't yet understand how some of the self-regulating populations manage to limit their own numbers, but they do, even though they have very high breeding rates and thus a potential for rapid expansion. Some of the small antelope of Africa are good examples. If we protect them for years they do not increase. If we try to shoot them out, as various tsetse fly eradication schemes attempted, they breed about as fast as they are shot.

Such antelope, which are solitary creatures, appear to have small but strict territories, which may be threatened when numbers reach a certain threshold. Quite possibly this threat stresses the animals in some way that inhibits breeding. No matter how abundant the food, cover, and other requirements, the population remains limited.

Self-regulating populations present little known difficulty in management. Nonself-regulating populations, on the other hand, present a very different picture, unless communities are intact and complex.

Some nonself-regulating populations do not appear as such as long as they exist in complex communities and remain relatively stable. Predation and other causes of attrition provide limits to population growth. Amongst animals, birds, and insects, most of the herding, flocking, or gregarious species seem to fall in this category.

Once predators in particular are removed, such populations can explode and face heavy periodic die-off or become severe pests. This danger threatens whenever we simplify any community.

A few species are notorious for their unrestricted growth potential— prickly pear and rabbits in Australia; quelea finches and locusts in Africa. The bison of North America and the springbok of South Africa are some of the best known. No matter how much predation they encountered from indigenous hunters and other predators, bison and springbok numbers grew so high that their survival depended on die-offs and high accident rates. Early travelers told of incredible numbers of bison that annually broke through the ice on rivers like the Yellowstone and drowned in whole herds.

In Africa a close friend of mine shot one buffalo with a light rifle. The ensuing stampede left twenty-seven dead. Excellent films on the migration of the wildebeest herds in the Serengeti plains of East Africa show something of the culling that occurs as they cross steep-banked rivers leaving many individuals crushed or drowned. One should not view this as bad, as such populations have gone beyond predation's capacity to control them.

Humanity, to its sorrow, belongs to the same category. For millions of years as hunter/gatherers our populations remained small and in balance with the communities that sustained us. No longer! We historically overcame so many limiting factors that our numbers exploded and continue to do so. Yet even today, some cultures, such as the Bushmen of Africa, depend on heavy infant mortality, slow breeding, and short lives for their very survival, because their world will not sustain greater numbers. Does one pity them and thus provide the basic hygiene and medicine that may eventually destroy them as a culture, or does one create a vast reservation for them and allow them to exist for many more years in harmony with their community, but as museum pieces in the modern world?

Since *Homo sapiens* cannot escape the successional principles of this planet, we have but two options:

1. Become self-regulating through birth control and family planning, or
2. Continue as a nonself-regulating population and allow massive death losses from war, accident, disease, and starvation to regulate our numbers.

Age Structure Means More Than Numbers in Assessing the Condition of Any Population

Figure 37-1 shows what is known as the sigmoid, or S-shaped, curve that describes the growth of virtually all populations. Starting at point A with very few individuals, a species increases gradually. By point B growth accelerates as the breeding population expands geometrically. At about point C further growth encounters difficulties of some kind and the rate falls off as numbers approach the community's capacity to support them. Although individuals may breed as quickly as ever, the pressure for food, cover, space, and so on becomes so extreme that accident, disease, malnutrition, increased success of predation, etc. impose heavy losses on the population. In the case of a self-regulating population breeding is somehow reduced, it appears.

The importance of the individual changes as this growth occurs. At

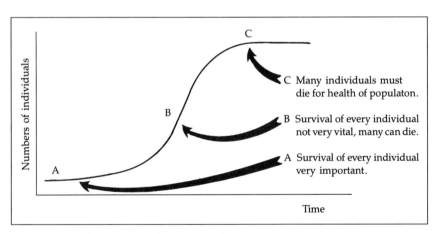

Figure 37-1. Sigmoid population growth curve.

point A the survival of each individual has a great influence on progress along the curve. By point B the occasional loss of an individual matters less. By point C the very survival of the population depends on the death of many individuals. Sometimes this occurs in ways that allow the population to remain high and relatively stable. Often, however, populations that reach point C become extremely unstable, and the limiting factors produce a catastrophic die-off that returns the whole process to point A.

The great naturalist Aldo Leopold called the limiting pressures on a population at point C environmental resistance because they come from the entire community. Unfortunately, when mankind upsets the built-in checks and balances, as he does by removing predators, some populations explode to higher numbers, which in turn exert great pressure on yet other populations and thus destabilize the whole. Predators, remember, consist of more than lions and coyotes. A spraying of insects also kills millions of their predators.

At each point on the growth curve the population has a characteristic age structure. Figure 37-2 shows in sketch 1 how at point A, though numbers are low, the proportion of young is high. At point B the age structure looks more like sketch 2. The young remain numerous and numbers decline regularly through all age classes.

Sketch 2 represents a very healthy population within a community. It will remain healthy if kept at that level by human management or predation (including human predation), which takes off individuals in a way that maintains the structure.

Sketch 3 shows the age structure at point C where broader environmental resistance becomes important. Because disease, starvation, and accidents affect the very young and the very old more than adults in their prime, the numbers dip sharply at point (a). This low reflects the high proportion of last year's young that did not survive. A herd of deer that bear young once a year, for example, might have relatively few two-year-olds. The age classes at point (b) are relatively abundant, however, because they represent individuals in their prime that can better withstand disease, starvation, etc. By point (c) the numbers drop off again as fewer individuals reach really old age under the stress of environmental resistance.

These diagrams of population age structure cover almost all situations where individuals in a population have any sort of prolonged life. Annual plant populations would not follow this pattern. There are anomalies.

Most living organisms acquire the age structure in sketch 3 when they reach the limit of their community to support them. Mankind, however, can get there prematurely. We are the only creature that can so damage its environment that it starts to die off before reaching its full potential. Ethiopia recently has provided a case example of this. Millions have starved, not because of overpopulation, but because conventional management has so

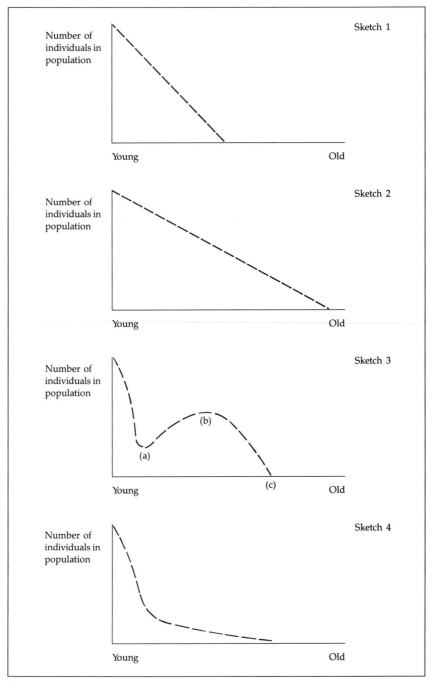

Figure 37-2. Population age structure at various points on a sigmoid growth curve.

damaged water and mineral cycles, successional processes, and energy flow in their largely brittle environment. Well-managed, it could sustain their present population, I believe.

Likewise in New Mexico, the four ecosystem processes have suffered as dramatically as I have seen anywhere on earth, and the rural population is in fact low and declining. If New Mexico had to support the sort of population that many developing countries must on a similar area of land, its chief export would also be gruesome photographs from relief agencies.

Second, humans occasionally kill off the prime age classes of their populations first. Warfare does this when the brunt falls on the actual soldiers as opposed to civilian populations. Now an epidemic of acquired immune deficiency syndrome (AIDS) threatens the adult sector of the population rather than the very young or the very old. A serious AIDS epidemic will give a human society the structure shown in sketch 4.

Because age structure reflects so precisely where on the S-curve a population lies, it provides much more useful information for management purposes than numbers ever can. First of all, numbers can be very misleading in regard to the potential carrying capacity of the environment, which is almost always subject to change. Second, knowing the size of a population seldom helps decide what to do about it, whereas the age structure often does. Third, accurate counts, especially of wild and mobile populations, are nearly impossible, whereas a simple random sample will tell a lot about age structure.

Field counts, even of plants, frequently fail to meet scientific standards. In Pakistan, for instance, I had no way to count those desert bushes. Even if I could have, I could not know how far from the village people under extreme pressure could organize to cut them. After sampling several sites, however, I can argue for the high degree of accuracy in the age structure shown by the solid line in figure 37-3. The dotted line represents what a

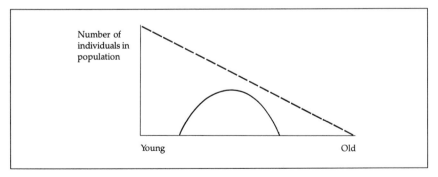

Figure 37-3.   Desert bush population age structure. Pakistan.

healthy brush community supplying firewood should be, as people do not pull out seedlings or young plants.

Even assuming the villagers manage holistically and set a landscape goal that includes productive brush, the situation does not require total protection. The age structure indicates that the population is regressing from point C but has not regressed to point A (figure 37-1) where the survival of every individual is crucial. In Chapter 48 I will discuss this case in more detail showing what management tools we could use to save the brush.

The failure of people to notice and act on such readily apparent information extends far beyond the developing world. When I first visited California in 1978 I traveled through miles of oak woodlands without seeing a single seedling or young tree, but no one voiced the slightest concern. Deer populations had produced a browse line on nearly every tree so early in the season that few fawns could possibly survive after weaning. Hunting, confined mainly to mature males, was clearly not helping to reduce pressure on the fawns. As local ranchers killed coyotes on sight, little besides an annual starvation of the fawn crop, accidents, and disease could keep the deer numbers in check.

Illustration 37-1. "Pristine" range site in New Mexico showing "desired" species of grasses but expanding bare ground and absence of any young plants for many years.

When major tree populations as well as game show no significant survival of young, bad trends already afflict all four ecosystem processes, and of course human prospects as well, but a simple count does not reveal this.

On rangelands plant age structure tells us much more about the health of the community than key species. Illustration 37-1 is a close-up view of a piece of range in New Mexico, which the Soil Conservation Service has used as the standard against which to measure similar sites as it reflects the potential they could reach. It contains the key species all right, but every plant is old and senile after sixteen years of total rest. Despite millions of seeds having been produced in those sixteen years, there is not one young plant. All four of the ecosystem foundation blocks are functioning at very low levels and the desertification process is well on its way.

The management of game provides many dramatic examples of the limitations of counting, though whenever people initiate a game management program they usually sink a large part of the initial budget into a census and base further decisions on that. Usually their results prove not only irrelevant but also faulty.

When construction began on one of the world's first megadams, the Kariba Dam on the Zambezi River between Zimbabwe and Zambia, I was working with the Game Department, which was responsible for rescuing game from the islands that formed as the lake filled. The large number of islands and the logistics involved required a high level of planning and good estimates of the game. The perfect hindsight possible as we took the last animal off the dwindling bits of land consistently revealed the utter inaccuracy of our best techniques.

I recall one island with a large, flat, thirty-five-acre top, grassy and easy to move over. It had large baobab trees scattered about, which made good viewing platforms, and the game had browsed off all leaves below about six feet, making visibility excellent. Our highly experienced crew, amounting to more than a man per acre, counted 60 kudu, 150 impala, and numerous other animals. But there were in fact 120 kudu and over 300 impala when all were finally captured.

How many people rely on the counting done by one or two people over a few days on a vast area of land?

The mystique of aerial counting has also proven hollow in my experience. I used to allow tourist planes to fly over my own game reserve regularly, when the public game reserves and national parks forbade them. If I was flying myself and happened to spot a herd of elephant or buffalo, I would contact the tour pilots and tell them where they could find the game, but often they could not see it until I flew overhead and dipped a wing. At times they would see herds and report to me, but I could not find them.

Few animals stand out better from the air than elephant and buffalo. With less conspicuous animals the situation was hopeless. I once circled four times very low over a herd of sable antelope in open woodland while four observers in the plane classified them as to sex and age. Only after the fourth turn did any of us notice the herd contained more zebra than sable. Four times we had circled without noticing a single one. The moment one was seen, many were seen. Such is the nature of aerial sighting.

On another occasion I took up some visitors who particularly wanted to see gemsbok and before long found a herd of about fifteen of these large animals standing well out in the open plains. I spotted them on my side of the plane as I passed low over them, but when I circled back, no gemsbok! Another pass. Nothing! My pride at stake, I criss-crossed the area for thirty minutes before giving up in embarrassment. Once back on the ground we drove to the site, and there they stood, fifteen gemsbok calmly grazing.

Large masses of game can render themselves practically invisible. I remember one twenty-thousand-acre tract in Zimbabwe where the owner planned to ranch game, particularly impala that we had assessed to number over five thousand. We flew the area at various altitudes searching all the places we knew them to spend the day without seeing a single one. The owner concluded in despair that since they obviously migrated on such days to neighboring land, he could not count on a commercial harvest. Then, driving back from the airstrip along the river, we saw several hundred standing there as usual.

Ultimately I came to mistrust aerial counting more than any other technique. We have learned the same lesson when trying to spot humans from the air. During Algeria's war for independence, the Algerians marched large bodies of men over open country right under French spotter planes. They had only to walk in ragged fashion, rather than in formation, and not look up at the planes. Just look at how we have to use spotter pigeons to find people lost in boats at sea. Ask any pilot how many of the blips on his radar screen he actually sees in the sky.

If aerial counting is hopeless, what about estimates by people who live amongst the game? Surely after many years on a ranch, a rancher knows roughly how many deer he has?

I recall spending a full week strip counting game on an African ranch in the company of the owner. In this procedure one covers roads and tracks morning and evening with several observers recording the distance traveled from the center of the track to the nearest animal sighted in each herd. Using the distance traveled and the average width of the sample strip one assumes a constant density over the whole area and computes total population figures, which, though better than most estimates, usually turn out low.

After spending a week at this, the rancher declared that in all his years on the place he had never actually seen so much of it. When we worked out the size of the sample, however, we had covered only 2 percent of his land. What did either of us really know?

Seat-of-the-pants guesses seldom rest on hard evidence. On many ranch tours I have recorded every cow and deer sighted. The rancher might tell me he had about three hundred deer. On questioning, he would agree that they lay up in cover most of the day and hid from the sound of vehicles, while the cattle hung around the roads and gates. What did it mean that in broad daylight we saw from the pickup 190 of his 300 deer and 430 of his 1,500 cattle?

In order of importance probably twenty other questions deserve more attention than numbers in the management of game. Besides age structure, other factors such as the sex ratio in adults; the feed, cover, and water requirements; home ranges; levels of use of feed plants; the age structures of those feed plants, and so on deserve far more attention than game counts.

One example illustrates how age-class sampling can be used to monitor a reduction in numbers.

Years ago an American wildlifer, Archie Mossman, and I assisted the Forestry Commission in Zimbabwe in starting a game management scheme that called for culling and marketing sable antelope and eland (our largest antelope). The forest was dense and large, and eland in particular avoid people. I personally did the first survey and found them impossible to even sample. Even though their tracks and dung indicated a large population, I saw only six after traveling the tracks for days and lying in wait countless hours at waterholes.

In this case we said "let there be X number of eland that we assume from evidence to be large enough to allow culling of two hundred animals." Although we had seen few from our vehicles, professional hunters had no trouble tracking and shooting that number. Then, of course, we had a sample, as the animals were shot on sight without regard to age, condition, or sex, as long as they appeared adult.

The age structure of such a sample can be worked out by weighing the eye lenses, which get heavier with age, or by noting tooth wear and replacement. Ranking the jaws of all two hundred eland on a scale of 1 to 10 produced the age structure shown in sketch 1 of figure 37-4. This, plus the signs of browsing on vegetation, confirmed that the X number of eland had arrived at point C in figure 37-4.

After three years of culling at this level, the curve changed to that shown in sketch 2 of figure 37-4. This indicated that the culling had begun to reduce mortality of the young and increase recruitment to the population. By steadily watching this age structure and sampling track density and vegetation response, we gradually refined herd management without ever knowing how many animals we had.

I have dwelt perhaps overlong on this matter of numbers because it so obsesses many people. My own examples come mostly from game management, because natural cases give the purest illustrations, but the same

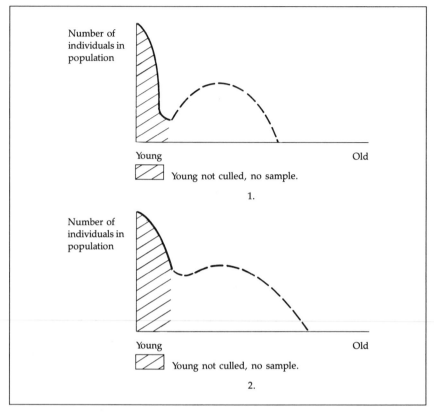

Figure 37-4. Age structure of eland population before and after culling operations.

principle applies to all plant, animal, fish, and bird populations on which we depend.

Particularly when dealing with nomadic cultures or indigenous people, the discussion of numbers of livestock may be an explosive issue. Many have encountered government-enforced stock reduction and see it as genocide. Traditionally, keeping the largest possible herd of female animals of whatever age has enabled them to rebound quickly after episodes of drought cost them a crop or two of young, and when general environmental decline threatens, they do not change this strategy. Thus they will fight any talk of reduction as hard as any overcapitalized Texas rancher.

On the other hand, most understand completely the principle of age structure and the environmental resistance that takes their young animals. That can be the opening for discussion of the second part of the population management guideline—the causes of population decline or increase.

Bottlenecks (the Weak Link Revisited)

I illustrated this principle in Chapter 21 with the case of the Mexican rancher who acquired a large population of toads by constructing ramps in his water troughs so that smaller creatures could reach water. This probably eliminated the weak link in their population growth.

The principle can work to reduce a population as well, but, granting the benefit of stability from greater complexity, be sure to test rigorously any action against the guidelines if it will simplify a community.

Water for crucial short periods often constitutes the weak link for populations that must drink frequently. They may have all the feed, cover, and water enough for enormous numbers, but if water lacks for several days at one point in the year, the entire population, if nonmobile, dies.

Even mobile species, however, may not escape. I had many sandgrouse in my game reserve in Zimbabwe. They not only needed water, they actually had to be able to walk into it each evening to thoroughly wet their breast feathers. In this manner, they carried water miles out into the dry country for their chicks, which could not survive without it. A simple drinking ramp, then, was not enough. I had to ensure that they could walk into water that was deep enough to wet their chests, but shallow enough to prevent drowning.

Many a rancher has told of placing waterpoints out on the land that can be used by birds, small animals, and game, but steep-sided stock troughs in sites of maximum disturbance and no cover don't serve those species and may even kill them. At low water levels, birds and other creatures frequently can clear the sides but drown when they can't get back out. I like to ask such ranchers how they would fare in hot weather if they crossed the desert toward the scent of water to find a ten-thousand-gallon reservoir six inches out of reach.

Many bottlenecks, however, require more diligent observation than that. I have a falconer friend in Scotland with whom I have enjoyed some good days of sport on his grouse moor. Once after many hours of trudging through the heather behind the pointers, he commented that the grouse population should be higher given the quantity of food, cover, and water—the most common bottlenecks. After mulling the evidence, we hit on the fact that a more productive moor nearby had graveled roadsides that might offer more grit for a bird's crop.

Soon afterwards he put out mounds of broken shells at several sites, but later reported that the grouse ignored them, so he abandoned the idea. Close inspection a few years later when I returned nevertheless showed that although the piles had not visibly diminished, some creature, presumably grouse, had methodically removed the tiniest bits of shell, leaving only larger, unusable pieces.

The bottleneck principle applies equally to plants. A good example are the potentially very productive vleis (grassy valleys) in much of southern Africa. Moisture, soil depth, and all other conditions for a highly complex successional community exist. However, every dry season the low-lying vlei can experience a frost or two that limits development to communities dominated by grasses and forbs. Beyond the frost line, the community can develop to woodland.

Absence of a particular trace mineral is another common bottleneck, or weak link, in plant growth. I recall a ranch in Africa on open, grassy country, which for no obvious reason lacked a good mixture of woody, deeper-rooted plants. One day while surveying the bleak countryside from the ranch house verandah, I noticed that the scraggly hedge the rancher's wife had tried to establish round the house was noticeably healthier at one point. Neither the rancher nor his wife could explain this, so we dug up the earth for evidence and discovered the copper ground of their lightning rod. As a consequence I recommended the addition of copper to the supplementary feed given the cattle so that they could begin to spread it on the land. Unfortunately, as the war heated up in Zimbabwe I was unable to get back to the ranch and never knew the outcome.

Managing for Diversity, Not Single Species

Whether the population in question is a desirable crop, forage grass, or a particular species of wild game, much damage flows from focusing on the health of a single population out of context. Agricultural producers have understandable incentives to question this principle, though it applies to all situations. Some of the most serious abuse, however, occurs in national parks and forests where management often concentrates on a particular game species or tourist attraction and imperils the whole.

Earlier I cited the culling of elephants in the Mana Pools National Park in Zimbabwe as one of my worst mistakes as a research officer. It illustrates this point very well.

National parks generally have eliminated or interfered with predators, including man, leaving communities far from intact as wholes. Most areas are too small for the large free-roaming herds of old, and many in brittle environments have suffered from the combination of low animal impact and overgrazing that leads to bare ground. Overgrazing, dependent as we now know on the exposure and reexposure of plants to grazing animals, reflects timing. That comes from movement, which in wild herds depends on size of home range or territory and predation. Home range or territory in turn is a function of population size and habitat. As populations become too large and flocks and herds too numerous, each population eventually finds its territory (and thus its ability to move) more restricted. An area might be very large but its various habitats may be poorly distributed. If this is so it may not serve the territorial requirements of some species. Population size and habitat are in turn affected by fire, road patterns, human disturbance, fences, and much more.

I recommended drastic reduction of elephant herds in order to protect a fine population of winterthorn trees (*Acacia albida*) that grew in the alluvial plains along the Zambezi River (shown in illustrations 19-17 and 19-18). Eventually, when this was done, complete families of elephants were destroyed, leaving no survivors that would pass a fear of man on to the tame animals that tourists liked to photograph.

Now the fewer, tame, elephants hang around the winterthorn trees on the alluvial plains and methodically destroy them. They feed high off the ground, so have no incentive to move off their own dung and urine. They can ignore the parade of tame humans, clicking cameras through the windows of their cars. They have no other predators, so why move?

Illustration 37-2 shows an elephant that had walked right through a tourist camp, oblivious to people, tents, washrooms, cars, camp tables, and

Illustration 37-2. Unaware of the heavy culling that has taken place, this elephant shows little concern for humans and ignores me standing eight yards from him with a clicking camera, 1985. Mana Pools National Park, Zimbabwe.

noise. This is as unnatural as an elephant can be. When I first worked there, just after the indigenous people had been removed because of sleeping sickness, wild, natural elephants in that wonderful setting reacted immediately and often violently to the slightest scent of humans. I was seriously charged myself as many as six times in a single day by anxious cow elephants.

All that change is nevertheless just part of the story. Away from the alluvial plains lies a vast area of bush that stays dry for much of the year. Three miles from the plains, illustration 37-3 shows one of the winterthorn trees that has germinated on the hard-crusted soil typical of a brittle environment with inadequate soil disturbance. It has struck root in the footprint of an elephant that broke the surface crust. Elephants that can break such soil crusts and open up dense brush, allowing grass and habitat to form for other species, are now being killed at a high rate to save the trees on the plains. If we kill almost all the elephants in this park, as we will have to in order to prevent tree damage where the remaining few lie up for hours daily, what of the effects on the surrounding areas and the other species?

The consequences of my misguided policy don't stop there. To carry out the kind of complete, instant eradication of herds necessary for keeping

Illustration 37-3. A young winterthorn tree establishing itself where an elephant has broken the hard cap on the soil, 1985. Mana Pools National Park, Zimbabwe.

other herds tame requires a capital intensive, military-style operation equipped with helicopters, radios, and equipment to process vast amounts of meat, tusks, and hides quickly. The local people, already displaced from the land to make way for the park, get next to nothing, yet without their good will, the park cannot survive.

Perhaps culling has to return to year-round hunting with man regarded as, and acting as, a predator. He has been the principal predator of some species for a long time and perhaps this cannot be discontinued without damage to the whole. Local guides could be used and the meat, hides, and tusks could be offered to the local people. If overseas visitors did much of the hunting, it would bring in far more foreign currency than bulk sales through an absentee contractor.

Conclusion

In summary, humanity depends entirely upon living organisms, which are indivisible components of communities of complexity beyond our comprehension. However, we must manage populations within those communities. In reality, we can only follow sound and long-established principles while monitoring the whole through the four fundamental processes that drive our ecosystem. Once management loses sight of the whole and concentrates on species, be it crops, insects, game, or man, tragedy looms just around the corner.

Now let's proceed to the guidelines developed for the use of that powerful and ancient tool, fire.

38

Burning

Fire is not unlike a carpenter's chisel. At times it is the only tool for the job, but it is dangerous in the hands of an inexperienced person. Because the key to management of all four ecosystem processes is the soil surface, which fire exposes so ruthlessly, burning requires extreme caution. The burning guideline serves to remind you of the dangers while providing appropriate safeguards.

Use fire only when the testing guidelines show it to be the best tool for achieving both landscape and production goals. Particularly avoid burning purely for the sake of tradition, accepted practice, or what other people say. Because results may vary considerably even in the best of circumstances, monitor closely after the burn.

Granted all those warnings, fire remains a powerful and often useful tool. If your landscape goal includes great diversity, then to maintain species that depend on periodic burns will require it. Nevertheless, many who advocate burning to invigorate grassland in brittle environments fail to understand that the benefit comes from disturbance in any form, not just fire. Any uniform type of disturbance will tend to produce a more uniform (less diverse) community than the same land under a variety of forms of disturbance.

The most common justifications for burning as a means to reach landscape goals are:

1. To invigorate and freshen mature perennial grass plants.
2. To invigorate and thicken up brush for wildlife cover.
3. To expose soils and create lower successional areas and mosaics of

different communities in order to support a greater diversity of species.

4. To reduce selected woody species that are fire-sensitive at certain stages of their lives.
5. To provide intense disturbance to an old senile community.

Before You Burn

Quickly review again the testing guidelines to make sure you have made the right decision.

Whole Ecosystem

This is vital, though a bit subjective. Look at the status of all four ecosystem foundation blocks. What degree of soil exposure do you have now? What litter will you lose? What might fire do to the mineral and water cycles envisioned in your goal? What will happen to the microenvironment at the soil surface, and how will that influence the succession you count on?

In considering these questions remember to think about the entire future community and age structure of its populations, not just adult plants and animals. In managing wholes don't think in terms of species but processes—water and mineral cycles, succession, and energy flow. In Chapter 17 I cited the example of the annual burning of teak forests early in the dry season to save the trees from more damaging fires later. The practice ignored the successional process, thus dooming the forest. No teak seedlings could establish on the bare, inorganic sand left by the frequent low-intensity fires set to save the forest.

Burning to eradicate brush (the most common reason given by extension services) almost always fails to pass the whole ecosystem guideline. Fire, rather than killing, invigorates many woody species, causing them to thicken up and send out multiple stems. Because it bares soil, it also tends to produce long-term damage to the grassland you might hope to enhance. The whole ecosystem guideline asks you to anticipate the impact on all four blocks, not just the brush.

Cause and Effect

If intending to burn to fight a symptom (effect), you must ensure that you simultaneously act to rectify the cause. If you don't, you could find yourself using fire to fight symptoms brought on by fire itself. Burning very rank fibrous grass to make it more palatable is a good example. The fire will freshen individual plants by clearing the old growth but it also tends to bare soil and increase the spacing between plants. This results in fewer, larger plants, which in turn become coarser and more fibrous. Repeated burning only exacerbates the problem as can be seen in the tall grass areas of Africa and South America and the alkali sacaton valleys of the American West.

Burning forbs considered weeds that spring from the cracks in bare, exposed soil is equally self-defeating. The successional process begins with such tap-rooted plants that take hold easily in the cracks left by the fire, and the material of their stems, leaves etc. will provide the soil cover enabling succession to advance. Burning them sets succession back to square one and defeats your goal.

Elsewhere I mentioned my belief that the tsetse fly population (*Glossina morsitans* in particular) increased when we burned because burning exposed soil and increased breeding sites. We burned in order to ease game hunting. The game was being hunted out in an attempt to remove the fly's blood supply and so eradicate the fly. These efforts proved useless in the end because enough small host animals remained to supply blood anyway and with the breeding sites created by our burning, the fly population was able to expand.

Marginal Reaction

We often view the tool of fire as cheap because the only investment involved is a box of matches. However, reckoning in lost forage and grazing time and the reduced effectiveness of rainfall may well show the true cost to be extremely high.

Weak Link

Burning to reduce a fire-sensitive woody species becomes most tempting in years of low forage production because the brush stands out amid the poor grass. However, in that case energy conversion (into forage) is the weak link between sunlight and solar dollar, and burning the range will *reduce* forage over the short term when you need it most. Ideally you would burn in a season that grows an excess of forage that livestock or wildlife can't use, i.e., when energy conversion is not the weak link in the sunlight to solar dollar chain.

Gross Margin Analysis, Energy/Wealth

As burning is seldom an enterprise that can be marketed, gross margin analysis would not normally apply. The energy/wealth test probably won't affect most decisions on burning either, but that doesn't mean you can forget either test. Like the pilot who keeps landing gear on his check list, even though he flies a fixed-wheel plane, by keeping all the tests on yours you too will avoid the chance of someday coming in wheels up.

Society and Culture

This test might be difficult to pass in certain situations in that not using fire can present problems where people hold certain beliefs about fire. I mentioned in Chapter 17, for instance, that in parts of Africa people believe that if certain areas are not burned the rains may fail to come. Years of burning undoubtedly will have led to a poor water cycle, which is bound to have harmful effects on the livelihood of those people. In such cases an effort must be made to educate the people to the dangers.

Planning

Once you have decided to burn, you must plan for the fire. Apart from the legalities that may apply in any particular area regarding warnings to neighbors, etc., you will probably need firebreaks. To avoid the eroding eyesores often created by burning or grading firebreaks, use animal impact to create them instead. As I mentioned in Chapter 29, you can spray a fine molasses/water or salt/water solution (when salt has been deprived) in a strip where you want the firebreak in order to attract stock to the area. They will remove enough flammable material for a break from which to backburn but without exposing the soil.

Next you must consider what kind of fire you need.

Types of Burn

Burns may be either hot or cool, depending on the amount of fuel, its moisture content, and atmospheric humidity. Hot burns occur when large amounts of combustible material and dry conditions produce large flames that persist for a long time and can seriously damage the aboveground parts of woody plants. In the tropics, where the year divides into wet and dry seasons, the best time for hot burns comes at the end of the dry season. In temperate zones opportunities may depend on several factors.

Cool burns (often called early burns in the tropics because they come at the start of the dry season) are done when forage is still partially green or damp and difficult to ignite. In this case the fire trickles along, barely scorching the woody plants. Where cool burns come at the beginning of a dry season, they expose soil longer before new growth can provide cover than a hot burn that comes later. This consideration also varies considerably according to local conditions.

Where hot fires, being more fierce, tend to burn uniformly, cool burns are generally patchy and broken, as not all the material burns well.

If you decide your situation calls for a hot burn for high heat, more uniform burning, and shorter soil exposure, you must ensure the presence of sufficient fuel by not grazing it down just before you need it. The biological planning technique covered in Chapter 40 and in the companion workbook deal with this in more detail. If you intend the hot burn to kill a fire-sensitive plant, then the burn date should come at its most vulnerable stage, be it during fast growth, dormancy, or just before dormancy. The stage of life of the plant, whether seedling or more mature, may also be crucial.

A cool burn requires less fuel, which may mean taking some grazing out before the burn. Again, biological planning should assure this well before the event.

For some years I tried to perfect another form of burn in the high rainfall areas of Zimbabwe and in the South American tropics, which I called a singe burn. It supposedly would consume the old oxidizing grass during the early rains when wet ground would keep litter from burning and thus not expose soil. Though attractive in theory, this idea proved impossible in practice. For fire to run over litter without burning it, perfect wind, temperature, and moisture conditions must coincide, and that may happen for only a few hours on one or two days. Without a mammoth labor force standing by to seize the moment, you cannot cover much ground.

For our experiments we would start the morning after an inch of rain and spend the morning battling to get the fire to run. If we decided to wait a few hours until the tops dried a bit more, the wretched fire often as not caught too well, dried out whole plants, and burned the litter anyway. To cover more ground we had lines of men on horseback dragging burning tires, but nothing proved workable over wide areas.

Though the idea failed as a substitute for grazing to rejuvenate grassland, it is worth mentioning because it did succeed in isolated patches, and that sometimes has value in itself.

Burning to Enhance Wildlife Habitat or Reinvigorate Communities

As so many plants and animals are to varying degrees fire-dependent, it can be a mistake in some environments to suppress fire altogether. A community depressed by excessive old, oxidizing material will commonly require a hot burn if animal impact cannot be used to reinvigorate it. However, the patchiness that characterizes cool burns often produces the most varied wildlife habitat.

Patchy burning increases the edge effect, often an important factor in supporting large and diverse populations of game animals, birds, and other creatures. For example, where forest meets meadow, animals find cover in the wood, visibility across the open land, and feed from two types of environment. Hunters know this well, as they most often find greatest success along the edge between major communities. Streams also provide an edge of great contrasts.

Thus the quantity of edge, together with water distribution, counts for much. Figure 38-1 shows two equal blocks of land, both containing two different habitats in equal measure. Block B, however, offers far more edge and thus more opportunities for wildlife.

If, with firebreaks and control, one can make a hot fire burn in patches, all the better. By eliminating more woody vegetation, at the risk of more erosion, it will increase the contrast with unburned areas. Repeated cool

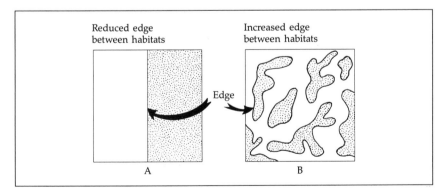

Figure 38-1.   Edge effect increased with a mosaic of habitats.

burns, although initially providing patchiness, may lead eventually to greatly increased woody communities of somewhat fire-tolerant species and loss of patchiness. This may reduce the contrast in habitat type significantly.

Following a Burn

Because fire exposes soil, most goals require advance planning to include a strategy for applying other tools immediately after the fire to speed restoration of ground cover. Commonly, high animal impact does the job most efficiently. Where the fire leaves large, bare, ash-covered spaces between plants, a concentrated herd breaks up these surfaces so that succession starts rapidly.

Big game species in Africa at times concentrate on the burned area even before the ground cools off, though they can move off to nearby areas for more abundant feed. You will usually have to wait for some regrowth before holding livestock on burned ground unless you can plan to graze burned and unburned paddocks as one, with herd effect concentrated on the burn. Alternatively, if it passes the testing guidelines, you can feed hay on the burn, though that consumes dollars and takes technology to produce and distribute (therefore, pay special attention to the marginal reaction guideline).

Unfortunately, so great is the fear of animal impact in range mangagement thinking that extension services routinely recommend (or insist) on keeping stock off burned land for up to two years. I have yet to discover any need for this, as long as the grazings are planned.

When an unexpected fire sweeps through your ranch, either by human accident or an act of Nature, you must replan at once. When you do, assess the soil surface needs relative to your landscape goal, and if they justify using the tool of animal impact, plan to bring on livestock as soon as possible using high concentration and herd effect. Normally you can do this as soon as enough forage grows to carry animals for a short time in the burned area. You can do it sooner if nearby unburned areas will support them while they have access to the burned land. Seldom will you have to induce animal impact from game animals as they tend to concentrate on the burn.

Finally, remember to ask yourself, "What if I was wrong in anything I've done up to now in connection with the burn? What data would give me the earliest measurable warning? Am I watching and noting in detail what I need to so that no great mistakes are made?"

Monitoring

Monitoring of the four ecosystem processes (as Chapter 41 will cover) is essential following a burn. Apart from helping avoid potential crises, it will help you gain a better working knowledge of the effects of fire on the land. Where fire itself does little damage in many situations, and often advances many goals, frequent use of fire can become very detrimental. Had we monitored the effect on basic processes during my game department days, we surely would never have set fires with such abandon. We never even considered the fundamentals of ecology nor realized their importance. Thinking only of adult trees, grasses, and animals we managed for species, not process or population structure.

But one must manage for the whole, not species, and therefore must monitor constantly the factors that reflect the health of the whole, such as litter cover, soil exposure, and plant spacings. Changes in these give the earliest warning of change in the water cycle through increased run-off and surface evaporation and decreased penetration. Changes in age structure of plant populations in particular show what is happening to succession. Which plants show the greatest influx of young that survive through the seedling stage? When they mature, will that be the community you want?

You must watch particularly for any early signs indicating need for another burn within a few years. If such develop, try to find an alternative tool to do the task, especially in more arid areas. The drier the climate, the more dramatic the effects of fire and the less frequent its use should be. But what is frequent?

For many years in Zimbabwe the four-paddock-three-herd grazing system was common practice. One paddock was burned each year and the animals rotated through the other three; thus each paddock was burned once every four years. In the early days of my search for better ways, I visited numerous ranches as well as the research stations promoting this practice, to see if it offered any hope. This took me to a variety of areas, which included both sandy and clay soils and rainfall averages that ranged from eight to seventy inches. Nowhere did I find land on which the water cycle was not deteriorating. Many published papers had attested to the tremendous results gained by burning every four years, but all were based on the plant species present, rather than what was happening to the soil surface and reflected in the ecosystem processes. Monitoring the soil surface for change will tell you how frequent a burn should be. Where a periodic fire every twenty to fifty years can do good, a burn every two to five years, by exposing soil, can lead to tragedy.

The monitoring methods explained in the companion workbook will cover most watershed and rangeland management situations in brittle environments. However, always think of your own case in detail. Think about your landscape goal and the present state of the ecosystem processes and their future desired state. Make sure that you are measuring, or at least photographing, situations that represent your progress.

Given the tremendous variation in weather, in the physical nature of any piece of land and its alternate and simultaneous uses, and many other factors, you will need considerable flexibility to ensure attainment of your goals. No matter how well we plan, emergencies do arise and these too call for flexibility in management. The next guideline covers the flexibility available to us in both the short and long term.

39

Flexibility

Putting holism into practice means among other things accepting the fact that any resource management problem has many solutions. Like so many other aspects of HRM this apparently trite homily, if taken seriously, has rather radical implications in the context of most modern cultures.

Our faith in science and the mechanistic view of our world that it has brought about in our societies has caused us to commit enormous effort and time trying to invent perfect systems ranging from teacher-proof materials for geography instruction to computer simulations of the world economy, and resource management has not escaped. But the ideal of the well-oiled machine maintained according to a manual of operations that precludes all need for further thought cannot exist, as the vagaries of life in general prove every second. Not only is every whole in the natural world unique today but it is also unique tomorrow in a different way.

In contrast to static ideal solutions, the flexibility guideline says simply this: As the natural world is composed of interdependent wholes in a state of constant change, a mechanical approach to its management can never succeed. This means that preconceived management systems have to end, as do quick fix answers.

Recently, for example, a farmer phoned me wanting to know what he should do about some fields inundated by volunteer plants from the previous year's crop. Because they looked messy, he felt he should either harrow the fields or arrange for sheep to graze them. If I had taken a mechanical approach to this, I would have given him an answer. In taking a holistic approach, I declined, saying that he was the expert. He knew what his goals were and that they pertained to a whole that included much more than the messy fields. With that in mind, he could use the HRM model to assess the best use of his dollars and effort toward those goals and then arrive at a decision. When he did this, he realized the unwanted plants could be ignored as they did not hinder progress toward his goals. In fact, the plants were assisting in their achievement!

Management always has to be based on that three-part goal and the whole it encompasses, and you must be free from rules, systems, and restraints to manage the whole effectively. Given this degree of flexibility, we often don't know what to do with it. Like the imprisoned bird whose cage has been opened suddenly, we remain on our perches, confused by the new possibilities. This chapter aims to clear some of that confusion.

As a practical matter we have come to divide flexibility into three broad levels for planning and management purposes.

1. Strategic—very long-term flexibility in determining and achieving our goals.
2. Tactical—flexibility in handling a crisis year or event while not being sidetracked from the long-term goals.
3. Operational—flexibility in dealing with day-to-day management toward our long-term goals while meeting our immediate needs.

The Strategic Level

At this level we plan those things that have truly long-term consequence and that cannot be changed easily on a whim. The most common examples are:

1. Formation of the more permanent three-part goals discussed in Chapter 46.
2. Planning for the conservation of wealth from generation to generation as mentioned in Chapter 44.
3. Planning the long-term physical layout of land for management to achieve the landscape and production aspects of the goal on farms, ranches, forests, tribal lands, national parks, and the like.

As this last item, land planning, is an infrequent operation—generally applied once in one hundred to two hundred years or so—with long-term consequences not covered by other guidelines, we normally deal with it under this one.

Land Planning

Until now we have rarely planned the land on farms and ranches, forests, national parks, or tribal lands with any long-term vision in mind. Forests were planned for easy extraction, and national parks for the needs of tourists. Farms were planned around the original home site and fields often dictated by the roads and tracks or hedgerows and more recently by the machinery used to work them. Ranches were planned around home sites and handling facilities as well. Fencing went in according to where the water was and, more recently, where range sites differed, the belief being that certain soils and plant communities needed different grazing regimens to limit damage from overgrazing/overtrampling. Nomadic tribes at one time planned their moves according to the needs of their animals for water and forage, and, more recently, as settlement was enforced, conformed to the same restraints as modern-day ranchers, often losing their cultural identity in the process.

Now land planning is based on the three-part goal and considerable forethought goes into it to ensure that it will lead you toward that. The previous restraints imposed by past developments or enforced by modern practices no longer hold sway. But with those limitations now removed, we're like that caged bird that clings to its perch in confusion. Where do we go and how do we begin?

To answer that I'd like to discuss the most difficult situation there is to plan — one involving livestock that have to move frequently and where crops, timber extraction, and recreation may also be features needing attention. Add to this a large number of people with different values and desires and land planning in any other situation becomes a simple task indeed.

First, no sensible planning or management can take place in conflict. For this reason where there are different values and desires in many people using the same land, as would be the case on a ranch that encompasses public land, absolutely nothing should be attempted until a three-part goal is formulated, as described in Chapter 46. This may well be a long process but then so too is strategic level land planning and it should not proceed until conflict is resolved and goals are clear and accepted by everyone involved.

Where planning fencing and other developments used to be fairly rigid thus inviting difficulties in the real world, the flexibility now available somehow has to be dealt with practically. When I started to tackle this some twenty-five years ago, I did not have the knowledge of holism we have today and was thrown in the deep end trying to help farmers pressed by war and the trade restrictions imposed against Rhodesia following its unilateral declaration of independence from Britain.

Most were having to diversify from what had become a traditional crop rotation of one year of tobacco and five years of grass. To make ends meet the continuous grass fallows had to yield to other crops interspersed between years of tobacco and grass. In addition, serious livestock raising entered the picture for the first time as a way to produce extra income off the remaining range, grass leys, and crop residues.

Prevailing wisdom required fencing off range sites of different types to prevent overgrazing or overtrampling of favored areas. Stock had to feed in certain paddocks at certain times according to a systematic pattern. However, this never succeeded in practice because most of the farms were in broken, hilly country where arable land lay in small pockets among a matrix of roads, tracks, rivers, grassy valleys, and woodland remnants. I had to find a new approach that would handle such complexity on the ground amid ever changing external circumstances.

After several years of trying out all sorts of fencing designs and planning techniques, I finally developed a combination of the land planning approach summarized here and the biological planning covered in the next chapter. The two go hand in glove where livestock run on any land.

My first breakthrough came out of better understanding of time management in the control of overgrazing and overtrampling. I realized that we no longer had to follow the old rules. We no longer had to fence in any particular manner or pay lavish attention to range site descriptions. As soon as we could minimize damage to all sites by timing the grazing, the reason for isolating different types of vegetation vanished, though of course intact communities in Nature had never known such divisions.

Solution of the overgrazing and overtrampling problem, not to mention the discovery that grazing and animal impact could serve as positive tools, allowed division of land according to entirely different considerations— animal handling, administration, and transport; management of wildlife, streamsides, and cropland; recreational use; and a host of other needs.

From success in planning complex farms we soon realized that we could assume a totally different attitude toward the management of the land and livestock of tribal people in livestock-oriented cultures. Since they herded their animals, any demarcation of land could serve the purpose of a fence.

Many a well-intentioned livestock and land management scheme has foundered because specific requirements for moving livestock in a set manner conflicted with the lifestyle of the people. To follow such grazing systems, nomads had to settle in static communities, and villagers could not keep livestock in the lower floor of their houses because the animals had to be in a certain pasture. When flexibility and the HRM model replace the system, however, possibilities open up. The people's unique goals take precedence, and their livestock becomes the tool for realizing them.

As one example, the radial fence layout can play a major role in fitting livestock management into the social and geographical structure of villages and many nomadic people. The design consists of separate paddocks radiating out from a focal point that might be a village, water point, handling facility, or merely a convenient point through which livestock can move from one paddock to any other, as illustrated in figure 39-1.

Many condemned this design. André Voisin, who first saw the significance of timing, had found it led to severe trampling where the fences converged. While that holds true under high densities on frequently wet soils such as those in France, it worked well in brittle environments. The drier soils compact less, and recovery periods last long enough for root growth to sustain a healthy community and a well-aerated soil. In fact, once timing is well-planned, the higher animal impact produces better water and mineral cycles, and thus energy flow, near the center where fences converge and high levels of dung and urine are deposited. Thus, in brittle environments where radial layouts have existed for prolonged time under heavy stocking, the growth of vegetation and stability is highest near the center.

Illustration 13-5 (Chapter 13) showed the excellent development of grassland where the fences had converged for many years in one such layout where higher than normal livestock numbers had been run. This contradicts

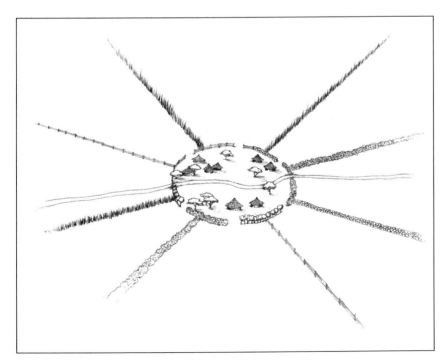

Figure 39-1. Radiating grazing areas from a village.

our experience going back thousands of years of dust bowls developing around livestock concentration points.

The process for developing long-term land plans in livestock situations, described fully in the companion workbook, follows along these lines:

1. The people involved prepare by considering all factors that bear on the situation, beginning with quality of life, production, and landscape goals and proceeding on to boundaries, croplands, crop rotations, topography, weather, wildlife, predation, recreational uses, etc. A short brainstorming session often uncovers factors that might otherwise be forgotten.

2. Special thought goes to the likely size of livestock herds and areas in which the herds probably will graze regularly in normal seasons. This gives an idea of the size of the "grazing cells"—the areas that we will plan as a unit to regulate plant exposure and reexposure.

3. Information on wildlife, weather, sources of water, croplands and rotations, timber extraction routes, recreational access areas, and so on is displayed on transparent overlays placed on clean maps. Separate overlays for each possible use of the same land help draw attention to important features to consider. One overlay will show clearly the essential features of the landscape projected in the landscape goal. Situations that involve a delineation of grazing areas but no fencing follow the same procedure, and this could even extend to the vast range of a nomadic people.

4. Next, a fast and furious brainstorming session is held to produce as many trial layouts as possible. Land can be subdivided in many ways, and all those remotely reasonable are recorded on paper or separate maps. Throughout this process all existing land divisions, fences, water points, and other developments for livestock are ignored in order not to stifle creativity. When all possibilities are exhausted, a plan is drawn up, which takes into account all the existing developments that the brainstorming ignored.

5. Finally the best plan is selected. This is necessarily a long process, covering every possible aspect and all the previously prepared overlays. It requires the participation of people very familiar with both the land and all of the many problems and considerations, but also it is necessary for them to understand the biological planning that will function through the final design. At this stage the chosen plan must also pass the society and culture guideline to see that it does not in any way affect the people or their quality of life adversely.

The final plan may or may not fit easily into existing improvements on many a ranch or public land area. If it does not, then planning must handle a phased changeover in much the same fashion as development of an ideal layout from scratch. The financial planning guideline in Chapter 44 discusses this in detail. Developing a ranch in such a manner should not cost money. On the contrary, the land should generate the capital for each step of development, and each investment should make the next step possible. The financial planning guideline, properly used, not only insures holistically sound developments, but also progress that does not cost outside money unless you choose to use it.

Who Should Plan?

I have seen far too many people who feel they know their land so well they don't need to go to the trouble of creating a long-term plan in such a way that involves other people and some effort. Consequently they simply grab the nearest old map and start drawing fencelines. When tested against the creative planning I have outlined, *very seldom* do those knowledgeable people produce the best plan, so they end up condemning themselves and future generations to an inferior and often more costly layout and poorer results. Much experience shows that the person who knows the land best, by having so many preconceptions, is least qualified to do the creative planning, but is the best and sometimes the only person capable of selecting the ideal plan.

When Herding

If the final plan involves herding rather than fences, any number of methods can demarcate land divisions and grazing areas. In the arid Baluchistan Province of Pakistan I have seen a line drawn on the ground by a donkey dragging a piece of iron. This sufficed for years as an intertribal boundary that herdsmen respected. Line-of-sight divisions, ridge lines, blaze-marked trees, and periodic rock piles (cairns) will also serve. Where a radial layout does not include fencing, short barriers of some kind near the center help funnel the herds as they approach, as shown in figure 39-1. Wire fencing, hedges, or stone walls provide better control, for example, near village boundaries where animals will concentrate 365 days a year and can beat out a sizable area if allowed to spill over and mill about outside the narrow end of a particular grazing area.

In summary, good land planning produces great savings in annual running costs and reduced livestock stress. At the same time, alongside biological planning, it leads to faster and more efficient achievement of goals and better integration of livestock into crops, crop rotations, and all other uses of the land.

Land planning is still advisable even when livestock are not involved. Where farms include row crops, orchards, and perhaps timber, soil types and their distribution may partially determine the layout, but there are other factors to consider. A good layout that takes into account prevailing winds, slopes and waterways, wildlife, and aesthetic and recreational goals as well as production and landscape goals will always be better than one that is laid out purely with the handling of large machinery in mind.

Many a farm is acquired with a layout that was dictated by the whims of a farmer in the distant past, the machines he chose to use, or the forms of transport available. As that layout influences all management toward that three-part goal, it is a good idea at some time to do the unthinkable and actually undertake the creative planning mentioned to see if there are better possibilities. Don't be put off by the fear of change or cost. You would only proceed with a new plan if in fact it did lead to better overall management.

National parks like so many farms and ranches developed from the first access track and administrative settlement. As tourist growth and demand expanded so did tracks, campsites, water points, and other developments, but almost always with no long-term landscape goal in mind. We just did not know that national parks would ever need management much beyond benign neglect. There is a real need now to look at such valued treasures holistically and to plan their management accordingly with long-range land plans that enable us to meet whatever goals are established.

Once you have completed your strategic planning—established your three-part goals, designed a land plan that will help you achieve them and an estate plan to ensure that the results of your efforts are preserved for future generations—what do you do when the worst drought in one hundred years hits and threatens your very survival?

Tactical Level

Tactical level flexibility is required in those infrequent but catastrophic years when we are forced to change routine practices and yet do not want to abandon any of our long-term goals. Where livestock are not involved, the greatest urgency is the need to replan financially what is now going to be a very different picture for the year than planned. Where livestock are involved, the biological plan gets attention first as it will have considerable bearing on financial replanning, and may in fact make it unnecessary.

Biological Planning and Replanning

First look at the flexibility available for handling livestock on land divided by fencing, as most ranches are today. Ranchers, like all humans, are creatures of habit and naturally settle into repeating the same practices year after year. For some reason the radial layout of fencing in grazing cells has an additional mesmerizing effect that lulls both people and livestock into an unshakable rotation schedule. That culminates in tragedy as we saw in Chapter 24 because it subverts any semblance of biological planning.

Even where ranchers do the necessary biological planning each year they will still usually favor a particular way of running their livestock on the land through most years. If the situation changes in any major way, however, you must snap out of the routine. If you have monitored progress well through the season, you should know early on when your planned moves have become improper due to some catastrophe—drought, flood, pest outbreak, fire, or whatever else. Do not continue with the plan-monitor-control procedure of normal years but *replan* immediately. This means a completely new look, rather than minor adjustments to an ongoing plan.

At such times you must drop altogether all preconceived ideas, remind yourself of your three-part goal, and apply the model from scratch to the resources available in the new circumstances. Emergencies such as flood, fire, etc. usually make the need for radical rethinking quite obvious. Droughts, however, creep up on people, and most consider them acts of God, and thus a matter for prayer instead of timely replanning. Where prayer may help, in reality each growing season, especially in brittle environments, is a potential drought, and we have seen impressive improvement of ranges and ranch economics when people planned and replanned according to this tactical flexibility guideline.

All initial planning should automatically include a "time" reserve against potential drought, as discussed in Chapter 25. That covers you if the early part of the growing season does not produce normally. However, if that drought persists, as it may, then you face a *whole growing season* that may not produce enough feed. You can do a lot about that *only if you replan without delay.*

Think particularly about all of the tools that you could apply to improve the effectiveness of any rain that should fall. Fire clearly should be avoided, likewise rest. Technology in its various forms usually will not pass the testing guidelines in such an emergency case except possibly for that technology used to increase animal impact (fences, water, and attractants). Very high animal impact without any overgrazing is commonly a good booster of the water cycle. Every ounce of forage grown per square yard amounts to over three million pounds on a twenty-thousand-acre ranch, no small return on the effort of amalgamating herds for additional animal impact and longer recovery periods.

Figure 39-2 gives an example of an actual six-thousand-acre ranch divided into four cells. Two one-thousand-acre cells of seven and nine paddocks hold herds of two-hundred and three hundred head. Two two-thou-

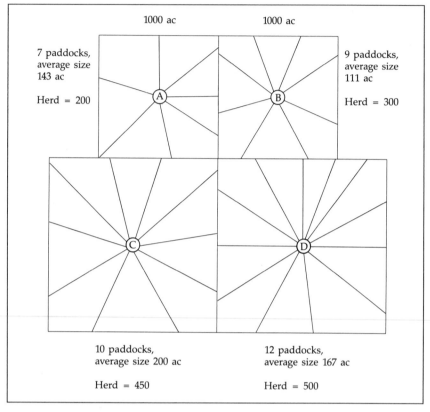

1000 ac   1000 ac

7 paddocks,
average size
143 ac

Herd = 200

9 paddocks,
average size
111 ac

Herd = 300

10 paddocks,
average size 200 ac

Herd = 450

12 paddocks,
average size 167 ac

Herd = 500

Figure 39-2. Drought planning.

sand-acre cells of ten and twelve paddocks carry herds of 450 and 500 head, respectively. For simplicity's sake, assume similar stock in all herds.

According to the grazing planned at the start of the growing season, the four herds follow the grazing period parameters in column 3 of figure 39-3. They take out the average ADA of forage shown in column 4, and over the remaining 130 days of growing season that have become drought they will take out the total ADA shown in column 5.

What happens if we combine the four herds into one for the remainder of the growing season and treat the whole ranch as one thirty-eight-paddock cell? Assuming that the drought causes slow growth, we could extend the ninety-day recovery periods previously used during slow growth to 130 days. The average grazing period for the single herd of 1,450 animals in a thirty-eight-paddock cell, however, would fall to 3.5 days from the 11.1 it would have been in four cells with ninety-day recovery periods. The average ADA remain the same.

1	2	3		
Cell	Recovery periods	Grazing periods	Average ADA per grazing period	Average total ADA per paddock over 130-day season
A	30 — 90	5 — 15 Av. 10	7 — 21	26
B	30 — 90	3.8 — 11.3 Av. 7.5	10 — 30	38
C	30 — 90	3.3 — 10 Av. 6.6	7 — 21	27
D	30 — 90	2.7 — 8.2 Av. 5.5	8 — 24	32

Average grazing periods, all herds all cells   = 7.4 days

Average animal days per acre forage consumed from all paddocks all cells   = 30.75 ADA

Cell	Recovery period	Grazing period	Average ADA per grazing period	Average ADA per paddock
A B C D	130	3.5	32	32

Figure 39-3.   Dramatic effect of combining herds.

It does not require a lot of imagination or experience to realize that higher impact, longer recovery periods, and shorter grazing periods without overgrazing will lead to considerably more forage growth in that season on whatever rain you happen to receive.

In this particular case, before 130 days pass and low temperatures kill any hope of further growth, you would plan the dormant season. This would take into account any additional forage grown in consequence of the herd amalgamation, and would plot its consumption right through to the time reserve allowed for the following season in case that too starts out dry.

The worse the drought and the less forage standing at the outset of the dormant season, the more important the planning, including a drought reserve, becomes. Most ranchers miss the cold fact that if available forage will not carry a herd through the dormant season, and numbers must be cut, *the earlier the decision, the less the reduction.* Decisions left too late can necessitate almost total livestock reduction or whopping feed bills, as the companion workbook explains in detail. In my experience, ranchers who follow conventional grazing practices without the biological planning and time reserve that give them flexibility routinely lose many hundreds of thousands of dollars in a drought needlessly.

My example gives but one alternative. A few hours with pencil and paper will give you many more. Perhaps you have two types of livestock that must stay apart. One herd might stay on continuous grazing in one or two paddocks while a large combined herd moves through many paddocks. Juggling time, numbers, and paddocks will turn up any number of policies that produce quite different effects.

In practice I recommend penciling out up to six or more alternatives before selecting one to follow through the problem period, because drought, being indeterminate in extent and severity, raises very complex questions. Where flood or fire has wiped out many paddocks but not adversely affected the entire ranch, you have all the facts on hand and can replan using the biological planning technique outlined in the next chapter. This should always be done before any stock reduction or panic measures are instituted.

Financial Planning and Replanning

Flexibility at the tactical level includes being ready at any time to change enterprises on a farm or ranch. In setting your goals at the strategic level you were purposely vague about the type of crop, livestock, or other enterprises you named so you would have the flexibility to change to suit markets and other factors, such as the consequences of some natural catastrophe you might face. When catastrophe strikes it is usually necessary to replan finances from scratch. You might be halfway through the year and already incurred your heaviest expenses, which means your present plan does not allow for the extra income you'll now need to cover them. Chapter 44 and the companion workbook show you how to deal with such events.

When replanning in these sorts of circumstances, you start with considerable advantage if you and those working with you formed your goals as a collaborative team. Nothing more than that will bring out the creativity and sacrifice that might be necessary to end the year and go into a new one still on your feet, albeit a bit leaner and harder.

Many farmers and ranchers have little idea of how many possible sources of income they have on their land. At one of the Center for Holistic Resource Management's financial planning courses recently, a Texas farmer currently enjoying income from two enterprises on his land brainstormed thirteen additional sources that had never occurred to him before. An Arizona rancher, again exploiting only two opportunities, thought up eighteen more with the help of a brainstorming group. Clearly no single manager could handle so many efficiently, and one would eliminate those least compatible with goals. Nevertheless, the average tradition-bound manager may overlook enormous resources, especially in times of emergency.

Operational Level

The degree of flexibility exercised at all levels is dependent on how free people are to express their creativity. At the operational (day-to-day) level of management this is critical. Too often, we give people the responsibility for the job without giving them the authority to exercise their creativity in executing it. Chapter 42 discusses the problems this leads to and suggests that when authority is given to managers at the operational level opportunities seen only by them can be seized that otherwise would have been lost, thus delaying the attainment of your goals.

Many of the livestock and range management approaches that we now see the need to alter included some flexibility at the strategic and tactical levels, but at the operational level most concentrated on doing just the opposite. Grazing systems, rotations, and most traditional practices intentionally reduce day-to-day decisions to fixed routines.

Perhaps the livestock business, by assuming the burden of protecting the land from the very animals it raises, while seeking maximum performance from those animals, falls into a particularly straitened form of this human tendency to stay in ruts. A person who sees his herds as agents of destruction does not want daily responsibility for engineering it. Chores are chores and that's that.

Seeing livestock as the primary tool for invigorating land, however, changes that viewpoint fundamentally. One does have responsibility to monitor and fine tune operations daily, and one can do this in four dimensions by manipulating volume (number of animals), area (size of paddocks), time (grazing periods), and behavior (herd effect).

To change the numbers of animals having an impact on the land at any given time you can combine herds or separate them, and you can apply the numbers to the land in several different ways. Multiple herds in a single cell may run together as one, follow each other in close succession through paddocks, or stay separate to allow for recovery between the exit of one herd and the entry of another.

By amalgamating herds or opening two or more paddocks at the same time you can change the area of land per animal, thus increasing or decreasing density. Often during calving, lambing, or kidding you will engineer lower densities, and more time, by allowing three or more paddocks to remain open so that mothers who leave their young hidden can return to them and bring them into the herd when ready.

To change time you simply open a gate sooner or leave it closed longer. Also, as seen in the tactical matter of replanning after drought, you can change timing dramatically by rearranging herds and cells.

And of course at any time you have the option of inducing herd effect through feeding of salt or supplements, or in cases of extreme need, even driving the stock.

All of these changes can stem from simple management decisions on any day and do not involve altering layouts or putting in more fencing. Years ago when I first perceived the enormous permutations our four dimensions of flexibility allow, I could not see how anyone could handle them simply. Fortunately the biological planning process that we look at next does it with ease.

The flexibility guideline constantly reminds us that systematic approaches to the management of our resources must become a thing of the past. Quick fix solutions applied from a limited perspective ultimately culminate in crisis management—*reacting* to the unexpected and unplanned. Now we proceed from clear goals, which we achieve through constant monitoring, control, and replanning when necessary.

40

Biological Planning

The biological planning used in conjunction with the HRM model grew out of planning processes developed for complex crop farms in Africa that included livestock production. Experience and knowledge of the four missing keys greatly refined these into the approach outlined here and in detail in the companion workbook.

Planning in the livestock business once applied principally to attempts to limit overgrazing by controlling stocking rates and the grazing pressure on desirable plant species. Discovery of the role of herding animals in succession, particularly in brittle environments, however, made the planning of grazing relevant to all sorts of other considerations. A good plan can deploy livestock to reduce or cure excessive growth of problem plants, reduce brush and remove its causes, heal a gully, or decrease the breeding sites of grasshoppers. Also, when stock management no longer reflects a desire to protect a given plant species, plans can include a host of other factors such as predation danger, calving convenience, etc.

In the near future, water, rather than meat, hide, or hair, may become the main "product," sought from watersheds in brittle environments. When people and governments realize the utter futility of using mechanical measures alone to conserve water where it falls, livestock grazing and herd effect, planned to minimize overgrazing, will assume even greater importance.

This does not mean neglect of the individual animal's needs. Since most livestock owners list profitability among their goals, their stock must enjoy the best possible plane of nutrition and the least possible need for supplements. Planning also must handle fires, flash floods, droughts, poisonous plant infestations, and other catastrophes.

Wildlife needs, too, must bear on any plan. Herding livestock can devastate ground nesting birds, and as stock management influences succession it plays the key role in maintenance of habitat, cover, and feed for all the diverse creatures that make up a healthy environment.

The list continues almost without end, but holistic management requires consideration of all factors simultaneously. Jokes about not being able to walk and chew gum aside, the human brain has difficulty working on two thoughts at once, and large numbers of animals, vast tracts of land, and long periods of time are particularly hard to conceptualize, even singly. You cannot achieve a specific landscape goal, using livestock as a major tool, without forethought and planned action. Clearly a methodical planning process, *on paper*, offers the only hope.

The Planning Approach

A large percentage of the farmers and ranchers who have heard my case for planning have volunteered vigorous arguments why their own situation would subvert any attempt to really do it. "Too many things change all the time," goes the excuse, or "I'm a practical person and have to be able to make decisions one day and change them the next."

When I encountered such remarks as a consultant in Africa, I happened to have parallel responsibilities as a reserve officer on active duty in a prolonged war, and I could not help making comparisons. What would a general think of a brigade commander in the field who gave the same reasons for not planning? "What do you mean plan, sir? I don't know what the hell the enemy's going to do next. I'm a practical soldier. I just deal with whatever comes when it gets here."

War had its own ways of eliminating such attitudes if the general didn't, and economic reality, like war, culls farmers and ranchers who don't plan. Slowly but surely they fall by the wayside blaming droughts, prices, and everything but themselves. A really professional soldier understands that the worse and more unpredictable events become, the more he must plan.

After researching the procedures of many professions, the parallels between agriculture and the military still impress me. Like farmers, generals not only must know how to plan thoroughly but also how to replan instantly if all should fail. In addition they have had to face the problem of large civilian call-ups and the need to train people rapidly in planning techniques. Whole nations, over centuries, have employed some of their best brains to perfect such techniques.

My academic specialty, biology, had no history of forward planning. Much of the business planning taught in schools has become very academic and thus requires considerable training. Consequently I have taken the simple planning procedure developed at the Royal Military Academy at Sandhurst, England, and adapted it to biological use. It thus represents several hundred years of experience in fields of battle, and several decades of use in agriculture have shown it as effective in managing the plowshare and cattle hoof as the sword.

The companion workbook goes through the whole biological planning procedure in detail. Here I will outline the principles and cover some of the points that concern most people at this stage.

The *Aide Memoire*

Since so many factors influence any plan, one cannot tackle them all at once. But as anyone who has reassembled a complicated machine knows, putting things in a sequence that is not carefully planned has risks too. Toward the end of the job one discovers a piece that won't fit without the disassembly of half the day's work, or worse, a piece that appears important but remains in the parts bucket when you're ready to clean up and go home.

The expression used at Sandhurst for a guide that prevents those problems is *aide memoire*, which is French for "memory aid." It is much more than a simple checklist because it gives a sequence for making decisions that takes into account the effect of one decision on another. It is also less than a checklist because it does not reduce management to a series of yes or no items. The questions raised in the *aide memoire* are often quite broad and demand a good deal of creative, detailed thought.

The specific *aide memoire* used for biological planning has undergone close to thirty years of adjustment and development by ranchers, farmers, foresters, wildlifers, tribal people, and others who have used livestock in the service of production and/or landscape goals. Every situation and problem experienced by hundreds of people on three continents has influenced the development of the *aide*. Even now if a practitioner encounters a problem not anticipated by it, we modify it at once, adding a footnote or changing a sequence to cover that case.

A main benefit of planning according to such a tested procedure is peace of mind. One can concentrate fully on one step at a time without worrying about something that might come first or get left out. At each step you record your work on a planning chart, wipe that from your mind, and move on to the next. This ability to concentrate completely and confidently on one point at a time bears fruit particularly in emergencies when a tendency to panic and lose focus can destroy you.

This point came home forcefully to me when I got a call one night from a client in Zimbabwe after a fire had raged through about half of his very fine ranch. It had struck worst in the areas where he had water for stock but spared some areas where water points had already dried up. He needed advice on whether to lease land to get him through the season or destock and, if the latter, by how much.

When he met me at the local airstrip he was eager to take me off to see the burned area and the cattle as soon as possible, but I asked to see his biological planning. "No," he said. How could that help, if I hadn't seen the fire damage or his livestock? He got extremely hot at the suggestion that one more look at blackened ground and idle cattle would waste my time and his money, so perhaps he'd rather muddle through by himself.

He did not of course have a plan. The various charts had disappeared, but by luck his wife retrieved the *aide memoire*, reeking of tomcat, from the bottom of her son's toy chest. I got out some fresh charts and insisted, against vigorous protest, that we now plan step by step. Gradually, however, his protests weakened as a picture of his ranch began to emerge on the planning chart he'd been taught how to use but hadn't thought important. His enthusiasm really began to mount after we laid out all the problems and began to plot actual cattle moves.

It was a very sheepish man who finally accompanied me to the burned areas to confirm some final judgments. Without any input from me, other than the knowledge that the longer he put off planning, the more hours I would add to my bill, he had proven to himself on paper that he could carry his whole herd through without risk or leased pasture.

In ranching, sad to say, losses due to lack of planning are the rule, not the exception. That stems only in part from ignorance of the planning tools available. In the main it results from a life-threatening allergy to paper that unfortunately afflicts many classes besides ranchers.

From the very first series of lectures I gave in the United States, I have stressed that this biological planning technique underpins all my work on grazing situations and all my claims for success. None of the academics and researchers who later criticized my work grasped that point. The vast majority of research projects conducted in America allegedly to study my methods ignored the heart of the matter—this planning (and replanning) process. Instead they set up short-duration grazing rotations with radial fence layouts involving no biological planning. In fact, not a single professional researcher has yet tried to test this biological planning procedure against any fixed system or rotation.

How can a planning procedure cover your specific needs? Let's look at the sort of things it includes.

- All livestock needs that we can perceive or have experienced, including numbers and physiological state—lactation, breeding, etc.

- Problem plants, crop rotations, hay cutting, simultaneous recreational use, forestry practices, wildlife management needs (nest protection, winter feed and cover, freedom from disturbance during mating, and so on).
- All weather-related problems known to have occurred on your land, including water sources drying out, heavy frosts (greatly reducing feed values in the tropics), snow cover, lightning, etc.

Obviously such planning ties in closely to the long-term land planning discussed earlier. For instance, a common concern for stream banks damaged by years of livestock presence can be addressed through a combination of a fencing or herding pattern developed especially for riparian management and the biological planning just described.

The Biological Planning Chart

As you cover each step in the *aide memoire*, you record the details on the biological planning chart, the principles of which are shown in figure 40-1 (detail follows in the companion workbook).

Across the body of the actual chart 365 tiny divisions account for time down to the day. Where figure 40-1 shows "area," on the actual chart separate rows represent areas of land, paddocks in a fenced cell (or herding areas where no fences are used). In this main planning portion enclosed by area and time, all problems and needs can be shown by color-coded marks. Orange shading in paddock 3 in May might show poisonous plant danger. Brown in paddock 4 in August might show lack of water. Red in November might show prime hunting sites. Then, within the context of all these factors, one engineers the livestock moves in a rational way using the slowest moves

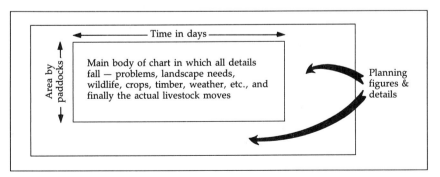

Figure 40-1. Principle of the biological planning chart.

that the stock are likely to make in periods of slow daily plant growth.

At the base of the chart and over on the right-hand side are space and format for various planning figures and calculations. The latter include procedures for changing grazing times in periods of rapid plant growth. Actual monitoring of growth rates, discussed in the next chapter, determines whether the longer periods plotted on the chart or the precomputed shorter ones apply.

Figures showing planned and actual animal days per acre (ADA) of forage harvested during each grazing period accompany entries for each paddock on the main body of the chart, showing at a glance how much on average every acre of ground contributes to total forage consumed. That allows for fine tuning of future plans and increasingly accurate assessments of forage availability. Charts for the northern and southern hemispheres differ in that each has the months laid out to put the main growing season in the middle of the chart.

When Do You Plan?

Holistic management by definition requires that you plan, monitor progress continuously, control deviations as soon as possible, and replan whenever necessary. Nevertheless, though this plan-monitor-control-replan sequence proceeds without gaps and covers emergency situations, normal practice in livestock operations calls for major planning twice a year.

Make the first plan at least a month before the onset of the growing season. It should project well ahead but remain open-ended as one cannot predict conditions precisely. Normally as the growing season continues we can anticipate more rather than less forage. However, if drought develops, that requires immediate replanning as described in the last chapter on tactical flexibility.

Make the second plan toward the end of the growing season when forage reserves available during the nongrowth period become known. Because the amount of forage will not change (unless catastrophe, such as fire, occurs), you can project the plan forward to a theoretical end point. Landscape and production goals will suffer from total consumption of forage and litter, so this *closed-ended plan* should cover the normal dormant period plus a prudent allotment for wildlife and a drought reserve and still leave a comfortable margin.

Figure 40-2 illustrates the open- and closed-ended plan principle, showing how the time reserve for drought fits in.

Record Keeping

The record of actual grazing times, places, and ADA harvested, plus the weather and growth rate information set down on the chart, probably will

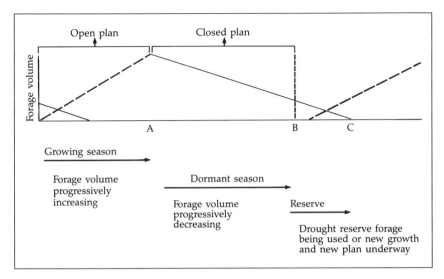

Figure 40-2. Biological planning across seasons.

provide all the information needed for future planning and will give an excellent picture of the strengths and weaknesses of each part of a whole cell.

That benefit notwithstanding, professional range people following my work frequently fall into the mistake of turning the planning chart into nothing but a record of the past, dropping the *aide memoire* and all forward planning. This is fatal. In fact most record keeping that I have come across on farms and ranches yields little profit for the time and effort given to it. Not infrequently the least profitable ranches had the most complete records. Thus, the grazing chart without the *aide memoire* is just a waste of paper.

I cannot make this point strongly enough. Planning compares to *looking forward* through the windshield of your car to see where you want to go; *monitoring* for curves that may put you in the ditch; and *controlling* speed, gears, and steering to keep you on the road until you reach your destination. Obviously you can't do this efficiently facing backwards. Excessive record keeping is like gazing out the rear window to savor where you have been when all you need is a glance in the rearview mirror.

Stocking Rate Assessment

Many critics have charged that holistic management ignores the fact that a given piece of land can feed only a limited number of creatures, but in reality that obvious truth affects many aspects of the HRM model. The misunderstanding arises because traditionally people equated high animal numbers and overgrazing. Therefore range scientists developed a variety of methods that linked stocking rates to the physiology of important grasses in ways that required a good deal of expertise and subjective judgment.

The discovery that overgrazing reflects timing, not numbers, means that we now determine stocking rate by much more straightforward criteria, chiefly the volume of forage, the time it must last, and the landscape and production goals. Almost by accident I hit on a way to make this assessment under normal working conditions in the field.

In the midst of a drought in Africa I got an emergency call to assist a ranch owner and two managers in deciding how much to destock. All the way to the assignment I puzzled over ways to add anything to the deep knowledge these three must already have of their land and local climate. As an outside advisor I could only fall back on the theoretical assumptions used in planning, but to everyone's relief they proved perfectly sound in practice.

If one can compute how many Animal Days per Acre of forage a herd will require for a whole season, then one also can figure out how many cows a single acre must feed for one day.

In this case the fifteen-thousand-acre ranch had 950 head of cattle, and from the threshold of the dry season they faced at least 180 days of no growth and conceivably forty more in a hard luck situation. No one, no matter how experienced, can visualize that many acres, cattle, and days simultaneously. However, a quick calculation shows that, including the drought reserve time, forage demand works out to 13.9 Animal Days per Acre.

We went out on the land and began to pace off a random sampling of one-acre plots and asked ourselves, "Could this acre feed fourteen cows for a day on the forage here now?" Consistently we agreed it could. Next we sampled areas we knew were poorer and came to the same happy conclusion. In the end the evidence pointed against any reduction at all. None was made and all went well.

Following this experience, which prevented the loss of thousands of dollars through unnecessary reduction, we refined the technique so that we had only to assess the area required to feed one animal for one day. Figure 40-3 shows the calculations. If one acre (or 4,048 square yards) must feed 13.9 cows for a day, then 348.2 square yards must feed one cow for one day. The square root of this (fortunately most calculators have a square root button) is 18.6. One only has to pace off a square about 18 yards on a side and judge whether it would feed a cow for a day.

The weaknesses in this technique are almost entirely due to a human tendency to fudge, first in selection of the samples and then in judging them. A truly random sample will include every kind of area—roads, hillsides, and brush. If your way of selecting samples does not allow for that, then before you start, reduce the total acreage by the amount of land tied up in roads and rough country that you don't intend to measure.

Ranch 15,000 ac

Herd = 950 animals
Days of dormancy = 180
Plus reserve of 40 days = 220 days

Animal days per acre of forage required

$$\frac{950 \text{ animals} \times 220 \text{ days}}{15,000 \text{ ac}} = 13.9 \text{ ADA}$$

Therefore, a square of 1 ac on average must be able to provide enough forage for 13.9 cows today.

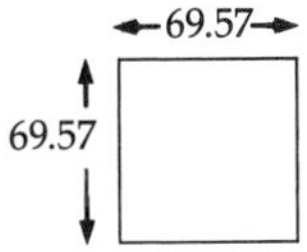

← 69.57 →

69.57 □ = 1 ac or 4,840 square yards

If this is the case then the area of land needed to provide forage for 1 cow today is:

$$\frac{4840}{13.9} = 348.2 \text{ square yards}$$

$$\sqrt{348.2} = 18.6 \text{ (square root)}$$

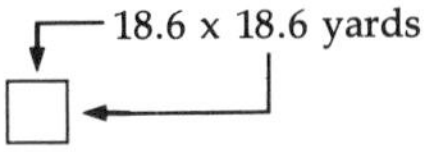

┌── 18.6 x 18.6 yards
□ ◄────────┘

Must feed 1 cow for 1 day

Figure 40-3.   Assessing stocking rate.

Likewise, in judging each sample, set yourself up to err on the conserv-ative side. First, estimate like a cow. Imagine yourself with a large bag around your neck and the job of filling it in eight hours using only one hand to pick leafy material a whole handful at a time. A cow, having teeth only in the lower jaw, cannot pick individual leaves and will avoid taking old, oxidizing stems among the leaves.

If you imagine any difficulty in this task, then a cow probably would have trouble too. Again, to keep all errors on the safe side, fail the sample if you have any doubt, however small. In other words, if you cannot see that full bag instantly when you look at the sample, record it as deficient.

Voisin first used this idea of filling the bag in evaluating nonbrittle pastures, but I've found it to be of even greater value in evaluating brittle rangelands. For all its apparent crudity it yields very good results. At training sessions we inevitably have academics who suggest that the grass be clipped, weighed, and recorded, but we do not encourage that for several reasons:

- Cattle do not clip grass. Their grazing far more resembles a human's harvesting by the handful and avoiding whole stems.
- Ranchers will not, and often cannot, clip, dry, and weigh grass, but they can make good estimates by eye like a cow.
- Clipping and weighing, though perhaps less subjective in terms of one sample, takes time, and thus reduces the number of samples. More samples, even if less precise, yield a more accurate overall picture.

In addition, you will find with experience that you can vary the question to suit your own needs. Given lactating cows it might go, "Would this sample feed one cow very well?" In another case it might go, "Will it keep a steer alive?" or "What could a pronghorn find tomorrow, after the cow has gone?"

The companion workbook adds embellishments to this general method for assessing stocking rates given a prolonged dormant period. The same techniques, however, will work during the growing season, even though regrowth occurs between grazings. Regrowth makes the problem tricky, however, because one cannot predict tomorrow's weather.

During the growing season when a herd depletes the forage in a given paddock before you plan to move it, that signals a warning that the stocking rate may be too high or the grazing period too long for the size of the paddock. Of course, one might ease the situation by cutting grazing days from a poor paddock and adding them to a better one. However, a series of slightly shortened grazing periods adds up to much shorter recovery periods and in slow growth conditions that assures severe overgrazing, the most common cause of failure in rotational grazing.

These judgments only prove right or wrong in retrospect because a good soaking rain can overcome a potentially disastrous mistake. However, the ADA assessment technique outlined above can determine the absolute theoretical limit for stocking rate on any given day, and that serves as a good benchmark for estimating the limits when conditions are less than perfect.

Obviously, continuous rapid growth conditions would give a cell maximum carrying capacity. The shortest possible grazing periods also would apply in that case. If you compute for each paddock the square of land necessary to feed one animal for one day during the short grazing period desirable during rapid growth, that represents the best you can hope for. Similar squares computed for slower growth and slower moves would all be smaller.

Whatever the current growth conditions are, if that largest square will not feed one animal for a day right now, you are overstocked, and if growth is less than ideal, you are seriously overstocked.

In this way stocking rates can be checked at any time of year on the basis of forage available at the time. Suppose for example you made this test midway through a very dry summer and found that the next paddock your herd entered did not have enough forage for even the shortest foreseeable grazing period. That would indicate overstocking *even if ideal conditions return tomorrow.*

Although ADA assessments are a vast improvement over old methods of assessing stocking rates, we need to refine this judgment, as both production and landscape goals depend on it. Low stocking rates allow old forage to accumulate, especially in brittle environments where decay occurs slowly. This usually leads to a shift toward woody species in the plant community.

Excessive stocking rates often cause animal performance to drop, and soil becomes exposed as animals attempt to fill out their diet by picking up litter.

Basing Stocking Rates on Annual Rainfall

Some have tried to use running averages of actual precipitation to determine stocking rates. The figure includes several past years and as each new year's rainfall total is added, the last is dropped. This is appealing but breaks down for the simple reason that running averages of actual rainfall do not reflect the *effectiveness* of that rainfall, which depends on many factors.

Some years ago I had a chance to demonstrate this point in the field to a group of World Bank officials on a tour of a Texas ranch. The night before their arrival, a soaking rain fell over the entire area. We first visited three sites where we had applied the tools of high animal impact with a large herd, many paddocks, and consistent biological planning for one, two, and three years respectively. Then we looked at an area protected from livestock for many years.

I claimed that grass in the last area had poor color due to the low effectiveness of the previous night's rain, but the visitors did not believe it. To settle the question I had them pick shocks of green growing grass themselves (so I wouldn't bias the result) from all four areas and arrange them in order of verdure along the roadside. They did range in fact from pale to rich green according to the treatment of the place where they had grown, although all were the same species and had received the same rain.

Had stocking rate been judged by volume of rain, it would have been meaningless as the resultant growth was so different in four areas receiving the same rain. Had we based our judgment on effectiveness of rain we would have recommended a stock reduction in the area that had no stock! The only realistic means of assessing stocking rates is on the actual forage grown in every season.

Conflicts with Wildlife

The biological planning process also helps overcome the age-old conflict between wildlife and livestock that widespread destruction of wildlife habitat by commercial grazing interests has made a political issue.

The planned grazing of concentrated herds gives positive control over where the livestock go on any given day and takes into account all of the known wildlife needs (nesting, cover, habitat, breeding privacy, etc.) so that livestock will not disturb crucial areas at critical times. The concentration of herds means that most sites have no livestock present up to 90 percent of the time, and even then are under close control. Fitting in wildlife considerations seldom presents as much difficulty as many people fear.

The one weakness remains the problem of assessing game numbers reliably enough to use in planning, as Chapter 37 explained. Sex and age structures provide some handle for management, but in terms of actual numbers and stocking rates, we can make only educated guesses on the basis of game condition, vegetation bulk, and browsing throughout the year. Unfortunately, where people can learn to observe signs of overbrowsing by game easily, it is not as easy to detect overgrazing. Also, while the former quickly leads to high mortality among juvenile browsers, which cannot reach as high as adults, overgrazing does not have this effect because even the youngest can reach the ground. This area requires research on better management techniques, and when that bears fruit, the biological planning process outlined here can put the new knowledge to work.

In summary, the biological planning procedure with the *aide memoire* offers the simplest way I have found for managing the complexity of any range, watershed, forest, farm, or other area shared by livestock and other uses. It will lead to the best possible plan in the most difficult and seemingly hopeless situations.

Ironically the greatest danger lies in the simpler cases that involve livestock alone and no complicated landscape goal to develop. Here the planning appears so routine that one is tempted to drop it and fall back to rotational grazing. The most costly errors I have seen have arisen from such cases.

In all situations, and those situations especially, continuous monitoring will warn of matters that need attention in order to reach your goals. The next chapter describes the monitoring approach developed thus far.

41

Biological Monitoring and Control

Aplan, no matter how sound, serves little purpose unless its application is monitored and deviations controlled. Otherwise, even assuming no lapses at all in administration, unpredictable events sooner or later render the best plan irrelevant or even destructive.

Once again, some will ask, "Then why plan in the first place?" We must plan simply because it is the only way to produce desired results in complex situations. If the situation is simple enough, a rough plan in our heads with common sense adjustments as we go is adequate. Unfortunately such simplicity is almost nonexistent in the management of biological resources.

With a plan that involves livestock and the production of a landscape goal, there are two aspects that need to be monitored and controlled. First, progress toward the landscape goal requires at the least annual monitoring of the four ecosystem foundation blocks. Second, the grazing of the livestock, if there are few paddocks or grazing areas (less than fifty to one hundred, depending on the situation), has to be monitored for the daily growth rate of the plants throughout the growing seasons. This monitoring enables you to change the periods of exposure and reexposure of the plants to the animals to minimize overgrazing.

Landscape Monitoring

Monitoring can mean many different things, but in holistic management it means looking for deviations from the plan *or* changing conditions *for the*

377

purpose of correcting or fine-tuning the application of tools. Though not obviously radical, this definition differs fundamentally from the understanding of monitoring used in many other situations, and the distinctions are critical.

Often so-called monitoring only amounts to quantifying already obvious situations. On our croplands we measure water run-off and changes in soil density and organic material long after obvious damage. In our national parks and wilderness areas we usually measure gross changes in game, bird, and plant species only after conspicuous changes have raised public outcry.

Wherever people think in terms of inflexible systems, whether a rest-rotation grazing system, a curriculum for a school, or a formula for buying stocks, they monitor to answer the question, "Does it work?" Range scientists often record changes in plant comunities toward undesirable species to prove the weakness of one system and then try to invent another system from scratch. Theoretically, such monitoring will give early warning of catastrophe, so one can find a new system without extreme loss. Frequently, however, a vested interest holds on until disaster strikes anyway, but always the process leads toward a drastic and costly succession of systems, fads, and programs that remain as inflexible as their predecessors.

All too often people monitored the individual performance of the livestock (heavily supplemented) and decided that a grazing system was working if daily weight gains and conception were good. The fact that the yield per acre was decreasing while the cost of production through increased supplemental feeding was rising was somehow ignored although it should have warned us the ecosystem was deteriorating. Many farmers do not even know that their croplands are deteriorating and do not stop to think whether they are applying less fertilizer, herbicide, or insecticide each year or more, which in itself would give an indication. Farmers, like ranchers, all too often monitor their production but not the rising costs of that production, which reflect the deterioration of the soil and increasing disruption of the four ecosytem foundation blocks.

In holistic management we monitor with the specific purpose of bringing about desired changes toward a predetermined goal rather than monitoring to see if a management system worked or failed. Our aim in monitoring is to ensure that we reach our long-term goals and that they will be sustained. It is not done to compare your piece of land to your neighbor's.

With our rising comprehension of the holistic nature of our ecosystem we are gaining some idea of its truly incredible complexity. Thus, we must take the attitude that much of what we do to our ecosystem may lead to unanticipated effects. In managing holistically *we always assume that we might be wrong as we decide to apply any tool to the ecosystem,* even when it has passed all of the testing guidelines.

If you have selected a tool that in fact doesn't alter the blocks in the manner required to achieve your goal, then you need to know as early as possible so you can alter your application of the tool or use another one.

By the time species have changed or costs of external inputs have risen to achieve the same production we once did without them, it is a bit too late. Great change has taken place already in succession, mineral and water cycles, and energy flow.

To avoid such late warnings as we contemplate any tool's use, we think about the four ecosystem foundation blocks and ask, "What measurement would give the earliest possible warning of impending change?" In almost all situations (farming, ranching, forestry, wildlife management, stream management, etc.) this will be the nature of the soil surface between the plants. Soil surface changes precede changes in water cycle, mineral cycle, energy flow, and succession. They are our earliest warning of impending change in populations of plants and animals. This is especially so with such problem insects as tsetse flies and grasshoppers, many species of which breed on bare, exposed soil sites or dry sand and silt sites.

There is no set rule as to what you monitor. The rule, if any, is think, think, think, and then monitor what you believe the earliest measurable change will be. It could be plant spacings, soil litter cover, soil density, soil organic content, earthworm populations, seedling success, nesting or breeding sites, quality of water run-off, and a host of other things.

In the companion workbook the technique we have developed over many years for the monitoring of brittle rangelands is covered in detail. We are constantly improving this technique—and the monitoring notes used with it—by incorporating ever simpler and more practical methods for measuring change. Ideally the monitoring should be done by the people managing the land and they usually lack the time or training to do a full-dress academic study.

Some of the simplest ways of noting change quickly have come from people with no formal scientific education at all. I once spent an afternoon in Zimbabwe with a rancher and his herdsman discussing the changes we planned to bring about on his granitic soil surface, which we happened to be sitting on, and how we could measure them. The rancher spotted my canteen and suggested I pour the water onto the soil and time how long it took to soak in on bare capped areas and litter-covered areas. In no time we had a simple technique of pouring a pint on randomly chosen sites and measuring the time it took to soak in and the spread of the wet patch. The quicker the water disappeared and the smaller the wet patch, the better the soil conditions for complex organic life.

The main thing to remember is that, rather than a mass of information that you don't know how to use in practical management, you want something you can measure and understand that indicates to you what changes are taking place. Soil surface changes are key because they precede most changes in populations that make up the community under your responsibility and allow you to preempt many problems.

Obviously, one does not start monitoring a week or a month or a year down the road. Start now, before implementing your plans. You need a good idea of the health of all four ecosystem foundation blocks right at the outset. From that baseline you can build toward a landscape goal. At the very minimum in the case of vital watersheds you should take a number of fixed point photos of the land as you implement the biological planning. Preferably these should be backed up with actual measurements as covered in the companion workbook.

Implementing Control

Depending upon what your monitoring indicates, either you will continue applying the tools as you have been or you will need to make adjustments. Obviously, if all is going as anticipated when the particular tool was selected for use then the tendency is as you expected and the use of the tool is leading you toward your goals. If the tool you selected is not having the tendency you expected you'll have to rethink. We usually apply the HRM model in the diagnostic mode, which I'll cover in Chapter 48, to assist us in this process.

In implementing some form of control to get you back on track you can now do one of several things:

1. Apply the same tool but in a different manner.
2. Apply another tool altogether.
3. Apply a combination of the tools at your disposal.

In some cases, the diagnosis may show that to correct the unwanted change, the model favors a tool or tools that the goal itself rules out. Generally this means that you need to reexamine the goal, which probably specified the inclusion or exclusion of one or more tools. Apart from the brief reference to forms of production, tools should never be mentioned in the goal, as Chapter 46 will cover. At goal formation that should have been clarified, but high emotionalism, low trust, or some other problem may have hindered full and proper goal formation at the outset.

An example of this sort of situation has occurred where a group of people has developed a production goal that was mainly aesthetic in nature and, by their definition, excluded livestock. At the same time the landscape goal involved a stable and productive watershed in a brittle environment area that was too small to support large predators and free-roaming large herding ungulates. Such a goal, made with good intention, thus excludes two possible tools—grazing and animal impact—that may be essential to achieve the intended landscape and thus the three-part goal.

In summary, both production and quality of life goals ultimately depend on the landscape, and thus on planning, monitoring, and controlling to reach that landscape goal. The monitoring may take many forms but must remain simple and practical so the field level operator will use it, be he forester, farmer, rancher, tribesman, engineer, veterinarian, wildlifer, or whatever. It also must give the earliest possible warning of change. Most commonly this will be some measurement of the soil—surface condition, density, or organic content—or of breeding sites or juvenile survival of plants, insects, birds, animals, etc.

Monitoring Daily Growth Rate

All situations require annual landscape monitoring—farms, ranches, forests, national parks, etc. Where livestock run with few paddocks per herd, you must monitor plant growth rates every few days during the growing season and control grazing and recovery periods in order to avoid overgrazing. Irrigated crops also require daily checks to prevent unnecessary costs and damage to the soil community.

In the livestock case you will recall that overgrazing occurs in two situations:

1. When animals stay long enough in one area to regraze fast-growing plants before they recover from a first grazing.
2. When animals return to graze slow-growing plants before they have had time to recover from a previous grazing.

You will also remember that a large number of paddocks or grazing areas allows short grazing periods and long recovery periods simultaneously and growth rate becomes less important in controlling overgrazing. Always remember that experience has shown us that greatest damage follows short grazing and recovery periods during slow daily rates of plant growth. With *bunch grass ranges* and few paddocks or grazing areas we judge growth rates on the basis of *severely grazed individual plants* and not on the general view of the range as a whole. In the case of *pure stands of runner-type grasses* in pastures, where the individual plant cannot be detected and much leaf remains on plants grazed low, we judge by the *general growth rate, or volume, in the pasture as a whole.*

On the bunch grass ranges that typify brittle grazing lands worldwide, the most straightforward monitoring procedure only involves finding and marking severely grazed plants alongside ungrazed plants of the same species just as livestock leave each paddock. A two- or three-foot wire carrying a fluorescent flag, such as surveyors use, makes finding the sample days or weeks later a simple matter, and a kink in the wire can record the grazed-down height.

As the livestock graze in the manner we have planned, we periodically return to the marked plants and assess their recovery rate using the nearby ungrazed plants as a yardstick. If the plants have barely grown weeks later and the livestock are due back in that paddock any day, then we know the move is too fast for the prevailing slow growth and overgrazing will occur as the livestock return to the unrecovered plants. The livestock, however, undoubtedly will perform well on the fast move.

If our inspection shows that the plants are growing so fast that they are already barely distinguishable from the ungrazed plants, and the plan shows that the livestock are not due back for a month or more, overgrazing is probably occurring in each of the paddocks grazed since marking (unless you have very high paddock numbers). Livestock performance, in this instance, will be poorer than it need be as they are being held longer than necessary on fouled ground already well-selected over.

People commonly ask *when* a plant has recovered and we don't really know. Much research confirms overgrazing as a function of the time plants are exposed to animals, but few have investigated the point at which a plant has recovered fully from a severe defoliation. In practice, however, this matters little because so many other factors obscure the question. A healthy range contains myriad species, all with different growth rates. And slope, soil variations, shade, aeration, and other things all affect the growth rate within species and within areas of the paddock. One can only observe the most severely grazed plants of whatever species and consider them recovered when they resemble ungrazed plants alongside them under virtually identical conditions and health. This apparently rough method has produced excellent results for close to thirty years.

Another common question runs, "When the general rule is fast growth fast move/slow growth slow move, what happens when some grasses grow slowly and some fast?" Fortunately this, too, does not prove as awkward as it first appears, and the answer demonstrates once again the flexibility and power of the holistic approach.

Figure 41-1 shows how you would pencil out such a situation and then make a decision. In this case you only have a few paddocks for your herd. As you see, with five paddocks you have grazing periods that are long, whatever the growth rate of the plants—seven or twenty-two days if you use recovery periods of thirty to ninety days. Let's assume that you are monitoring in the period toward the end of April (Point A) and detect slow growth on some severely grazed, warm season grasses and fast growth on severely grazed, cool season grasses.

Ask yourself these questions and work out the answers. What if I move fast? Clearly with the seven-day grazing period you are doing the best you can with five paddocks in the grazing period for either type of grass. What of the recovery period? Looking at the diagram you can see that the cool

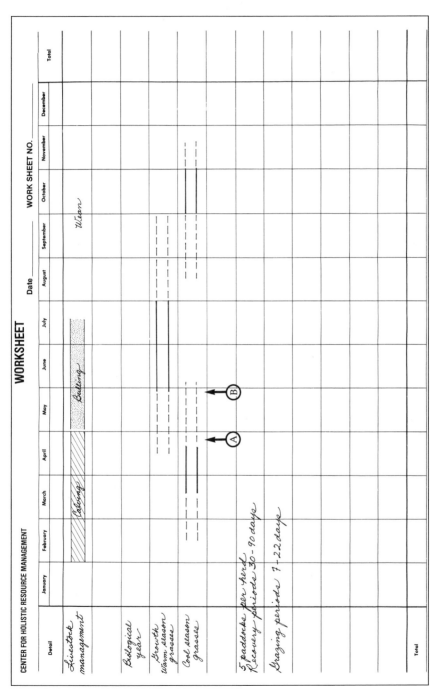

Figure 41-1. Varying grazing/recovery periods with simultaneously differing growth rates.

season grasses are likely to be in dormancy on your return in thirty days (Point B), but that the warm season grasses could be growing fast. If the warm season grasses have continued to grow at a slow rate then you are likely to overgraze those plants that were bitten severely. Your alternative was to go to the slow move, but then you would have increased the chances of overgrazing some of the cool season plants that were growing fast.

Now what of the animals? Holism implies a consideration of all factors. A look at the livestock management year (top row) shows lactating cows in late April and bulls going in May first. This might justify faster moves to gain higher animal performance at this short but crucial time of year, even though it means accepting the chance of overgrazing of warm season plants if growth continues slow into June.

How serious will that be? Not very if you are applying high animal impact and good planning. This is not even near the degree of overgrazing that we accept daily under conventional grazing management. It will affect one period only enough to set back the vigor of those plants that get bitten twice before recovery. We are not talking about repeated overgrazing to the point of plant distortion or death. However, since some evidence suggests that a grass grazed repeatedly at the same time of the year, especially during early spring growth, may suffer, one of the *aide memoire* planning steps covered in the companion workbook specifically addresses that problem.

The above situation would look somewhat different with thirty-five or more paddocks per herd. Recovery periods of thirty to ninety days would mean grazing periods of only one to three days. Even the fastest growing plant will not suffer overgrazing during the longest grazing period of three days, so slow moves might work. Again, however, livestock factors could qualify that decision. The thirty-five paddocks mean much higher stock density and faster consumption of ADA in each paddock. Holding stock too long at a crucial time could cause a drop in conception rates. Moving faster to gain on conception rates and calf/lamb/kid weights might result in coming back onto plants after thirty days but at high stock density, thus overgrazing many warm season plants if growth rates continue to be slow. A management decision has to be made and the consequences accepted.

In either of these cases, and in most cases generally, the land will forgive a reasonable compromise as long as you have a good biological plan and keep applying high animal impact. You only truly overcome the dilemma of how to deal with simultaneous fast and slow growth at very high paddock (or grazing area) numbers—i.e., approaching fifty to one hundred. At ultra-high paddock numbers, remember, stock density is also high, animal impact is usually high, and exposure of the plants and animals to one another very short. This tends to keep the proportion of leaf to fiber in the plants high and this, together with the short grazing periods, allows better animal performance on longer-rested grass.

The Importance of Monitoring Individual Plants

Do not make assumptions about growth rates just because rain has fallen or the temperature seems right. Remember the story in the last chapter of the World Bank team in Texas that found four shades of green in grass plants that had all received the same rain the night before. The darker color represented faster growth, which stemmed from a better water cycle.

Some years ago on a New Mexico ranch I saw demonstrated the liability of assuming that rain always translates into rapid growth. Under pressure from lengthening drought, this rancher had put four eight-paddock cells into one thirty-five-paddock plan and combined his herds into one. Three-day moves gave each paddock over ninety days' recovery time.

Both his thinking and planning were sound, but when two inches of rain fell and the view from his pickup looked a bit greener, he assumed immediate fast growth and cut back to daily moves and a thirty-day recovery period. I visited nine days after the rain, and we actually checked plants. We found no evidence of fast growth. Out on the range, the general level of soil capping and consequent poor aeration had suppressed the growth rate. Only the roadsides, which had better aeration, were showing fast daily growth.

The wrong assumption had led to a plan that would soon put cattle at quadruple normal density on paddocks that had had only a third of the required recovery time, the most rapid path to disaster he could have chosen in a drought.

New Zealand sheep farmers have a great awareness of the attention one must pay to plant growth rates, and in some districts the radio announces daily growth rates as a service to them. There and elsewhere the daily evaporation rate is broadcast as well so farmers can compute transpiration rates for crops and alter irrigation schedules accordingly.

Personally I worry about such approaches for the reasons given—that soils, slopes, and plants vary too much to fit a general formula. In New Zealand, where generous and predictable rainfall and heavy fertilization make a fairly homogeneous environment, perhaps it pays. On brittle ranges I believe it wise to judge from actual plant daily growth rates.

Earlier I commented that irrigated crops also require a similar level of monitoring. The growth rate of most crops depends directly on the balance of air and water in the soil and an excess of either will slow it down appreciably. On my own farm, where I used overhead irrigation, I monitored soil moisture ahead of each spray line continually throughout the year. I found that the general advice put out on daily evapotranspiration rates consistently led to depressed yields at higher costs from overirrigation. Finally, to achieve highest yields at lowest cost, I not only monitored ahead of the spray lines but made a decision for each sprinkler in the line. Where the pipe would stay set for eight hours, I would pull some of the sprinklers after anywhere between four and seven hours because land that appeared uniform obviously was not so underground.

Monitoring growth rates under irrigation requires a simultaneous check of soil moisture. In Chapter 48 I mention a serious mistake I almost made in assuming that poor growth and a dry, cracked soil surface meant too little water. Below the surface the problem was in fact the opposite—waterlogging.

Obviously certain plants, like rice or prickly pear, do not prosper under ideal water/air balance. Others, like cotton, will not necessarily give the highest yield at optimum growth rate. On my own farm maximum growth on irrigated cotton gave too much leaf and too little boll, while slow growth produced the opposite. In that case as growth rate and yield were different I monitored the proportion of boll to leaf as a guide to watering.

Such careful monitoring of growth rates and soil moisture is important under irrigation because, as in all our technological interventions in Nature, small decisions can have massive consequences. Overirrigation, a predominating practice, damages soil in many ways and costs money while depressing yields.

In summary, useful monitoring must look at individual plants, not general information or area rainfall reports. In managing livestock, control of overgrazing without a large number of paddocks or grazing areas depends on daily knowledge of growth rates. A large number of paddocks lessens this need. Irrigated crops also need close monitoring of individual plants and the surrounding soil in order to cut costs and prevent soil damage.

Such close attention to the land and the critical decision making that flows from it in turn depends on conscientious and committed people. Nagging supervision may force a certain level of competence, but at great cost. On the other hand a willing, caring, and creative work force will do it far better and cheaper. The largest ranch or the smallest farm can foster that by becoming more collaborative in nature. The next chapter makes clear how that affects cost, human stress, and success or failure.

42

Organization

Organizing is an instinctive habit. All higher forms of animal life and a good many rather primitive ones do it in ways ranging from simple pecking orders and territorial patterns to highly complex divisions of labor. Organization in a flying wedge of geese, a colony of beavers, a hive of bees, or a pride of lions defines the species as much as feather, fur, stinger, or claw. Survival depends on it.

Mankind, of course, is no exception. No creature whose offspring spend so long in helpless infancy could persist for long without the caring family structure from which in time grew the myriad clan, tribal, and national structures that occupy anthropologists today.

One of the simplest forms of human organization, and therefore perhaps the most primitive, is the hierarchy, the chain of command down which orders travel from a boss to successive layers of subordinates. Stone Age hunting and raiding parties no doubt had their versions of colonels, captains, sergeants, and privates, and all modern armies preserve this structure. The argument for organizing in this way rests on the assumption that the person or people at the top have greater wisdom or can see the bigger picture because of access to more information. Therefore, lower levels must obey for the good of the whole.

Structure, however, does not always determine how an organization functions. In the case of hierarchies, that generally depends on how much wisdom or access to information the commanding layer actually has. Wise commands depend on good communication of intelligence, but commanding and communicating differ so fundamentally that in the functioning of many hierarchies they become mutually exclusive. Commands are messages that go in one direction only and accept no reply but "mission completed." Though that has a definite place, an environment built only on commands is unlikely to foster the open and fearless two-way communication between people necessary for informed actions by the commanders.

Hierarchies have served humanity well in many situations throughout history, but they fail conspicuously in the management of resources. There the need for communication becomes paramount. Survival, not to mention management, depends on creativity, humanity's unique and most potent attribute. But our creative power shrivels without open and fearless transfer of thoughts between people.

We use the organization guideline to aid us in enhancing creativity through organizational structure and function, seeking those that foster the most open, fearless, and genuine communication. We call such a working environment collaborative—an atmosphere where individuals can work with one another rather than for or against one another.

Specifically, an organization, regardless of its official structure, is functioning collaboratively if it does three things:

1. Provides an environment for collaboration in the truest sense.
2. Allows the latent creativity and ability in people to come to bear on personal and organizational goals.
3. Deals with the *whole* as a whole organization and not as an agglomeration of departments each addressing aspects of the whole.

This last point applies to government particularly. It is my present belief, based on experience both as a civil servant and a member of parliament, that no government currently is structured to manage the resources of any nation soundly. None, even at the highest level, can view the nation in its care holistically, and yet only treatment of the whole as the only reality will lead to long-term success. Now every aspect of government is broken down to a portfolio represented in the cabinet by a secretary or minister, generally in charge of a narrowly focused and turf-conscious bureaucracy. Only in budgeting does the allocation of limited money force a certain degree of coordination and general discussion of priorities, but never true collaborative management of the nation's wealth and resources.

Over centuries we have struggled through much bloodshed to find the best forms of government in which all people feel well-represented and secure. It has been said that unless all the people of a nation feel well-governed and secure none are. For the future we must now add that without sound management of resources nobody is secure, least of all the government. Depleted and damaged resources lead to poverty, and poor people mean social upheaval and political unrest. We still lack means for entire governments to view the whole, whether a president, prime minister, ayatollah, or dictator sits at the helm.

This brings us to consideration of the characteristics of three main groups of organizations.

1. Hierarchical-Dictatorial—this would include totalitarian governments and many families, the best known and perhaps oldest of structures.
2. Hierarchical/Democratic—Includes governments and many companies and families; much used and well-known.
3. Collaborative—Some families, social groups, and companies; least used and known as it is still evolving. Collaborative refers to function rather than structure and thus a number of different structures, including hierarchical, theoretically could be collaborative.

Hierarchically-Functioning Organizations

The typical hierarchical organization mentioned earlier quite possibly developed around hunting and defense needs. Such organizations currently tend to be noncollaborative, manipulative, and competitive. Communication gets little reward compared to great emphasis on obedience to commands. The atmosphere does not encourage individual creativity and often actively stifles it.

While such structures have served us well for defense purposes, even armies now question them, as success in both modern and guerrilla warfare turns on quick and effective communication. Since the days of the American Revolution numerous conflicts have shown that a greater freedom to use their intellect has allowed small, less rigidly structured irregular militia to run circles around regular and highly-disciplined armies. However, because of their tradition and rigid hierarchical natures, regular armies have taken hundreds of years to learn that lesson. When the trench, tank, and machine gun became features of warfare, traditional cavalry units became obsolete overnight, yet combatants in World War I maintained these units, made even more cumbersome by the necessity of supplying them with thousands of tons of feed, and many brave men galloped to certain and senseless death.

In addition, because of endemic poor communication and the need to follow commands, even when clearly stupid, armies can make spectacular blunders. Bungled orders produced the gallant but disastrous charge of the British Light Brigade in the Battle of Balaklava, which prompted a French observer to exclaim, "It's magnificent, but it's not war." The sickening stupidity of the repeated charges by the Australian infantry against the Turks at Gallipoli is unbelievable to an intelligent person, but intelligent people in hierarchical organizations were responsible for those charges. Those and a host of other examples have caused modern pundits to cite military intelligence as a contradiction in terms.

While regular armies may provide the bloodiest examples of the spectacular errors caused by stifled creativity, they have no monopoly on that weakness. Bureaucracies of all kinds, public or private, that function hierarchically supply an inexhaustible catalog of parallel glitches.

Again, the weakness of most hierarchies lies in an inherent inability to handle communication. Apart from the near impossibility of establishing, in a competitive and manipulative environment, the necessary degree of trust between people to allow communication, ideas must pass through several levels before approval. A low-ranking person risks reprimand with every open and honest communication he makes.

Though the boss at the top may have the big picture in mind, he cannot see the detail familiar to the worker at the bottom. But when that worker sees a way to do his job better he has to ask permission, and that goes up from supervisor to supervisor because none can take responsibility for a command. What the person at the top actually hears depends on how his minions on each level feel and how they relate to those above and below.

An old army joke tells of how the urgent request "Send reinforcements. We're going to advance." got rendered by this process into "Send refreshments. We're going to a dance." When that kind of thing happens, the message understandably comes back down the chain to reprimand the hapless individual who started the wave. The majority of us simply have no idea of the extent to which we distort messages because of our state of mind, our reaction to the message itself, or our relationship to the messenger.

Often as I lecture on these deficiencies in rigid hierarchical structures I see ranchers or farmers smugly thinking, "Well, this does not concern me. I am not part of a bureaucracy. There is just me, my wife, and the two kids!" They no doubt would diagram this relationship as in figure 42-1, which depicts, of course, a strict hierarchy. Many is the farm family leaving the land because of poor communication in such a structure and the rigidity and lack of creativity of the top person, commonly male.

Even universities generally have fallen into a rigid hierarchical pattern,

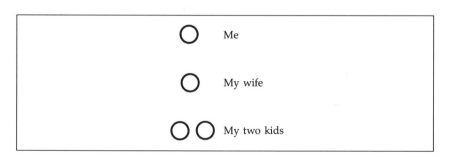

Figure 42-1. Hierarchical autocratic family.

and thus they too often stifle the creativity they exist to promote. According to historian Daniel Boorstin in *The Discoverers*, universities originated when wandering scholars, using Latin as their common language, got together to escape the rigidity and dogma enforced by church and state hierarchies. Now we have come full circle and many is the independent scholar working outside the university system in order to pursue creative ideas. The HRM model was developed in such a manner and the Center's degree program runs for the same reasons.

Though certainly many academics recognize this problem and do promote independent scholarship, creative people in a university all too often must risk losing tenure and security. When they threaten the institution's source of funding the powers that be act quickly to bring them in line. Interdisciplinary communication too will succumb in an atmosphere of competition and manipulation. That universities themselves have done some of the best work on ways to improve organizations does not contradict the fact that they also are among the best laboratories for that effort.

In all of the above discussion I have intentionally not distinguished between totalitarian and democratic hierarchies. Unfortunately, in the matter of stifling communication and creativity, the differences tend to be only a matter of degree. Control cloys, and even where rather benevolent people exercise it, the lower levels come to fear rejection, fear what others may think, fear going against the mainstream, and none of this leads to the openness ideally required for good resource management.

As hierarchical structures show no sign of vanishing soon, we must learn to make them function more collaboratively.

Collaboratively-Functioning Organizations

A collaborative organization first and foremost treats people as human beings rather than as machines of production. In structure it may resemble other organizations, but it functions quite differently. Organizational diagrams and formal job descriptions generally don't exist and the emphasis has changed. The autocratic boss has disappeared, but there is a leader who bears ultimate responsibility for getting the job done. Now, however, that includes encouraging leadership skills in those who work alongside him or her. Leadership in fact becomes a shared responsibility rather than something that one person alone acquires by virtue of rank.

Leadership style distinguishes a collaborative organization. It requires different beliefs, practices, and skills from those traditionally emphasized. People have more leeway to manage for themselves and those structurally in charge do not overmanage, a tendency cited by organization development specialist Jack Gibb as "the most critical organizational disease in America."

| *Leadership Beliefs*

According to management researcher and consultant Jay Hall in *The Competence Process*, competent leaders in collaborative organizations hold four core beliefs about their people:

1. People can do what needs to be done. Most have a need and desire to exercise and display personal competence. People are creative and, far from disliking their work, see it as an opportunity for growth. (Only 16.7 percent of America's managers actually believe this, according to Hall's surveys).

2. Most people put forward their best efforts as collaborators in the tasks before them. When they see their own needs and objectives best met by achieving the goals of their organization, the majority will give whatever effort is required. (Hall found only 30 percent of American managers agree.)

3. Most people work at their highest level when they find meaning and challenge in their work. When they derive a sense of personal identity and self-esteem from doing a task well, they give more to the job and get more from it. In a community of mutual respect and support, people enjoy both greater health and more productive relationships. (Hall found only 18 percent concurrence among managers.)

4. Most people, to perform at full potential, need opportunity for authentic and open communication and comparison with co-workers. The clarity gained from honest discussion enables people to get on with their work without anxieties about failure. The undercurrents of unexpressed feelings or opinions, which rob people of their energy, will recede. Trust, respect, and mutual support will raise the vital energy and creativity in the organization. (Only 7.6 percent of American managers credit this according to Hall.)[1]

Quite possibly the preponderance of managers who don't hold these beliefs essential to collaborative organizations contributes mightily to the crisis in American management today.

Management consultant Doug Raynor writes in the *Organization Development Journal:*

> The fact of the matter is that most American businesses in the mid 1980's continue to manage themselves in the same way they did in the 1930's and 1940's: top-down, hierarchical, and frequently autocratic. Despite radical changes taking place all around us, the majority of American managers have steadfastly refused to consider altering their style of management. The result of this resistance to change has been

falling productivity, shrinking profits, and an ever-widening polarity between workers and managers. Not the least of the problems plaguing old-style managers is the loss of individuality and human dignity suffered by both manager and worker as they remain trapped in traditional roles.[2]

Hall's management survey looked at urban industrial leaders. If it had included the agricultural sector he would have found a still smaller fraction of managers holding beliefs essential to collaborative management. People in the resource management fields have generally not matched the pace of development in other industries. Many ranchers and farmers do not even see themselves as managers or admit any weakness in this area—this at a time when poor management rather than any other single factor, in my experience, accounts for hundreds of thousands of farm families leaving the land.

An individual's management style derives from personal beliefs, which the next chapter on personal growth treats more directly. For myself, however, one major experience colored my management style ever after.

Qualified only by a pristine undergraduate degree in botany and zoology and instructions on filling out a government purchase order for ammunition and fuel, I entered the workaday world as a lowly game ranger. Then at age twenty-one, after less than a year in the bush, I suddenly was promoted to Provincial Game Officer in charge of two provinces containing eight thousand square miles of one of the world's richest game reserves and two hundred widely scattered employees. I arrived in heavy rain in my mud-spattered Land Rover, had a brief handover from my superior, and did not see another superior in the provinces for nearly two years.

In the course of the transfer formalities I learned that a ranger was being transferred in to my headquarters to do the necessary elephant control work from there. When I questioned the need for that in the light of other priorities, my superior added in confidence that the man in question was a dishonest, lazy, drunken thief. If he worked from my headquarters, perhaps I could catch him out and fire him.

Soon the fellow arrived in a three-ton lorry loaded down to the blocks with furniture and family, and we had a candid talk. I couldn't imagine how, in my panic to learn the ropes of my new post, I could waste energy spying on one ranger, so I told him the true agenda.

The news shattered him, but he wondered aloud why I had told him. In fact, however justified his reputation, I couldn't afford to believe it. Quite aside from the petty distraction of watching someone day and night, when antagonists must share such isolated surroundings, very strange things can happen. In any case I confessed I had a tremendous task to accomplish and too few good men to help. One more could really make a difference.

I said he had the chance to prove himself by starting a lechwe antelope control unit in the Banguelo swamps. At the moment I had no house for him and no staff and no money. He would have to find a suitable place to camp with his family and start from there and trust that as soon as I got word of his location I would start sending him all the men and money I could find.

He never let me down, doing a superb job on very little. He caught more poachers than all the rest of my staff together. The Game Department had argued over lack of funds for years while the fine lechwe antelope of the swamps were slaughtered by the thousands, but he succeeded in establishing a control unit nonetheless. No doubt under my superior his sins did match the accusations, but because I had no time to give to following that suspicion, I learned a greater truth about human nature.

Leadership Skills and Practices

In building a collaborative organization, leaders first of all must open their minds to new knowledge, actively seek it, and then put it to use. We have found that a management team can do this better than an individual acting alone because the dynamics of the group speed learning and the process of learning together promotes collaboration in other areas.

The very next priority is to commit plenty of time to work together on more trusting, open, and caring relationships among team members. Initially that means meeting frequently, as team members may feel a lot of anxiety about the tasks before them and not speak freely in short, pressured talks. You, as leader, must create an emotional climate where people really are free and encouraged to speak not only of what they think but, more important, of what they feel.

Often feelings precede clear understanding of crucial issues. You may plan a project that no one criticizes, although many may feel antagonistic or doubtful. Normally such a project would go ahead, sometimes to disaster as those who feel doubts they can't articulate keep silent. Often only one person speaking out will open the way for others to express strong feelings, and then it behooves the leader to address the cause. When people don't feel good about a project, they have a reason, but more than that they are unlikely to put shoulders to the wheel as zealously as they could.

I have seen many examples of this on farms and ranches. One time in particular a couple in one of our management training courses insisted that their staff supported them all the way, like family. Later an accident prevented them from attending a session on grazing planning, and they sent their two foremen in their stead.

That indeed proved enlightening. Throughout the course the two men displayed an attitude best described as passive resistance. Gradually, however, they began to see some sense in the new way of controlling overgrazing by time rather than by numbers and in planning grazing well ahead of droughts and other contingencies. Eventually they became quite enthusiastic. At that point they revealed that, yes, indeed they had felt like family to the extent that they had taken it on themselves to protect the owner and his wife against this nutty fad from Africa by making sure it did not work. Here was a ranch family certain of openness and good communication where there was in fact little. Had it not been detected, failure would have been inevitable.

Above all in holistic management the formation of goals touching the quality of life of all parties involves a significant level of collaboration. From this, the remainder of the goal—production and landscape—flows easily, and what we call goal ownership can take root. This ownership of the goal runs far deeper than mere participation as I will cover in Chapter 46.

The leader venturing into collaborative management will have, as I did, a number of fears and doubts. I still by no means have overcome all of these concerns, but I have experienced enough of collaboration to know that I never want to go back to more autocratic leadership.

The benefits from collaborative work are immediate and many. Collaboration spreads the normal worries, concerns, and anxiety of management among many more people who really care for goals they own. Control over the business actually increases in contradiction of a common fear of leaders who contemplate assuming a more collaborative style.

This happens because people within the organization start to "go that extra mile" both in dealing with customers and other outsiders and in helping each other. Almost miraculously people start to grow just like plants suddenly given the right environment, and exhibit talents and creativity you never realized they had. I have now seen many people charitably described as mediocre in a rigid hierarchical organization suddenly blossom in the warmth of a collaborative team. This experience made me truly comprehend that as a rule the people aren't bad in our failing hierarchical organizations. They may function badly, however, under what we increasingly recognize as bad leadership.

While I have seen such changes in others working with me, I, too, unconsciously changed in the eyes of others who had known me for years. Yet such changes typify the kind of growth this relatively new approach to management brings about. I had always worked in democratic and liberal hierarchies that in retrospect were rigid nonetheless. In trying to bring a collaborative style to my own organization I fell into all the snares likely to entrap others pursuing that ideal. These are:

1. Fear of letting go the reins. "Surely I would lose the tight control I

have at present? Perhaps I will let go just a little and see how it goes." This will not work. Leading a collaborative team is a little bit like pregnancy. You cannot be a little bit pregnant. You have to commit yourself totally to collaborative management because to those around you, your actions speak far louder than any words. Mutual learning with your team helps more than anything I can think of until you overcome this short-lived fear. From increased knowledge comes more readiness to commit.

2. Lip service by the leader. This grows from the first point. It is fatal as everyone sees through your false sincerity and commitment. They cannot believe or trust you and so hang back in their actions while rendering loyal lip service to match yours.

3. Not enough time spent learning leadership skills and getting help. "I can make my organization more collaborative without any outside guidance," runs the thinking. A few may pull this off, but most of us cannot and would do better committing time and effort to attending courses and getting help from others involved in change and better management.

4. Not enough time spent on maintenance of the team's human relationships and feelings for each other and too much on immediate tasks and crisis management. I made this mistake often and have seen many others do the same. When work has piled up, how can we waste time just chatting, playing, and getting to know each other? Illogical as it may seem, not one minute of that time is wasted. The investment in building trust, caring, and collaboration pays off richly in smoother work and less crisis management.

Initially I, like others, felt that collaborative organizations had to have a special structure unfettered by organization charts and job descriptions. However, I am coming to see that function means more than structure, and thus many different structures, including those previously highly autocratic and hierarchical, could function collaboratively under more enlightened leadership.

Although a collaborative structure is best, the HRM model can be used in a hierarchical structure as a first step toward holistic management. Since use of the model itself facilitates collaboration, applying it can be a first step toward larger change.

Conclusion

To summarize, leaders must take responsibility for establishing a collaborative environment, and success depends on their beliefs and values. As

Hall states, "Values are very personal, but most of their effects are inter-personal. What we believe as individuals directly affects how we relate to others." Our actions always communicate our beliefs more deeply than words and policy statements, hence leaders can go only as far as their beliefs allow. Yet, these can change as we open ourselves to new learning and gain confidence. Leaders must be open and collaborative for associates to become so. As Gandhi said it, "You have to *be* the change you expect."

At the Center we have come to understand through many hardships and errors that sound holistic management depends on collaborative organizations, or what develops beyond them. I realize this means acceptance of many many years of faltering progress on the part of governments and individuals as we approach the ideal, but, knowing the right direction, we have no choice but to start as we would in climbing any great mountain, one step at a time.

Much research, learning, and experimenting in many countries now goes into organizational development as this changing field of management is called. A number of places, including the Center for Holistic Resource Management, provide courses and assistance, but attending a course doesn't guarantee change. That comes through a continual process involving complex human dynamics. It requires care and maintenance by all but especially the leadership, be it the head of a family or a corporation.

The Center, because of its worldwide efforts and vision, by definition strives for better collaboration between individuals and organizations. As a nonprofit entity heavily dependent on volunteer manpower, we could not function if the work did not give the people involved the kind of personal satisfaction that comes from collaboration. Although still far from the ideal, all of us have grown and developed in exceptional ways, as you will also as you open to change.

As this guideline concerns the working environment, it is almost inseparable from the one on individual development and personal growth that follows. In truly collaborative organizations everyone to varying degrees plays a leadership role at times. The extent to which each individual can assume this role depends upon an openness to learning and change, and the key to this is personal growth. Once again the final functioning of the people in any organization directly reflects the beliefs and personal growth of the leader.

43
Personal Growth

"There is in every organism, at whatever level, an underlying flow of movement toward constructive fulfillment of its inherent possibilities," said psychologist Carl Rogers. In the life of a biological community we call this process succession, but its psychological parallel, the natural human urge toward more complex and complete intellectual, emotional, and spiritual development, concerns us just as much. Rogers and others have referred to the human successional process as the "actualizing tendency," and note that it may be thwarted but cannot be destroyed without destroying the whole person.

In managing personal growth we take responsibility as individuals for our own growth and as leaders (whether as head of a family or a large corporation) for setting a climate in which those around us can thrive in theirs. This does not mean just avoiding destruction, but assuring that you and those around you *flourish*.

The personal growth guideline applies specifically to the tool of human creativity. As mentioned in Chapter 16, the successful application of holistic management depends entirely on your ability to think and be creative, and this in turn depends chiefly on your mental, emotional, and physical health. As the last chapter discussed, the environment in which you live and work powerfully influences all of these factors. In addition, your relationship to others affects both your creativity and theirs and thus the group as a whole. In applying this guideline you try to judge how much self-improvement in all areas of your lives you and those within your influence can achieve. Such personal growth should go on throughout your life. If you feel it thwarted or see it thwarted in others, all your efforts will suffer.

Books, articles, cassette programs, and workshops abound on the subject of personal growth, and I give a partial listing of some in the references at the end of this book. In practice, however, the subject is extremely personal, so I can illustrate its importance only from experience. At this point in my understanding I see three areas that need most emphasis: self-awareness, self-direction, and support (both giving and getting). Growth in these three areas often leads to a creative outpouring and generates momentum for the journey toward one's goals.

Self-Awareness

Personal growth begins in the struggle against attitudes such as "ignorance is bliss," or "What you don't know can't hurt you." Comfortable as these homilies may seem as a way to avoid difficulties, in the end they ensure stress and prevent growth or change. The walls that we build to avoid discomfort may seem like a good idea, but all too often they imprison us.

"Know thyself, and you will be free," said Aristotle and other sages in similar words. For me, knowing oneself means being aware of one's values, attitudes, and beliefs. Many a ranch or government program has failed because the people involved roiled in confusion over these fundamentals.

Values

Values are the "oughts" and "shoulds" for both yourself and others that govern your actions. Research at the Menninger Foundation, the world's largest psychiatric training center, shows that both mental and physical well-being and growth benefit from a clear understanding both of one's own values and of their relative priority. People who can't articulate this tend to be apathetic, uncertain, indecisive, and inconsistent. On the other hand, those who have worked to identify things that matter to them personally, and their relative order of importance, draw from that insight vigor, decisiveness, and consistency.

Values evolve in large part from personal experiences with family, friends, and co-workers in the context of social and cultural forces, none of which we originate or control. Values also change, so it's little wonder that few people have a sharp sense of what they themselves stand for at any given time. Finding such clarity of values often means working through a lot of frustration and confusion, but doing it is the essential first step in personal growth to a richer, fuller, and more satisfying and productive life.

In our courses we start people on this process by asking them to recall particularly pleasant, rewarding, enjoyable, and productive experiences — ones that bring back warm memories and good feelings even now. We find our values among those feelings and thus gain a deeper understanding of what motivates us.

Merely understanding values, however, does not suffice. Actions and decisions must flow from them. When what we do does not violate the integrity of what we believe and feel, we enjoy an inner harmony that gives us a strength of character that enhances all our relationships and our leadership abilities as well. The Menninger researchers managed to document this effect through clinical findings. People who based their lives on well-articulated values became more fully functioning individuals.

Values sometimes conflict of course, which explains why their order of importance takes on a significance equal to the values themselves. Typically in our society work satisfaction competes against family harmony, and pressure to put work first often becomes extreme. Though periodically circumstances may justify that, in most cases putting family first enhances your own health and theirs and thus that of the community. That almost certainly benefits your work more than putting that one more assignment first would have done.

We do not see these things without great personal effort and often outside help as well. I have always said that I placed family at the top of my list and have always defended that value, but when I finally scrutinized my values under the professional guidance of one of our course leaders, it became clear that I actually placed some other values higher. As I examined my actions throughout life in retrospect, they did reflect this order.

Attitudes

Life is change, and our attitude determines whether we will grow in new situations or succumb to them, whether we act in helplessness or hope, cynicism or optimism, bitterness and anger or openness and caring. In a study of business executives, cited by Joan Borysenko in her book *Minding the Body, Mending the Mind*, researchers found that even under tremendous life stress those who held certain attitudes avoided physical consequences. This "stress-hardy" personality included:

1. Commitment — An attitude of curiosity and involvement in whatever happens, an opposite attitude to alienation or withdrawal.
2. Control — The belief that we can influence events, coupled with a willingness to act on that belief rather than be a victim of circumstances. (If we try to control too tightly, we're also stressed. We need

to develop the ability to tell when to hold on and when to let go, a key to escaping past conditioning and responding freshly to life's challenges).

3. Challenge—The belief that life's changes stimulate personal growth instead of threatening the status quo.[1]

Committed people who believe they are in control and expect challenge, says Borysenko, usually react to stressful events by *increasing* their involvement, exploring, controlling, and learning from difficulty. "This attitude transforms the event into something less stressful by placing it in a broader frame of reference that revolves around continued personal growth and understanding."[2]

Persons who take the attitude of helplessness tend to back away from stress. "Their attitudes are the opposite of hardiness," says Borysenko. "They are alienated from activities, feel powerless to change things, and are therefore threatened by anything that rocks the boat. These people are the ones who are most likely to fall ill when stressful events arise."[3] Tragically, many an apparently hardy farmer falls into this category.

If we can acquire the attitude that lets us see opportunity in every crisis, we can only grow. In fact, crises often lead to situations much more satisfying than the old rut. As you'll see in the next chapter on financial planning, personal attitude can make or break an operation.

Belief Systems

Our belief systems include our values and attitudes and govern the ways we relate to all parts of our world. We begin forming our belief systems in early childhood, but they develop throughout our lives. Everything and everyone surrounding us, particularly our families, contributes to the process. Some childhood beliefs fall away as we acquire an adult perspective, but many do not except through experiences from which we consciously or subconsciously extract a lesson. Failing that, we often hang onto beliefs that limit us. For instance, we may be quite needlessly fearful in our daily dealings with certain people or situations, but we don't admit this weakness, even to ourselves. Rather, we elect to stay comfortable and resign ourselves to going through life slightly crippled.

A learning journal can be used as a crutch to help one overcome this disability. What I'm talking about is not a mere diary that keeps a daily record of events, but a personal record of feelings and why you have them, and experiences and what you learn from them. I resisted keeping a journal for many years because I did not know that it could be used in such a way or what value it had. I had merely seen a journal as the self-conscious record people in high places kept so they could write their memoirs one day, and I found that somewhat distasteful. In recent years, others, including those with whom I work, convinced me otherwise and after using one habitually, I'm more than ever behind the idea.

Many of the problems that I had been unable to deal with throughout my life, no matter how hard I struggled, have started to melt away. Previously my mind simply would not focus on the very deep beliefs underlying these problems and thus I could never solve them. The journal made me do this. The magic was in the act of *writing* things down in the form of a dialogue with myself. This somehow made it easier to face what I was afraid of facing and didn't know it. Once I saw the beliefs that had held me captive for so long down on paper, my fears seemed ridiculous and it was easy to change the beliefs, even when they had handicapped me for forty years or more.

Most of us remain unaware of our own belief systems even when those living and working around us see them clearly. Our everyday actions and management style convey them much more honestly than our verbal expressions. As everyone has both limiting and enhancing belief systems, it would seem to follow that, if we knew how, we would accentuate the positive and eliminate the negative. Indeed, nothing less can unfetter personal growth.

Jerome Lund, in *The Last Self-Help Book*, describes a specific process for identifying and evaluating belief systems that one might well use in addition to a learning journal. First, you figure out which belief systems are limiting or faulty. Second, you look at the ways you consciously or unconsciously create and reinforce them. Then you change them into something more workable. This process, which Lund describes in detail, addresses the second step first. "We need to deal with what we are doing to reinforce faulty belief systems first," he writes, "because unless we are able to take corrective measures in this area, we will have difficulty in dealing with the actual belief system in a constructive way."[4]

In the same way as a leader's beliefs about others affect all members of an organization, so too do our beliefs influence all our actions. All who achieve great things have the common characteristic of strong belief in both themselves and in what they are doing. If, on the other hand, we believe we cannot do something, that limiting belief ensures that we don't.

To some degree the belief systems of our community also influence us. One charismatic speaker, such as a Hitler or a Churchill, can sway a nation's beliefs and actions. Forecasts of recession actually can bring one on. For us as individuals, the initial task is not to change society's belief systems, even those of our local communities, but our own, which limit our potential, and if need be to rise above the social belief systems that may entrap us.

Self-Direction

Self-direction refers to the approach one takes to acquiring knowledge. It means not waiting around for the teacher or waiting to be taught, but actively seeking knowledge. If you depend on the teacher you embrace obsolescence because what is taught today may be out-of-date tomorrow. That does not imply that teachers themselves are obsolete, only that you must now take more of the responsibility for learning upon yourself.

Self-direction grows naturally from self-awareness and reinforces it. Taking responsibility for acquiring knowledge means learning more about yourself, constantly identifying strengths and weaknesses, and developing the former while minimizing the effects of the latter. When feelings of self-worth ebb (and that happens to everyone), you become defensive about weaknesses and blind to your strengths. When feelings of self-worth rise, your vision sharpens. In addition, you are far more likely to take the risks necessary for growth, the biggest, for many, being simply an openness to learning.

Becoming Teachable

With practice, you will find that each experience in life affords an opportunity for learning. If you're not making mistakes, in fact, you will come to feel you're not extending yourself enough. In his book *Growing Young*, Ashley Montagu stresses that human beings, alone in the animal kingdom, have the capacity *and the responsibility* to grow and develop all the days of their lives. Unfortunately, we tend to let the traits that make this possible atrophy as we grow older.

Curiosity, along with imagination, playfulness, open-mindedness, willingness to experiment, flexibility, humor, energy, receptiveness to new ideas, honesty, eagerness to learn, and, perhaps most persuasive and most valuable of all, love, comprise the arsenal of characteristics that make a person teachable, writes Montague.

> All normal children, unless they have been corrupted by their elders, show these qualities every day of their childhood years. . . . They want to know everything about everything. . . . They accept changes without defensiveness. When they try to accomplish something and fail, they are able to try to do it another way, and another, until they find that it works. . . . Unless they suspect they may be punished for it, they tell the truth; they call the shots as they see them. And they soak up

knowledge and information like sponges; they are learning all the time; every moment is filled with learning.[5]

By no coincidence have many of the world's great innovators been labeled childlike in their quest for knowledge. Those of us who have forgotten we had these innate capacities must relearn them. Sometimes a mentor—a talented, special person who enters into mutually beneficial experiences with younger, eager people—can innoculate us against the tendency to ossify. I had such luck myself.

Generally, we do not seek out mentors deliberately, but rather at some point almost by fate we encounter individuals who affect our lives dramatically. I had several mentors, but did not see them as such until many years later.

As a university student I took a vacation job with the Rhodesian Forestry Commission and found myself working under Blake Goldsmith in the Gwampa Forest Reserve. Blake had entered World War II at the minimum age and afterward learned a little botany in forestry school. By his own initiative, however, he had become a brilliant and dedicated botanist from whom I later recognized I learned more in three months than in three years at university. As we enthusiastically collected plants together we did not stop at naming them. We learned all we could about where they grew and why, what human uses they had, what ate them, and how their Latin names had been derived. We studied the earliest recordings of the plants and their distribution in Africa. From Blake I first learned that Jan Smuts, whom I had known as a wartime leader, was also a botanist of note.

The year after university I worked some months under Frank Ansell in the Northern Rhodesia Game Department. Frank, like Blake, had gone to war directly following high school. So fanatical a mammalogist was he that while fighting with "Peacock Force" behind Japanese lines in Burma he wrote a paper on the status of the Burmese rhino and had it published. Once more I found myself in the company of an outstanding scientist from whom I later realized I learned a great deal in a subtle way. Isolated in the bush, away from any stimulus or competition from his peers, he still studied and wrote daily with painstaking care that never let up. It could not help but rub off onto me a little. From Frank I learned more about the rigorous discipline necessary to any scientific endeavor than I ever got from the classroom.

Several other mentors passed through my life at about the same stage. Two American wildlifers, Raymond Dasmann and Archie Mossman, came to do research in Rhodesia when I worked in the Game Department there. I instantly realized that they already knew far more about game management in Rhodesia than all of us Rhodesians put together. Where I had local knowledge, they had principles that I could not have learned at any African university of the day. Every day we worked together became a lesson.

The mentor I value most I've known the longest, my godfather Eustace Poles with whom I worked in the Northern Rhodesian Game Department. Over the long span of our friendship we have clashed at nearly every meeting like two cantankerous rhino bulls, but early on I learned to love him as a parent. He has always been my harshest and most blunt critic, but I've never doubted that every harsh judgment was uttered out of deep caring. From him I learned simple values like steadfastness, integrity, loyalty, and above all generosity.

Surely if you think about it, you have encountered mentors in your own life whom you did not set out to find but you realize in retrospect performed that role. Where I would have been without mine, I do not know. I gained different things from each. Two started me on the path to self-directed learning without ever explicitly saying so. Two gave me a wildlife training on the job, and one gave me values that have sustained me.

Self-direction entails a commitment to lifelong learning, a necessity for survival in a rapidly changing world. As Anthony Robbins in *Unlimited Power* states, "The power of the future lies in knowledge rather than in capital or birthright."

Giving and Getting Support

While mentors contribute greatly to your growth, you also contribute to theirs. The relationship, to be meaningful, is always mutually beneficial. If you succeed, I have a better chance of succeeding myself. If you fail, I may well fail, too. The laws of nature keep us all deeply connected. Stressing the importance of "self" in *self*-awareness and *self*-direction risks falling into selfishness. Here I want to emphasize that interdependence is just as important as independence, if not more so. How you interrelate with others bears directly on how and when you reach your goals.

Relationships can be defined by the degree to which the parties are able to communicate, and the depth of communication, in turn, is governed by the extent to which the parties are aware of themselves and their impact on others. High awareness permits you to share perceptions accurately, without distortion to yourself or to others. Low awareness produces double messages. Your voice says one thing, and the rest of you says something else. Everyone on occasion does this when self-worth is threatened. Family therapist Virginia Satir has observed a pattern in what we do to avoid the stress of revealing "weakness":

- We *placate* so the other person doesn't get mad. ("Whatever you say is okay with me.")

- We *blame* so the other person will regard us as strong. ("You never do anything right!")
- We become *super-rational*, in an attempt to deal with the threat as though it were harmless. ("Let's be rational about this; if one were to observe carefully, one might see things differently.")
- We *distract*, changing the subject to irrelevant matters, avoiding eye contact, or behaving as though the threat were not there. ("If I ignore this long enough, maybe it will go away.")
- When for various reasons we find communication with another person difficult, we may also seek out a third party, thus forming a *triangle* ("I told him this, and he said that, and what do you think?")[6]

I have fallen into all those patterns countless times throughout my life and know as well as any that they never produce the desired effect. They undermine the trust essential for good communication and growth-producing relationships.

In contrast, high awareness allows you to respond to a threatening situation with what Satir calls *congruence*, or genuineness. You can let the other person know "where you are" emotionally. It accepts a risk in talking about how you feel, and it takes self-confidence to do it without concern for "scoring points."

Meaningful communication also entails listening effectively and again that ability is related to your level of awareness. When it is high you can hear the message clearly; when it is low you have trouble hearing the message at all.

Listening effectively means listening with empathy, having the ability to enter the skin of someone else, to understand them on their terms, not yours. When something you say threatens them, you can avoid reacting to their double-level messages simply by understanding the messages for what they are. The sensitive understanding offered by an empathic listener often provides illumination, healing, and eventually deep communication. If you can develop your skills as an empathic listener, it is a wonderful gift to those with whom you are associated and also enhances your own life.

Carl Rogers had much to say on this subject, and perhaps defines the quality of empathic listening best:

> When I say that I enjoy hearing someone, I mean, of course, hearing deeply. I mean that I hear the words, the thoughts, the feeling tones, the personal meaning, even the meaning that is below the conscious intent of the speaker. Sometimes too, in a message which superficially is not very important, I hear a deep human cry that lies buried and unknown far below the surface of the person. . . .
>
> So I have learned to ask myself, can I hear the sounds and sense the shape of this other person's inner world? Can I resonate to what

he is saying so deeply that I sense the meanings he is afraid of yet would like to communicate, as well as those he knows?[7]

The Need for a Vision Beyond Ourselves

No one arrives at personal growth. It remains a journey to some wonderful destination always just around the next bend or over the next hill. It is a lifelong process that has its good and bad days. Self-awareness, self-direction, giving and getting support. We can only work on those things without letup and try to keep them high, trusting that they will make life more meaningful and fulfilling.

Our lifetime goals become more realistic when we know our own strengths and weaknesses and the effects of our behavior on others, and appreciate our dependence on others. Yet most people still need convincing that personal growth really justifies the tremendous effort called for. For me that conviction has come from a dedication to a vision that was beyond myself.

In times of great national emergency or catastrophe the magnitude and utter desperation of the task often unites us as a people. Small grievances and worries are forgotten in the rush to defend, protect, or rescue, and many people accomplish things way beyond the capabilities they believed they had.

In quieter times we must replace the binding force of catastrophe with a shared vision. The goals we set together as an organization—whether as two of us running a farm, or dozens of us running a great conglomerate— can provide that vision. Without that vision, collaboration in the truest sense is impossible.

The vision that guided me personally changed as I grew. As a youngster my only aim in life was to live in the wildest African bush forever. Within a few years that aim expanded as I sought to save the wildlife that was my reason for being in the bush. When my puny efforts proved futile, I realized I could no longer make my life in the bush if I would save the wildlife I loved. I moved to the city and entered Parliament to change the laws of the land. But even that proved futile. I saw that before laws could change, new knowledge and belief systems had to take root. Then I saw the scale of the problem, that land was not only deteriorating in my beloved Africa, but everywhere. The magnitude of the task was indeed overwhelming, but it only made me more determined.

I unintentionally instilled in my sons the same almost fanatical love of the bush and unfortunately for them, they would grow up with an ardent longing to live out their days in truly wild areas that no longer exist. My sense of despair was, and is, not unlike that of many a parent who cannot leave the farm to the next generation better than he found it.

As I have watched the inheritance of my own children and their children deteriorate or disappear altogether, I could not stand by and do nothing. The vision I had of seeing a turnaround in my lifetime became a driving force. It has kept me going through much adversity. It has guided my pursuit of knowledge and will continue to spur whatever personal growth I manage to make as long as I breathe.

44

Financial Planning and Wealth Generation

M any ranchers and farmers struggle for mere financial survival, and that alone should justify acute attention to all questions of money and wealth. However, agricultural producers also carry a much bigger social burden than simply providing for their own families.

The protection of the ecosystem throughout most of the world cannot depend on government regulation or industrial conscience but on individual farmers, ranchers, nomads, foresters, and others. The necessity in a rather basic sense to both save the world and make a profit is not a condition people who make a living directly from the soil freely choose out of moral sensibility. Nature forces it upon them and upon society as a whole.

Nature is doing this now. The bill for years of industrial pollution, and for treating agriculture as an industry independent of Nature, comes due in the form of lost or lifeless soil, water, and air pollution. No magical "they" will stop the degeneration of the rural foundation that one way or another supports other forms of wealth. Even if we develop incredible technology, cities and industry can only add to pollution. They cannot assist Nature to purify the air, water, and soil on the vast scale that is needed around our planet. As agriculture in all its forms—croplands, forests, and rangelands— is occupying such vast surface areas of the earth, it must discontinue adding to pollution as it is at present and return to the vital role of purification while producing for mankind's needs.

This guideline restates in financial terms how all actions in the management of land must render genuine profit to both people and land. To do this you must plan thoroughly according to attitudes, priorities, and considerations not normally included in most prevailing business strategies.

The annual planning of expenses determines both how you will generate wealth from the land and produce that long-term landscape goal and its sound water and mineral cycles, stable successional level, and high energy flow. The process of producing that landscape starts with annual financial planning. Ranchers in particular tend not to see expenses as generating wealth. They feel incorrectly that only the livestock and other items on the income side of the planning sheets generate wealth. In the chain of events from sun to ultimate solar dollar, the livestock represent but one link and that is the production link. The often more critical link of converting sunlight energy into edible forage on the other hand does respond to investment (preferably reinvestment of solar dollars) in fencing, better herding, better livestock training, biological planning, brush clearing, and so on.

Farmers have reason to see relationships more clearly as the crops they market convert solar energy directly. On the other hand they often err in trying to force more energy conversion through use of fossil-fuel-based energy at the expense of the ecosystem's natural potential. The costs associated with the use of chemicals such as fertilizers, herbicides, and pesticides usually escalate and become self-perpetuating costs that lead eventually to the bankruptcy of the farmer (no matter what size) and serious damage to humanity and our environment.

Proper financial planning can put all of these problems, and some others, in perspective.

Time of Annual Planning

Annual planning should be initiated just before the financial year starts. Thereafter it should be done two or three months before the financial year ends because in following the plan and control procedure you will become profitable and will need time at year's end for measures to minimize taxation. Whatever moves you make will affect the final stages of the current year as well as the coming one. Sensibly planning to reduce taxation and allow for the consequences in the coming year does not flow from last-minute crisis planning.

Nothing during the year counts more than this annual planning. It takes precedence over vacations, interruptions, or excuses of any kind. It also requires a quiet, well-ordered work space. How many times I have seen a rancher wrestle vainly over the most crucial decisions of his family's life while screaming children spill tea and jam over his papers and dogs fight under the table.

All who are involved in management at any level should attend the annual planning and the monthly control meetings that follow from it. This means all people who make decisions and are held responsible. Think of reasons to include people, not to exclude them. Most farms and ranches can justify including everyone. A very large business might require dividing the planning among groups structured so that people at all levels of management could participate in producing a holistically-sound plan.

I developed my approach to financial planning while working on farms, ranches, and game ranches, so it necessarily reflects rural, land-related considerations, but certainly much of it applies to any business.

In Chapter 15 I commented on the origins of wealth and the importance of basing financial thinking on sources of wealth rather than the symbols— i.e., you must distinguish among solar, mineral, and paper dollars. That distinction bears directly on the annual steps you plan to achieve your three-part goal. All proposed actions involving the use of any tools will be tested through the testing guidelines at this stage.

The completed physical layout of this planning, either on paper or computer spreadsheet, looks like the familiar cash flow, but here the resemblance ends.

The cash flow planning common in agribusinesses and elsewhere has three stages. First comes an estimate of income from enterprises determined most profitable. Then expenses are budgeted in columns for capital investment, variable costs, loan repayments, etc. One tries to keep cost below the anticipated gross income by using past records and information from experts and other sources and adjusting for inflation and cost trends. On top of that goes the cost of borrowed money, and out comes a bottom line in red or black. If the result is not satisfactory to the bank one redoes this and that and juggles the figures until the outlook appears satisfactory. As long as all endeavors appear cost-effective and the plan "cash flows" well, in that it predicts no cash shortages that the bank won't cover, all should go well.

For many years I did such financial planning in great detail and taught it to clients. With the discovery of practical holism and the realization that it was dramatically different from the interdisciplinary effort that had gone into our most sophisticated financial planning, I realized how far short this approach fell from what was attainable with holistic management.

Cash flow planning fails because it does not rest on certain principles that underlie the whole of any operation. The companion workbook covers the mechanical aspect of putting holism into financial practice, the filling out of forms, the sequence of operations according to financial planning notes, etc. In these respects it is similar to cash flow planning. However, what we need to do goes far further and embodies the essence of two other principles.

- Effective planning requires an attitude of mind bent on creativity and success, especially where the goal includes profit. As bloodless and mathematically determined as the planning process may seem, psychology rules it.
- The sequence of the HRM model—goals, ecosystem processes, tools, and guidelines—applies to all thinking before dollar figures attach to it.

Psychological Attitude

After years of consulting in many countries for clients who managed many different enterprises, and whose sophistication varied greatly, I came to the conclusion that the majority of farmers and ranchers actually plan non-profitability, and then complain loudly when they achieve it!

How could this be? Interdisciplinary background research and rigorous computation of cost-effectiveness seemed to make little difference. People of every description finished the year in the same nail-biting suspense over their bottom line. No matter what state, country, or currency; no matter what size of farm or ranch or type of geography, in peace and war; no matter what market or price condition, always the same picture. Planned income, $200,000; expenses $195,000. Planned income, $350,000; expenses, $345,000. Like the unanimous elections in totalitarian countries, it defied logic. Margins simply could not be so uniform across so many situations.

Eventually it dawned on me that the problem must lie in the only common factor, human nature.

That price received for a product governs profit is a myth comfortably accepted by nearly everyone. In reality, cost of production has far more influence on profit and that, more than we care to believe, is a function of psychology.

According to the myth, producers raise a bushel of wheat or a pound of beef at a certain cost, and if the price is right they make a profit. When the price falls, they lose. The whole political argument over agricultural price supports in the United States and many other countries rests on the belief that producers should receive a certain margin over a common cost of production in order to have an income at parity with other industries.

The belief that overproduction and consequent low prices underlie the massive tragedy of American farmers leaving the land stems from the same myth, but the facts argue otherwise. For years American farmers, thanks to price supports, have enjoyed excellent prices for their product by world standards. Compared to the world market, they also have enjoyed, and still do, incredibly low input item prices. Where else do fuel, machinery, vehicles, herbicides, pesticides, and fertilizers cost so little? Nowhere that I know.

Why then do American farmers continue to go broke at an alarming rate?

The problem obviously is one of management, of allowing production costs to rise unnecessarily. Even the evidence of massive deterioration of the ecosystem and the mistaken desire to compensate by increasing chemical inputs has not weakened the farm economy as much as the failure of people in the industry to see that *cost of production governs profit.*

Cost of production differs fundamentally from the price of the input items. Prices may be low, as in America, but excessive use still results in high cost. Though many producers will argue this point to death, in fact all evidence shows that producers usually have tremendous flexibility in controlling input costs, but fail to exercise it.

I admit to suffering from this weakness myself and believe it comes from a common habit of the human mind.

Point A in figure 44-1 shows my condition on graduating from university. The left-hand bar of the graph shows my income from which I buy the essentials of life at a cost represented by the right-hand bar. The minuscule surplus surprises me as I had thought that earning real money after years of scrounging through school would put me in clover, so I looked forward to getting a raise.

Point B shows my situation after getting the raise. I still don't have any extra money and wouldn't even say I'm living better. On the other hand I traded my motorbike and some cash for a car so I could take out girls, and I really did need that color TV set like my friend had.

Points C and D represent further raises but each time the expected savings account never materializes. Most people manage life in this way

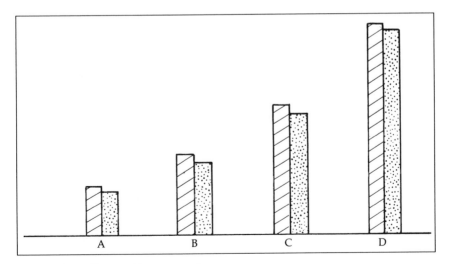

Figure 44-1. Personal income and expenses.

until they have to make do on a pension. If you look back over the years at what you earned and what you saved, they probably bear little relationship. Far more important were the things you bought because of peer pressure, advertising, or simply because the material culture around you made it seem necessary.

"Ah," say you the farmer. "That does describe people on a salary, but that does not apply to the cost of growing a bushel of wheat."

Not so. Look at the case in figure 44-2. At point A, based on prevailing prices, you project the income shown in the left-hand column. You now contemplate a production plan, but in an atmosphere of salespeople, advertisements, neighbor's advice, and extension service pamphlets. You do not have much money in the bank because the crop is neither sown nor are the new calves on the ground yet, but you've got credit.

You borrow, and presto the costs of production and running the farm and your life rise to the level of the right-hand column.

When prices rise a year or so later, you project the income shown in the left-hand column at point B. Now you experience an acute need for a bigger tractor. You have read how very efficient and cost-effective they are. The pickup also looks suddenly old. The newer ones have super cabs, air conditioning, and stereo, which your work-bent body deserves.

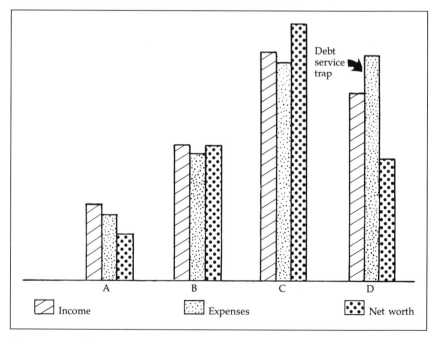

Figure 44-2. Farm/ranch income and expenses.

In addition, the condition of your soil has deteriorated so it needs mechanical ripping and a bigger dose of fertilizer because last year's application didn't stay fixed. Before you know it, cost of production has overtaken income once more, but you can borrow what you need because land prices have risen, as shown in the right-hand column.

Fortunately, prices go up again at point C, and on the strength of this trend, land values also rise further, reassuringly bolstering your net worth. Thank goodness. You needed so much. Your home needed work. Your two kids needed cars. You have seen how quickly your neighbor gets over his fields in his air-conditioned, four-wheel-drive Steiger tractor, and figure that if you had one you would have time at last to learn the futures market, or go fishing occasionally.

Your debt at the bank bothers you a bit, but your son has returned from college saying "get big or get out." Trends in land prices and inflation indicate that you can borrow to buy land and pay back later in cheaper dollars, even as your asset grows in value. Everything will "cash flow" as long as the commodity market holds, and your banker wants to lend. In fact he gives you that final persuasive push. He expects a mighty profit from your loan.

Your projected costs rise to match projected income. Then commodity prices break (point D), as they always do after every period of growth, because you, and thousands of others, have speculated on a rising price trend to invest money you didn't have in production that no one needed. Now you may try to cut costs, but you can't for several reasons.

1. You have a tremendous debt to service at high interest rates.
2. You have expensive machinery that you can't sell and, in any case, its value has dropped.
3. You have expensive land that you can't sell.
4. You have killed the natural fertility of the soil, so to grow the crop to get the cash to service the debt, let alone reduce it, you have to sustain, or even ratchet up, production through still larger technological inputs, at greater cost.

How does anyone get out of this pit dug by bad management, aggressive lending, and the advice of academic and government experts? Many argue that no strategy can save the individual producer, but agriculture in general might survive when more people leave the land and larger, more technologically sophisticated outfits can capitalize on economies of scale. The advocates of such solutions, however, again speculate that true economies of scale will flow from as yet unproven advances in chemical, genetic, and mechanical engineering.

If you intend to bank on that faith, good luck. You will need a lot of it.

Government subsidies and price supports tend to worsen the long-term prospects. They underwrite the shift to production methods that depend on costly technological inputs from an industry that itself depends on agricultural demand and has every reason to charge every penny the market will bear. Thus, however much producers may belatedly desire to increase margins by cutting costs, suppliers have the motivation and considerable power to push them to the limit. Once again the standard solution addresses the symptom, not the cause.

Nevertheless the HRM thought model can assist you to a step-by-step realization of goals, including profitability. The first step, however, is to appreciate that the prices of input items and the cost of production are not the same thing. Without thorough respect for this fact and iron discipline in planning and spending, costs will rise through purchase of unnecessary items and wasteful quantities.

You as operator and manager control production costs and therefore hold the key to profitability. High prices for products, low input prices, and easy credit are a trap for the unwary. Because of the natural human tendency to fall into this trap, we approach annual planning in the following way.

1. We project anticipated income.
2. *We cut planned income in half.*
3. We plan the running of the farm, ranch, or business, letting the total cost of production rise to that 50 percent figure as shown in figure 44-3.

This reduction of the money available for all expenses is a vital mental exercise. It probably will horrify you, and most people at first blush consider it impossible. Nevertheless, collective creativity and concentrated effort can pro-

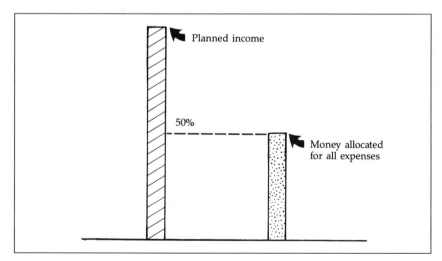

Figure 44-3. Overall expense allocation.

duce amazing results. People in training at the Center, especially in the financial planning courses, commonly report both increased income and decreased costs as a result of this discipline, and the rest of this chapter should make the reasons clear.

The Center's Northern Plains Regional Director Roland Kroos found that some people with very high debt servicing payments became demoralized and gave up any desire to plan further when they looked at half their gross income and took all their debt payments off that. Figure 44-4 shows why a person might find this depressing. Therefore Roland advised taking out the debt servicing expenses first, then dividing the remainder in half. This gives an amount to allocate to production and living that is hard but still achievable and thus does not demoralize the heavily indebted farmer completely.

In doing this Roland had a purely psychological motive supported by no theories of accounting. He meant to keep people trying to find creative solutions that would give them a start on climbing out of the debt quicksand.

Overcoming Reluctance to Plan

In teaching I have come to joke about the rancher/farmer disease. Most commonly seen in males, the clinical symptoms include a violent shaking

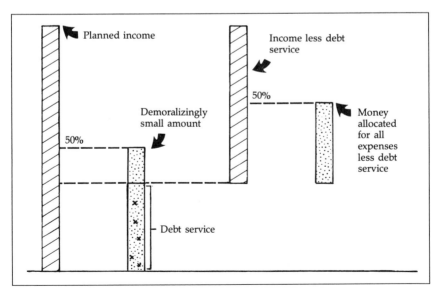

Figure 44-4. Overall expense allocation with heavy debt servicing.

of the hand in the presence of paper and pencil, sometimes followed by a cold sweat and dementia that only responds to a rapid drive to the local coffee shop and group therapy involving complaints about prices or bragging about weaner weights and crop yields. The syndrome has ill-defined causes but in the absence of a reliable cure is usually fatal. Aside from the coffee shop treatment, victims also may seek relief in fixing fences, greasing the tractor, or other irrelevant physical and mentally therapeutic work.

Rural people especially thrive on hard physical work but shy away from paper. Males may even feel guilty sitting behind a desk while "the real work" goes begging outside. I suffer from the affliction as badly as anyone. On leaving university I became a game ranger, hoping to escape the consequences. When I became a farmer it nearly destroyed me, and only by a wrenching dose of self-discipline, fueled by the horror of bankruptcy and failure to support my family, did I suppress the symptoms enough to survive.

There is no other way around this problem that has contributed so much to the travails of agriculture, and family farms in particular. They never fail because the fences don't run straight, nor because the machinery was neglected a little or their crops had more weeds than their neighbor's. They fail because planning fell short or just was never done. Under that vital guideline in the HRM model of marginal reaction to dollars, time, and labor, seldom does any activity outrank the time a manager spends in planning.

The old saying that "the finest fertilizer in the world is a farmer's footprints" carried real meaning in days gone by. Its corollary, which survives in the corporate world says that the best management is MBWA (management by wandering around). For the farmer of today I would say that the best fertilizer is the farmer's fingerprints on paper and computer keyboard.

Do You Really Want to Be a Manager?

If you inherit a farm or ranch, it does not mean you have to manage it. If that would commit you to a life you do not enjoy, you could hire a manager. Many people in such a position act from fear of family scorn or their own sense of tradition or duty. But if managing lies outside your well-defined goals, you might serve all parties better by avoiding it.

I am reminded of various people who sought my advice on purchasing game ranches in Africa. Usually they had sold a business or inherited money and thought game ranching represented a greener pasture. I would ask why they wanted to change, and the answers usually ran something like, "I'm sick of town life and long for the hunt and the camp life. I have always enjoyed just being in the bush and sitting by the campfire at night."

I then would offer them a list of game ranchers who might hire a hunter, a suggestion they usually found insulting when they had sought my help to buy a game ranch. But they had described a hunter's life of physical activity in the bush, and not the reality of an owner/manager's life of planning finances, worrying about markets, arranging long-distance refrigerated transport, meeting health requirements in butcheries, finding refrigerated storage in town, selling, arranging permits in a bureaucratic swamp, and sweating out financial survival.

Goal confusion of that kind is common, and usually leads to tragedy. Unfortunately this is not the only form of goal confusion with managers that leads to disaster. Ranchers commonly have an unstated goal of high calving rates and large calves and then go broke because of no profit. Had the goal been profit and been kept clearly in mind, then the high costs associated with producing the calving rate and calf weight would have been detected and rectified. Farmers likewise will have an unstated goal of high yield per acre and lose sight of profit being governed by the costs of producing that high yield.

In summary, planning means little, especially in hard times, unless the goals are very clear and the attitude is right. A downhearted, mentally defeated person will be defeated. Optimism and determination, followed by smart (and sometimes hard) work, always produces lucky results. Bad luck attends those who assume defeat and do not plan.

Attitude alone, however, does not suffice without enough self-discipline to carry out the necessary work on paper. If you cannot do this, then you should rethink your goals and role seriously before you lose the farm or ranch as an asset.

Generation of Wealth Using the HRM Model

Now we turn to the manner of planning that will ensure the maximum marginal reaction of labor, time, and dollars as you move toward your three-part goal in a holistic way.

Chapter 33 described the nature of the challenge in the example that weighed the expense of spraying noxious weeds against an investment in fencing. The spraying, though the normally recommended policy, gave insignificant return, while the fencing at that time could return 200 percent a year for each of the next fifty years. Such is the nature of holism that on the same property in the very next year, if energy conversion was not the weak link in the sun to solar dollar chain, then an investment in fencing would have been the wrong thing to do. In planning holistically you cannot step into the same river twice because the water is always moving, just as your situation is. Different decisions will be made every year as you use the model's guidelines to assist you in seeing the whole at any moment in time.

As a great many facets of your life are nonquantifiable, you will not always have great precision in the figures. What the model will enable you to do, however, is to avoid gross errors involving thousands of dollars and put most of the effort in the right place most of the time.

To do the job right, the management team must have time for uninterrupted thought, discussion, and brainstorming. The process may take considerable time broken by many recesses. Few people can concentrate on something for more than a couple of hours without some break.

Production and Income

As always you will start by deciding what you will produce to provide income, but rather than letting tradition or custom guide you, you must rethink everything from scratch, as trends and markets change each year.

The style of this rethinking seriously influences everything that follows. An oppressive, hurried, or politically charged atmosphere will kill good ideas before they ever see light. Opportunities abound for weeding out bad ideas later. At this point you can and should entertain all suggestions, no matter how farfetched they appear initially.

Structure a brainstorming session for as many people as you reasonably can involve, including some not familiar with the business or its history. Such people do not know *what cannot be done!*—an attitude that always stifles creative thinking. Warm up on a totally unrelated and playful task such as listing uses for old golf balls or ways to get an audience with the Sultan of Oman or writing headlines for a hypothetical tabloid, so that the group begins to pick and build on ideas in a relaxed and humorous manner.

Only then appoint a record keeper and give the team ten minutes to toss up every possible idea for generating income. Do *not* stop to judge any idea or elaborate much. Just jot down the crux of it in telegraphic form and go on. The most ridiculous idea gets the same treatment as any other.

The million-dollar idea that saves the ranch can come from such a session. I have seen owners respond in shock to the suggestion that ultimately rescued them. If someone hadn't shocked them into fresh thinking, they would have gone down with their ship, clinging to the traditional mast.

When the clamor of brainstorming settles down, discuss the list and select workable ideas. Consider trends in the community and markets, and other influences. In past decades large sectors of American manufacturing, including the automotive industry, failed to notice when consumers began to buy for quality rather than price and quantity. Agriculture, too, has responded sluggishly to increasing demand for leaner, fresher, less chemically-adulterated products and shorter preparation times. In markets, like guerrilla warfare, the people always win in the end. Individual producers, however, can capitalize on such trends independently, and where economies of scale apply they can collaborate to seize that opportunity too.

Given now a list of what you could produce, be it crops, livestock, recreational hiking and camping, hunting, birdwatching, or whatever, next carry out a gross margin analysis of each enterprise. What can each contribute to your immediate overhead? How do they fit into your present production and goals?

Some families will find this wrenching, especially those producing registered livestock that may represent generations of love, pride, and toil. Even when they see that the herd runs at a loss (adds to overhead expenses), they naturally want to stick by the breed. Goals, as explained in Chapter 8 on that subject, must be broad enough to preclude self-contradiction. If profit comes first, then profit from livestock or crops is specific enough. Circumstances may arise when a particular kind of livestock or crop simply can't render a profit, and to stay in business you will have to change.

Gross margin analysis *does not decide* which enterprises to operate, however; it is only one of the tests. You must pass any idea through all of them. Gross margin analysis is an economic concept that is not in itself holistic. If the product that contributes most toward paying overhead cost also damages the ecosystem or violates some social value, drop it, as it ultimately will defeat the quality of life you strive for.

Finally, however, you will decide which enterprises to pursue and through various calculations on worksheets, make month-by-month income projections. These you will enter *in pencil* on a master planning sheet (see the companion workbook) or computer spreadsheet program, either of which you can alter as more detail emerges from the planning.

Expenses and Goal Attainment

At this point, in the interest of self discipline you cut the total projected income figure in half and allocate that amount to the administration and production for the year. This will alter the present way we look at many expense items. For example, instead of working out what supplements cows need and then what they will cost, you will find yourself now allocating a given amount to supplement and then finding the best value for those dollars.

All expenses will have amounts allocated that you deem will carry you in the most effective way toward your goals. Those who have grown up in an affluent, materialistic culture will find this hard, ruthless, and perhaps impossible. But it isn't impossible. Do not use the word can't, even in your mind. Be creative. Collaborate with all involved and do it!

To work up a normal cash flow statement you would go through your overhead items, capital investments, and operating expenses for projected enterprises one by one and work out the amount and timing of costs. Here, however, you must step further back in order to see the whole picture. That will cause you to allocate income in a different sequence according to a new ranking of priorities.

The matter of sequence is critical, and to understand the reason, consider the parallel case of allocating time. So often you hear the phrase, "I haven't got time." In fact you have 100 percent of your time until you start allocating it, and you could give it all to your first priority. The common phrase really means, "I don't think this is important."

The same thing applies as you now allocate the money you are allowing for the year's running of the business. You have to get the expense items in a strict order of priorities regarding wealth generation and then allocate in that order. To do this we plan in this sequence:

1. Allocate funds for those expenses that *actually generate new wealth.*
2. Allocate funds to cover *inescapable costs* such as debt services, taxes, etc.
3. Allocate funds to provide for all of the *maintenance costs* that are essential but will not generate new wealth.
4. Make adjustments to see that all necessary costs are covered.
5. Reckon the cost of borrowed money and make a final profitability assessment.
6. Do immediate replanning if profitability is not adequate.

The approaches to all of these steps need some explanation, because once again they combine the psychological factor, the concept of holism, and some hard-nosed calculations. You cannot create a standardized list of costs in the three categories (wealth-generating, inescapables, maintenance) for planning as each year is different. A cost item that will generate wealth in one year may fall into the maintenance category the next year—i.e., you cannot step into the same river twice.

Creating Wealth

Of the items that you might spend money on, which actually *generate solar dollars*? Answering this question takes a lot of thought and quite likely will reorder old priorities drastically. Training and education provide a striking example. In the old cash flow planning approach, any money left at the end (a rare event) might support a little training, but that would *never* happen in hard times. However, of all investments in almost any business, none returns more than knowledge. Thus, even in hard times, make allocations for basic training and education right up front when you have 100 percent of your funds to play with.

On a worksheet reckon the cost, the number of people, type of training, transportation, and accommodation, then put the figures on the main planning chart in a special column according to the months when payments fall due. Then go on to other items that will enhance the generation of real solar wealth. Areas related to training, because they affect the performance of people, may include:

- Establishing a collaborative environment, free from fear and interpersonal stress.
- Improving time management.
- Use of computers and other aids to cut drudgery and enhance creativity.

Next turn to other items that touch the land directly such as:

- Fencing. By allowing better manipulation of time, herd effect, and grazing, fencing can increase energy flow greatly. In a year when energy conversion is considered the weak link in the solar dollar chain, and if fencing passes all of the other testing guidelines, it should be a high priority.
- Improved subterranean drainage (in croplands rather than wetlands). In croplands this may enhance energy flow far more than annual applications of fertilizer and has the added benefit of long-term effect.
- Improved irrigation efficiency. Unnecessary watering costs money and reduces productivity.
- Expanding herds and buying winter feed instead of tying up land to grow hay. The feed for carrying cattle through the snow season is a variable cost. The more cattle you have, the more feed you need, but sometimes you can carry enough extra cattle by grazing the hay fields to more than pay for buying winter feed, especially if you can eliminate the machinery and labor cost of haying.
- Purchase of or improvement in livestock when product conversion is the weak link.

In each of these cases all testing guidelines should be considered. If one does not apply, simply bypass it, but all should be given some thought. As you see, the solar chain crops up repeatedly.

Where to Invest in the Solar Chain

At the start of each year's planning, you will have to think about the position in that year and in particular remind yourself that you are in the business of generating solar dollars. Where in that chain of events from sun to solar dollar is the weak link in your operation this year? I recall once listening to an excellent speaker who was researching the transfer of embryos from outstanding cows to foster mothers. In this way greater production per cow could be achieved. He supported his case with many figures and appealed to the ranchers to get their industry to support the work financially. In particular he told the cattlemen to wake up to the fact that they had to compete with the pig and poultry producers who produced their meat at lower cost. The presentation was good and the appeal strong, but was it right?

The pig and poultry producers have the breeding animal or bird in small pens. The sunlight from which we generate solar dollars was a variable cost for them in that feed was grown elsewhere and brought in. This entire energy conversion link in their cases was a purchased item. For them the yield per fowl or pig is vital for profitability. The ranchers have their breeding cows not in pens but on the land. A cow needs anywhere between a couple of acres and a couple of hundred acres depending on the productivity of the land. The sunlight in this case is an overhead cost and not a variable. The money is tied up in the area of land and it has to generate solar dollars per acre at low cost, not per cow at low cost. In this case the entire energy conversion link is within the rancher's control. He has money tied up in capital and requires investments in various ways annually to convert the maximum energy.

Is the land owned or not? If it is not owned, how is the leasing based? Each of these considerations makes a big difference to what the right measure is for you. Remember that owned land produces no more than leased land and yet it ties up infinitely more working capital.

When you are trying to decide which expense items will generate the most new wealth each year, bear the solar chain in mind. The weakest link in the chain shifts constantly and for maximum returns (or to generate the most new wealth) you have to make sure your investment is constantly strengthening the weakest. An expense that would fall into the category of generating wealth last year may not fall in the same category this year. Is the weak link this year the same as last? Is it in the energy conversion, product conversion, or marketing link?

Energy conversion weak link. If energy conversion is weakest, what expense items actually convert more energy?

On a ranch running livestock as the product, the things that tend to convert more energy are fencing and herd amalgamation, which increase the ratio of recovery period to grazing period on the plants grazed; increased animal impact (using the herd effect guideline) to improve water and mineral cycles; and management measures that increase concentration and decrease time on the land.

Improved biological planning can produce excellent results at almost no cost provided the knowledge is there (this would be a training expense).

Brush clearing and erosion control measures can increase energy flow. As you try to determine which of these measures to spend money on, use the remaining testing guidelines—whole ecosystem, society and culture, marginal reaction, cause and effect, energy/wealth source and use. Those ideas that do not pass the testing should be dropped for now. In a year or two they may pass and become a justifiable expense.

In one year, brush clearing, erosion control, and fencing all might convert more energy, but only one is likely to pass all tests at any one time. When it comes to marginal reaction per dollar, for example, one has to be better than the others.

When you have finally decided where best to spend your money the next step is to allocate it. Do the detailed planning of this allocation on worksheets and carry the penciled amount to the planning sheets. Remember, nothing is final yet; you'll take time to juggle figures later.

On croplands, high input costs (machinery and chemicals) often point to a weak link in energy conversion. Possible responses could be to increase crop acreage, improve soil drainage or irrigation technique, reduce chemical use while introducing multicropping in various forms (interspersed crops, including legumes, alley cropping between rows of trees), simple rotations, a changed attitude toward weeds.

Make sure that before you take any action you run the tools involved through the testing guidelines to ensure that you are on track toward your goals. If your soil has become chemically-dependent, changes will be harder to effect.

Increased knowledge also can improve energy conversion. As part of your training investment, join organizations that strive for sustainable cropland agriculture (see References) and look for university programs in this area. Attend field days and keep challenging thinking through the testing guidelines as none of these organizations yet takes a fully holistic approach. They are moving in the right direction, however, and you can gain much from collaboration with them.

Finally, make your allocations once more after planning the details on the worksheets.

Other forms of production from the land—timber, fish, wildlife, and recreation—also depend on energy conversion, and if that appears to be the weak link, then determine which tools will maximize energy conversion for these forms of production, test them through the guidelines, and make allocations accordingly.

Production weak link. If this is where the weak link in the solar chain lies this year, you need to think about those expense items that will enhance the formation of a marketable product from that energy already converted in plants.

If you engage in wildlife production, what will produce more trophy animals or fish? Perhaps reduced populations, better biological planning? A fire? Temporary introduction of a large herd of cattle to improve habitat? Brainstorm for answers and check them against all the guidelines.

The stock grower seeking to strengthen his operation at the production link might consider higher stocking rate, better breeding and culling, better biological planning or production policies.

The crop farmer perhaps would look for harvesting techniques that cut waste and spoilage, better storage, handling, and transport. Are you proud of what you sell? Are you putting in that little extra effort that makes the difference between an adequate product and an exceptional one?

Do all of the proposed changes pass all of the tests? Plan the detail on worksheets and allocate money.

Marketing weak link. The production link naturally overlaps with the marketing link and you'll always need to consider the two together. Marketing decisions you make at this stage may affect your initial income projections and you may now have to relook at those figures.

Are you doing the best you can in marketing? Many a farmer or rancher works like a slave only to hand the vital marketing to an entrepreneur who makes a living by expanding his margins at the expense of yours. Feedlot owners and other processors also may serve particular niches in the market and ignore the unique potential of your product. If, for example, you might sell lean, chemical-free beef when the public demands it, why pay a feeder to turn it into a fat- and chemical-laden product the public resists?

Are you watching trends? Are you sensitive to your customers? Are you going that extra mile that makes for excellence and success? Are you making the maximum effort to find and collaborate with others of like mind where bulk markets have to be serviced?

Making investment decisions. Before you finally decide where to invest your dollars, you may have to plan still further. This is almost always the case when you are considering fencing versus supplementary feed. Supplementary feed and many other costs routinely fall into the maintenance category and do not actually generate wealth. These costs always should be cut to the bone in order to free up money for generating wealth.

Once energy conversion is identified as the weak link and fencing is considered a possibility for allocation of money, then it will need to pass the guidelines, marginal reaction in particular. Any fence you build should correspond to your long-term plan (Chapter 39). But which of the numerous fences envisioned do you build now? You must assess each area and each fence, because all possibilities give a different marginal reaction per dollar spent.

Figure 44-5 illustrates this point. Three fences are planned, but you only have enough money to build two. Which two would give you the highest return based on the marginal reaction test? To answer that you have to work

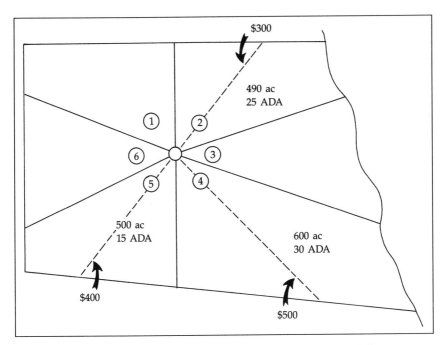

Figure 44-5. Selecting fences on basis of marginal reaction per dollar.

out how many animal days of grazing you would get for each dollar invested in the new fence. Estimate the possible ADA of forage in each paddock (or use actual figures based on past performance), then calculate the size of the new paddocks, and figure the cost of the fence. Now use these figures to arrive at a decision.

Paddock 2: A 490-acre paddock divided by 2 gives a new paddock of 245 acres. This multiplied by 25 ADA gives 6,125 animal days (AD). of forage and this divided by the fence cost of $300 gives 20.4 animal days per dollar (AD/$).

Paddock 4: $\left(\dfrac{600 \text{ acres} \times 30 \text{ ADA}}{2} \right) \div \$500 = 18 \text{ AD/\$}$

Paddock 5: $\left(\dfrac{500 \text{ acres} \times 15 \text{ ADA}}{2} \right) \div \$400 = 9.4 \text{ AD/\$}$

Obviously, in this example you would put your limited funds into splitting paddock 2 first, then 4, and 5 last. In this manner the whole of the ranch plan can be worked up step-by-step as the solar dollars are generated from the land with each dollar going back where it gives the greatest boost toward the goals.

Needless to say, real cases seldom work out so neatly as the one given here. You don't always split paddocks exactly in half, and other factors enter in. Perhaps splitting paddock 5 would reduce predation by giving better control of breeding stock. Use your common sense in considering such factors and build fences that provide the highest marginal reaction toward all three parts of your goal, not just dollars.

In all events you want to lean away from short-term solutions and base judgments not on the immediate bottom line, but on progress toward long-term goals. This isn't always easy and it's one of the reasons why goal formation is so vital. If all involved really own and take responsibility for those goals, it makes potentially hard decisions that much easier.

Inescapable Costs

Debt service, taxes, and some other costs may seem as inevitable as death. Sometimes they are, but an aggressive imagination may prove otherwise.

In American agriculture, a very unhealthy proportion of producers in the recent past assumed crushing debt obligations that overwhelmed them when land and commodity prices fell, while interest stayed high. Irresponsible and greedy lending contributes to such problems, but most lenders do not benefit by driving you off your land because they can neither sell it at a profit nor manage it as well as you can. Nevertheless, the customs and procedures that govern financial institutions often cause them to act against this logic.

Breaking the old conventions takes a creative imagination, thorough written planning, and salesmanship, and it may save the family farm.

At this stage of planning you have an idea of your gross income and the cost of items crucial to generating more in the future. If the immediate impact of debt service still threatens your survival, you must brainstorm again to devise better ways to repay the debt that will benefit both you and your lender.

Can you collaborate as management agent with your lender under a new relationship? You have know-how and detailed planning through the HRM model at your fingertips. The lender has capital but wants his money back. How you define a collaborative relationship will vary from country to country and even state to state in America, because laws and regulations differ, so a good solution will demand creativity.

The payment of compound interest and capital at the same time creates a particularly fatal situation because it leaves so little working money to generate the income you need to get you off the treadmill. Can you use your planning for a greater income base of solar wealth to persuade your lender to accept only interest payments for a certain period?

In Canada, authorities are looking at some innovative ideas that would allow some heavily indebted farmers to incorporate themselves and pay the bank in shares of stock, the dividends from which replace interest. In many instances the lender would earn more in this way than by taking over the land, and eventually the farmer could buy back his shares.

All such arrangements require trust and reliability on both sides, and few things impress a lender more than the kind of planning outlined in this chapter when carried out through diligent monitoring and control procedures. As part of any agreement the lender probably should insist on such planning and control, and that outside discipline might encourage more farmers to actually do the paper work they dread so much.

Finally, when you're back on your feet, you can buy out your lender and not look back.

Maintenance Costs

I use this expression for all expenses of general administration and other applications that do not directly generate income. Phone bills, office supplies, transport, advertising, supplementary feed, fertilizers, salaries, seasonal help, and your own withdrawings are commonly maintenance costs.

Remember that, depending upon shifts in the position of the weak link in the solar dollar chain, some items can change from generating wealth to maintenance and vice versa.

Most producers question putting fertilizers and supplementary feed for livestock in this category since it comes at the low end of priorities. Conventional management considers them vital to producing income, and they loom large in most budgets. They nonetheless represent imported energy, not solar energy converted on the land. Though supplements may aid in product conversion, by definition they constitute a net loss of energy, in that it takes more energy to grow and transport them than they add to the product. The same applies to fertilizer and most other chemicals, but in the majority of cases they degrade the local ability to convert energy as well.

Any portion of such maintenance cost that could go toward enhancing the intrinsic local potential for harnessing solar energy would better serve your long-term goals. Unlike the previous categories, the challenge lies not in how to allocate for the best marginal reaction, but how to cut so that your operation can still run and you can put more into things that do give the biggest boost toward your long-range goals.

This will take all the creativity and brainstorming you can command, and once more you should do it properly, giving time for a warm-up exercise as before. Whatever your initial prejudice against this, a good brainstorming session on cutting maintenance costs commonly generates thirty or more fairly reasonable ideas.

Collaboration and joint undertakings with neighbors offer a particularly rich lode of opportunity. Join others in bulk purchases. Share vehicles and heavy equipment, marketing costs and trips to town, repair tools, hunting permits, and advertising. Farmers of old knew this and made barn raising a social occasion. Community support and sharing among the Amish is one more reason why they stand among the buyers when the most independent, technologically-sophisticated farms nearby go on the auction block.

In our materialistic age we have forgotton how to work with others for the common good, but sharing luxury items also can cut the cost of the good life. Boats, planes, ski resort condos, motor homes, etc. seldom get full use from a single family. If you have overindulged in the past, selling shares to friends beats giving these things to the bank and can reduce the burden on your finances immensely without affecting your enjoyment.

Smarter predator control also may yield big savings. Biological planning to assure that calves come in protected areas, culling in favor of good mothering, use of guard donkeys and imprinted dogs among sheep all may help at little cost. Lambing boards that keep small lambs or kids from jumping out of cell centers to follow their mothers assure that only fairly fleet and hardy animals are exposed to predation.

New techniques may take a bit of trial and error. One member of the Center found his newly imprinted sheep dog calmly eating fresh lamb while a coyote munched dog food nearby. But one can't learn without trying.

Incentives for labor also can produce radical savings. I have seen predation losses cut, for example, simply by switching from paying herders a small bonus for each lamb weaned to paying a large bonus, say $50, for each lamb over a certain threshold number. Thus throughout the season all lambs have a potential value of $50, and vigilance increases proportionately.

On my own farm I brought manual weeding way below the cost of chemical and mechanical weeding by assigning competing teams to equal areas of land. Winners got recognition and prizes. I also cut labor costs dramatically by seeking laborers' ideas and rewarding successful ones.

People in labor gangs respond differently to supervision, and costs drop if you can find people who keep working without it. In Africa I would set as many as forty men to a task without supervision all day, but watched from afar with binoculars. Each day some left to seek work on other farms, and I took on replacements. Before long I had a crew of independent natural workers who performed better than any sullen gang that required the expensive and degrading presence of a full-time supervisor.

Equipment maintenance costs likewise drop when operators have reason to take responsibility. When I did my own repairs, I soon discovered that almost every stoppage stemmed from slack prevention (cause and effect guideline), though drivers always had reasons for the cut tire, jammed roller in the bulldozer tracks, broken fanbelt, or lost bolt. That changed instantly, however, when I dropped them from the payroll and hired them as independent contractors.

As such they earned a small daily fee and a large daily bonus that gave them more potential income than before. However, the contract included a long list of items to attend to on their machines and a corresponding penalty in daily bonuses if anything turned up deficient. Once they understood the terms, my time spent in supervision and maintenence dropped to an occasional random inspection.

Somehow, even in the dark, they saw every stump that could stab a tire. I never found a dirty air filter or an oil filter full of gum. Lubricants and coolants stayed at proper levels and no grease nipple became dry. The drivers' income rose, but the drop in repair costs more than paid for it. I had more time, and work proceeded faster.

When we went into twenty-four-hour operations the system worked even better. Each machine had a little book, and when the shift changed, the new driver had to sign that he had received his machine in perfect condition. Never had these machines had such thorough and regular inspections.

I give these examples because from my own undercapitalized farming experience in extremely hard times, I know what can happen when you refuse to say can't.

Before all maintenance costs are completed, it is wise to add one more actual expense column and plan for it. This vital expense is depreciation. Depreciation is no abstract writing down of assets according to a legislated schedule. It must represent real cash set aside to replace real machines when you actually expect them to wear out. How many farmers take the depreciation allowance each year at tax time, but have no money when the old John Deere finally throws a rod? Make a realistic allowance for the depreciation of machinery and items that do wear out so that by the time you estimate you will have to replace them you will have the cash and not borrow to do so. This money actually should be invested to one side earning interest until required.

Net Managerial Income

The concept of net managerial income (NMI) provides a direct and immediate measure of management success in keeping income up and costs down. When used as a basis on which managers can participate in the results financially, it is far superior to the outdated and ineffective concept of bonuses, which may produce movement, but not motivation (people who move themselves to receive a bonus are very different from people who motivate themselves internally). Whether or not NMI is used to help allocate financial rewards, it keeps management focused on profitability much as the bathroom scale inspires the weight watcher. NMI works in the following way.

On the planning sheet, expense and income columns under the direct control of particular managers are defined and grouped for easy analysis. All income within the power of management to control less all costs within the power of management to control equals net managerial income. This often does not represent all costs or income. An owner or another branch of management may control some expenses, and income from mineral leases, market trading, etc. handled by others does not count. However, when a management team can see graphically what it contributes to the success of the whole, its members become more effective.

The injunction to include all levels of people in creative planning and its rewards bears repeating. The lowest on the totem pole see things on the job that you do not, and if included in the team, rewarded and acknowledged, they will surprise you.

Readjustment of Allocations

At this point—toward the end of the planning—you quite likely will want to juggle and adjust some allocations. Some of those higher priorities probably did absorb more than you can afford right now. Maintenance, though considered last, is essential. Gears won't turn without oil.

Cost of Borrowed Money and Final Assessment

Finally, the planning sheet includes columns on the right-hand side for calculating and reckoning interest on monthly credit balances. From this you can see the total cost of borrowing, spot peaks of indebtedness, and compute that final bottom-line figure. The workbook shows the details.

Now you decide if the profit picture meets your requirements.

This bottom-line figure on the planning chart does not compare to the figures prepared for tax purposes for several reasons. Mainly, it does not show changes in net worth due to outside influences such as land price changes. On the other hand, do not forget to include real increases in worth represented by such things as breeding stock held back from sale or bulk supplies on hand at year's end. These, as opposed to increased worth of property that you have no desire to sell, have a value that directly affects operations. Relevance to operations is the touchstone.

If you have a professional accountant help you determine profitability at the end of your planning, be sure to remind him that you do it for management purposes only, and his tax preparation job has other criteria. While on this matter it is important that you realize that you as manager do the annual financial planning and not the accountant whose task is completely different.

If your bottom line does not work, then do not implement the plan. You must replan immediately from the beginning and continue to do so until the bottom line meets your expectation. *You, as manager, must plan profit and know what profit you plan before the financial year begins.*

When you realize the kind of juggling of allocations and replanning necessary to do this in most cases, you will understand instantly why I recommend buying a computer. Now especially, you must be fresh and creative and the amount of computing, erasing, finding totals, and following the ripples through myriad columns will wear you out quickly. A single replanning by hand, not to mention two or three, can take hours.

Modern electronics lets you change a figure anywhere in the plan, punch a button, and in seconds the screen shimmers slightly, giving you perfect figures right to the end. Seeing that happen after a short attempt to do the same job on paper will cure the worst computer phobia instantly. Computers require little skill to operate and by taking hours of tedious work out of planning time they free up your mind for its task of creative and alert planning. They cost less than a pickup and are safer to drive. A $2,000 machine can easily save you $20,000 and two days' work in an hour.

With that said, you should still proceed cautiously in computerizing your planning. Always initiate your first plan on paper so you know exactly what part the computer is playing—it only crunches numbers, it does not think for you. Many, myself included, become mesmerized on occasion by the computer's lightning speed and credit it with an intelligence it does not have. It will take several months before you have debugged your programs and become thoroughly familiar with operating the computer. Plan with paper and pencil until you reach this stage and until you have a thorough understanding of the planning process.

Conserving Wealth

It is important that farm and ranch families not only generate wealth toward achieving their three-part goals, but that they also conserve it for future generations.

An unfortunate feature of many such businesses is that they are land rich but, upon death of an owner, lack the liquidity to avoid catastrophic breakup to meet death dues and taxes. The complications of the many laws affecting estates are beyond the understanding of most of us and thus it is essential that professional help be sought and proper estate planning be undertaken. Even when the situation appears hopeless, a professional planner usually can find ways to overcome most obstacles. The earlier you seek one out, the more ways there are.

Summary

The annual planning for attainment of goals and genuine wealth is driven by three principles: 1) the mechanical process detailed in the companion workbook; 2) the psychological attitude vital to success and the recognition that cost control means more to profit than selling price; and 3) the use of the model and human creativity to generate new solar wealth while achieving the goals.

Expenses fall into three categories—those that actually generate new wealth and build the landscape goal, those that must be paid, and maintenance that keeps the wheels turning but does not directly generate income.

When you have worked through all of this you will have an incredibly sound plan for the year's operations. Still, the most perfect plan achieves nothing unless followed and adjusted until the end.

The next chapter talks about monitoring and controlling your plan.

45

Financial Monitoring
and Control

A plan, no matter how detailed, serves little purpose unless it is followed. This chapter outlines procedures to make sure it is. There are only two, monitoring progress and controlling deviations. Occasionally, circumstances will render a whole plan inappropriate and necessitate a thorough replanning, but basic monitoring will give early warning when that need arises.

As an extension of planning, the job of keeping a plan on track requires a priority allocation of time and the participation of all the people concerned. Monitoring involves organizing an efficient way to gather and compile data. Controlling means formally scheduling from a half to a full day at least once a month for discussing deviations from the plan and organizing corrective action.

Monitoring

The form we use for recording the financial plan has columns for each income and expense item and four rows for each month. The planned figures occupy the first row. (For closer monitoring of items purchased in bulk these may represent actual amounts consumed rather than cash paid out.) The other three rows serve to record and display the results of monitoring.

Actual income, expense, or consumption of bulk supplies goes in the second row at the end of each month. The positive or negative variation from plan goes in row three. The cumulative difference, computed by combining the variations from month to month, goes on row four. By showing total deviation for the year to date, it highlights trends away from plan.

Figure 45-1 illustrates a portion of a sample form showing how the four rows work in practice.

To make the form give a graphic impression of how reality does or doesn't follow the plan, items adverse to plan must carry some visible negative sign. On charts done by hand, income shortfalls or expense/consumption overruns recorded in red ink will make the overall picture evident at a glance. Most computers will put these negative figures in parentheses, but an additional touch of red felt pen on the printout will help draw attention to items requiring control.

Frequency of monitoring is important and should reflect the degree of stress and worry about the business. Normally no less than once a month *within the first week of the month* will suffice. Monitoring quickly and on time matters more than perfect accuracy. Use round dollars to save time and space. You don't need to nail down every cent as a tax accountant must to make management decisions.

Managers who hire outside accountants sometimes do not get printouts back until the month following the actual accounting. This will not work. Arrange to record the raw data for your monitoring at the same time the accountant collects it for his more refined processes.

If survival prospects look critical, then obtain monitoring figures daily and project them to month's end daily to see where they stand relative to the plan.

In developing a sugar farm from virgin bush in Africa, I myself came to the point of daily monitoring and the ability to see expenses mounting toward the planned monthly limit saved me more than once. Short of capital and heavily in debt, a rapid fall in prices pushed me to the edge of desperation. Planning a way out took ages. My main crop, sugar cane, would not return any income until eighteen months from the date it was planted, and the price trend and interest rate destroyed any chance of borrowing more against that.

Eventually I managed to plan survival around a series of crops—cane, cotton, corn, potatoes, and cabbages—which would mature at different stages and pay the development costs, but all aspects of the plan simply had to work. Even one month of over-budget expenses on any crop would have put me out of business. Only daily monitoring allowed me to take corrective action in time. Some of the more creative ways to cut costs mentioned in the last chapter arose from that tight monitoring and ruthless control.

A financial planning sheet, flecked here and there by red ink, will show at a glance what needs attention.

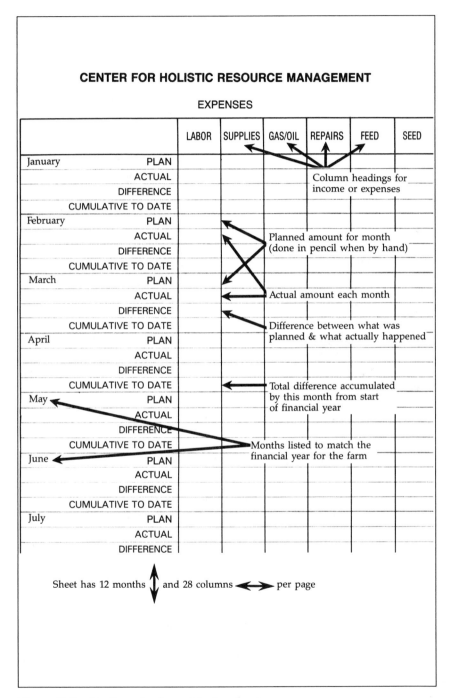

CENTER FOR HOLISTIC RESOURCE MANAGEMENT

EXPENSES

		LABOR	SUPPLIES	GAS/OIL	REPAIRS	FEED	SEED
January	PLAN						
	ACTUAL			Column headings for			
	DIFFERENCE			income or expenses			
	CUMULATIVE TO DATE						
February	PLAN						
	ACTUAL			Planned amount for month			
	DIFFERENCE			(done in pencil when by hand)			
	CUMULATIVE TO DATE						
March	PLAN						
	ACTUAL			Actual amount each month			
	DIFFERENCE						
	CUMULATIVE TO DATE			Difference between what was			
April	PLAN			planned & what actually happened			
	ACTUAL						
	DIFFERENCE						
	CUMULATIVE TO DATE			Total difference accumulated			
May	PLAN			by this month from start			
	ACTUAL			of financial year			
	DIFFERENCE						
	CUMULATIVE TO DATE			Months listed to match the			
June	PLAN			financial year for the farm			
	ACTUAL						
	DIFFERENCE						
	CUMULATIVE TO DATE						
July	PLAN						
	ACTUAL						
	DIFFERENCE						

Sheet has 12 months ↕ and 28 columns ◄──► per page

Figure 45-1.   Portion of a financial plan sheet.

Control

According to the governing principle of control, *each item* must be brought into line with the plan. Except in exceptional circumstances, a surplus in one area does not balance a deficit in another from the standpoint of management. You cannot allow yourself the luxury of saying, "Well, I used too much fuel this month, but we're okay because it didn't snow and we're ahead on feed grain and hay." Just be grateful for every item that goes better than planned. Balancing across columns will lead to sloppy management and erode profits, and every surplus you can retain will soften the shock of emergencies you don't foresee.

An income item that falls short of plan creates a more complicated situation. You can seldom control it against itself as there may be no further income from that source in that year. You can only respond by reducing expenses, and that means reworking as many expense items as it takes to find the money while figuring how to prevent the same problem in the future.

Such control is vital to success, and warrants a formal process, recorded in writing, of recognizing a problem, analyzing it, deciding on corrective action, and naming the individuals responsible for seeing that through.

Figure 45-2 shows a control sheet that covers all the steps and can serve both as a record of meetings on control issues and as a reminder to those taking responsibility. It has five columns:

1. Item and column number.
2. Amount of deviation in dollars or bulk measure.
3. Cause of deviation, simply stated.
4. Proposed action to return to plan in clear, brief language.
5. Person responsible—name or initials.

Small deviations in large items do not require such full dress review unless they represent a trend. The fourth line under the monthly headings on the planning chart (figure 45-1), which shows cumulative deviations, will show up such cases. When small deficits mount continually, the situation needs attention.

Control is the hardest part of planning and management. Though you might have spent a week or more making the best possible plan, when your monitoring turns up a few adverse figures you have to do better than your best. That may push you to despair and to simply ignore the signs and grind on in hopes that fate will err in your favor somewhere down the road. If you are serious about making profit part of your goal, do not do this. Knuckle down and do that seemingly impossible control.

Once again attitude makes the difference. Winston Churchill is alleged

Center for Holistic Resource Management

CONTROL SHEET

Name: ______________ Date: June 1988 Sheet #: 1.

Plan Column #	Amount Adverse to Date	Cause of Deviation from Plan	Proposed Action to Return to Plan	ACT
I-5	$5000	Sales prices lower than	- Plan reductions in all areas —	
		expected.	each person to prepare & come up	All
			with suggested reductions by next	
			control meeting.	
			- Sell as pairs next year & market	B.J.
			wider afield.	
E-16	$1500	Labor used earlier than planned.	- No action - will balance in August.	—
E-26	360	Poor use of heavy transport.	- Reduce to 1 trip to town each month.	B.J.
	gallons	Too many unnecessary trips.	Keep purchase requests at office.	
E-37	$ 636	Farrier charges have risen	- Horses will not be shod. All hooves	
		as has transport cost.	will be rasped & checked weekly.	J.S.
			Send Jack on course in November.	
E-39	200 gals.	Too much pickup use.	- Supplies will be bulked in small	
	gas		storage sheds at strategic sites on	
			ranch.	
			- Use 4-wheelers - no pickup use	M.K.
			in good weather except emergency.	
E-42	$2000	Several unexpected breakdowns	- Arrange brainstorming party	
		with machinery, pickups	Tuesday next week at Bill's	B.J.
		& tractor.	house 6 p.m. All staff present.	

Figure 45-2. Control sheet.

to have said, "If something has to be done, and all of your experts convince you that it cannot be, then change your experts and do it!" *Do not accept can't. Do not make or accept excuses. Do it.* Cut those costs. Cut those costs. Cut those costs. Air-conditioned cabs are not essential. Motorbikes cost less per mile than pickups, but more than bicycles in terms of cutting costs and remaining fit. Maybe a few weeds will not cut yields as much as people say. They provide diversity in the community and thus help reduce insect damage, which will offset reduced yields. If the neighbors buy a new tractor, take pride in the condition of an old one and brag about that. Can maintenance be improved still further? What about another brainstorming session?

The process of controlling will quickly show the advantage of involving everyone possible in both goal formation and planning. The more people at the operational level who took part in the initial planning, the more ownership and responsibility felt for those figures and the more personal the stakes involved in meeting the planned amounts. Picture yourself as a cowboy assigned to put up a cabin for a summer camp at the end of the ranch. If the boss simply allocates some money and tells you to build it, will you approach the job in the same manner as you would if you knew the overall profit picture and the boss asked you to estimate what you could build the cabin for?

No. In the first case you actually may have an interest in spending the absolute limit of your allocation and stand a good chance of overrunning it in the process. In the second case your pride rests on demonstrating the economy and efficiency you yourself promised, and you will do everything possible to achieve that.

In my consulting days I watched hired hunters nearly break a big game ranch and destroy their jobs in the process because they had had no part in the planning. Despite long hours in the field they brought in less and less game, often a sign of falling game numbers. Yield from the ranch had dropped so low that the owners hired me to determine if they had overharvested and needed to cut back.

My game surveys showed thriving herds. A surreptitious check of the hunters, however, turned up the real problem. They habitually went out early, shot a few animals from the first herd but, after loading them, did not go in to the handling facilities and out again to hunt. They parked their loaded vehicles in the shade and lay back with a portable radio to listen to music and sleep, timing their actual return just late enough to make a second run impractical and excusing themselves by lamenting the scarcity of game.

The hunters had no criminal intent to defraud the landlord of his rightful due and no abnormal inclination to laziness. In fact they had estimated the gross income generated by their labor and concluded that it sufficed to feed them and the owner well enough. Having never seen any other aspect of the business in detail, they had no idea how close to bankruptcy the whole enterprise had come. They left out of their estimates the cost of refrigerated transport, breakdowns, spoiled meat, refrigerated storage in the field and rented in town, taxes, permits, and a host of other costs. Had they some appreciation for that, their attitude might have been quite different.

As a consultant I solved the problem by recommending payment of hunters on results alone without a basic salary. Their productivity soared overnight. However, I have learned enough since to see a better way. Today I would include the hunters in the planning and control process and reward their success on the basis of net managerial income. That way they would have some stake in controlling costs as well as production, and a reason to care about the total performance of the enterprise as well as their own income.

Good monitoring and the subsequent challenge of control has taught us a good deal about cost cutting on ranches and farms. It has led to some of the most creative uses of biological planning in conjunction with investment in fencing as ways to cut supplementary feed costs. As earlier chapters described, high paddock numbers allow a reduction in the number of times animals select from each one during dormant periods. That gives better distribution of available nutrition throughout the season and dramatically cuts the need for supplementation, a very high annual cost on many ranches and a significant brake on profits.

Once more, when facing apparently impossible control tasks, use creativity and do not hesitate to brainstorm, beginning on a playful exercise, as one of the most successful ways to really get ideas flowing.

Replanning

Monitoring may show drastic problems of course, as will happen when income slumps because of some catastrophe in the business itself or externally. Then mere control makes little sense. Get all concerned together immediately and spend the necessary time to replan entirely. This may mean going right back to the first steps and going through the entire process discussed in the last chapter.

If you really have to do this—a thankfully rare occurence when initial planning and control was done—mental attitude becomes, if possible, more critical than before. Ideally you would take a break and tackle the terrible task fresh. I myself could never do that. The proximity of disaster so dominated every thought that I simply couldn't sleep until I had worked out a solution on paper. It made no sense to toss and turn pretending to rest when the same energy might produce answers that would let me really sleep later. But whatever your personal style, do not despair, replan.

Drought and catastrophic fires create the most common replanning situations on ranches. While they quite often make biological replanning necessary, normally the financial plan will need only moderate adjustment. Therefore, do the biological plan first. Only then can you see the whole picture clearly enough to assess the financial impact.

When you carry this off, you will have acquired experience in all the guidelines, tools, and processes of holistic management and presumably can see the way toward your goals. If you can't, and you remain cynical about this approach and all its analysis, planning, monitoring, controlling, and replanning, what alternative can you offer?

If you have come so far and yet begin to doubt, look again to your goals. Chapter 8 on goal formation discussed the need for three-part temporary goals as a prerequisite for starting the process of holistic management. Now that you and those working with you have studied the whole HRM model you can refine and clarify those goals, and in the process discover a growing sense of ownership that will inspire your efforts further.

Temporary goals serve a true purpose. The next chapter talks about defining more permanent ones.

PART VII

Goals

46

Goals II: Setting More Permanent Goals

Nearly every chapter of this book repeats in some way the notion that serious management, and holistic management in particular, can only exist in the context of a journey toward goals. Chapter 8 on goal setting discussed this in some detail and briefly described the rationale for setting quality of life, production, and landscape goals. However, since thorough goal setting requires some understanding of the model and what it can potentially render, we could not discuss the goal-setting process in depth until this point.

Although events often demand that you initiate your use of the HRM model with temporary goals, within a year you must reopen the goal-setting process and formulate more permanent ones. This may not actually change the goals themselves, but it will deepen the commitment of the people whose lives revolve about them and foster smoother and more creative management of the whole.

When people in the same canoe paddle in different directions, conflict and confusion prevail. Arriving at a state of harmony may take time and effort, and the sequence of working through the three-part goal may well determine success or failure.

First, find a quality of life statement that all parties support. Next, determine the form of production required to support the desired quality of life. Only at the last work out a description of the landscape that will support the production and sustain the quality of life. This order often leads to resolution of long-standing conflict over the management of land, because the people drawn to the same piece of land often seek similar personal reward, despite different approaches.

A typical temporary goal, set without much consultation by ranch or farm owners when starting holistic management, might run thus. "We want to remain on the land, enjoying a rural way of life and relative security. We want to raise livestock and crops profitably and also enjoy some profit from utilization of our wildlife. Our land at the moment is covered in dense brush and has many eroding gullies. We want to see it develop to open grassland that still contains brush, but is not dominated by it, and to heal the gullies and stop the erosion."

This will support initial changes in the process of management, but assume the existence of an extended family who all own shares in the ranch and of several employees as well. All of them eventually should take part in the formation of a more permanent and detailed statement.

The idea of a three-part goal worked out in a definite order grew out of much trial and error, not logical analysis. Initially, the HRM model did not even include goal setting, and one began applying it by analyzing the four ecosystem processes. Such myopia seems incredible today, but few scientists with my training talk of goals even now. In fact Einstein, who unlike most of his heirs understood the full implications of atomic energy, is one of the few scientists of any kind who ever made a formal comment on the danger of pursuing scientific endeavors without goals for mankind.

In our case, experience on the land rapidly revealed the futility of manipulating the ecosystem foundation blocks without some idea of what we wanted to produce. Thus the production goal became part of the model. Very soon we encountered the problem that so afflicts modern agriculture, of production goals achieved at the expense of the landscape that supports them. Adding the landscape goal focused the application of the model marvelously, but still the people involved often argued to a standstill over forms of production and thus the desired landscape. Some time passed before it appeared that such conflict could only be resolved by finding a common vision of quality of life from which to proceed. Fortunately, most people within a community in fact tend to have remarkably similar desires and can overcome seemingly impossible divisions when they recognize and build on that.

The strength of the three-part goal derives from the way the parts limit as well as complement each other. For instance, where a particular quality of life implies great material demands, the discipline of describing a landscape that can meet them without sacrificing its ecological health checks the possibility of exploitation. Some environments simply cannot produce enough of a given commodity to assuage unlimited greed or need, and in reconciling quality of life, production, and landscape, the goal-setting process must address that.

The self-regulating nature of the three parts of the goal virtually guarantees that if they can be articulated, they also can be achieved through application of the model.

The same kind of logic should govern most human endeavor. After all, if I do not know what I want to make, then what use are a hammer and saw to me? Unfortunately, very few of us as individuals or families have any written goals. Even fewer communities have such clear goals. And yet, as humans can affect their planet in ever more drastic ways, the lack of clear goals becomes increasingly dangerous.

Three common errors in goal setting as it does exist result in what Chapter 8 referred to as nongoals:

- Setting production goals without reference to either the ecosystem (landscape) or quality of life.
- Confusing tools and goals.
- Making exceedingly narrow goal definitions such as safeguarding or eradicating a particular species, protecting watersheds by mechanical means, stopping desertification by planting trees, and the like.

Mainstream American agriculture, as mentioned frequently already, now makes the first error by technologically forcing production at the expense of the landscape and quality of life.

Environmentalists whose declared goal is removal of livestock from public lands in the United States commit a mistake of the second order, as animal impact, grazing, and rest are all tools. To declare a goal of applying rest to all public lands may utterly defeat the possibility of attaining a desired landscape goal. Environmentalists would do better to put the landscape goal first and then use whatever tools necessary to achieve it.

I have particular sympathy for their reluctance to embrace livestock as a possible tool for land restoration, because I used to share it. I once bought a piece of land in Zimbabwe, intending to preserve it as an outdoor school for the study of conservation. The land, graced by hills of broken granite, was so astonishingly lovely that Cecil Rhodes had chosen to be buried there, and I hoped by keeping out domestic stock to restore its primordial splendor.

Conditions in the whole area had changed, however. Old herds had diminished and human activity restricted their movement. I soon realized I had only two options; bring on carefully managed livestock as a tool or face continual decline and the eventual loss of the large animal component altogether.

A more current example is the conservation reserve program (CRP) in America, which has taken millions of acres of croplands out of production to restore soil and reduce erosion while cutting production and thus raising commodity prices. However good the intent, legislating rest as a tool will subvert it on brittle lands that require disturbance to advance succession and the other ecosystem processes. Had they understood the model, legislators no doubt could have found a fair way to allow beneficially managed livestock production in areas where the land requires it.

Examples abound of goals defined too narrowly. State programs for eradicating noxious weeds or problem trees fall into this category, as do most campaigns to protect certain endangered species. The monotonous record of failure of such efforts illustrates the inadequacy of goals that do not include a futuristic description of the landscape required. The underlying intention has merit, but even the most heroic efforts will fail if they do not create an environment where the targeted pest will not thrive and the endangered species will.

Other common goals that defeat themselves by their narrowness are:

- Establishing wilderness and park areas by leaving them to Nature when many species and key predators, including primitive man, have already disappeared.
- Stopping erosion by building earthworks across gullies and arroyos while ignoring the general condition of the watershed.
- Reversing desertification by planting trees where the general state of succession has fallen to a level where trees cannot establish seedlings and maintain the community.
- Protecting higher successional fish populations by poisoning predators and competing species that inevitably flourish when succession, as determined by conditions across the whole watershed, descends to their level.

Unfortunately, the list of similarly deficient projects has no end, and developed countries routinely lead undeveloped countries into forming the same sorts of goals.

The following chapter will cover application of the HRM model in other modes besides management. One of these is policy analysis that will reveal in advance when and why a particular program may founder or fail due to narrow goals.

Goal Ownership

Aside from the necessity of reviewing temporary goals in order to winnow out and replace the kind of nongoals discussed above, reworking and defining permanent goals creates an opportunity to give more people a share in goal ownership from which they derive a sense of responsibility and commitment that helps mightily in achieving success. Such a flowering of participation does not happen, however, except in an atmosphere of trust and collaboration and only top leadership such as an owner or department head can create the environment for that. That person must have the confidence to consider his or her ownership a technical issue and allow others to take part in formulating goals for themselves and the land.

If you as owner worry that opening the business of setting a three-part goal for your land will let others force revolutionary changes down your throat, you can try the following exercise to allay your fears.

Write down your own three-part goal and seal it in an envelope along with similar statements from other owners or people whom you do trust. Then start afresh and conduct an open discussion that includes all levels of people who make decisions and are held responsible, including yourself. When you have combined all opinions into a three-part goal that everyone can accept, open your envelope. Chances are very good that your original goals will not differ much from those articulated by the group, but those defined by the team undoubtedly will reflect more thorough understanding and deeper commitment.

Quality of Life

Goal formation always starts from discussion of quality of life by all parties involved in the use of land or other resources in question. Approaching the matter from this side tends to foster collaboration, as people associated with the same piece of land almost by definition have related interests. Particularly in cases involving public lands, conflicts are already present over tools—i.e., rest versus livestock—before goals have been set. Rehashing those areas of conflict can quickly destroy any hope of finding common ground. On the other hand discussing quality of life first can dissolve many a hard attitude.

Some may take the pessimistic view that holistic management will not work, and that it's better to leave things as they are. Such attitudes usually come from people who perceive the HRM model as a management system imposed upon them rather than as a tool of thought useful in setting a course and arriving at any freely chosen goal. A sensitive use of the model to analyze their work and predict the outcome may make the point, if one can avoid offending pride in the process.

No matter how long it takes, however, people must determine the goals for themselves. As said before, you cannot apply holistic management to others and their resources, or apply it anywhere in the long run, without true ownership of the goals by the people involved. If any mistrust lingers, work on that weak link first and leave goal formation until greater agreement and understanding prevails.

When you arrive at a point where all can communicate freely on the quality of life question, start with a blank sheet of paper. Never prepare an outline or try to build on any temporary goal used before; either approach could chill the atmosphere of trust and participation from the outset.

Ultimately everyone should think deeply about their lives and the community of which they are a part. I personally like to ask everyone to write what they would like to see for their children and/or the community if they should return in one hundred years. Ponderous paragraphs aren't necessary. Telegraphic phrases or headlines will convey the picture, and it should be broad. Religion, freedom, security, cultural activities, educational and recreational opportunities, and aesthetics all play a part. A good understanding of your own values is useful.

Normally, people in the same community, even though of radically different religious and ethnic backgrounds, have remarkably similar opinions on these matters. We have not compiled any research on this phenomenon, but it would not surprise me to discover that people in different cultures, continents apart, in fact don't differ very much.

To keep the discussion on track and prevent domination by any individual, a neutral facilitator often helps, but whether or not this person comes from outside the group, his or her first duty is *to keep the discussion from turning to tools at any point.* One of our staff members, Roland Kroos, keeps discussion focused by encouraging people to talk about what they *hope to accomplish,* rather than *how* they will accomplish it. When tools are allowed to creep into the discussion, conflict will likely ensue, even though any discussion of tools is meaningless until goals have been set. It takes no genius to see this, but people have argued over tools for so long that by habit they fall into that mire and stick there.

Only from a base of solid agreement on quality of life should you proceed to production and landscape goals. But ranchers and farmers in particular tend to begin and end with production, addressing quality of life and landscape goals only in passing. Poor working relationships, high staff turnover, and short-lived family businesses result from this habit.

Production

Although of course central to every operation, production must follow quality of life in order of discussion for a very practical reason in addition to the reasons just mentioned. Usually the process of working out a quality of life statement shows the necessity of several forms of production most people otherwise overlook. Farmers and ranchers tend to equate production and profit and see no further. Quality of life depends on more than cash, however, and single-minded pursuit of profit can make life miserable, as many people in materialistic societies are discovering.

Production goals need be no more than a list of things that count. The following one is fairly typical:

Profit from crops

Profit from livestock

Food production for home consumption

Profit from wildlife

Profit from recreation

Profit from timber

Recreation (personal, without profit)

Aesthetic environment (restful and pleasing to eye and soul)

Work of cultural value (development of a way or life, preservation of ancient relics or sites, etc.)

Recreational resources (clear and prolific trout streams or woods abounding in wildlife)

As an understanding of the model should make clear, you should not specify what form of livestock, crop, or recreational income you will produce. That may have to change according to the market if profit truly counts most. Cultural, aesthetic, and recreational values not tied to profit also may change, but usually they do so less often.

Many are the ranchers I have advised who do not grasp that profit as a goal must stand alone. They bragged on their bloodlines, the size of fall calves, and show trophies, ignoring high costs of production that inevitably would drive them out of business altogether. The perfect heifer and the prize bull may represent legitimate products in their own right, sometimes related to, but always considered separately from, profit.

In cases involving public or communal ownership of any land, naturally the production goal must spell out, under relevant headings, all forms of production necessary to maintain the quality of life of the various constituencies using that land. Some may merely want to enjoy the scenery periodically while others hope to make homes and live there. The former do not want to find the trout streams fouled by lounging cattle. The latter don't want litter, opened gates, dangerous campfires, or reckless hunters. The apparently divergent needs in such cases nevertheless can be resolved on the basis of common quality of life goals, if all parties can work out mutual landscape goals. Once again no discussion of tools must cloud the issue.

Unfortunately, tools must at least be mentioned in the production goal if profit is involved. If we aren't specific in mentioning profit from crops, livestock, or whatever, we do not know what the landscape has to sustain and thus cannot formulate the landscape goal. This also holds true in some tribal situations where livestock may take on a deeply religious or cultural significance and be mentioned in the quality of life goal. The use of a skilled facilitator would be crucial in such cases to keep discussion away from the tools until the full goal is formulated.

Landscape

Unlike production, landscape demands very deep and detailed thinking, for the whole structure rests on what happens to the four ecosystem processes. Without a precise description of exactly what you mean to render on the land, you cannot reasonably choose tools or monitor progress. A farm or ranch takes thought enough, but far less than a public area serving multiple interests.

The landscape description is not what you have today but what you intend to produce. It should include a map and a detailed written commentary. Figures 46-1, 46-2, 46-3, and 46-4 show sketch maps of a typical ranching case and a national game park. To draw the distinction between the present situation and the future vision, I have included maps of the former. Practice, however, only calls for the latter, and that can include detail right down to individual groves of trees.

Think of it in the same terms you would apply to a new house. You wouldn't just get some sticks or bricks and go at it like one of the three little pigs. You would draw blueprints that showed which way the front door would open, where the pipes would run, and laid out rooms to serve different purposes, so you could then acquire the supplies and tools to build just that.

A written commentary should accompany the map, adding yet more detail about each area in terms of the four ecosystem processes. An example might be:

Grassland (all shaded areas on the map):

Succession: Highly complex with many species of grasses, forbs, small mammals, birds, and insects. Area broken with interspersed patches of brush to provide cover for wildlife and livestock.

Water cycle: As effective as possible with clean run-off that remains gradual except in extreme rainfalls. Maximum soil cover with close plant spacings to hold litter.

Mineral cycle: As effective as possible with good soil cover and a wide range of plants with root systems of varying depths. High organic material in a biologically active soil.

Energy flow: This will be maximized to wildlife and livestock through the whole complex of vegetation rather than through additional inputs. To this end plant spacings will be close and soil aeration good with good crumb structure at the surface. Though the plant composition will be as complex as possible, it will have a preponderance of broad-leaved (mesophytic) grasses.

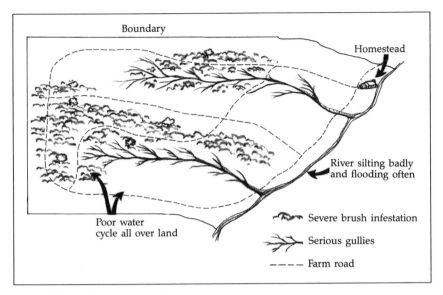

Figure 46-1. Present ranch landscape.

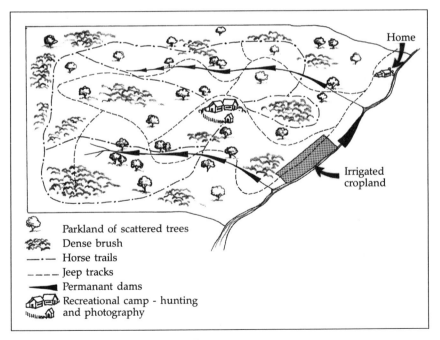

Figure 46-2. Ranch landscape goal.

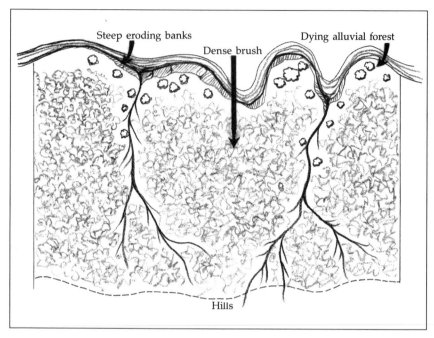

Figure 46-3. National park present situation.

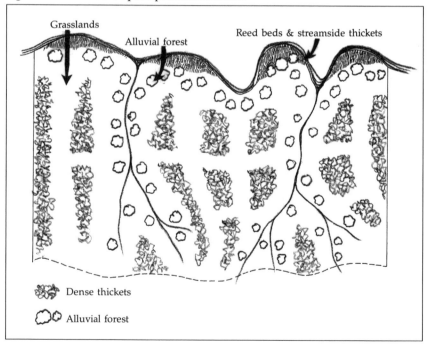

Figure 46-4. National park landscape goal.

Other areas—woodlands, croplands, rivers, and wetlands—would warrant the same kind of written description.

To do all this, you will have to review meticulously all the points of quality of life and production previously set down, analyzing each in terms of how, where, and how much the four ecosystem processes can deliver.

Only here and not before do such objectives as preservation of a rare or endangered species enter the picture in a serious way, but interestingly enough, not by name. The laws of the land may set aside an area for the preservation of a dwindling population, but that definition, as explained earlier, is too narrow for a management goal. However, the landscape description would ensure the production and maintenance of the successional community believed optimal for the endangered organism. Protection and regulation can achieve nothing without that. For example, a landscape description designed to maintain a population of desert tortoises perhaps would stipulate poor water cycle and a successional community likely to provide ideal feed and cover. It would recognize the need for good breeding sites and include areas successionally uncomfortable for animals known to prey on the eggs and young of the tortoise. Naturally, the more you know about the needs of tortoises or any other species, the better you can describe the ideal successional community. But that cannot exist, of course, without simultaneous attention to water and mineral cycles and energy flow since all four function as a whole. Write out the intended condition of each one to avoid missing any important point.

Goals can change, but where crops can change from season to season, a landscape represents a long-term commitment. Make every possible effort to be sure that the one you envision will indeed support all that people demand from it.

The drawing up of landscape goals will reveal any conflicts among interests touching the land that have a serious basis. Irrelevant arguments over tools can still interfere. Production goals that include crops and livestock imply tools of some kind that some may challenge a priori. Now, however, you can analyze such challenges one by one by taking the various production goals and thinking through what tools applied to the landscape could achieve them. Do they in fact produce inevitable conflict?

They may. Continuing the example of livestock on public lands, in certain cases analysis through the HRM model may expose running livestock as both undesirable and unnecessary and likely to cause problems on the land and inconvenience and offense to other users. In other cases removal of livestock may precipitate worse deterioration than even the badly-managed herds do now. In the latter case removing livestock advances no purpose, but understanding of that fact can provide a strong incentive to improve management.

When analysis reveals goals to be mutually exclusive or unattainable, but people persist in asserting their respective claims, then sound resource management cannot succeed in the long run, and legal and political maneuvering takes over. Even at such a pass, however, creativity may find a way, through including larger areas in a plan, innovative use of technology, new definitions of property rights, etc. In retrospect much of the past conflict over such matters as urban growth and development, water rights, mine reclamation, and air and water pollution could have turned out differently had the people involved believed in finding solutions rather than negotiating trade-offs on the basis of money and power.

Summary

The goals you set after understanding the potential of the HRM model, though not set in concrete, should be as stable as possible granted the evolutionary nature of events.

Quality of life goals may shift and develop with the pace of unfolding life. While broad production goals do not often change, detail may change from year to year according to markets and fashions. Landscape goals should seldom change.

Goals should be general and, as they describe quality of life and production, not too detailed. Landscape goals, however, require as much detail as possible.

At present mankind lives in societies largely devoid of goals, and our inexperience in setting them rationally leads to much confusion—nongoals, partial goals, unattainable goals, tools confused with goals, and so on—and yet without goals, resources cannot be managed sensibly, let alone holistically.

Holistic resource management depends on well-formulated goals. Without them the model will not work, and until we manage resources holistically, I believe we will see rising international conflict and increasing poverty and strife in all countries.

The most critical ingredient in preventing this is goal ownership, the fullest possible participation, acceptance, and responsibility of people involved in management or affected by the outcome. Every time a group is excluded from goal formulation the ensuing problems can rise in a hundred different guises. Modern management science offers many more sophisticated methods than I have described for setting long-range goals for diverse participants, and no doubt many of them would adapt to the areas of quality of life, production, and landscape. That sequence, however, remains key to ultimate success.

This chapter concludes the explanation of Holistic Resource Management in its management mode. We have covered the general concept of holistic management and the use of the HRM model, though without some of the detail included in the companion workbook. The model functions in three other modes as well, however, to diagnose problems, analyze policy, and direct research. The following chapters will explain those uses and how they complement each other.

PART VIII

The Modes of Application

47

Introduction

Many years ago, when I set out to find a solution to the environmental degradation occurring in Africa, I had no idea where the quest would lead.

Obviously, haphazard remedies did not work, but neither did uniform systems of management that ground away independently of actual conditions. I wanted to find a methodical way to think through real cases and make plans that led to specific improvements. To that end I developed an *aide memoire* and planning chart for livestock grazing that also took into account wildlife, crops, and numerous other biological factors that differ in every situation.

This early work was the root stock of today's HRM model and survives in the model as the biological plan/monitor/control guideline. It followed the discovery of the first two keys (the role of herding animals and their predators in maintaining grassland communities, and the importance of the time factor). In hindsight, this one guideline was hopelessly inadequate for solving the large problems we faced, but it was a start. From there we kept building in response to each obstacle struck in striving for a solution that truly worked, could apply anywhere, and give sustained results.

The model in what we now recognize as its management mode was based initially on actual management application, mostly in Africa. When I moved to America and began teaching professional resource managers, the pace of development accelerated with the volume of constructive criticism. That, plus consulting experiences and continual reviews of the scientific

462 HOLISTIC RESOURCE MANAGEMENT

literature, filled in many gaps. In the last few years progress has accelerated again due to the contributions of the staff and members of the Center for Holistic Resource Management.

My early aim had been merely to understand what caused the deterioration of resources and successfully tailor a response, but as the model evolved into an ever better tool for doing this, the breadth of its power became evident.

The core of the model's application in management is the plan-monitor-control-replan procedure. As this was put increasingly into practice I found a need to diagnose what was going wrong when monitoring showed that we were deviating from our intended result. From this the diagnostic mode, described in Chapter 48, developed.

In some management applications we found instances where we lacked knowledge of certain finer points—the establishment conditions for certain plants, for example, or the exact breeding requirements of certain species of wildlife. This pinpointed areas for further investigation that Chapter 50 develops as the research orientation mode.

Finally, as the model matured we began to see that any use of any tools classified in the tools row of the model constituted a management policy in some form. If we could assume or deduce the goals or get the people concerned to state what they were trying to achieve, then we could analyze such a policy. We did not need to wait for the result to learn that yet another effort to halt deserts, save farmers, kill brush, or whatever had failed. We could determine before application whether or not a policy enjoyed any likelihood of success and if not why. From this came the policy analysis mode described in Chapter 49.

These four modes of use—management, diagnosis, research orientation, and policy analysis—no doubt will all evolve further over time. This book and its companion workbook concentrate mainly on the management mode, but the other three may have equal importance in the future.

48
Diagnostic Mode

The HRM model as a diagnostic tool serves two purposes, to ascertain the causes of deviations from a management plan and to find the reasons behind distortions in the functioning of the ecosystem (increased floods, droughts, outbreaks of problem plants and insects, disease, etc.). In principle, diagnosis using the HRM model rests on knowing the effects the various tools tend to have on the four ecosystem processes.

Diagnosis During Management Monitoring and Controlling

Consider a large ranch in a fairly brittle area of the tropics that receives twenty inches of rainfall on average. The rancher's production goal is profit from livestock and game. Because profit from wildlife (through hunting and photographic concessions) is a production goal, and because the rancher and his family have described their desire for aesthetic surroundings in their quality of life goal, there is a high aesthetic requirement. The landscape goal for the ranch is mapped out in detail and the family is in its seventh year of applying Holistic Resource Management.

Unfortunately, this year's monitoring shows that bare ground has increased due to both lessened litter and widening plant spacing. Other disturbing signs include increased capping and decreased insect and small animal activity. Obviously, tools in at least one category have produced a trend that runs counter to plan. A look at the available tools one by one should reveal which one(s) and indicate what control steps to take.

463

464   HOLISTIC RESOURCE MANAGEMENT

| *Rest*

No rest was deliberately used.

| *Fire*

Fire could have produced the disturbing symptoms, but none was used.

| *Grazing*

Overgrazing tends to widen plant spacings, decrease litter, and expose soil, but actual monitoring of plants shows no signs of overgrazing and a review of the biological plan shows this to be an unlikely factor.

| *Animal Impact*

Suspicious, as this tool if applied at a low level would have the tendency to increase the amount of mature capping on the bared soil and quite possibly could account for the decrease in litter and the widening plant spacings as well. Could any change of practice within the last year have reduced animal impact? Possibly. The herd was split in two in order to breed some of the cows to a new bull.

| *Living Organisms*

Other than the livestock and the wildlife on the land in use, no other form was actually used in management. Any outbreaks of small mammals or insects? None was noted, but a decrease in insect and small animal activity was noted. Any other changes in respect to livestock or game? Yes, as noted above, the livestock ran in two herds.

| *Technology*

Only fencing, water pipes, and supplementary feeding (classed as technology, because the minerals, cubes, etc. were manufactured) fell into this category. Did any practices change? Yes; supplements were fed at the water points this year rather than out on the land, which could have affected animal impact. Were any chemicals used on the livestock (dosing, dipping, spraying, or tagging)? No.

From the above review two possibilities stand out, animal impact and rest. Although not deliberately applied, low animal impact usually results in partial rest. Partial rest in a brittle environment does tend to decrease litter and increase capping. In combination with low animal impact, it could produce wider plant spacings.

One more run-through ensures that nothing has been missed. Therefore, animal impact and rest need some attention. As a first step the family could return to feeding supplements away from the water and in a manner designed to excite the stock for maximum herd effect. If they could find no way to recombine the herds without sacrificing the breeding program, they might consider splitting all their paddocks to return stock density to the former level. As this would require considerable investment, the breeding program would have to pass the various tests in the guidelines (gross margin analysis, marginal reaction, and weak link in particular).

The plan-monitor-control-replan procedure depends on this kind of diagnosis, and one more example should show its power.

Consider a ranch in West Texas, also in a brittle environment, where monitoring shows up increased bare ground and a decrease in litter as well. This time, however, capped soil has decreased and plant spacing has not changed.

Once more, as the landscape goal requires more ground cover, not less, the rancher would review, one after another, all the tools and their influences on the ecosystem blocks to ferret out the problem and change management to get back on track.

Rest

An unlikely cause. Though rest does decrease litter and increase bare ground, it also causes increased soil capping. Capping decreased, however, and no rest was deliberately applied.

Fire

No fire was used.

Grazing

Monitoring does not show overgrazed plants, and biological plans appear sound on this point. Depending on degree of brittleness and other climatic factors, overgrazing could produce widening plant spacings or a sod-bound mat, but changes in either direction would not show up in a single year.

Animal Impact

This was applied well with plenty of herd effect induced on selected sites. The decrease in mature capping reflects this, as does the fact that plant spacing is no wider. Such good animal impact nevertheless should have increased litter, and yet declining litter cover appears to have created the bare ground problem.

Living Organisms

Outside the game and livestock none came under specific management. An outbreak of small mammals, insects, etc. could explain the decrease in litter, but none was noted. Monitoring, in fact, indicated a small decrease in insect activity. Did livestock or game change significantly in any way? Yes, livestock numbers were increased and a high fawn mortality was recorded in the deer population.

Technology

Apart from fencing, supplements, and water, none was used. Practices remained unchanged from prior years, and would be unlikely to produce the symptoms in question.

This first review of the tools does not throw an answer into high relief, but the heart of the problem seems to lie in the reduction of litter. As no major catastrophe such as unusual weather or superhighway construction would explain that, a closer look at the tools should.

Fire played no part in this case. Rest, partial or otherwise, did not occur as supported by the decrease in capping. Animal impact light enough to cause decreasing litter would be likely to increase capping. Grazing did not cause overgrazing, but how did it measure up in other respects? Also, did the change in stocking rate noted in the review of living organisms have any significant effect?

In fact a look at the biological planning record shows that livestock ran short of forage in late winter, and grazings were shortened to maintain animal condition until spring growth started. This did not result in overgrazing, as the grass was dormant, but it did leave less plant material behind for litter, and might have caused stock to actually eat litter already on the ground. Thus, overstocking appears to explain the situation best.

Control then would involve cutting back on livestock, more attention to Animal Days per Acre of forage in the biological planning, and closer attention to field sampling of planned offtake to allow for higher fawn survival.

Future monitoring soon should show rebuilding of litter, reduced bare ground, more insect activity, and no overgrazing if the diagnosis was correct. If not, the whole process is repeated annually until successful.

The same process of analysis also will diagnose problems on cropland, differing only by a more thorough monitoring of soil conditions both above and below ground. Surface cover and litter breakdown, soil movement due to wind or water, compaction, organic content, and biological activity in response to various tools need attention. Keep reminding yourself that all changes outside of major events do result from application of one or more tools. Avoid snap judgments and reason through the six categories one by one.

I had my own hard lessons in hasty diagnosis many years ago on my sugar farm. My irrigated fields had patches of stunted, pale cane. The streaked and blotched leaves indicated various trace mineral deficiencies that led consulting agronomists to recommend amendments to make up the lack, and, judging from the dry, cracked soil surface, they prescribed more frequent watering.

The advice did not add up for several reasons. The black basalt soil had extremely high mineral content, and if the cane could not use that, why would additives help? Also, the clay soil in the sickly patches theoretically would require less frequent irrigation, not more, and I could not give them more without overwatering the healthy parts of the field.

Finally a man of no formal training but vast practical experience told me to make a longer testing auger and check the situation deeper underground. While the surface was dry and cracking, there was a deeper layer about five feet down impeding the drainage and these plants had their roots in waterlogged conditions. On his advice I pulled the sprinklers out of the spray lines that ran over these poor patches for the next few sprayings.

The surface cracks opened up so wide I could put my hand into them, but gradually the cane plants regained color and lost their blotchy streaks until they grew as well as any in the field. Thereafter we gave them half the amount of water sprayed on the rest of the field.

Diagnosing Resource Problems Generally

Great mystery and speculation surround the sudden disappearance of the people who once inhabited Chaco Canyon in New Mexico. The canyon itself runs through the middle of the San Juan Basin, a treeless expanse of land over one hundred miles in diameter and blessed by about nine inches of precipitation a year. There an unknown tribe built communal buildings of stone that housed a high civilization of many thousands of people. They engaged in irrigated agriculture, hunting, and, judging from goods found in the ruins, extensive and complex trade as well. The Chaco culture grew slowly for five hundred years, peaked spectacularly in the early twelfth century, then vanished totally within about sixty years, leaving no signs of violence or civil strife.

Scientific speculation on the decline of the Chacoans has posed theories of catastrophic drought, climate change, a cycle of arroyo cutting that would have hampered irrigation, disease, and destruction of soils from overcropping.

Evidence shows that many shifts occurred in plant and animal populations in the surrounding community during their occupation of the site.

Applying the HRM model to this problem suggests that their survival would have been a greater mystery than their decline.

The surrounding environment is extremely brittle, but long ago it obviously had a good water cycle that could sustain agriculture and water-loving plants such as sedges, whose pollen still persists in the soil. Though all four ecosystem processes function as a whole, a look at the water cycle reveals why the Chaco demise was inevitable.

The tools of the Chaco people, though in some measure less sophisticated than ours, fell into the same six categories, with the exception of grazing and animal impact. They had no livestock, but large herding game, particularly pronghorn and elk, abounded, so that those influences did exist in the context of the living organisms category as they settled.

They commanded rest, fire, and technology (to the extent of farming tools, simple irrigation, bows, spears, traps, etc.). How then did they use these tools?

Rest

Being a settled people who hunted locally and carried out their trade along well-trafficked routes, they no doubt forced big game away from their population centers, thus inadvertently applying the tool of partial rest to an extensive area of watershed most critical to their agriculture. In such a brittle environment this in itself, over time, could damage the water cycle seriously, causing enough flash flooding, arroyo cutting, dessication, and lowering of water tables to starve them out.

Fire

Quite likely, they used fire frequently over large areas, as written accounts show later tribes in similar areas did. Remains of ancient corral traps show that they drove and captured big game in large numbers. They could have used fire both to attract herds to new growth or to drive herds into traps. Smoking bees, flushing rabbits, controlled burning to prevent big fires around settlements are other ways many native peoples used fire.

The more arid the land, the more prolonged the influence of fire. In Chaco, even infrequent use would affect the soil surface and all four eco-system processes profoundly, the water cycle in particular.

Living Organisms

In their production goals, the Chaco people used various crop plants, timber, and wildlife. They farmed only in favored areas, not over the watershed as a whole. As mentioned before, they almost certainly pushed large game far enough from their settlements to subject substantial areas to partial rest. Evidence also shows that during the later years of occupation, mule deer and jackrabbits had largely replaced the earlier pronghorn, elk, and cottontails in their diet, which suggests successional shifts on a large scale.

Quite clearly, they harvested large amounts of brush for firewood. Big trees, remains of which have been found, largely disappeared early on. Many timbers in later buildings are high altitude species from a mountain range seventy-five miles away. Abundant evidence from the present shows what excessive firewood gathering alone can do to the water cycle in such an area.

Technology

With the possible exception of the antelope trap, Chaco technology probably had little impact. Irrigation ditches that became gullies would have increased lateral drainage and lowered the water table, but that probably followed greater changes.

As both partial rest and fire could independently have damaged the water cycle enough to doom an irrigation-based civilization, the two influences together virtually guaranteed disaster.

Some claim that an abnormal run of dry years caused the exodus. Tree rings show a long period of rapid growth indicative of good rain, followed by narrow rings reflecting insufficient water and slow growth. As trees respond not to total rainfall but to effective rainfall (water penetration of the soil together with aeration), the ring data only lets us know growth conditions were poor over many years. A series of lower rainfall years combined with a poor water cycle could well be the straw that broke the camel's back.

Finally, inspection of the land now, after some fifty years of total rest imposed by the u.s. Park Service, confirms the continued deterioration of the water cycle under this tool alone. What else could explain Chaco? No evidence points to a better theory, and even a disease or political upheaval that left no trace on the land would not explain as well the lack of recolonization and continued decline of the critical water cycle. We do not have any record of the degree of recovery, if any, before the Park Service applied total rest.

Such diagnosis only suggests a probability, of course, never total certainty. To assume the latter in complex natural systems is arrogant and dangerous. Nevertheless, the desire for sophisticated solutions often obscures the obvious.

In Chapter 10 I mentioned a newspaper headline from Zimbabwe that read "Scientists Puzzled by 40% Increase in Flow over Victoria Falls Since 1948." Again, a look at the question through the HRM model reveals that it would be a greater mystery if the flow had not increased over these years.

Since 1948 vast areas of the watershed feeding the falls have been burned as a matter of government policy for game and forest management, in addition to the accidental fires set by the local population. This tool alone, when applied on such a scale, degrades the water cycle and increases runoff.

In this particular case I could confirm the drastic degree of damage because I owned a large block of land near the Victoria Falls. Just four years of curbing fire while encouraging animal impact, through wildlife alone, reduced both the run-off itself and the silt load by an unbelievable amount. Unlike Chaco Canyon I had the benefit of relatively intact wild herds and their attendant predators, including man (as represented by myself).

Our first night on the place my family camped by a large pool on the Katchachete River. As measured by the water in the coffee mugs the next morning we got two inches of rain during the night. All night long the river roared in full flood, but by dawn it had subsided, leaving behind only mud and flattened vegetation.

Four years later we returned to the site after a similar storm that dropped four inches of rain during the night. The stream ran high for a long, long time, and when it subsided the banks were clean, a wonderful reward for four years of effort and faith.

The case cited in Chapter 37 of the desert bushes in Pakistan that did not regenerate also yields to diagnosis through the model. A healthy population should have had the age curve shown by the dotted line in figure 48-1. These had the profile shown by the solid line that indicates no young plants whatever. The government was seeking to redress the situation by forbidding brush harvesting, when the real problem to be tackled was the lack of regeneration, which had little to do with harvesting of the adult bushes.

In diagnosing this problem, once again we look at what tools were being applied and how, and the effects we would expect them to produce.

Rest

Total rest was applied in isolated areas under government protection. Because it was a low rainfall brittle environment in which succession moved beyond algae and mosses with difficulty, this resulted in mature capping on the ground between bushes, which was utterly inhospitable to new seedlings. Partial rest was applied on the bulk of the land although it was grazed by many small flocks. This had produced enough capping, both mature and immature, to keep succession at a low level.

Near villages, markets, and water points, where livestock periodically

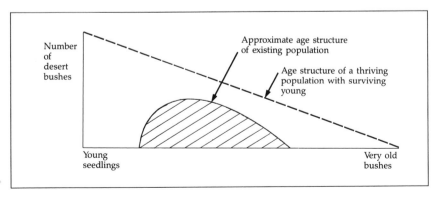

Figure 48-1.   Population of desert bushes.

provided considerable disturbance, I found plenty of seedlings, despite the lack of adult bushes, confirming my suspicion that the smooth, capped surfaces elsewhere were not suitable sites on which desert bushes could establish.

Fire

Fire had not been used for a very long time.

Grazing

The grazing tool had widespread impact in the form of overgrazing/over-browsing. Although animals were herded, herders had inadequate knowledge to herd in such a manner as to minimize overgrazing. Where desert bush seedlings managed to establish, they were quickly overbrowsed to death.

Animal Impact

Apart from those areas near villages, marketplaces, or watering points, animal impact was always applied at a low level. Although animals were herded, herd effect was never induced.

Living Organisms

Apart from the livestock and desert bushes, no other living organisms were used in management. Discussions with the people on the land and observation revealed no evidence of disease in the bushes, nor any major insect problems over the millions of acres.

Technology

None was used, other than the primitive digging implements used in harvesting bushes.

No other changes, such as weather or natural catastrophe, occurred that might have contributed to the seedling failure on all areas but for those adequately disturbed by animals.

In sum, the evidence clearly showed that the problem stemmed from a combination of low animal impact and overgrazing, either of which alone could account for the failure of the bushes to establish new seedlings. Any remedy that did not address both problems would surely fail, most decisively if it involved fire or increased rest.

In this case a social question enters the picture, as no solution can succeed without the full support of the villagers. A demonstration plot set up by outside experts, even if it succeeded, would carry the message, "Look how clever I am compared to you." But that is a subject for resolution through the policy analysis mode of the HRM model.

Common Problems, Common Cause in Brittle Environments

From the diagnosis of many problems in the field in a number of countries, two facts emerge. Many seemingly unrelated problems in brittle environments have a common cause, and therefore when we correctly address one problem, others heal without additional action.

With monotonous regularity, the following list of woes applies to Africa, South America, the Middle East, Pakistan, India, China, the United States, and elsewhere.

- Desertification
- Increasing frequency and severity of floods and droughts
- Noxious forbs (weeds)
- Outbreaks of grasshoppers, quelea finches, army worm, and other problem organisms
- Brush encroachment
- Soil erosion and gullying
- Silting of rivers and dams
- Financial difficulties in agriculture from overcapitalization and excessive supplementation of animals
- Vast areas reduced to near monocultures of sod-bound, matted, short grass
- Drying up of springs and underground water supplies

Just as in the Pakistan case discussed above, the common cause of all of the situations more often than not turns out to be low animal impact and overgrazing, unfortunately the normal treatment for millions of acres of brittle land throughout the world.

Changing practices to produce high animal impact and minimal over-grazing tends to have the following effects:

- Reduction of plant spacings
- Improvement of grassland health through greater diversity, deeper root systems, and more porous soil
- Restoration of water cycles raising water tables and reestablishing perennial flow of streams and springs
- Reduction of noxious forbs and brush
- Reduction of breeding sites of pest organisms and stabilization of populations through greater diversity of species
- Reduction of capital and supplemental feed demands
- Reversal of desertification

Monitoring of the soil surface in particular should ensure that any changes in practice really do lead to these results.

Just as the HRM model can diagnose problems of this nature, it also serves to evaluate any policy designed to correct them. The next chapter on the model in its policy analysis mode does this.

49

Policy Analysis Mode

Management of any nation's resources takes place at two basic levels:

1. On the ground, where individuals, groups, companies, tribes, and government agencies actually carry out operations day-by-day on forests, farms, refuges, tribal lands, and so on.
2. At the policy level, where governments and other bodies influence management through policy statements, laws, taxation, education, and extension services.

The holistically-sound management of any nation's resources can occur when people at both levels understand what that implies and enjoy some degree of harmony in seeking it. Having been a government research officer, farmer, rancher, consultant, and politician, I have viewed resource management from many angles and can imagine no better way to ensure sound overall national resource management than to use the HRM model in a management mode on the ground and in a policy analysis mode at cabinet level.

The absence of such a broad and consistent approach has wrought great damage to the health and wealth of the world and continues to do so. Funds squandered on faulty resource policies contribute to national deficits. Destruction on the ground has disrupted people's lives, extinguished species, and reduced our resource base. Thus the need to give governments and international agencies in particular an understanding of holistic management has become urgent.

Since, at the operational level, we can predict the influence of any tool on the ecosystem, we obviously can evaluate any policy that mentions or implies the use of specific tools. We need only know what the policy intends to do and the nature of the environment concerned (the state of the four ecosystem processes and the degree of brittleness). Unfortunately few policies at present express goals in the necessary three parts or make allowance for their expression before policies are implemented. All too often dangerously narrow nongoals such as "increase in production," "eradication (or protection) of species," "reduction of erosion," etc. are the only ones specified.

Because these sorts of goals never lead to holistic solutions, the first step in policy analysis is to articulate a three-part goal that reflects the intent of the policy in terms of quality of life, production, and landscape.

In the last chapter on the diagnostic mode, we worked back from the current state of each ecosystem foundation block to discover which tools had produced it and which could change it. In analyzing policy we use the testing guidelines to discover if tools chosen to change a situation actually will serve our goals.

The inability or the failure of people in policy-making positions to reason through the implications of their decisions despite the damage they may cause has several explanations. As a member of Parliament I deeply believed in the great British statesman Edmund Burke's dictum that "The only thing necessary for the triumph of evil is for good men to do nothing." Nevertheless, I found myself keeping silent about many assuredly destructive policies, not for lack of political courage, but because I myself could offer no constructive alternatives.

As a politician I came under extreme pressure to do something about the deterioration of land, but as an ecologist working actively on the country's environmental problems I had serious doubts about the long-term effects of the laws we passed and in particular the regulations those laws empowered civil servants to impose without informed debate or parliamentary approval. In fact, until we had those four missing keys and thoroughly understood them, none of us really knew why the land was deteriorating, and to act as if we did violated my sense of ethics.

The proliferation of Environmental Impact Statements and National Conservation Strategies reflects the same policy level dilemma. They can only document the most blatant flaws and offer no solutions that will actually work. Now the HRM model, being based on the four missing keys, provides a way out. Looking back on my own experience in politics, I can see that only by analyzing holistically all policies and the laws and regulations passed under them could we have achieved sound results.

I now believe in analyzing *all* policies, ideally in the planning stages. Many people responsible for policies will insist that they do analyze, and often they do in a conventional sense. The HRM model, however, brings a whole new order of accuracy and simplicity to the challenge. Not only the governments and international agencies who implement policy should use it, but so should the universities, environmental organizations, economic think tanks, and others who generate the ideas that become policy.

A typical example of how a nonholistic approach to policy subverts the initial intent is the spraying of grasshopper outbreaks on the western rangelands of America.

When certain rainfall and temperatures coincide, massive quantities of eggs hatch and the young nymphs survive to bound about in great swarms. Alarmed farmers and ranchers call for help as they see their crops and forage about to disappear. The press gets word and out goes a reporter and cameraman. Soon the clamor for action reaches such a pitch that politicians feel called upon to demonstrate their sensitivity and power.

Unfortunately, politicians can do little except allocate money for solutions proposed by technical advisors in various agencies, which they nevertheless expect to produce immediate results. Emergency appropriations of $35 million to spray pesticides on offending grasshoppers are not unusual.

Even a cursory examination of such a policy through the HRM model shows it about as effective in the long run as extinguishing a fire with kerosene.

The Goal

The spraying program calls for applying a tool, technology, without an adequate goal. The objective of killing adult grasshoppers makes no mention of the whole such a program will affect or of any long-term conditions it might create. As a practical matter it has no meaning in the context of the successional process that produced the outbreak. It only suppresses a symptom of the successional community's present level of development or regression, and the plague can and will return whenever weather permits.

In order to proceed any further one must develop a three-part goal that covers the intent of the proposed spraying program. A likely one would be to help rural people stay in business and enjoy a rural way of life, supported by production of crops and livestock in an environment of complex plant and animal life and healthy soils. On the basis of such a simple goal statement, one can then use the testing guidelines to discover if the proposed tools actually will give desirable results.

The Tools

The spraying policy proposes to use only one of the six classes of tools available—technology in the form of chemicals.

| The Guidelines

The testing guidelines can be applied in any order, but a given case might suggest some in particular. Since spraying acts against an outbreak that is bound to have a cause, we might well start with the cause and effect guideline. In fact, when grasshopper populations rise drastically above the normal point, indicated by C on the growth curve in figure 49-1, one would expect to find that use of certain management tools has reduced what Leopold called environmental resistance. Something has altered the ecosystem processes in favor of massive grasshopper survival. As their life cycle is most critical at the egg and nymph stage, probably either egg laying sites have increased or disease and predation on eggs and nymphs have declined, or both.

Once nymphs assume the adult form, they require about fourteen days before they can reproduce, and most probably have done so before any sprayers can mobilize. The bulk of the adult population will die at the end of the growing season, as shown in figure 49-1. Thus, most spraying programs kill grasshoppers doomed to die shortly anyway without affecting future generations. Because the spraying does nothing to treat the cause, it clearly fails the cause and effect test.

We also might predict a negative verdict on the whole ecosystem guideline. The whole may include more than two hundred organisms that prey on grasshoppers in their various stages and help limit outbreaks, but spraying does not offer the slightest possibility of benefiting any of them. In fact, it

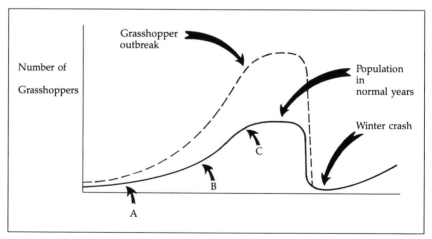

Figure 49-1.   Annual grasshopper buildup.

will kill off high proportions of many and thus promote the hatching and survival of more grasshoppers.

Though advocates of chemical solutions like to discount the influence of natural organisms, u.s. Department of Agriculture research documents its importance. Working in Montana, J. A. Onsager has shown that natural populations of grasshoppers in a reasonably healthy environment suffer 2 to 13 percent daily mortality at the nymph stage and 3 to 40 percent as adults. He calculates that a 2 percent increase in the daily mortality rate of young can result in a 50 percent reduction of adults. At 13 percent mortality, fewer than 1 percent survive to maturity.[1]

An earlier chapter that discussed the characteristic S-shaped growth curve of populations explained this extreme significance of early mortality, but spraying that also decimates a broad range of predators unleashes the full power of the principle in the wrong direction. According to the Voltera Principle mentioned in Chapter 37, prey populations always recover before the predators. The next time ideal conditions prevail, an abundant egg supply and reduced predators will guarantee another outbreak.

Poisoning adult grasshoppers at best will save some crops and forage; however, the poison never kills all individuals. Some survive to breed even if timely spraying catches the bulk before they get a chance. Successive generations of survivors produce ever more pesticide-tolerant strains, and this buildup of resistance may occur as well in hundreds of untargeted species, such as mosquitoes.

Clearly most grasshopper spraying programs fail the whole ecosystem guideline, not to mention the direct threat that chemical pollution poses to humans.

At this point we can definitely call this policy unsound. The typical spraying program sets back succession by simplifying populations, people face increased pollution danger, and a country struggling to balance its budget wastes $35 million. Obviously, we should seek other solutions.

Unfortunately, today most people still look for further remedies through further technology such as more specific pesticides or genetic engineering. A developing concept called integrated pest management (IPM) promises to reduce reliance on pesticides through the use of diseases, predators, biological controls, and other factors. While this represents a move in the right direction, applications still tend to focus on symptoms rather than causes, lack well-defined goals, and ignore the needs of the whole. Many techniques developed through IPM, however, open up powerful possibilities for using the living organisms tool as governed by the model.

The real challenge lies in using the model to generate good policies as well as to eliminate bad ones. As already indicated, everything depends first of all on addressing problems in the context of three-part goals. Ideally, the various groups involved would define this very precisely for each land unit. For the present example, the temporary goal we just used to illustrate the grasshopper case could be fleshed out by a quality of life description that detailed urban/rural relationships, aesthetic criteria for public land, and a landscape described in terms of the four ecosystem foundation blocks. Assuming no great changes, however, consider how you as a politician might approach the grasshopper problem holistically.

As a primary rule you would try to keep public attention centered on the goal and avoid confusing that by debate over IPM or any other tool. Then, given the possibility of a $35-million appropriation, you might propose allocating it in the following way.

1. To soften the immediate impact of the grasshoppers, you might use some of the money to compensate people directly who truly suffered damage to their livelihood. If IPM or any other method of controlling adult populations could pass the guidelines, funds might go to that as well. Suppose this cost $20 million.

2. Of the remaining $15 million, $5 million could go to training extension agents, farmers, and ranchers in management techniques that would promote the overall landscape goal. Increased ground cover would reduce egg laying sites. Increased ground cover plus a better water cycle would enhance the population of fungi and microorganisms that destroy grasshopper eggs, and healthy succession would keep predation levels high.

That would provide a long-term solution. More species of grasshopper might inhabit the complex community but in lower numbers characterized by smaller outbreaks.

3. You could return $10 million to the treasury to help balance the budget and reduce taxation. If such a common sense solution proved hard to sell, $1 million might go toward a public awareness campaign.

From my own political experience I believe it possible to sell such a program to voters far more easily than the poisoning that will add to taxation, endanger human health, and ultimately lead to more grasshoppers. In an extreme case, where spraying just had to employ all of the money to prevent excessive crop damage, it would not make sense to do this without simultaneously taking measures to prevent a recurrence. Any policy that concentrates on cure rather than prevention and at the same time exacerbates the cause must contribute to ever mounting crisis management.

Grasshoppers represent only one of thousands of problems throughout the world consistently exacerbated by the same patterns of thought. Altogether, many nations spend millions annually on futile attempts to combat soil erosion and the spread of deserts, noxious plants, and so on, without clear goals and in situations that would pass few if any of the testing guidelines in the HRM model.

The Importance of Policy Analysis

To the best of my knowledge all governments inadvertently shoot themselves in the foot through bad resource management policy. Quite recently the United States instituted the Conservation Reserve Program, which sets aside croplands to reduce production and soil erosion, but it will prove counterproductive in many brittle areas because it legislates the tool of rest. The World Bank and other international agencies continually underwrite similarly well-intentioned policies that we now can see will damage whole nations that they seek to develop.

From our experience in training people involved in policy formulation, it appears that nothing remotely resembling the HRM model directs policy at any level nationally or internationally.

In the HRM introductory courses we've run over the past five years for university and government educators, researchers, and advisors—those who most often provide technical advice to politicians—we've asked the participants to comment on the following policies actually practiced in America:

1. With the aim of rescuing a vanishing breed of trout in a wilderness area, a predatory trout is being poisoned.

2. To stave off the day when a large and vital dam inevitably fills with silt, its wall is being raised. There is some controversy on whether to raise it a few feet at a time (so as not to destroy eagle nesting sites immediately) or all at once (the cheaper course).

3. To help rid rangelands of noxious plants, livestock numbers are being reduced and the plants poisoned. At the same time ranchers are being encouraged, with cost-sharing programs, to invest in more fencing and water points.

4. To destroy grasshoppers that threaten crop and forage yields, an aerial spraying program is being implemented.

5. To reduce brush encroachment (mesquite trees) a liquid herbicide is being applied.

6. In order to heal the land after a severe drought, extension agents are advising a prolonged rest period.

Every case except the last involves technology, and in nearly all situations the HRM model would show it to be counterproductive. All the proposed solutions address a symptom and fail under the cause and effect guideline. None happens to pass the whole ecosystem test either. Where profitability and ecosystem stability are factors, the weak link, gross margin, and marginal reaction tests also would eliminate them all.

After the brief exposure to HRM given in the courses, all the participants—which currently number over one thousand—have come to similar conclusions. They have responded to the following six questions with a remarkably unanimous voice.

1. *After studying these policies do you think that the holistic resource management model applies to all of them? Could it have been applied before these policies were implemented?*

One hundred percent of the course participants have agreed that the model did apply and could have been used before implementation.

2. *Are any of these policies likely to lead to lasting success?*

Everyone has agreed that none of the policies could succeed. A few have expressed the view that some were essential Band-Aids required in emergencies but incapable of producing permanent success.

This reply has particular significance as the participants included some of the very people who masterminded the policies in question. Prior to their exposure to HRM they had believed they would succeed.

3. *Are public funds being spent wisely?*

Unanimous opinion has held that public funds have been wasted on these policies.

4. *How common are such policies in the United States? Is this sample of policies biased in your opinion?*

Again, 100 percent without hesitation have found such policies typical and the sample not biased. One class of thirty-five, after some discussion, actually stated as a group that they could now recognize that unsound resource management was universal in the United States.

5. *How common do you think such policies might be in the Third World or developing countries following American technological leadership through the United Nations, World Bank, Agency for International Development (USAID), other consultants (including professors on sabbatical), and through education of their people in the United States?*

Once more, 100 percent of the participants have replied "very common." Most classes also have discussed the irony of a nation of massive goodwill and largesse inadvertently doing damage. If it is recognized that damaged resources lead to poverty, social upheaval, and political unrest, America's role becomes even more ironic. In fact, however, the same criticism probably applies to all developed countries.

6. *Who or what produces such policies? The politicians? The bankers? The public? The professionals (foresters, wildlifers, range management specialists, ecologists, etc. who serve as educators or advisors in private, academic, or government institutions)? The media? Industrial firms with vested financial interests?*

This is the only question on which course participants have not expressed 100 percent agreement. All have said initially that such policies are produced by all of the above. When asked to probe deeper and think about where we might start to rectify such a situation, discussion ranged widely, but most participants have arrived at a similar breakdown. About 75 percent have stated that the policies ultimately emanate from our educational system and professional people. About 25 percent have felt that though this accounts for most cases, vested interests also influence a certain proportion of our policies.

Even assuming that some participants might have accepted the majority opinion publicly, while not entirely agreeing, the overwhelming consensus indicates a real need to rethink our approach to resource management policies.

Also significant is the conclusion that procedures presently enforced in America to screen out bad policies apparently do not work. In the United States neither public nor private undertakings that might have significant effects on the land may proceed without an Environmental Impact Statement that presents an interdisciplinary study of the policy according to very strict guidelines. That holistically-unsound and damaging projects routinely slip through this filter indicates again the weakness of the interdisciplinary approach.

Official Environmental Impact Statements usually consist of a compendium of various viewpoints, unconnected by any goal or vision or any point of reference for relating one view to another. Thus their interpretation remains a matter of negotiation between forces in which vested power, academic seniority, and political expediency usually count more than logic.

I recall once being asked to run through the model with a large group of foresters. They had encountered many problems with the public in trying to manage their jurisdiction for multiple uses: timber, recreation, fishing, hunting, and grazing. In a room of sixty foresters, all in the same agency, I began as always by raising the question of goals. The ensuing confusion and conflict showed quickly that the problem lay within the agency itself, not the public. Those responsible for timber harvest had no idea of the needs of those responsible for clear streams and recreation, and all guarded a blissful ignorance of any responsibility to people and other forms of life further down the watershed.

Over fifty years of management and millions of dollars had not touched the heart of the problem as profoundly as an hour of analysis. Until a single agency can get its own house in order and see itself as a whole instead of an aggregation of competing parts, it will not provide constructive services, no matter what the public does or thinks. The public can only perpetuate the same divisions.

In analyzing national policies, it is relatively easy to spot where they are going wrong, but the process of revising them to ensure success is difficult at best. Many governments, for instance, have soil conservation policies in place, but rarely are they successful. In most cases, these policies must be revised every few years to cater for a worsening situation. The need for sound soil conservation policies is pressing as our survival and prosperity as nations depend on healthy soils. How could we revise national soil conservation policies to make them successful?

In using the HRM model we know that for resource management to be successful, we have to have three-part goals. Does a government's desire to foster better soil conservation constitute a three-part goal? Obviously not. We would need to begin by establishing three-part goals for thousands of units of land, but who should do this? The government? Or the people who actually manage the land?

In most instances only the people who actually manage the land *can* do this. Those people are farmers, ranchers, tribesmen, foresters, wildlifers, etc., who will require three-part goals for the management of their families, communities, and finances, as well as the land. The landscape descriptions they develop will almost certainly involve healthy, stable soils.

Next, we would need to decide, at least annually, which tools to apply to achieve those goals. Again, who should have responsibility for this decision? The government? Or the people on the land? The government would be incapable of making such decisions on the thousands of land units involved, therefore they would have to be made by the people who manage those units.

What role then should a government play in fostering successful soil conservation? Clearly, it should facilitate the process.

What resources does it have to do this? Traditionally it has education, research, extension programs, and financial inducements that it can direct toward that end. Education in resource management would need to be less vocational and more holistic. Extension agents would have to refrain from advocating specific management tools and, rather, collaborate with land managers in the development of their three-part goals and the steps taken to achieve them. Research would need to steer away from management systems and toward the basic biology of soils and living organisms, and the effects tools tend to have on ecosystem processes. Financial inducements, if provided at all, would need to be based on *results* rather than on the application of various tools—i.e., a farmer would be rewarded for cleaner, less silt-laden water coming off the land rather than for using any specific tool, such as rest, or some form of technology.

Ranchers who have established clear, three-part goals and are using the HRM model to select the necessary tools to achieve them have shown that they can decrease the space between plants, decrease mature soil capping, increase soil cover, and often triple species diversity while greatly increasing production and lowering the costs of production. This embraces all that any government could wish for in its desire for better soil conservation. In the meantime, ranchers given financial inducements to apply recommended tools rarely achieve such results.

When policies specify the tools for management, just as when goals specify them, conflict and crisis management result. Few people, however, argue against having clear goals, a thorough testing process to select the tools to achieve them, and sound monitoring of results. A politically important point is that government policies that advocate such a process are likely to enjoy strong public support.

In summary, when analysis of any policy runs into difficulty, almost always the whole has been defined too narrowly, if at all, and no clear goals guide the process. The rest of the HRM model notwithstanding, recognition of this fact alone could prevent many of the disastrous policies visited on the world every day.

Again, national resources deserve holistic management at two levels — on the ground by the operators and at the policy level by governments. The HRM model serves at both levels. At the policy level it works to analyze policies in the planning stage before implementation and thus prevent costly, destructive programs.

Some in government advisory positions find a tool as simple as the HRM model somewhat suspect. In most cases I see behind that complaint only an infatuation for mounds of paperwork, data, and jargon. That common bureaucratic and professional ailment also causes people to equate simplicity, ignorance, and naiveté.

On the contrary. Ignorance often masks itself in a surplus of data. Anyone who has put pen to paper seriously knows the difficulty of condensing five pages of rambling prose into a few clear, concise paragraphs. The HRM model helps us attain that essential simplicity and clarity and permits us to see a path through the jungle of detail. At some stage we may need exhausting detail, but we fail most frequently for *failing to define for ourselves a clear vision of the whole.*

When we use the model in management and in diagnosis or policy analysis, it generally indicates the route to more successful and holistically sound results. However, in all of these modes it also points to areas of weakness in our knowledge. It thus helps us to direct research into important areas unrecognized before. The next chapter discusses the HRM model in the research orientation mode.

50

Research Orientation Mode

Academics have frequently denounced Holistic Resource Management as unsupported by research. Actually, exhaustive research in many countries supports all the principles underlying the HRM model, but the criticism does point up the fundamental difference between holism as it applies to management, and the long-hallowed and often necessary procedures of scientific research.

This difference in fact puts holistic management and the tradition of modern science in a healthy and complementary relationship. Modern science, which I call reductionist, seeks by controlling all variables to reduce phenomena to a simple form for study. It must do this to show that one factor and not another contributes to a given result. Anyone repeating the study must be able to produce the same results, and theories proven must apply in all situations.

By contrast, holistic management applies to situations that are by definition unique. It undertakes to manage innumerable variables simultaneously without artificially limiting any of them, but it can only do so successfully on the basis of knowledge about those variables that must come in large measure from reductionist science.

As applied to resources, management and scientific research up to now have coincided to such an extent that the distinction often disappeared. This occurred because resource management in the past meant little more than production. If a laboratory discovered a new seed-fertilizer combination, then management became only a question of exploiting it on a commercial scale. If managers encountered a problem, such as a falling water table, then in order to maintain production, they enlisted scientists to address that specific obstacle by designing better irrigation systems or engineering less thirsty crops.

Other fields have developed beyond this stage. Architecture and the science of engineering, for example, once meant virtually the same thing. Today however, architecture involves far more than enclosing space, because a building is a whole, and the community context of the building is a greater whole. The engineer may figure out ways to make stronger trusses or bake tougher bricks, but the architect must understand how to realize the complex purpose (goal) for the building from a whole that includes finances, social impact, construction costs, labor skill and availability, properties of materials, and aesthetics.

Scientific research in the strictest sense has a definite function in all these areas but remains distinct from architecture, as does the interdisciplinary approach. Suppose that to build a railroad station one assembled an interdisciplinary team of structural engineers, concrete experts, electricians, plumbers, earth movers, bankers, and train dispatchers, and told them to get to work. What a mess!

Architecture by its nature has to understand wholes even as modern science reduces. Similarly, holistic management functions to bring together isolated elements of research to advance a complex whole toward a goal, but even more than the architect, the resource manager must show sensitivity for dynamic, living organisms and their role in a series of wholes that grow increasingly complex. Since context affects their behavior, the relationship between holistic management and reductionist science often does blur but should still remain constructive. Figure 50-1 illustrates this developing relationship.

The HRM model serves both to show gaps in our knowledge that science

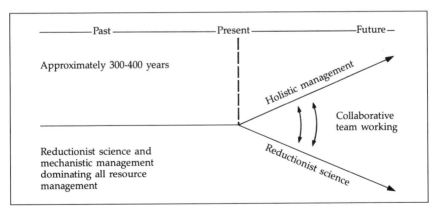

Figure 50-1. Future relationship between scientific research and resource management.

can fill and to show the relevance of research proposals to current needs. A number of examples show how this works in practice.

From my first articulation of the four keys, many scientists have sought to prove that hoof action does the things I say it does, and their largely unsuccessful attempts reveal the grey area where holistic practice and rigorous experimental science appear to conflict, but shouldn't.

Isolated from the whole in the simplified context of a laboratory experiment, simulated hoof action will compact barren soil in just the same manner as a sheep's foot roller compacts an earthen dam. In practice, however, hooves seldom function in this way. The action itself varies according to the behavior of the animals, which may reflect territorial restrictions, fences, predators, avoidance of fouled ground, etc. It never occurs independently of dung and urine or other organisms, litter, root action, and climate. Livestock that move according to a proper biological plan rarely linger long enough to compact soil severely, and assuming that the plan minimizes overgrazing, the root growth of vigorous plants will loosen what compaction does occur.

Over the last twenty-five years a succession of academic papers have claimed that hoof action does all kinds of damage, and yet overwhelming evidence shows it to be beneficial in the context of holistic practice. Such apparent contradictions should not threaten anyone, however. The natural world abounds in them.

By way of illustration consider the difficulty of scientifically describing the suitable climate for a given crop, at first glance a far simpler task. By most measurements eastern Maryland and the Puget Sound region of Washington State have very similar climate, but exhaustive data on this point means little from the standpoint of a winter oat crop. For some reason juries composed of oats consistently find the weather in Maryland unquestionably harsher. Similarly, Swedish varieties of winter wheat consistently suffer winter kill in the winter wheat areas of America, though in several respects the Swedish climate is statistically more severe.

Climate consists of dozens of factors, length of day, precipitation, extremes of temperature, duration of extreme temperature, length of season, ambient humidity, and many others, any combination of which might affect a particular species or cultivar in ways complex enough to frustrate academic rigor for years to come.

The lesson of such cases is not that the holistic approach should replace reductionist science across the board, but that one must appreciate the limitations and strengths of both. Knowing that a certain research finding comes from reductionist methodology simply warns us to observe carefully as we apply it in the whole. Because all wholes are unique, the results may not follow predictions or even be replicable. Unwillingness to recognize this possibility accounts for the dismal failure of reductionist science, even when applied by the most advanced integrated teams, to reverse the spread of deserts or the decline of the agricultural base in both developed and undeveloped countries.

On the other hand some of the most powerful aspects of the HRM model came straight out of standard research. For example, laboratory tests showed that severe and repeated defoliation of perennial grass plants causes their root systems to diminish. Research also showed how much the health of the plant depends on adequate recovery periods between defoliations. That knowledge plus twenty years of trial and error application led to the development of the biological planning used in Holistic Resource Management. This planning and the monitoring it entails of changes in growth rate, litter, reserve requirements, etc. produce the desired results while minimizing both overgrazing and root damage.

Research in Support of Management

In farming situations, when many practices involving current agricultural technology fail to pass the testing guidelines, it means in blunt terms that the farmers using them will not attain their goals. They may survive financially over the short term, but the sacrifice of natural soil-based capital and the allocation of funds for unsustainable production eventually will force them off the land. However, even if they recognize this, they face an agonizing dilemma because the research on more sustainable practices in a mechanized culture is woefully thin, and the study of ways to wean a farm onto them paltry.

The very fact that we now distinguish in America between mainstream agriculture and sustainable agriculture implies a latter-day realization that perhaps we have followed the wrong path for a long time. Clearly we need to direct the energy of modern science to the development of practices and machinery that will enable farmers to produce without exposing soils for very long periods, if at all, and not destroy the life and structure of the soil.

Fortunately people have begun to accept this challenge and some American universities have even created departments of sustainable agriculture for the purpose. However, if in the allocation of budgets, departmental chairmen have to choose between work on a new herbicide for bindweed or development of a perennial wheat variety, the HRM model clearly indicates which should take priority.

In both farming and ranching, the HRM model indicates countless important but far less grandiose research challenges as well. Quite frequently the biological planning of a ranching operation calls for information about wildlife or forestry that simply doesn't exist. Ideally, if your goal includes robust wildlife populations you will note on the planning charts all relevant information concerning breeding times, nesting sites, habitat, and feed for various species. Gaps in this information indicate a specific research need.

Similarly, precise research information on the establishment conditions for various plants makes it possible through holistic management to increase populations of desired plants and decrease undesirable ones. In its diagnostic mode the HRM model points to our poverty of such knowledge even as we spend vast sums on research and effort to kill adult plants while unwittingly fostering their regeneration.

The previous chapter described how extensive research on optimal survival conditions for grasshopper eggs and nymphs enables us to manage in a way that minimizes bare ground suitable for egg laying sites and maximizes the organisms that prey on eggs and nymphs. Had the basic research not already existed, the model would have shown a need to discover the weak link in the grasshopper's life cycle.

We can expect often in the diagnosis of a problem to find that we just do not know enough about a problem to address it effectively, particularly in the case of heretofore unknown or recently introduced fungi, bacteria, and viruses, and these are areas for urgent research. To date, management as well as research on such problems has tended to be reductionist with isolated calls for a broader approach, which generally went unheeded.

It is highly unlikely that such simple organisms defy the successional process and ecosystem functioning generally. Where we create ideal survival conditions for an organism, or where we introduce one without the predators and diseases that restrained it, an invading organism can flourish to problem levels—as rabbits and prickly pear did in Australia, or as syphilis did in Renaissance Europe and measles and smallpox in North America. Present-day epidemics, such as Dutch elm disease, or even Acquired Immune Deficiency Syndrome (AIDS), exist because an environment exists that supports them. Our task is to find what we have done to produce that environment. In our passion to cure with technological nonsolutions rather than prevent, we often overlook this basic question. Let me cite three instances that would support this.

1. *The Great Plague.* Today we know that the bubonic plague that devastated Europe's population in medieval times was derived from a bacteria that was spread by fleas living on rats. The plague reached epidemic proportions when overcrowded urban slums produced the right conditions for a massive increase in the rat population, which in turn provided the right environment for a massive increase in fleas. Attempts to tackle the disease head-on by seeking a cure for the individuals afflicted by the plague were unsuccessful. It wasn't until the slum conditions were rectified, and thus the environment made less conducive to rat and flea, that the disease was contained.

2. *Foot and Mouth Disease.* This viral disease, which mainly affects cattle, is indirectly responsible for the destruction of game in Africa on a massive scale. American and European importers of African beef insist that the meat come from disease-free areas, which is a reasonable demand as the virus takes on a particularly virulent form when it reaches northern climes. Veterinarians believe the virus is carried by wildlife, buffalo in particular, and spread to cattle through close contact. To prevent any contact they fence livestock areas to exclude game, sometimes shoot out the game, and vaccinate the livestock as well.

In tackling the problem head-on, today's veterinarians have failed to address the larger questions, the most obvious one being what kind of environment is conducive to the virus?

In India during the 1930s British researcher Sir Albert Howard demonstrated repeatedly that cattle running on healthy soils and maintaining a healthy diet could actually rub noses with infected animals and not contract the disease.

My own experience backs this up. The outbreaks that occurred in Zimbabwe always showed a far greater correlation with nutritionally stressed livestock, certain soil types, and a deteriorating environment than they ever did with game populations. In fact in our areas of greatest buffalo-to-cattle contact, outbreaks were almost unknown. When one did occur in a small cattle herd in the middle of a large game reserve, the veterinarians jumped on it as proof that buffalo were spreading the virus. When we investigated further, we found that immediately before the outbreak the area had been visited by a veterinary officer who had come from a foot-and-mouth area in nearby Zambia.

Whenever an outbreak occurred, a cordon was placed around the area, which meant that all roads leading out of it had checkpoints where shoes and tires were sprayed. This control of human movement effectively controlled the spread of the disease. Many species of game, including buffalo, still moved freely back and forth, which indicated that game were not the main agent in spreading the disease. Despite this, fences continued to be built and game shot to keep them away from livestock.

Clearly we need to research the relationship between health and infection—not only health of the cattle but also of the soil and plant communities. Much as the urban slums of medieval times contributed to outbreaks of plague, I believe livestock living in "slum conditions" are more susceptible to foot-and-mouth disease. In the meantime, hundreds of thousands of game animals are dying of thirst because fences deny them access to water, and whole buffalo herds are shot when fences don't contain them.

3. *The Irish Potato Famine.* Over a million people starved as a result of the blight that struck Ireland's staple crop in the nineteenth century. Today, we understand why the blight's spread was so extensive: We had created

an environment that was ideal for that particular fungus to flourish. Not only were the potatos grown as near monocultures, they were virtually all derived from the same seedstock and thus lacked genetic diversity. Therefore, the blight encountered little or no resistance in that environment and spread readily. The same principle is at work today wherever monoculture cropping is practiced, but we put large-scale blights off to a later day by poisoning the offending fungus, virus, or bacteria. Tragically, research efforts still concentrate on instant cures such as poisons, rather than the longer-term prevention brought about by greater diversity in the environment.

In the future it is hoped that we will concentrate on whole communities rather than the offending organism in our endeavors both to understand and to prevent major disease outbreaks. We cannot continue on our present course, which seeks the instant cure rather than the underlying cause. Once the cause is determined and rectified, we commonly find we need do nothing further.

Research in New Areas

Quite often the HRM model leads to ways of addressing a problem that fall far enough outside the traditional way of doing things to indicate a research priority in areas that may appear unrelated to the goal initially. The need to find alternatives to wire fences in order to stabilize both a rural economy and urban water supplies is a case in point.

In a 1986 publication, *Research for Tomorrow*, the u.s. Department of Agriculture gives a pretty good idea about the evolution of conventional priorities and includes many projects that may serve the holistic manager well in years to come, ranging from development of natural pesticides to biological controls and the decoding of insect chemical communications. Such projects represent a healthy advance beyond the era of unqualified faith in toxic chemicals, but they are still an attempt to cure problems directly through reductionist science, often ignoring cause and effect.

The agency does not have a goal stated in holistic terms, but in a foreword to the book the u.s. Secretary of Agriculture writes, "Our current challenge in agriculture is to remain competitive in the world market. u.s. producers must be able to produce their crops at a price that will allow them to be marketed successfully in this global economy. Research will help us discover more efficient and more cost-effective means of doing this."

For the sake of analyzing his research objectives through the HRM model, I might extrapolate from that the following three-part goal:

Quality of life—a stable rural population that produces high quality food and water for the national good and supports healthy communities that provide adequate educational, cultural, and economic opportunities from locally-generated commerce.

Production—profit from livestock and crops, clean water for urban uses, and an aesthetically pleasing recreational environment for both local and urban populations.

Landscape—to achieve this production goal, all four ecosystem processes should generally function at maximum potential, but in the light of national priorities, a highly productive water cycle has particular importance and thus it is here that we should focus our attention (although all four blocks are one).

It is a fact that many past civilizations of great urban and rural sophistication have fallen, never to rise again, because their watersheds deteriorated, and the United States is exposing itself to the same fate. An evaluation of the four ecosystem foundation blocks as they apply to the above goal makes this clear.

Over 50 percent of our watersheds, millions of square miles of land, fall between four and ten on a scale where ten represents maximum brittleness. Perhaps as much as ninety percent of this vast area is subjected to livestock continuously in a manner that assures both overgrazing and overrest, an application of two powerful tools so as to guarantee soil exposure and water cycle damage (along with damage to the other ecosystem foundation blocks).

The HRM model leads us to the unavoidable conclusion that the long-range goal depends on restoring and maintaining the water cycle over an enormous area by means appropriate to its brittleness. When the Chaco culture in New Mexico, like us, so disrupted the wild game that the Chaco's sustaining watersheds began to deteriorate from overrest and periodic burning, they had no remedy. We can see through the HRM model, however, that livestock, properly concentrated and moved on a carefully planned regimen as described in the biological plan/monitor/control guideline, offer a cost-effective solution.

At this point, however, we must recognize that we don't know enough about handling animals. Apart from minor exceptions, the professional herder has vanished from American culture. Fencing technology took quantum leaps with the American invention of barbed wire in the nineteenth century and more recently with the New Zealand invention of energizers that could power slick wire effectively. It nevertheless remains fencing, and the thought of enmeshing billions of acres of North America in wire horrifies many people, including me, for both aesthetic reasons and the impact on wildlife. Besides that, fencing, though less expensive than land destruction, does not come cheap.

Nothing, therefore, might serve the future of the nation, or perhaps even the world, better than research into ways to control livestock without fences, and yet out of budgets that total in the billions, no American research institution has allocated a dollar to this end. Surely a nation that can confine dogs with radio-triggered shock collars and develop lasers to shoot down missiles could solve this problem.

This is only one example of how holistic thinking can jolt research orientation out of the ruts that often confine it. A similar exercise applied to goals for a national park, wilderness area, duck breeding refuge, or a United Nations program to halt desertification might turn up equally unforeseen gaps in our knowledge.

Summary

While management must be holistic to succeed, most research must remain reductionist, but this difference is complementary and strengthens both areas of endeavor. HRM is research-driven, but any research data applied in management must be monitored to ensure that the expected results do materialize in the whole.

When used in the management and diagnostic modes, the HRM model constantly points to new areas where research is needed. When applied in the research orientation mode, the model helps set research priorities. This ensures that areas of greatest need get the most attention and gives countries with small research budgets a powerful decision-making tool.

Now that I have taken you through the development of Holistic Resource Management as a means of reversing the deterioration of resources and the desertification of the world, I would like to venture a look into the future. HRM is still in its infancy but it is developing exponentially. In our awakening to what holism means for mankind and our planet we are like a litter of puppies staring dazzled at the wide world around them. As one of those puppies whose eyes have just opened, what do I see ahead, and what lead, if any, can I give?

PART IX

Conclusion

51
The Future

Our lovely planet now staggers under massive human impact, and fast-rising populations that, if unchecked, can only lead to war, disease, and starvation. Invoking the names of religious leaders who preached tolerance, we fight and kill each other to claim small patches of the earth that sustain us, destroying in the process its fruitfulness. Nevertheless, I am optimistic about the future as I see a real, practical way forward.

Until recently not a single scientist, including myself, whether he commanded the wealth of Texas or the poverty of sub-Saharan Africa, understood why agriculture and resource management was running into crisis everywhere. On the other hand, for ten thousand years mankind dreamed of flying and not a single person knew how, although other creatures had done it for millions of years. Then, within seventy years of the first successful flight, men walked on the moon.

Practical holism promises the same kind of phenomenal advance. Though we have advanced the destruction of our planet over many millennia, we now can hope to restore it at ever increasing speed. The primitive but successful holistic model treated in this book will surely be improved and extended by thousands of people. As long as it remains simple enough for ordinary people to use, the power of the ideas behind it will encounter few limits.

Alongside the deterioration of land, water, and air one other problem haunts our future; the explosion of the human population that has paralleled the degradation of our resources. We cannot manage resources holistically according to the natural laws of our ecosystem if we continue to act as if those laws did not apply to humanity as well.

497

Various cultures and religions favor large families for reasons deeply rooted in historical conditions in which security in old age, or survival of a race, depended on many children. Now, however, uncontrolled population growth threatens our survival, and we have other means to provide old age security.

We do have examples of cultures that already depend on limited numbers. To survive in the Kalahari desert the African Bushmen must maintain low birthrates, enforced by high mortality whenever they approach the limits of their harsh world. Modern medicine and economic incentives have upset this balance, and though as individuals the Bushmen may incorporate themselves into modern society, the world will be the poorer for the loss of a rich and ancient culture. They and their culture could be saved if we could accept that as hunter-gatherers they depend on low population and adequate territory. We have the knowledge to help them preserve the ancient harmony of man and desert, but do we have the wisdom and compassion to do it? The planet Earth, in the context of space no less limited than the Kalahari, hands mankind as a whole the same mortal challenge.

The institutionalized religions in modern society that encourage high numbers of children do not reflect the present state of the world. The sages who founded them spoke out of the conditions of the times in which they lived, but in all cases their universal message was compassion. I find it difficult to believe that, were they preaching today, they would ever suggest that we continue to produce high numbers of children knowing that by doing so we threaten the wonderful creation of our planet and its myriad forms of life.

I myself am not a conventionally religious man. However, I do feel infinitely small and powerless in the presence of the wonders of Nature and our universe. Such a marvelous creation did not occur by chance. There is a power that is greater than all mankind, and out of deference to it we should respect each other and the ecosystem that sustains us all.

This means controlling our population and respecting the diversity of cultures, tribes, nations, and spiritual beliefs as a great gift to all mankind, and the same duty includes the companion task of halting the deterioration of the Earth.

Fortunately we do not have to wait for an era of world peace and collaboration to make a start because Holistic Resource Management will function for any people in any place, and the HRM model will work regardless of religion, system of government, economic base, or climate. Using it, however, makes us take the human factors into full account. It can only lead to greater consciousness and action on all fronts.

A great many of our conflicts arise directly out of the deterioration of resources and ignorance about the tools we have to manage them, but even such a materialistic explanation has a philosophical aspect. I heard recently of a Navajo medicine man who, in mediating a grazing dispute between two families, said, "You are neighbors whether you want to be or not, because the land itself unites you. It links you as you both walk on it today, and you will both lie in it together when you die. Then the plants that grow in the soil you become will infect your children with either your hatred or affection as you can choose now. If you bless your land, it will return the blessing and your present argument will become insignificant."

To the prayers, songs, and practical gestures the medicine man had in mind, I would add holistic management. In case after case we have already witnessed what it can contribute to conflict resolution, and this role will surely become ever greater.

Making the world think holistically will not be easy, but the path of holism carries no risk, and survival of modern man depends on taking the first steps along it soon. I have spent over thirty adult years struggling to learn how we humans might reverse the deterioration of our life-support system, during which time I have worn many hats in societies from the most simple to the most complex, and within the whole task I see many subwholes where we must advance the holistic idea.

Language

Our language itself reflects mechanistic logic and thus hinders holistic thought. In this book two cases have bothered me in particular. The term ecosystem implies an entity distinct from us as humans, and to say we are part of it raises a second problem. Part is a mechanical term, while in the natural world there are no parts, only wholes within wholes.

I might have coined a word such as "ecosystemselves" to convey the notion of humanity and the ecosystem as one whole, jarring as it would have been to read. The parts problem, however, seems to lie beyond the reach of English altogether. We lack words to describe a lesser whole, nature's equivalent of a mechanical part. We talk of the parts of the human body, for example, when we mean whole arms, legs, lungs, and other organs that developed as wholes in a whole human.

The understanding of holism will evolve more quickly if our vocabulary can expand to match it.

Education

Our experience at the Center in trying to explain holism to people of all ages, educational levels, and professional backgrounds indicates that our weak link in resource management lies within our education system. From kindergarten through graduate school it injects a mechanistic world view into every aspect of our society.

If humanity is to enjoy a prosperous and secure future we must develop our understanding of holism throughout all our years of formal education and beyond by acquiring the habit of lifelong learning. I am reminded here of the comment of a dean of agriculture at an American university who said, "We have no disagreement with Holistic Resource Management and can see that this is the direction in which we have to go, but what do we teach tomorrow?" He did have a problem as all his textbooks were written, and his staff trained, to present agriculture as an isolated mechanical process.

I spent a sleepless night or two over that dilemma, for one shouldn't criticize without offering constructive alternatives. At the Center we have had to acknowledge our lack of knowledge as teachers and learn as equals with our students in a much more self-directed way than more tradition-bound institutions permit. At the cutting edge of discovery, pupils cannot "sit at the feet of the master" because there isn't one. In public education a whole generation of young people has begun to vote with its feet or disrupt schools outright in instinctive protest against a system that doesn't explain the world these people see. And their parents, who produced that world, cannot understand because they only learned to see it in disconnected parts.

The reductionist education of today, which after all did put men on the moon, has a place, but not untempered by respect for holism. We cannot afford the luxury of granting leadership to politicians, technocrats, or entrepreneurs in any system of government who cannot grasp that humanity and our ecosystem function as one.

The discovery that holism is essential in resource management and how radically it differs from our reductionist, mechanical approach to world resource management deals a death blow to the kind of vocational training our universities traditionally offer. Nevertheless, like the mounted officers who ordered the charge long after the machine gun had rendered the cavalry obsolete, the professors who instruct our range managers, foresters, wildlife managers, etc. will be the last to change. Only the most broad-minded will dare question their own education. The rest will have to be pushed by their students.

Agriculture

The realization that agricultural practices cannot defy the limitations of the four fundamental ecosystem processes will change the production of food and fiber in many ways. From all that we know today it appears that we will have to manage our croplands in smaller units of greater complexity. Crops in polycultures with animals will likely prove better and more stable than rotations of monocultures without animals. Societies heavily dependent on machinery will have to develop the technology to handle complex operations, such as harvesting one crop intersewn with others requiring different treatment.

Even as cropland management focuses on smaller units, our watersheds (ranches, tribal lands, national parks, wilderness areas, forests, and mountains) will likely require management as larger units. This is not to confuse ownership and management, as large land holdings can be broken into smaller administrative units and vice versa.

Agricultural production will need to serve the three-part goals of local communities rather than political expediency in order to build long-term national security.

At the research level, the various attempts at more ecologically sound practices, such as integrated pest management, will have to recognize people's three-part goals and a holistic model in order to succeed. Though encouraging moves away from the old single-discipline approach, they are still reductionist and mechanistic, and will thus lead to disappointing results.

Agricultural extension services (of governments, international organizations, universities, and consultants) will have to stop giving advice from the perspective of narrow disciplines and training whether in integrated teams or not. Their prime task will become helping people in whole communities set their own three-part goals.

Holistic management by definition must come from the people most intimately connected to the resources they possess, and nowhere does this rule apply more completely than in the case of international aid. The major aid organizations such as The World Bank, United Nations Food and Agriculture Organization, Asian Development Bank, and the various agencies of wealthy countries must cease imposing their ideas of progress on weaker nations. People at farm and village levels must determine their three-part goals, not bureaucrats in Washington, Moscow, Stockholm, or London.

The so-called developed nations moreover must put their own houses in order first, as not one presently handles its own resources in a sustainable way. Until that changes they should not presume to tell others what to do, and they remain vulnerable to the charge that their development philosophy masks an attempt to plunder abroad to offset lost capacity at home. The wholesale logging of fragile rain forests and the replacement of subsistence farms by plantations of cash crops for export are but two examples.

Water

Modern urban society, dependent on vast amounts of water and energy, has become extremely vulnerable to any disruption of its sources. As fresh water can only come from healthy, unpolluted watersheds, it soon will become the main product of forests, mountains, ranches, national parks, wilderness areas, and nomadic ranges. All other uses will have lower priority. Thus water cycles must function well over billions of acres of our planet's land surface.

The old panacea, building dams, does not solve the problem, as it does not address the issue of the quality, quantity, and speed of the water actually coming off the land. That, more than any other measure, reflects the health of the whole ecosystem, including its urban, industrial members. Some of our megadams have proven disastrous for a variety of additional reasons. Though national pride will no doubt intervene, the most famous of them all, the Aswan High Dam, should be destroyed to save the Egyptian economy. It has blocked the annual silt deposits that maintained her agriculture and fisheries for over six thousand years. That same silt eventually must destroy the dam itself, but in the meantime farmers downstream must spend hard currency on dangerous chemical fertilizers to feed the nation.

Though I have not mentioned oceans in this book, they also suffer from the exploitation and chemical pollution of our watersheds. One has only to watch every rainy season how the terrific silt loads carried down by southern Africa's rivers discolor the sea for miles to know that the mismanagement of land is destroying salt water life in the most productive zones. Such destruction has become widespread around all continents as we continue to send horrible burdens of chemicals and silt into the oceans.

National Parks and Wilderness

These are national and international treasures more precious than any human work of art, and they cannot be managed with the benign neglect represented by the standard regime of law enforcement in support of tourism. As enclaves isolated for the benefit of outsiders, they cannot withstand the pressure of local populations who see no value in them for their community. This holds as true in the United States, where poor rural people would rather see parks mined for coal or logged to provide employment, as in Africa, where poachers steal meat and ivory.

Integrated scientific teams studying the use and management of these lands will not provide answers, because as always they will look at the situation from the outside, and their opinions, however numerous, represent narrow and often mutually exclusive points of view.

Three-part goals and holistic management automatically will begin to rectify many of the current problems that loom in such preserves. These include complex social issues as well as simpler matters such as the impact of tourist and administrative facilities on vital habitat, static and unnatural game populations, excessive use or suppression of fire, and other crisis management reactions to constant deterioration.

We will have to work on ways to reintroduce crucial predators into some of our national parks, and this may involve the reintroduction of man as the most important predator of the last million years. Tourism, truly a vital element, will benefit from much more careful planning in relationship to goals.

As a hungry man knows no boundaries, we cannot expect to maintain some of the world's greatest treasures by fortified perimeters against human populations struggling for survival. Such harsh divisions must soften and tangible benefits must go to the local human populations so that they appreciate the treasures as much as any wealthy person in a developed country far away. In Africa in particular the benefits of foreign currency must flow directly to local people and not to politicians in far-off cities. They must see that wild land provides schools, clinics, and other infrastructure for neighboring villagers rather than Mercedes cars for bureaucrats in Nairobi, Lusaka, or Harare.

Ultimately the worth of parklands surpasses calculation. When one painting done by a human hand brings millions of dollars at auction, the world's entire monetary supply could not approach the value of one national park. To protect such wealth we may well have to look to administrative structures besides government bureaucracies subject to political whim.

Cities

Megacities have come to burden our ecosystem only in relatively recent times but already they have produced some megaproblems. They not only demand incredible concentrations of water and energy as mentioned, but also they require the extraction of very high volumes of nutrients from surrounding rural lands and create an overload of wastes too concentrated for an ecosystem already staggering under agricultural and industrial abuse to absorb.

We will have to start looking at cities as wholes in the context of their surrounding rural environments. A quality of life goal sought by all, a hard look at the production required to sustain it as defined by aesthetics, cultural and recreational opportunities as well as economic activity, and definition of the landscape needed to support that, might well lead us to some radical conclusions.

Such goals allow the application of the HRM model and the testing of policies before implementation, but that may reveal a need to reduce city concentrations and size, distribute humans more widely, and enable large numbers of people to return to a rural life. As the current expansion precipitates crisis management and failure to face underlying problems, cities risk becoming ecologically unmanageable.

Unplanned urban sprawl onto valued food-producing lands can only continue at our peril, as China has discovered to its sorrow. Its population, already the largest among nations, doubled over the last twenty-five years, and much of it was allowed to sprawl onto incredibly large acreages of valued food-producing lands. At the same time the rest of China's rural lands continue to desertify at a terrific rate.

Near my home in the Rio Grande Valley in impoverished New Mexico, I see mile upon mile of tremendously valuable agricultural land and wildlife habitat buried under housing and double highways, while not half a mile away poor land that could have supported those developments equally well desertifies badly.

Around many a city, wealthy people and retirees have settled on small plots of land where they can keep one horse in the back yard. Economically justifiable on brittle watersheds, such fragmentation courts disaster. Though each family only holds three or four acres, ten thousand such lots control thirty to forty thousand acres of vital watershed. Between the horses and the fences, overrest and overgrazing of plants have degraded the watershed seriously within only a few years. Is this to be a case of the "Tragedy of the Commons" in reverse? Clearly it will be unless ownership is not confused with management and such communities can set goals and manage holistically.

Economies

Few economists yet take account of the ecosystem processes that ultimately produce the bulk of our wealth. Clearly the revolution in education must take effect before we can expect economic models that have any chance of working in practice.

According to Peter Drucker in *The Frontiers of Management*, less than one-thirtieth of the volume of world transactions today is in actual goods and services. The bulk is financial institution borrowing and currency trading.[1] Nations individually are no better. This indicates how far we have removed our daily experience from the generation of actual wealth. Little wonder then that we hardly notice when management of the resources that produce it lapses into haphazard reactions to crises.

I see a great need to rethink economic models on the basis of our ecosystem, clear human goals, and energy flows for individual nations and the world as a whole. The HRM model at present cannot handle the immense ramifications of financial transactions at the national or international level, but it does indicate a direction for development because it recognizes the forgotten relationship between wealth and the ecosystem and includes all currently known tools. As suggested in earlier chapters, new economic modeling based on the HRM model might create submodels in the guidelines row to handle such things as international transactions and the economies of nations and cities.

At the Center we have made a good start at getting individual ranches and farms to plan their economies holistically. Since governments don't lead but follow, as underground economies have repeatedly taught us, reforms may reach that level eventually. In developed economies, however, a third sector also could provide leadership—the philanthropic network. Large philanthropic organizations and individuals can influence whole nations through their choices of what to support. It is my hope that they will learn how effectively the HRM model can serve them in determining what endeavors truly serve humanity.

Nations

Selfish national interest in a world inextricably linked by geography, economics, and communications subverts progress in resource management as much as any other force. Few things indicate this more clearly than our willingness to let pollutants that we would not tolerate drift downwind or downstream to bedevil foreigners. Similarly, the American appetite for hamburger or the Japanese demand for lumber is somehow allowed to justify the destruction of tropical forests that the world as a whole cannot afford to lose.

I do not believe that as currently formed, any government is structured to manage its own resources holistically, let alone control its international impact. In the thousands of years of struggle to find ways to govern ourselves, we have acted in terms of power, wealth, defense, religion, tribe, or race but never out of concern for living within the confines of our life-support system. Only in this century have we encountered the harsh necessity to even think about that.

An axiom of politics that impressed me early in my own political career says that unless all feel secure and well-governed, none are. As long as we continue to undermine our resource base, few, if any, governments can truly govern their citizens well.

Where might we start looking for ways to govern ourselves holistically? As I said earlier, I believe that governments will have to be restructured before they can govern along holistic lines. While many may find this disturbing, it may prove our only salvation.

I do not believe that we can look to any present government or institute in the world for leadership in this necessary change. The magnitude of world desertification alone, taking but one of our problems, has already grown beyond the power of any human organization to handle. So great is the problem that now only ordinary people can deal with it—you and I—teachers, farmers, ranchers, tribesmen, foresters, mothers, fathers, business people, or whatever we are outside of our institutional identities.

We can only do what is necessary by working collaboratively and supporting one another with a vision of a world greater than ourselves. None of our institutions, government or otherwise, has this. No sooner do we form them and promulgate lofty goals than human nature takes over and the ego of the institution assumes an identity more important than its mission. Our Center has attempted to form a collaborative structure that will not threaten any established institution, but it remains to be seen if our experiment will succeed. We envision at least creating a diffuse and friendly network through which individuals from many institutions can help one another learn, understand, apply, and develop holistic management. Eventually, as people change, governments and institutions will change to meet their needs.

Ultimately we will have to manage our planet as one whole through a vast series of lesser wholes. Only in this manner can we prosper. Earlier in my life, the magnitude of problems without solutions depressed me utterly. Now, at last, I see the possibility of wonderful times ahead as we both enjoy the fruits of technology and learn to live within our ecosystem's rules. Had I another stock of years to replace those I've spent already, I could not imagine a more exciting time to live them than now.

APPENDIX
The Center for Holistic
Resource Management

In order to increase knowledge of Holistic Resource Management and to develop the HRM model further, the Center for HRM was established as an international nonprofit corporation in 1984. Based in Albuquerque, New Mexico, the Center has as its goal the improvement of the human environment and quality of life through better resource management. In 1988 membership was approximately two thousand, representing fourteen different countries. Branches had been formed in Texas, New Mexico, Oregon/ Washington, Nebraska, Arizona, Colorado, Montana, North Dakota, Canada, and Mexico.

The Center offers a variety of programs designed to help families, communities, and governments use the HRM model to analyze their position and proceed toward their goals in an ecologically and financially sound way. Courses are held three to four times each month in various locations and are attended by approximately one thousand farmers, ranchers, foresters, wildlifers, environmentalists, and government and university extension agents each year. A two- or three-year degree program is also offered to twenty-five students per year with the Center acting as a "university without walls."

The Center sponsors an international intensive training program, which works with foreign governments and international agencies to train teachers and extension advisors in the use of the HRM model. Representatives from Zimbabwe, Tunisia, Morocco, Jordan, Algeria, and the Navajo Nation have participated in this program funded by the United Nations, the U.S. Agency for International Development, the Ford Foundation, or private individuals.

A quarterly newsletter links members and practitioners together and provides a forum in which they can share problems and exchange ideas. Five regional directors also assist practitioners in the field and work closely with state and regional branches to organize local management clubs (self-help groups) and provide local introductory seminars.

For further information, contact Center for Holistic Resource Management, P.O. Box 7128, Albuquerque, New Mexico 87194, (505) 242-9272.

GLOSSARY

ANIMAL DAYS PER ACRE (ADA). A term used to express simply the volume of forage taken from an area in a specified time. It can relate to one grazing in a PADDOCK or to several, in that more grazings than one can be added to give a total ADA figure. The figure is arrived at by a simple calculation as follows:

$$\frac{\text{animal numbers x days of grazing}}{\text{area of land}} = \text{ADA}$$

ANIMAL IMPACT. The sum total of the direct physical influences herding animals have on the land—trampling, dunging, urinating, salivating, rubbing, digging, etc.

BRITTLE AND NONBRITTLE ENVIRONMENTS. All environments, regardless of total rainfall, fall somewhere on a continuous scale from *brittle* to *nonbrittle*. Completely *nonbrittle environments* are mainly characterized by 1) reliable precipitation regardless of volume; 2) good atmospheric moisture distribution through the year as a whole; 3) a high rate of biological decay in old plant and animal material, which is fastest near the soil surface; 4) speedy successional community development from smooth and sloped soil surfaces; 5) the development of complex and relatively stable communities with a lack of disturbance for many years.

Completely *brittle environments*, on the other hand, are characterized by 1) unreliable precipitation, regardless of volume; 2) poor distribution of atmospheric moisture through the year as a whole; 3) a high rate of chemical (oxidation) and physical (weathering) decay in old plant and animal material, which is generally slow and from upper parts downward; 4) **very** slow successional development from bare and smooth soil sur-

509

faces, often stopping at algal capping and on steep slopes not even reaching algal stages; and 5) with a lack of adequate physical disturbance for some years, successional communities become simpler, less diversified, and less stable.

CAPPING, IMMATURE. A soil surface that has sealed with the last rainfall and on which there is no visible sign of successional movement. Capping is initiated by raindrop impact on bare soil that causes soil crumb structure to be lost.

CAPPING, MATURE. An exposed soil surface on which SUCCESSION has proceeded to the level of an algae-, lichen-, and/or moss-dominated community and stalled there.

DESERTIFICATION. A process characterized by complete shifts in plant, animal, and soil communities. Symptoms include increased incidence of flood and drought, declining levels of soil organic matter, increased soil surface exposure, and erosion.

GRAZING CELL. An area of land planned for grazing management purposes, normally as one unit to ensure adequate timing of grazing and recovery periods. In its most common form a *grazing cell* is divided into smaller units of land (PADDOCKS) by radiating fences (or markers herders can use) from a central point. A *grazing cell* can, however, utilize any design of fencing and shape of PADDOCKS. A *grazing cell* will normally contain stock year-round, or at least for prolonged periods of time.

GRAZING, FREQUENT. Grazing in the growing season that takes place with short intervals between the actual grazings on the plant. With most plants *frequent grazing* is not harmful as long as the degree of defoliation is light.

GRAZING, SEVERE. Grazing that removes a high proportion of a plant's leaf in either the growing or the nongrowing season. In the growing season this causes a temporary growth setback to the plant. In BRITTLE ENVIRONMENTS *severe grazing* at some stage in the year is often essential for grass health.

HERD EFFECT. The impact on soil and vegetation produced by a large herd of animals in an excited state. *Herd effect* is not to be confused with STOCK DENSITY, as they are different although often linked. You can have high *herd effect* with very low STOCK DENSITY (e.g., the bison of old that ran in large herds at very low STOCK DENSITY, as the whole of North America was the PADDOCK). You can have very high STOCK DENSITY with no *herd effect*, such as when two steers are placed in a one-acre PADDOCK. *Herd effect* is generally produced by concentration with excitement such as at supplements or other attractants, and then applied to areas of the range where required. It does not follow automatically that a cell with a large herd and high STOCK DENSITY will receive good herd effect.

Note: *Herd effect* is due to animal behavior and usually has to be brought about by some actual management action and is mainly used as a means of applying high ANIMAL IMPACT. Applied too long it will result on many soils in surface powdering, which is undesirable.

LOW-DENSITY GRAZING (sometimes referred to as PATCH or SELECTIVE GRAZING). This refers to the grazing of certain areas while others are left ungrazed to become stale and moribund. Normally it is caused by stock grazing at too low a STOCK DENSITY, too small a herd, or a combination of these with too short a time in the PADDOCK. Once it has started, even by only one grazing, it tends to get progressively worse, as the nutritional contrast between grazed and ungrazed areas increases with time. It is commonly corrected by forcing the stock to graze nonselectively. This is wrong and causes stock stress. It is *low-density grazing* and is rectified by increasing STOCK DENSITY rather than grazing pressure in the long run. In the short term it can be corrected through a number of palliatives, such as HERD EFFECT, fire, and grazing planning. Bear in mind that the productive and more stable ranges of the past had no problem with selective grazing even though they evolved with herding animals, which were as selective in their diets as their domestic relatives.

OVERGRAZING. Grazing during active growth that is both severe and frequent. Generally, this results in eventual death of the plant. In intermediate stages, it results in reduced production. *Overgrazing* damages plants to varying degrees by utilizing energy temporarily obtained by the plant from roots sacrificed for that purpose.

OVERREST. Rest of any perennial plant that is so prolonged that accumulating old material hampers growth and/or kills the plant. It occurs mainly in BRITTLE ENVIRONMENTS where the decay process is slow.

PADDOCK. A smaller division of land within a GRAZING CELL in which stock are grazed for short periods of time. (The American term, pasture, is deliberately not used, as in most countries it means a planted grass sward). *Paddocks* can be fenced permanently, temporarily, or marked in various ways for herding without fencing.

REST. Prolonged nondisturbance to soils and plant/animal communities. A lack of physical disturbance and/or fire. PARTIAL REST takes place when grazing and browsing herding animals are on the land, but without a full complement of predators to excite them. It commonly results in damaged algae/lichen communities but no successional advance beyond to more complex, stable communities.

STOCK DENSITY. The number of animals run on a small unit of land (PADDOCK) at a given moment of time. This could be from one day or less to several days. Usually expressed as the number of animals (of any size or age) run on one acre.

STOCKING RATE. The number of animals run on a unit of land expressed usually in the number of acres required to run one full-grown animal throughout the year or part thereof.

SUCCESSION. The process of change and development in communities of living organisms. Low SUCCESSIONAL: Simple communities composed of populations of only a few species. Usually highly unstable and vulnerable. Prone to serious upheavals and fluctuations in numbers. HIGH SUCCESSIONAL: Complex communities composed of populations of a great many different species of plants, animals, birds, insects, and microorganisms. Usually highly stable and not prone to high fluctuations in numbers of individual populations.

REFERENCES

The nature of holism is such that I have referred to few research papers. It is not that there isn't a wealth of information available in the voluminous mass of research conducted in all disciplines; it is just that the knowledge is reductionist. While it is of limited application to the HRM concept as a whole, it is often of great importance in cases of detailed specific application.

Chapter 1. What Is Holistic Resource Management?

Readers who have fallen into the trap of believing that science is a hard, mathematical, and exact field would do well to read Albert Einstein's *Out of My Later Years*. Secaucus, N.J.: Lyle Stuart, 1973. One of our most revered scientists, Einstein gave considerable thought to the future of humanity and the consequences of science. Of particular significance is the clarity with which he saw the need for goals and the inability of science per se to produce such goals. Regrettably, most scientists have come to view science and technology as the goal of human endeavor.

Chapter 2. Political and Economic Ramifications

I am not aware, apart from the Green Movement initiated in Germany, of any concerted effort to bring ecological thinking into government. I entered

Parliament in Zimbabwe in a very difficult period of civil war but did endeavor to bring about ecological coordination of government policies. Interested readers will find one debate in the Record of Parliamentary Debates, Rhodesia, House of Assembly, First Session, Twelfth Parliament, 1970. Hansard columns 737 to 741.

My idea was to have an "ecological coordination council" at cabinet level through which all actions of government would have to pass. My efforts at the time were overrun by war and by my crossing the floor in Parliament to rebuild and lead the opposition. But I believe the idea still has merit although today I would expand it with what we have learned about holism since 1970.

Chapter 3. Introduction

Readers interested in the long history of ideas in science and how humans consistently have reacted to new knowledge will find much material in such books as W. I. B. Beveridge. 1957. *The Art of Scientific Investigation*. New York: Random House; Daniel Boorstin. 1983. *The Discoverers*. New York: Random House; and Marilyn Ferguson. 1980. *The Aquarian Conspiracy*. Boston: Houghton Mifflin.

Chapter 4. Management Must Be Holistic

Holism is one of the most misunderstood concepts in science. It has been given lesser meanings through use in such terms as holistic health, holistic medicine, holistic ranch management (a term I was guilty of coining in my ignorance). With this has gone some adverse publicity and reaction as though it were not "respectable science." Interested readers would do well to study the thinking of Jan Christian Smuts in *Holism and Evolution*. Westport, Conn.: Greenwood Press, 1973, and the biography written by his son, J. C. Smuts, *Jan Christian Smuts*. London: Cassell & Company Ltd., 1952.

Understanding of the difference between the integrated approach and the holistic approach is crucial, and readers are encouraged to read Maurice Berman's *Reenchantment of the World*. Ithaca, N.Y.: Cornell University Press, 1981. Where I concluded that the integrated approach and holism are opposites from the practical failures in management of my own and other integrated teams, Berman arrived at this conclusion from an academic and philosophical perspective.

Currently there are few references to the failure of the integrated approach, as it is still too new an observation and experience. Naveh and Lieberman refer to it in *Landscape Ecology*. New York: Springer-Verlag, 1983.

Chapter 5. Brittle and Nonbrittle Environments

The following sources outline the fate of earlier civilizations in which soil erosion took its toll: W. C. Lowdermilk, "Conquest of the Land Through 7,000 Years," Agriculture Information Bulletin No. 99, u.s. Department of Agriculture, Soil Conservation Service, issued in 1953 and slightly revised in 1975; Hugh Bennett's *Soil Conservation*. New York: McGraw-Hill, 1939; and Raymond Dasmann's *Environmental Conservation*. New York: John Wiley & Sons, 1959.

Where earlier plant ecologists tended to see plant communities independent of large animal populations and disturbance, and viewed such things as essentially unnatural, publications like S. T. A. Pickett and P. S. White's *The Ecology of Natural Disturbance and Patch Dynamics*. New York: Academic Press, Harcourt Brace Jovanovich, 1985, are now starting to appear. Eventually, I believe we will look at *communities* rather than plant communities where animal organisms are viewed as something extraneous.

Information on the collapse of wildlife populations in the brittle environment Tuli Circle area of Zimbabwe is contained in the following reports and papers, which I authored: "Range assessment—Tuli Circle (National Land)," unpublished report to Game Ranchers Association of Rhodesia, 1966; "Game utilization in Rhodesia." *Zoologica Africana*, 2 (1964); "The utilization of wildlife on Rhodesian marginal lands and its relationship to humans, domestic stock and land deterioration." *Proceedings of the First Congress of the Associated Scientific Societies of Rhodesia Symposium on Drought and Development*, Bulawayo, 1966; "Crisis in Rhodesia." *Oryx, Journal of The Fauna Preservation Society*, May 1969.

These papers represent some of my early observations and thinking. The most significant, "Efforts in Rhodesia to apply an ecological philosophy and practice to the human environment to avert semidesert formation," regrettably is not available. Presented at the Symposium on Terrestrial Animal Ecology, Pretoria, South Africa, 1967, it was not published with the proceedings because the findings and views expressed offended the scientific thinking of the day. Attempts to have the same work published in America in the *Journal of Range Management* met with the same fate. It was unacceptable in those years that livestock could even be considered as constructive agents in the reversal of desertification.

Chapter 6. The Role of Herding Animals and Their Predators in Brittle Environments

Nothing has generated as much controversy in the development of Holistic Resource Management to date as the use of large herding animals to produce desired landscapes in management of our watersheds and deserts. For this reason I list the books and papers I have been able to locate that describe observations on the role of large herding animals in grasslands:

Bell, Richard. 1971. A grazing ecosystem in the Serengeti. *Scientific American* 225(1):86–93.

Davies, William. 1938. Vegetation of grass verges and other excessively trodden habitats. *Journal of Ecology* XXVI: 38–49.

Geist, Valerius. 1974. On the relationship of social evolution and ecology in ungulates. *American Zoologist* 14:205–220.

Gordon, Iain, and Patrick Duncan. 1988. Pastures new for conservation. *New Scientist*, vol. 117, no. 1604, 54–59.

McNaughton, S. J. 1979. Grazing as an optimization process: Grass-ungulate relationships in the Serengeti. *The American Naturalist* 5:691–703.

McNaughton, S. J., M. B. Coughenour, and L. L. Wallace. 1982. Interactive processes in grassland ecosystems, in *Grasses and Grasslands: Systematics and Ecology*. Norman: University of Oklahoma Press.

McNaughton, S. J. 1984. Grazing lawns: Animals in herds, plant form, and coevolution. *The American Naturalist* 6:863–83.

Voisin, André. 1966. *Better Grassland Sward*. London: Crosby Lockwood & Son Ltd.

Paige, Ken, and Whitham Thomas. 1987. Overcompensation in response to mammalian herbivory: The advantage of being eaten. *American Naturalist* 129:407–16.

Bell and McNaughton in particular draw attention to the importance of large herding ungulates on the grasslands of East Africa (largely brittle environments). In all cases, unfortunately, the role of herd behavior and predation was missed. Predators are a vital component in communities. McNaughton theorizes that the herding ungulates in some manner learned that their concentration produced a more palatable form on the grass plants upon which they fed and thus the herding/moving pattern developed. I believe that predators produce the tendency to concentrate and that concentrated dung and urine deposition produces the tendency for animals feeding close to the ground to move. Where large predators have been removed, their prey remain scattered more often and more widely and become more static. Another reason for my belief is the observation concerning different hoof action and placement under excitement not produced while feeding as a herd—hence the requirement for the management guideline of "herd effect" in the HRM model.

The recent work by Iain Gordon and Patrick Duncan indicates that the impact of large herbivores is greater than we realized, even in nonbrittle environments. They report the loss of species diversity in wetlands with the removal of livestock.

Chapter 7. The Time Dimension in Soil, Plant, and Animal Relationships

Considerable research in a number of countries has illustrated the damage to grass root systems from defoliation but no one has observed the connection between time rather than animal numbers more clearly than André Voisin, who reported his findings in *Grass Productivity*, first published in 1959, and *Better Grassland Sward*, 1960, both London: Crosby Lockwood & Son Ltd.

American researcher Franklin Crider also discussed the fate of grass roots under severe and frequent grazing in his paper, "Root Growth Stoppage," Technical Bulletin No. 1102, United States Department of Agriculture, Washington, D.C., 1955. It was from his work that the U.S. Soil Conservation Service developed the idea of stocking at a rate that would have the livestock "take half and leave half" of key indicator plants. Simultaneously, in Africa, H. Weinmann confirmed the damage to roots following severe defoliation and wrote "The chemistry and physiology of grasses," in *The Grasses and Pastures of South Africa*, edited by D. Meredith, Cape Town: Central News Agency, 1955, as well as "Effects of defoliation on veld pastures," in *Proceedings of the Veld Management Conference*, Bulawayo. Department of Conservation & Extension, Salisbury, Rhodesia, May 1969.

The work of John Acocks can be found in his own writings: "Nonselective grazing as a means of veld reclamation," *Proceedings Grassland Association of South Africa* 1:33–39, 1966; and in articles such as that by Len Howell, "The development of multi-camp systems on a farm in the Southern Orange Free State," *Proceedings Grassland Society of South Africa*, 1976, 11:53–57.

For the student of conventional range management, such books as Laurence Stoddart and Arthur Smith's *Range Management*. New York: McGraw-Hill, 1955, and Harold Heady's *Rangeland Management*. New York: McGraw-Hill, 1975, contain information on the effects of grazing and browsing on plants. However, the authors interpret the data to mean that when overuse occurs, too many animals are the problem.

Chapter 9. Introduction
Chapter 10. Water Cycle
Chapter 11. Succession
Chapter 12. Mineral Cycle
Chapter 13. Energy Flow

It is hard to find any single publication where the four ecosystem processes covered in these chapters are stated and described simply. Knowledge about them has to be gleaned from many sources and I have thus listed a number of books and papers below with comments where they seem appropriate.

Albrecht, William A. 1982. *The Albrecht Papers*, Vol. I. Ed. by Charles Walters, Jr. Kansas: Acres u.s.a.

Allee, W. C., Alfred E. Emerson, Orlando Park, Thomas Park, and Karl P. Schmidt. 1958. *Principles of Animal Ecology*. Philadelphia and London: W. B. Saunders Co.

Branson, Farrel A., Gerald F. Gifford, Kenneth G. Renard, and Richard F. Hadley. 1981. *Rangeland Hydrology*. Ed. by Elbert H. Reid. Dubuque, Iowa: Kendall/Hunt Publishing Co.

Dasmann, Raymond F. 1975. *Environmental Conservation*, fourth edition. New York: John Wiley & Sons.

Ehrlich, Paul. 1986. *The Machinery of Nature: The Living World Around Us and How it Works*. New York: Simon & Schuster.

Odum, Eugene P. 1963. *Fundamentals of Ecology*. Philadelphia and London: W. B. Saunders Co.

Russell, Sir E. John. 1961. *Soil Conditions and Plant Growth*. London: Longmans.

Satterlund, Donald R. 1972. *Wildland Watershed Management*. New York: John Wiley & Sons.

These books give a good general outline of the concept of the ecosystem and how nutrients, and water cycle, and energy flows within it. None refers to the different nature of the decay and successional processes in brittle and nonbrittle environments, which is a more recent discovery.

A good feel for the successional process and total interdependence of our atmosphere, mineral matter, living soils, plants, and animals in complex communities can be gleaned from the above books as well as the following.

Albrecht, William A. 1975. *Soil Fertility and Animal Health*, Vol. II. Ed. by Charles Walters, Jr. Kansas: Acres u.s.a.

Berger, Patricia J., Norman C. Negus, and Carol N. Rowsemitt. 1987. Effect of 6-methoxybenzoxazolinone on sex ratio and breeding performance in *Microtus montanus*. *Biology of Reproduction* 36:255–260.

Dice, Lee R. 1955. *Natural Communities*. Ann Arbor: University of Michigan Press.

Elton, Charles. 1956. *Animal Ecology*. London: Sidgewick & Jackson, Ltd.

Fukuoka, Masanobu. 1978. *The One Straw Revolution: An Introduction to Natural Farming*. Emmaus, Pa.: Rodale Press.

Howard, Sir Albert. 1975. *The Soil and Health*. New York: Schocken Books.

Leopold, A. 1966. *A Sand County Almanac: With Essays on Conservation from Round River*. New York: Ballantine Books.

Leopold, A. 1986. *Game Management*. Madison, Wisc.: University of Wisconsin Press.

Lovelock, J. E. 1979. *Gaia: A New Look at Life on Earth*. New York: Oxford University Press. Few publications approach this for giving meaning to the concept of our planet as a living organism.

Maser, Chris, and James M. Trappe, eds. 1985. The seen and unseen world of the fallen tree. General Technical Report PNW-164, March 1984. Washington, D.C.: Forest Service, U.S. Department of Agriculture.

Maser, Zane, Chris Maser, and James M. Trappe. 1985. Food habits of the northern flying squirrel (*Glaucomys sabrinus*). *Canadian Journal of Zoology* 63:1084–1088.

Moore, John. 1985. Science as a way of knowing—human ecology. *American Zoologist* 25(2):486–637.

Tansley, A.G. 1949. *Introduction to Plant Ecology*. London: George Allen & Unwin Ltd.

Trappe, James M., and Chris Maser. 1977. Ectomycorrhizal fungi: Interactions of mushrooms and truffles with beasts and trees. *Mushrooms and Man, an Interdisciplinary Approach to Mycology*. Ed. by Tony Walters. Washington, D.C.: Forest Service, U.S. Department of Agriculture.

Weaver, John E., and Frederic E. Clements. 1938. *Plant Ecology*. New York: McGraw-Hill.

Chapter 15. Money and Labor

It is hard indeed to find good economic works that take any cognizance of the real world. Although real wealth is totally dependent on the sound functioning of our ecosystem and although we have witnessed civilization after civilization collapse because it destroyed its foundation (soil), I have yet to read any economic text that even mentions the essential processes whereby our ecosystem functions, even though the two words, economy and ecology, share the same Greek root.

Books I suggest are:

Drucker, Peter F. 1986. *The Frontiers of Management: Where Tomorrow's Decisions are Being Made Today*. New York: E.P. Dutton.

Hawken, Paul. 1983. *The Next Economy*. New York: Ballantine Books.

Hazlitt, Henry. 1979. *Economics in One Lesson*. New York: Arlington House.

Henderson, Hazel. 1981. *The Politics of the Solar Age: Alternatives to Economics*. Garden City, N.Y.: Anchor Press/Doubleday.

Chapter 16. Human Creativity

Books that help people to get better control of their time are the two by Edwin Bliss, *Getting Things Done* (1976) and *Doing it Now* (1983), Bantam Books, and *How to Get Control of Your Time and Your Life* by Alan Lakein (Signet, 1973).

After many years of investigating various commercial time management systems, I have found none better than that of Time Systems Inc., 5353 North 16th Street, Suite 400, Phoenix, Arizona 85016. Their system involves training courses or audio cassettes that enable you to learn how to use the system until habit, and thus trust, is established.

There are many references that are of great help in releasing human creativity in the home and workplace, which will be found in the chapters on organization and personal growth.

Chapter 17. Fire

There are a number of publications on fire such as "Fire: Its effects on the ecology of the vegetation in Rhodesia and its application in grazing management," by Oliver West, in *Proceedings of the Veld Management Conference*, Bulawayo, May 1969 (Department of Conservation & Extension, Salisbury, Rhodesia); and "Veld management in the dry, summer-rainfall bushveld," also by Oliver West, in *The Grasses and Pastures of South Africa*, D. Meredith editor, Central News Agency, Cape Town, 1955, pp. 624–46.

In these papers, West describes the role of fire in endeavors to maintain healthy grassland with a combination of grazing and fire. The grazing management was the "four-paddock, three-herd system" and fire was used following the fourth rest year to try to offset the encroachment of woody plants. For many years of my early life, this management approach was standard practice in Rhodesia. Observation of these results both on the many ranches and on the experimental stations over a wide variety of soils and rainfall led me to realize the damage to all four of the ecosystem foundation blocks with a burning frequency of once in four years.

Alston Chase in *Playing God in Yellowstone: The Destruction of America's*

First National Park, The Atlantic Monthly Press, Boston, 1986, and *The Journals of Lewis and Clark*, by John Bakeless, New American Library, New York, 1964, provide information on the early Native American use of fire and a number of other references. Apparently burning was extensive and this parallels my own experience in Africa where much of the same extensive burning is still taking place.

Henry A. Wright and Arthur W. Bailey, in *Fire Ecology* (John Wiley & Sons, New York, 1982), cover the role and management of fire in some detail but not holistically. Unfortunately the very title of the book suggests that the subject is not well understood, as fire that involves the rapid oxidation of material has no "ecology." Despite this it is worth reading for the wealth of detailed information, much of which can be used in holistic management.

In the references for Chapter 19 I have mentioned the work being done in the famous Kruger National Park in South Africa. This work will be pertinent to the reader interested in national park management and the use of fire to offset the adverse effects of low animal numbers.

Chapter 18. Rest

So deeply ingrained is our human belief that rest is always beneficial to land and plants that little serious investigation has been done. Where plots of land were fenced to exclude grazing animals during the 1930s by government agencies and universities to prove the response to rest, which they generally did initially, no one bothered to follow up the recordings. Where established in brittle environments, such plots that still survive suffer varying degrees of deterioration in the ecosystem processes. Publications are almost non-existent as it appears people relied on the early pictures as proof of the known.

Several papers are available describing the situation in long-rested land in Utah described in the text:

Kleiner, Edgar F., and K. T. Harper. 1972. Environment and community organization in grasslands of Canyonlands National Park. *Ecology* 53(2):209–309.

Kleiner, Edgar F., and K. T. Harper. 1977. Soil properties in relation to cryptogamic groundcover in Canyonlands National Park. *Journal of Range Management* 33(3):202–205.

Kleiner, Edgar F., and K. T. Harper. 1977. Occurence of four major perennial grasses in relation to edaphic factors in a pristine community. *Journal of Range Management* 30(4):286–289.

These observations in a brittle environment grassland never reached by large game animals and livestock note the high prevalence of algae and lichens (cryptogamic communities) as a major part of the soil cover. The authors refer several times to its being a "climax community" because of the absence of large animals. It is my belief that the surrounding rock formations that have accidentally precluded the large animals that so characterized the brittle environments of North America have made it a less than natural community to which the term climax cannot be attributed. The implication is that if this is truly climax then large ungulates were unnatural, which clearly is not the case.

Throughout, Virginia Park is compared with Chesler Park, which has been subjected over the years to overgrazing of plants and partial rest brought about by prolonged light stocking with livestock. We now know that these two influences are detrimental to the health of brittle environment grassland communities and do not approximate the manner in which natural populations of ungulates functioned in such environments. It follows that any comparative conclusions drawn are of limited value, as two unnatural situations in effect are under comparison. It is important to note the relative flatness of the land in Virginia Park. Where equally brittle environment is not flat (i.e., sloping canyon walls in the immediate area), the community under equal rest has been unable to stabilize at even the algae level.

An interesting study conducted in a somewhat brittle environment shows the adverse effects of excessive mulch accumulation, such as occurs with inadequate disturbance where breakdown is slow: Weaver, J. E., and N. W. Rowland. 1952. Effects of excessive natural mulch on development, yield, and structure of native grassland. *Botanical Gazette* 114(1):1–19.

Along the Beale Trail, by H.C. Lockett (a publication of the Education Division, u.s. Office of Indian Affairs, Printing Department, Haskell Institute, Lawrence, Kansas, 1940), is a small booklet with photographs of actual sites described in his travels by Lieutenant Edward Fitzgerald Beale who was commissioned by the War Department to survey a wagon road from Fort Defiance, Arizona, to the Colorado River in 1857. Alongside Beale's description of each site is a picture of it as it appeared eighty-one years later. Many of the early photographs now used to illustrate changes over the years were taken around permanent mining or army campsites where the ground was trampled out. In this case Beale's descriptions of the open country serve us better for comparison purposes because they were not disturbed by people or their domestic animals. The adverse changes in these brittle environment areas subjected to livestock overgrazing and partial rest over these years is dramatic indeed.

In my observations of the reduced health and premature death of brittle environment bunched grasses that are not grazed, trampled, or burned, I had assumed it was the lack of total light reaching growth points that mattered. But research conducted in Argentina suggests that it is the *quality* of the light that matters. The researchers report their findings in:

Casal, J. J., V. A. Deregibus, and R. A. Sanchez. 1985. Variations in tiller dynamics and morphology in *Lolium multiflorum* Lam. Vegetative and reproductive plants as affected by differences in red/far-red irradiation. *Annals of Botany* 56:553–559.

Deregibus, V. A., R. A. Sanchez, and J. J. Casal. 1983. Effects of light quality on tiller production in *Lolium* spp. *Plant Physiology* 72:900–902.

Deregibus, V. A., R. A. Sanchez, J. J. Casal, and M. J. Trlica. 1985. Tillering in responses to enrichment of red light beneath the canopy in a humid natural grassland. *Journal of Applied Ecology* 22:199–206.

Desertification of the United States, by David Sheridan (Council on Environmental Quality, 1981, U.S. Government Printing Office, Washington, D.C.), contains much useful information on the serious desertification that is taking place in America. It is short on solutions because of our belief that overstocking with livestock is causing the desertification of our rangeland watersheds. The author states on page 22, "The way to stop overgrazing is to reduce the number of livestock on the land." In the same breath he states that this is politically difficult to achieve. As pointed out earlier, he also neglected to look at the evidence available on the totally destocked plots set up in the 1930s and still available for inspection.

Chapter 19. Grazing

The references cited in Chapter 7 are all pertinent to this chapter. In addition, those readers grappling with the severe difficulties of managing game animals now confined to relatively small national parks, often with inadequate predation and home ranges, will find the approach of the biologists in the Kruger National Park of interest. Two good papers are those by U. de V. Pienaar, "Management by intervention: The pragmatic/economic option" (pp. 23–36) and V. de Vos, R. G. Bengis, and H. J. Coetzee, "Population control of large mammals in the Kruger National Park" (pp. 213–231), both in *Management of Large Mammals in African Conservation Areas*, 1983. Edited by R. Norman Owen-Smith (Pretoria: Haum Educational Publishers).

The fact that the park is no longer natural is accepted, along with the realization that it has to be scientifically managed. A policy of holding animal numbers down through culling has been adopted in preference to periodic high die-off in dry years. This park lies in a moderate rainfall brittle environment and thus large quantities of forage accumulate (through the slow decay process present) when animal numbers are deliberately held at a low level. The fact that this lack of adequate grazing and trampling of perennial grasses leads to successional shifts to undesired woody communities (which will alter the grazing game habitat undesirably) has led to burning every two to four years in places. This frequency is accepted as natural and there is no evidence presented to indicate that the ecological processes are being monitored. The authors are apparently unaware of why the one-herd, four-paddock grazing system, with its burn every four years, was abandoned in nearby Zimbabwe. Such frequent burning adversely affected all four eco-system processes in an area receiving similar rainfall.

Chapter 20. Animal Impact

The references cited in Chapter 6 are appropriate in this chapter. Due to our deep antagonism to livestock trampling over prolonged time, we have little in the literature of its possible benefits over short time periods.

André Voisin saw the benefits and mentions them many times in *Grass Productivity* (1961) and *Better Grassland Sward* (1960), London: Crosby Lockwood & Son Ltd. He refers also to early references to the "golden hooves" of sheep. One of the few people in America to see the importance of livestock trampling was August L. Hormay, who wrote "Principles of Rest Rotation Grazing and Multiple-Use Land Management" (1971), Washington, D.C.: U.S. Department of the Interior, Bureau of Land Management; U.S. Department of Agriculture, Forest Service.

Hormay's work represents, I believe, one of the best grazing systems devised, as he saw the beneficial as well as the potentially harmful role of the animal.

Harold F. Heady (1975), in *Rangeland Management*, New York: McGraw-Hill, has devoted a chapter to the physical effects of grazing animals, with a number of references to the observations of others. In all cases the importance of the time dimension was missed, which renders most of the observations meaningless. Trampling without reference to how long a period it took place over and how soon it was repeated is without meaning. Time and trampling, like time and grazing, are inseparable. Despite this, Heady mentions some beneficial effects of trampling in breaking capped algal soil surfaces and allowing better seed establishment, as well as laying dead material on the surface where decomposition increases and the minerals return to the soil.

Chapter 21. Living Organisms

Many of the publications mentioned in connection with Chapters 9 through 14 concerning the complexities of living communities are applicable to this chapter. Here I have repeated a few that are particularly applicable to the use of living organisms in production or landscape goals:

Machinery of Nature: The Living World Around Us and How It Works (1986), by Paul R. Ehrlich, New York: Simon & Schuster.

An excellent book with many good examples of the complexity of and interdependency of living organisms in communities. It is weak, however, when it comes to solutions for such problems as the desertification occurring in Africa, as unfortunately Ehrlich was not familiar with the new discoveries concerning this problem.

Several authors write on many aspects of the screwworm control program initiated in the United States in *The Screwworm Problem* (1979), edited by R. H. Richardson, Austin: University of Texas Press. This biological control program was based on the release of sterilized males to mate with the wild females, thus reducing the population, and has been a huge success. Of particular importance is the warning given in the book on the need for continual vigilance and a well-planned strategy combining ecological knowledge and biological control due to the ability of organisms to constantly make genetic changes. With biological control as with chemical control there is no quick fix that will always work.

The following papers arose from the second annual session of "Science as a Way of Knowing," a project of the education committee of the American Society of Zoologists and eleven other organizations. They are a good source of information on human ecology, as it is called. As mentioned elsewhere with my remarks on animal ecology, plant ecology, and fire ecology, I do not accept the term human ecology. Sooner or later we will come to realize that there is only one ecology and only one ecosystem and only then will we truly begin to understand the full oneness of our planet and beyond. Despite this remark these papers are excellent and represent much far-sighted wisdom.

Breslow, Lester. 1985. Trends in health—ecological consequences for the human population. *American Zoologist* 25:433–439.

Ehrlich, Paul R. 1985. Human ecology for introductory biology courses: An overview. *American Zoologist* 25:379–394.

Moore, John. 1985. Science as a way of knowing—human ecology. *American Zoologist* 25:483–637.

The following references contain many observations of the complexity inherent in our ecosystem, which has to be understood for humans to manage other organisms successfully for our own use.

Altieri, Miguel A. 1986. *Agroecology: The Scientific Basis of Alternative Agriculture.* Boulder, Colo.: Westview Press.

Gabel, Medard. 1986. *Empty Breadbasket: The Coming Challenge to America's Food Supply and What We Can do About It, A Study of the u.s. Food System by The Cornucopia Project.* Emmaus, Pa.: Rodale Press.

Howard, Sir Albert. 1943. *An Agricultural Testament*. New York: Oxford University Press.

Howard, Sir Albert. 1975. *The Soil and Health*. New York: Schocken Books.

In addition, the following papers all published in a special edition of *Biological Agriculture and Horticulture*. 1986. 3:2 and 3 are important: "Sustainable agriculture: The microbial potential—The micro-biologist's challenge" (pp. 87–94), by J. M. Lopez-Real; "The microbiology of soil structure" (pp. 95–114), by Richard G. Burns and Julie A. Davies; "Recycling of organic wastes for a sustainable agriculture" (pp. 115–30), by J. F. Parr, R. I. Papendick, and D. Colacicco; "Crop residue management for improved soil productivity" (pp. 131–42), by L. F. Elliott and R. I. Papendick; "Rhizospere microbiology and its manipulation" (pp. 143–52), by J. M. Lynch; "Nitrogen fixation in sustainable agriculture" (pp. 153–66), by J. I. Sprent; "Biological husbandry and the 'nitrogen problem' " (pp. 167–90), by David G. Patriquin; "Mycorrhiza in a sustainable agriculture" (pp. 191–210), by Barbara Mosse; "Plant health and the sustainability of agriculture with special reference to disease control by beneficial microorganisms" (pp. 211–32), by R. James Cook; "The contributions of fungi, bacteria and physical processes in the development of aggregate stability of a cultivated soil" (pp. 233–50), by M. B. Malope and E. R. Page.

The following three books contain a wealth of good information on the underlying principles of population management.

Allen, Durward L. 1966. *Our Wildlife Legacy*. New York: Funk & Wagnalls.

Dasmann, Raymond F. 1960. *Wildlife Biology*. New York: John Wiley & Sons.

Leopold, Aldo. 1986. *Game Management*. Madison: University of Wisconsin Press.

Chapter 22. Technology

Rachel Carson's *Silent Spring* (Boston: Houghton-Mifflin, 1962) and Barry Commoner's *The Closing Circle: Nature Man and Technology* (New York: Alfred A. Knopf, 1971) more than any other works alerted us to the dangers in our zealous use of technology to solve problems. Since then there have been isolated cases of improvement, but in general the situation has worsened simply because enough people don't care. We all achieve immediate personal gain while the social costs are spread over everybody later (the tragedy of the commons). Two organizations serving as watchdogs over the unfolding tragedy provide information on a regular basis: The National Wildlife Federation (1412 16th Street N.W., Washington, D.C. 20036) and the Northwest Coalition for Alternatives to Pesticides (P.O. Box 1393, Eugene, Oregon 97440).

Samuel S. Epstein's paper "Losing the war against cancer," in *The Ecologist*, 17(2/3):91–101, 1987, explains the connection between cancer and environmental factors but in particular carcinogenic pollutants in our air, water, and food. It contains a wealth of additional references.

An interesting study of the effects of our technology on decreasing mineral cycles and thus health of American watersheds is G. T. Fincher's paper, "Importation, colonization, and release of dung-burying scarabs," in *Biological Control of Muscoid Flies*, Miscellaneous Publication No. 61. USDA Agricultural Research Service, Veterinary Toxicology and Entomology Research Laboratory, College Station, Texas, 1985.

The author states:

> In the U.S. dung beetles have not increased in proportion to the increased production of livestock feces. Widespread use of insecticides, herbicides, fungicides, or anthelmintics and systemic insecticides in the feces on which the beetles feed may be responsible.
>
> The accumulation of feces on pasture hinders maximum livestock productivity which reduces profits for livestock producers. Dung accumulation takes many hectares of pasture out of production annually by smothering the herbage under each deposit and by creating areas of rank growth around each deposit that is not normally eaten by cattle.

I am inclined to believe the author's suggestion that the heavy use of chemicals in agriculture in America may underlie this serious destruction of so vital an organism in nutrient cycling. I say this as in my work in an area of Mexico far removed from chemical agricultural practices I have observed very dense deposits of cattle dung completely removed in six days by a variety of dung beetles during a period of no rain.

Despite statements from scientists such as that mentioned in this book's preface indicating a need for more holistic approaches and not merely more of the same that is not working, the literature is full of more of the same. *Research For Tomorrow: 1986 Yearbook of Agriculture* (USDA), Government Printing Office, indicates that a continued reductionist approach to American agriculture is on the drawing boards.

Other developed nations and international organizations appear to exhibit the same thrust of "technology first" with little attempt to consider the needs of people and their goals. A document illustrating this is *World Conservation Strategy: Living Resource Conservation for Sustainable Development* (1980), prepared in a collaborative effort by the International Union for the Conservation of Nature and Natural Resources, the United Nations Environmental Program, the World Wildlife Fund, and the U.N. Food & Agriculture Organization. This well-meaning document outlines four strategic principles, the first being "To Integrate": "The separation of conservation from development together with narrow sectorial approaches to living resource management are at the root of current living resource problems. Many of the priority requirements demand a cross-sectorial interdisciplinary approach." While looking to technology and this interdisciplinary approach, the document attributes much of the problem to high populations and poverty. This ignores the case of America where with all of the technology available and interdisciplinary teams to supervise its application, her semiarid western states (in the rural areas, where population is lowest) are desertifying as badly as in any other country.

Two other such documents were produced as part of the "World Conservation Strategy." They are *Proceedings of the Conference/Workshop on the Implementation of a National Conservation Strategy in Zimbabwe* (November 4–8, 1985) and *Towards a Regional Conservation Strategy for the Serengeti* (Report of a workshop held at Serengeti Wildlife Research Centre Seronera, Tanzania December 2–4, 1985, compiled by R. Malpas and S. Perkin, International Union for Conservation of Nature and Natural Resources). Another such document was produced by Mostafa K. Tolba, executive director of the u.n. environmental program, *Sands of Change: Why Land Becomes Desert and What Can Be Done About It* (unep Environmental Brief No. 2, 1987). All of these vital programs have nothing new to offer but more of the same technology that produced the dismal picture they are attempting to rectify.

In general the literature is well studded with papers and articles on how technology will enable us to do incredible things with human bodies and crops in the future but with little or no reference to any need for more holistic thinking. The exceptions are few but these are two examples: In "Alley cropping: Trees as sources of green manure and mulch in the tropics," in *Biological Agriculture and Horticulture*, 3(2/3):251–268, 1986, G. F. Wilson, B. T. Kang, and K. Mulongoy report on a promising new approach in which mixed crops are grown in rows between trees. In *The Soul of the Soil: A Guide to Ecological Soil Management*, 2nd Edition (Quebec: Gaia Services, 1986), Grace Gershuny and Joseph Smillie show great sensitivity to the nature of soil. They have a delightful sentence on page four: "Find out what soils *live in your area*, how they are classified and described by soil scientists, and how that compares with what you observe about them yourself [emphasis added]." They point out how hard it is to find literature that is helpful to the farmer but is not dominated by technology use and sales interests.

Chapter 24. Time in Cropping, Grazing, Browsing, and Trampling

Masanobu Fukuoka has many good observations on the vital importance of timing in his two books *The One Straw Revolution*, Emmaus, Pa.: Rodale Press, 1978, and *The Natural Way of Farming: The Theory & Practice of Green*

Philosophy, New York: Japan Publications Inc., 1985. Good management of the timing of various operations, together with his deep understanding of succession, has enabled Fukuoka apparently to increase yields and decrease insect damage in his crops.

André Voisin, in *Grass Productivity*, London: Crosby Lockwood and Son Ltd., 1961, explains in great detail and clarity the better management of time to minimize overgrazing in pastures and greatly increase yield.

Chapter 25. Time and Energy Flow

In this chapter I mention my observations on the correlation of certain soils with better livestock nutrition. Two others who have recorded such observations are Sir Albert Howard, in *An Agricultural Testament*, New York: Oxford University Press, 1943, and William A. Albrecht, in *The Albrecht Papers*, Vol. II, Ed. by Charles Walters, Jr., Kansas: Acres u.s.a., 1975.

Many practical ranchers in Africa and North America have observed the same connection between soils and nutrition. For example, in southern African countries it is a common observation that cattle do not perform well for some time after being moved from lowveld (sweetveld) to highveld (sourveld), although they can be moved the other way without major setback.

Chapter 26. Time and Livestock Nutrition

A good source of information on livestock nutrition is the two volumes of *Hanbuch der Tier Ernahrung*, edited by Walter Lenkeit, Knut Breirem, and Edgar Crasemann, Hamburg und Berlin: Verlag Paul Parey, 1969.

These voluminous works, with papers by many researchers in a number of countries, contain a great deal of information. However, it appears that there is a great deal more unknown than known in this field.

Two papers describing the marked change in diet with successive days in a paddock are "A comparison of intake, digestive ability, and diet selection by bison-hybrid and crossbred cattle" by Doak Elledge (unpublished thesis submitted to the Graduate College of Texas A & M University in partial fulfullment of the requirements for the degree of master of science, December 1979) and "Diet selection by cattle under high-intensity low-frequency, short duration, and Merrill grazing systems" by Charles A. Taylor, M. M. Kothmann, L. B. Merrill, and Doak Elledge, *Journal of Range Management*, 33(6):428–434, 1980.

The free choice mineral supplementation program mentioned is available as a commercial product from two sources: Feed Service Corporation, Box 348, Crete, Nebraska 68333, and Free Choice Enterprises Inc., P.O. Box 154, Richland, Iowa 52585. My own observations with the use of the Feed Service Corporation product indicated a very significant response in situations of moderate to high rainfall, low fertility leached soils, and a lesser response on low rainfall, low leaching highly mineralized soils. This ability of animals to select even macro and micro minerals and balance their own diets is a fertile field for investigation in pastures, rangelands, and feedlots.

Chapter 27. Time and Game Management

The first culling of large game in Zimbabwe's game reserves was instigated by my "Report on the status of game and management needs in the Urungwe non-hunting area" (unpublished report to the Department of Wildlife Conservation, Southern Rhodesia, 1961).

This official report on the extensive damage that was taking place in what is today the Mana Pools National Park of Zimbabwe contained my recommedations to undertake heavy culling of elephant, buffalo, and some other species. At the time, any suggestion that deliberate culling of animals should take place in areas set aside for their preservation was anathema to most people. There was considerable opposition to this report, which led to my leaving government service and continuing my work privately. Eventually the culling took place and is still being practiced. With the knowledge we have today, I now realize that although culling should take place, there is far more that we need to be aware of and to take into account in management of such areas. This is a typical moderate rainfall brittle environment but we had not discovered that concept at the time of the report. In brief, this means that we have a great need to maintain high animal numbers in such areas but to ensure predation and adequate movement.

That new thinking in African national park management is emerging is indicated in such papers as "Matching conservation goals to diverse conservation areas: A global perspective," by K. R. Miller, and "Management and conservation areas as ecological baseline controls," by A. R. E. Sinclair, both in *Management of Large Mammals in African Conservation Areas*, edited by R. Norman Owen-Smith, Pretoria: Haum Educational Publishers, 1983.

Both these papers express refreshing ideas about management of conservation areas such as national parks. The authors show a willingness to accept that management by default will not suffice and that we have to take a more active role and show greater political awareness of the situation in developing countries with high populations and land pressures.

The role and functioning of home ranges and territories, as well as semirandom movement, is of the greatest importance to managing game animals so as to minimize overgrazing. The following works amongst others contain information about home ranges and territories:

Allee, W. C., Alfred E. Emerson, Orlando Park, Thomas Park, and Karl P. Schmidt. 1955. *Principles of Animal Ecology*. Philadelphia and London: W. B. Saunders Company.

Dasmann, Raymond, F. 1966. *Wildlife Biology*. New York, London, Sydney: John Wiley & Sons, Inc.

Dice, Lee, R. 1955. *Natural Communities*. Ann Arbor: University of Michigan Press.

Ehrlich, Paul. 1986. *The Machinery of Nature: The Living World Around Us and How It Works*. New York: Simon & Schuster.

Hesse, Richard, W. C. Allee, and Karl P. Schmidt. 1951. *Ecological Animal Geography*. New York: John Wiley and Sons, Inc.

Leopold, Aldo. 1986. *Game Management*. Madison: University of Wisconsin Press.

With modern marking techniques and the knowledge we now have of overgrazing, such work should be capable of vast expansion in the years ahead.

Chapter 29. Herd Effect

Where I lived with and experienced some of the vast game herds of Africa their equivalents had gone from the North American continent before most of today's scientists could witness them. There are however some references to the large herds that once existed in North America.

The journals of Lewis and Clark in the original probably have many accounts. I have read *The Journals of Lewis and Clark: A New Selection with an Introduction by John Bakeless* (New York: New American Library, 1964) and there are several accounts particularly of the large numbers of buffalo breaking through the river ice and drowning. Another good source of material about past numbers is David A. Dary's *The Buffalo Book: The Full Saga of the American Animal*, Sage Books, Chicago: The Swallow Press, Inc., 1974, which has a number of references to the enormous herds and their accompanying predators that characterized the vast and productive prairies as settlers from Europe found them.

Chapter 30. Whole Ecosystem

In my early life as a professional having to deal with problem lions, elephants, hippo, and other large game turned killer, we all knew that it was useless to get any but the actual rogue animal. Little has been written on this aspect of predator control in the scientific journals.

However, two authors who had to deal with such problems wrote fascinating books. *Man-Eaters of Kumaon*, by Jim Corbett, New York: Oxford University Press, 1946, tells of Corbett's experiences in having to kill man-eating tigers in India. In *The Man-Eaters of Tsavo*, New York: St. Martin's Press, 1986, Lt. Col. J. H. Patterson recounts the story of two lions that killed many railway workers and brought railway construction to a halt until he was able to identify and kill the lions. Apart from these, the only reference I have found to actual research is the paper "Lamb predation in Australia: Incidence, predisposing conditions, and the identification of wounds," by Ian Rowley, CSIRO *Wildlife Research* 15:79–123, 1970. The author found that the feared dingo actually was doing more good for Australian sheep farmers than harm.

Chapter 32. Cause and Effect

We use the term "cause and effect" often and casually but few comprehend how much we ignore it in daily life. An excellent example of a writer comprehending the concept is Henry Hazlitt, who wrote *Economics in One Lesson*, New York: Arlington House Publishers, 1979. This is a new edition of his earlier work published in 1946. Hazlitt gives a very clear explanation of many of the economic principles affecting our daily lives. One of the strong points of this book is that Hazlitt really does understand the simple concept of cause and effect. He goes to great pains to prevent the various common smoke screens from clouding the principle and the simple connections from an action to its consequences. He points out with many examples how missing the simple cause and effect relationships leads to increasing depths of crisis management as we react to the unexpected.

Our economic systems, complex as they appear, are infinitely more simple and mechanical than natural ecological systems. If we cannot get on top of understanding our own homemade economic systems better than we are doing today then our future of living with our complex planet is bleak indeed.

Chapter 34. Gross Margin Analysis

A good account of gross margin analysis is to be found in "Planning the Farm," by D. B. Wallace and H. Burr, Farm Economics Branch Report No.

60, Farm Economics Branch, School of Agriculture, Cambridge University, June 1963. Wallace's choice of the name described in the text is from correspondence.

Chapter 35. Energy/Wealth Source and Use

Entropy: A New World View, by Jeremy Rifkin, New York: Bantam Books, 1981, is an excellent thought-provoking book about our current attitude toward energy. The author also provides a wealth of references.

The reader interested in energy use in agriculture in the United States is advised to read "Energy and agriculture" by Amory B. Lovins, L. Hunter Lovins, and Marty Bender in *Meeting the Expectations of the Land: Essays in Sustainable Agriculture and Stewardship*, edited by Wes Jackson, Wendell Berry, and Bruce Colman, San Francisco: North Point Press, 1984.

Chapter 37. Population Management

The situation of the desert bushes dying out is contained in my report "Holistic Resource Management in Pakistan" of November 1983 to the United Nations (FAO) TCP/PAK/2305 PROJECT. Assistance to Rangeland and Livestock Development Survey in Baluchistan.

A number of the readings suggested for Chapters 9 to 13 contain valuable information on population dynamics and principles. Aldo Leopold's *Game Management* is still one of the best books for clarity and simplicity, and is even good reading for people who are not considering game management as many of the principles are universal. Anne H. Ehrlich's "The human population: Size and dynamics," in *American Zoologist*, 25:395–406 (1985) is also good reading.

Chapter 39. Flexibility

An excellent book concerning landscaping our environment is Ian L. McHarg's *Design with Nature*, New York: Doubleday, 1971. The author shows a great sensitivity to our natural systems and the full interdependence of the whole. Essential reading for anyone involved in greater landscaping for entire communities.

Chapter 42. Organization

There is considerable literature in this field, which has proliferated in recent years. The readings below are suggested for those interested in learning more.

Bennis, Warren, and Burt Nanus. 1985. *Leaders, The Strategies for Taking Charge.* New York: Harper & Row.

Gibb, Jack. 1978. *Trust: A New View of Personal and Organizational Development.* La Jolla, Calif.: Omicron Press.

Hall, Jay. 1982. *The Competence Process.* The Woodlands, Tex.: Teleometrics International.

Herzburg, Frederick. 1982. *The Managerial Choice: To Be Efficient and to Be Human.* Salt Lake City: Olympus Publishing Company.

Naisbitt, John, and Patricia Aburdene. 1985. *Reinventing the Corporation.* New York: Warner Books.

Peters, Thomas J., and Robert H. Waterman. *In Search of Excellence.* New York: Warner Books.

Chapter 43. Personal Growth

Like organizational development, there is a wealth of material available in the field of personal growth these days. I have listed some of the sources, a number of which were used in the text and are used in the Center's training programs. Where appropriate I have commented in the hope that it helps you select from so wide a range of books.

Bliss, Edwin. 1976. *Getting Things Done.* New York: Bantam Books. An easy-to-read "how to" book on personal time management.

Bliss, Edwin. 1983. *Doing it Now.* New York: Bantam Books. A follow-up to *Getting Things Done.* Contains a twelve-step program for moving beyond procrastination.

Bolles, Richard. 1987. *What Color is Your Parachute?* Berkeley, Calif.: Ten Speed Press. Guidance in how to find the right job and the right kind of work.

Borysenko, Joan. 1987. *Minding the Body, Mending the Mind.* Reading, Mass.: Addison-Wesley. A rich study in the connections between mind and body that are severed all too often, and how to reunite them.

Bridges, William. 1980. *Transitions—Making Sense of Life's Changes.* Reading, Mass.: Addison-Wesley. Very readable book about the many adult transitions.

Gross, Ronald. 1977. *The Lifelong Learner.* New York: Simon & Schuster. Excellent description of the "invisible university"—a wealth of new and informal arenas for continuous learning.

Gross, Ronald. 1982. *The Independent Scholar's Handbook.* Reading, Mass.: Addison-Wesley. A continuation of *The Lifelong Learner.* Illustrates the important contributions made by people outside of academia, makes clear that anyone can become an independent scholar, and gives tips on how to go about it.

Houston, Jean. 1982. *The Possible Human, A Course in Enhancing Your Physical, Mental, and Creative Abilities.* Los Angeles: J. P. Tarcher, Inc. Introduction to a comprehensive theory and program to help you develop your creativity. The best part is that it's fun.

Krupnick, Louis B., and Elizabeth Krupnick. *From Despair to Decision.* Minneapolis: CompCare Publications (2415 Annapolis Lane, Minneapolis, Minnesota 55441). A thorough, well-researched, and highly readable report on chemical dependency and its far-reaching effects on the family. The authors give a step-by-step method for intervention (a caring confrontation planned and carried out by a professional and a team of others close to the chemically-dependent person).

Lakein, Alan. 1973. *How to Get Control of Your Time and Your Life.* New York: Signet. Good, quick course in rational goal setting and time management.

Lund, Jerome. 1983. *The Last Self-Help Book.* San Francisco: The Barclay Press (to order, write: Self-Help, P.O. Box 31813, Aurora, CO 80041). A step-by-step process that helps one identify the limiting emotions and beliefs that are blocking his/her development. Jerome Lund lectures at some of the Center's courses.

Montagu, Ashley. 1981. *Growing Young.* New York: McGraw-Hill. The goal of adulthood is not to grow up, but to develop what are considered childlike traits. Based on scientific evidence and years of research, this revolutionary book shows that we are actually supposed to grow and develop all our lives.

Pearsall, Paul. 1987. *Superimmunity.* New York: McGraw-Hill. Delightful reading, emphasizing holism from the human point of view. Aimed at a general audience, the message is nevertheless powerful.

Rainer, Tristine. 1978. *The New Diary.* Boston: Houghton Mifflin. An excellent guide for developing the skills of journal writing.

Robbins, Anthony. 1986. *Unlimited Power.* New York: Simon & Schuster. A comprehensive "how to" book on personal development and control.

Rogers, Carl. 1980. *A Way of Being.* Boston: Houghton Mifflin. An eloquent discussion, based on personal experience, of communication at its deepest levels, living with life's changes now and in the future, and, in passing, a reference to Rogers's discovery of Smuts.

Rokeach, Milton. 1973. *The Nature of Human Values.* New York: Free Press. A classic work on the measurement of values and value systems.

Satir, Virginia. 1972. *Peoplemaking.* Palo Alto: Science and Behavior Books. Very readable and informative book about family dynamics containing exercises to enhance self-awareness and ideas to stimulate family discussion.

Sperry, Len, et al. 1977. *You Can Make it Happen*. Reading, Mass.: Addison-Wesley. A guide to both self-actualization and organization change. Good chapters on personal development strategy, implementing a development program, and strategies for self-change.

Viscott, David. 1974. *How to Live with Another Person*. New York: Simon & Schuster. Thought-provoking work on relationships. Contrary to its title, it is not a "how to" book. It poses a number of important questions for couples.

Viscott, David. 1976. *The Language of Feelings*. Simon & Schuster. On the importance of tuning in to one's feelings.

Viscott, David. 1977. *Risking*. New York: Simon & Schuster. Very helpful in understanding the necessity for and the "how to" of taking chances without which life will never be really lived.

Wegscheider, Sharon. 1981. *Another Chance*. Palo Alto: Science and Behavior Books. A must book for anyone who lives in a family with a chemically-dependent (alcohol or drugs) person. Author talks about the roles that various family members develop in trying to adjust to a chemically-dependent person. The theme of the book is that chemical dependency is a family disease that negatively affects every family member.

Chapter 44. Financial Planning and Wealth Generation

With holistic management, we take such a different approach to generating wealth and financial planning that much of the literature is of little help.

Henry Hazlitt's *Economics in One Lesson*, New York: Arlington House Publishers, 1979, is a good source for understanding the effects of such things as price supports and the larger economic picture in simple terms. As planning is always best done with knowledge of larger trends, I suggest reading Peter F. Drucker's *The Frontiers of Management: Where Tomorrow's Decisions are Being Shaped Today*, New York, E. P. Dutton, 1986.

It is inevitable that farmers will have to turn increasingly to scientifically-sound and sustainable agricultural practices. Few investments on the farm or ranch will yield the same return as investment in education and training and I urge that practitioners in particular subscribe to several farming magazines. One of the best in the United States, *The New Farm*, the magazine of the Regenerative Agriculture Association, is published seven times a year and is available from the Rodale Institute, Emmaus, Pennsylvania 18049.

There is a growing group of people and universities in America becoming involved in sustainable cropland practices, and comprehensive lists for various areas of the country are available from the Rodale Institute. This institute is also helpful in putting people in other countries in touch with organizations working on sustainable agriculture.

In Canada there is an active group of people working on the same lines around Dr. Stuart Hill, who puts out a monthly report. The address is Macdonald College, P.O. Box 21, 111 Lakeshore Road, Ste-Anne de Bellevue, QC, Canada, H9X 1CO.

Chapter 48. Diagnostic Mode

Readers interested in the Chaco Canyon situation used to demonstrate diagnosis of a problem will find further information in the following:

Environment and subsistence of Chaco Canyon, New Mexico. 1985. Ed. by Frances Joan Mathien. National Park Service Publications in Archeology, Chaco Canyon Studies 18E.

Cully, Anne C. 1979. Some aspects of pollen analysis in relation to archeology. *The Kiva* 44:2–3.

Love, David W. 1979. Quaternary fluvial geomorphic adjustments in Chaco Canyon, in *Adjustments of the Fluvial System.* Ed. by D. D. Rhodes and G. P. Williams. Dubuque, Iowa: Kendall/Hunt Publishing Co.

Akins, Nancy J. 1982. Perspectives on faunal resource utilization, Chaco Canyon, New Mexico. *New Mexico Archeological Newsletter* 5 & 6:23–29.

Love, David W. 1977. Dynamics of sedimentation and geomorphic history of Chaco Canyon National Monument, New Mexico. *New Mexico Geologic Society Guidebook,* 28th Field Conference, San Juan Basin.

Gillespie, William B. 1985. The environment of the Chaco Anasazis, in *New Light on Chaco Canyon.* Ed. by David Grant Noble. Santa Fe, N.M.: School of American Research.

The Ecologist, 1987. Nos. 2 & 3 contain some good articles on major development projects, which would have benefited from sound holistic policy analysis before implementation: The Bodhghat Project and the World Bank, by S. K. Roy; Brazil's Greater Carajas Programme, by David Treece; and The Sizewell Report: A foregone conclusion, by J. W. Jeffery.

From China we only hear about the four-thousand-year-old croplands that have been sustained in good condition. An excellent source of information on the Chinese situation currently is Smil, Vaclav. 1984. *The Bad Earth: Environmental Degradation in China.* Armonk, N.Y.: M. E. Sharpe, Inc. The desertification in China is as bad as in many countries about which we hear far more. China is looking for help to the technologically developed Western countries like America, which themselves are beginning to face the fact that their agriculture is unsustainable. Desertifying developed countries with no solutions to their own problems are not well-placed to help anyone. The Chinese, like peoples of other nations, will have to develop holistic resource management for their own needs.

Chapter 49. Policy Analysis Mode

The work that provided some of the information used in the grasshopper spraying policy analysis was done by a group of researchers in Montana and published in the following papers:

Onsager, J. A., and G. B. Hewitt. 1982. Rangeland grasshoppers: Average longevity and daily rate of mortality among six species in nature. *Environ. Entomol.* 10:127–33.

Onsager, J. A. 1985. An ecological basis for prudent control of grasshoppers in the western United States. *Proceedings 3rd Triennial Mtg Pan American Acrid. Soc.* July 5–10, 1981, 97–104.

Onsager, Jerome A. 1986. Current tactics for suppression of grasshoppers on range. *Symposium Proceedings, IPM on Rangeland: State of the Art in the Sagebrush Ecosystem.* Bozeman, Mont.: Rangeland Insect Laboratory, Agricultural Research Service, USDA.

On page 11 of the latter paper the author states:

> In summary, it appears that any range management practice that significantly opens up the plant canopy, either temporarily or permanently, will tend to improve the microhabitat, either temporarily or permanently, for important pest species of grasshoppers. Decreased relative humidity, increased temperature, and increased solar radiation all will tend to enhance grasshopper development, and all will tend to debilitate important grasshopper pathogens.

Chapter 50. Research Orientation Mode

Two publications that give an idea of proposed research and policy in the United States Department of Agriculture are *Research for Tomorrow*, 1986 Yearbook of Agriculture, USDA, Washington D.C., and *Technology, Public Policy, and the Changing Structure of American Agriculture*, Summary, Congress of the United States, Office of Technology Assessment, Washington D.C., OTA-F-286, March 1986.

Chambers, Robert, and Janice Jiggins. 1986. Agricultural research for resource poor farmers: A parsimonious paradigm. Institute of Development Studies, University of Sussex, DP 220, is a refreshing look at research for developing countries from the perspective of a social anthropologist who considers the needs of the people themselves. The authors' ideas approach the findings of the Center for HRM. Management cannot be imposed but must flow from the desires of the people themselves, i.e., we cannot apply holistic management to others.

NOTES

Preface

1. Judge James M. Burns, p. 39. NRDC et al., vs. Donald P. Hodel, as Secretary of the U.S. Department of the Interior, et al, Civil No. R-84-13-ECR, U.S. District Court, District of Nevada, January 2, 1985.

2. L. Stiles, "Pros Ask Validity of Dry Land Measures," p. 2 in *Lo Que Pasa* (University of Arizona, Tucson), Vol. 9, No. 11, 1985.

Chapter 1. What Is Holistic Resource Management?

1. Albert Einstein, *Out of My Later Years* (Secaucus, N.J.: Lyle Stuart, 1973), 113.

2. Amory B. Lovins, "Energy and Agriculture," in *Meeting the Expectations of the Land*, Wes Jackson, Wendell Berry, and Bruce Coleman (eds.) (San Francisco: North Point Press, 1984), 1.

Chapter 3. Introduction

1. W. I. Beveridge, *The Art of Scientific Investigation* (New York: Random House, 1957), 144.

Chapter 4. Management Must Be Holistic

1. J. C. Smuts, *Jan Christian Smuts* (London: Cassell & Co. Ltd., 1952), 290.
2. J. C. Smuts, *Holism and Evolution* (Westport, Conn.: Greenwood Press, 1973), 336.
3. Zev Naveh and Arthur Lieberman, *Landscape Ecology* (New York: Springer-Verlag, 1984), 56.

Chapter 10. Water Cycle

1. "Better than Tiling," *The New Farm*, 1986, vol. 8, no. 1, 48.
2. Ben Osborn, "Range Cover Tames the Raindrop: A Summary of Range Cover Evaluations, 1949." Internal report prepared by the Operations and Research Branches of the Soil Conservation Service, Fort Worth, Texas, 1950.
3. P. A. Yeomans, *Water for Every Farm: Using the Keyline Plan* (Katoomba, Australia: Second Back Row Press Pty Ltd., 1981), 247 pp.

Chapter 11. Succession

1. Roderick M. MacDonald, "Extraction of Microorganisms from the Soil," *Biological Agriculture and Horticulture*, 1986, no. 3, 361–65.
2. Robert van den Bosch, *The Pesticide Conspiracy* (Garden City, N.Y.: Anchor Books, 1980), 24.
3. Robert T. Paine, "Food Web Complexity and Species Diversity," *American Naturalist*, 1966, no. 910, 65–75.

Chapter 18. Rest

1. David Sheridan, *Desertification of the United States* (Washington, D.C.: Council on Environmental Quality, 1981), 21.

Chapter 21. Living Organisms

1. C. W. Gay, D. D. Dwyer, C. Allison, S. Hatch, and J. Schickedanz, *New Mexico Range Plants*, New Mexico State University Cooperative Extension Circular 374, January 1980, 43.

2. Paul R. Ehrlich, *The Machinery of Nature: The Living World Around Us and How It Works* (New York: Simon & Schuster 1986), 162.

Chapter 22. Technology

1. The Tragedy of the Commons concept was first expressed by the Rev. William Forster Lloyd in *Two Lectures on the Checks to Population, Delivered Before the University of Oxford, Michaelmas Term, 1832* (Oxford: Collingwood, 1933). This rare text was reprinted in Augustus M. Kelly Economic Classics, New York, 1968. American economist Garrett Hardin revived the idea and expounded on it in his famous essay, "The Tragedy of the Commons," which has been reprinted in numerous anthologies. Hardin's *Exploring New Ethics for Survival: The Voyage of the Spaceship Beagle* (New York: Viking, 1972) is a booklength elaboration of the essay.

2. Kathleen Minje, "Pesticide Opponents Point to '84 EPA Memo," *The Oregonian*, May 2, 1986, B-1.

3. Robert Rodale, "Importance of Resource Generation," *Resource Efficient Farming Methods for Tanzania* (Emmaus, Pa.: Rodale Press, 1983), 21.

Chapter 24. Time in Cropping, Grazing, Browsing, and Trampling

1. Paul R. Ehrlich, *The Machinery of Nature*, 163.

Chapter 25. Time and Energy Flow

1. My assertion that it was easy to double conventional stocking rates with planned grazing generated enormous controversy and condemnation in the early days. To put the matter to rest once and for all, the Minister of Agriculture in Rhodesia challenged me to demonstrate this in a trial. The "Charter Trial," named after the company that provided the land for it, ran for eight years and was monitored by the University of Rhodesia and the Marandellas Research Station. We successfully ran double the conventional stocking rate without any deterioration of the land, as I had predicted. The conclusion was written up in "Results of the Botanical Analyses in the Charter Trial," by J. N. Clatworthy for the Rhodesian branch of the South African Society of Animal Production in 1976 and published in the *Zimbabwe Agricultural Journal* in 1984.

No great change was measured on the ground, despite vast man-hours spent in collecting data, as only plant species composition was considered, not ecological processes. However, as the effects on ecosystem processes were sufficiently pronounced, Clatworthy felt the need to add additional comment on observations that were not reflected in species composition:

Under the conservative stocking rate of the Charter system [the control] the grass grew tall and dead top hamper accumulated so that periodic burning was necessary to remove this. On the rotationally grazed plots the heavier stocking rate kept the grass short and there was no build-up of dead material. This gave the sward a very healthy appearance.

Incidentally, this trial "to end all controversy" merely increased resistance amongst range scientists. Common sense suggests that a demonstration "to show people" will influence their opinion. It does influence a few, usually when they are far removed from it. To those closely involved, the underlying message of demonstrations is, "Look how clever we are and how stupid you are." Following the Charter Trial experience, I have consistently refused to be involved in demonstrations "to show people." Collaborating with others in mutual learning situations has proven far more effective as it does not create the psychological barriers that demonstrations of this sort do.

Chapter 26. Time and Livestock Nutrition

1. USDA News WR-58-81, 1/9/81, Science and Education Administration, U.S. Department of Agriculture. This news release reported on the poor performance established for livestock at various research stations in the Great Plains area when they were rotated from pasture to pasture "as the forage was depleted."

Chapter 28. Stock Density

1. This discovery was made after the initiation of the Charter Trial mentioned in the note under Chapter 25. As the trial was set up with the customary rigidity, we could not bring the new knowledge to bear on the trial. Thus, throughout it, individual livestock performance at the higher stocking rate suffered in comparison with the control where stocking rate was much lower. Profit, however, was consistently higher at the higher stocking rate as yield per acre was still greater than it was in the control. Simultaneously, on ranches where we were not constrained by the rigidity of the trial, we were able to learn from our mistakes and replanned until we did experience higher individual animal performance under higher stocking rates.

Chapter 29. Herd Effect

1. D. M. Gammon and B. R. Roberts, "Aspects of defoliation during short duration grazing of the Matopos Sandveld of Zimbabwe," *Zimbabwe Journal of Agricultural Research*, 1980, vol. 18, 29.

When I visited the Matopos Research Station, where this study on my work took place, I found that only two steers were being used to constitute the herd. The researchers would not accept that two steers can never simulate the effects that a real herd of 200 or more steers produced, and thus the research trial continued despite the defect that rendered the results meaningless.

Chapter 32. Cause and Effect

1. John D. Hamaker and Donald A.Weaver, *The Survival of Civilization* (Michigan and California: Hamaker-Weaver Publishers, 1982), 14.
2. Mostafa K. Tolba, "Desertification is stoppable," *Arid Lands Newsletter*, 1984, no. 21, 5.

Chapter 35. Energy/Wealth Sources and Use

1. Dennis Hayes, *Rays of Hope* (New York: Norton, 1977), 139.
2. "A Nation Troubled by Toxics," *National Wildlife*, February/March 1987, 39.
3. "Sands of Change," UNEP Environmental Brief No. 2, 1987, United Nations Environmental Program, Nairobi, Kenya.

Chapter 42. Organization

1. Jay Hall, *The Competence Process* (The Woodlands, Tex.: Teleometrics International, 1982), 226–29.
2. Doug Raynor, "The Need for Transformation in Management Theory and Practice," *Organizational Development Journal*, 1985, vol. 3, no. 4, 9.

Chapter 43. Personal Growth

1. Joan Borysenko, with Larry Rothstein, *Minding the Body, Mending the Mind* (Reading, Mass.: Addison-Wesley, 1987), 24.
2. Ibid.
3. Ibid.
4. Jerome Lund, *The Last Self-Help Book: Before Getting Results* (San Francisco: The Barclay Press, 1983), 62.

5. Ashley Montagu, *Growing Young* (New York: McGraw-Hill, 1983), 2–3.

6. Virginia Satir, *Peoplemaking* (Palo Alto, Calif.: Science and Behavior Books, 1972), 63.

7. Carl Rogers, *A Way of Being* (Boston: Houghton Mifflin, 1980), 8.

Chapter 49. Policy Analysis Mode

1. J. A. Onsanger, "An Ecological Basis for Prudent Control of Grasshoppers in the Western United States," *Proc. 3rd. Triennial Mtg., Pan Amer. Acrid. Soc., 5–10 July 1981*, 1985, 98.

Chapter 51. The Future

1. Peter F. Drucker, *The Frontiers of Management: Where Tomorrow's Decisions Are Being Shaped Today* (New York: E. P. Dutton, 1986), 37–8. In his book, Drucker supplies the following detail:

> World trade in goods is larger, much larger, than it has ever been before. And so is the invisible trade, the trade in services. Together the two amount to around $2.5 to $3 trillion a year. But the London Eurodollar market, in which the world's financial institutions borrow from and lend to each other, turns over $300 billion each working day, or $75 trillion a year.
>
> In addition, there are the (largely separate) foreign-exchange transactions in the world's main money centers, in which one currency is traded against another (for example, u.s. dollars against the Japanese yen). These run around $150 billion a day, or about $35 trillion a year: twelve times the worldwide trade in goods and services.

Index

Acocks, John, 48–49
Actualizing tendency, 398
ADA. *See* Animal days per acre
Aeration of soil, 67–68
Aerial counting, 333–334
Age-class sampling, monitoring
    reduction in numbers, 335–336
Age structure, assessment of
    population condition, 328–336
Agricultural extension services, 501
Agriculture, future and, 500–501
Algal crust, 78, 79, 178
American Dust Bowl of 1930s, 181
Animal(s). *See also* Game management;
    Game ranching; Predators
    behavior
        effect on land, 42
        herd effect and, 265
    culling of, 169, 246
    destruction caused by, 45
    diet selection, 159–160, 214, 234–235,
        239
        plant condition and, 254–255
    dung sites of, 157, 159
    in energy pyramid, 96
    eradication of pests, effect on
        succession, 88–89
    fire and, 129–130
    fouling by, 247
    grazing styles of, 163
    herded, advantages of many
        paddocks or grazing areas, 237–239

herding, 41
    significance to soil and plants, 42–
        43
    maintenance of environment against
        successional advance, 78
    performance, 260
        stock density and, 253–254
    production connection with soil, 230
    protected game, destruction under
        conventional grazing, 275
    ruminants, 241
    self-regulating vs. nonself-regulating
        populations, 164, 326–328
    species, favoring of, succession and,
        87
    succession and, 74
    training, reduction of stress of
        frequent livestock moves, 244–245
    wild, 246
Animal day, 211–212
Animal days per acre (ADA)
    assessment technique, 374
    definition, 509
    grazing planning and, 212–216, 259
    livestock nutrition and, 236
    stocking rate assessment and, 372,
        374
Animal impact
    in brittle environments, 174, 181–182
    definition of, 173, 509
    in diagnosing resource problems, 471
    diagnostic evaluation, 464

review of effect on ecosystem, 466
herd effect. *See* Herd effect
immediate benefit from, 181
indications for usage, 174–176
insufficient, 106
mineral cycle and, 93
misconception of, 176
as natural influence, 147
in nonbrittle environments, 182–183
overtrampling
  animal numbers and, 45, 46
  time management and, 354–355
plant densities and, 103
power and versatility of, 173–176
salient aspects of, 176
on soil and plants, 51
stock density and, 178
timing and, 177–178
trampling, 179–180
  time and, 206–207
water cycle and, 174
Animal Unit Months (AUM), 211
Attitudes, self-awareness and, 400–401

Banking, 116
Belief systems, self-awareness and,
  401–402
Biological controls, 188
Biological planning
  aide memoire (memory aid), 367–369
  basing stocking rates on annual
    rainfall, 375–376
  chart for, 369–370
  conflicts with wildlife, 376
  importance of, 365–366
  monitoring and control, 377–386
    daily growth rate monitoring, 381–
      386
    of landscape, 377–381
  open- and closed-ended principle,
    370, 371
  record keeping, 370–371
  and replanning, 358–362
  stocking rate assessment, 371–375
  timing for, 370, 371
Biological resources, 280–281
Brittle environment(s)
  animal impact in, 174
  causes, common, 473
  definition of, 35, 509–510
  desertification of, 94

effects of high animal impact and
  overgrazing, 474
evidence of poor water cycles, 71
features of, 37–39
fire and, 131
germination conditions, 289–290
grazing impact, 154
maintenance by herding animals and
  predators, 173
movement of minerals above ground
  to soil surface, 92–93
overgrazing vs. total rest, 159–160
overrest and, 173
pasture evaluation, 373–374
plant spacings in, 103
predator-induced herd effect and, 264
rest period, 150, 237
  effects of, 135–138
soil cover, 66
soil disturbance for, 42–43
succession in, 79–81, 82
technological management, 111–112
ungrazed plants in, 230
vulnerability, 77
Browsing, 164–166
Brush
  clearing of, 324
    marginal reaction guideline, 301–
      304
  desert, overharvesting for fuel, 326
  encroachment, 70, 288–289
  eradication, 57–58
  impenetrable, animal impact and, 174
Burning. *See also* Fire
  edge effect, 347
  to enhance wildlife habitat or
    reinvigorate communities, 347–348
  following a burn, 348
  indications and justifications, 342–343
  monitoring of ecosystem processes
    after, 348–350
  patchy, 347
  planning for, 345–348
  review of decision to burn
    cause and effect of, 343–344
    effect on whole ecosystem, 343
    energy/wealth and, 345
    gross margin analysis and, 345
    marginal reaction, 344
    society and culture, 345
    weak link, 344
  types of burns, 345–347

Capping
    air exchange and, 94
    in desert, animal impact and, 176
    immature, 510
    mature, 510
Carbon cycle, 95. *See also* Energy flow
Cash flow planning, 411
Cattle. *See* Livestock
Cause and effect guideline
    brush encroachment and, 288–289
    burning and, 343–344
    desertification and, 294–298
    dipping of cattle for ticks and, 292–294
    shift from grassland to tap-rooted plants and, 289–292
    simple, 287–288
Center for Holistic Resource Management, 507–508
    formation, 11
    organizational development, 397
Cities, future and, 503–504
Collaboration
    inescapable costs and, 428
    maintenance costs and, 429–430
Collaboratively-functioning organizations, 391–396
Computers, 433
Conservation Reserve Program, 448, 481
Cool burns, 346
Cost-sharing, government, 284–285
Creativity, human, 121–124
    money derived from, 118
    organization and, 388
Crisis management, for land under rest, initiation of, 144–150
Croplands
    in brittle environment, 181
    energy flow goals, 108
    succession in, 83–86
Cropping, time and, 202–203
CRP (Conservation Reserve Program), 447, 481
Culling of animals, 169, 246
Culture, effects of holistic management, 320–324

Daily growth rate, monitoring of, 381–386
Darling, Sir Frank Fraser, 12–13

DDT, 194
Desertification
    brush encroachment and, 288
    definition of, 510
    herding effect and, 264
    perennial grass, fate of, 152
    quick fixes for, 294–295
Desertification in the United States, 143–144
Destocking, total, 142
Developed countries, 321, 501
Developing countries, 482
Diagnostic mode
    common problems, 473–474
    diagnosing resource problems, generally, 468–473
    during management monitoring and control, 463–468
Dipping, chemical, for ticks, 292
Domestic cattle, destructive trampling and intense grazing, 41
Dormant periods, 239
Double-cropping, 203
Drought planning, 359–362
Drought reserve, grazing and, 231–233
Duration grazing, 240

Earthworms, soil porosity and, 66
Ecological relationships, time and, 45–52
Economies, future and, 504–505
Economists
    need to learn new ways to address problems, 13–16
    role of, 13
Ecosystem
    definition, 61
    environments within, 61
    processes of, 6–7
    tools for managing, 111–113
    unity of, 61
    weak link in, 279–286
    whole
        effect of burning on, 343
        guideline, 273–278
Ecosystem foundation blocks. *See* Energy flow; Mineral cycle; Succession; Water cycle
Education, future and, 499–500
Elephants
    heavy culling of, 169–170

herds, 47
reduction of herds to protect
    winterthorn trees, 339–340
Energy
    conversion
        financial planning and, 424–425
        of sunlight, 282
        ways to increase, 302
    sources and patterns of use, 316–317
Energy flow
    area of leaf and, 104–107
    in brittle environment
        animal impact and, 182
        fire and, 131
        grazing impact, 154
        rest, effects of, 150
    definition, 8
    drought reserves of forage and, 231
    duration of growth and, 100–102
    energy tetrahedron, 98–99
    fire and, 274
    goals, 107–108
    in grassland, description of goals, 452
    increasing, by use of technology, 107
    misplaced technical solutions and,
        193
    in nonbrittle environment
        animal impact and, 183
        fire and, 132
        grazing impact, 153–154
        rest, effects of, 150
    pyramid, 95–97
    ramifications of, 99
    as tetrahedron, 98–99
    time and, 100–102, 227–233
    volume of plants and, 102–104
Energy pyramid, 95–97
Energy/wealth, consideration in
    decision to burn, 345
Environmental deterioration, causes, 22
Environmental Impact Statement, 483
Environmental resistance, 329
Erosion, in brittle environments, 72
Eucalyptus trees, 295

Farm costs
    fixed vs. variable, 311–313
    overhead, 310, 311
    variable or direct, 311
Fencing
    to control livestock number, 246

creation of wealth and, 423
    livestock movement and, 244
    marginal reaction and, 304–306
    planning, 353–354
    radial fence layout, 354–355
    selection based on marginal reaction
        per dollar, 426–428
    soil distrubance and, 42
Fertilizers, dangers of, 94
Financial planning
    cash flow planning, 411
    conserving wealth, 433–434
    control, 436–441
    cost of borrowed money and final
        assessment, 432–434
    financial planning sheet, 436, 437
    generation of wealth using HRM
        model, 419–428
        creation of wealth, 422–423
        expenses and goal attainment, 421–
            422
        production and income, 420–421
        where to invest in solar chain, 423–
            428
    inescapable costs, 428–429
    investment decisions, making, 426–
        428
    maintenance costs, 429–432
    monitoring, 435–442
        frequency of, 436
    net managerial income and, 431–432
    psychological attitude and, 412–419
        manager, goal confusion of, 418–
            419
        overcoming reluctance to plan,
            417–418
    purpose, 409–410
    readjustment of allocations, 432
    replanning and, 362–363, 441–442
    time for, 410–411
    and wealth generation, 409–434
Financial resources, 282–286
Fire. See also Burning
    animals and, 129–130
    in brittle environment, 131
    cool, 129
    in diagnosing resource problems,
        469, 472
    diagnostic evaluation, 464
        review of effect on ecosystem, 465
    energy flow and, 274

Fire *(continued)*
    extent of destruction caused by, 130–
        131
    hot, 129
    increased frequency of, effect on soil
        surface, 125
    microenvironment and, 128
    mineral cycle and, 93, 274
    natural, 125
    in nonbrittle environment, 132
    prescribed burnings, 126
    soil exposure and, 127
    succession and, 274
    water cycle and, 274
Firebreak, 174
Fish management, animal impact and,
    174
Flexibility
    operational level, 363–364
    strategic level, 352–358
    tactical level, 358–363
Foot and mouth disease, 491
Forage consumption
    measurement, time and, 211–215
    time and, 211–215
Forbs, 154*n*, 166, 344. *See also* Weeds
Four-paddock-three-herd grazing
    system, 349
Freezing, effect on environment, 43
Fukuoka, Masanobu, 85, 186, 203
Future
    agriculture and, 500–501
    cities and, 503–504
    economies and, 504–505
    education and, 499–500
    and HRM model, nations, 505–506
    language and, 499
    national parks and wilderness and,
        502–503
    water and, 501–502

Game management
    by cutting off water periodically, 248
    removal of game, 46
    time and, 246–250
Game ranching, 47
Genetic engineering, 188–189
Germination, 289
Goal(s)
    energy flow, 107–108
    for holistic resource management, 4,
        6
    importance of, 55
    lack of sharing or clarity, 57
    landscape, 452–456
    management, flexibility and, 352
    narrowly defined, 447–448
    ownership of, 448–449
    parts of
        landscape, 56
        production, 56
        quality of life, 55–56
    permanent, setting more, 445–457
    production, 450–451
    quality of life and, 449–450
    setting, common errors in, 447
    temporary, 446
    three-part, 446
    well-formulated, 456
Goats, 225–226
Government
    collaborative functioning of, 388
    compartmentalized, 16–18
Government agencies, nongoals of, 57–
    58
Government subsidies, 415
Grain crops, perennial, 181
Grasses
    clipping and weighing, stocking rate
        assessment and, 374
    establishment, aiding in, 78, 80
    overbrowsing of, 166
    overgrazing of, 162
    palatability, animal impact and, 174
    types, daily growth rates, 381
Grasshoppers
    integrated pest management, 479–481
    spraying programs, 292–293
    policy analysis, 477–479
Grasslands
    description of goals, 452
    invasion of woody species into, 157
    shift to tap-rooted plants, 289
Grazing
    animal day per acre and, 213
    in brittle environment, 154–172
    in diagnosing resource problems, 472
    diagnostic evaluation, 464
        review of effect on ecosystem, 466
    drought reserve of, 231–233
    on fixed rotations, 259
    frequent, 510
    land damaged by, restoration of, 36
    light, 153

low-density, 255–256
  definition, 511
  overcoming with planned grazing,
    259
  with rotational grazing, 256–257
nonbrittle environment, impact on,
  153–154
nonselective, 48–49, 159, 214
overgrazing. *See* Overgrazing
patterns, animal nutrition and, 235–
  236
periods, computation from
  preselected recovery period, 209–
  211
planned, 217–219
  stock density and, 255
proper, 151
recovery periods and, 207–209
rigid rotation, 256
rotational, 216–222, 258
schedules, inflexible, dangers of, 216–
  222
severe, 152, 153, 159, 160, 229, 510
  prejudice against, 155
Grazing areas, 209, 237–239
Grazing cells
  advanced, 220
  in computation of grazing periods,
    209, 210
  definition of, 510
  size of, 356
Grazing succession, 248–249
The Great Plague, 490
Green Revolution, 186, 188, 189, 277
Gross margin analysis, 310–314
  consideration in decision to burn, 345
  creation of wealth and, 421
Gross profit, 310
Groundwater, falling supplies, 70
Growth, duration of, energy flow and,
  100–102
Guidelines for management. *See* specific
  guidelines

Habit
  reduction of stress of frequent
    livestock moves and, 244–245
  time management and, 124
Hedging, 165
Herbicides. *See* Pesticides

Herd effect
  animal behavior and, 265
  animal impact and, 178
  in brittle environment, 42
  definition of, 263, 510–511
  induction of, 263
  predator-induced, 264
  requirements for, 265
  simulation of predator-induced
    behavior, 266
  size of herd and, 270–272
  soil disturbance and, 42–44
  type of livestock and, 268–270
Herding
  importance to land, 42
  land planning and, 357–358
  natural vs. domesticated, 41–42
  patterns of, 157
Hierarchically functioning
  organizations, 387–391
High successional communities, 512
Historic preservation, 56
Holistic management model, 33–34
Holism
  concept of, 8
  in resource management, essential
    nature of, 23–24
Holistic resource management model
  acceptance of, impediment to, 21–22
  application, 461–462. *See also* specific
    application mode
  description of, 4, 5–12
  diagnostic mode, 463–474
  ecosystem foundation blocks, 6, 61–
    62
    energy flow. *See* Energy flow
    mineral cycle. *See* Mineral cycle
    succession. *See* Succession
    water. *See* Water
  failure to form goals and, 57
  impediments to acceptance, brittle
    and nonbrittle environments, 35–40
  policy analysis mode, 475–485
  questions and answers, common,
    482–483
  vs. modern science tradition, 486
Hot burns, 345–346
Human endeavors, 24, 25
Human population
  creativity. *See* Creativity, human
  in energy pyramid, 96–97

Human population *(continued)*
  organization of, 387–388
  personal growth, 398–408
  psychological attitude in financial
    planning, 412–419
  self-regulating vs. nonself-regulating,
    328
  successional process, 398
  uncontrolled growth, 498
Humidity
  brittleness and, 37
  seasonal pattern, 38
Hydrophytic plants, 104, 105

Implementation, 4
Inflation, 116
Insects, noneffective water cycle and,
  77–78
Integrated pest management (IPM),
  479–481
Irish potato famine, 491–492
Irrigation, 16

"Key indicator" plants, 47, 48, 159
Knowledge
  growth of, 24
  new, approach to, 21–22

Labor, 8, 111
Labor and money, 114–120
Land, differences between naturally
  herded areas and domesticated stock,
  41–42
Land degradation
  Acocks's theory and, 49
  from overgrazing and overtrampling,
    45
  problems from, 15–16
Land management, succession and, 86–
  89
Land planning
  herding and, 357–358
  process of, 353–357
  reduction of stress of frequent
    livestock moves, 244–245
  who should plan, 357
Landscape
  description of, 4
  goals, 56, 452–456
  succession and, 87
  monitoring of, 377–381

implementing control, 380–381
  new areas for research, 492
Language, future and, 499
Leaching, 93–94
Leadership
  beliefs, 392–394
  skills and practices, 394–396
  style, 391–392
Leopold, Aldo, 329
Lichens, encrustation of soil, 78, 79
Livestock
  cattle production, 306–309
  flexibility of management, operational
    level, 363–364
  frequent moves
    reduction of stress from, 244–245
    stimulation from, 243–244
  induction of movement of other
    animal species, 248–249
  long-term plans for, 356–357
  management, 35–36
  nutrition and time, 234–245
  performance, stock density and, 255
  planning, 365
  profiting from, succession and, 87
  training of, 266
  trampling and grazing by, 41
  type of, herd effect and, 268–270
Living organisms tool
  description of, 184–189
  in diagnosing resource problems,
    469, 472
  diagnostic evaluation, 464
  review of effect on ecosystem, 466
Locoweed, 298, 304
Loudecia grasses, 107
Low-density grazing, definition, 511
Low successional communities, 512

Management decisions, perspective of
  the whole, 32
Management guidelines, 200–201
Marginal reaction, 299–309
  consideration in decision to burn, 344
  definition of, 299
  example of, 299–300
  fencing selection and, 426–428
Marketing, 285–286, 426
Mentors, 404–405
Mesophytic plants, 104, 105–106
Microenvironment, fire and, 128

Mineral cycle
  in brittle environment
    animal impact and, 182
    fire and, 131
    grazing impact, 154
    rest, effects of, 150
  definition of, 7
  energy pyramid and, 97
  fire and, 274
  in grassland, description of goals, 452
  importance of, 90–91
  misplaced technical solutions and,
    192–193
  movement above ground to soil
    surface, 92–93
  movement from surface to
    underground, 93–94
  movement to soil surface, 92
  in nonbrittle environment
    animal impact and, 183
    fire and, 132
    grazing impact, 153
    rest, effects of, 150
  soil surface, importance of, 94
Mineral dollars, 118
Mob grazing. See Nonselective grazing
Money
  categories of, 117–119
  establishment of, 115
  labor and, 111
  wealth and, 114
Monoculture
  crops, 85
  instability of, 89, 219
  management of, 278
  problems from, 294
  problems with, 87

National parks and wilderness, future
  and, 502–503
Nations, future and HRM model, 505–
  506
Net decay process, 40
Net managerial income, 431–432
Nonbrittle environment(s)
  characteristics, 37
  definition of, 509–510
  disturbances in growing season, 228
  fire in, 132
  germination conditions, 289
  grazing, impact of, 153–154

movement of minerals above ground
  to soil surface, 92
pasture evaluation, 373
rest, effects of, 134–135, 150
soil cover, 66
spacing between plants, 102–103
succession in, 35, 81–83
time manipulation based on
  perennial grass component, 205–
  206
ungrazed plants in, 230
vs. brittle environment, 38, 39
Nongoals, 57–58, 447
Nonrenewable resources, 14
Nonselective grazing, 48–49, 159, 214
Nonself-regulating populations, 164,
  326–328

Organic material, 94
Organizations
  characteristics of, 389
  collaborative, 396–397
  collaboratively-functioning, 388, 391–
    396
  hierarchically-functioning, 389–391
  purpose, 388
Overbrowsing
  responses to, 165–166
  time and, 203–205
Overgrazing
  animal numbers and, 43–46
  in brittle environment, 154
  causes, 381
  characteristics of, 290
  definition of, 511
  effects of, 153
  of grass species, 162
  inflexible rotation grazing and, 216–
    217
  in nonbrittle environment, 153–154
  with partial rest, land deterioration
    and, 178–179
  plant damage from, 155
  plant recovery period and, 152
  preventive measures, 47–48
  soil compaction and exposed
    surfaces, 288–289
  succession and, 151
  time and, 51, 157, 203–205
  time management and, 354–355
  in wild herds, 162

Overhead, 310, 311
Overrest
  in brittle environments, 173
  definition of, 511
  plants and, 157, 290
  from rotational grazing, 262
Overstocking, 161, 375
Overtrampling
  animal numbers and, 45, 46
  time management and, 354–355
Oxidation, 92, 93

Paddock(s)
  definition of, 209, 511
  eight per grazing cell, 210
  high number of, 260
    advantages, 237–239
    danger derived from high stock
      density, 219
    decreasing risk and, 215–216
    decreasing size, effect on grazing
      pressure in cell, 213–214
    shorter grazing and, 252
  low number of, 241
  movement throughout, effect on
    animal nutrition, 235–236
  number, distribution of grazing on
    plants and, 229
  nutrition, rate of drop-off in, 258
  relationship to grazing and recovery
    period, 207–209
  short duration grazing system in, 240
  size reduction of, 214–215
  splitting, stock density and, 252–253
Paine, Robert, 88
Paper dollars, 118–119
Parasites, biological controls for, 188
Partial rest, 178
Patch grazing. See Low-density grazing
Patchiness, low-density grazing and,
  260
Perennial grasses
  in brittle environments, 228
  overgrazing and, 162
  prolonged rest and, 230–231
  time management from, fate of
    woody plants and, 222–226
  time manipulation based on, 205–206
Personal growth
  creativity and, 398
  giving and getting support, 405–407

  need for vision beyond ourselves,
    407–408
  self-awareness, 399–402
  self-direction and, 403–405
Pesticides
  chemical dipping for ticks, 292
  dangers of, 94
  DDT, 194
  for grasshoppers, 292, 294
  human safety and, 193
  marginal reaction and, 304–305
Planned grazing, 217–219
Planned rigidity, 256
Planning, 4, 6
Plant(s)
  absorption of water, 67
  adaptation to growing conditions, 104
  age structure of, 333
    degree of brittleness and, 148
  bitten, effects on, 152. See also
    Grazing
  daily growth rate monitoring, 381–
    386
    importance of monitoring
      individual plants, 385–386
  in energy pyramid, 96
  fire and, 127–128
  herbicide resistant, 189
  key indicator species, 159
  leaf area, energy flow and, 104–107
  recovery period, 382–384
  regrowing, overgrazing and, 155,
    159, 217
  roots, porosity of soil and, 66
  spacing between, 102–103, 228
    degree of brittleness and, 148
  species, favoring of, succession and,
    87
  tap-rooted, shift to, 289
  ungrazed, 261–262
    problem of, 229–231
  vegetation type and selection of
    livestock, 270
  volume of, energy flow and, 102–104
  weed eradication, effect on
    succession, 88–89
  woody
    browsing and, 166
    fate of, 222–226
    invasion into grasslands, 157
  xerophytic, 104, 105

Plant roots, lifting of minerals to soil surface, 92
Policy analysis mode, 475–476
  goal, 477
  importance of, 481–485
  testing guidelines, 478–481
  tools and, 477
Political and economic ramifications, 12–18
Politicians
  need to learn new ways to address problems, 13–16
  role of, 13
Polycultures, 85
Population management
  age structure, 328–336
  bottleneck principle, 337–338
  diversity management vs. single species management, 338–341
  goals and, 325
  knowledge needed for, 326
  reduction of populations, 337–338
  self-regulating and nonself-regulating populations, 326–328
Precipitation
  distribution, brittleness and, 37
  effectiveness of, 64–65
  stocking rates based on annual rainfall, 375–376
Predator-induced behavior, simulation of, 266
Predators
  destruction of, effect on environment, 43
  humans as, 247
  nonself-regulating populations and, 327
  production of herd effect, 263
  protection against, problems of, 276–277
  removal of main, consequences, 247–248
  single species of, prey animals dependent on, 277
  soil disturbance and, 42, 43
  time prey spends in proximity of plants and, 247
Price supports, 415
Production
  goals for resource management and, 56

new areas for research, 493
profitability, gross margin analysis and, 310–314
as weak link, financial planning and, 425–426
Production costs
  control of, 416
  profit and, 412–413
Production goals, 446, 450–451
Profit
  cost of production and, 412–413
  production goals and, 56

Quality of life
  in goal for resource management, 55–56
  goals and, 449–450
  goal setting and, 56–57
  in national goals, 322–323
  relationship between scientific research and resource management, 487
  research in new areas and, 492–493
Quality of life statement, 4

Rainfall. See Precipitation
Ranch management, holistic, 28–29
Range management research, 48
Range science, 204
Recovery period(s)
  grazing and, 207–209
  lengthening of, 241
  and paddock size and number, 237, 252–253
  preselected, computation of grazing periods from, 209–211
  selection, 217
Red range, 106
Reductionist science, 486–488
Reinvestment cycle, 284
Renewable resources, 14
Research orientation mode, 486–489
  research in new areas, 492–494
  research in support of management, 489–492
Resource management
  definition of, 3
  levels of, 475
  narrow perspective, problems with, 29

Resources
    biological, 280–281
    financial, 282–286
    human, 281–282
Rest. *See also* Overrest
    in brittle environment, 150
    delayed effect of, 141–144
    effects of, 135–138
    definition of, 511
    in diagnosing resource problems,
        468–469, 471–473
    diagnostic evaluation, 464
    review of effect on ecosystem, 465
    as ecosystem tool, 133–150
    effects on ecosystem foundation
        blocks, 150
    germination conditions and, 289–290
    as goal, problem of, 447
    land under, initiation of crisis
        management of, 144–150
    in nonbrittle environment, 134–135,
        150
    partial, 133, 178
        definition of, 511
    prolonged, perennial grasses and,
        230–231
    in semibrittle environments, 139–141
    total, 133
Rooiveld, 106
Rotational grazing, 216–222, 258
Rumenal flora populations, 241

Scientific method, 4
Screwworms, 188
Selective grazing. *See* Low-density
    grazing
Self-awareness, 399–402
Self-direction, personal growth and,
    403–405
Self-regulating populations, 164, 326–
    328
Semibrittle environments, rest, effects
    of, 139–141
Sheep, hooves of, relationship to health
    of soil, 43
Singe burn, 346
Smuts, Jan Christian, 26–27
Society, 322–324
    consideration in decision to burn, 345
    cultural complexity in, 320–321

Soil
    aeration, 67–68
    algal encrustation of, 78, 79, 128
    bare, 71
    capped
        aeration and, 94
        animal impact and, 176
        immature, 510
        mature, 510
    compacted, 289
    damage on rangeland, 318
    exposure from fire, 127
    fouled, browsing and, 167–168
    living, 90
    loss off farms, 318
    porosity, 66
    surface
        crumb structure, 94, 181
        movement of minerals to, 92
        penetration, decreased, 70
        water cycle and, 65
Soil cover, 65–66
Soil disturbance, by herding animals,
    benefits of, 42
Solar chain, investment in, 423–428
Solar dollars, 119
Solar energy, 8
Solution, 7
South Africa, abundance of wild herds,
    46
Spot grazing, 251–252
Spraying policy
    goal, 477
    testing guidelines, 478–481
    tools, 477
Springbok, 46
Standard Animal Units, 212
Stock density
    definition of, 178, 251, 510, 511
    high, 237
        on brittle environment, 220–221
        with high paddock number, 219
    increasing
        effect of, 305
        with shortened grazing periods,
            253
    low, 251–252, 251–262
        patchiness and, 251
        trailing and, 251
    paddock size reduction and number,
        214, 215

and time, 260
vs. herd effect, 265
Stocking rate
   assessment in biological planning,
      371–375
   based on annual rainfall, 375–376
   definition of, 178, 511
   doubled, 167
   light, 155
   proper, 170
Stress-hardy personality, 400–401
Subterranean drainage, 423
Success, as short-term high production,
   danger of, 48
Succession
   advancement, management of species
      against, 78
   animals and, 74
   in brittle environment, 79–81, 82
      animal impact and, 181–182
      fire and, 131
      grazing impact, 154
      rest, effects of, 150
   complexity of, relationship to relative
      stability, 76–77
   creation of herbicide-resistant crop
      plants and, 189
   in croplands, 83–86
   definition of, 7, 73–74, 512
   energy pyramid and, 97
   fire and, 274
   in grassland, description of goals, 452
   growing time and, 101
   in human populations, 398
   importance of, 75
   landscape goals and, 87
   living organisms tool and, 185–186
   management and, 86–89
   misplaced technical solutions and,
      192
   in nonbrittle environment, 81–83
      animal impact and, 182–183
      fire and, 132
      grazing impact, 153
      rest, effects of, 150
   process of, 75–77
   shift toward monoculture, 219
   technology and, 188–189

Technology
   assessment, 195

   in diagnosing resource problems,
      469–470, 472–473
   diagnostic evaluation, 464–465
      review of effect on ecosystem, 466–
         467
   future and, 190
   misguided, 194
   misplacment in ecosystem foundation
      blocks, 192–193
   nonsolutions, 191–192
   as solution, pitfalls of, 191
   succession and, 188–189
Testing guidelines, 200, 323–324
Thawing, effect on environment, 43
Ticks, chemical dipping for, 292
Time
   animal impact and, 177–178
   control, increasing paddock number
      and decreasing risk, 215–216
   in cropping, grazing, browsing, and
      trampling, 202–226
   energy flow and, 100–102, 227–233
   game management and, 246–250
   livestock nutrition and, 234–245
   manipulation based on perennial
      grass component, 205–206
   marginal reaction and, 300–301
   overbrowsing and, 203–205
   overgrazing and, 157, 203–205
   role in measuring forage
      consumption, 211–215
   role in soil, plant, and animal
      relationship, 45–52
   trampling and, 206–207
Time management
   based on perennial grasses, fate of
      woody plants and, 222–226
   control of number of grazing
      selections and, 239–242
   in mixed crops, 203
   overtrampling and overgrazing, 354–
      355
   stifling of creativity and, 123–124
Tools. See also specific tools
   for ecosystem management, 111–113
   grazing, 151–168
   guidelines for usage, 199–201
   management guidelines, 200–201
   selection for whole ecosystem
      management, 274–275
   testing guidelines, 200

Trampling. *See* Animal impact
Trees, planted in desert, 185–186
Trust, time management and, 124
Tsetse fly, 36, 130, 194, 344
Tuli Circle, 36, 38

Underdeveloped countries, 321

Values, self-awareness and, 399–400
Variable costs, 311
Voisin, André, 47, 50, 157, 204, 213, 355
von Kleist, Heinrich, 32–33

Wallace, David, 310
Water
    future and, 501–502
    interaction with soil, animals, and
        plants, 66–67
    penetration into soil surface, 65–66
    run-off, increased, 70
Water cycle
    animal impact and, 174
    basic pattern of, 63–64
    in brittle environment
        animal impact and, 182
        fire and, 131
        grazing impact, 154
        rest, effects of, 150
    capping and, 65
    definition of, 7
    effective, 66–69
    and effective precipitation, 64–65
    energy pyramid and, 97
    fire and, 274
    in grassland, description of goals, 452
    growing time and, 101
    importance of, 72
    misplaced technical solutions and,
        192
    nature of soil surface and, 65

    in nonbrittle environment
        animal impact and, 183
        fire and, 132
        grazing impact, 153
        rest, effects of, 150
        noneffective, 68–70
        consequences of, 70–71
        insects and, 77–78
        recognition of, 71–72
        succession and, 77–78
Water points, 45
Weak link concept, consideration in
    decision to burn, 344
Wealth
    conserving, 433–434
    creation of, 422–423
    mineral dollar, 118
    money and, 114
    paper dollar, 118–119
    solar dollar, 119
    sources and patterns of use, 317–319
Weather, effect on environment, 43
Weathering, mineral cycle and, 93
Weeds. *See also* Forbs
    encroachment by, 70
    or forbs, 154*n*
    value of, 85
White range, 106
Wildlife, conflict with livestock,
    biological planning and, 376
Winterfat, 167, 169
Witveld, 106
Woody plants
    browsing and, 166
    fate when time management is based
        on perennial grasses, 222–226
    invasion into grasslands, 157

Xerophytic plants, 104, 105

Also Available from Island Press

Land and Resource Planning in the National Forests
By Charles F. Wilkinson and H. Michael Anderson
Foreword by Arnold W. Bolle

This comprehensive, in-depth review and analysis of planning, policy, and law in the National Forest System is the standard reference source on the National Forest Management Act of 1976 (NFMA). This clearly written, non-technical book offers an insightful analysis of the Fifty Year Plans and how to participate in and influence them.

1987. xii, 396 pp., index.
Paper ISBN 0-933280-38-6. **$19.95**

Reforming the Forest Service
By Randal O'Toole

Reforming the Forest Service contributes a completely new view to the current debate on the management of our national forests. O'Toole argues that poor management is an institutional problem; he shows that economic inefficiencies and environmental degradation are the inevitable result of the well-intentioned but poorly designed laws that govern the Forest Service. This book proposes sweeping reforms in the structure of the agency and new budgetary incentives as the best way to improve management.

1988. xii, 256 pp., graphs, tables, notes.
Cloth, ISBN 0-933280-49-1. **$34.95**
Paper, ISBN 0-933280-45-9. **$19.95**

Last Stand of the Red Spruce
By Robert A. Mello
Published in cooperation with Natural Resources Defense Council

Acid rain—the debates rage between those who believe that the cause of the problem is clear and identifiable and those who believe that the evidence is inconclusive. In *Last Stand of the Red Spruce*, Robert A. Mello has written an ecological detective story that unravels this confusion and explains how air pollution is killing our nation's forests. Writing for a lay audience, the author traces the efforts of scientists trying to solve the mystery of the dying red spruce trees on Camels Hump in Vermont. Mello clearly and succinctly presents both sides of an issue on which even the scientific community is split and concludes that the scientific evidence uncovered on Camels Hump elevates the issues of air pollution and acid rain to new levels of national significance.

1987. xx, 156 pp., illus., references, bibliography.
Paper, ISBN 0-933280-37-8. **$14.95**

Western Water Made Simple, by the editors of **High Country News**
Edited by Ed Marston

Winner of the 1986 George Polk Award for environmental reporting, these four special issues of *High Country News* are here available for the first time in book form. Much has been written about the water crisis in the West, yet the issue remains confusing and difficult to understand. *Western Water Made Simple*, by the editors of *High Country News*, lays out in clear language the complex issues of Western water. This survey of the West's three great rivers—the Colorado, the Columbia, and the Missouri—includes material that reaches to the heart of the West—its ways of life, its politics, and its aspirations. *Western Water Made Simple* approaches these three river basins in terms of overarching themes combined with case studies—the Columbia in an age of reform, the Colorado in the midst of a fight for control, and the Missouri in search of its destiny.

1987. 224 pp., maps, photographs, bibliography, index.
Paper, ISBN 0-933280-39-4.   **$15.95**

**The Report of the President's Commission on Americans Outdoors:
The Legacy, The Challenge**
With Case Studies
Preface by William K. Reilly

"If there is an example of pulling victory from the jaws of disaster, this report is it. The Commission did more than anyone expected, especially the administration. It gave Americans something serious to think about if we are to begin saving our natural resources."
—Paul C. Pritchard, President,
National Parks and Conservation Association

This report is the first comprehensive attempt to examine the impact of a changing American society and its recreation habits since the work of the Outdoor Recreation Resource Review Commission, chaired by Laurance Rockefeller in 1962. The President's Commission took more than two years to complete its study; the Report contains over sixty recommendations, such as the preservation of a nationwide network of "greenways" for recreational purposes and the establishment of an annual $1 billion trust fund to finance the protection and preservation of our recreational resources. The Island Press edition provides the full text of the report, much of the additional material compiled by the Commission, and twelve selected case studies.

1987. xvi, 426 pp., illus., appendixes, case studies.
Paper, ISBN 0-933280-36-X.   **$24.95**

Public Opinion Polling: A Handbook for Public Interest and Citizen Advocacy Groups
By Celinda C. Lake, with Pat Callbeck Harper

"Lake has taken the complex science of polling and written a very usable 'how-to' book. I would recommend this book to both candidates and organizations interested in professional, low-budget, in-house polling." —Stephanie Solien, Executive Director, Women's Campaign Fund.

Public Opinion Polling is the first book to provide practical information on planning, conducting, and analyzing public opinion polls as well as guidelines for interpreting polls conducted by others. It is a book for anyone— candidates, state and local officials, community organizations, church groups, labor organizations, public policy research centers, and coalitions focusing on specific economic issues—interested in measuring public opinion.

1987. x, 166 pp., bibliography, appendix, index.
Paper, ISBN 0-933280-32-7.   **$19.95**
Companion software now available.

Green Fields Forever: The Conservation Tillage Revolution in America
By Charles E. Little

"*Green Fields Forever* is a fascinating and lively account of one of the most important technological developments in American agriculture. . . . Be prepared to enjoy an exceptionally well-told tale, full of stubborn inventors, forgotten pioneers, enterprising farmers—and no small amount of controversy." —Ken Cook, World Wildlife Fund and The Conservation Foundation.

Here is the book that will change the way Americans think about agriculture. It is the story of "conservation tillage"—a new way to grow food that, for the first time, works *with*, rather than against, the soil. Farmers who are revolutionizing the course of American agriculture explain here how conservation tillage works. Some environmentalists think there are problems with the methods, however; author Charles E. Little demonstrates that on this issue both sides have a case, and the jury is still out.

1987. 189 pp., illus., appendixes, index, bibliography.
Cloth, ISBN 0-933280-35-1.   **$24.95**
Paper, ISBN 0-933280-34-3.   **$14.95**

Federal Lands: A Guide to Planning, Management, and State Revenues
By Sally K. Fairfax and Carolyn E. Yale

"An invaluable tool for state land managers. Here, in summary, is everything that one needs to know about federal resource management policies." — Rowena Rogers, President, Colorado State Board of Land Commissioners.

Federal Lands is the first book to introduce and analyze in one accessible volume the diverse programs for developing resources on federal lands. Offshore and onshore oil and gas leasing, coal and geothermal leasing, timber sales, grazing permits, and all other programs that share receipts and revenues with states and localities are considered in the context of their common historical evolution as well as in the specific context of current issues and policy debates.

1987. xx, 252 pp., charts, maps, bibliography, index.
Paper, ISBN 0-933280-33-5.   **$24.95**

Hazardous Waste Management: Reducing the Risk
By Benjamin A. Goldman, James A. Hulme, and Cameron Johnson for the Council on Economic Priorities

Hazardous Waste Management: Reducing the Risk is a comprehensive sourcebook of facts and strategies that provides the analytic tools needed by policy makers, regulating agencies, hazardous waste generators, and host communities to compare facilities on the basis of site, management, and technology. The Council on Economic Priorities' innovative ranking system applies to real-world, site-specific evaluations, establishes a consistent protocol for multiple applications, assesses relative benefits and risks, and evaluates and ranks ten active facilities and eight leading commercial management corporations.

1986. xx, 316 pp., notes, tables, glossary, index.
Cloth, ISBN 0-933280-30-0.   **$64.95**
Paper, ISBN 0-933280-31-9.   **$34.95**

An Environmental Agenda for the Future
By Leaders of America's Foremost Environmental Organizations

". . . a substantive book addressing the most serious questions about the future of our resources." — John Chafee, U.S. Senator, Environmental and Public Works Committee. "While I am not in agreement with many of the positions the authors take, I believe this book can be the basis for constructive dialogue with industry representatives seeking solutions to environmental problems."—Louis Fernandez, Chairman of the Board, Monsanto Corporation.

The chief executive officers of ten major environmental and conservation organizations launched a joint venture to examine goals that the environmental movement should pursue now and into the twenty-first century. This book presents policy recommendations for implementing the changes needed to bring about a healthier, safer world. Topics discussed include nuclear issues, human population growth, energy strategies, toxic waste and pollution control, and urban environments.

1985. viii, 155 pp., bibliography.
Paper, ISBN 0-933280-29-7. **$9.95**

Water in the West
By Western Network

Water in the West is an essential reference tool for water managers, public officials, farmers, attorneys, industry officials, and students and professors attempting to understand the competing pressures on our most important natural resource: water. Here is an in-depth analysis of the effects of energy development, Indian rights, and urban growth on other water users.

1985. *Vol. III: Western Water Flows to the Cities*
v, 217 pp., maps, table of cases, documents, bibliography, index.
Paper, ISBN 0-933280-28-9. **$25.00**

These titles are available directly from Island Press, Box 7, Covelo, CA 95428. Please enclose $2.00 shipping and handling for the first book and $1.00 for each additional book. California and Washington, DC residents add 6% sales tax. A catalog of current and forthcoming titles is available free of charge. Prices subject to change without notice.